IBO Financial Management & Currency Risk

PEARSON

We work with leading authors to develop the strongest learning experiences, bringing cutting-edge thinking and best learning practice to a global market. We craft our print and digital resources to do more to help learners not only understand their content, but to see it in action and apply what they learn, whether studying or at work.

Pearson is the world's leading learning company. Our portfolio includes Penguin, Dorling Kindersley, the Financial Times and our educational business, Pearson International. We are also a leading provider of electronic learning programmes and of test development, processing and scoring services to educational institutions, corporations and professional bodies around the world.

We enable our customers to access a wide and expanding range of market-leading content from world-renowned authors and develop their own tailor-made book. You choose the content that meets your needs and Pearson produces a high-quality printed book.

Every day our work helps learning flourish, and wherever learning flourishes, so do people.

To learn more please visit us at: www.pearsoned.co.uk/personalised

IBO Financial Management & Currency Risk

Compiled from:

Cost Accounting: A Managerial Emphasis
Fourteenth Edition
Charles T. Horngren, Srikant M. Datar & Madhav V. Rajan

Fundamentals of Multinational Finance
Fourth Edition
Michael H. Moffett, Arthur I. Stonehill & David K. Eiteman

PEARSON

Harlow, England • London • New York • Boston • San Francisco • Toronto • Sydney • Auckland • Singapore • Hong Kong
Tokyo • Seoul • Taipei • New Delhi • Cape Town • Sao Paulo • Mexico City • Madrid • Amsterdam • Munich • Paris • Milan

Pearson Education Limited
Edinburgh Gate
Harlow
Essex CM20 2JE

And associated companies throughout the world

Visit us on the World Wide Web at:
www.pearson.com/uk

© Pearson Education Limited 2014

Compiled from:

Cost Accounting: A Managerial Emphasis
Fourteenth Edition
Charles T. Horngren, Srikant M. Datar & Madhav V. Rajan
ISBN 978 0 273 75387 2
© Pearson Education Limited 2012

Fundamentals of Multinational Finance
Fourth Edition
Michael H. Moffett, Arthur I. Stonehill & David K. Eiteman
ISBN 978 0 13282 991 5
© Pearson Education Limited 2011

All rights reserved. No part of this publication may be reproduced, stored in a retrieval system, or transmitted in any form or by any means, electronic, mechanical, photocopying, recording or otherwise, without either the prior written permission of the publisher or a licence permitting restricted copying in the United Kingdom issued by the Licensing Agency Ltd, Saffron House, 6–10 Kirby Street, London EC1N 8TS.

ISBN 978 1 78365 944 9

Contents

Activity-Based Costing and Activity-Based Management   02
Chapter 5 in *Cost Accounting: A Managerial Emphasis* Fourteenth Edition
Charles T. Horngren, Srikant M. Datar & Madhav V. Rajan

Strategy, Balanced Scorecard, and Strategic Profitability Analysis   46
Chapter 13 in *Cost Accounting: A Managerial Emphasis* Fourteenth Edition
Charles T. Horngren, Srikant M. Datar & Madhav V. Rajan

Management Control Systems, Transfer Pricing, and Multinational Considerations   82
Chapter 22 in *Cost Accounting: A Managerial Emphasis* Fourteenth Edition
Charles T. Horngren, Srikant M. Datar & Madhav V. Rajan

Performance Measurement, Compensation, and Multinational Considerations   114
Chapter 23 in *Cost Accounting: A Managerial Emphasis* Fourteenth Edition
Charles T. Horngren, Srikant M. Datar & Madhav V. Rajan

Foreign Exchange Theory and Markets   148
Chapter 6 in *Fundamentals of Multinational Finance* Fourth Edition
Michael H. Moffett, Arthur I. Stonehill & David K. Eiteman

International Parity Conditions   175
Chapter 7 in *Fundamentals of Multinational Finance* Fourth Edition
Michael H. Moffett, Arthur I. Stonehill & David K. Eiteman

Foreign Currency Derivatives and Swaps   206
Chapter 8 in *Fundamentals of Multinational Finance* Fourth Edition
Michael H. Moffett, Arthur I. Stonehill & David K. Eiteman

Foreign Exchange Rate Determination and Forecasting   236
Chapter 9 in *Fundamentals of Multinational Finance* Fourth Edition
Michael H. Moffett, Arthur I. Stonehill & David K. Eiteman

Transaction and Translation Exposure 265
Chapter 10 in *Fundamentals of Multinational Finance* Fourth Edition
Michael H. Moffett, Arthur I. Stonehill & David K. Eiteman

Operating Exposure 301
Chapter 11 in *Fundamentals of Multinational Finance* Fourth Edition
Michael H. Moffett, Arthur I. Stonehill & David K. Eiteman

IBO Financial Management & Currency Risk

5 Activity-Based Costing and Activity-Based Management

Learning Objectives

1. Explain how broad averaging undercosts and overcosts products or services

2. Present three guidelines for refining a costing system

3. Distinguish between simple and activity-based costing systems

4. Describe a four-part cost hierarchy

5. Cost products or services using activity-based costing

6. Evaluate the costs and benefits of implementing activity-based costing systems

7. Explain how activity-based costing systems are used in activity-based management

8. Compare activity-based costing systems and department costing systems

A good mystery never fails to capture the imagination.

Money is stolen or lost, property disappears, or someone meets with foul play. On the surface, what appears unremarkable to the untrained eye can turn out to be quite a revelation once the facts and details are uncovered. Getting to the bottom of the case, understanding what happened and why, and taking action can make the difference between a solved case and an unsolved one. Business and organizations are much the same. Their costing systems are often mysteries with unresolved questions: Why are we bleeding red ink? Are we pricing our products accurately? Activity-based costing can help unravel the mystery and result in improved operations, as LG Electronics discovers in the following article.

LG Electronics Reduces Costs and Inefficiencies Through Activity-Based Costing[1]

LG Electronics is one of the world's largest manufacturers of flat-screen televisions and mobile phones. In 2009, the Seoul, South Korea-based company sold 16 million liquid crystal display televisions and 117 million mobile phones worldwide.

To make so many electronic devices, LG Electronics spends nearly $40 billion annually on the procurement of semiconductors, metals, connectors, and other materials. Costs for many of these components have soared in recent years. Until 2008, however, LG Electronics did not have a centralized procurement system to leverage its scale and to control supply costs. Instead, the company had a decentralized system riddled with wasteful spending and inefficiencies.

To respond to these challenges, LG Electronics hired its first chief procurement officer who turned to activity-based costing ("ABC") for answers. ABC analysis of the company's procurement system revealed that most company resources were applied to administrative and not strategic tasks. Furthermore, the administrative tasks were done manually and at a very high cost.

The ABC analysis led LG Electronics to change many of its procurement practices and processes, improve efficiency and focus

---

[1] *Sources:* Carbone, James. 2009. LG Electronics centralizes purchasing to save. *Purchasing*, April. http://www.purchasing.com/article/217108-LG_Electronics_centralizes_purchasing_to_save.php; Linton's goals. 2009. Supply Management, May 12. http://www.supplymanagement.com/analysis/features/2009/lintons-goals/; Yoou-chul, Kim. 2009. CPO expects to save $1 billion in procurement. *The Korea Times*, April 1. http://www.koreatimes.co.kr/www/news/biz/2009/04/123_42360.html

on the highest-value tasks such as managing costs of commodity products and negotiating with suppliers. Furthermore, the company developed a global procurement strategy for its televisions, mobile phones, computers, and home theatre systems by implementing competitive bidding among suppliers, standardizing parts across product lines, and developing additional buying capacity in China.

The results so far have been staggering. In 2008 alone, LG Electronics reduced its materials costs by 16%, and expects to further reduce costs by $5 billion by the end of 2011.

Most companies—such as Dell, Oracle, JP Morgan Chase, and Honda—offer more than one product (or service). Dell Computer, for example, produces desktops, laptops, and servers. The three basic activities for manufacturing computers are (a) designing computers, (b) ordering component parts, and (c) assembly. The different products, however, require different quantities of the three activities. For example, a server has a more complex design, many more parts, and a more complex assembly than a desktop.

To measure the cost of producing each product, Dell separately tracks activity costs for each product. In this chapter, we describe activity-based costing systems and how they help companies make better decisions about pricing and product mix. And, just as in the case of LG Electronics, we show how ABC systems assist in cost management decisions by improving product designs, processes, and efficiency.

Broad Averaging and Its Consequences

Historically, companies (such as television and automobile manufacturers) produced a limited variety of products. Indirect (or overhead) costs were a relatively small percentage of total costs. Using simple costing systems to allocate costs broadly was easy, inexpensive, and reasonably accurate. However, as product diversity and indirect costs have increased, broad averaging has resulted in greater inaccuracy of product costs. For example, the use of a single, plant-wide manufacturing overhead rate to allocate costs to products often produces unreliable cost data. The term *peanut-butter costing* (yes, that's what it's called) describes a particular costing approach that uses broad averages for assigning (or spreading, as in spreading peanut butter) the cost of resources uniformly to cost

Learning Objective 1

Explain how broad averaging undercosts and overcosts products or services

... this problem arises when reported costs of products do not equal their actual costs

objects (such as products or services) when the individual products or services, may in fact, use those resources in nonuniform ways.

Undercosting and Overcosting

The following example illustrates how averaging can result in inaccurate and misleading cost data. Consider the cost of a restaurant bill for four colleagues who meet monthly to discuss business developments. Each diner orders separate entrees, desserts, and drinks. The restaurant bill for the most recent meeting is as follows:

	Emma	James	Jessica	Matthew	Total	Average
Entree	$11	$20	$15	$14	$ 60	$15
Dessert	0	8	4	4	16	4
Drinks	4	14	8	6	32	8
Total	$15	$42	$27	$24	$108	$27

If the $108 total restaurant bill is divided evenly, $27 is the average cost per diner. This cost-averaging approach treats each diner the same. Emma would probably object to paying $27 because her actual cost is only $15; she ordered the lowest-cost entree, had no dessert, and had the lowest-cost drink. When costs are averaged across all four diners, both Emma and Matthew are overcosted, James is undercosted, and Jessica is (by coincidence) accurately costed.

Broad averaging can lead to undercosting or overcosting of products or services:

- **Product undercosting**—a product consumes a high level of resources but is reported to have a low cost per unit (James's dinner).
- **Product overcosting**—a product consumes a low level of resources but is reported to have a high cost per unit (Emma's dinner).

What are the strategic consequences of product undercosting and overcosting? Think of a company that uses cost information about its products to guide pricing decisions. Undercosted products will be underpriced and may even lead to sales that actually result in losses—sales bring in less revenue than the cost of resources they use. Overcosted products lead to overpricing, causing these products to lose market share to competitors producing similar products. Worse still, product undercosting and overcosting causes managers to focus on the wrong products, drawing attention to overcosted products whose costs may in fact be perfectly reasonable and ignoring undercosted products that in fact consume large amounts of resources.

Product-Cost Cross-Subsidization

Product-cost cross-subsidization means that if a company undercosts one of its products, it will overcost at least one of its other products. Similarly, if a company overcosts one of its products, it will undercost at least one of its other products. Product-cost cross-subsidization is very common in situations in which a cost is uniformly spread—meaning it is broadly averaged—across multiple products without recognizing the amount of resources consumed by each product.

In the restaurant-bill example, the amount of cost cross-subsidization of each diner can be readily computed *because all cost items can be traced as direct costs to each diner.* If all diners pay $27, Emma is paying $12 more than her actual cost of $15. She is cross-subsidizing James who is paying $15 less than his actual cost of $42. Calculating the amount of cost cross-subsidization takes more work when there are indirect costs to be considered. Why? Because when the resources represented by indirect costs are used by two or more diners, we need to find a way to allocate costs to each diner. Consider, for example, a $40 bottle of wine whose cost is shared equally. Each diner would pay $10 ($40 ÷ 4). Suppose Matthew drinks 2 glasses of wine while Emma, James, and Jessica drink one glass each for a total of 5 glasses. Allocating the cost of the bottle of wine on the basis of the glasses of wine that each diner drinks would result in Matthew paying $16 ($40 × 2/5) and each of the others $8 ($40 × 1/5). In this case, by sharing the cost equally, Emma, James, and Jessica are each paying $2 ($10 − $8) more and are cross-subsidizing Matthew who is paying $6 ($16 − $10) less for the wine he consumes.

To see the effects of broad averaging on direct and indirect costs, we consider Plastim Corporation's costing system.

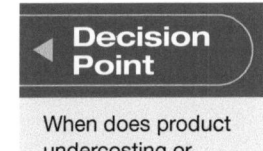

Decision Point

When does product undercosting or overcosting occur?

Simple Costing System at Plastim Corporation

Plastim Corporation manufactures lenses for the rear taillights of automobiles. A lens, made from black, red, orange, or white plastic, is the part of the lamp visible on the automobile's exterior. Lenses are made by injecting molten plastic into a mold to give the lamp its desired shape. The mold is cooled to allow the molten plastic to solidify, and the lens is removed.

Under its contract with Giovanni Motors, a major automobile manufacturer, Plastim makes two types of lenses: a complex lens, CL5, and a simple lens, S3. The complex lens is a large lens with special features, such as multicolor molding (when more than one color is injected into the mold) and a complex shape that wraps around the corner of the car. Manufacturing CL5 lenses is more complex because various parts in the mold must align and fit precisely. The S3 lens is simpler to make because it has a single color and few special features.

Design, Manufacturing, and Distribution Processes

The sequence of steps to design, produce, and distribute lenses, whether simple or complex, is as follows:

- **Design products and processes.** Each year Giovanni Motors specifies some modifications to the simple and complex lenses. Plastim's design department designs the molds from which the lenses will be made and specifies the processes needed (that is, details of the manufacturing operations).
- **Manufacture lenses.** The lenses are molded, finished, cleaned, and inspected.
- **Distribute lenses.** Finished lenses are packed and sent to Giovanni Motors.

Plastim is operating at capacity and incurs very low marketing costs. Because of its high-quality products, Plastim has minimal customer-service costs. Plastim's business environment is very competitive with respect to simple lenses. At a recent meeting, Giovanni's purchasing manager indicated that a new supplier, Bandix, which makes only simple lenses, is offering to supply the S3 lens to Giovanni at a price of $53, well below the $63 price that Plastim is currently projecting and budgeting for 2011. Unless Plastim can lower its selling price, it will lose the Giovanni business for the simple lens for the upcoming model year. Fortunately, the same competitive pressures do not exist for the complex lens, which Plastim currently sells to Giovanni at $137 per lens.

Plastim's management has two primary options:

- Plastim can give up the Giovanni business in simple lenses if selling simple lenses is unprofitable. Bandix makes only simple lenses and perhaps, therefore, uses simpler technology and processes than Plastim. The simpler operations may give Bandix a cost advantage that Plastim cannot match. If so, it is better for Plastim to not supply the S3 lens to Giovanni.
- Plastim can reduce the price of the simple lens and either accept a lower margin or aggressively seek to reduce costs.

To make these long-run strategic decisions, management needs to first understand the costs to design, make, and distribute the S3 and CL5 lenses.

While Bandix makes only simple lenses and can fairly accurately calculate the cost of a lens by dividing total costs by units produced, Plastim's costing environment is more challenging. The processes to make both simple and complex lenses are more complicated than the processes required to make only simple lenses. Plastim needs to find a way to allocate costs to each type of lens.

In computing costs, Plastim assigns both variable costs and costs that are fixed in the short run to the S3 and CL5 lenses. Managers cost products and services to guide long-run strategic decisions (for example, what mix of products and services to produce and sell and what prices to charge for them). In the long-run, managers want revenues to exceed total costs (variable and fixed) to design, make, and distribute the lenses.

To guide their pricing and cost-management decisions, Plastim's managers assign all costs, both manufacturing and nonmanufacturing, to the S3 and CL5 lenses. If managers had wanted to calculate the cost of inventory, Plastim's management accountants would have assigned only manufacturing costs to the lenses, as required by generally accepted accounting principles. Surveys of company practice across the globe overwhelmingly indicate that the vast majority of companies use costing systems not just for inventory costing but also for strategic purposes such as pricing and product-mix decisions and decisions about cost reduction, process improvement, design, and planning and budgeting. As a result, even merchandising-sector companies (for whom inventory costing is straightforward) and service-sector companies (who have no inventory) expend considerable resources in designing and operating their costing systems. In this chapter, we take this more strategic focus and allocate costs in all functions of the value chain to the S3 and CL5 lenses.

Simple Costing System Using a Single Indirect-Cost Pool

Plastim has historically had a simple costing system that allocates indirect costs using a single indirect-cost rate, the type of system described in Chapter 4. We calculate budgeted costs for each type of lens in 2011 using Plastim's simple costing system and later contrast it with activity-based costing. (Note that instead of jobs, as in Chapter 4, we now have products as the cost objects.) Exhibit 5-1 shows an overview of Plastim's simple costing system. Use this exhibit as a guide as you study the following steps, each of which is marked in Exhibit 5-1.

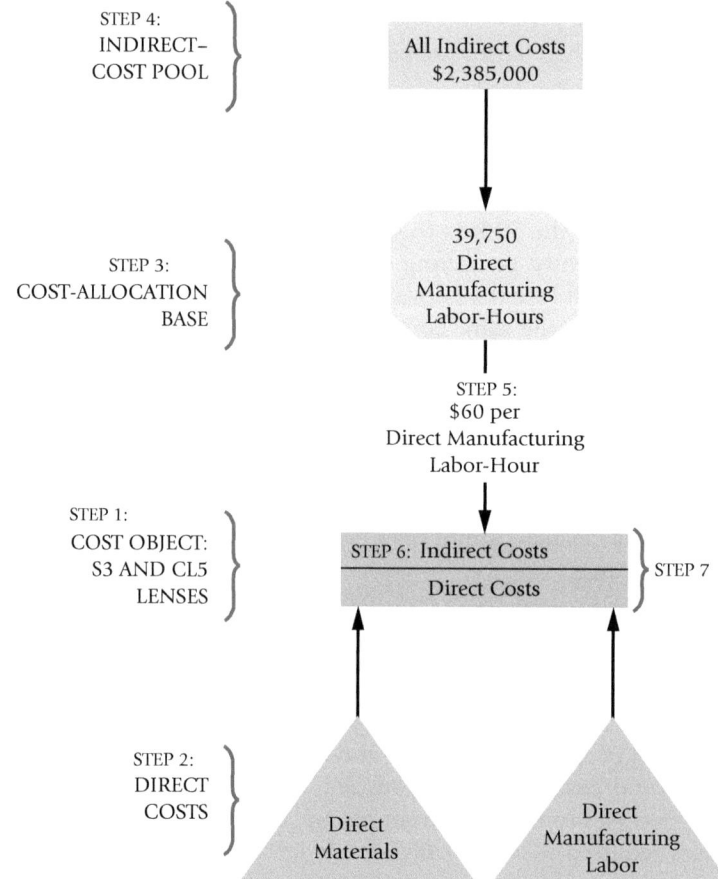

Exhibit 5-1

Overview of Plastim's Simple Costing System

Step 1: **Identify the Products That Are the Chosen Cost Objects.** The cost objects are the 60,000 simple S3 lenses and the 15,000 complex CL5 lenses that Plastim will produce in 2011. Plastim's goal is to first calculate the total costs and then the unit cost of designing, manufacturing, and distributing these lenses.

Step 2: **Identify the Direct Costs of the Products.** Plastim identifies the direct costs—direct materials and direct manufacturing labor—of the lenses. Exhibit 5-2 shows the direct and indirect costs for the S3 and the CL5 lenses using the simple costing system. The direct cost calculations appear on lines 5, 6, and 7 of Exhibit 5-2. Plastim classifies all other costs as indirect costs.

Step 3: **Select the Cost-Allocation Bases to Use for Allocating Indirect (or Overhead) Costs to the Products.** A majority of the indirect costs consist of salaries paid to supervisors, engineers, manufacturing support, and maintenance staff, all supporting direct manufacturing labor. Plastim uses direct manufacturing labor-hours as the only allocation base to allocate all manufacturing and nonmanufacturing indirect costs to S3 and CL5. In 2011, Plastim plans to use 39,750 direct manufacturing labor-hours.

Step 4: **Identify the Indirect Costs Associated with Each Cost-Allocation Base.** Because Plastim uses only a single cost-allocation base, Plastim groups all budgeted indirect costs of $2,385,000 for 2011 into a single overhead cost pool.

Step 5: **Compute the Rate per Unit of Each Cost-Allocation Base.**

$$\text{Budgeted indirect-cost rate} = \frac{\text{Budgeted total costs in indirect-cost pool}}{\text{Budgeted total quantity of cost-allocation base}}$$

$$= \frac{\$2,385,000}{39,750 \text{ direct manufacturing labor-hours}}$$

$$= \$60 \text{ per direct manufacturing labor-hour}$$

Step 6: **Compute the Indirect Costs Allocated to the Products.** Plastim expects to use 30,000 total direct manufacturing labor-hours to make the 60,000 S3 lenses and 9,750 total direct manufacturing labor-hours to make the 15,000 CL5 lenses. Exhibit 5-2 shows indirect costs of $1,800,000 ($60 per direct manufacturing labor-hour × 30,000 direct manufacturing labor-hours) allocated to the simple lens and $585,000 ($60 per direct manufacturing labor-hour × 9,750 direct manufacturing labor-hours) allocated to the complex lens.

Step 7: **Compute the Total Cost of the Products by Adding All Direct and Indirect Costs Assigned to the Products.** Exhibit 5-2 presents the product costs for the simple and complex lenses. The direct costs are calculated in Step 2 and the indirect costs in Step 6. Be sure you see the parallel between the simple costing system overview diagram (Exhibit 5-1)

Exhibit 5-2 Plastim's Product Costs Using the Simple Costing System

	A	B	C	D	E	F	G
1		\multicolumn{2}{c}{60,000}		\multicolumn{2}{c}{15,000}	
2		Simple Lenses (S3)			Complex Lenses (CL5)		
3		Total	per Unit		Total	per Unit	Total
4		(1)	(2) = (1) ÷ 60,000		(3)	(4) = (3) ÷ 15,000	(5) = (1) + (3)
5	Direct materials	$1,125,000	$18.75		$ 675,000	$45.00	$1,800,000
6	Direct manufacturing labor	600,000	10.00		195,000	13.00	795,000
7	Total direct costs (Step 2)	1,725,000	28.75		870,000	58.00	2,595,000
8	Indirect costs allocated (Step 6)	1,800,000	30.00		585,000	39.00	2,385,000
9	Total costs (Step 7)	$3,525,000	$58.75		$1,455,000	$97.00	$4,980,000
10							

and the costs calculated in Step 7. Exhibit 5-1 shows two direct-cost categories and one indirect-cost category. Hence, the budgeted cost of each type of lens in Step 7 (Exhibit 5-2) has three line items: two for direct costs and one for allocated indirect costs. The budgeted cost per S3 lens is $58.75, well above the $53 selling price quoted by Bandix. The budgeted cost per CL5 lens is $97.

Applying the Five-Step Decision-Making Process at Plastim

To decide how it should respond to the threat that Bandix poses to its S3 lens business, Plastim's management works through the five-step decision-making process introduced in Chapter 1.

Step 1: Identify the problem and uncertainties. The problem is clear: If Plastim wants to retain the Giovanni business for S3 lenses and make a profit, it must find a way to reduce the price and costs of the S3 lens. The two major uncertainties Plastim faces are (1) whether Plastim's technology and processes for the S3 lens are competitive with Bandix's and (2) whether the S3 lens is overcosted by the simple costing system.

Step 2: Obtain information. Management asks a team of its design and process engineers to analyze and evaluate the design, manufacturing, and distribution operations for the S3 lens. The team is very confident that the technology and processes for the S3 lens are not inferior to those of Bandix and other competitors because Plastim has many years of experience in manufacturing and distributing the S3 with a history and culture of continuous process improvements. If anything, the team is less certain about Plastim's capabilities in manufacturing and distributing complex lenses, because it only recently started making this type of lens. Given these doubts, management is happy that Giovanni Motors considers the price of the CL5 lens to be competitive. It is somewhat of a puzzle, though, how at the currently budgeted prices, Plastim is expected to earn a very large profit margin percentage (operating income ÷ revenues) on the CL5 lenses and a small profit margin on the S3 lenses:

	60,000 Simple Lenses (S3)		15,000 Complex Lenses (CL5)		
	Total (1)	per Unit (2) = (1) ÷ 60,000	Total (3)	per Unit (4) = (3) ÷ 15,000	Total (5) = (1) + (3)
Revenues	$3,780,000	$63.00	$2,055,000	$137.00	$5,835,000
Total costs	3,525,000	58.75	1,455,000	97.00	4,980,000
Operating income	$ 255,000	$ 4.25	$ 600,000	$ 40.00	$ 855,000
Profit margin percentage		6.75%		29.20%	

As it continues to gather information, Plastim's management begins to ponder why the profit margins (and process) are under so much pressure for the S3 lens, where the company has strong capabilities, but high on the newer, less-established CL5 lens. Plastim is not deliberately charging a low price for S3, so management starts to believe that perhaps the problem lies with its costing system. Plastim's simple costing system may be overcosting the simple S3 lens (assigning too much cost to it) and undercosting the complex CL5 lens (assigning too little cost to it).

Step 3: Make predictions about the future. Plastim's key challenge is to get a better estimate of what it will cost to design, make, and distribute the S3 and CL5 lenses. Management is fairly confident about the direct material and direct manufacturing labor costs of each lens because these costs are easily traced to the lenses. But management is quite concerned about how accurately the simple costing system measures the indirect resources used by each type of lens. It believes it can do much better.

At the same time, management wants to ensure that no biases enter its thinking. In particular, it wants to be careful that the desire to be competitive on the S3 lens should not lead to assumptions that bias in favor of lowering costs of the S3 lens.

Step 4: **Make decisions by choosing among alternatives.** On the basis of predicted costs, and taking into account how Bandix might respond, Plastim's managers must decide whether they should bid for Giovanni Motors' S3 lens business and if they do bid, what price they should offer.

Step 5: **Implement the decision, evaluate performance, and learn.** If Plastim bids and wins Giovanni's S3 lens business, it must compare actual costs, as it makes and ships S3 lenses, to predicted costs and learn why actual costs deviate from predicted costs. Such evaluation and learning form the basis for future improvements.

The next few sections focus on Steps 3, 4, and 5—how Plastim improves the allocation of indirect costs to the S3 and CL5 lenses, how it uses these predictions to bid for the S3 lens business, and how it makes product design and process improvements.

Refining a Costing System

A **refined costing system** reduces the use of broad averages for assigning the cost of resources to cost objects (such as jobs, products, and services) and provides better measurement of the costs of indirect resources used by different cost objects—no matter how differently various cost objects use indirect resources.

Reasons for Refining a Costing System

There are three principal reasons that have accelerated the demand for such refinements.

1. **Increase in product diversity.** The growing demand for customized products has led companies to increase the variety of products and services they offer. Kanthal, the Swedish manufacturer of heating elements, for example, produces more than 10,000 different types of electrical heating wires and thermostats. Banks, such as the Cooperative Bank in the United Kingdom, offer many different types of accounts and services: special passbook accounts, ATMs, credit cards, and electronic banking. These products differ in the demands they place on the resources needed to produce them, because of differences in volume, process, and complexity. The use of broad averages is likely to lead to distorted and inaccurate cost information.

2. **Increase in indirect costs.** The use of product and process technology such as computer-integrated manufacturing (CIM) and flexible manufacturing systems (FMS), has led to an increase in indirect costs and a decrease in direct costs, particularly direct manufacturing labor costs. In CIM and FMS, computers on the manufacturing floor give instructions to set up and run equipment quickly and automatically. The computers accurately measure hundreds of production parameters and directly control the manufacturing processes to achieve high-quality output. Managing more complex technology and producing very diverse products also requires committing an increasing amount of resources for various support functions, such as production scheduling, product and process design, and engineering. Because direct manufacturing labor is not a cost driver of these costs, allocating indirect costs on the basis of direct manufacturing labor (which was the common practice) does not accurately measure how resources are being used by different products.

3. **Competition in product markets.** As markets have become more competitive, managers have felt the need to obtain more accurate cost information to help them make important strategic decisions, such as how to price products and which products to sell. Making correct pricing and product mix decisions is critical in competitive markets because competitors quickly capitalize on a company's mistakes.

Whereas the preceding factors point to reasons for the increase in *demand* for refined cost systems, *advances in information technology* have enabled companies to implement these refinements. Costing system refinements require more data gathering and more analysis, and improvements in information technology have drastically reduced the costs to gather, validate, store, and analyze vast quantities of data.

> **Learning Objective 2**
>
> Present three guidelines for refining a costing system
>
> ... classify more costs as direct costs, expand the number of indirect-cost pools, and identify cost drivers

Guidelines for Refining a Costing System

There are three main guidelines for refining a costing system. In the following sections, we delve more deeply into each in the context of the Plastim example.

1. **Direct-cost tracing.** Identify as many direct costs as is economically feasible. This guideline aims to reduce the amount of costs classified as indirect, thereby minimizing the extent to which costs have to be allocated, rather than traced.

2. **Indirect-cost pools.** Expand the number of indirect-cost pools until each pool is more homogeneous. All costs in a *homogeneous cost pool* have the same or a similar cause-and-effect (or benefits-received) relationship with a single cost driver that is used as the cost-allocation base. Consider, for example, a single indirect-cost pool containing both indirect machining costs and indirect distribution costs that are allocated to products using machine-hours. This pool is not homogeneous because machine-hours are a cost driver of machining costs but not of distribution costs, which has a different cost driver, number of shipments. If, instead, machining costs and distribution costs are separated into two indirect-cost pools (with machine-hours as the cost-allocation base for the machining cost pool and number of shipments as the cost-allocation base for the distribution cost pool), each indirect-cost pool would become homogeneous.

3. **Cost-allocation bases.** As we describe later in the chapter, whenever possible, use the cost driver (the cause of indirect costs) as the cost-allocation base for each homogenous indirect-cost pool (the effect).

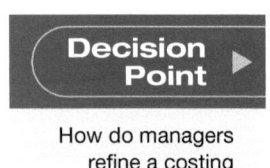

Decision Point

How do managers refine a costing system?

Learning Objective 3

Distinguish between simple and activity-based costing systems

. . . unlike simple systems, ABC systems calculate costs of individual activities to cost products

Activity-Based Costing Systems

One of the best tools for refining a costing system is activity-based costing. **Activity-based costing (ABC)** refines a costing system by identifying individual activities as the fundamental cost objects. An **activity** is an event, task, or unit of work with a specified purpose—for example, designing products, setting up machines, operating machines, and distributing products. More informally, activities are verbs; they are things that a firm does. To help make strategic decisions, ABC systems identify activities in all functions of the value chain, calculate costs of individual activities, and assign costs to cost objects such as products and services on the basis of the mix of activities needed to produce each product or service.[2]

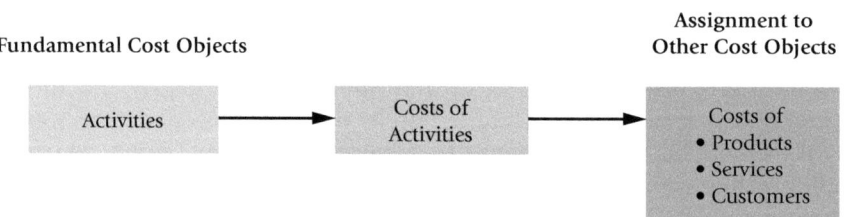

Plastim's ABC System

After reviewing its simple costing system and the potential miscosting of product costs, Plastim decides to implement an ABC system. Direct material costs and direct manufacturing labor costs can be traced to products easily, so the ABC system focuses on refining the assignment of indirect costs to departments, processes, products, or other cost objects. Plastim's ABC system identifies various activities that help explain why Plastim incurs the costs it currently classifies as indirect in its simple costing system. In other words, it breaks up the current indirect cost pool into finer pools of costs related to various activities. To identify these activities, Plastim organizes a team comprised of managers from design, manufacturing, distribution, accounting, and administration.

---

[2] For more details on ABC systems, see R. Cooper and R. S. Kaplan, *The Design of Cost Management Systems* (Upper Saddle River, NJ: Prentice Hall, 1999); G. Cokins, *Activity-Based Cost Management: An Executive's Guide* (Hoboken, NJ: John Wiley & Sons, 2001); and R. S. Kaplan and S. Anderson, *Time-Driven Activity-Based Costing: A Simpler and More Powerful Path to Higher Profits* (Boston: Harvard Business School Press, 2007).

Defining activities is not a simple matter. The team evaluates hundreds of tasks performed at Plastim before choosing the activities that form the basis of its ABC system. For example, it decides if maintenance of molding machines, operations of molding machines, and process control should each be regarded as a separate activity or should be combined into a single activity. An activity-based costing system with many activities becomes overly detailed and unwieldy to operate. An activity-based costing system with too few activities may not be refined enough to measure cause-and-effect relationships between cost drivers and various indirect costs. Plastim's team focuses on activities that account for a sizable fraction of indirect costs and combines activities that have the same cost driver into a single activity. For example, the team decides to combine maintenance of molding machines, operations of molding machines, and process control into a single activity—molding machine operations—because all these activities have the same cost driver: molding machine-hours.

The team identifies the following seven activities by developing a flowchart of all the steps and processes needed to design, manufacture, and distribute S3 and CL5 lenses.

a. Design products and processes
b. Set up molding machines to ensure that the molds are properly held in place and parts are properly aligned before manufacturing starts
c. Operate molding machines to manufacture lenses
d. Clean and maintain the molds after lenses are manufactured
e. Prepare batches of finished lenses for shipment
f. Distribute lenses to customers
g. Administer and manage all processes at Plastim

These activity descriptions form the basis of the activity-based costing system—sometimes called an *activity list* or *activity dictionary*. Compiling the list of tasks, however, is only the first step in implementing activity-based costing systems. Plastim must also identify the cost of each activity and the related cost driver. To do so, Plastim uses the three guidelines for refining a costing system described on page 168.

1. **Direct-cost tracing.** Plastim's ABC system subdivides the single indirect cost pool into seven smaller cost pools related to the different activities. The costs in the cleaning and maintenance activity cost pool (item d) consist of salaries and wages paid to workers who clean the mold. These costs are direct costs, because they can be economically traced to a specific mold and lens.

2. **Indirect-cost pools.** The remaining six activity cost pools are indirect cost pools. Unlike the single indirect cost pool of Plastim's simple costing system, each of the activity-related cost pools is homogeneous. That is, each activity cost pool includes only those narrow and focused set of costs that have the same cost driver. For example, the distribution cost pool includes only those costs (such as wages of truck drivers) that, over time, increase as the cost driver of distribution costs, cubic feet of packages delivered, increases. In the simple costing system, all indirect costs were lumped together and the cost-allocation base, direct manufacturing labor-hours, was not a cost driver of the indirect costs.

    Determining costs of activity pools requires assigning and reassigning costs accumulated in support departments, such as human resources and information systems, to each of the activity cost pools on the basis of how various activities use support department resources. This is commonly referred to as *first-stage allocation*, a topic which we discuss in detail in Chapters 14 and 15. We focus here on the *second-stage allocation*, the allocation of costs of activity cost pools to products.

3. **Cost-allocation bases.** For each activity cost pool, the cost driver is used (whenever possible) as the cost-allocation base. To identify cost drivers, Plastim's managers consider various alternatives and use their knowledge of operations to choose among them. For example, Plastim's managers choose setup-hours rather than the number of setups as the cost driver of setup costs, because Plastim's managers believe that more complex setups take more time and are more costly. Over time, Plastim's managers can use data to test their beliefs. (Chapter 10 discusses several methods to estimate the relationship between a cost driver and costs.)

The logic of ABC systems is twofold. First, structuring activity cost pools more finely with cost drivers for each activity cost pool as the cost-allocation base leads to more accurate costing of activities. Second, allocating these costs to products by measuring the cost-allocation bases of different activities used by different products leads to more accurate product costs. We illustrate this logic by focusing on the setup activity at Plastim.

Setting up molding machines frequently entails trial runs, fine-tuning, and adjustments. Improper setups cause quality problems such as scratches on the surface of the lens. The resources needed for each setup depend on the complexity of the manufacturing operation. Complex lenses require more setup resources (setup-hours) per setup than simple lenses. Furthermore, complex lenses can be produced only in small batches because the molds for complex lenses need to be cleaned more often than molds for simple lenses. Thus, relative to simple lenses, complex lenses not only use more setup-hours per setup, but they also require more frequent setups.

Setup data for the simple S3 lens and the complex CL5 lens are as follows:

		Simple S3 Lens	Complex CL5 Lens	Total
1	Quantity of lenses produced	60,000	15,000	
2	Number of lenses produced per batch	240	50	
3 = (1) ÷ (2)	Number of batches	250	300	
4	Setup time per batch	2 hours	5 hours	
5 = (3) × (4)	Total setup-hours	500 hours	1,500 hours	2,000 hours

Of the $2,385,000 in the total indirect-cost pool, Plastim identifies the total costs of setups (consisting mainly of depreciation on setup equipment and allocated costs of process engineers, quality engineers, and supervisors) to be $300,000. Recall that in its simple costing system, Plastim uses direct manufacturing labor-hours to allocate all indirect costs to products. The following table compares how setup costs allocated to simple and complex lenses will be different if Plastim allocates setup costs to lenses based on setup-hours rather than direct manufacturing labor-hours. Of the $60 total rate per direct manufacturing labor-hour (p. 165), the setup cost per direct manufacturing labor-hour amounts to $7.54717 ($300,000 ÷ 39,750 total direct manufacturing labor-hours). The setup cost per setup-hour equals $150 ($300,000 ÷ 2,000 total setup-hours).

	Simple S3 Lens	Complex CL5 Lens	Total
Setup cost allocated using direct manufacturing labor-hours:			
$7.54717 × 30,000; $7.54717 × 9,750	$226,415	$ 73,585	$300,000
Setup cost allocated using setup-hours:			
$150 × 500; $150 × 1,500	$ 75,000	$225,000	$300,000

As we have already discussed when presenting guidelines 2 and 3, setup-hours, not direct manufacturing labor-hours, are the cost driver of setup costs.. The CL5 lens uses substantially more setup-hours than the S3 lens (1,500 hours ÷ 2,000 hours = 75% of the total setup-hours) because the CL5 requires a greater number of setups (batches) and each setup is more challenging and requires more setup-hours.

The ABC system therefore allocates substantially more setup costs to CL5 than to S3. When direct manufacturing labor-hours rather than setup-hours are used to allocate setup costs in the simple costing system, it is the S3 lens that is allocated a very large share of the setup costs because the S3 lens uses a larger proportion of direct manufacturing labor-hours (30,000 ÷ 39,750 = 75.47%). As a result, the simple costing system overcosts the S3 lens with regard to setup costs.

Note that setup-hours are related to batches (or groups) of lenses made, not the number of individual lenses. Activity-based costing attempts to identify the most relevant cause-and-effect relationship for each activity pool, without restricting the cost driver to only units of output or variables related to units of output (such as direct manufacturing labor-hours). As our discussion of setups illustrates, limiting cost-allocation bases in this manner weakens the cause-and-effect relationship between the cost-allocation base and the costs in a cost pool.

Decision Point

What is the difference between the design of a simple costing system and an activity-based costing (ABC) system?

Cost Hierarchies

A **cost hierarchy** categorizes various activity cost pools on the basis of the different types of cost drivers, or cost-allocation bases, or different degrees of difficulty in determining cause-and-effect (or benefits-received) relationships. ABC systems commonly use a cost hierarchy with four levels—output unit-level costs, batch-level costs, product-sustaining costs, and facility-sustaining costs—to identify cost-allocation bases that are cost drivers of the activity cost pools.

Output unit-level costs are the costs of activities performed on each individual unit of a product or service. Machine operations costs (such as the cost of energy, machine depreciation, and repair) related to the activity of running the automated molding machines are output unit-level costs. They are output unit-level costs because, over time, the cost of this activity increases with additional units of output produced (or machine-hours used). Plastim's ABC system uses molding machine-hours—an output-unit level cost-allocation base—to allocate machine operations costs to products.

Batch-level costs are the costs of activities related to a group of units of a product or service rather than each individual unit of product or service. In the Plastim example, setup costs are batch-level costs because, over time, the cost of this setup activity increases with setup-hours needed to produce batches (groups) of lenses. As described in the table on page 170, the S3 lens requires 500 setup-hours (2 setup-hours per batch × 250 batches). The CL5 lens requires 1,500 setup-hours (5 setup-hours per batch × 300 batches). The total setup costs allocated to S3 and CL5 depend on the total setup-hours required by each type of lens, not on the number of units of S3 and CL5 produced. (Setup costs being a batch-level cost cannot be avoided by producing one less unit of S3 or CL5.) Plastim's ABC system uses setup-hours—a batch-level cost-allocation base—to allocate setup costs to products. Other examples of batch-level costs are material-handling and quality-inspection costs associated with batches (not the quantities) of products produced, and costs of placing purchase orders, receiving materials, and paying invoices related to the number of purchase orders placed rather than the quantity or value of materials purchased.

Product-sustaining costs (**service-sustaining costs**) are the costs of activities undertaken to support individual products or services regardless of the number of units or batches in which the units are produced. In the Plastim example, design costs are product-sustaining costs. Over time, design costs depend largely on the time designers spend on designing and modifying the product, the mold, and the process. These design costs are a function of the complexity of the mold, measured by the number of parts in the mold multiplied by the area (in square feet) over which the molten plastic must flow (12 parts × 2.5 square feet, or 30 parts-square feet for the S3 lens, and 14 parts × 5 square feet, or 70 parts-square feet for the CL5 lens). As a result, the total design costs allocated to S3 and CL5 depend on the complexity of the mold, regardless of the number of units or batches of production. Design costs cannot be avoided by producing fewer units or running fewer batches. Plastim's ABC system uses parts-square feet—a product-sustaining cost-allocation base—to allocate design costs to products. Other examples of product-sustaining costs are product research and development costs, costs of making engineering changes, and marketing costs to launch new products.

Facility-sustaining costs are the costs of activities that cannot be traced to individual products or services but that support the organization as a whole. In the Plastim example, the general administration costs (including top management compensation, rent, and building security) are facility-sustaining costs. It is usually difficult to find a good cause-and-effect relationship between these costs and the cost-allocation base. This lack of a cause-and-effect relationship causes some companies not to allocate these costs to products and instead to deduct them as a separate lump-sum amount from operating income. Other companies, such as Plastim, allocate facility-sustaining costs to products on some basis—for example, direct manufacturing labor-hours—because management believes all costs should be allocated to products. Allocating all costs to products or services becomes important when management wants to set selling prices on the basis of an amount of cost that includes all costs.

> **Learning Objective 4**
>
> Describe a four-part cost hierarchy
>
> ... a four-part cost hierarchy is used to categorize costs based on different types of cost drivers—for example, costs that vary with each unit of a product versus costs that vary with each batch of products

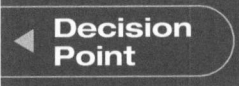

What is a cost hierarchy?

Learning Objective 5

Cost products or services using activity-based costing

... use cost rates for different activities to compute indirect costs of a product

Implementing Activity-Based Costing

Now that you understand the basic concepts of ABC, let's use it to refine Plastim's simple costing system, compare it to alternative costing systems, and examine what managers look for when deciding whether or not to develop ABC systems.

Implementing ABC at Plastim

In order to apply ABC to Plastim's costing system, we follow the seven-step approach to costing and the three guidelines for refining costing systems (increasing direct-cost tracing, creating homogeneous indirect-cost pools, and identifying cost-allocation bases that have cause-and-effect relationships with costs in the cost pool). Exhibit 5-3 shows an overview of Plastim's ABC system. Use this exhibit as a guide as you study the following steps, each of which is marked in Exhibit 5-3.

Step 1: Identify the Products That Are the Chosen Cost Objects. The cost objects are the 60,000 S3 and the 15,000 CL5 lenses that Plastim will produce in 2011. Plastim's goal is to first calculate the total costs and then the per-unit cost of designing, manufacturing, and distributing these lenses.

Step 2: Identify the Direct Costs of the Products. Plastim identifies as direct costs of the lenses: direct material costs, direct manufacturing labor costs, and mold cleaning and maintenance costs because these costs can be economically traced to a specific lens or mold.

Exhibit 5-5 shows the direct and indirect costs for the S3 and CL5 lenses using the ABC system. The direct costs calculations appear on lines 6, 7, 8, and 9 of Exhibit 5-5. Plastim classifies all other costs as indirect costs, as we will see in Exhibit 5-4.

Step 3: Select the Activities and Cost-Allocation Bases to Use for Allocating Indirect Costs to the Products. Following guidelines 2 and 3 for refining a costing system, Plastim identifies six activities—(a) design, (b) molding machine setups, (c) machine operations, (d) shipment setup, (e) distribution, and (f) administration—for allocating indirect costs to products. Exhibit 5-4, column 2, shows the cost hierarchy category, and column 4

Exhibit 5-3 Overview of Plastim's Activity-Based Costing System

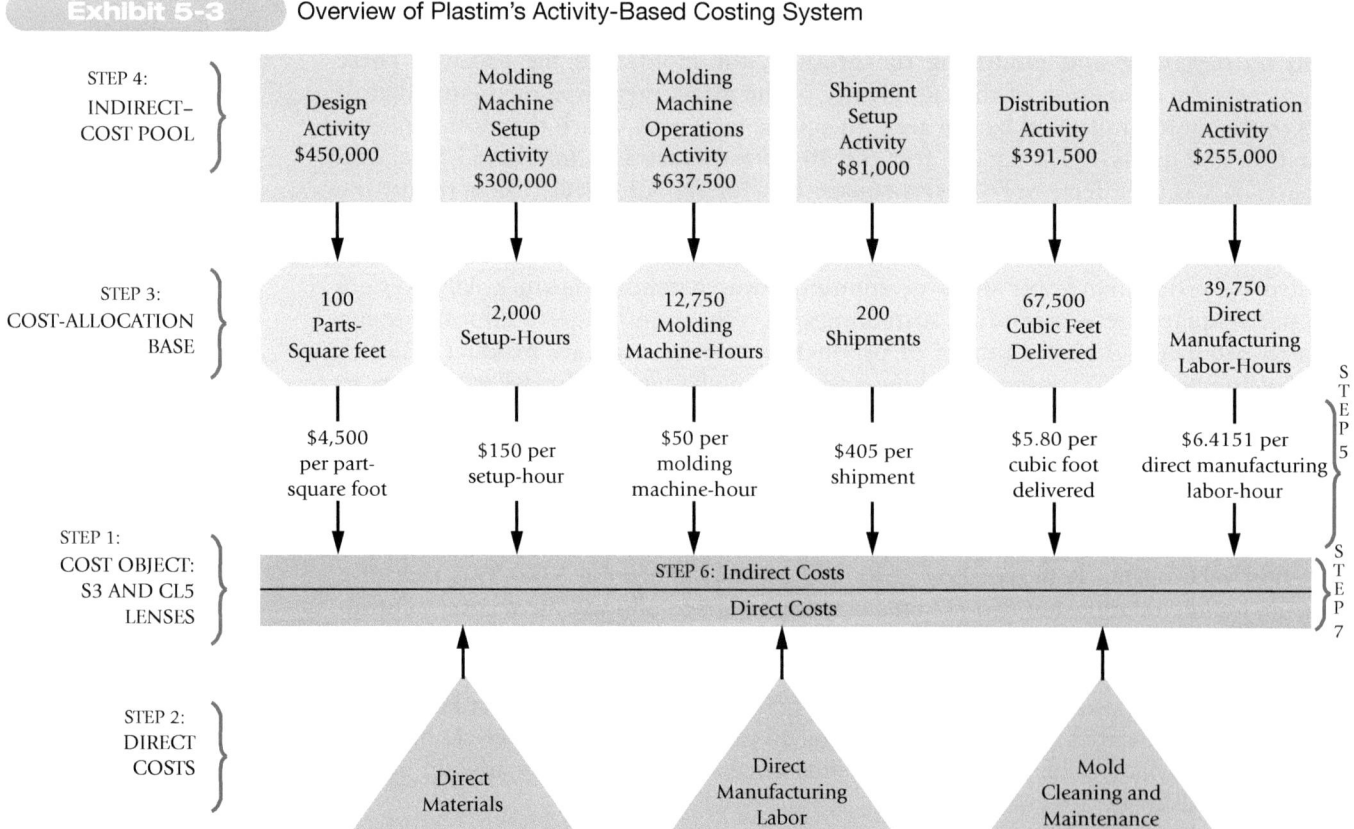

Exhibit 5-4 Activity-Cost Rates for Indirect-Cost Pools

	A	B	C	D	E	F	G	H
1			(Step 4)	(Step 3)		(Step 5)		
2	Activity	Cost Hierarchy Category	Total Budgeted Indirect Costs	Budgeted Quantity of Cost-Allocation Base		Budgeted Indirect Cost Rate		Cause-and-Effect Relationship Between Allocation Base and Activity Cost
3	(1)	(2)	(3)	(4)		(5) = (3) ÷ (4)		(6)
4	Design	Product-sustaining	$450,000	100	parts-square feet	$4,500	per part-square foot	Design Department indirect costs increase with more complex molds (more parts, larger surface area).
5	Setup molding machines	Batch-level	$300,000	2,000	setup-hours	$150	per setup-hour	Indirect setup costs increase with setup-hours.
6	Machine operations	Output unit-level	$637,500	12,750	molding machine-hours	$50	per molding machine-hour	Indirect costs of operating molding machines increases with molding machine-hours.
7	Shipment setup	Batch-level	$81,000	200	shipments	$405	per shipment	Shipping costs incurred to prepare batches for shipment increase with the number of shipments.
8	Distribution	Output-unit-level	$391,500	67,500	cubic feet delivered	$5.80	per cubic foot delivered	Distribution costs increase with the cubic feet of packages delivered.
9	Administration	Facility sustaining	$255,000	39,750	direct manuf. labor-hours	$6.4151	per direct manuf. labor-hour	The demand for administrative resources increases with direct manufacturing labor-hours.

shows the cost-allocation base and the budgeted quantity of the cost-allocation base for each activity described in column 1.

Identifying the cost-allocation bases defines the number of activity pools into which costs must be grouped in an ABC system. For example, rather than define the design activities of product design, process design, and prototyping as separate activities, Plastim defines these three activities together as a combined "design" activity and forms a homogeneous design cost pool. Why? Because the same cost driver, the complexity of the mold, drives costs of each design activity. A second consideration for choosing a cost-allocation base is the availability of reliable data and measures. For example, in its ABC system, Plastim measures mold complexity in terms of the number of parts in the mold and the surface area of the mold (parts-square feet). If these data are difficult to obtain or measure, Plastim may be forced to use some other measure of complexity, such as the amount of material flowing through the mold that may only be weakly related to the cost of the design activity.

Step 4: Identify the Indirect Costs Associated with Each Cost-Allocation Base. In this step, Plastim assigns budgeted indirect costs for 2011 to activities (see Exhibit 5-4, column 3), to the extent possible, on the basis of a cause-and-effect relationship between the cost-allocation base for an activity and the cost. For example, all costs that have a cause-and-effect relationship to cubic feet of packages moved are assigned to the distribution cost pool. Of course, the strength of the cause-and-effect relationship between the cost-allocation base and the cost of an activity varies across cost pools. For example, the cause-and-effect relationship between direct manufacturing labor-hours and administration activity costs is not as strong as the relationship between setup-hours and setup activity costs.

Some costs can be directly identified with a particular activity. For example, cost of materials used when designing products, salaries paid to design engineers, and depreciation of equipment used in the design department are directly identified with the design activity. Other costs need to be allocated across activities. For example, on the basis of interviews or time records, manufacturing engineers and supervisors estimate the time they will spend on design, molding machine setup, and machine operations. The time to be spent on these activities serves as a basis for allocating each manufacturing engineer's and supervisor's salary

Exhibit 5-5: Plastim's Product Costs Using Activity-Based Costing System

	A	B	C	D	E	F	G
1		60,000			15,000		
2		Simple Lenses (S3)			Complex Lenses (CL5)		
3		Total	per Unit		Total	per Unit	Total
4	Cost Description	(1)	(2) = (1) ÷ 60,000		(3)	(4) = (3) ÷ 15,000	(5) = (1) + (3)
5	Direct costs						
6	Direct materials	$1,125,000	$18.75		$ 675,000	$ 45.00	$1,800,000
7	Direct manufacturing labor	600,000	10.00		195,000	13.00	795,000
8	Direct mold cleaning and maintenance costs	120,000	2.00		150,000	10.00	270,000
9	Total direct costs (Step 2)	1,845,000	30.75		1,020,000	68.00	2,865,000
10	Indirect Costs of Activities						
11	Design						
12	S3, 30 parts-sq.ft. × $4,500	135,000	2.25				} 450,000
13	CL5, 70 parts-sq.ft. × $4,500				315,000	21.00	
14	Setup of molding machines						
15	S3, 500 setup-hours × $150	75,000	1.25				} 300,000
16	CL5, 1,500 setup-hours × $150				225,000	15.00	
17	Machine operations						
18	S3, 9,000 molding machine-hours × $50	450,000	7.50				} 637,500
19	CL5, 3,750 molding machine-hours × $50				187,500	12.50	
20	Shipment setup						
21	S3, 100 shipments × $405	40,500	0.67				} 81,000
22	CL5, 100 shipments × $405				40,500	2.70	
23	Distribution						
24	S3, 45,000 cubic feet delivered × $5.80	261,000	4.35				} 391,500
25	CL5, 22,500 cubic feet delivered × $5.80				130,500	8.70	
26	Administration						
27	S3, 30,000 dir. manuf. labor-hours × $6.4151	192,453	3.21				} 255,000
28	CL5, 9,750 dir. manuf. labor-hours × $6.4151				62,547	4.17	
29	Total indirect costs allocated (Step 6)	1,153,953	19.23		961,047	64.07	2,115,000
30	Total Costs (Step 7)	$2,998,953	$49.98		$1,981,047	$132.07	$4,980,000
31							

costs to various activities. Still other costs are allocated to activity-cost pools using allocation bases that measure how these costs support different activities. For example, rent costs are allocated to activity cost pools on the basis of square-feet area used by different activities.

The point here is that all costs do not fit neatly into activity categories. Often, costs may first need to be allocated to activities (Stage 1 of the 2-stage cost-allocation model) before the costs of the activities can be allocated to products (Stage 2).

Step 5: Compute the Rate per Unit of Each Cost-Allocation Base. Exhibit 5-4, column 5, summarizes the calculation of the budgeted indirect cost rates using the budgeted quantity of the cost-allocation base from Step 3 and the total budgeted indirect costs of each activity from Step 4.

Step 6: Compute the Indirect Costs Allocated to the Products. Exhibit 5-5 shows total budgeted indirect costs of $1,153,953 allocated to the simple lens and $961,047 allocated to the complex lens. Follow the budgeted indirect cost calculations for each lens in Exhibit 5-5. For each activity, Plastim's operations personnel indicate the total quantity of the cost-allocation base that will be used by each type of lens (recall that Plastim operates at capacity). For example, lines 15 and 16 of Exhibit 5-5 show that of the 2,000 total setup-hours, the S3 lens is budgeted to use 500 hours and the CL5 lens 1,500 hours. The budgeted indirect cost rate is $150 per setup-hour (Exhibit 5-4, column 5, line 5). Therefore, the total budgeted cost of the setup activity allocated to the S3 lens is $75,000 (500 setup-hours × $150 per setup-hour) and to the CL5 lens is $225,000 (1,500 setup-hours × $150 per setup-hour). Budgeted setup cost per unit equals $1.25 ($75,000 ÷ 60,000 units) for the S3 lens and $15 ($225,000 ÷ 15,000 units) for the CL5 lens.

Step 7: Compute the Total Cost of the Products by Adding All Direct and Indirect Costs Assigned to the Products. Exhibit 5-5 presents the product costs for the simple and complex lenses. The direct costs are calculated in Step 2, and the indirect costs are calculated in Step 6. The ABC system overview in Exhibit 5-3 shows three direct-cost categories and six indirect-cost categories. The budgeted cost of each lens type in Exhibit 5-5 has nine line items, three for direct costs and six for indirect costs. The differences between the ABC product costs of S3 and CL5 calculated in Exhibit 5-5 highlight how each of these products uses different amounts of direct and indirect costs in each activity area.

We emphasize two features of ABC systems. First, these systems identify all costs used by products, whether the costs are variable or fixed in the short run. When making long-run strategic decisions using ABC information, managers want revenues to exceed total costs. Second, recognizing the hierarchy of costs is critical when allocating costs to products. It is easiest to use the cost hierarchy to first calculate the total costs of each product. The per-unit costs can then be derived by dividing total costs by the number of units produced.

◀ **Decision Point**

How do managers cost products or services using ABC systems?

Comparing Alternative Costing Systems

Exhibit 5-6 compares the simple costing system using a single indirect-cost pool (Exhibit 5-1 and Exhibit 5-2) Plastim had been using and the ABC system (Exhibit 5-3 and Exhibit 5-5). Note three points in Exhibit 5-6, consistent with the guidelines for

Exhibit 5-6

Comparing Alternative Costing Systems

	Simple Costing System Using a Single Indirect-Cost Pool (1)	ABC System (2)	Difference (3) = (2) − (1)
Direct-cost categories	2	3	1
	Direct materials	Direct materials	
	Direct manufacturing labor	Direct manufacturing labor	
		Direct mold cleaning and maintenance labor	
Total direct costs	$2,595,000	$2,865,000	$270,000
Indirect-cost pools	1	6	5
	Single indirect-cost pool allocated using direct manufacturing labor-hours	Design (parts-square feet)[1]	
		Molding machine setup (setup-hours)	
		Machine operations (molding machine-hours)	
		Shipment setup (number of shipments)	
		Distribution (cubic feet delivered)	
		Administration (direct manufacturing labor-hours)	
Total indirect costs	$2,385,000	$2,115,000	($270,000)
Total costs assigned to simple (S3) lens	$3,525,000	$2,998,953	($526,047)
Cost per unit of simple (S3) lens	$58.75	$49.98	($8.77)
Total costs assigned to complex (CL5) lens	$1,455,000	$1,981,047	$526,047
Cost per unit of complex (CL5) lens	$97.00	$132.07	$35.07

[1]Cost drivers for the various indirect-cost pools are shown in parentheses.

refining a costing system: (1) ABC systems trace more costs as direct costs; (2) ABC systems create homogeneous cost pools linked to different activities; and (3) for each activity-cost pool, ABC systems seek a cost-allocation base that has a cause-and-effect relationship with costs in the cost pool.

The homogeneous cost pools and the choice of cost-allocation bases, tied to the cost hierarchy, give Plastim's managers greater confidence in the activity and product cost numbers from the ABC system. The bottom part of Exhibit 5-6 shows that allocating costs to lenses using only an output unit-level allocation base—direct manufacturing labor-hours, as in the single indirect-cost pool system used prior to ABC—overcosts the simple S3 lens by $8.77 per unit and undercosts the complex CL5 lens by $35.07 per unit. The CL5 lens uses a disproportionately larger amount of output unit-level, batch-level, and product-sustaining costs than is represented by the direct manufacturing labor-hour cost-allocation base. The S3 lens uses a disproportionately smaller amount of these costs.

The benefit of an ABC system is that it provides information to make better decisions. But this benefit must be weighed against the measurement and implementation costs of an ABC system.

Considerations in Implementing Activity-Based-Costing Systems

Learning Objective 6

Evaluate the costs and benefits of implementing activity-based costing systems

... measurement difficulties versus more accurate costs that aid in decision making

Managers choose the level of detail to use in a costing system by evaluating the expected costs of the system against the expected benefits that result from better decisions. There are telltale signs of when an ABC system is likely to provide the most benefits. Here are some of these signs:

- Significant amounts of indirect costs are allocated using only one or two cost pools.
- All or most indirect costs are identified as output unit-level costs (few indirect costs are described as batch-level costs, product-sustaining costs, or facility-sustaining costs).
- Products make diverse demands on resources because of differences in volume, process steps, batch size, or complexity.
- Products that a company is well-suited to make and sell show small profits; whereas products that a company is less suited to produce and sell show large profits.
- Operations staff has substantial disagreement with the reported costs of manufacturing and marketing products and services.

When a company decides to implement ABC, it must make important choices about the level of detail to use. Should it choose many finely specified activities, cost drivers, and cost pools, or would a few suffice? For example, Plastim could identify a different molding machine-hour rate for each different type of molding machine. In making such choices, managers weigh the benefits against the costs and limitations of implementing a more detailed costing system.

The main costs and limitations of an ABC system are the measurements necessary to implement it. ABC systems require management to estimate costs of activity pools and to identify and measure cost drivers for these pools to serve as cost-allocation bases. Even basic ABC systems require many calculations to determine costs of products and services. These measurements are costly. Activity cost rates also need to be updated regularly.

As ABC systems get very detailed and more cost pools are created, more allocations are necessary to calculate activity costs for each cost pool. This increases the chances of misidentifying the costs of different activity cost pools. For example, supervisors are more prone to incorrectly identify the time they spent on different activities if they have to allocate their time over five activities rather than only two activities.

At times, companies are also forced to use allocation bases for which data are readily available rather than allocation bases they would have liked to use. For example, a company might be forced to use the number of loads moved, instead of the degree of difficulty and distance of different loads moved, as the allocation base for

Concepts in Action: Successfully Championing ABC

Successfully implementing ABC systems requires more than an understanding of the technical details. ABC implementation often represents a significant change in the costing system and, as the chapter indicates, it requires a manager to make major choices with respect to the definition of activities and the level of detail. What then are some of the behavioral issues that the management accountant must be sensitive to?

1. **Gaining support of top management and creating a sense of urgency for the ABC effort.** This requires management accountants to lay out the vision for the ABC project and to clearly communicate its strategic benefits (for example, the resulting improvements in product and process design). It also requires selling the idea to end users and working with members of other departments as business partners of the managers in the various areas affected by the ABC project. For example, at USAA Federal Savings Bank, project managers demonstrated how the information gained from ABC would provide insights into the efficiency of bank operations, which was previously unavailable. Now the finance area communicates regularly with operations about new reports and proposed changes to the financial reporting package that managers receive.
2. **Creating a guiding coalition of managers throughout the value chain for the ABC effort.** ABC systems measure how the resources of an organization are used. Managers responsible for these resources have the best knowledge about activities and cost drivers. Getting managers to cooperate and take the initiative for implementing ABC is essential for gaining the required expertise, the proper credibility, and the necessary leadership.

    Gaining wider participation among managers has other benefits. Managers who feel more involved in the process are likely to commit more time to and be less skeptical of the ABC effort. Engaging managers throughout the value chain also creates greater opportunities for coordination and cooperation across the different functions, for example, design and manufacturing.
3. **Educating and training employees in ABC as a basis for employee empowerment.** Disseminating information about ABC throughout an organization allows workers in all areas of a business to use their knowledge of ABC to make improvements. For example, WS Industries, an Indian manufacturer of insulators, not only shared ABC information with its workers but also established an incentive plan that gave employees a percentage of the cost savings. The results were dramatic because employees were empowered and motivated to implement numerous cost-saving projects.
4. **Seeking small short-run successes as proof that the ABC implementation is yielding results.** Too often, managers and management accountants seek big results and major changes far too quickly. In many situations, achieving a significant change overnight is difficult. However, showing how ABC information has helped improve a process and save costs, even if only in small ways, motivates the team to stay on course and build momentum. The credibility gained from small victories leads to additional and bigger improvements involving larger numbers of people and different parts of the organization. Eventually ABC and ABM become rooted in the culture of the organization. Sharing short-term successes may also help motivate employees to be innovative. At USAA Federal Savings Bank, managers created a "process improvement" mailbox in Microsoft Outlook to facilitate the sharing of process improvement ideas.
5. **Recognizing that ABC information is not perfect because it balances the need for better information against the costs of creating a complex system that few managers and employees can understand.** The management accountant must help managers recognize both the value and the limitations of ABC and not oversell it. Open and honest communication about ABC ensures that managers use ABC thoughtfully to make good decisions. Critical judgments can then be made without being adversarial, and tough questions can be asked to help drive better decisions about the system.

material-handling costs, because data on degree of difficulty and distance of moves are difficult to obtain. When erroneous cost-allocation bases are used, activity-cost information can be misleading. For example, if the cost per load moved decreases, a company may conclude that it has become more efficient in its materials-handling operations. In fact, the lower cost per load move may have resulted solely from moving many lighter loads over shorter distances.

Many companies, such as Kanthal, the Swedish manufacturer of heating elements, have found the strategic and operational benefits of a less-detailed ABC system to be good enough to not warrant incurring the costs and challenges of operating a more-detailed system. Other organizations, such as Hewlett-Packard, implement ABC in chosen divisions or functions. As improvements in information technology and accompanying

Decision Point

What should managers consider when deciding to implement ABC systems?

declines in measurement costs continue, more-detailed ABC systems have become a practical alternative in many companies. As such trends persist, more detailed ABC systems will be better able to pass the cost–benefit test.

Global surveys of company practice suggest that ABC implementation varies among companies. Nevertheless, its framework and ideas provide a standard for judging whether any simple costing system is good enough for a particular management's purposes. Any contemplated changes in a simple costing system will inevitably be improved by ABC thinking. The Concepts in Action box on page 177 describes some of the behavioral issues that management accountants must be sensitive to as they seek to immerse an organization in ABC thinking.

Using ABC Systems for Improving Cost Management and Profitability

Learning Objective 7

Explain how activity-based costing systems are used in activity-based management

. . . such as pricing decisions, product-mix decisions, and cost reduction

The emphasis of this chapter so far has been on the role of ABC systems in obtaining better product costs. However, Plastim's managers must now use this information to make decisions (Step 4 of the 5-step decision process, p. 167) and to implement the decision, evaluate performance, and learn (Step 5, p. 167). **Activity-based management (ABM)** is a method of management decision making that uses activity-based costing information to improve customer satisfaction and profitability. We define ABM broadly to include decisions about pricing and product mix, cost reduction, process improvement, and product and process design.

Pricing and Product-Mix Decisions

An ABC system gives managers information about the costs of making and selling diverse products. With this information, managers can make pricing and product-mix decisions. For example, the ABC system indicates that Plastim can match its competitor's price of $53 for the S3 lens and still make a profit because the ABC cost of S3 is $49.98 (see Exhibit 5-5).

Plastim's managers offer Giovanni Motors a price of $52 for the S3 lens. Plastim's managers are confident that they can use the deeper understanding of costs that the ABC system provides to improve efficiency and further reduce the cost of the S3 lens. Without information from the ABC system, Plastim managers might have erroneously concluded that they would incur an operating loss on the S3 lens at a price of $53. This incorrect conclusion would have probably caused Plastim to reduce its business in simple lenses and focus instead on complex lenses, where its single indirect-cost-pool system indicated it is very profitable.

Focusing on complex lenses would have been a mistake. The ABC system indicates that the cost of making the complex lens is much higher—$132.07 versus $97 indicated by the direct manufacturing labor-hour-based costing system Plastim had been using. As Plastim's operations staff had thought all along, Plastim has no competitive advantage in making CL5 lenses. At a price of $137 per lens for CL5, the profit margin is very small ($137.00 − $132.07 = $4.93). As Plastim reduces its prices on simple lenses, it would need to negotiate a higher price for complex lenses with Giovanni Motors.

Cost Reduction and Process Improvement Decisions

Manufacturing and distribution personnel use ABC systems to focus on how and where to reduce costs. Managers set cost reduction targets in terms of reducing the cost per unit of the cost-allocation base in different activity areas. For example, the supervisor of the distribution activity area at Plastim could have a performance target of decreasing distribution cost per cubic foot of products delivered from $5.80 to $5.40 by reducing distribution labor and warehouse rental costs. The goal is to reduce these costs by improving the way work is done without compromising customer service or the actual or perceived value (usefulness) customers obtain from the product or service. That is, Plastim will attempt to take out only those costs that are *nonvalue added*. Controlling physical cost drivers, such as setup-hours or cubic feet delivered, is another fundamental way that operating personnel manage costs. For example, Plastim can decrease distribution costs by packing the lenses in a way that reduces the bulkiness of the packages delivered.

The following table shows the reduction in distribution costs of the S3 and CL5 lenses as a result of actions that lower cost per cubic foot delivered (from $5.80 to $5.40) and total cubic feet of deliveries (from 45,000 to 40,000 for S3 and 22,500 to 20,000 for CL5).

	60,000 (S3) Lenses		15,000 (CL5) Lenses	
	Total (1)	per Unit (2) = (1) ÷ 60,000	Total (3)	per Unit (4) = (3) ÷ 15,000
Distribution costs (from Exhibit 5-5)				
S3, 45,000 cubic feet × $5.80/cubic foot	$261,000	$4.35		
CL5, 22,500 cubic feet × $5.80/cubic foot			$130,500	$8.70
Distribution costs as a result of process improvements				
S3, 40,000 cubic feet × $5.40/cubic foot	216,000	3.60		
CL5, 20,000 cubic feet × $5.40/cubic foot			108,000	7.20
Savings in distribution costs from process improvements	$ 45,000	$0.75	$ 22,500	$1.50

In the long run, total distribution costs will decrease from $391,500 ($261,000 + $130,500) to $324,000 ($216,000 + $108,000). In the short run, however, distribution costs may be fixed and may not decrease. Suppose all $391,500 of distribution costs are fixed costs in the short run. The efficiency improvements (using less distribution labor and space) mean that the same $391,500 of distribution costs can now be used to distribute 72,500 $\left(\dfrac{\$391,500}{\$5.40 \text{ per cubic foot}}\right)$ cubic feet of lenses. In this case, how should costs be allocated to the S3 and CL5 lenses?

ABC systems distinguish *costs incurred* from *resources used* to design, manufacture, and deliver products and services. For the distribution activity, after process improvements,

Costs incurred = $391,500

Resources used = $216,000 (for S3 lens) + $108,000 (for CL5 lens) = $324,000

On the basis of the resources used by each product, Plastim's ABC system allocates $216,000 to S3 and $108,000 to CL5 for a total of $324,000. The difference of $67,500 ($391,500 − $324,000) is shown as costs of unused but available distribution capacity. Plastim's ABC system does not allocate the costs of unused capacity to products so as not to burden the product costs of S3 and CL5 with the cost of resources not used by these products. Instead, the system highlights the amount of unused capacity as a separate line item to signal to managers the need to reduce these costs, such as by redeploying labor to other uses or laying off workers. Chapter 9 discusses issues related to unused capacity in more detail.

Design Decisions

Management can evaluate how its current product and process designs affect activities and costs as a way of identifying new designs to reduce costs. For example, design decisions that decrease complexity of the mold reduce costs of design, materials, labor, machine setups, machine operations, and mold cleaning and maintenance. Plastim's customers may be willing to give up some features of the lens in exchange for a lower price. Note that Plastim's previous costing system, which used direct manufacturing labor-hours as the cost-allocation base for all indirect costs, would have mistakenly signaled that Plastim choose those designs that most reduce direct manufacturing labor-hours when, in fact, there is a weak cause-and-effect relationship between direct manufacturing labor-hours and indirect costs.

Planning and Managing Activities

Many companies implementing ABC systems for the first time analyze actual costs to identify activity-cost pools and activity-cost rates. To be useful for planning, making decisions, and managing activities, companies calculate a budgeted cost rate for each activity and use these budgeted cost rates to cost products as we saw in the Plastim example. At year-end, budgeted costs and actual costs are compared to provide feedback on how well activities were managed and to make adjustments for underallocated or overallocated indirect costs for each activity using methods described in Chapter 4. As activities and processes are changed, new activity-cost rates are calculated.

We will return to activity-based management in later chapters. Management decisions that use activity-based costing information are described in Chapter 6, in which we discuss activity-based budgeting; Chapter 11, in which we discuss outsourcing and adding or dropping business segments; in Chapter 12, in which we evaluate alternative design choices to improve efficiency and reduce nonvalue-added costs; in Chapter 13, in which we cover reengineering and downsizing; in Chapter 14, in which we explore managing customer profitability; in Chapter 19, in which we explain quality improvements; and in Chapter 20, in which we describe how to evaluate suppliers.

Decision Point

How can ABC systems be used to manage better?

Activity-Based Costing and Department Costing Systems

Companies often use costing systems that have features of ABC systems—such as multiple cost pools and multiple cost-allocation bases—but that do not emphasize individual activities. Many companies have evolved their costing systems from using a single indirect cost rate system to using separate indirect cost rates for each department (such as design, manufacturing, distribution, and so on) or each subdepartment (such as machining and assembly departments within manufacturing) that can be thought of as representing broad tasks. ABC systems, with its focus on specific activities, are a further refinement of department costing systems. In this section, we compare ABC systems and department costing systems.

Plastim uses the design department indirect cost rate to cost its design activity. Plastim calculates the design activity rate by dividing total design department costs by total parts-square feet, a measure of the complexity of the mold and the driver of design department costs. Plastim does not find it worthwhile to calculate separate activity rates within the design department for the different design activities, such as designing products, making temporary molds, and designing processes. Why? Because complexity of a mold is an appropriate cost-allocation base for costs incurred in each design activity. Design department costs are homogeneous with respect to this cost-allocation base.

In contrast, the manufacturing department identifies two activity cost pools—a setup cost pool and a machine operations cost pool—instead of a single manufacturing department overhead cost pool. It identifies these activity cost pools for two reasons. First, each of these activities within manufacturing incurs significant costs and has a different cost driver, setup-hours for the setup cost pool and machine-hours for the machine operations cost pool. Second, the S3 and CL5 lenses do not use resources from these two activity areas in the same proportion. For example, CL5 uses 75% (1,500 ÷ 2,000) of the setup-hours but only 29.4% (3,750 ÷ 12,750) of the machine-hours. Using only machine-hours, say, to allocate all manufacturing department costs at Plastim would result in CL5 being undercosted because it would not be charged for the significant amounts of setup resources it actually uses.

Based on what we just explained, using department indirect cost rates to allocate costs to products results in similar information as activity cost rates if (1) a single activity accounts for a sizable proportion of the department's costs; or (2) significant costs are incurred on different activities within a department, but each activity has the same cost driver and hence cost-allocation base (as was the case in Plastim's design department). From a purely product costing standpoint, department and activity indirect cost rates

Learning Objective 8

Compare activity-based costing systems and department costing systems

... activity-based costing systems are a refinement of department costing systems into more-focused and homogenous cost pools

will also result in the same product costs if (1) significant costs are incurred for different activities with different cost-allocation bases within a department but (2) different products use resources from the different activity areas in the same proportions (for example, if CL5 had used 65%, say, of the setup-hours and 65% of the machine-hours). In this case, though, not identifying activities and cost drivers within departments conceals activity cost information that would be valuable for cost management and design and process improvements.

We close this section with a note of caution. Do not assume that because department costing systems require the creation of multiple indirect cost pools that they properly recognize the drivers of costs within departments as well as how resources are used by products. As we have indicated, in many situations, department costing systems can be refined using ABC. Emphasizing activities leads to more-focused and homogeneous cost pools, aids in identifying cost-allocation bases for activities that have a better cause-and-effect relationship with the costs in activity cost pools, and leads to better design and process decisions. But these benefits of an ABC system would need to be balanced against its costs and limitations.

◀ **Decision Point**

When can department costing systems be used instead of ABC systems?

ABC in Service and Merchandising Companies

Although many of the early examples of ABC originated in manufacturing, ABC has many applications in service and merchandising companies. In addition to manufacturing activities, the Plastim example includes the application of ABC to a service activity—design—and to a merchandising activity—distribution. Companies such as the Cooperative Bank, Braintree Hospital, BCTel in the telecommunications industry, and Union Pacific in the railroad industry have implemented some form of ABC system to identify profitable product mixes, improve efficiency, and satisfy customers. Similarly, many retail and wholesale companies—for example, Supervalu, a retailer and distributor of grocery store products, and Owens and Minor, a medical supplies distributor—have used ABC systems. Finally, as we describe in Chapter 14, a large number of financial services companies (as well as other companies) employ variations of ABC systems to analyze and improve the profitability of their customer interactions.

The widespread use of ABC systems in service and merchandising companies reinforces the idea that ABC systems are used by managers for strategic decisions rather than for inventory valuation. (Inventory valuation is fairly straightforward in merchandising companies and not needed in service companies.) Service companies, in particular, find great value from ABC because a vast majority of their cost structure comprises indirect costs. After all, there are few direct costs when a bank makes a loan, or when a representative answers a phone call at a call center. As we have seen, a major benefit of ABC is its ability to assign indirect costs to cost objects by identifying activities and cost drivers. As a result, ABC systems provide greater insight than traditional systems into the management of these indirect costs. The general approach to ABC in service and merchandising companies is similar to the ABC approach in manufacturing.

The Cooperative Bank followed the approach described in this chapter when it implemented ABC in its retail banking operations. It calculated the costs of various activities, such as performing ATM transactions, opening and closing accounts, administering mortgages, and processing Visa transactions. It then used the activity cost rates to calculate costs of various products, such as checking accounts, mortgages, and Visa cards and the costs of supporting different customers. ABC information helped the Cooperative Bank to improve its processes and to identify profitable products and customer segments.

Activity-based costing raises some interesting issues when it is applied to a public service institution such as the U.S. Postal Service. The costs of delivering mail to remote locations are far greater than the costs of delivering mail within urban areas. However, for fairness and community-building reasons, the Postal Service cannot charge higher prices to customers in remote areas. In this case, activity-based costing is valuable for understanding, managing, and reducing costs but not for pricing decisions.

Concepts in Action: Pincky: Capacity Costs and Time-Driven Activity-Based Costing

Pincky is a small Australian company with humble beginnings. In December 2000, young entrepreneur Ed Sparrow began selling soft serve and prepacked ice cream from a lone ice cream van on the weekends. Time-driven activity-based costing (TDABC) was used by Pincky for pricing its unused capacities, analyzing its profits from different operations, and managing its costs.

In 2004, Pincky's available capacities included 6 vans, 6 ice cream machines, 10 freezers, and a large building for storage (over 1,000 square meters). The respective approximate total values were $72,000, $42,000, $15,000, and $195,000, respectively.

Pincky only operated on Saturdays and Sundays from 1 P.M. to 6 P.M. with six ice cream vans driving through Australian suburbs selling a wide variety of ice creams. Given the nature of the business, managing the costs and performing an accurate profit analysis for Pincky's different operations were deemed crucial for the company. During this, the calculation of costs of unused capacities (including freezers, vans, ice cream machines, and property) during the weekdays was an important issue for Pincky.

In 2003, Pincky received several offers from a few small businesses who wanted to utilize its unused capacities during the weekdays. Using TDABC was an appropriate method to calculate the costs of supplying resources such as the cost of individual vans, freezers, ice cream machines, and the property per hour during the weekdays.

By dividing supplying resources costs (depreciation costs of vans, ice cream machines, and property) by practical capacities of facilities (expected available hours for each facility), the company was able to determine an accurate hourly price rate for each facility for pricing its unused capacities, analyzing its profits from different operations, and managing its costs. Using TDABC information, Pincky was also able to increase its yearly profits by 30% by lowering its operational costs through outsourcing some activities (e.g., driving the vans, cleaning the ice cream machines, and delivery of goods to the company), reducing its opportunity costs through renting out some unused capacities (e.g., vans and ice cream machines) during the weekdays, and by indentifying and focusing on more profitable services (e.g., selling more soft serve rather than prepacked ice creams).

Source: Based on D. Askarany. 2009. Atlas Ice Cream case: capacity issues, just in time, profitability and decision making. In *Cases in Management: Indian and International Perspectives,* eds. V. Jham and Bindu Gupta, Wiley India.

Problem for Self-Study

Family Supermarkets (FS) has decided to increase the size of its Memphis store. It wants information about the profitability of individual product lines: soft drinks, fresh produce, and packaged food. FS provides the following data for 2011 for each product line:

	Soft Drinks	Fresh Produce	Packaged Food
Revenues	$317,400	$840,240	$483,960
Cost of goods sold	$240,000	$600,000	$360,000
Cost of bottles returned	$ 4,800	$ 0	$ 0
Number of purchase orders placed	144	336	144
Number of deliveries received	120	876	264
Hours of shelf-stocking time	216	2,160	1,080
Items sold	50,400	441,600	122,400

FS also provides the following information for 2011:

Activity (1)	Description of Activity (2)	Total Support Costs (3)	Cost-Allocation Base (4)
1. Bottle returns	Returning of empty bottles to store	$ 4,800	Direct tracing to soft-drink line
2. Ordering	Placing of orders for purchases	$ 62,400	624 purchase orders
3. Delivery	Physical delivery and receipt of merchandise	$100,800	1,260 deliveries
4. Shelf-stocking	Stocking of merchandise on store shelves and ongoing restocking	$ 69,120	3,456 hours of shelf-stocking time
5. Customer support	Assistance provided to customers, including checkout and bagging	$122,880	614,400 items sold
Total		$360,000	

Required

1. Family Supermarkets currently allocates store support costs (all costs other than cost of goods sold) to product lines on the basis of cost of goods sold of each product line. Calculate the operating income and operating income as a percentage of revenues for each product line.
2. If Family Supermarkets allocates store support costs (all costs other than cost of goods sold) to product lines using an ABC system, calculate the operating income and operating income as a percentage of revenues for each product line.
3. Comment on your answers in requirements 1 and 2.

Solution

1. The following table shows the operating income and operating income as a percentage of revenues for each product line. All store support costs (all costs other than cost of goods sold) are allocated to product lines using cost of goods sold of each product line as the cost-allocation base. Total store support costs equal $360,000 (cost of bottles returned, $4,800 + cost of purchase orders, $62,400 + cost of deliveries, $100,800 + cost of shelf-stocking, $69,120 + cost of customer support, $122,880). The allocation rate for store support costs = $360,000 ÷ $1,200,000 (soft drinks $240,000 + fresh produce $600,000 + packaged food, $360,000) = 30% of cost of goods sold. To allocate support costs to each product line, FS multiplies the cost of goods sold of each product line by 0.30.

	Soft Drinks	Fresh Produce	Packaged Food	Total
Revenues	$317,400	$840,240	$483,960	$1,641,600
Cost of goods sold	240,000	600,000	360,000	1,200,000
Store support cost ($240,000; $600,000; $360,000) × 0.30	72,000	180,000	108,000	360,000
Total costs	312,000	780,000	468,000	1,560,000
Operating income	$ 5,400	$ 60,240	$ 15,960	$ 81,600
Operating income ÷ Revenues	1.70%	7.17%	3.30%	4.97%

2. Under an ABC system, FS identifies bottle-return costs as a direct cost because these costs can be traced to the soft drink product line. FS then calculates cost-allocation rates for each activity area (as in Step 5 of the seven-step costing system, described in the chapter, p. 174). The activity rates are as follows:

Activity (1)	Cost Hierarchy (2)	Total Costs (3)	Quantity of Cost-Allocation Base (4)	Overhead Allocation Rate (5) = (3) ÷ (4)
Ordering	Batch-level	$ 62,400	624 purchase orders	$100 per purchase order
Delivery	Batch-level	$100,800	1,260 deliveries	$80 per delivery
Shelf-stocking	Output unit-level	$ 69,120	3,456 shelf-stocking-hours	$20 per stocking-hour
Customer support	Output unit-level	$122,880	614,400 items sold	$0.20 per item sold

Store support costs for each product line by activity are obtained by multiplying the total quantity of the cost-allocation base for each product line by the activity cost rate. Operating income and operating income as a percentage of revenues for each product line are as follows:

	Soft Drinks	Fresh Produce	Packaged Food	Total
Revenues	$317,400	$840,240	$483,960	$1,641,600
Cost of goods sold	240,000	600,000	360,000	1,200,000
Bottle-return costs	4,800	0	0	4,800
Ordering costs				
(144; 336; 144) purchase orders × $100	14,400	33,600	14,400	62,400
Delivery costs				
(120; 876; 264) deliveries × $80	9,600	70,080	21,120	100,800
Shelf-stocking costs				
(216; 2,160; 1,080) stocking-hours × $20	4,320	43,200	21,600	69,120
Customer-support costs				
(50,400; 441,600; 122,400) items sold × $0.20	10,080	88,320	24,480	122,880
Total costs	283,200	835,200	441,600	1,560,000
Operating income	$ 34,200	$ 5,040	$ 42,360	$ 81,600
Operating income ÷ Revenues	10.78%	0.60%	8.75%	4.97%

3. Managers believe the ABC system is more credible than the simple costing system. The ABC system distinguishes the different types of activities at FS more precisely. It also tracks more accurately how individual product lines use resources. Rankings of relative profitability—operating income as a percentage of revenues—of the three product lines under the simple costing system and under the ABC system are as follows:

Simple Costing System		ABC System	
1. Fresh produce	7.17%	1. Soft drinks	10.78%
2. Packaged food	3.30%	2. Packaged food	8.75%
3. Soft drinks	1.70%	3. Fresh produce	0.60%

The percentage of revenues, cost of goods sold, and activity costs for each product line are as follows:

	Soft Drinks	Fresh Produce	Packaged Food
Revenues	19.34%	51.18%	29.48%
Cost of goods sold	20.00	50.00	30.00
Bottle returns	100.00	0	0
Activity areas:			
Ordering	23.08	53.84	23.08
Delivery	9.53	69.52	20.95
Shelf-stocking	6.25	62.50	31.25
Customer-support	8.20	71.88	19.92

Soft drinks have fewer deliveries and require less shelf-stocking time and customer support than either fresh produce or packaged food. Most major soft-drink suppliers deliver merchandise to the store shelves and stock the shelves themselves. In contrast, the fresh produce area has the most deliveries and consumes a large percentage of shelf-stocking time. It also has the highest number of individual sales items and so requires the most customer support. The simple costing system assumed that each product line used the resources in each activity area in the same ratio as their respective individual cost of goods sold to total cost of goods sold. Clearly, this assumption is incorrect. Relative to cost of goods sold, soft drinks and packaged food use fewer resources while fresh produce uses more resources. As a result, the ABC system reduces the costs assigned to soft drinks and packaged food and increases the costs assigned to fresh produce. The simple costing system is an example of averaging that is too broad.

FS managers can use the ABC information to guide decisions such as how to allocate a planned increase in floor space. An increase in the percentage of space allocated to soft drinks is warranted. Note, however, that ABC information should be but one input into decisions about shelf-space allocation. FS may have minimum limits on the shelf space allocated to fresh produce because of shoppers' expectations that supermarkets will carry products from this product line. In many situations, companies cannot make product decisions in isolation but must consider the effect that dropping or deemphasizing a product might have on customer demand for other products.

Pricing decisions can also be made in a more informed way with ABC information. For example, suppose a competitor announces a 5% reduction in soft-drink prices. Given the 10.78% margin FS currently earns on its soft-drink product line, it has flexibility to reduce prices and still make a profit on this product line. In contrast, the simple costing system erroneously implied that soft drinks only had a 1.70% margin, leaving little room to counter a competitor's pricing initiatives.

Decision Points

The following question-and-answer format summarizes the chapter's learning objectives. Each decision presents a key question related to a learning objective. The guidelines are the answer to that question.

Decision	Guidelines
1. When does product undercosting or overcosting occur?	Product undercosting (overcosting) occurs when a product or service consumes a high (low) level of resources but is reported to have a low (high) cost. Broad averaging, or peanut-butter costing, a common cause of undercosting or overcosting, is the result of using broad averages that uniformly assign, or spread, the cost of resources to products when the individual products use those resources in a nonuniform way. Product-cost cross-subsidization exists when one undercosted (overcosted) product results in at least one other product being overcosted (undercosted).
2. How do managers refine a costing system?	Refining a costing system means making changes that result in cost numbers that better measure the way different cost objects, such as products, use different amounts of resources of the company. These changes can require additional direct-cost tracing, the choice of more-homogeneous indirect cost pools, or the use of cost drivers as cost-allocation bases.
3. What is the difference between the design of a simple costing system and an activity-based costing (ABC) system?	The ABC system differs from the simple system by its fundamental focus on activities. The ABC system typically has more-homogeneous indirect-cost pools than the simple system, and more cost drivers are used as cost-allocation bases.

4. What is a cost hierarchy?	A cost hierarchy categorizes costs into different cost pools on the basis of the different types of cost-allocation bases or different degrees of difficulty in determining cause-and-effect (or benefits-received) relationships. A four-part hierarchy to cost products consists of output unit-level costs, batch-level costs, product-sustaining or service-sustaining costs, and facility-sustaining costs.	
5. How do managers cost products or services using ABC systems?	In ABC, costs of activities are used to assign costs to other cost objects such as products or services based on the activities the products or services consume.	
6. What should managers consider when deciding to implement ABC systems?	ABC systems are likely to yield the most decision-making benefits when indirect costs are a high percentage of total costs or when products and services make diverse demands on indirect resources. The main costs of ABC systems are the difficulties of the measurements necessary to implement and update the systems.	
7. How can ABC systems be used to manage better?	Activity-based management (ABM) is a management method of decision making that uses ABC information to satisfy customers and improve profits. ABC systems are used for such management decisions as pricing, product-mix, cost reduction, process improvement, product and process redesign, and planning and managing activities.	
8. When can department costing systems be used instead of ABC systems?	Activity-based costing systems are a refinement of department costing systems into more-focused and homogeneous cost pools. Cost information in department costing systems approximates cost information in ABC systems only when each department has a single activity (or a single activity accounts for a significant proportion of department costs), a single cost driver for different activities, or when different products use the different activities of the department in the same proportions.	

Terms to Learn

This chapter and the Glossary at the end of this book contain definitions of the following important terms:

activity
activity-based costing (ABC)
activity-based management (ABM)
batch-level costs
cost hierarchy
facility-sustaining costs
output unit-level costs
product-cost cross-subsidization
product overcosting
product-sustaining costs
product undercosting
refined costing system
service-sustaining costs

Assignment Material

Questions

5-1 What is broad averaging and what consequences can it have on costs?
5-2 Why should managers worry about product overcosting or undercosting?
5-3 What is costing system refinement? Describe three guidelines for refinement.
5-4 What is an activity-based approach to designing a costing system?
5-5 Describe four levels of a cost hierarchy.
5-6 Why is it important to classify costs into a cost hierarchy?
5-7 What are the key reasons for product cost differences between simple costing systems and ABC systems?
5-8 Describe four decisions for which ABC information is useful.
5-9 "Department indirect-cost rates are never activity-cost rates." Do you agree? Explain.
5-10 Describe four signs that help indicate when ABC systems are likely to provide the most benefits.

5-11 What are the main costs and limitations of implementing ABC systems?

5-12 "ABC systems only apply to manufacturing companies." Do you agree? Explain.

5-13 "Activity-based costing is the wave of the present and the future. All companies should adopt it." Do you agree? Explain.

5-14 "Increasing the number of indirect-cost pools is guaranteed to sizably increase the accuracy of product or service costs." Do you agree? Why?

5-15 The controller of a retail company has just had a $50,000 request to implement an ABC system quickly turned down. A senior vice president, in rejecting the request, noted, "Given a choice, I will always prefer a $50,000 investment in improving things a customer sees or experiences, such as our shelves or our store layout. How does a customer benefit by our spending $50,000 on a supposedly better accounting system?" How should the controller respond?

Exercises

5-16 Cost hierarchy. Hamilton, Inc., manufactures boom boxes (music systems with radio, cassette, and compact disc players) for several well-known companies. The boom boxes differ significantly in their complexity and their manufacturing batch sizes. The following costs were incurred in 2011:

a. Indirect manufacturing labor costs such as supervision that supports direct manufacturing labor, $1,450,000

b. Procurement costs of placing purchase orders, receiving materials, and paying suppliers related to the number of purchase orders placed, $850,000

c. Cost of indirect materials, $275,000

d. Costs incurred to set up machines each time a different product needs to be manufactured, $630,000

e. Designing processes, drawing process charts, making engineering process changes for products, $775,000

f. Machine-related overhead costs such as depreciation, maintenance, production engineering, $1,500,000 (These resources relate to the activity of running the machines.)

g. Plant management, plant rent, and plant insurance, $925,000

1. Classify each of the preceding costs as output unit-level, batch-level, product-sustaining, or facility-sustaining. Explain each answer.

2. Consider two types of boom boxes made by Hamilton, Inc. One boom box is complex to make and is produced in many batches. The other boom box is simple to make and is produced in few batches. Suppose that Hamilton needs the same number of machine-hours to make each type of boom box and that Hamilton allocates all overhead costs using machine-hours as the only allocation base. How, if at all, would the boom boxes be miscosted? Briefly explain why.

3. How is the cost hierarchy helpful to Hamilton in managing its business?

5-17 ABC, cost hierarchy, service. (CMA, adapted) Vineyard Test Laboratories does heat testing (HT) and stress testing (ST) on materials and operates at capacity. Under its current simple costing system, Vineyard aggregates all operating costs of $1,190,000 into a single overhead cost pool. Vineyard calculates a rate per test-hour of $17 ($1,190,000 ÷ 70,000 total test-hours). HT uses 40,000 test-hours, and ST uses 30,000 test-hours. Gary Celeste, Vineyard's controller, believes that there is enough variation in test procedures and cost structures to establish separate costing and billing rates for HT and ST. The market for test services is becoming competitive. Without this information, any miscosting and mispricing of its services could cause Vineyard to lose business. Celeste divides Vineyard's costs into four activity-cost categories.

a. Direct-labor costs, $146,000. These costs can be directly traced to HT, $100,000, and ST, $46,000.

b. Equipment-related costs (rent, maintenance, energy, and so on), $350,000. These costs are allocated to HT and ST on the basis of test-hours.

c. Setup costs, $430,000. These costs are allocated to HT and ST on the basis of the number of setup-hours required. HT requires 13,600 setup-hours, and ST requires 3,600 setup-hours.

d. Costs of designing tests, $264,000. These costs are allocated to HT and ST on the basis of the time required for designing the tests. HT requires 3,000 hours, and ST requires 1,400 hours.

1. Classify each activity cost as output unit-level, batch-level, product- or service-sustaining, or facility-sustaining. Explain each answer.

2. Calculate the cost per test-hour for HT and ST. Explain briefly the reasons why these numbers differ from the $17 per test-hour that Vineyard calculated using its simple costing system.

3. Explain the accuracy of the product costs calculated using the simple costing system and the ABC system. How might Vineyard's management use the cost hierarchy and ABC information to better manage its business?

5-18 Alternative allocation bases for a professional services firm. The Walliston Group (WG) provides tax advice to multinational firms. WG charges clients for (a) direct professional time (at an hourly rate) and (b) support services (at 30% of the direct professional costs billed). The three professionals in WG and their rates per professional hour are as follows:

Professional	Billing Rate per Hour
Max Walliston	$640
Alexa Boutin	220
Jacob Abbington	100

WG has just prepared the May 2011 bills for two clients. The hours of professional time spent on each client are as follows:

	Hours per Client	
Professional	San Antonio Dominion	Amsterdam Enterprises
Walliston	26	4
Boutin	5	14
Abbington	39	52
Total	70	70

Required

1. What amounts did WG bill to San Antonio Dominion and Amsterdam Enterprises for May 2011?
2. Suppose support services were billed at $75 per professional labor-hour (instead of 30% of professional labor costs). How would this change affect the amounts WG billed to the two clients for May 2011? Comment on the differences between the amounts billed in requirements 1 and 2.
3. How would you determine whether professional labor costs or professional labor-hours is the more appropriate allocation base for WG's support services?

5-19 Plant-wide, department, and ABC indirect cost rates. Automotive Products (AP) designs and produces automotive parts. In 2011, actual variable manufacturing overhead is $308,600. AP's simple costing system allocates variable manufacturing overhead to its three customers based on machine-hours and prices its contracts based on full costs. One of its customers has regularly complained of being charged noncompetitive prices, so AP's controller Devon Smith realizes that it is time to examine the consumption of overhead resources more closely. He knows that there are three main departments that consume overhead resources: design, production, and engineering. Interviews with the department personnel and examination of time records yield the following detailed information:

	A	B	C	D	E	F
1			Variable Manufacturing Overhead in 2011	Usage of Cost Drivers by Customer Contract		
2	Department	Cost Driver		United Motors	Holden Motors	Leland Vehicle
3	Design	CAD-design-hours	$ 39,000	110	200	80
4	Production	Engineering-hours	29,600	70	60	240
5	Engineering	Machine-hours	240,000	120	2,800	1,080
6	Total		$308,600			

Required

1. Compute the variable manufacturing overhead allocated to each customer in 2011 using the simple costing system that uses machine-hours as the allocation base.
2. Compute the variable manufacturing overhead allocated to each customer in 2011 using department-based variable manufacturing overhead rates.
3. Comment on your answers in requirements 1 and 2. Which customer do you think was complaining about being overcharged in the simple system? If the new department-based rates are used to price contracts, which customer(s) will be unhappy? How would you respond to these concerns?

4. How else might AP use the information available from its department-by-department analysis of variable manufacturing overhead costs?
5. AP's managers are wondering if they should further refine the department-by-department costing system into an ABC system by identifying different activities within each department. Under what conditions would it not be worthwhile to further refine the department costing system into an ABC system?

5-20 Plant-wide, department, and activity-cost rates. Tarquin's Trophies makes trophies and plaques and operates at capacity. Tarquin does large custom orders, such as the participant trophies for the Mishawaka Little League. The controller has asked you to compare plant-wide, department, and activity-based cost allocation.

Tarquin's Trophies
Budgeted Information
For the Year Ended November 30, 2011

Forming Department	Trophies	Plaques	Total
Direct materials	$13,000	$11,250	$24,250
Direct labor	15,600	9,000	24,600
Overhead Costs			
Setup			12,000
Supervision			10,386

Assembly Department	Trophies	Plaques	Total
Direct materials	$ 2,600	$ 9,375	$11,975
Direct labor	7,800	10,500	18,300
Overhead costs			
Setup			23,000
Supervision			10,960

Other information follows:

Setup costs vary with the number of batches processed in each department. The budgeted number of batches for each product line in each department is as follows:

	Trophies	Plaques
Forming department	40	116
Assembly department	43	103

Supervision costs vary with direct labor costs in each department.

1. Calculate the budgeted cost of trophies and plaques based on a single plant-wide overhead rate, if total overhead is allocated based on total direct costs.
2. Calculate the budgeted cost of trophies and plaques based on departmental overhead rates, where forming department overhead costs are allocated based on direct labor costs of the forming department, and assembly department overhead costs are allocated based on total direct costs of the assembly department.
3. Calculate the budgeted cost of trophies and plaques if Tarquin allocates overhead costs in each department using activity-based costing.
4. Explain how the disaggregation of information could improve or reduce decision quality.

5-21 ABC, process costing. Parker Company produces mathematical and financial calculators and operates at capacity. Data related to the two products are presented here:

	Mathematical	Financial
Annual production in units	50,000	100,000
Direct material costs	$150,000	$300,000
Direct manufacturing labor costs	$ 50,000	$100,000
Direct manufacturing labor-hours	2,500	5,000
Machine-hours	25,000	50,000
Number of production runs	50	50
Inspection hours	1,000	500

Total manufacturing overhead costs are as follows:

	Total
Machining costs	$375,000
Setup costs	120,000
Inspection costs	105,000

Required

1. Choose a cost driver for each overhead cost pool and calculate the manufacturing overhead cost per unit for each product.
2. Compute the manufacturing cost per unit for each product.

5-22 Activity-based costing, service company. Quikprint Corporation owns a small printing press that prints leaflets, brochures, and advertising materials. Quikprint classifies its various printing jobs as standard jobs or special jobs. Quikprint's simple job-costing system has two direct-cost categories (direct materials and direct labor) and a single indirect-cost pool. Quikprint operates at capacity and allocates all indirect costs using printing machine-hours as the allocation base.

Quikprint is concerned about the accuracy of the costs assigned to standard and special jobs and therefore is planning to implement an activity-based costing system. Quikprint's ABC system would have the same direct-cost categories as its simple costing system. However, instead of a single indirect-cost pool there would now be six categories for assigning indirect costs: design, purchasing, setup, printing machine operations, marketing, and administration. To see how activity-based costing would affect the costs of standard and special jobs, Quikprint collects the following information for the fiscal year 2011 that just ended.

	A	B	C	D	E – H Cause-and-Effect Relationship Between Allocation Base and Activity Cost
1		Standard Job	Special Job	Total	
2	Number of printing jobs	400	200		
3	Price per job	$1,200	$1,500		
4	Cost of supplies per job	$200	$250		
5	Direct labor costs per job	$180	$200		
6	Printing machine-hours per job	10	10		
7	Cost of printing machine operations			$150,000	Indirect costs of operating printing machines
8					increase with printing machine hours
9	Setup-hours per job	4	7		
10	Setup costs			$90,000	Indirect setup costs increase with setup hours
11	Total number of purchase orders	400	500		
12	Purchase order costs			$36,000	Indirect purchase order costs increase with
13					number of purchase orders
14	Design costs	$8,000	$32,000	$40,000	Design costs are allocated to standard and special
15					jobs based on a special study of the design department
16	Marketing costs as a percentage of revenues	5%	5%	$39,000	
17	Administration costs			$48,000	Demand for administrative resources increases with direct labor costs

Required

1. Calculate the cost of a standard job and a special job under the simple costing system.
2. Calculate the cost of a standard job and a special job under the activity-based costing system.
3. Compare the costs of a standard job and a special job in requirements 1 and 2. Why do the simple and activity-based costing systems differ in the cost of a standard job and a special job?
4. How might Quikprint use the new cost information from its activity-based costing system to better manage its business?

5-23 Activity-based costing, manufacturing. Open Doors, Inc., produces two types of doors, interior and exterior. The company's simple costing system has two direct cost categories (materials and labor) and one indirect cost pool. The simple costing system allocates indirect costs on the basis of machine-hours. Recently, the owners of Open Doors have been concerned about a decline in the market share for their interior doors, usually their biggest seller. Information related to Open Doors production for the most recent year follows:

	Interior	Exterior
Units sold	3,200	1,800
Selling price	$ 125	$ 200
Direct material cost per unit	$ 30	$ 45
Direct manufacturing labor cost per hour	$ 16	$ 16
Direct manufacturing labor-hours per unit	1.50	2.25
Production runs	40	85
Material moves	72	168
Machine setups	45	155
Machine-hours	5,500	4,500
Number of inspections	250	150

The owners have heard of other companies in the industry that are now using an activity-based costing system and are curious how an ABC system would affect their product costing decisions. After analyzing the indirect cost pool for Open Doors, six activities were identified as generating indirect costs: production scheduling, material handling, machine setup, assembly, inspection, and marketing. Open Doors collected the following data related to the indirect cost activities:

Activity	Activity Cost	Activity Cost Driver
Production scheduling	$95,000	Production runs
Material handling	$45,000	Material moves
Machine setup	$25,000	Machine setups
Assembly	$60,000	Machine-hours
Inspection	$ 8,000	Number of inspections

Marketing costs were determined to be 3% of the sales revenue for each type of door.

Required

1. Calculate the cost of an interior door and an exterior door under the existing simple costing system.
2. Calculate the cost of an interior door and an exterior door under an activity-based costing system.
3. Compare the costs of the doors in requirements 1 and 2. Why do the simple and activity-based costing systems differ in the cost of an interior and exterior door?
4. How might Open Door, Inc., use the new cost information from its activity-based costing system to address the declining market share for interior doors?

5-24 ABC, retail product-line profitability. Family Supermarkets (FS) operates at capacity and decides to apply ABC analysis to three product lines: baked goods, milk and fruit juice, and frozen foods. It identifies four activities and their activity cost rates as follows:

Ordering	$100 per purchase order
Delivery and receipt of merchandise	$ 80 per delivery
Shelf-stocking	$ 20 per hour
Customer support and assistance	$ 0.20 per item sold

The revenues, cost of goods sold, store support costs, the activities that account for the store support costs, and activity-area usage of the three product lines are as follows:

	Baked Goods	Milk and Fruit Juice	Frozen Products
Financial data			
Revenues	$57,000	$63,000	$52,000
Cost of goods sold	$38,000	$47,000	$35,000
Store support	$11,400	$14,100	$10,500
Activity-area usage (cost-allocation base)			
Ordering (purchase orders)	30	25	13
Delivery (deliveries)	98	36	28
Shelf-stocking (hours)	183	166	24
Customer support (items sold)	15,500	20,500	7,900

Under its simple costing system, FS allocated support costs to products at the rate of 30% of cost of goods sold.

Required

1. Use the simple costing system to prepare a product-line profitability report for FS.
2. Use the ABC system to prepare a product-line profitability report for FS.
3. What new insights does the ABC system in requirement 2 provide to FS managers?

5-25 ABC, wholesale, customer profitability. Ramirez Wholesalers operates at capacity and sells furniture items to four department-store chains (customers). Mr. Ramirez commented, "We apply ABC to determine product-line profitability. The same ideas apply to customer profitability, and we should find out our customer profitability as well." Ramirez Wholesalers sends catalogs to corporate purchasing departments on a monthly basis. The customers are entitled to return unsold merchandise within a six-month period from the purchase date and receive a full purchase price refund. The following data were collected from last year's operations:

	Chain			
	1	2	3	4
Gross sales	$55,000	$25,000	$100,000	$75,000
Sales returns:				
Number of items	101	25	65	35
Amount	$11,000	$ 3,500	$ 7,000	$ 6,500
Number of orders:				
Regular	45	175	52	75
Rush	11	48	11	32

Ramirez has calculated the following activity rates:

Activity	Cost-Driver Rate
Regular order processing	$25 per regular order
Rush order processing	$125 per rush order
Returned items processing	$15 per item
Catalogs and customer support	$1,100 per customer

Customers pay the transportation costs. The cost of goods sold averages 70% of sales.

Required Determine the contribution to profit from each chain last year. Comment on your solution.

5-26 ABC, activity area cost-driver rates, product cross-subsidization. Idaho Potatoes (IP) operates at capacity and processes potatoes into potato cuts at its highly automated Pocatello plant. It sells potatoes to the retail consumer market and to the institutional market, which includes hospitals, cafeterias, and university dormitories.

IP's simple costing system, which does not distinguish between potato cuts processed for retail and institutional markets, has a single direct-cost category (direct materials, i.e. raw potatoes) and a single indirect-cost pool (production support). Support costs, which include packaging materials, are allocated on the basis of pounds of potato cuts processed. The company uses 1,200,000 pounds of raw potatoes to process 1,000,000 pounds of potato cuts. At the end of 2011, IP unsuccessfully bid for a large institutional contract. Its bid was reported to be 30% above the winning bid. This feedback came as a shock because IP included only a minimum profit margin on its bid and the Pocatello plant was acknowledged as the most efficient in the industry.

As a result of its review process of the lost contract bid, IP decided to explore ways to refine its costing system. The company determined that 90% of the direct materials (raw potatoes) related to the retail market and 10% to the institutional market. In addition, the company identified that packaging materials could be directly traced to individual jobs ($180,000 for retail and $8,000 for institutional). Also, the company used ABC to identify three main activity areas that generated support costs: cleaning, cutting, and packaging.

- **Cleaning Activity Area**—The cost-allocation base is pounds of raw potatoes cleaned.
- **Cutting Activity Area**—The production line produces (a) 250 pounds of retail potato cuts per cutting-hour and (b) 400 pounds of institutional potato cuts per cutting-hour. The cost-allocation base is cutting-hours on the production line.
- **Packaging Activity Area**—The packaging line packages (a) 25 pounds of retail potato cuts per packaging-hour and (b) 100 pounds of institutional potato cuts per packaging-hour. The cost-allocation base is packaging-hours on the production line.

The following table summarizes the actual costs for 2011 before and after the preceding cost analysis:

	Before the cost analysis	After the cost analysis Production Support	Retail	Institutional	Total
Direct materials used					
Potatoes	$ 150,000		$135,000	$15,000	$ 150,000
Packaging			180,000	8,000	188,000
Production support	983,000				
Cleaning		$120,000			120,000
Cutting		231,000			231,000
Packaging		444,000			444,000
Total	$1,133,000	$795,000	$315,000	$23,000	$1,133,000

Required

1. Using the simple costing system, what is the cost per pound of potato cuts produced by IP?
2. Calculate the cost rate per unit of the cost driver in the (a) cleaning, (b) cutting, and (c) packaging activity areas.
3. Suppose IP uses information from its activity cost rates to calculate costs incurred on retail potato cuts and institutional potato cuts. Using the ABC system, what is the cost per pound of (a) retail potato cuts and (b) institutional potato cuts?
4. Comment on the cost differences between the two costing systems in requirements 1 and 3. How might IP use the information in requirement 3 to make better decisions?

5-27 Activity-based costing. The job costing system at Smith's Custom Framing has five indirect cost pools (purchasing, material handling, machine maintenance, product inspection, and packaging). The company is in the process of bidding on two jobs; Job 215, an order of 15 intricate personalized frames, and Job 325, an order of 6 standard personalized frames. The controller wants you to compare overhead allocated under the current simple job-costing system and a newly-designed activity-based job-costing system. Total budgeted costs in each indirect cost pool and the budgeted quantity of activity driver are as follows:

	Budgeted Overhead	Activity Driver	Budgeted Quantity of Activity Driver
Purchasing	$ 70,000	Purchase orders processed	2,000
Material handling	87,500	Material moves	5,000
Machine maintenance	237,300	Machine-hours	10,500
Product inspection	18,900	Inspections	1,200
Packaging	39,900	Units produced	3,800
	$453,600		

Information related to Job 215 and Job 325 follows. Job 215 incurs more batch-level costs because it uses more types of materials that need to be purchased, moved, and inspected relative to Job 325.

	Job 215	Job 325
Number of purchase orders	25	8
Number of material moves	10	4
Machine-hours	40	60
Number of inspections	9	3
Units produced	15	6

1. Compute the total overhead allocated to each job under a simple costing system, where overhead is allocated based on machine-hours.
2. Compute the total overhead allocated to each job under an activity-based costing system using the appropriate activity drivers.
3. Explain why Smith's Custom Framing might favor the ABC job-costing system over the simple job-costing system, especially in its bidding process.

5-28 ABC, product costing at banks, cross-subsidization. National Savings Bank (NSB) is examining the profitability of its Premier Account, a combined savings and checking account. Depositors receive a 7% annual interest rate on their average deposit. NSB earns an interest rate spread of 3% (the difference between the rate at which it lends money and the rate it pays depositors) by lending money for home loan purposes at 10%. Thus, NSB would gain $60 on the interest spread if a depositor had an average Premier Account balance of $2,000 in 2011 ($2,000 × 3% = $60).

The Premier Account allows depositors unlimited use of services such as deposits, withdrawals, checking accounts, and foreign currency drafts. Depositors with Premier Account balances of $1,000 or more receive unlimited free use of services. Depositors with minimum balances of less than $1,000 pay a $22-a-month service fee for their Premier Account.

NSB recently conducted an activity-based costing study of its services. It assessed the following costs for six individual services. The use of these services in 2011 by three customers is as follows:

	Activity-Based Cost per "Transaction"	Account Usage		
		Holt	Turner	Graham
Deposit/withdrawal with teller	$ 2.30	42	48	5
Deposit/withdrawal with automatic teller machine (ATM)	0.70	7	19	17
Deposit/withdrawal on prearranged monthly basis	0.40	0	13	62
Bank checks written	8.40	11	1	3
Foreign currency drafts	12.40	4	2	6
Inquiries about account balance	1.40	12	20	9
Average Premier Account balance for 2011		$1,100	$700	$24,600

Assume Holt and Graham always maintain a balance above $1,000, whereas Turner always has a balance below $1,000.

Required
1. Compute the 2011 profitability of the Holt, Turner, and Graham Premier Accounts at NSB.
2. Why might NSB worry about the profitability of individual customers if the Premier Account product offering is profitable as a whole?
3. What changes would you recommend for NSB's Premier Account?

Problems

5-29 Job costing with single direct-cost category, single indirect-cost pool, law firm. Wigan Associates is a recently formed law partnership. Ellery Hanley, the managing partner of Wigan Associates, has just finished a tense phone call with Martin Offiah, president of Widnes Coal. Offiah strongly complained about the price Wigan charged for some legal work done for Widnes Coal.

Hanley also received a phone call from its only other client (St. Helen's Glass), which was very pleased with both the quality of the work and the price charged on its most recent job.

Wigan Associates operates at capacity and uses a cost-based approach to pricing (billing) each job. Currently it uses a simple costing system with a single direct-cost category (professional labor-hours) and a single indirect-cost pool (general support). Indirect costs are allocated to cases on the basis of professional labor-hours per case. The job files show the following:

	Widnes Coal	St. Helen's Glass
Professional labor	104 hours	96 hours

Professional labor costs at Wigan Associates are $70 an hour. Indirect costs are allocated to cases at $105 an hour. Total indirect costs in the most recent period were $21,000.

Required
1. Why is it important for Wigan Associates to understand the costs associated with individual jobs?
2. Compute the costs of the Widnes Coal and St. Helen's Glass jobs using Wigan's simple costing system.

5-30 Job costing with multiple direct-cost categories, single indirect-cost pool, law firm (continuation of 5-29). Hanley asks his assistant to collect details on those costs included in the $21,000 indirect-cost pool that can be traced to each individual job. After analysis, Wigan is able to reclassify $14,000 of the $21,000 as direct costs:

Other Direct Costs	Widnes Coal	St. Helen's Glass
Research support labor	$1,600	$ 3,400
Computer time	500	1,300
Travel and allowances	600	4,400
Telephones/faxes	200	1,000
Photocopying	250	750
Total	$3,150	$10,850

Hanley decides to calculate the costs of each job as if Wigan had used six direct cost-pools and a single indirect-cost pool. The single indirect-cost pool would have $7,000 of costs and would be allocated to each case using the professional labor-hours base.

Required

1. What is the revised indirect-cost allocation rate per professional labor-hour for Wigan Associates when total indirect costs are $7,000?
2. Compute the costs of the Widnes and St. Helen's jobs if Wigan Associates had used its refined costing system with multiple direct-cost categories and one indirect-cost pool.
3. Compare the costs of Widnes and St. Helen's jobs in requirement 2 with those in requirement 2 of Problem 5-29. Comment on the results.

5-31 Job costing with multiple direct-cost categories, multiple indirect-cost pools, law firm (continuation of 5-29 and 5-30). Wigan has two classifications of professional staff: partners and associates. Hanley asks his assistant to examine the relative use of partners and associates on the recent Widnes Coal and St. Helen's jobs. The Widnes job used 24 partner-hours and 80 associate-hours. The St. Helen's job used 56 partner-hours and 40 associate-hours. Therefore, totals of the two jobs together were 80 partner-hours and 120 associate-hours. Hanley decides to examine how using separate direct-cost rates for partners and associates and using separate indirect-cost pools for partners and associates would have affected the costs of the Widnes and St. Helen's jobs. Indirect costs in each indirect-cost pool would be allocated on the basis of total hours of that category of professional labor. From the total indirect cost-pool of $7,000, $4,600 is attributable to the activities of partners, and $2,400 is attributable to the activities of associates.

The rates per category of professional labor are as follows:

Category of Professional Labor	Direct Cost per Hour	Indirect Cost per Hour
Partner	$100.00	$4,600 ÷ 80 hours = $57.50
Associate	50.00	$2,400 ÷ 120 hours = $20.00

Required

1. Compute the costs of the Widnes and St. Helen's cases using Wigan's further refined system, with multiple direct-cost categories and multiple indirect-cost pools.
2. For what decisions might Wigan Associates find it more useful to use this job-costing approach rather than the approaches in Problem 5-29 or 5-30?

5-32 Plant-wide, department, and activity-cost rates. Allen's Aero Toys makes two models of toy airplanes, fighter jets, and cargo planes. The fighter jets are more detailed and require smaller batch sizes. The controller has asked you to compare plant-wide, department, and activity-based cost allocations.

Allen's Aero Toys
Budgeted Information per unit
For the Year Ended 30 November 2010

Assembly Department	Fighters	Cargo	Total
Direct materials	$2.50	$3.75	$ 6.25
Direct manufacturing labor	3.50	2.00	5.50
Total direct cost per unit	$6.00	$5.75	$11.75

Painting Department	Fighters	Cargo	
Direct materials	$0.50	$1.00	$ 1.50
Direct manufacturing labor	2.25	1.50	3.75
Total direct cost per unit	$2.75	$2.50	$ 5.25
Number of units produced	800	740	

The budgeted overhead cost for each department is as follows:

	Assembly Department	Painting Department	Total
Materials handling	$1,700	$ 900	$ 2,600
Quality inspection	2,750	1,150	3,900
Utilities	2,580	2,100	4,680
	$7,030	$4,150	$11,180

Other information follows:

Materials handling and quality inspection costs vary with the number of batches processed in each department. The budgeted number of batches for each product line in each department is as follows:

	Fighters	Cargo	Total
Assembly department	150	48	198
Painting department	100	32	132
Total	250	80	330

Utilities costs vary with direct manufacturing labor cost in each department.

Required

1. Calculate the budgeted cost per unit for fighter jets and cargo planes based on a single plant-wide overhead rate, if total overhead is allocated based on total direct costs.
2. Calculate the budgeted cost per unit for fighter jets and cargo planes based on departmental overhead rates, where assembly department overhead costs are allocated based on direct manufacturing labor costs of the assembly department and painting department overhead costs are allocated based on total direct costs of the painting department.
3. Calculate the budgeted cost per unit for fighter jets and cargo planes if Allen's Aero Toys allocates overhead costs using activity-based costing.
4. Explain how activity-based costing could improve or reduce decision quality.

5-33 Department and activity-cost rates, service sector. Roxbury's Radiology Center (RRC) performs X-rays, ultrasounds, CT scans, and MRIs. RRC has developed a reputation as a top Radiology Center in the state. RRC has achieved this status because it constantly reexamines its processes and procedures. RRC has been using a single, facility-wide overhead allocation rate. The VP of Finance believes that RRC can make better process improvements if it uses more disaggregated cost information. She says, "We have state of the art medical imaging technology. Can't we have state of the art accounting technology?"

Roxbury's Radiology Center
Budgeted Information
For the Year Ended May 30, 2011

	X-rays	Ultrasound	CT scan	MRI	Total
Technician labor	$ 64,000	$104,000	$119,000	$106,000	$ 393,000
Depreciation	136,800	231,000	400,200	792,000	1560,000
Materials	22,400	16,500	23,900	30,800	93,600
Administration					19,000
Maintenance					260,000
Sanitation					267,900
Utilities					121,200
	$223,200	$351,500	$543,100	$928,800	$2,714,700
Number of procedures	2,555	4,760	3,290	2,695	
Minutes to clean after each procedure	10	10	20	40	
Minutes for each procedure	5	20	15	40	

RRC operates at capacity. The proposed allocation bases for overhead are as follows:

Administration	Number of procedures
Maintenance (including parts)	Capital cost of the equipment (use Depreciation)
Sanitation	Total cleaning minutes
Utilities	Total procedure minutes

Required

1. Calculate the budgeted cost per service for X-rays, Ultrasounds, CT scans, and MRIs using direct technician labor costs as the allocation basis.
2. Calculate the budgeted cost per service of X-rays, Ultrasounds, CT scans, and MRIs if RRC allocated overhead costs using activity-based costing.
3. Explain how the disaggregation of information could be helpful to RRC's intention to continuously improve its services.

5-34 Choosing cost drivers, activity-based costing, activity-based management. Annie Warbucks runs a dance studio with childcare and adult fitness classes. Annie's budget for the upcoming year is as follows:

Annie Warbuck's Dance Studio
Budgeted Costs and Activities
For the Year Ended June 30, 2010

Dance teacher salaries	$62,100
Child care teacher salaries	24,300
Fitness instructor salaries	39,060
Total salaries	$125,460
Supplies (art, dance accessories, fitness)	21,984
Rent, maintenance, and utilities	97,511
Administration salaries	50,075
Marketing expenses	21,000
Total	$316,030

Other budget information follows:

	Dance	Childcare	Fitness	Total
Square footage	6,000	3,150	2,500	11,650
Number of participants	1,485	450	270	2,205
Teachers per hour	3	3	1	7
Number of advertisements	26	24	20	70

Required

1. Determine which costs are direct costs and which costs are indirect costs of different programs.
2. Choose a cost driver for the indirect costs and calculate the budgeted cost per unit of the cost driver. Explain briefly your choice of cost driver.
3. Calculate the budgeted costs of each program.
4. How can Annie use this information for pricing? What other factors should she consider?

5-35 Activity-based costing, merchandising. Pharmacare, Inc., a distributor of special pharmaceutical products, operates at capacity and has three main market segments:

a. General supermarket chains
b. Drugstore chains
c. Mom-and-Pop single-store pharmacies

Rick Flair, the new controller of Pharmacare, reported the following data for 2011:

	A	B	C	D	E
1					
2	Pharmacare, 2011	General Supermarket Chains	Drugstore Chains	Mom-and-Pop Single Stores	Pharmacare
5	Revenues	$3,708,000	$3,150,000	$1,980,000	$8,838,000
6	Cost of goods sold	3,600,000	3,000,000	1,800,000	8,400,000
7	Gross margin	$ 108,000	$ 150,000	$ 180,000	438,000
8	Other operating costs				301,080
9	Operating income				$ 136,920

For many years, Pharmacare has used gross margin percentage [(Revenue − Cost of goods sold) ÷ Revenue] to evaluate the relative profitability of its market segments. But, Flair recently attended a seminar on activity-based costing and is considering using it at Pharmacare to analyze and allocate "other operating costs." He meets with all the key managers and several of his operations and sales staff and they agree that there are five key activities that drive other operating costs at Pharmacare:

Activity Area	Cost Driver
Order processing	Number of customer purchase orders
Line-item processing	Number of line items ordered by customers
Delivering to stores	Number of store deliveries
Cartons shipped to store	Number of cartons shipped
Stocking of customer store shelves	Hours of shelf-stocking

Each customer order consists of one or more line items. A line item represents a single product (such as Extra-Strength Tylenol Tablets). Each product line item is delivered in one or more separate cartons. Each store delivery entails the delivery of one or more cartons of products to a customer. Pharmacare's staff stacks cartons directly onto display shelves in customers' stores. Currently, there is no additional charge to the customer for shelf-stocking and not all customers use Pharmacare for this activity. The level of each activity in the three market segments and the total cost incurred for each activity in 2011 is as follows:

	A	B	C	D	E
13					
14	Activity-based Cost Data		Activity Level		
15	Pharmacare 2011	General			Total Cost
16		Supermarket	Drugstore	Mom-and-Pop	of Activity
17	Activity	Chains	Chains	Single Stores	in 2011
18	Orders processed (number)	140	360	1,500	$ 80,000
19	Line-items ordered (number)	1,960	4,320	15,000	63,840
20	Store deliveries made (number)	120	360	1,000	71,000
21	Cartons shipped to stores (number)	36,000	24,000	16,000	76,000
22	Shelf stocking (hours)	360	180	100	10,240
23					$301,080

Required

1. Compute the 2011 gross-margin percentage for each of Pharmacare's three market segments.
2. Compute the cost driver rates for each of the five activity areas.
3. Use the activity-based costing information to allocate the $301,080 of "other operating costs" to each of the market segments. Compute the operating income for each market segment.
4. Comment on the results. What new insights are available with the activity-based costing information?

5-36 Choosing cost drivers, activity-based costing, activity-based management. Pumpkin Bags (PB) is a designer of high quality backpacks and purses. Each design is made in small batches. Each spring, PB comes out with new designs for the backpack and for the purse. The company uses these designs for a year, and then moves on to the next trend. The bags are all made on the same fabrication equipment that is expected to operate at capacity. The equipment must be switched over to a new design and set up to prepare for the production of each new batch of products. When completed, each batch of products is immediately shipped to a wholesaler. Shipping costs vary with the number of shipments. Budgeted information for the year is as follows:

Pumpkin Bags
Budget for costs and Activities
For the Year Ended February 28, 2011

Direct materials—purses	$ 379,290
Direct materials—backpacks	412,920
Direct manufacturing labor—purses	98,000
Direct manufacturing labor—backpacks	120,000
Setup	65,930
Shipping	73,910
Design	166,000
Plant utilities and administration	243,000
Total	$1,559,050

Other budget information follows:

	Backpacks	Purses	Total
Number of bags	6,050	3,350	9,400
Hours of production	1,450	2,600	4,050
Number of batches	130	60	190
Number of designs	2	2	4

Required

1. Identify the cost hierarchy level for each cost category.
2. Identify the most appropriate cost driver for each cost category. Explain briefly your choice of cost driver.
3. Calculate the budgeted cost per unit of cost driver for each cost category.
4. Calculate the budgeted total costs and cost per unit for each product line.
5. Explain how you could use the information in requirement 4 to reduce costs.

5-37 ABC, health care. Uppervale Health Center runs two programs: drug addict rehabilitation and aftercare (counseling and support of patients after release from a mental hospital). The center's budget for 2010 follows:

Professional salaries:		
4 physicians × $150,000	$600,000	
12 psychologists × $75,000	900,000	
16 nurses × $30,000	480,000	$1,980,000
Medical supplies		220,000
Rent and clinic maintenance		126,000
Administrative costs to manage patient charts, food, laundry		440,000
Laboratory services		84,000
Total		$2,850,000

Muriel Clayton, the director of the center, is keen on determining the cost of each program. Clayton compiled the following data describing employee allocations to individual programs:

	Drug	Aftercare	Total Employees
Physicians	4		4
Psychologists	4	8	12
Nurses	6	10	16

Clayton has recently become aware of activity-based costing as a method to refine costing systems. She asks her accountant, Huey Deluth, how she should apply this technique. Deluth obtains the following budgeted information for 2010:

	Drug	Aftercare	Total
Square feet of space occupied by each program	9,000	12,000	21,000
Patient-years of service	50	60	110
Number of laboratory tests	1,400	700	2,100

Required

1. a. Selecting cost-allocation bases that you believe are the most appropriate for allocating indirect costs to programs, calculate the budgeted indirect cost rates for medical supplies; rent and clinic maintenance; administrative costs for patient charts, food, and laundry; and laboratory services.
   b. Using an activity-based costing approach to cost analysis, calculate the budgeted cost of each program and the budgeted cost per patient-year of the drug program.
   c. What benefits can Uppervale Health Center obtain by implementing the ABC system?
2. What factors, other than cost, do you think Uppervale Health Center should consider in allocating resources to its programs?

5-38 Unused capacity, activity-based costing, activity-based management. Nivag's Netballs is a manufacturer of high quality basketballs and volleyballs. Setup costs are driven by the number of batches. Equipment and maintenance costs increase with the number of machine-hours, and lease rent is paid per square foot. Capacity of the facility is 12,000 square feet and Nivag is using only 70% of this capacity. Nivag records the cost of unused capacity as a separate line item, and not as a product cost. The following is the budgeted information for Nivag:

Nivag's Netballs
Budgeted Costs and Activities
For the Year Ended August 31, 2012

Direct materials—basketballs	$ 209,750
Direct materials—volleyballs	358,290
Direct manufacturing labor—basketballs	107,333
Direct manufacturing labor—volleyballs	102,969
Setup	143,500
Equipment and maintenance costs	109,900
Lease rent	216,000
Total	$1,247,742

Other budget information follows:

	Basketballs	Volleyballs
Number of balls	66,000	100,000
Machine-hours	11,000	12,500
Number of batches	300	400
Square footage of production space used	3,360	5,040

Required

1. Calculate the budgeted cost per unit of cost driver for each indirect cost pool.
2. What is the budgeted cost of unused capacity?
3. What is the budgeted total cost and the cost per unit of resources used to produce (a) basketballs and (b) volleyballs?
4. What factors should Nivag consider if it has the opportunity to manufacture a new line of footballs?

5-39 Activity-based job costing, unit-cost comparisons.

The Tracy Corporation has a machining facility specializing in jobs for the aircraft-components market. Tracy's previous simple job-costing system had two direct-cost categories (direct materials and direct manufacturing labor) and a single indirect-cost pool (manufacturing overhead, allocated using direct manufacturing labor-hours). The indirect cost-allocation rate of the simple system for 2010 would have been $115 per direct manufacturing labor-hour.

Recently a team with members from product design, manufacturing, and accounting used an ABC approach to refine its job-costing system. The two direct-cost categories were retained. The team decided to replace the single indirect-cost pool with five indirect-cost pools. The cost pools represent five activity areas at the plant, each with its own supervisor and budget responsibility. Pertinent data are as follows:

Activity Area	Cost-Allocation Base	Cost-Allocation Rate
Materials handling	Parts	$ 0.40
Lathe work	Lathe turns	0.20
Milling	Machine-hours	20.00
Grinding	Parts	0.80
Testing	Units tested	15.00

Information-gathering technology has advanced to the point at which the data necessary for budgeting in these five activity areas are collected automatically.

Two representative jobs processed under the ABC system at the plant in the most recent period had the following characteristics:

	Job 410	Job 411
Direct material cost per job	$ 9,700	$59,900
Direct manufacturing labor cost per job	$750	$11,250
Number of direct manufacturing labor-hours per job	25	375
Parts per job	500	2,000
Lathe turns per job	20,000	59,250
Machine-hours per job	150	1,050
Units per job (all units are tested)	10	200

Required

1. Compute the manufacturing cost per unit for each job under the previous simple job-costing system.
2. Compute the manufacturing cost per unit for each job under the activity-based costing system.
3. Compare the per-unit cost figures for Jobs 410 and 411 computed in requirements 1 and 2. Why do the simple and the activity-based costing systems differ in the manufacturing cost per unit for each job? Why might these differences be important to Tracy Corporation?
4. How might Tracy Corporation use information from its ABC system to better manage its business?

5-40 ABC, implementation, ethics.

(CMA, adapted) Applewood Electronics, a division of Elgin Corporation, manufactures two large-screen television models: the Monarch, which has been produced since 2006 and sells for $900, and the Regal, a newer model introduced in early 2009 that sells for $1,140. Based on the following income statement for the year ended November 30, 2010, senior management at Elgin have decided to concentrate Applewood's marketing resources on the Regal model and to begin to phase out the Monarch model because Regal generates a much bigger operating income per unit.

Applewood Electronics
Income Statement
For the Fiscal Year Ended November 30, 2010

	Monarch	Regal	Total
Revenues	$19,800,000	$4,560,000	$24,360,000
Cost of goods sold	12,540,000	3,192,000	15,732,000
Gross margin	7,260,000	1,368,000	8,628,000
Selling and administrative expense	5,830,000	978,000	6,808,000
Operating income	$ 1,430,000	$ 390,000	$ 1,820,000
Units produced and sold	22,000	4,000	
Operating income per unit sold	$65.00	$97.50	

Details for cost of goods sold for Monarch and Regal are as follows:

	Monarch		Regal	
	Total	Per unit	Total	Per unit
Direct materials	$ 4,576,000	$208	$2,336,000	$584
Direct manufacturing labor[a]	396,000	18	168,000	42
Machine costs[b]	3,168,000	144	288,000	72
Total direct costs	$ 8,140,000	$370	$2,792,000	$698
Manufacturing overhead costs[c]	$ 4,400,000	$200	$ 400,000	$100
Total cost of goods sold	$12,540,000	$570	$3,192,000	$798

[a] Monarch requires 1.5 hours per unit and Regal requires 3.5 hours per unit. The direct manufacturing labor cost is $12 per hour.
[b] Machine costs include lease costs of the machine, repairs, and maintenance. Monarch requires 8 machine-hours per unit and Regal requires 4 machine-hours per unit. The machine hour rate is $18 per hour.
[c] Manufacturing overhead costs are allocated to products based on machine-hours at the rate of $25 per hour.

Applewood's controller, Susan Benzo, is advocating the use of activity-based costing and activity-based management and has gathered the following information about the company's manufacturing overhead costs for the year ended November 30, 2010.

Activity Center (Cost-Allocation Base)	Total Activity Costs	Units of the Cost-Allocation Base		
		Monarch	Regal	Total
Soldering (number of solder points)	$ 942,000	1,185,000	385,000	1,570,000
Shipments (number of shipments)	860,000	16,200	3,800	20,000
Quality control (number of inspections)	1,240,000	56,200	21,300	77,500
Purchase orders (number of orders)	950,400	80,100	109,980	190,080
Machine power (machine-hours)	57,600	176,000	16,000	192,000
Machine setups (number of setups)	750,000	16,000	14,000	30,000
Total manufacturing overhead	$4,800,000			

After completing her analysis, Benzo shows the results to Fred Duval, the Applewood division president. Duval does not like what he sees. "If you show headquarters this analysis, they are going to ask us to phase out the Regal line, which we have just introduced. This whole costing stuff has been a major problem for us. First Monarch was not profitable and now Regal."

"Looking at the ABC analysis, I see two problems. First, we do many more activities than the ones you have listed. If you had included all activities, maybe your conclusions would be different. Second, you used number of setups and number of inspections as allocation bases. The numbers would be different had you used setup-hours and inspection-hours instead. I know that measurement problems precluded you from using these other cost-allocation bases, but I believe you ought to make some adjustments to our current numbers to compensate for these issues. I know you can do better. We can't afford to phase out either product."

Benzo knows that her numbers are fairly accurate. As a quick check, she calculates the profitability of Regal and Monarch using more and different allocation bases. The set of activities and activity rates she had used results in numbers that closely approximate those based on more detailed analyses. She is confident that headquarters, knowing that Regal was introduced only recently, will not ask Applewood to phase it out. She is also aware that a sizable portion of Duval's bonus is based on division revenues. Phasing out either product would adversely affect his bonus. Still, she feels some pressure from Duval to do something.

Required

1. Using activity-based costing, calculate the gross margin per unit of the Regal and Monarch models.
2. Explain briefly why these numbers differ from the gross margin per unit of the Regal and Monarch models calculated using Applewood's existing simple costing system.
3. Comment on Duval's concerns about the accuracy and limitations of ABC.
4. How might Applewood find the ABC information helpful in managing its business?
5. What should Susan Benzo do in response to Duval's comments?

Collaborative Learning Problem

5-41 Activity-based costing, activity-based management, merchandising. Super Bookstore (SB) is a large city bookstore that sells books and music CDs, and has a café. SB operates at capacity and allocates selling, general, and administration (S, G & A) costs to each product line using the cost of merchandise of each product line. SB wants to optimize the pricing and cost management of each product line. SB is wondering if its accounting system is providing it with the best information for making such decisions.

Super Bookstore
Product Line Information
For the Year Ended December 31, 2010

	Books	CDs	Café
Revenues	$3,720,480	$2,315,360	$736,216
Cost of merchandise	$2,656,727	$1,722,311	$556,685
Cost of café cleaning	—	—	$ 18,250
Number of purchase orders placed	2,800	2,500	2,000
Number of deliveries received	1,400	1,700	1,600
Hours of shelf stocking time	15,000	14,000	10,000
Items sold	124,016	115,768	368,108

Super Bookstore incurs the following selling, general, and administration costs:

Super Bookstore
Selling, General, & Administration (S, G & A) Costs
For the Year Ended December 31, 2010

Purchasing department expenses	$ 474,500
Receiving department expenses	432,400
Shelf stocking labor expense	487,500
Customer support expense (cashiers and floor employees)	91,184
	$1,485,584

Required

1. Suppose Super Bookstore uses cost of merchandise to allocate all S, G & A costs. Prepare product line and total company income statements.
2. Identify an improved method for allocating costs to the three product lines. Explain. Use the method for allocating S, G & A costs that you propose to prepare new product line and total company income statements. Compare your results to the results in requirement 1.
3. Write a memo to Super Bookstore's management describing how the improved system might be useful for managing Super Bookstore.

13 Strategy, Balanced Scorecard, and Strategic Profitability Analysis

▶ Learning Objectives

1. Recognize which of two generic strategies a company is using

2. Understand what comprises reengineering

3. Understand the four perspectives of the balanced scorecard

4. Analyze changes in operating income to evaluate strategy

5. Identify unused capacity and how to manage it

Olive Garden wants to know.

So do Barnes and Noble, PepsiCo, and L.L.Bean. Even your local car dealer and transit authority are curious. They all want to know how well they are doing and how they score against the measures they strive to meet. The balanced scorecard can help them answer this question by evaluating key performance measures. Many companies have successfully used the balanced scorecard approach. Infosys Technologies, one of India's leading information technology companies, is one of them.

Balanced Scorecard Helps Infosys Transform into a Leading Consultancy[1]

In the early 2000s, Infosys Technologies was a company in transition. The Bangalore-based company was a market leader in information technology outsourcing, but needed to expand to meet increased client demand. Infosys invested in many new areas including business process outsourcing, project management, and management consulting. This put Infosys in direct competition with established consulting firms, such as IBM and Accenture.

Led by CEO Kris Gopalakrishnan, the company developed an integrated management structure that would help align these new, diverse initiatives. Infosys turned to the balanced scorecard to provide a framework the company could use to formulate and monitor its strategy. The balanced scorecard measures corporate performance along four dimensions—financial, customer, internal business process, and learning and growth.

The balanced scorecard immediately played a role in the transformation of Infosys. The executive team used the scorecard to guide discussion during its meetings. The continual process of adaptation, execution, and management that the scorecard fostered helped the team respond to, and even anticipate, its clients' evolving needs. Eventually, use of the scorecard for performance measurement spread to the rest of the organization, with monetary incentives linked to the company's performance along the different dimensions.

Over time, the balanced scorecard became part of the Infosys culture. In recent years, Infosys has begun using the balanced

---

[1] *Source*: Asis Martinez-Jerez, F., Robert S. Kaplan, and Katherine Miller. 2011. Infosys's relationship scorecard: Measuring transformational partnerships. Harvard Business School Case No. 9-109-006. Boston: Harvard Business School Publishing.

scorecard concept to create "relationship scorecards" for many of its largest clients. Using the scorecard framework, Infosys began measuring its performance for key clients not only on project management and client satisfaction, but also on repeat business and anticipating clients' future strategic needs.

The balanced scorecard helped successfully steer the transformation of Infosys from a technology outsourcer to a leading business consultancy. From 1999 to 2007, the company had a compound annual growth rate of 50%, with sales growing from $120 million in 1999 to more than $3 billion in 2007. Infosys was recognized for its achievements by making the *Wired* 40, *BusinessWeek* IT 100, and *BusinessWeek* Most Innovative Companies lists.

This chapter focuses on how management accounting information helps companies such as Infosys, Merck, Verizon, and Volkswagen implement and evaluate their strategies. Strategy drives the operations of a company and guides managers' short-run and long-run decisions. We describe the balanced scorecard approach to implementing strategy and methods to analyze operating income to evaluate the success of a strategy. We also show how management accounting information helps strategic initiatives, such as productivity improvement, reengineering, and downsizing.

What Is Strategy?

Strategy specifies how an organization matches its own capabilities with the opportunities in the marketplace to accomplish its objectives. In other words, strategy describes how an organization can create value for its customers while differentiating itself from its competitors. For example, Wal-Mart, the retail giant, creates value for its customers by locating stores in suburban and rural areas, and by offering low prices, a wide range of product categories, and few choices within each product category. Consistent with its strategy, Wal-Mart has developed the capability to keep costs down by aggressively negotiating low prices with its suppliers in exchange for high volumes and by maintaining a no-frills, cost-conscious environment.

In formulating its strategy, an organization must first thoroughly understand its industry. Industry analysis focuses on five forces: (1) competitors, (2) potential entrants into the market, (3) equivalent products, (4) bargaining power of customers, and (5) bargaining power of input suppliers.[2] The collective effect of these forces shapes an organization's profit potential. In general, profit potential decreases with greater competition, stronger potential entrants, products that are similar, and more-demanding customers and suppliers. We illustrate these five forces for Chipset, Inc., maker of linear integrated circuit

Learning Objective 1

Recognize which of two generic strategies a company is using

... product differentiation or cost leadership

---

[2] M. Porter, *Competitive Strategy* (New York: Free Press, 1980); M. Porter, *Competitive Advantage* (New York: Free Press, 1985); and M. Porter, "What Is Strategy?" *Harvard Business Review* (November–December 1996): 61–78.

devices (LICDs) used in modems and communication networks. Chipset produces a single specialized product, CX1, a standard, high-performance microchip, which can be used in multiple applications. Chipset designed CX1 with extensive input from customers.

1. **Competitors.** The CX1 model faces severe competition with respect to price, timely delivery, and quality. Companies in the industry have high fixed costs, and persistent pressures to reduce selling prices and utilize capacity fully. Price reductions spur growth because it makes LICDs a cost-effective option in new applications such as digital subscriber lines (DSLs).
2. **Potential entrants into the market.** The small profit margins and high capital costs discourage new entrants. Moreover, incumbent companies such as Chipset are further down the learning curve with respect to lowering costs and building close relationships with customers and suppliers.
3. **Equivalent products.** Chipset tailors CX1 to customer needs and lowers prices by continuously improving CX1's design and processes to reduce production costs. This reduces the risk of equivalent products or new technologies replacing CX1.
4. **Bargaining power of customers.** Customers, such as EarthLink and Verizon, negotiate aggressively with Chipset and its competitors to keep prices down because they buy large quantities of product.
5. **Bargaining power of input suppliers.** To produce CX1, Chipset requires high-quality materials (such as silicon wafers, pins for connectivity, and plastic or ceramic packaging) and skilled engineers, technicians, and manufacturing labor. The skill-sets suppliers and employees bring gives them bargaining power to demand higher prices and wages.

In summary, strong competition and the bargaining powers of customers and suppliers put significant pressure on Chipset's selling prices. To respond to these challenges, Chipset must choose one of two basic strategies: *differentiating its product* or *achieving cost leadership*.

Product differentiation is an organization's ability to offer products or services perceived by its customers to be superior and unique relative to the products or services of its competitors. Apple Inc. has successfully differentiated its products in the consumer electronics industry, as have Johnson & Johnson in the pharmaceutical industry and Coca-Cola in the soft drink industry. These companies have achieved differentiation through innovative product R&D, careful development and promotion of their brands, and the rapid push of products to market. Differentiation increases brand loyalty and the willingness of customers to pay higher prices.

Cost leadership is an organization's ability to achieve lower costs relative to competitors through productivity and efficiency improvements, elimination of waste, and tight cost control. Cost leaders in their respective industries include Wal-Mart (consumer retailing), Home Depot and Lowe's (building products), Texas Instruments (consumer electronics), and Emerson Electric (electric motors). These companies provide products and services that are similar to—not differentiated from—their competitors, but at a lower cost to the customer. Lower selling prices, rather than unique products or services, provide a competitive advantage for these cost leaders.

What strategy should Chipset follow? To help it decide, Chipset develops the customer preference map shown in Exhibit 13-1. The *y*-axis describes various attributes of the product desired by customers. The *x*-axis describes how well Chipset and Visilog, a competitor of Chipset that follows a product-differentiation strategy, do along the various attributes desired by customers from 1 (poor) to 5 (very good). The map highlights the trade-offs in any strategy. It shows the advantages CX1 enjoys in terms of price, scalability (the CX1 technology allows Chispet's customer to achieve different performance levels by simply altering the number of CX1 units in their product), and customer service. Visilog's chips, however, are faster and more powerful, and are customized for various applications such as different types of modems and communication networks.

CX1 is somewhat differentiated from competing products. Differentiating CX1 further would be costly, but Chipset may be able to charge a higher price. Conversely, reducing the cost of manufacturing CX1 would allow Chipset to lower price, spur growth, and increase market share. The scalability of CX1 makes it an effective solution for meeting

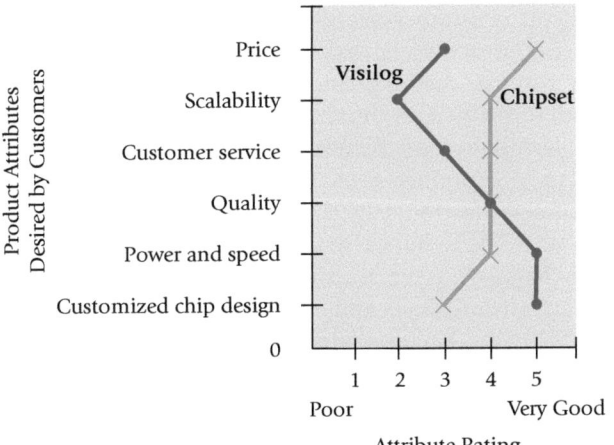
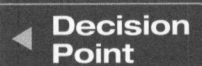

Customer Preference Map for LICDs

varying customer needs. Also, Chipset's current engineering staff is more skilled at making product and process improvements than at creatively designing new products and technologies. Chipset decides to follow a cost-leadership strategy.

To achieve its cost-leadership strategy, Chipset must improve its own internal capabilities. It must enhance quality and reengineer processes to downsize and eliminate excess capacity. At the same time, Chipset's management team does not want to make cuts in personnel that would hurt company morale and hinder future growth.

Building Internal Capabilities: Quality Improvement and Reengineering at Chipset

To improve product quality—that is, to reduce defect rates and improve yields in its manufacturing process—Chipset must maintain process parameters within tight ranges based on real-time data about manufacturing-process parameters, such as temperature and pressure. Chipset must also train its workers in quality-management techniques to help them identify the root causes of defects and ways to prevent them and empower them to take actions to improve quality.

A second element of Chipset's strategy is reengineering its order-delivery process. Some of Chipset's customers have complained about the lengthening time span between ordering products and receiving them. **Reengineering** is the fundamental rethinking and redesign of business processes to achieve improvements in critical measures of performance, such as cost, quality, service, speed, and customer satisfaction.[3] To illustrate reengineering, consider the order-delivery system at Chipset in 2010. When Chipset received an order from a customer, a copy was sent to manufacturing, where a production scheduler began planning the manufacturing of the ordered products. Frequently, a considerable amount of time elapsed before production began on the ordered product. After manufacturing was complete, CX1 chips moved to the shipping department, which matched the quantities of CX1 to be shipped against customer orders. Often, completed CX1 chips stayed in inventory until a truck became available for shipment. If the quantity to be shipped was less than the number of chips requested by the customer, a special shipment was made for the balance of the chips. Shipping documents moved to the billing department for issuing invoices. Special staff in the accounting department followed up with customers for payments.

The many transfers of CX1 chips and information across departments (sales, manufacturing, shipping, billing, and accounting) to satisfy a customer's order created delays. Furthermore, no single individual was responsible for fulfilling a customer order. To respond to these challenges, Chipset formed a cross-functional team in late 2010 and implemented a reengineered order-delivery process in 2011.

Decision Point

What are two generic strategies a company can use?

Learning Objective 2

Understand what comprises reengineering

... redesigning business processes to improve performance by reducing cost and improving quality

---

[3] See M. Hammer and J. Champy, *Reengineering the Corporation: A Manifesto for Business Revolution* (New York: Harper, 1993); E. Ruhli, C. Treichler, and S. Schmidt, "From Business Reengineering to Management Reengineering—A European Study," *Management International Review* (1995): 361–371; and K. Sandberg, "Reengineering Tries a Comeback—This Time for Growth, Not Just for Cost Savings," *Harvard Management Update* (November 2001).

Under the new system, a customer-relationship manager is responsible for each customer and negotiates long-term contracts specifying quantities and prices. The customer-relationship manager works closely with the customer and with manufacturing to specify delivery schedules for CX1 one month in advance of shipment. The schedule of customer orders and delivery dates is sent electronically to manufacturing. Completed chips are shipped directly from the manufacturing plant to customer sites. Each shipment automatically triggers an electronic invoice and customers electronically transfer funds to Chipset's bank.

Companies, such as AT&T, Banca di America e di Italia, Cigna Insurance, Cisco, PepsiCo, and Siemens Nixdorf, have realized significant benefits by reengineering their processes across design, production, and marketing (just as in the Chipset example). Reengineering has only limited benefits when reengineering efforts focus on only a single activity such as shipping or invoicing rather than the entire order-delivery process. To be successful, reengineering efforts must focus on changing roles and responsibilities, eliminating unnecessary activities and tasks, using information technology, and developing employee skills.

Take another look at Exhibit 13-1 and note the interrelatedness and consistency in Chipset's strategy. To help meet customer preferences for price, quality, and customer service, Chipset decides on a cost-leadership strategy. And to achieve cost leadership, Chipset builds internal capabilities by reengineering its processes. Chipset's next challenge is to effectively implement its strategy

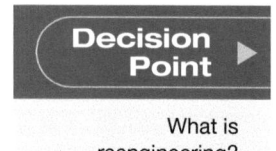

Decision Point

What is reengineering?

Strategy Implementation and the Balanced Scorecard

Learning Objective 3

Understand the four perspectives of the balanced scorecard

... financial, customer, internal business process, and learning and growth

Many organizations, such as Allstate Insurance, Bank of Montreal, BP, and Dow Chemical, have introduced a *balanced scorecard* approach to track progress and manage the implementation of their strategies.

The Balanced Scorecard

The **balanced scorecard** translates an organization's mission and strategy into a set of performance measures that provides the framework for implementing its strategy.[4] The balanced scorecard does not focus solely on achieving short-run financial objectives. It also highlights the nonfinancial objectives that an organization must achieve to meet and sustain its financial objectives. The scorecard measures an organization's performance from four perspectives: (1) financial, the profits and value created for shareholders; (2) customer, the success of the company in its target market; (3) internal business processes, the internal operations that create value for customers; and (4) learning and growth, the people and system capabilities that support operations. A company's strategy influences the measures it uses to track performance in each of these perspectives.

Why is this tool called a balanced scorecard? Because it balances the use of financial and nonfinancial performance measures to evaluate short-run and long-run performance in a single report. The balanced scorecard reduces managers' emphasis on short-run financial performance, such as quarterly earnings, because the key strategic nonfinancial and operational indicators, such as product quality and customer satisfaction, measure changes that a company is making for the long run. The financial benefits of these long-run changes may not show up immediately in short-run earnings; however, strong improvement in nonfinancial measures usually indicates the creation of future economic value. For example, an increase in customer satisfaction, as measured by customer surveys and repeat purchases, signals a strong likelihood of higher sales and income in the future. By balancing the mix of financial and nonfinancial measures, the balanced scorecard

---

[4] See R. S. Kaplan and D. P. Norton, *The Balanced Scorecard* (Boston: Harvard Business School Press, 1996); R. S. Kaplan and D. P. Norton, *The Strategy-Focused Organization: How Balanced Scorecard Companies Thrive in the New Business Environment* (Boston: Harvard Business School Press, 2001); R. S. Kaplan and D. P. Norton, *Strategy Maps: Converting Intangible Assets into Tangible Outcomes* (Boston: Harvard Business School Press, 2004); and R. S. Kaplan and D. P. Norton, *Alignment: Using the Balanced Scorecard to Create Corporate Synergies* (Boston: Harvard Business School Press, 2006).

For simplicity, this chapter, and much of the literature, emphasizes long-run financial objectives as the primary goal of for-profit companies. For-profit companies interested in long-run financial, environmental, and social objectives adapt the balanced scorecard to implement all three objectives.

broadens management's attention to short-run *and* long-run performance. *Never lose sight of the key point. In for-profit companies, the primary goal of the balanced scorecard is to sustain long-run financial performance. Nonfinancial measures simply serve as leading indicators for the hard-to-measure long-run financial performance.*

Strategy Maps and the Balanced Scorecard

We use the Chipset example to develop strategy maps and the four perspectives of the balanced scorecard. The objectives and measures Chipset's managers choose for each perspective relates to the action plans for furthering Chipset's cost leadership strategy: *improving quality* and *reengineering processes*.

Strategy Maps

A useful first step in designing a balanced scorecard is a *strategy map*. A **strategy map** is a diagram that describes how an organization creates value by connecting strategic objectives in explicit cause-and-effect relationships with each other in the financial, customer, internal business process, and learning and growth perspectives. Exhibit 13-2 presents Chipset's strategy map. Follow the arrows to see how a strategic objective affects other strategic objectives. For example, empowering the workforce helps align employee and organization goals and improves processes. Employee and organizational alignment also helps improve processes that improve manufacturing quality and productivity, reduce customer delivery time, meet specified delivery dates, and improve post-sales service, all of which increase customer satisfaction. Improving manufacturing quality and productivity

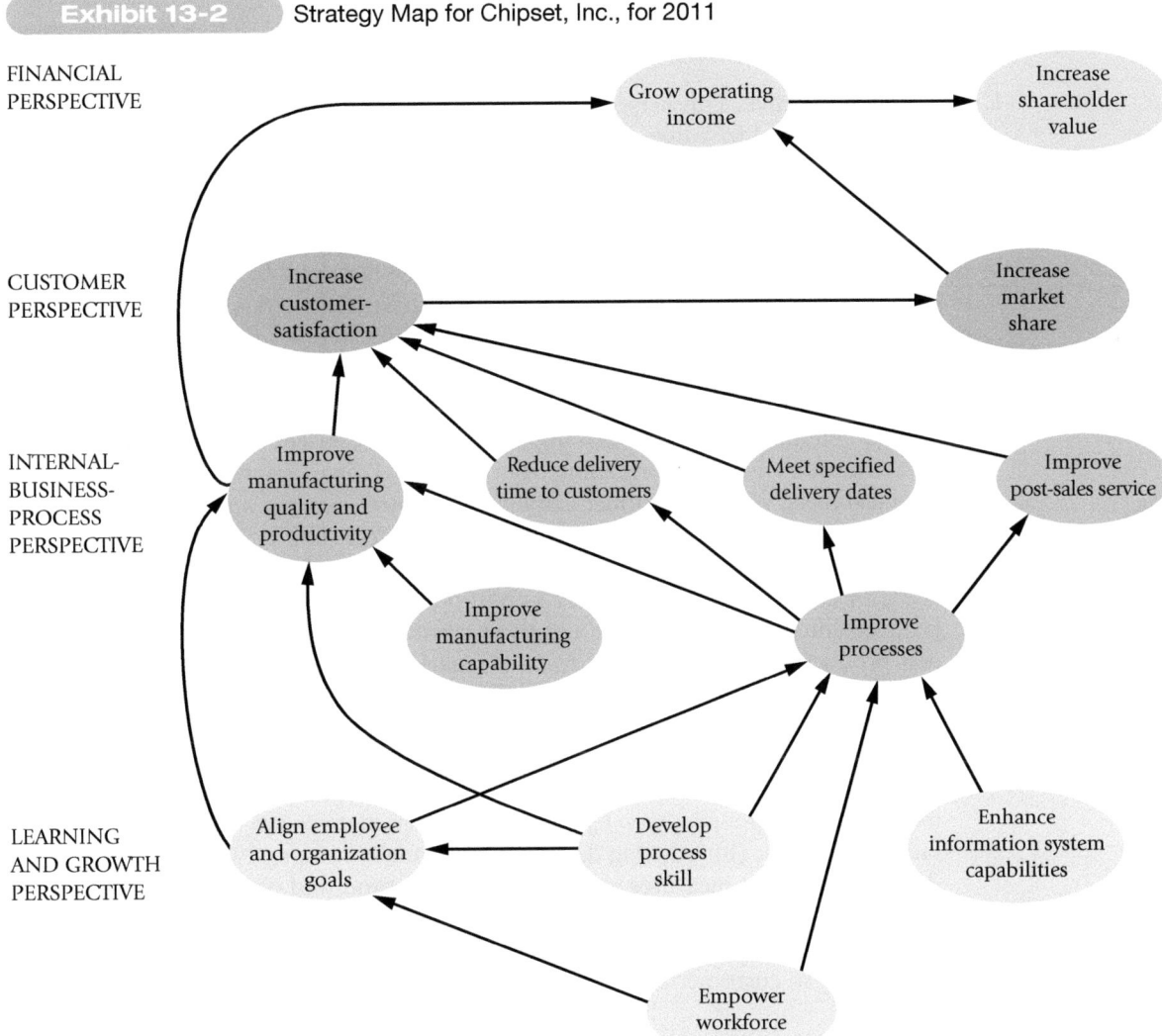

Exhibit 13-2 Strategy Map for Chipset, Inc., for 2011

grows operating income and increases customer satisfaction that, in turn, increases market share, operating income, and shareholder value.

Chipset operates in a knowledge-intensive business. To compete successfully, Chipset invests in its employees, implements new technology and process controls, improves quality, and reengineers processes. Doing these activities well enables Chipset to build capabilities and intangible assets, which are not recorded as assets in its financial books. The strategy map helps Chipset evaluate whether these intangible assets are generating financial returns.

Chipset could include many other cause-and-effect relationships in the strategy map in Exhibit 13-2. But, Chipset, like other companies implementing the balanced scorecard, focuses on only those relationships that it believes to be the most significant.

Chipset uses the strategy map from Exhibit 13-2 to build the balanced scorecard presented in Exhibit 13-3. The scorecard highlights the four perspectives of performance: financial, customer, internal business process, and learning and growth. The first column presents the strategic objectives from the strategy map in Exhibit 13-2. At the beginning of 2011, the company's managers specify the strategic objectives, measures, initiatives (the actions necessary to achieve the objectives), and target performance (the first four columns of Exhibit 13-3).

Chipset wants to use the balanced scorecard targets to drive the organization to higher levels of performance. Managers therefore set targets at a level of performance that is achievable, yet distinctly better than competitors. Chipset's managers complete the fifth column, reporting actual performance at the end of 2011. This column compares Chipset's performance relative to target.

Four Perspectives of the Balanced Scorecard

We next describe the perspectives in general terms and illustrate each perspective using the measures chosen by Chipset in the context of its strategy.

1. **Financial perspective.** This perspective evaluates the profitability of the strategy and the creation of shareholder value. Because Chipset's key strategic initiatives are cost reduction relative to competitors' costs and sales growth, the financial perspective focuses on how much operating income results from reducing costs and selling more units of CX1.

2. **Customer perspective.** This perspective identifies targeted customer and market segments and measures the company's success in these segments. To monitor its customer objectives, Chipset uses measures such as market share in the communication-networks segment, number of new customers, and customer-satisfaction ratings.

3. **Internal-business-process perspective.** This perspective focuses on internal operations that create value for customers that, in turn, help achieve financial performance. Chipset determines internal-business-process improvement targets after benchmarking against its main competitors using information from published financial statements, prevailing prices, customers, suppliers, former employees, industry experts, and financial analysts. The internal-business-process perspective comprises three subprocesses:
   - **Innovation process:** Creating products, services, and processes that will meet the needs of customers. This is a very important process for companies that follow a product-differentiation strategy and must constantly design and develop innovative new products to remain competitive in the marketplace. Chipset's innovation focuses on improving its manufacturing capability and process controls to lower costs and improve quality. Chipset measures innovation by the number of improvements in manufacturing processes and percentage of processes with advanced controls.
   - **Operations process:** Producing and delivering existing products and services that will meet the needs of customers. Chipset's strategic initiatives are (a) improving manufacturing quality, (b) reducing delivery time to customers, and (c) meeting specified delivery dates so it measures yield, order-delivery time, and on-time deliveries.
   - **Postsales-service process:** Providing service and support to the customer after the sale of a product or service. Chipset monitors how quickly and accurately it is responding to customer-service requests.

Exhibit 13-3 The Balanced Scorecard for Chipset, Inc., for 2011

Strategic Objectives	Measures	Initiatives	Target Performance	Actual Performance
Financial Perspective				
Grow operating income	Operating income from productivity gain	Manage costs and unused capacity	$1,850,000	$1,912,500
Increase shareholder value	Operating income from growth	Build strong customer relationships	$2,500,000	$2,820,000
	Revenue growth		9%	10%[a]
Customer Perspective				
Increase market share	Market share in communication-networks segment	Identify future needs of customers	6%	7%
Increase customer satisfaction	Number of new customers	Identify new target-customer segments	1	1[b]
	Customer-satisfaction ratings	Increase customer focus of sales organization	90% of customers give top two ratings	87% of customers give top two ratings
Internal-Business-Process Perspective				
Improve postsales service	Service response time	Improve customer-service process	Within 4 hours	Within 3 hours
Improve manufacturing quality and productivity	Yield	Identify root causes of problems and improve quality	78%	79.3%
Reduce delivery time to customers	Order-delivery time	Reengineer order-delivery process	30 days	30 days
Meet specified delivery dates	On-time delivery	Reengineer order-delivery process	92%	90%
Improve processes	Number of major improvements in manufacturing and business processes	Organize teams from manufacturing and sales to modify processes	5	5
Improve manufacturing capability	Percentage of processes with advanced controls	Organize R&D/manufacturing teams to implement advanced controls	75%	75%
Learning-and-Growth Perspective				
Align employee and organization goals	Employee-satisfaction ratings	Employee participation and suggestions program to build teamwork	80% of employees give top two ratings	88% of employees give top two ratings
Empower workforce	Percentage of line workers empowered to manage processes	Have supervisors act as coaches rather than decision makers	85%	90%
Develop process skill	Percentage of employees trained in process and quality management	Employee training programs	90%	92%
Enhance information-system capabilities	Percentage of manufacturing processes with real-time feedback	Improve online and offline data gathering	80%	80%

[a] (Revenues in 2011 − Revenues in 2010) ÷ Revenues in 2010 = ($25,300,000 − $23,000,000) ÷ $23,000,000 = 10%.
[b] Number of customers increased from seven to eight in 2011.

4. **Learning-and-growth perspective.** This perspective identifies the capabilities the organization must excel at to achieve superior internal processes that in turn create value for customers and shareholders. Chipset's learning and growth perspective emphasizes three capabilities: (1) information-system capabilities, measured by the percentage of manufacturing processes with real-time feedback; (2) employee capabilities, measured by the percentage of employees trained in process and quality management; and (3) motivation, measured by employee satisfaction and the percentage of manufacturing and sales employees (line employees) empowered to manage processes.

The arrows in Exhibit 13-3 indicate the *broad* cause-and-effect linkages: how gains in the learning-and-growth perspective lead to improvements in internal business processes, which lead to higher customer satisfaction and market share, and finally lead to superior financial performance. Note how the scorecard describes elements of Chipset's strategy implementation. Worker training and empowerment improve employee satisfaction and lead to manufacturing and business-process improvements that improve quality and reduce delivery time. The result is increased customer satisfaction and higher market share. These initiatives have been successful from a financial perspective. Chipset has earned significant operating income from its cost leadership strategy, and that strategy has also led to growth.

A major benefit of the balanced scorecard is that it promotes causal thinking. Think of the balanced scorecard as a *linked scorecard* or a *causal scorecard*. Managers must search for empirical evidence (rather than rely on faith alone) to test the validity and strength of the various connections. A causal scorecard enables a company to focus on the key drivers that steer the implementation of the strategy. Without convincing links, the scorecard loses much of its value.

Implementing a Balanced Scorecard

To successfully implement a balanced scorecard requires commitment and leadership from top management. At Chipset, the team building the balanced scorecard (headed by the vice president of strategic planning) conducted interviews with senior managers, probed executives about customers, competitors, and technological developments, and sought proposals for balanced scorecard objectives across the four perspectives. The team then met to discuss the responses and to build a prioritized list of objectives.

In a meeting with all senior managers, the team sought to achieve consensus on the scorecard objectives. Senior management was then divided into four groups, with each group responsible for one of the perspectives. In addition, each group broadened the base of inputs by including representatives from the next-lower levels of management and key functional managers. The groups identified measures for each objective and the sources of information for each measure. The groups then met to finalize scorecard objectives, measures, targets, and the initiatives to achieve the targets. Management accountants played an important role in the design and implementation of the balanced scorecard, particularly in determining measures to represent the realities of the business. This required management accountants to understand the economic environment of the industry, Chipset's customers and competitors, and internal business issues such as human resources, operations, and distribution.

Managers made sure that employees understood the scorecard and the scorecard process. The final balanced scorecard was communicated to all employees. Sharing the scorecard allowed engineers and operating personnel, for example, to understand the reasons for customer satisfaction and dissatisfaction and to make suggestions for improving internal processes directly aimed at satisfying customers and implementing Chipset's strategy. Too often, scorecards are seen by only a select group of managers. By limiting the scorecard's exposure, an organization loses the opportunity for widespread organization engagement and alignment.

Chipset (like Cigna Property, Casualty Insurance, and Wells Fargo) also encourages each department to develop its own scorecard that ties into Chipset's main scorecard described in Exhibit 13-3. For example, the quality control department's scorecard has measures that its department managers use to improve yield—number of quality circles, statistical process control charts, Pareto diagrams, and root-cause analyses (see

Chapter 19, pp. 697–699 for more details). Department scorecards help align the actions of each department to implement Chipset's strategy.

Companies frequently use balanced scorecards to evaluate and reward managerial performance and to influence managerial behavior. Using the balanced scorecard for performance evaluation widens the performance management lens and motivates managers to give greater attention to nonfinancial drivers of performance. Surveys indicate, however, that companies continue to assign more weight to the financial perspective (55%) than to the other perspectives—customer (19%), internal business process (12%), and learning and growth (14%). Companies cite several reasons for the relatively smaller weight on nonfinancial measures: difficulty evaluating the relative importance of nonfinancial measures; challenges in measuring and quantifying qualitative, nonfinancial data; and difficulty in compensating managers despite poor financial performance (see Chapter 23 for a more detailed discussion of performance evaluation). Many companies, however, are giving greater weight to nonfinancial measures in promotion decisions because they believe that nonfinancial measures (such as customer satisfaction, process improvements, and employee motivation) better assess a manager's potential to succeed at senior levels of management. For the balanced scorecard to be effective, managers must view it as fairly assessing and rewarding all important aspects of a manager's performance and promotion prospects.

Aligning the Balanced Scorecard to Strategy

Different strategies call for different scorecards. Recall Chipset's competitor Visilog, which follows a product-differentiation strategy by designing custom chips for modems and communication networks. Visilog designs its balanced scorecard to fit its strategy. For example, in the financial perspective, Visilog evaluates how much of its operating income comes from charging premium prices for its products. In the customer perspective, Visilog measures the percentage of its revenues from new products and new customers. In the internal-business-process perspective, Visilog measures the number of new products introduced and new product development time. In the learning-and-growth perspective, Visilog measures the development of advanced manufacturing capabilities to produce custom chips. Visilog also uses some of the measures described in Chipset's balanced scorecard in Exhibit 13-3. For example, revenue growth, customer satisfaction ratings, order-delivery time, on-time delivery, percentage of frontline workers empowered to manage processes, and employee-satisfaction ratings are also important measures under the product-differentiation strategy. The goal is to align the balanced scorecard with company strategy.[5] Exhibit 13-4 presents some common measures found on company scorecards in the service, retail, and manufacturing sectors.

Features of a Good Balanced Scorecard

A well-designed balanced scorecard has several features:

1. It tells the story of a company's strategy, articulating a sequence of cause-and-effect relationships—the links among the various perspectives that align implementation of the strategy. In for-profit companies, each measure in the scorecard is part of a cause-and-effect chain leading to financial outcomes. Not-for-profit organizations design the cause-and-effect chain to achieve their strategic service objectives—for example, number of people no longer in poverty, or number of children still in school.

2. The balanced scorecard helps to communicate the strategy to all members of the organization by translating the strategy into a coherent and linked set of understandable and measurable operational targets. Guided by the scorecard, managers and employees take actions and make decisions to achieve the company's strategy. Companies that have distinct strategic business units (SBUs)—such as consumer

---

[5] For simplicity, we have presented the balanced scorecard in the context of companies that have followed either a cost-leadership or a product-differentiation strategy. Of course, a company may have some products for which cost leadership is critical and other products for which product differentiation is important. The company will then develop separate scorecards to implement the different product strategies. In still other contexts, product differentiation may be of primary importance, but some cost leadership must also be achieved. The balanced scorecard measures would then be linked in a cause-and-effect way to this strategy.

Exhibit 13-4
Frequently Cited Balanced Scorecard Measures

Financial Perspective
Income measures: Operating income, gross margin percentage
Revenue and cost measures: Revenue growth, revenues from new products, cost reductions in key areas
Income and investment measures: Economic value added ª(EVA®), return on investment

Customer Perspective
Market share, customer satisfaction, customer-retention percentage, time taken to fulfill customers' requests, number of customer complaints

Internal-Business-Process Perspective
Innovation Process: Operating capabilities, number of new products or services, new-product development times, and number of new patents
Operations Process: Yield, defect rates, time taken to deliver product to customers, percentage of on-time deliveries, average time taken to respond to orders, setup time, manufacturing downtime
Postsales Service Process: Time taken to replace or repair defective products, hours of customer training for using the product

Learning-and-Growth Perspective
Employee measures: Employee education and skill levels, employee-satisfaction ratings, employee turnover rates, percentage of employee suggestions implemented, percentage of compensation based on individual and team incentives
Technology measures: Information system availability, percentage of processes with advanced controls

---
ªThis measure is described in Chapter 23.

products and pharmaceuticals at Johnson & Johnson—develop their balanced scorecards at the SBU level. Each SBU has its own unique strategy and implementation goals; building separate scorecards allows each SBU to choose measures that help implement its distinctive strategy.

3. In for-profit companies, the balanced scorecard must motivate managers to take actions that eventually result in improvements in financial performance. Managers sometimes tend to focus too much on innovation, quality, and customer satisfaction as ends in themselves. For example, Xerox spent heavily to increase customer satisfaction without a resulting financial payoff because higher levels of satisfaction did not increase customer loyalty. Some companies use statistical methods, such as regression analysis, to test the anticipated cause-and-effect relationships among nonfinancial measures and financial performance. The data for this analysis can come from either time series data (collected over time) or cross-sectional data (collected, for example, across multiple stores of a retail chain). In the Chipset example, improvements in nonfinancial factors have, in fact, already led to improvements in financial factors.

4. The balanced scorecard limits the number of measures, identifying only the most critical ones. Chipset's scorecard, for example, has 16 measures, between 3 and 6 measures for each perspective. Limiting the number of measures focuses managers' attention on those that most affect strategy implementation. Using too many measures makes it difficult for managers to process relevant information.

5. The balanced scorecard highlights less-than-optimal trade-offs that managers may make when they fail to consider operational and financial measures together. For example, a company whose strategy is innovation and product differentiation could achieve superior short-run financial performance by reducing spending on R&D. A good balanced scorecard would signal that the short-run financial performance might have been achieved by taking actions that hurt future financial performance because a leading indicator of that performance, R&D spending and R&D output, has declined.

Pitfalls in Implementing a Balanced Scorecard

Pitfalls to avoid in implementing a balanced scorecard include the following:

1. Managers should not assume the cause-and-effect linkages are precise. They are merely hypotheses. Over time, a company must gather evidence of the strength and timing of the linkages among the nonfinancial and financial measures. With experience,

organizations should alter their scorecards to include those nonfinancial strategic objectives and measures that are the best leading indicators (the causes) of financial performance (a lagging indicator or the effect). Understanding that the scorecard evolves over time helps managers avoid unproductively spending time and money trying to design the "perfect" scorecard at the outset. Furthermore, as the business environment and strategy change over time, the measures in the scorecard also need to change.

2. Managers should not seek improvements across all of the measures all of the time. For example, strive for quality and on-time performance but not beyond the point at which further improvement in these objectives is so costly that it is inconsistent with long-run profit maximization. Cost-benefit considerations should always be central when designing a balanced scorecard.

3. Managers should not use only objective measures in the balanced scorecard. Chipset's balanced scorecard includes both objective measures (such as operating income from cost leadership, market share, and manufacturing yield) and subjective measures (such as customer- and employee-satisfaction ratings). When using subjective measures, though, managers must be careful that the benefits of this potentially rich information are not lost by using measures that are inaccurate or that can be easily manipulated.

4. Despite challenges of measurement, top management should not ignore nonfinancial measures when evaluating managers and other employees. Managers tend to focus on the measures used to reward their performance. Excluding nonfinancial measures when evaluating performance will reduce the significance and importance that managers give to nonfinancial measures.

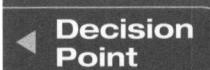

Decision Point

How can an organization translate its strategy into a set of performance measures?

Evaluating the Success of Strategy and Implementation

To evaluate how successful Chipset's strategy and its implementation have been, its management compares the target- and actual-performance columns in the balanced scorecard (Exhibit 13-3). Chipset met most targets set on the basis of competitor benchmarks in 2011 itself. That's because, in the Chipset context, improvements in the learning and growth perspective quickly ripple through to the financial perspective. Chipset will continue to seek improvements on the targets it did not achieve, but meeting most targets suggests that the strategic initiatives that Chipset identified and measured for learning and growth resulted in improvements in internal business processes, customer measures, and financial performance.

How would Chipset know if it had problems in strategy implementation? If it did not meet its targets on the two perspectives that are more internally focused: learning and growth and internal business processes.

What if Chipset performed well on learning and growth and internal business processes, but customer measures and financial performance in this year and the next did not improve? Chipset's managers would then conclude that Chipset did a good job of implementation (the various internal nonfinancial measures it targeted improved) but that its strategy was faulty (there was no effect on customers or on long-run financial performance and value creation). Management failed to identify the correct causal links. It implemented the wrong strategy well! Management would then reevaluate the strategy and the factors that drive it.

Now what if Chipset performed well on its various nonfinancial measures, and operating income over this year and the next also increased? Chipset's managers might be tempted to declare the strategy a success because operating income increased. Unfortunately, management still cannot conclude with any confidence that Chipset successfully formulated and implemented its strategy. Why? Because operating income can increase simply because entire markets are expanding, not because a company's strategy has been successful. Also, changes in operating income might occur because of factors outside the strategy. For example, a company such as Chipset that has chosen a cost-leadership strategy may find that its operating-income increase actually resulted from, say, some degree of product differentiation. *To evaluate the success of a strategy, managers and management accountants need to link strategy to the sources of operating-income increases.*

For Chipset to conclude that it was successful in implementing its strategy, it must demonstrate that improvements in its financial performance and operating income over time resulted from achieving targeted cost savings and growth in market share. Fortunately, the top two rows of Chipset's balanced scorecard in Exhibit 13-3 show that operating-income gains from productivity ($1,912,500) and growth ($2,820,000) exceeded targets. The next section of this chapter describes how these numbers were calculated. Because its strategy has been successful, Chipset's management can be more confident that the gains will be sustained in subsequent years.

Chipset's management accountants subdivide changes in operating income into components that can be identified with product differentiation, cost leadership, and growth. Why growth? Because successful product differentiation or cost leadership generally increases market share and helps a company to grow. Subdividing the change in operating income to evaluate the success of a strategy is conceptually similar to the variance analysis discussed in Chapters 7 and 8. One difference, however, is that management accountants compare actual operating performance over two different periods, not actual to budgeted numbers in the same time period as in variance analysis.[6]

Strategic Analysis of Operating Income

Learning Objective 4

Analyze changes in operating income to evaluate strategy

... growth, price recovery, and productivity

The following illustration explains how to subdivide the change in operating income from one period to *any* future period. The individual components describe company performance with regard to product differentiation, cost leadership, and growth.[7] We illustrate the analysis using data from 2010 and 2011 because Chipset implemented key elements of its strategy in late 2010 and early 2011 and expects the financial consequences of these strategies to occur in 2011. Suppose the financial consequences of these strategies had been expected to affect operating income in only 2012. Then we could just as easily have compared 2010 to 2012. If necessary, we could also have compared 2010 to 2011 and 2012 taken together.

Chipset's data for 2010 and 2011 follow:

		2010	2011
1.	Units of CX1 produced and sold	1,000,000	1,150,000
2.	Selling price	$23	$22
3.	Direct materials (square centimeters of silicon wafers)	3,000,000	2,900,000
4.	Direct material cost per square centimeter	$1.40	$1.50
5.	Manufacturing processing capacity (in square centimeters of silicon wafer)	3,750,000	3,500,000
6.	Conversion costs (all manufacturing costs other than direct material costs)	$16,050,000	$15,225,000
7.	Conversion cost per unit of capacity (row 6 ÷ row 5)	$4.28	$4.35

Chipset provides the following additional information:

1. Conversion costs (labor and overhead costs) for each year depend on production processing capacity defined in terms of the quantity of square centimeters of silicon wafers that Chipset can process. These costs do not vary with the actual quantity of silicon wafers processed.
2. Chipset incurs no R&D costs. Its marketing, sales, and customer-service costs are small relative to the other costs. Chipset has fewer than 10 customers, each purchasing roughly the same quantities of CX1. Because of the highly technical nature of the product, Chipset uses a cross-functional team for its marketing, sales, and customer-service activities. This cross-functional approach ensures that, although marketing, sales, and customer-service costs are small, the entire Chipset organization, including manufacturing engineers, remains focused on increasing customer satisfaction and

---

[6] Other examples of focusing on actual performance over two periods rather than comparisons of actuals with budgets can be found in J. Hope and R. Fraser, *Beyond Budgeting* (Boston, MA: Harvard Business School Press, 2003).

[7] For other details, see R. Banker, S. Datar, and R. Kaplan, "Productivity Measurement and Management Accounting," *Journal of Accounting, Auditing and Finance* (1989): 528–554; and A. Hayzen and J. Reeve, "Examining the Relationships in Productivity Accounting," *Management Accounting Quarterly* (2000): 32–39.

market share. (The Problem for Self-Study at the end of this chapter describes a situation in which marketing, sales, and customer-service costs are significant.)
3. Chipset's asset structure is very similar in 2010 and 2011.
4. Operating income for each year is as follows:

	2010	2011
Revenues		
($23 per unit × 1,000,000 units; $22 per unit × 1,150,000 units)	$23,000,000	$25,300,000
Costs		
Direct material costs		
($1.40/sq. cm. × 3,000,000 sq. cm.; $1.50/sq. cm. × 2,900,000 sq. cm.)	4,200,000	4,350,000
Conversion costs		
($4.28/sq. cm. × 3,750,000 sq. cm.; $4.35/sq. cm. × 3,500,000 sq. cm.)	16,050,000	15,225,000
Total costs	20,250,000	19,575,000
Operating income	$ 2,750,000	$ 5,725,000
Change in operating income		$2,975,000 F

The goal of Chipset's managers is to evaluate how much of the $2,975,000 increase in operating income was caused by the successful implementation of the company's cost-leadership strategy. To do this, management accountants start by analyzing three main factors: growth, price recovery, and productivity.

The **growth component** measures the change in operating income attributable solely to the change in the quantity of output sold between 2010 and 2011.

The **price-recovery component** measures the change in operating income attributable solely to changes in Chipset's prices of inputs and outputs between 2010 and 2011. The price-recovery component measures change in output price compared with changes in input prices. A company that has successfully pursued a strategy of product differentiation will be able to increase its output price faster than the increase in its input prices, boosting profit margins and operating income: It will show a large positive price-recovery component.

The **productivity component** measures the change in costs attributable to a change in the quantity of inputs used in 2011 relative to the quantity of inputs that would have been used in 2010 to produce the 2011 output. The productivity component measures the amount by which operating income increases by using inputs efficiently to lower costs. A company that has successfully pursued a strategy of cost leadership will be able to produce a given quantity of output with a lower cost of inputs: It will show a large positive productivity component. Given Chipset's strategy of cost leadership, we expect the increase in operating income to be attributable to the productivity and growth components, not to price recovery. We now examine these three components in detail.

Growth Component of Change in Operating Income

The growth component of the change in operating income measures the increase in revenues minus the increase in costs from selling more units of CX1 in 2011 (1,150,000 units) than in 2010 (1,000,000 units), *assuming nothing else has changed*.

Revenue Effect of Growth

$$\text{Revenue effect of growth} = \left(\begin{array}{c}\text{Actual units of} \\ \text{output sold} \\ \text{in 2011}\end{array} - \begin{array}{c}\text{Actual units of} \\ \text{output sold} \\ \text{in 2010}\end{array}\right) \times \begin{array}{c}\text{Selling} \\ \text{price} \\ \text{in 2010}\end{array}$$

$$= (1{,}150{,}000 \text{ units} - 1{,}000{,}000 \text{ units}) \times \$23 \text{ per unit}$$

$$= \$3{,}450{,}000 \text{ F}$$

This component is favorable (F) because the increase in output sold in 2011 increases operating income. Components that decrease operating income are unfavorable (U).

Note that Chipset uses the 2010 price of CX1 and focuses only on the increase in units sold between 2010 and 2011, because the revenue effect of growth component measures how much revenues would have changed in 2010 if Chipset had sold 1,150,000 units instead of 1,000,000 units.

Cost Effect of Growth

The cost effect of growth measures how much costs would have changed in 2010 if Chipset had produced 1,150,000 units of CX1 instead of 1,000,000 units. To measure the cost effect of growth, Chipset's managers distinguish variable costs such as direct material costs from fixed costs such as conversion costs, because as units produced (and sold) increase, variable costs increase proportionately but fixed costs, generally, do not change.

$$\text{Cost effect of growth for variable costs} = \left(\begin{array}{c}\text{Units of input required to produce 2011 output in 2010}\end{array} - \begin{array}{c}\text{Actual units of input used to produce 2010 output}\end{array}\right) \times \begin{array}{c}\text{Input price in 2010}\end{array}$$

$$\text{Cost effect of growth for direct materials} = \left(3{,}000{,}000 \text{ sq. cm.} \times \frac{1{,}150{,}000 \text{ units}}{1{,}000{,}000 \text{ units}} - 3{,}000{,}000 \text{ sq. cm.}\right) \times \$1.40 \text{ per sq. cm.}$$

$$= (3{,}450{,}000 \text{ sq. cm.} - 3{,}000{,}000 \text{ sq. cm.}) \times \$1.40 \text{ per sq. cm.} = \$630{,}000 \text{ U}$$

The units of input required to produce 2011 output in 2010 can also be calculated as follows:

$$\text{Units of input per unit of output in 2010} = \frac{3{,}000{,}000 \text{ sq. cm.}}{1{,}000{,}000 \text{ units}} = 3 \text{ sq. cm./unit}$$

Units of input required to produce 2011 output of 1,150,000 units in 2010 = 3 sq. cm. per unit × 1,150,000 units = 3,450,000 sq. cm.

$$\text{Cost effect of growth for fixed costs} = \left(\begin{array}{c}\text{Actual units of capacity in 2010 because adequate capacity exists to produce 2011 output in 2010}\end{array} - \begin{array}{c}\text{Actual units of capacity in 2010}\end{array}\right) \times \begin{array}{c}\text{Price per unit of capacity in 2010}\end{array}$$

$$\text{Cost effect of growth for conversion costs} = (3{,}750{,}000 \text{ sq. cm.} - 3{,}750{,}000 \text{ sq. cm.}) \times \$4.28 \text{ per sq. cm.} = \$0$$

Conversion costs are fixed costs at a given level of capacity. Chipset has manufacturing capacity to process 3,750,000 square centimeters of silicon wafers in 2010 at a cost of $4.28 per square centimeter (rows 5, and 7 of data on p. 500). To produce 1,150,000 units of output in 2010, Chipset needs to process 3,450,000 square centimeters of direct materials, which is less than the available capacity of 3,750,000 sq. cm. Throughout this chapter, we assume adequate capacity exists in the current year (2010) to produce next year's (2011) output. Under this assumption, the cost effect of growth for capacity-related fixed costs is, by definition, $0. Had 2010 capacity been inadequate to produce 2011 output in 2010, we would need to calculate the additional capacity required to produce 2011 output in 2010. These calculations are beyond the scope of the book.

In summary, the net increase in operating income attributable to growth equals the following:

Revenue effect of growth		$3,450,000 F
Cost effect of growth		
Direct material costs	$630,000 U	
Conversion costs	0	630,000 U
Change in operating income due to growth		$2,820,000 F

Price-Recovery Component of Change in Operating Income

Assuming that the 2010 relationship between inputs and outputs continued in 2011, the price-recovery component of the change in operating income measures solely the effect of price changes on revenues and costs to produce and sell the 1,150,000 units of CX1 in 2011.

Revenue Effect of Price Recovery

$$\text{Revenue effect of price recovery} = \left(\text{Selling price in 2011} - \text{Selling price in 2010}\right) \times \text{Actual units of output sold in 2011}$$

$$= (\$22 \text{ per unit} - \$23 \text{ per unit}) \times 1{,}150{,}000 \text{ units}$$

$$= \$1{,}150{,}000 \text{ U}$$

Note that the calculation focuses on revenue changes caused by changes in the selling price of CX1 between 2010 and 2011.

Cost Effect of Price Recovery

Chipset's management accountants calculate the cost effects of price recovery separately for variable costs and for fixed costs, just as they did when calculating the cost effect of growth.

$$\text{Cost effect of price recovery for variable costs} = \left(\text{Input price in 2011} - \text{Input price in 2010}\right) \times \text{Units of input required to produce 2011 output in 2010}$$

$$\text{Cost effect of price recovery for direct materials} = (\$1.50 \text{ per sq.cm.} - \$1.40 \text{ per sq.cm.}) \times 3{,}450{,}000 \text{ sq.} = \$345{,}000 \text{ U}$$

Recall that the direct materials of 3,450,000 square centimeters required to produce 2011 output in 2010 had already been calculated when computing the cost effect of growth (p. 502).

$$\text{Cost effect of price recovery for fixed costs} = \left(\text{Price per unit of capacity in 2011} - \text{Price per unit of capacity in 2010}\right) \times \text{Actual units of capacity in 2010 (because adequate capacity exists to produce 2011 output in 2010)}$$

Cost effect of price recovery for fixed costs is as follows:

Conversion costs: ($4.35 per sq. cm. − $4.28 per sq. cm.) × 3,750,000 sq. cm. = $262,500 U

Note that the detailed analyses of capacities were presented when computing the cost effect of growth (p. 502).

In summary, the net decrease in operating income attributable to price recovery equals the following:

Revenue effect of price recovery		$1,150,000 U
Cost effect of price recovery		
Direct material costs	$345,000 U	
Conversion costs	262,500 U	607,500 U
Change in operating income due to price recovery		$1,757,500 U

The price-recovery analysis indicates that, even as the prices of its inputs increased, the selling prices of CX1 decreased and Chipset could not pass on input-price increases to its customers.

Productivity Component of Change in Operating Income

The productivity component of the change in operating income uses 2011 input prices to measure how costs have decreased as a result of using fewer inputs, a better mix of inputs, and/or less capacity to produce 2011 output, compared with the inputs and capacity that would have been used to produce this output in 2010.

The productivity-component calculations use 2011 prices and output. That's because the productivity component isolates the change in costs between 2010 and 2011 caused solely by the change in the quantities, mix, and/or capacities of inputs.[8]

$$\text{Cost effect of productivity for variable costs} = \left(\begin{array}{c} \text{Actual units of input used to produce 2011 output} \end{array} - \begin{array}{c} \text{Units of input required to produce 2011 output in 2010} \end{array} \right) \times \begin{array}{c} \text{Input price in 2011} \end{array}$$

Using the 2011 data given on page 500 and the calculation of units of input required to produce 2011 output in 2010 when discussing the cost effects of growth (p. 502),

$$\text{Cost effect of productivity for direct materials} = (2{,}900{,}000 \text{ sq. cm.} - 3{,}450{,}000 \text{ sq. cm.}) \times \$1.50 \text{ per sq. cm}$$

$$= 550{,}000 \text{ sq. cm.} \times \$1.50 \text{ per sq. cm.} = \$825{,}000 \text{ F}$$

Chipset's quality and yield improvements reduced the quantity of direct materials needed to produce output in 2011 relative to 2010.

$$\text{Cost effect of productivity for fixed costs} = \left(\begin{array}{c} \text{Actual units of capacity in 2011} \end{array} - \begin{array}{c} \text{Actual units of capacity in 2010 because adequate capacity exists to produce 2011 output in 2010} \end{array} \right) \times \begin{array}{c} \text{Price per unit of capacity in 2011} \end{array}$$

To calculate the cost effect of productivity for fixed costs, we use the 2011 data given on page 500, and the analyses of capacity required to produce 2011 output in 2010 when discussing the cost effect of growth (p. 502).

Cost effects of productivity for fixed costs are

Conversion costs: $(3{,}500{,}000 \text{ sq. cm} - 3{,}750{,}000 \text{ sq. cm.}) \times \$4.35 \text{ per sq. cm.} = \$1{,}087{,}500 \text{ F}$

Chipset's managers decreased manufacturing capacity in 2011 to 3,500,000 square centimeters by selling off old equipment and laying off workers.

In summary, the net increase in operating income attributable to productivity equals,

Cost effect of productivity	
Direct material costs	$ 825,000 F
Conversion costs	1,087,500 F
Change in operating income due to productivity	1,912,500 F

The productivity component indicates that Chipset was able to increase operating income by improving quality and productivity and eliminating capacity to reduce costs. The appendix to this chapter examines partial and total factor productivity changes between 2010 and 2011 and describes how the management accountant can obtain a deeper understanding of Chipset's cost-leadership strategy. Note that the productivity component focuses exclusively on costs, so there is no revenue effect for this component.

Exhibit 13-5 summarizes the growth, price-recovery, and productivity components of the changes in operating income. Generally, companies that have been successful at cost leadership will show favorable productivity and growth components. Companies that

---

[8] Note that the productivity-component calculation uses actual 2011 input prices, whereas its counterpart, the efficiency variance in Chapters 7 and 8, uses budgeted prices. (In effect, the budgeted prices correspond to 2010 prices). Year 2011 prices are used in the productivity calculation because Chipset wants its managers to choose input quantities to minimize costs in 2011 based on currently prevailing prices. If 2010 prices had been used in the productivity calculation, managers would choose input quantities based on irrelevant input prices that prevailed a year ago! Why does using budgeted prices in Chapters 7 and 8 not pose a similar problem? Because, unlike 2010 prices that describe what happened a year ago, budgeted prices represent prices that are expected to prevail in the current period. Moreover, budgeted prices can be changed, if necessary, to bring them in line with actual current-period prices.

Exhibit 13-5 Strategic Analysis of Profitability

	Income Statement Amounts in 2010 (1)	Revenue and Cost Effects of Growth Component in 2011 (2)	Revenue and Cost Effects of Price-Recovery Component in 2011 (3)	Cost Effect of Productivity Component in 2011 (4)	Income Statement Amounts in 2011 (5) = (1) + (2) + (3) + (4)
Revenues	$23,000,000	$3,450,000 F	$1,150,000 U	—	$25,300,000
Costs	20,250,000	630,000 U	607,500 U	$1,912,000 F	19,575,000
Operating income	$ 2,750,000	$2,820,000 F	$1,757,500 U	$1,912,500 F	$ 5,725,000

$2,975,000 F
Change in operating income

have successfully differentiated their products will show favorable price-recovery and growth components. In Chipset's case, consistent with its strategy and its implementation, productivity contributed $1,912,500 to the increase in operating income, and growth contributed $2,820,000. Price-recovery contributed a $1,757,500 decrease in operating income, however, because, even as input prices increased, the selling price of CX1 decreased. Had Chipset been able to differentiate its product and charge a higher price, the price-recovery effects might have been less unfavorable or perhaps even favorable. As a result, Chipset's managers plan to evaluate some modest changes in product features that might help differentiate CX1 somewhat more from competing products.

Further Analysis of Growth, Price-Recovery, and Productivity Components

As in all variance and profit analysis, Chipset's managers want to more closely analyze the change in operating income. Chipset's growth might have been helped, for example, by an increase in industry market size. Therefore, at least part of the increase in operating income may be attributable to favorable economic conditions in the industry rather than to any successful implementation of strategy. Some of the growth might relate to the management decision to decrease selling price, made possible by the productivity gains. In this case, the increase in operating income from cost leadership must include operating income from productivity-related growth in market share in addition to the productivity gain.

We illustrate these ideas, using the Chipset example and the following additional information. *Instructors who do not wish to cover these detailed calculations can go to the next section on "Applying the Five-Step Decision-Making Framework to Strategy" without any loss of continuity.*

- The market growth rate in the industry is 8% in 2011. Of the 150,000 (1,150,000 − 1,000,000) units of increased sales of CX1 between 2010 and 2011, 80,000 (0.08 × 1,000,000) units are due to an increase in industry market size (which Chipset should have benefited from regardless of its productivity gains), and the remaining 70,000 units are due to an increase in market share.
- During 2011, Chipset could have maintained the price of CX1 at the 2010 price of $23 per unit. But management decided to take advantage of the productivity gains to reduce the price of CX1 by $1 to grow market share leading to the 70,000-unit increase in sales.

The effect of the industry-market-size factor on operating income (not any specific strategic action) is as follows:

Change in operating income due to growth in industry market size

$$\$2,820,000 \text{ (Exhibit 13-5, column 2)} \times \frac{80,000 \text{ units}}{150,000 \text{ units}} = \$1,504,000 \text{ F}$$

Concepts in Action: The Growth Versus Profitability Choice at Facebook

Competitive advantage comes from product differentiation or cost leadership. Successful implementation of these strategies helps a company to be profitable and to grow. Many Internet start-ups pursue a strategy of short-run growth to build a customer base, with the goal of later benefiting from such growth by either charging user fees or sustaining a free service for users supported by advertisers. However, during the 1990s dot-com boom (and subsequent bust), the most spectacular failures occurred in dot-com companies that followed the "get big fast" model but then failed to differentiate their products or reduce their costs.

Today, many social networking companies (Web-based communities that connect friends, colleagues, and groups with shared interests) face this same challenge. At Facebook, the most notable of the social networking sites, users can create personal profiles that allow them to interact with friends through messaging, chat, sharing Web site links, video clips, and more. Additionally, Facebook encourages other companies to build third-party programs, including games and surveys, for its Web site and mobile applications on the iPhone and BlackBerry devices. From 2007 to 2010, Facebook grew from 12 million users to more than 400 million users uploading photos, sharing updates, planning events, and playing games in the Facebook ecosystem.

During this phenomenal growth, the company wrestled with one key question: How could Facebook become profitable? In 2009, experts estimate that Facebook had revenues of $635 million, mostly through advertising and the sale of virtual gifts (as a private company, Facebook does not publicly disclose its financial information). But the company still did not turn a profit. Why not? To keep its global Web site and mobile applications operating, Facebook requires a massive amount of electricity, Internet bandwidth, and storage servers for digital files. In 2009, the company earmarked $100 million to buy 50,000 new servers, along with a new $2 million network storage system per week.

The cost structure of Facebook means that the company must generate tens of millions a month in revenue to sustain its operations over the long term. But how? Facebook has implemented the following popular methods of online revenue generation:

- Additional advertising: To grow its already significant advertising revenue, Facebook recently introduced "Fan Pages" for brands and companies seeking to communicate directly with its users. The company is also working on a tool that will let users share information about their physical whereabouts via the site, which will allow Facebook to sell targeted advertisements for nearby businesses.

- Transactions: Facebook is also testing a feature that would expand Facebook Credits, its transactions platform that allows users to purchase games and gifts, into an Internet-wide "virtual currency," that could be accepted by any Web site integrating the Facebook Connect online identity management platform. Facebook currently gets a 30% cut of all transactions conducted through Facebook Credits.

Despite rampant rumors, Facebook has rejected the idea of charging monthly subscription fees for access to its Web site or for advanced features and premium content.

With increased growth around the world, Facebook anticipates 2010 revenues to exceed $1 billion. Despite the opportunity to become the "world's richest twenty-something," Facebook's 25-year-old CEO Mark Zuckerberg has thus far resisted taking the company public through an initial public offering (IPO). "A lot of companies can go off course because of corporate pressures," says Mr. Zuckerberg. "I don't know what we are going to be building five years from now." With his company's focus on facilitating people's ability to share almost any- and everything with anyone, at any time, via the Internet, mobile phones, and even videogames, Facebook expects to offer users a highly personal and differentiated online experience in the years ahead and expects that this product differentiation will drive its future growth and profitability.

Sources: Vascellaro, Jessica E. 2010. Facebook CEO in no rush to 'friend' wall street. *Wall Street Journal*, March 3. http://online.wsj.com/article/SB10001424052748703787304575075942803630712.html; Eldon, Eric. 2010. Facebook revenues up to $700 million in 2009, on track towards $1.1 billion in 2010. *Inside Facebook*. Blog, March 2. http://www.insidefacebook.com/2010/03/02/facebook-made-up-to-700-million-in-2009-on-track-towards-1-1-billion-in-2010/; Arrington, Michael. 2010. Facebook may be growing too fast. And hitting the capital markets again. *Tech Crunch*. Blog, October 31. http://techcrunch.com/2010/10/31/facebooks-growing-problem/

Lacking a differentiated product, Chipset could have maintained the price of CX1 at $23 per unit even while the prices of its inputs increased.

The effect of product differentiation on operating income is as follows:

Change in prices of inputs (cost effect of price recovery)	607,500 U
Change in operating income due to product differentiation	$607,500 U

To exercise cost and price leadership, Chipset made the strategic decision to cut the price of CX1 by $1. This decision resulted in an increase in market share and 70,000 units of additional sales.

The effect of cost leadership on operating income is as follows:

Productivity component	$1,912,500 F
Effect of strategic decision to reduce price ($1/unit × 1,150,000 units)	1,150,000 U
Growth in market share due to productivity improvement and strategic decision to reduce prices	
$2,820,000 (Exhibit 13-5, column 2) × $\frac{70,000 \text{ units}}{150,000 \text{ units}}$	1,316,000 F
Change in operating income due to cost leadership	$2,078,500 F

A summary of the change in operating income between 2010 and 2011 follows.

Change due to industry market size	$1,504,000 F
Change due to product differentiation	607,500 U
Change due to cost leadership	2,078,500 F
Change in operating income	$2,975,000 F

Consistent with its cost-leadership strategy, the productivity gains of $1,912,500 in 2011 were a big part of the increase in operating income from 2010 to 2011. Chipset took advantage of these productivity gains to decrease price by $1 per unit at a cost of $1,150,000 to gain $1,316,000 in operating income by selling 70,000 additional units. The Problem for Self-Study on page 510 describes the analysis of the growth, price-recovery, and productivity components for a company following a product-differentiation strategy. The Concepts in Action feature (p. 506) describes the unique challenges that dot-com companies face in choosing a profitable strategy.

Under different assumptions about the change in selling price, the analysis will attribute different amounts to the different strategies.

Applying the Five-Step Decision-Making Framework to Strategy

We next briefly describe how the five-step decision-making framework, introduced in Chapter 1, is also useful in making decisions about strategy.

1. *Identify the problem and uncertainties.* Chipset's strategy choice depends on resolving two uncertainties—whether Chipset can add value to its customers that its competitors cannot emulate, and whether Chipset can develop the necessary internal capabilities to add this value.

2. *Obtain information.* Chipset's managers develop customer preference maps to identify various product attributes desired by customers and the competitive advantage or disadvantage it has on each attribute relative to competitors. The managers also gather data on Chipset's internal capabilities. How good is Chipset in designing and developing innovative new products? How good are its process and marketing capabilities?

3. *Make predictions about the future.* Chipset's managers conclude that they will not be able to develop innovative new products in a cost-effective way. They believe that Chipset's strength lies in improving quality, reengineering processes, reducing costs, and delivering products faster to customers.

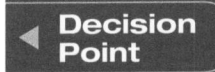

Decision Point

How can a company analyze changes in operating income to evaluate the success of its strategy?

4. *Make decisions by choosing among alternatives.* Chipset's management decides to follow a cost leadership rather than a product differentiation strategy. It decides to introduce a balanced scorecard to align and measure its quality improvement and process reengineering efforts.

5. *Implement the decision, evaluate performance, and learn.* On its balanced scorecard, Chipset's managers compare actual and targeted performance and evaluate possible cause-and-effect relationships. They learn, for example, that increasing the percentage of processes with advanced controls improves yield. As a result, just as they had anticipated, productivity and growth initiatives result in increases in operating income in 2011. The one change Chipset's managers plan for 2012 is to make modest changes in product features that might help differentiate CX1 somewhat from competing products. In this way, feedback and learning help in the development of future strategies and implementation plans.

Downsizing and the Management of Processing Capacity

Learning Objective 5

Identify unused capacity

... capacity available minus capacity used for engineered costs but difficult to determine for discretionary costs

and how to manage it

... downsize to reduce capacity

As we saw in our discussion of the productivity component, fixed costs are tied to capacity. Unlike variable costs, fixed costs do not change automatically with changes in activity level (for example, fixed conversion costs do not change with changes in the quantity of silicon wafers started into production). How then can managers reduce capacity-based fixed costs? By measuring and managing unused capacity. **Unused capacity** is the amount of productive capacity available over and above the productive capacity employed to meet consumer demand in the current period. To understand unused capacity, it is necessary to distinguish *engineered costs* from *discretionary costs*.

Engineered and Discretionary Costs

Engineered costs result from a cause-and-effect relationship between the cost driver—output—and the (direct or indirect) resources used to produce that output. Engineered costs have a detailed, physically observable, and repetitive relationship with output. In the Chipset example, direct material costs are *direct engineered costs*. Conversion costs are an example of *indirect engineered costs*. Consider 2011. The output of 1,150,000 units of CX1 and the efficiency with which inputs are converted into outputs result in 2,900,000 square centimeters of silicon wafers being started into production. Manufacturing-conversion-cost resources used equal $12,615,000 ($4.35 per sq. cm. × 2,900,000 sq. cm.), but actual conversion costs ($15,225,000) are higher because Chipset has manufacturing capacity to process 3,500,000 square centimeters of silicon wafer ($4.35 per sq. cm. × 3,500,000 sq. cm. = $15,225,000). Although these costs are fixed in the short run, over the long run there is a cause-and-effect relationship between output and manufacturing capacity required (and conversion costs needed). In the long run, Chipset will try to match its capacity to its needs.

Discretionary costs have two important features: (1) They arise from periodic (usually annual) decisions regarding the maximum amount to be incurred, and (2) they have no measurable cause-and-effect relationship between output and resources used. There is often a delay between when a resource is acquired and when it is used. Examples of discretionary costs include advertising, executive training, R&D, and corporate-staff department costs such as legal, human resources, and public relations. Unlike engineered costs, the relationship between discretionary costs and output is a blackbox because it is nonrepetitive and nonroutine. A noteworthy aspect of discretionary costs is that managers are seldom confident that the "correct" amounts are being spent. The founder of Lever Brothers, an international consumer-products company, once noted, "Half the money I spend on advertising is wasted; the trouble is, I don't know which half!"[9]

Identifying Unused Capacity for Engineered and Discretionary Overhead Costs

Identifying unused capacity is very different for engineered costs compared to discretionary costs. Consider engineered conversion costs.

At the start of 2011, Chipset had capacity to process 3,750,000 square centimeters of silicon wafers. Quality and productivity improvements made during 2011 enabled Chipset to produce 1,150,000 units of CX1 by processing 2,900,000 square centimeters of silicon wafers. Unused manufacturing capacity is 850,000 (3,750,000 − 2,900,000) square centimeters of silicon-wafer processing capacity at the beginning of 2011. At the 2011 conversion cost of $4.35 per square centimeter,

$$\text{Cost of unused capacity} = \text{Cost of capacity at the beginning of the year} - \text{Manufacturing resources used during the year}$$

$$= (3{,}750{,}000 \text{ sq. cm.} \times \$4.35 \text{ per sq. cm.}) - (2{,}900{,}000 \text{ sq. cm.} \times \$4.35 \text{ per sq. cm.})$$

$$= \$16{,}312{,}500 - \$12{,}615{,}000 = \$3{,}697{,}500$$

The absence of a cause-and-effect relationship makes identifying unused capacity for discretionary costs difficult. For example, management cannot determine the R&D resources used for the actual output produced. And without a measure of capacity used, it is not possible to compute unused capacity.

Managing Unused Capacity

What actions can Chipset management take when it identifies unused capacity? In general, it has two alternatives: eliminate unused capacity, or grow output to utilize the unused capacity.

In recent years, many companies have *downsized* in an attempt to eliminate unused capacity. **Downsizing** (also called **rightsizing**) is an integrated approach of configuring processes, products, and people to match costs to the activities that need to be performed to operate effectively and efficiently in the present and future. Companies such as AT&T, Delta Airlines, Ford Motor Company, and IBM have downsized to focus on their core businesses and have instituted organization changes to increase efficiency, reduce costs, and improve quality. However, downsizing often means eliminating jobs, which can adversely affect employee morale and the culture of a company.

Consider Chipset's alternatives with respect to its unused manufacturing capacity. Because it needed to process 2,900,000 square centimeters of silicon wafers in 2011, it could have reduced capacity to 3,000,000 square centimeters (Chipset can add or reduce manufacturing capacity in increments of 250,000 sq. cm.), resulting in cost savings of $3,262,500 [(3,750,000 sq. cm. − 3,000,000 sq. cm.) × $4.35 per sq. cm.]. Chipset's strategy, however, is not just to reduce costs but also to grow its business. So early in 2011, Chipset reduces its manufacturing capacity by only 250,000 square centimeters—from 3,750,000 square centimeters to 3,500,000 square centimeters—saving

---

[9] Managers also describe some costs as infrastructure costs—costs that arise from having property, plant, and equipment and a functioning organization. Examples are depreciation, long-run lease rental, and the acquisition of long-run technical capabilities. These costs are generally fixed costs because they are committed to and acquired before they are used. Infrastructure costs can be engineered or discretionary. For instance, manufacturing-overhead cost incurred at Chipset to acquire manufacturing capacity is an infrastructure cost that is an example of an engineered cost. In the long run, there is a cause-and-effect relationship between output and manufacturing-overhead costs needed to produce that output. R&D cost incurred to acquire technical capability is an infrastructure cost that is an example of a discretionary cost. There is no measurable cause-and-effect relationship between output and R&D cost incurred.

$1,087,500 ($4.35 per sq. cm. × 250,000 sq. cm.). It retains some extra capacity for future growth. By avoiding greater reductions in capacity, it also maintains the morale of its skilled and capable workforce. The success of this strategy will depend on Chipset achieving the future growth it has projected.

Because identifying unused capacity for discretionary costs, such as R&D costs, is difficult, downsizing or otherwise managing this unused capacity is also difficult. Management must exercise considerable judgment in deciding the level of R&D costs that would generate the needed product and process improvements. Unlike engineered costs, there is no clear-cut way to know whether management is spending too much (or too little) on R&D.

Decision Point

How can a company identify and manage unused capacity?

Problem for Self-Study

Following a strategy of product differentiation, Westwood Corporation makes a high-end kitchen range hood, KE8. Westwood's data for 2010 and 2011 follow:

		2010	2011
1.	Units of KE8 produced and sold	40,000	42,000
2.	Selling price	$100	$110
3.	Direct materials (square feet)	120,000	123,000
4.	Direct material cost per square foot	$10	$11
5.	Manufacturing capacity for KE8	50,000 units	50,000 units
6.	Conversion costs	$1,000,000	$1,100,000
7.	Conversion cost per unit of capacity (row 6 ÷ row 5)	$20	$22
8.	Selling and customer-service capacity	30 customers	29 customers
9.	Selling and customer-service costs	$720,000	$725,000
10.	Cost per customer of selling and customer-service capacity (row 9 ÷ row 8)	$24,000	$25,000

In 2011, Westwood produced no defective units and reduced direct material usage per unit of KE8. Conversion costs in each year are tied to manufacturing capacity. Selling and customer service costs are related to the number of customers that the selling and service functions are designed to support. Westwood has 23 customers (wholesalers) in 2010 and 25 customers in 2011.

Required

1. Describe briefly the elements you would include in Westwood's balanced scorecard.
2. Calculate the growth, price-recovery, and productivity components that explain the change in operating income from 2010 to 2011.
3. Suppose during 2011, the market size for high-end kitchen range hoods grew 3% in terms of number of units and all increases in market share (that is, increases in the number of units sold greater than 3%) are due to Westwood's product-differentiation strategy. Calculate how much of the change in operating income from 2010 to 2011 is due to the industry-market-size factor, cost leadership, and product differentiation.
4. How successful has Westwood been in implementing its strategy? Explain.

Solution

1. The balanced scorecard should describe Westwood's product-differentiation strategy. Elements that should be included in its balanced scorecard are as follows:
   - **Financial perspective.** Increase in operating income from higher margins on KE8 and from growth
   - **Customer perspective.** Customer satisfaction and market share in the high-end market
   - **Internal business process perspective.** New product features, development time for new products, improvements in manufacturing processes, manufacturing quality, order-delivery time, and on-time delivery
   - **Learning-and-growth perspective.** Percentage of employees trained in process and quality management and employee satisfaction ratings

2. Operating income for each year is as follows:

	2010	2011
Revenues		
($100 per unit × 40,000 units; $110 per unit × 42,000 units)	$4,000,000	$4,620,000
Costs		
Direct material costs		
($10 per sq. ft. × 120,000 sq. ft.; $11 per sq. ft. × 123,000 sq. ft.)	1,200,000	1,353,000
Conversion costs		
($20 per unit × 50,000 units; $22 per unit × 50,000 units)	1,000,000	1,100,000
Selling and customer-service cost		
($24,000 per customer × 30 customers;		
$25,000 per customer × 29 customers)	720,000	725,000
Total costs	2,920,000	3,178,000
Operating income	$1,080,000	$1,442,000
Change in operating income		$362,000 F

Growth Component of Operating Income Change

$$\text{Revenue effect of growth} = \left(\begin{array}{c}\text{Actual units of}\\ \text{output sold}\\ \text{in 2011}\end{array} - \begin{array}{c}\text{Actual units of}\\ \text{output sold}\\ \text{in 2010}\end{array}\right) \times \begin{array}{c}\text{Selling}\\ \text{price}\\ \text{in 2010}\end{array}$$

$$= (42{,}000 \text{ units} - 40{,}000 \text{ units}) \times \$100 \text{ per unit} = \$200{,}000 \text{ F}$$

$$\text{Cost effect of growth for variable costs} = \left(\begin{array}{c}\text{Units of input}\\ \text{required to produce}\\ \text{2011 output in 2010}\end{array} - \begin{array}{c}\text{Actual units of input}\\ \text{used to produce}\\ \text{2010 output}\end{array}\right) \times \begin{array}{c}\text{Input}\\ \text{price}\\ \text{in 2010}\end{array}$$

$$\text{Cost effect of growth for direct materials} = \left(120{,}000 \text{ sq. ft.} \times \frac{42{,}000 \text{ units}}{40{,}000 \text{ units}} - 120{,}000 \text{ sq. ft.}\right) \times \$10 \text{ per sq. ft.}$$

$$= (126{,}000 \text{ sq. ft.} - 120{,}000 \text{ sq. ft.}) \times \$10 \text{ per sq. ft.} = \$60{,}000 \text{ U}$$

$$\text{Cost effect of growth for fixed costs} = \left(\begin{array}{c}\text{Actual units of capacity in}\\ \text{2010, because adequate capacity}\\ \text{exists to produce 2011 output in 2010}\end{array} - \begin{array}{c}\text{Actual units}\\ \text{of capacity}\\ \text{in 2010}\end{array}\right) \times \begin{array}{c}\text{Price per}\\ \text{unit of}\\ \text{capacity}\\ \text{in 2010}\end{array}$$

Cost effects of growth for fixed costs are as follows:

Conversion costs: (50,000 units − 50,000 units) × $20 per unit = $0

Selling and customer-service costs: (30 customers − 30 customers) × $24,000 per customer = $0

In summary, the net increase in operating income attributable to growth equals the following:

Revenue effect of growth		$200,000 F
Cost effect of growth		
Direct material costs	$60,000 U	
Conversion costs	0	
Selling and customer-service costs	0	60,000 U
Change in operating income due to growth		$140,000 F

Price-Recovery Component of Operating-Income Change

$$\begin{pmatrix} \text{Revenue effect of} \\ \text{price recovery} \end{pmatrix} = \begin{pmatrix} \text{Selling price} \\ \text{in 2011} \end{pmatrix} - \begin{pmatrix} \text{Selling price} \\ \text{in 2010} \end{pmatrix} \times \begin{pmatrix} \text{Actual units} \\ \text{of output} \\ \text{sold in 2011} \end{pmatrix}$$

$$= (\$110 \text{ per unit} - \$100 \text{ per unit}) \times 42{,}000 \text{ units} = \$420{,}000 \text{ F}$$

$$\begin{pmatrix} \text{Cost effect of} \\ \text{price recovery} \\ \text{for variable costs} \end{pmatrix} = \begin{pmatrix} \text{Input} \\ \text{price} \\ \text{in 2011} \end{pmatrix} - \begin{pmatrix} \text{Input} \\ \text{price} \\ \text{in 2010} \end{pmatrix} \times \begin{pmatrix} \text{Units of input} \\ \text{required to produce} \\ \text{2011 output in 2010} \end{pmatrix}$$

Direct material costs: ($11 per sq. ft. − $10 per sq. ft.) × 126,000 sq. ft. = $126,000 U

$$\begin{pmatrix} \text{Cost effect of} \\ \text{price recovery} \\ \text{for fixed costs} \end{pmatrix} = \begin{pmatrix} \text{Price per} \\ \text{unit of} \\ \text{capacity} \\ \text{in 2011} \end{pmatrix} - \begin{pmatrix} \text{Price per} \\ \text{unit of} \\ \text{capacity} \\ \text{in 2010} \end{pmatrix} \times \begin{pmatrix} \text{Actual units of capacity in} \\ \text{2010, because adequate capacity} \\ \text{exists to produce 2011 output in 2010} \end{pmatrix}$$

Cost effects of price recovery for fixed costs are as follows:

Conversion costs: ($22 per unit − 20 per unit) × 50,000 units = $100,000 U

Selling and cust.-service costs: ($25,000 per cust. − $24,000 per cust.) × 30 customers = $30,000 U

In summary, the net increase in operating income attributable to price recovery equals the following:

Revenue effect of price recovery		$420,000 F
Cost effect of price recovery		
Direct material costs	$126,000 U	
Conversion costs	100,000 U	
Selling and customer-service costs	30,000 U	256,000 U
Change in operating income due to price recovery		$164,000 F

Productivity Component of Operating-Income Change

$$\begin{pmatrix} \text{Cost effect of} \\ \text{productivity for} \\ \text{variable costs} \end{pmatrix} = \begin{pmatrix} \text{Actual units of} \\ \text{input used to produce} \\ \text{2011 output} \end{pmatrix} - \begin{pmatrix} \text{Units of input} \\ \text{required to produce} \\ \text{2011 output in 2010} \end{pmatrix} \times \begin{pmatrix} \text{Input} \\ \text{price in} \\ \text{2011} \end{pmatrix}$$

$$\begin{pmatrix} \text{Cost effect of} \\ \text{productivity for} \\ \text{direct materials} \end{pmatrix} = (123{,}000 \text{ sq. ft.} - 126{,}000 \text{ sq. ft.}) \times \$11 \text{ per sq. ft.} = \$33{,}000 \text{ F}$$

$$\begin{pmatrix} \text{Cost effect of} \\ \text{productivity for} \\ \text{fixed costs} \end{pmatrix} = \begin{pmatrix} \text{Actual units} \\ \text{of capacity} \\ \text{in 2011} \end{pmatrix} - \begin{pmatrix} \text{Actual units of capacity in} \\ \text{2010, because adequate} \\ \text{capacity exists to produce} \\ \text{2011 output in 2010} \end{pmatrix} \times \begin{pmatrix} \text{Price per} \\ \text{unit of} \\ \text{capacity} \\ \text{in 2011} \end{pmatrix}$$

Cost effects of productivity for fixed costs are as follows:

Conversion costs: (50,000 units − 50,000 units) × $22 per unit = $0

Selling and customer-service costs: (29 customers − 30 customers) × $25,000/customer = $25,000 F

In summary, the net increase in operating income attributable to productivity equals the following:

Cost effect of productivity:	
Direct material costs	$33,000 F
Conversion costs	0
Selling and customer-service costs	25,000 F
Change in operating income due to productivity	$58,000 F

A summary of the change in operating income between 2010 and 2011 follows:

	Income Statement Amounts in 2010 (1)	Revenue and Cost Effects of Growth Component in 2011 (2)	Revenue and Cost Effects of Price-Recovery Component in 2011 (3)	Cost Effect of Productivity Component in 2011 (4)	Income Statement Amounts in 2011 (5) = (1) + (2) + (3) + (4)
Revenue	$4,000,000	$200,000 F	$420,000 F	—	$4,620,000
Costs	2,920,000	60,000 U	256,000 U	$58,000 F	3,178,000
Operating income	$1,080,000	$140,000 F	$164,000 F	$58,000 F	$1,442,000
			362,000 F		

Change in operating income

3. **Effect of the Industry-Market-Size Factor on Operating Income**
   Of the increase in sales from 40,000 to 42,000 units, 3%, or 1,200 units (0.03 × 40,000), is due to growth in market size, and 800 units (2,000 − 1,200) are due to an increase in market share. The change in Westwood's operating income from the industry-market-size factor rather than specific strategic actions is as follows:

   $140,000 \text{ (column 2 of preceding table)} \times \frac{1,200 \text{ units}}{2,000 \text{ units}}$ $84,000 F$

Effect of Product Differentiation on Operating Income

Increase in the selling price of KE8 (revenue effect of the price-recovery component)	$420,000 F
Increase in prices of inputs (cost effect of the price-recovery component)	256,000 U
Growth in market share due to product differentiation	
$140,000 \text{ (column 2 of preceding table)} \times \frac{800 \text{ units}}{2,000 \text{ units}}$	56,000 F
Change in operating income due to product differentiation	$220,000 F

Effect of Cost Leadership on Operating Income

Productivity component	$ 58,000 F

A summary of the net increase in operating income from 2010 to 2011 follows:

Change due to the industry-market-size factor	$ 84,000 F
Change due to product differentiation	220,000 F
Change due to cost leadership	58,000 F
Change in operating income	$362,000 F

4. The analysis of operating income indicates that a significant amount of the increase in operating income resulted from Westwood's successful implementation of its product-differentiation strategy. The company was able to continue to charge a premium price for KE8 while increasing market share. Westwood was also able to earn additional operating income from improving its productivity.

Decision Points

The following question-and-answer format summarizes the chapter's learning objectives. Each decision presents a key question related to a learning objective. The guidelines are the answer to that question.

Decision	Guidelines
1. What are two generic strategies a company can use?	Two generic strategies are product differentiation and cost leadership. Product differentiation is offering products and services that are perceived by customers as being superior and unique. Cost leadership is achieving low costs relative to competitors. A company chooses its strategy based on an understanding of customer preferences and its own internal capabilities, while differentiating itself from its competitors.
2. What is reengineering?	Reengineering is the rethinking of business processes, such as the order-delivery process, to improve critical performance measures such as cost, quality, and customer satisfaction.
3. How can an organization translate its strategy into a set of performance measures?	An organization can develop a balanced scorecard that provides the framework for a strategic measurement and management system. The balanced scorecard measures performance from four perspectives: (1) financial, (2) customer, (3) internal business processes, and (4) learning and growth. To build their balanced scorecards, organizations often create strategy maps to represent the cause-and-effect relationships across various strategic objectives.
4. How can a company analyze changes in operating income to evaluate the success of its strategy?	To evaluate the success of its strategy, a company can subdivide the change in operating income into growth, price-recovery, and productivity components. The growth component measures the change in revenues and costs from selling more or less units, assuming nothing else has changed. The price-recovery component measures changes in revenues and costs solely as a result of changes in the prices of outputs and inputs. The productivity component measures the decrease in costs from using fewer inputs, a better mix of inputs, and reducing capacity. If a company is successful in implementing its strategy, changes in components of operating income align closely with strategy.
5. How can a company identify and manage unused capacity?	A company must first distinguish engineered costs from discretionary costs. Engineered costs result from a cause-and-effect relationship between output and the resources needed to produce that output. Discretionary costs arise from periodic (usually annual) management decisions regarding the amount of cost to be incurred. Discretionary costs are not tied to a cause-and-effect relationship between inputs and outputs. Identifying unused capacity is easier for engineered costs and more difficult for discretionary costs. Downsizing is an approach to managing unused capacity that matches costs to the activities that need to be performed to operate effectively.

Appendix

Productivity Measurement

Productivity measures the relationship between actual inputs used (both quantities and costs) and actual outputs produced. The lower the inputs for a given quantity of outputs or the higher the outputs for a given quantity of inputs, the higher the productivity. Measuring productivity improvements over time highlights the specific input-output relationships that contribute to cost leadership.

Partial Productivity Measures

Partial productivity, the most frequently used productivity measure, compares the quantity of output produced with the quantity of an individual input used. In its most common form, partial productivity is expressed as a ratio:

$$\text{Partial productivity} = \frac{\text{Quantity of output produced}}{\text{Quantity of input used}}$$

The higher the ratio, the greater the productivity.

Consider direct materials productivity at Chipset in 2011.

$$\begin{aligned}\frac{\text{Direct materials}}{\text{partial productivity}} &= \frac{\text{Quantity of CX1 units produced during 2011}}{\text{Quantity of direct materials used to produce CX1 in 2011}} \\ &= \frac{1{,}150{,}000 \text{ units of CX1}}{2{,}900{,}000 \text{ sq. cm. of direct materials}} \\ &= 0.397 \text{ units of CX1 per sq. cm. of direct materials}\end{aligned}$$

Note direct materials partial productivity ignores Chipset's other input, manufacturing conversion capacity. Partial-productivity measures become more meaningful when comparisons are made that examine productivity changes over time, either across different facilities or relative to a benchmark. Exhibit 13-6 presents partial-productivity measures for Chipset's inputs for 2011 and the comparable 2010 inputs that would have been used to produce 2011 output, using information from the productivity-component calculations on page 504. These measures compare actual inputs used in 2011 to produce 1,150,000 units of CX1 with inputs that would have been used in 2011 had the input–output relationship from 2010 continued in 2011.

Evaluating Changes in Partial Productivities

Note how the partial-productivity measures differ for variable-cost and fixed-cost components. For variable-cost elements, such as direct materials, productivity improvements measure the reduction in input resources used to produce output (3,450,000 square centimeters of silicon wafers to 2,900,000 square centimeters). For fixed-cost elements such as manufacturing conversion capacity, partial productivity measures the reduction in overall capacity from 2010 to 2011 (3,750,000 square centimeters of silicon wafers to 3,500,000 square centimeters) regardless of the amount of capacity actually used in each period.

An advantage of partial-productivity measures is that they focus on a single input. As a result, they are simple to calculate and easily understood by operations personnel. Managers and operators examine these numbers and try to understand the reasons for the productivity changes—such as, better training of workers, lower labor turnover, better incentives, improved methods, or substitution of materials for labor. Isolating the relevant factors helps Chipset implement and sustain these practices in the future.

For all their advantages, partial-productivity measures also have serious drawbacks. Because partial productivity focuses on only one input at a time rather than on all inputs simultaneously, managers cannot evaluate the effect on overall productivity, if (say) manufacturing-conversion-capacity partial productivity increases while direct materials partial productivity decreases. Total factor productivity (TFP), or total productivity, is a measure of productivity that considers all inputs simultaneously.

Exhibit 13-6 Comparing Chipset's Partial Productivities in 2010 and 2011

Input (1)	Partial Productivity in 2011 (2)	Comparable Partial Productivity Based on 2010 Input–Output Relationships (3)	Percentage Change from 2010 to 2011 (4)
Direct materials	$\frac{1{,}150{,}000}{2{,}900{,}000} = 0.397$	$\frac{1{,}150{,}000}{3{,}450{,}000} = 0.333$	$\frac{0.397 - 0.333}{0.333} = 19.2\%$
Manufacturing conversion capacity	$\frac{1{,}150{,}000}{3{,}500{,}000} = 0.329$	$\frac{1{,}150{,}000}{3{,}750{,}000} = 0.307$	$\frac{0.329 - 0.307}{0.307} = 7.2\%$

Total Factor Productivity

Total factor productivity (TFP) is the ratio of the quantity of output produced to the costs of all inputs used based on current-period prices.

$$\text{Total factor productivity} = \frac{\text{Quantity of output produced}}{\text{Costs of all inputs used}}$$

TFP considers all inputs simultaneously and the trade-offs across inputs based on current input prices. Do not think of all productivity measures as physical measures lacking financial content—how many units of output are produced per unit of input. TFP is intricately tied to minimizing total cost—a financial objective.

Calculating and Comparing Total Factor Productivity

We first calculate Chipset's TFP in 2011, using 2011 prices and 1,150,000 units of output produced (based on information from the first part of the productivity-component calculations on p. 504).

$$\frac{\text{Total factor productivity}}{\text{for 2011 using 2011 prices}} = \frac{\text{Quantity of output produced in 2011}}{\text{Costs of inputs used in 2011 based on 2011 prices}}$$

$$= \frac{1{,}150{,}000}{(2{,}900{,}000 \times \$1.50) + (3{,}500{,}000 \times \$4.35)}$$

$$= \frac{1{,}150{,}000}{\$19{,}575{,}000}$$

$$= 0.058748 \text{ units of output per dollar of input cost}$$

By itself, the 2011 TFP of 0.058748 units of CX1 per dollar of input costs is not particularly helpful. We need something to compare the 2011 TFP against. One alternative is to compare TFPs of other similar companies in 2011. However, finding similar companies and obtaining accurate comparable data are often difficult. Companies, therefore, usually compare their own TFPs over time. In the Chipset example, we use as a benchmark TFP calculated using the inputs that Chipset would have used in 2010 to produce 1,150,000 units of CX1 at 2011 prices (that is, we use the costs calculated from the second part of the productivity-component calculations on p. 504). Why do we use 2011 prices? Because using the current year's prices in both calculations controls for input-price differences and focuses the analysis on adjustments the manager made in quantities of inputs in response to changes in prices.

$$\frac{\text{Benchmark}}{\text{TFP}} = \frac{\text{Quantity of output produced in 2011}}{\text{Costs of inputs at 2011 prices that would have been used in 2010 to produce 2011 output}}$$

$$= \frac{1{,}150{,}000}{(3{,}450{,}000 \times \$1.50) + (3{,}750{,}000 \times \$4.35)}$$

$$= \frac{1{,}150{,}000}{\$21{,}487{,}500}$$

$$= 0.053519 \text{ units of output per dollar of input cost}$$

Using 2011 prices, TFP increased 9.8% [(058748 − 0.053519) ÷ 0.053519 = 0.098, or 9.8%] from 2010 to 2011. Note that the 9.8% increase in TFP also equals the $1,912,500 gain (Exhibit 13-5, column 4) divided by the $19,575,000 of actual costs incurred in 2011 (Exhibit 13-5, column 5). Total factor productivity increased because Chipset produced more output per dollar of input cost in 2011 relative to 2010, measured in both years using 2011 prices. The gain in TFP occurs because Chipset increases the partial productivities of individual inputs and, consistent with its strategy, combines inputs to lower costs. Note that increases in TFP cannot be due to differences in input prices because we used 2011 prices to evaluate both the inputs that Chipset would have used in 2010 to produce 1,150,000 units of CX1 and the inputs actually used in 2011.

Using Partial and Total Factor Productivity Measures

A major advantage of TFP is that it measures the combined productivity of all inputs used to produce output and explicitly considers gains from using fewer physical inputs as well as substitution among inputs. Managers can analyze these numbers to understand the reasons for changes in TFP—for example, better human resource management practices, higher quality of materials, or improved manufacturing methods.

Although TFP measures are comprehensive, operations personnel find financial TFP measures more difficult to understand and less useful than physical partial-productivity measures. For example, companies that are more labor intensive than Chipset use manufacturing-labor partial-productivity measures. However, if productivity-based bonuses depend on gains in manufacturing-labor partial productivity alone, workers have incentives to substitute materials (and capital) for labor. This substitution improves their own productivity measure, while possibly decreasing the overall productivity of the company as measured by TFP. To overcome these incentive problems, some companies—for example, TRW, Eaton, and Whirlpool—explicitly adjust bonuses based on manufacturing-labor partial productivity for the effects of other factors such as investments in new equipment and higher levels of scrap. That is, they combine partial productivity with TFP-like measures.

Many companies such as Behlen Manufacturing, a steel fabricator, and Dell Computers use both partial productivity and total factor productivity to evaluate performance. *Partial productivity and TFP measures work best together because the strengths of one offset the weaknesses of the other.*

Terms to Learn

This chapter and the Glossary at the end of the book contain definitions of the following important terms:

- balanced scorecard
- cost leadership
- discretionary costs
- downsizing
- engineered costs
- growth component
- partial productivity
- price-recovery component
- product differentiation
- productivity
- productivity component
- reengineering
- rightsizing
- strategy map
- total factor productivity (TFP)
- unused capacity

Assignment Material

Questions

13-1 Define strategy.
13-2 Describe the five key forces to consider when analyzing an industry.
13-3 Describe two generic strategies.
13-4 What is a customer preference map and why is it useful?
13-5 What is reengineering?
13-6 What are four key perspectives in the balanced scorecard?
13-7 What is a strategy map?
13-8 Describe three features of a good balanced scorecard.
13-9 What are three important pitfalls to avoid when implementing a balanced scorecard?
13-10 Describe three key components in doing a strategic analysis of operating income.
13-11 Why might an analyst incorporate the industry-market-size factor and the interrelationships among the growth, price-recovery, and productivity components into a strategic analysis of operating income?
13-12 How does an engineered cost differ from a discretionary cost?
13-13 What is downsizing?
13-14 What is a partial-productivity measure?
13-15 "We are already measuring total factor productivity. Measuring partial productivities would be of no value." Do you agree? Comment briefly.

Exercises

13-16 Balanced scorecard. Ridgecrest Corporation manufactures corrugated cardboard boxes. It competes and plans to grow by selling high-quality boxes at a low price and by delivering them to customers quickly after receiving customers' orders. There are many other manufacturers who produce similar boxes. Ridgecrest believes that continuously improving its manufacturing processes and having satisfied employees are critical to implementing its strategy in 2012.

Required

1. Is Ridgecrest's 2012 strategy one of product differentiation or cost leadership? Explain briefly.
2. Kearney Corporation, a competitor of Ridgecrest, manufactures corrugated boxes with more designs and color combinations than Ridgecrest at a higher price. Kearney's boxes are of high quality but require more time to produce and so have longer delivery times. Draw a simple customer preference map as in Exhibit 13-1 for Ridgecrest and Kearney using the attributes of price, delivery time, quality, and design.

3. Draw a strategy map as in Exhibit 13-2 with two strategic objectives you would expect to see under each balanced scorecard perspective.
4. For each strategic objective indicate a measure you would expect to see in Ridgecrest's balanced scorecard for 2012.

13-17 Analysis of growth, price-recovery, and productivity components (continuation of 13-16). An analysis of Ridgecrest's operating-income changes between 2011 and 2012 shows the following:

Operating income for 2011	$1,850,000
Add growth component	85,000
Deduct price-recovery component	(72,000)
Add productivity component	150,000
Operating income for 2011	$2,013,000

The industry market size for corrugated cardboard boxes did not grow in 2012, input prices did not change, and Ridgecrest reduced the prices of its boxes.

Required
1. Was Ridgecrest's gain in operating income in 2012 consistent with the strategy you identified in requirement 1 of Exercise 13-16?
2. Explain the productivity component. In general, does it represent savings in only variable costs, only fixed costs, or both variable and fixed costs?

13-18 Strategy, balanced scorecard, merchandising operation. Roberto & Sons buys T-shirts in bulk, applies its own trendsetting silk-screen designs, and then sells the T-shirts to a number of retailers. Roberto wants to be known for its trendsetting designs, and it wants every teenager to be seen in a distinctive Roberto T-shirt. Roberto presents the following data for its first two years of operations, 2010 and 2011.

		2010	2011
1	Number of T-shirts purchased	200,000	250,000
2	Number of T-shirts discarded	2,000	3,300
3	Number of T-shirts sold (row 1 – row 2)	198,000	246,700
4	Average selling price	$25.00	$26.00
5	Average cost per T-shirt	$10.00	$8.50
6	Administrative capacity (number of customers)	4,000	3,750
7	Administrative costs	$1,200,000	$1,162,500
8	Administrative cost per customer (row 8 ÷ row 7)	$300	$310

Administrative costs depend on the number of customers that Roberto has created capacity to support, not on the actual number of customers served. Roberto had 3,600 customers in 2010 and 3,500 customers in 2011.

Required
1. Is Roberto 's strategy one of product differentiation or cost leadership? Explain briefly.
2. Describe briefly the key measures Roberto should include in its balanced scorecard and the reasons it should do so.

13-19 Strategic analysis of operating income (continuation of 13-18). Refer to Exercise 13-18.

Required
1. Calculate Roberto's operating income in both 2010 and 2011.
2. Calculate the growth, price-recovery, and productivity components that explain the change in operating income from 2010 to 2011.
3. Comment on your answers in requirement 2. What does each of these components indicate?

13-20 Analysis of growth, price-recovery, and productivity components (continuation of 13-19). Refer to Exercise 13-19. Suppose that the market for silk-screened T-shirts grew by 10% during 2011. All increases in sales greater than 10% are the result of Roberto's strategic actions.

Required Calculate the change in operating income from 2010 to 2011 due to growth in market size, product differentiation, and cost leadership. How successful has Roberto been in implementing its strategy? Explain.

13-21 Identifying and managing unused capacity (continuation of 13-18). Refer to Exercise 13-18.

Required
1. Calculate the amount and cost of unused administrative capacity at the beginning of 2011, based on the actual number of customers Roberto served in 2011.
2. Suppose Roberto can only add or reduce administrative capacity in increments of 250 customers. What is the maximum amount of costs that Roberto can save in 2011 by downsizing administrative capacity?
3. What factors, other than cost, should Roberto consider before it downsizes administrative capacity?

13-22 Strategy, balanced scorecard. Stanmore Corporation makes a special-purpose machine, D4H, used in the textile industry. Stanmore has designed the D4H machine for 2011 to be distinct from its competitors. It has been generally regarded as a superior machine. Stanmore presents the following data for 2010 and 2011.

	2010	2011
1. Units of D4H produced and sold	200	210
2. Selling price	$40,000	$42,000
3. Direct materials (kilograms)	300,000	310,000
4. Direct material cost per kilogram	$8	$8.50
5. Manufacturing capacity in units of D4H	250	250
6. Total conversion costs	$2,000,000	$2,025,000
7. Conversion cost per unit of capacity (row 6 ÷ row 5)	$8,000	$8,100
8. Selling and customer-service capacity	100 customers	95 customers
9. Total selling and customer-service costs	$1,000,000	$940,500
10. Selling and customer-service capacity cost per customer (row 9 ÷ row 8)	$10,000	$9,900

Stanmore produces no defective machines, but it wants to reduce direct materials usage per D4H machine in 2011. Conversion costs in each year depend on production capacity defined in terms of D4H units that can be produced, not the actual units produced. Selling and customer-service costs depend on the number of customers that Stanmore can support, not the actual number of customers it serves. Stanmore has 75 customers in 2010 and 80 customers in 2011.

Required

1. Is Stanmore's strategy one of product differentiation or cost leadership? Explain briefly.
2. Describe briefly key measures that you would include in Stanmore's balanced scorecard and the reasons for doing so.

13-23 Strategic analysis of operating income (continuation of 13-22). Refer to Exercise 13-22.

Required

1. Calculate the operating income of Stanmore Corporation in 2010 and 2011.
2. Calculate the growth, price-recovery, and productivity components that explain the change in operating income from 2010 to 2011.
3. Comment on your answer in requirement 2. What do these components indicate?

13-24 Analysis of growth, price-recovery, and productivity components (continuation of 13-23). Suppose that during 2011, the market for Stanmore's special-purpose machines grew by 3%. All increases in market share (that is, sales increases greater than 3%) are the result of Stanmore's strategic actions.

Required

Calculate how much of the change in operating income from 2010 to 2011 is due to the industry-market-size factor, product differentiation, and cost leadership. How successful has Stanmore been in implementing its strategy? Explain.

13-25 Identifying and managing unused capacity (continuation of 13-22). Refer to Exercise 13-22.

Required

1. Calculate the amount and cost of (a) unused manufacturing capacity and (b) unused selling and customer-service capacity at the beginning of 2011 based on actual production and actual number of customers served in 2011.
2. Suppose Stanmore can add or reduce its manufacturing capacity in increments of 30 units. What is the maximum amount of costs that Stanmore could save in 2011 by downsizing manufacturing capacity?
3. Stanmore, in fact, does not eliminate any of its unused manufacturing capacity. Why might Stanmore not downsize?

13-26 Strategy, balanced scorecard, service company. Westlake Corporation is a small information-systems consulting firm that specializes in helping companies implement standard sales-management software. The market for Westlake's services is very competitive. To compete successfully, Westlake must deliver quality service at a low cost. Westlake presents the following data for 2010 and 2011.

	2010	2011
1. Number of jobs billed	60	70
2. Selling price per job	$50,000	$48,000
3. Software-implementation labor-hours	30,000	32,000
4. Cost per software-implementation labor-hour	$60	$63
5. Software-implementation support capacity (number of jobs it can do)	90	90
6. Total cost of software-implementation support	$360,000	$369,000
7. Software-implementation support-capacity cost per job (row 6 ÷ row 5)	$4,000	$4,100

Software-implementation labor-hour costs are variable costs. Software-implementation support costs for each year depend on the software-implementation support capacity Westlake chooses to maintain each year (that is the number of jobs it can do each year). It does not vary with the actual number of jobs done that year.

78   IBO Financial Management & Currency Risk

Required
1. Is Westlake Corporation's strategy one of product differentiation or cost leadership? Explain briefly.
2. Describe key measures you would include in Westlake's balanced scorecard and your reasons for doing so.

13-27 Strategic analysis of operating income (continuation of 13-26). Refer to Exercise 13-26.

Required
1. Calculate the operating income of Westlake Corporation in 2010 and 2011.
2. Calculate the growth, price-recovery, and productivity components that explain the change in operating income from 2010 to 2011.
3. Comment on your answer in requirement 2. What do these components indicate?

13-28 Analysis of growth, price-recovery, and productivity components (continuation of 13-27). Suppose that during 2011 the market for implementing sales-management software increases by 5%. Assume that any decrease in selling price and any increase in market share more than 5% are the result of strategic choices by Westlake's management to implement its strategy.

Required Calculate how much of the change in operating income from 2010 to 2011 is due to the industry-market-size factor, product differentiation, and cost leadership. How successful has Westlake been in implementing its strategy? Explain.

13-29 Identifying and managing unused capacity (continuation of 13-26). Refer to Exercise 13-26.

Required
1. Calculate the amount and cost of unused software-implementation support capacity at the beginning of 2011, based on the number of jobs actually done in 2011.
2. Suppose Westlake can add or reduce its software-implementation support capacity in increments of 15 units. What is the maximum amount of costs that Westlake could save in 2011 by downsizing software-implementation support capacity?
3. Westlake, in fact, does not eliminate any of its unused software-implementation support capacity. Why might Westlake not downsize?

Problems

13-30 Balanced scorecard and strategy. Music Master Company manufactures an MP3 player called the Mini. The company sells the player to discount stores throughout the country. This player is significantly less expensive than similar products sold by Music Master's competitors, but the Mini offers just four gigabytes of space, compared with eight offered by competitor Vantage Manufacturing. Furthermore, the Mini has experienced production problems that have resulted in significant rework costs. Vantage's model has an excellent reputation for quality, but is considerably more expensive.

Required
1. Draw a simple customer preference map for Music Master and Vantage using the attributes of price, quality, and storage capacity. Use the format of Exhibit 13-1.
2. Is Music Master's current strategy that of product differentiation or cost leadership?
3. Music Master would like to improve quality and decrease costs by improving processes and training workers to reduce rework. Music Master's managers believe the increased quality will increase sales. Draw a strategy map as in Exhibit 13-2 describing the cause-and-effect relationships among the strategic objectives you would expect to see in Music Master's balanced scorecard.
4. For each strategic objective suggest a measure you would recommend in Music Master's balanced scorecard.

13-31 Strategic analysis of operating income (continuation of 13-30). Refer to Problem 13-30. As a result of the actions taken, quality has significantly improved in 2011 while rework and unit costs of the Mini have decreased. Music Master has reduced manufacturing capacity because capacity is no longer needed to support rework. Music Master has also lowered the Mini's selling price to gain market share and unit sales have increased. Information about the current period (2011) and last period (2010) follows:

		2010	2011
1.	Units of Mini produced and sold	8,000	9,000
2.	Selling price	$45	$43
3.	Ounces of direct materials used	32,000	33,000
4.	Direct material cost per ounce	$3.50	$3.50
5.	Manufacturing capacity in units	12,000	11,000
6.	Total conversion costs	$156,000	$143,000
7.	Conversion cost per unit of capacity (row 6 ÷ row 5)	$13	$13
8.	Selling and customer-service capacity	90 customers	90 customers
9.	Total selling and customer-service costs	$45,000	$49,500
10.	Selling and customer-service capacity cost per customer (row 9 ÷ row 8)	$500	$550

Conversion costs in each year depend on production capacity defined in terms of units of Mini that can be produced, not the actual units produced. Selling and customer-service costs depend on the number of customers that Music Master can support, not the actual number of customers it serves. Music Master has 70 customers in 2010 and 80 customers in 2011.

Required

1. Calculate operating income of Music Master Company for 2010 and 2011.
2. Calculate the growth, price-recovery, and productivity components that explain the change in operating income from 2010 to 2011.
3. Comment on your answer in requirement 2. What do these components indicate?

13-32 Analysis of growth, price-recovery, and productivity components (continuation of 13-31). Suppose that during 2011, the market for MP3 players grew 3%. All decreases in the selling price of the Mini and increases in market share (that is, sales increases greater than 3%) are the result of Music Master's strategic actions.

Required

Calculate how much of the change in operating income from 2010 to 2011 is due to the industry-market-size factor, product differentiation, and cost leadership. How does this relate to Music Master's strategy and its success in implementation? Explain.

13-33 Identifying and managing unused capacity (continuation of 13-31) Refer to the information for Music Master Company in 13-31.

Required

1. Calculate the amount and cost of (a) unused manufacturing capacity and (b) unused selling and customer-service capacity at the beginning of 2011 based on actual production and actual number of customers served in 2011.
2. Suppose Music Master can add or reduce its selling and customer-service capacity in increments of five customers. What is the maximum amount of costs that Music Master could save in 2011 by downsizing selling and customer-service capacity?
3. Music Master, in fact, does not eliminate any of its unused selling and customer-service capacity. Why might Music Master not downsize?

13-34 Balanced scorecard. Following is a random-order listing of perspectives, strategic objectives, and performance measures for the balanced scorecard.

Perspectives	Performance Measures
Internal business process	Percentage of defective-product units
Customer	Return on assets
Learning and growth	Number of patents
Financial	Employee turnover rate
Strategic Objectives	Net income
Acquire new customers	Customer profitability
Increase shareholder value	Percentage of processes with real-time feedback
Retain customers	Return on sales
Improve manufacturing quality	Average job-related training-hours per employee
Develop profitable customers	Return on equity
Increase proprietary products	Percentage of on-time deliveries by suppliers
Increase information-system capabilities	Product cost per unit
Enhance employee skills	Profit per salesperson
On-time delivery by suppliers	Percentage of error-free invoices
Increase profit generated by each salesperson	Customer cost per unit
Introduce new products	Earnings per share
Minimize invoice-error rate	Number of new customers
	Percentage of customers retained

Required

For each perspective, select those strategic objectives from the list that best relate to it. For each strategic objective, select the most appropriate performance measure(s) from the list.

13-35 Balanced scorecard. (R. Kaplan, adapted) Caltex, Inc., refines gasoline and sells it through its own Caltex Gas Stations. On the basis of market research, Caltex determines that 60% of the overall gasoline market consists of "service-oriented customers," medium- to high-income individuals who are willing to pay a higher price for gas if the gas stations can provide excellent customer service, such as a clean facility, a convenience store, friendly employees, a quick turnaround, the ability to pay by credit card, and high-octane premium gasoline. The remaining 40% of the overall market are "price shoppers" who look to buy the cheapest gasoline available. Caltex's strategy is to focus on the 60% of service-oriented customers. Caltex's balanced scorecard for 2011 follows. For brevity, the initiatives taken under each objective are omitted.

Objectives	Measures	Target Performance	Actual Performance
Financial Perspective			
Increase shareholder value	Operating-income changes from price recovery	$90,000,000	$95,000,000
	Operating-income changes from growth	$65,000,000	$67,000,000
Customer Perspective			
Increase market share	Market share of overall gasoline market	10%	9.8%
Internal-Business-Process Perspective			
Improve gasoline quality	Quality index	94 points	95 points
Improve refinery performance	Refinery-reliability index (%)	91%	91%
Ensure gasoline availability	Product-availability index (%)	99%	100%
Learning-and-Growth Perspective			
Increase refinery process capability	Percentage of refinery processes with advanced controls	88%	90%

Required

1. Was Caltex successful in implementing its strategy in 2011? Explain your answer.
2. Would you have included some measure of employee satisfaction and employee training in the learning-and-growth perspective? Are these objectives critical to Caltex for implementing its strategy? Why or why not? Explain briefly.
3. Explain how Caltex did not achieve its target market share in the total gasoline market but still exceeded its financial targets. Is "market share of overall gasoline market" the correct measure of market share? Explain briefly.
4. Is there a cause-and-effect linkage between improvements in the measures in the internal business-process perspective and the measure in the customer perspective? That is, would you add other measures to the internal-business-process perspective or the customer perspective? Why or why not? Explain briefly.
5. Do you agree with Caltex's decision not to include measures of changes in operating income from productivity improvements under the financial perspective of the balanced scorecard? Explain briefly.

13-36 Balanced scorecard. Lee Corporation manufactures various types of color laser printers in a highly automated facility with high fixed costs. The market for laser printers is competitive. The various color laser printers on the market are comparable in terms of features and price. Lee believes that satisfying customers with products of high quality at low costs is key to achieving its target profitability. For 2011, Lee plans to achieve higher quality and lower costs by improving yields and reducing defects in its manufacturing operations. Lee will train workers and encourage and empower them to take the necessary actions. Currently, a significant amount of Lee's capacity is used to produce products that are defective and cannot be sold. Lee expects that higher yields will reduce the capacity that Lee needs to manufacture products. Lee does not anticipate that improving manufacturing will automatically lead to lower costs because Lee has high fixed costs. To reduce fixed costs per unit, Lee could lay off employees and sell equipment, or it could use the capacity to produce and sell more of its current products or improved models of its current products.

Lee's balanced scorecard (initiatives omitted) for the just-completed fiscal year 2011 follows:

Objectives	Measures	Target Performance	Actual Performance
Financial Perspective			
Increase shareholder value	Operating-income changes from productivity improvements	$1,000,000	$400,000
	Operating-income changes from growth	$1,500,000	$600,000
Customer Perspective			
Increase market share	Market share in color laser printers	5%	4.6%
Internal-Business-Process Perspective			
Improve manufacturing quality	Yield	82%	85%
Reduce delivery time to customers	Order-delivery time	25 days	22 days
Learning-and-Growth Perspective			
Develop process skills	Percentage of employees trained in process and quality management	90%	92%
Enhance information-system capabilities	Percentage of manufacturing processes with real-time feedback	85%	87%

1. Was Lee successful in implementing its strategy in 2011? Explain.
2. Is Lee's balanced scorecard useful in helping the company understand why it did not reach its target market share in 2011? If it is, explain why. If it is not, explain what other measures you might want to add under the customer perspective and why.
3. Would you have included some measure of employee satisfaction in the learning-and-growth perspective and new-product development in the internal-business-process perspective? That is, do you think employee satisfaction and development of new products are critical for Lee to implement its strategy? Why or why not? Explain briefly.
4. What problems, if any, do you see in Lee improving quality and significantly downsizing to eliminate unused capacity?

13-37 Partial productivity measurement. Gerhart Company manufactures wallets from fabric. In 2011, Gerhart made 2,520,000 wallets using 2,000,000 yards of fabric. In 2011, Gerhart has capacity to make 3,307,500 wallets and incurs a cost of $9,922,500 for this capacity. In 2012, Gerhart plans to make 2,646,000 wallets, make fabric use more efficient, and reduce capacity.

Suppose that in 2012 Gerhart makes 2,646,000 wallets, uses 1,764,000 yards of fabric, and reduces capacity to 2,700,000 wallets, incurring a cost of $8,370,000 for this capacity.

1. Calculate the partial-productivity ratios for materials and conversion (capacity costs) for 2012, and compare them to a benchmark for 2011 calculated based on 2012 output.
2. How can Gerhart Company use the information from the partial-productivity calculations?

13-38 Total factor productivity (continuation of 13-37). Refer to the data for Problem 13-37. Assume the fabric costs $3.70 per yard in 2012 and $3.85 per yard in 2011.

1. Compute Gerhart Company's total factor productivity (TFP) for 2012.
2. Compare TFP for 2012 with a benchmark TFP for 2011 inputs based on 2012 prices and output.
3. What additional information does TFP provide that partial productivity measures do not?

Collaborative Learning Problem

13-39 Strategic analysis of operating income. Halsey Company sells women's clothing. Halsey's strategy is to offer a wide selection of clothes and excellent customer service and to charge a premium price. Halsey presents the following data for 2010 and 2011. For simplicity, assume that each customer purchases one piece of clothing.

	2010	2011
1. Pieces of clothing purchased and sold	40,000	40,000
2. Average selling price	$60	$59
3. Average cost per piece of clothing	$40	$41
4. Selling and customer-service capacity	51,000 customers	43,000 customers
5. Selling and customer-service costs	$357,000	$296,700
6. Selling and customer-service capacity cost per customer (row 5 ÷ row 4)	$7 per customer	$6.90 per customer
7. Purchasing and administrative capacity	980 designs	850 designs
8. Purchasing and administrative costs	$245,000	$204,000
9. Purchasing and administrative capacity cost per distinct design (row 8 ÷ row 7)	$250 per design	$240 per design

Total selling and customer-service costs depend on the number of customers that Halsey has created capacity to support, not the actual number of customers that Halsey serves. Total purchasing and administrative costs depend on purchasing and administrative capacity that Halsey has created (defined in terms of the number of distinct clothing designs that Halsey can purchase and administer). Purchasing and administrative costs do not depend on the actual number of distinct clothing designs purchased. Halsey purchased 930 distinct designs in 2010 and 820 distinct designs in 2011.

At the start of 2010, Halsey planned to increase operating income by 10% over operating income in 2011.

1. Is Halsey's strategy one of product differentiation or cost leadership? Explain.
2. Calculate Halsey's operating income in 2010 and 2011.
3. Calculate the growth, price-recovery, and productivity components of changes in operating income between 2010 and 2011.
4. Does the strategic analysis of operating income indicate Halsey was successful in implementing its strategy in 2011? Explain.

22 Management Control Systems, Transfer Pricing, and Multinational Considerations

Learning Objectives

1. Describe a management control system and its three key properties
2. Describe the benefits and costs of decentralization
3. Explain transfer prices and four criteria used to evaluate alternative transfer-pricing methods
4. Illustrate how market-based transfer prices promote goal congruence in perfectly competitive markets
5. Understand how to avoid making suboptimal decisions when transfer prices are based on full cost plus a markup
6. Describe the range of feasible transfer prices when there is unused capacity
7. Apply a general guideline for determining a minimum transfer price
8. Incorporate income tax considerations in multinational transfer pricing

Transfer pricing is the price one subunit of a company charges for the services it provides another subunit of the same company.

Top management uses transfer prices to focus managers' attention on the performance of their own subunits and to plan and coordinate the actions of different subunits to maximize the company's income as a whole. While transfer pricing is productive, it can also be contentious as managers of different subunits often differ on how transfer prices should be set. Some managers prefer the prices to be based on market prices. Others prefer prices to be based on costs alone. There may also be some disputes on what should be included in the cost of the products or services transferred between subunits and also different tax rates applied to subunits.

Controversy also arises when multinational corporations seek to reduce their overall income tax burden by charging high transfer prices to units located in countries with high tax rates. Many countries attempt to restrict this practice.

Transfer Pricing Disputes and Tax Issues Stop Collaborations Between Subunits of Mehr Co.[1]

Merh Co. is a multinational corporation (MNC) which operates in several countries with a decentralized organizational structure and subsidiaries as investment centers. The group is active in several business sectors including automobile parts, textiles, and food. Fajr-e-Taale and Food Vision Europe are two of its subsidiaries.

Fajr-e-Taale (FeT) is an import/export company based in the Middle East and active in exporting food, groceries, and similar products from the Middle East, Asia, and Africa to Europe. To expand its business, it targeted the UK as a potential market and approached the management of Food Vision Europe (FVE), which was a newly established subsidiary of the group in the UK. FVE's remit, among its other potential businesses, was to market, store, and sell other subsidiaries' products. The first business experience of FVE within the Mehr Co. group was with FeT. The parties agreed on marketing and other operational activities, including the percentage of profit sharing between them. They also identified target markets, and initial agreements were made with some chain stores, which could lead to long term contracts.

---

[1] Source: Dr. Hassan Yazdifar. The role of performance measurement in complex organizations. A funded research project in the Middle East (2005–11).

The first shipment of products to the UK was in early 2007. Consequently, FeT invoiced FVE. The invoice included (a portion of) FeT's purchasing department expenses as part of the product costs. This was the beginning of a challenge between both parties—they had generally agreed on how to share the profit but not on the details of how the profit should be worked out and the transfer price of the products between parties. FVE realized that it should have given proper thought to the detailed costs involved and the transfer price between

parties in the agreement. A further concern of FVE was the tax rate in the UK, as it was higher than the rate in the Middle East, which would be applied to FeT. FVE (the UK subunit) wanted to consider the effect of tax in both regions when sharing profits between parties, but this was challenged by the Middle East subunit.

The parties could not solve the preceding disputes and the products that had arrived in the UK were not removed from the port by FVE, which caused further custom charges. Eventually, and with the involvement of the company headquarters, the two parties agreed to consider the purchase price of the product for this shipment and to not consider the effect of tax, but to then terminate the contract. The parties both suffered some losses and also were left with unsatisfied customers (the chain stores) due to the delays with their order delivery. FVE then ceased its operation and the chain stores lost faith in FeT for any future business.

Though not all companies face multinational tax concerns, transfer-pricing issues are common to many companies. In these companies, transfer pricing is part of the larger management control system. This chapter develops the links between strategy, organization structure, management control systems, and accounting information. In this chapter we'll examine the benefits and costs of centralized and decentralized organization structures, and we'll look at the pricing of products or services transferred between subunits of the same company. We emphasize how accounting information, such as costs, budgets, and prices, helps in planning and coordinating actions of subunits.

Management Control Systems

A **management control system** is a means of gathering and using information to aid and coordinate the planning and control decisions throughout an organization and to guide the behavior of its managers and other employees. Some companies design their management control system around the concept of the balanced scorecard. For example, ExxonMobil's management control system contains financial and nonfinancial information in each of the four perspectives of the balanced scorecard (see Chapter 13 for details). Well-designed management control systems use information both from within the company, such as net income and employee satisfaction, and from outside the company, such as stock price and customer satisfaction.

Formal and Informal Systems

Management control systems consist of formal and informal control systems. The formal management control system of a company includes explicit rules, procedures, performance measures, and incentive plans that guide the behavior of its managers and other employees. The formal control system is comprised of several systems, such as the

Learning Objective 1

Describe a management control system

... gathers information for planning and control decisions

and its three key properties

... aligns with strategy, supports organizational responsibility of managers, and motivates employees

management accounting system, which provides information regarding costs, revenues, and income; the human resources systems, which provide information on recruiting, training, absenteeism, and accidents; and the quality systems, which provide information on yield, defective products, and late deliveries to customers.

The informal management control system includes shared values, loyalties, and mutual commitments among members of the organization, company culture, and the unwritten norms about acceptable behavior for managers and other employees. Examples of company slogans that reinforce values and loyalties are "At Ford, Quality Is Job 1," and "At Home Depot, Low Prices Are Just the Beginning."

Effective Management Control

To be effective, management control systems should be closely aligned with the organization's strategies and goals. Two examples of strategies at ExxonMobil are (1) providing innovative products and services to increase market share in key customer segments (by targeting customers who are willing to pay more for faster service, better facilities, and well-stocked convenience stores) and (2) reducing costs and targeting price-sensitive customers. Suppose ExxonMobil decides to pursue the former strategy. The management control system must then reinforce this goal, and ExxonMobil should tie managers' rewards to achieving the targeted measures.

Management control systems should also be designed to support the organizational responsibilities of individual managers. Different levels of management at ExxonMobil need different kinds of information to perform their tasks. For example, top management needs stock-price information to evaluate how much shareholder value the company has created. Stock price, however, is less important for line managers supervising individual refineries. They are more concerned with obtaining information about on-time delivery of gasoline, equipment downtime, product quality, number of days lost to accidents and environmental problems, cost per gallon of gasoline, and employee satisfaction. Similarly, marketing managers are more concerned with information about service at gas stations, customer satisfaction, and market share.

Effective management control systems should also motivate managers and other employees. **Motivation** is the desire to attain a selected goal (the *goal-congruence* aspect) combined with the resulting pursuit of that goal (the *effort* aspect).

Goal congruence exists when individuals and groups work toward achieving the organization's goals—that is, managers working in their own best interest take actions that align with the overall goals of top management. Suppose the goal of ExxonMobil's top management is to maximize operating income. If the management control system evaluates the refinery manager *only* on the basis of costs, the manager may be tempted to make decisions that minimize cost but overlook product quality or timely delivery to retail stations. This oversight is unlikely to maximize operating income of the company as a whole. In this case, the management control system will not achieve goal congruence.

Effort is the extent to which managers strive or endeavor in order to achieve a goal. Effort goes beyond physical exertion, such as a worker producing at a faster rate, to include mental actions as well. For example, effort includes the diligence or acumen with which a manager gathers and analyzes data before authorizing a new investment. It is impossible to directly observe or reward effort. As a result, management control systems motivate employees to exert effort by rewarding them for the achievement of observable goals, such as profit targets or stock returns. This induces managers to exert effort because higher levels of effort increase the likelihood that the goals are achieved. The rewards can be monetary (such as cash, shares of company stock, use of a company car, or membership in a club) or nonmonetary (such as a better title, greater responsibility, or authority over a larger number of employees).

What is a management control system and how should it be designed?

Decentralization

Management control systems must fit an organization's structure. An organization whose structure is decentralized has additional issues to consider for its management control system to be effective.

Decentralization is the freedom for managers at lower levels of the organization to make decisions. **Autonomy** is the degree of freedom to make decisions. The greater the freedom, the greater the autonomy. As we discuss the issues of decentralization and autonomy, we use the term "subunit" to refer to any part of an organization. A subunit may be a large division, such as the refining division of ExxonMobil, or a small group, such as a two-person advertising department of a local clothing chain.

Until the mid-twentieth century, many firms were organized in a centralized, hierarchical fashion. Power was concentrated at the top and there was relatively little freedom for managers at the lower levels to make decisions. Perhaps the most famous example of a highly centralized structure is the Soviet Union, prior to its collapse in the late 1980s. Today, organizations are far more decentralized and many companies have pushed decision-making authority down to subunit managers. Examples of firms with decentralized structures include Nucor, the U.S. steel giant, which allows substantial operational autonomy to the general managers of its plants, and Tesco, Britain's largest retailer, which offers great latitude to its store managers. Of course, no firm is completely decentralized. At Nucor headquarters management still retains responsibility for overall strategic planning, company financing, setting base salary levels and bonus targets, purchase of steel scrap, etc. How much decentralization is optimal? Companies try to choose the degree of decentralization that maximizes benefits over costs. From a practical standpoint, top management can seldom quantify either the benefits or the costs of decentralization. Still, the cost-benefit approach helps management focus on the key issues.

> **Learning Objective 2**
>
> Describe the benefits of decentralization
>
> ... responsiveness to customers, faster decision making, management development
>
> and the costs of decentralization
>
> ... loss of control, duplication of activities

Benefits of Decentralization

Supporters of decentralizing decision making and granting responsibilities to managers of subunits advocate the following benefits:

1. **Creates greater responsiveness to needs of a subunit's customers, suppliers, and employees.** Good decisions cannot be made without good information. Compared with top managers, subunit managers are better informed about their customers, competitors, suppliers, and employees, as well as about local factors that affect performance, such as ways to decrease costs, improve quality, and be responsive to customers. Eastman Kodak reports that two advantages of decentralization are an "increase in the company's knowledge of the marketplace and improved service to customers."

2. **Leads to gains from faster decision making by subunit managers.** Decentralization speeds decision making, creating a competitive advantage over centralized organizations. Centralization slows decision making as responsibility for decisions creeps upward through layer after layer of management. Interlake, a manufacturer of materials handling equipment, cites this benefit of decentralization: "We have distributed decision-making powers more broadly to the cutting edge of product and market opportunity." Interlake's materials-handling equipment must often be customized to fit customers' needs. Delegating decision making to the sales force allows Interlake to respond faster to changing customer requirements.

3. **Increases motivation of subunit managers.** Subunit managers are more motivated and committed when they can exercise initiative. Hawei & Hawei, a highly decentralized company, maintains that "Decentralization = Creativity = Productivity."

4. **Assists management development and learning.** Giving managers more responsibility helps develop an experienced pool of management talent to fill higher-level management positions. The company also learns which people are unlikely to be successful top managers. According to Tektronix, an electronics instruments company, "Decentralized units provide a training ground for general managers and a visible field of combat where product champions can fight for their ideas."

5. **Sharpens the focus of subunit managers, broadens the reach of top management.** In a decentralized setting, the manager of a subunit has a concentrated focus. The head of Yahoo Japan, for example, can develop country-specific knowledge and expertise (local advertising trends, cultural norms, payment forms, etc.) and focus attention on maximizing Yahoo's profits in Japan. At the same time, this relieves Yahoo's top

management in Sunnyvale, CA from the burden of controlling day-to-day operating decisions in Japan. The American managers can now spend more time and effort on strategic planning for the entire organization.

Costs of Decentralization

Advocates of more-centralized decision making point to the following costs of decentralizing decision making:

1. **Leads to suboptimal decision making.** This cost arises because top management has given up control over decision making. If the subunit managers do not have the necessary expertise or talent to handle this responsibility, the company, as a whole, is worse off.

   Even if subunit managers are sufficiently skilled, **suboptimal decision making**—also called **incongruent decision making** or **dysfunctional decision making**—occurs when a decision's benefit to one subunit is more than offset by the costs to the organization as a whole. This is most prevalent when the subunits in the company are highly interdependent, such as when the end product of one subunit is used or sold by another subunit. For example, suppose that Nintendo's marketing group receives an order for additional Wii consoles in Australia following the release of some unexpectedly popular new games. A manufacturing manager in Japan who is evaluated on the basis of costs may be unwilling to arrange this rush order since altering production schedules invariably increases manufacturing costs. From Nintendo's viewpoint, however, supplying the consoles may be optimal, both because the Australian customers are willing to pay a premium price and because the current shipment is expected to stimulate orders for other Nintendo games and consoles in the future.

2. **Focuses manager's attention on the subunit rather than the company as a whole.** Individual subunit managers may regard themselves as competing with managers of other subunits in the same company as if they were external rivals. This pushes them to view the relative performance of the subunit as more important than the goals of the company. Consequently, managers may be unwilling to assist when another subunit faces an emergency (as in the Nintendo example) or share important information. In the recent Congressional hearings on the recall of Toyota vehicles, it was revealed that it was common for Toyota's Japan unit to not share information about engineering problems or reported defects between its United States, Asian, and European operations. Toyota has since asserted that this dysfunctional behavior will no longer be tolerated.

3. **Results in duplication of output.** If subunits provide similar products or services, their internal competition could lead to failure in the external markets. The reason is that divisions may find it easier to steal market share from one another, by mimicking each other's successful products, rather than from outside firms. Eventually, this leads to confusion in the minds of customers, and the loss of each division's distinctive strengths. The classic example is General Motors, which has had to wind down its Oldsmobile, Pontiac, and Saturn divisions and is now in bankruptcy reorganization. Similarly, Condé Nast Publishing's initially distinct (and separately run) food magazines, *Bon Appétit* and *Gourmet*, eventually ended up chasing the same readers and advertisers, to the detriment of both. *Gourmet* magazine stopped publication in November 2009.[2]

4. **Results in duplication of activities.** Even if the subunits operate in distinct markets, several individual subunits of the company may undertake the same activity separately. In a highly decentralized company, each subunit may have personnel to carry out staff functions such as human resources or information technology. Centralizing these functions helps to streamline and use fewer resources for these activities, and eliminates wasteful duplication. For example, ABB (Switzerland), a global leader in power and automation technology, is decentralized but has generated significant cost savings of late by centralizing its sourcing decisions across business units for parts, such as pipe pumps and fittings, as well as engineering and erection services. The

---

[2] For an intriguing comparison of the failure of decentralization in these disparate settings, see Jack Shafer's article, "How Condé Nast is Like General Motors: The Magazine Empire as Car Wreck," Slate, October 5, 2009, www.slate.com/id/2231177/.

growing popularity of the "shared service center" model, especially for financial transactions and human resources, is predicated on the 30%–40% savings enabled by the consolidation of such functions, rather than allowing them to be controlled by the subunits.[3]

Comparison of Benefits and Costs

To choose an organization structure that will implement a company's strategy, top managers must compare the benefits and costs of decentralization, often on a function-by-function basis. Surveys of U.S. and European companies report that the decisions made most frequently at the decentralized level are related to product mix and product advertising. In these areas, subunit managers develop their own operating plans and performance reports and make faster decisions based on local information. Decisions related to the type and source of long-term financing and income taxes are made least frequently at the decentralized level. Corporate managers have better information about financing terms in different markets and can obtain the best terms. Centralizing income tax strategies allows the organization to trade off and manage income in a subunit with losses in others. The benefits of decentralization are generally greater when companies face uncertainties in their environments, require detailed local knowledge for performing various jobs, and have few interdependencies among divisions.

Decentralization in Multinational Companies

Multinational companies—companies that operate in multiple countries—are often decentralized because centralized control of a company with subunits around the world is often physically and practically impossible. Also, language, customs, cultures, business practices, rules, laws, and regulations vary significantly across countries. Decentralization enables managers in different countries to make decisions that exploit their knowledge of local business and political conditions and enables them to deal with uncertainties in their individual environments. For example, Philips, a global electronics company headquartered in the Netherlands, delegates marketing and pricing decisions for its television business in the Indian and Singaporean markets to the managers in those countries. Multinational corporations often rotate managers between foreign locations and corporate headquarters. Job rotation combined with decentralization helps develop managers' abilities to operate in the global environment.

There are drawbacks to decentralizing multinational companies. One of the most important is the lack of control and the resulting risks. Barings PLC, a British investment banking firm, went bankrupt and had to be sold when one of its traders in Singapore caused the firm to lose more than £1 billion on unauthorized trades that were not detected until after the trades were made. Similarly, a trader at Sumitomo Corporation racked up $2.6 billion in copper-trading losses because poor controls failed to detect the magnitude of the trader's activities. Multinational corporations that implement decentralized decision making usually design their management control systems to measure and monitor division performance. Information and communications technology helps the flow of information for reporting and control.

Choices About Responsibility Centers

Recall from Chapter 6 that a responsibility center is a segment or subunit of the organization whose manager is accountable for a specified set of activities. To measure the performance of subunits in centralized or decentralized companies, the management control system uses one or a mix of the four types of responsibility centers:

1. *Cost center*—the manager is accountable for costs only.
2. *Revenue center*—the manager is accountable for revenues only.
3. *Profit center*—the manager is accountable for revenues and costs.
4. *Investment center*—the manager is accountable for investments, revenues, and costs.

Centralization or decentralization is not mentioned in the descriptions of these centers because each type of responsibility center can be found in either centralized or decentralized companies.

---

[3] For more on this topic, see http://www.sap.com/solutions/business-suite/erp/pdf/BWP_WP_Shared_Services.pdf.

Decision Point

What are the benefits and costs of decentralization?

A common misconception is that *profit center*—and, in some cases, *investment center*—is a synonym for a decentralized subunit, and *cost center* is a synonym for a centralized subunit. *Profit centers can be coupled with a highly centralized organization, and cost centers can be coupled with a highly decentralized organization.* For example, managers in a division organized as a profit center may have little freedom in making decisions. They may need to obtain approval from corporate headquarters for introducing new products and services, or to make expenditures over some preset limit. When Michael Eisner ran Walt Disney Co., the giant media and entertainment conglomerate, the strategic-planning division applied so much scrutiny to business proposals that managers were reluctant to even pitch new ideas.[4] In other companies, divisions such as Information Technology may be organized as cost centers, but their managers may have great latitude with regard to capital expenditures and the purchase of materials and services. In short, the labels "profit center" and "cost center" are independent of the degree of centralization or decentralization in a company.

Transfer Pricing

Learning Objective 3

Explain transfer prices

... price one subunit charges another for product

and four criteria used to evaluate alternative transfer-pricing methods

... goal congruence, management effort, subunit performance evaluation, and subunit autonomy

In decentralized organizations, much of the decision-making power resides in its individual subunits. In these cases, the management control system often uses *transfer prices* to coordinate the actions of the subunits and to evaluate their performance.

As you may recall from the opener, a **transfer price** is the price one subunit (department or division) charges for a product or service supplied to another subunit of the same organization. If, for example, a car manufacturer has a separate division that manufactures engines, the transfer price is the price the engine division charges when it transfers engines to the car assembly division. The transfer price creates revenues for the selling subunit (the engine division in our example) and purchase costs for the buying subunit (the assembly division in our example), affecting each subunit's operating income. These operating incomes can be used to evaluate subunits' performances and to motivate their managers. The product or service transferred between subunits of an organization is called an **intermediate product**. This product may either be further worked on by the receiving subunit (as in the engine example) or, if transferred from production to marketing, sold to an external customer.

In one sense, transfer pricing is a curious phenomenon. Activities within an organization are clearly nonmarket in nature; products and services are not bought and sold as they are in open-market transactions. Yet, establishing prices for transfers among subunits of a company has a distinctly market flavor. The rationale for transfer prices is that subunit managers (such as the manager of the engine division), when making decisions, need only focus on how their decisions will affect their subunit's performance without evaluating their impact on company-wide performance. In this sense, transfer prices ease the subunit managers' information-processing and decision-making tasks. In a well-designed transfer-pricing system, a manager focuses on optimizing subunit performance (the performance of the engine division) and in so doing optimizes the performance of the company as a whole.

Criteria for Evaluating Transfer Prices

As in all management control systems, transfer prices should help achieve a company's strategies and goals and fit its organization structure. We describe four criteria to evaluate transfer pricing: (1) Transfer prices should promote goal congruence. (2) They should induce managers to exert a high level of effort. Subunits selling a product or service should be motivated to hold down their costs; subunits buying the product or service should be motivated to acquire and use inputs efficiently. (3) The transfer price should help top management evaluate the performance of individual subunits. (4) If top management favors a high degree of decentralization, transfer prices should preserve a high degree of subunit autonomy in decision making. That is, a subunit manager seeking to maximize the operating income of the subunit should have the freedom to transact with other subunits of the company (on the basis of transfer prices) or to transact with external parties.

---

[4] When Robert Iger replaced Eisner as CEO in 2005, one of his first acts was to disassemble the strategic-planning division, thereby giving more authority to Disney's business units (parks and resorts, consumer products, and media networks).

Calculating Transfer Prices

There are three broad categories of methods for determining transfer prices. They are as follows:

1. **Market-based transfer prices.** Top management may choose to use the price of a similar product or service publicly listed in, say, a trade association Web site. Also, top management may select, for the internal price, the external price that a subunit charges to outside customers.

2. **Cost-based transfer prices.** Top management may choose a transfer price based on the cost of producing the product in question. Examples include variable production cost, variable and fixed production costs, and full cost of the product. Full cost of the product includes all production costs plus costs from other business functions (R&D, design, marketing, distribution, and customer service). The cost used in cost-based transfer prices can be actual cost or budgeted cost. Sometimes, the cost-based transfer price includes a markup or profit margin that represents a return on subunit investment.

3. **Hybrid transfer prices.** Hybrid transfer prices take into account both cost and market information. Top management may administer such prices, for example by specifying a transfer price that is an average of the cost of producing and transporting the product internally and the market price for comparable products. At other times, a hybrid transfer price may take the form where the revenue recognized by the selling unit is different from the cost recognized by the buying unit. The most common form of hybrid prices arise via negotiation—the subunits of a company are asked to negotiate the transfer price between them and to decide whether to buy and sell internally or deal with external parties. The eventual transfer price is then the outcome of a bargaining process between selling and buying subunits. Even though there is no requirement that the chosen transfer price bear any specific relationship to cost or market-price data, information regarding costs and prices plays a critical role in the negotiation process. Negotiated transfer prices are often employed when market prices are volatile and change constantly.

To see how each of the three transfer-pricing methods works and to see the differences among them, we examine transfer pricing at Horizon Petroleum against the four criteria of promoting goal congruence, motivating management effort, evaluating subunit performance, and preserving subunit autonomy (if desired).

An Illustration of Transfer Pricing

Horizon Petroleum has two divisions, each operating as a profit center. The transportation division purchases crude oil in Matamoros, Mexico, and transports it from Matamoros to Houston, Texas. The refining division processes crude oil into gasoline. For simplicity, we assume gasoline is the only salable product the Houston refinery makes and that it takes two barrels of crude oil to yield one barrel of gasoline.

Variable costs in each division are variable with respect to a single cost driver: barrels of crude oil transported by the transportation division, and barrels of gasoline produced by the refining division. The fixed cost per unit is based on the budgeted annual fixed costs and practical capacity of crude oil that can be transported by the transportation division, and the budgeted fixed costs and practical capacity of gasoline that can be produced by the refining division. Horizon Petroleum reports all costs and revenues of its non-U.S. operations in U.S. dollars using the prevailing exchange rate.

- The transportation division has obtained rights to certain oil fields in the Matamoros area. It has a long-term contract to purchase crude oil produced from these fields at $72 per barrel. The division transports the oil to Houston and then "sells" it to the refining division. The pipeline from Matamoros to Houston has the capacity to carry 40,000 barrels of crude oil per day.
- The refining division has been operating at capacity (30,000 barrels of crude oil a day), using oil supplied by Horizon's transportation division (an average of 10,000 barrels per day) and oil bought from another producer and delivered to the Houston refinery (an average of 20,000 barrels per day at $85 per barrel).
- The refining division sells the gasoline it produces to outside parties at $190 per barrel.

Exhibit 22-1 summarizes Horizon Petroleum's variable and fixed costs per barrel of crude oil in the transportation division and variable and fixed costs per barrel of gasoline in the refining division, the external market prices of buying crude oil, and the external market price of selling gasoline. What's missing in the exhibit is the actual transfer price from the transportation division to the refining division. This transfer price will vary depending on the transfer-pricing method used. Transfer prices from the transportation division to the refining division under each of the three methods are as follows:

1. Market-based transfer price of $85 per barrel of crude oil based on the competitive market price in Houston.
2. Cost-based transfer prices at, say, 105% of full cost, where full cost is the cost of the crude oil purchased in Matamoros plus the transportation division's own variable and fixed costs (from Exhibit 22-1): 1.05 × ($72 + $1 + $3) = $79.80.
3. Hybrid transfer price of, say, $82 per barrel of crude oil, which is between the market-based and cost-based transfer prices. We describe later in this section the various ways in which hybrid prices can be determined.

Exhibit 22-2 presents division operating incomes per 100 barrels of crude oil purchased under each transfer-pricing method. Transfer prices create income for the selling division and corresponding costs for the buying division that cancel out when division results are consolidated for the company as a whole. The exhibit assumes all three transfer-pricing methods yield transfer prices that are in a range that does not cause division managers to change the business relationships shown in Exhibit 22-1. That is, Horizon Petroleum's total operating income from purchasing, transporting, and refining the 100 barrels of crude oil and selling the 50 barrels of gasoline is the same, $1,200, *regardless of the internal transfer prices used.*

$$\text{Operating income} = \text{Revenues} - \text{Cost of crude oil purchases in Matamoros} - \text{Transportation Division costs} - \text{Refining Division costs}$$

$$= (\$190 \times 50 \text{ barrels of gasoline}) - (\$72 \times 100 \text{ barrels of crude oil})$$

$$- (\$4 \times 100 \text{ barrels of crude oil}) - (\$14 \times 50 \text{ barrels of gasoline})$$

$$= \$9,500 - \$7,200 - \$400 - \$700 = \$1,200$$

Note further that under all three methods, summing the two division operating incomes equals Horizon Petroleum's total operating income of $1,200. By keeping total operating

Exhibit 22-1 Operating Data for Horizon Petroleum

	A	B	C	D	E	F	G	H
1								
2				**Transportation Division**				
3	Contract price per barrel of crude oil supplied in Matamoros			Variable cost per barrel of crude oil	$1			
4		= $72	→	Fixed cost per barrel of crude oil	3			
5				Full cost per barrel of crude oil	$4			
6								
7								
8				Barrels of crude oil transferred				
9								
10								
11				**Refining Division**				
12	Market price per barrel of crude oil supplied to Houston refinery			Variable cost per barrel of gasoline	$ 8		Market price per barrel of gasoline sold to external parties	
13		= $85	→	Fixed cost per barrel of gasoline	6	→		= $190
14				Full cost per barrel of gasoline	$14			
15								

Exhibit 22-2 — Division Operating Income of Horizon Petroleum for 100 Barrels of Crude Oil Under Alternative Transfer-Pricing Methods

	A	B	C	D	E	F	G	H
1	**Production and Sales Data**							
2	Barrels of crude oil transferred = 100							
3	Barrels of gasoline sold = 50							
4								
5		Internal Transfers at			Internal Transfers at			
6		Market Price =			105% of Full Cost =		Hybrid Price =	
7		$85 per Barrel			$79.80 per Barrel		$82 per Barrel	
8	**Transportation Division**							
9	Revenues, $85, $79.80, $82 × 100 barrels of crude oil	$8,500			$7,980		$8,200	
10	Costs							
11	Crude oil purchase costs, $72 × 100 barrels of crude oil	7,200			7,200		7,200	
12	Division variable costs, $1 × 100 barrels of crude oil	100			100		100	
13	Division fixed costs, $3 × 100 barrels of crude oil	300			300		300	
14	Total division costs	7,600			7,600		7,600	
15	Division operating income	$ 900			$ 380		$ 600	
16								
17	**Refining Division**							
18	Revenues, $190 × 50 barrels of gasoline	$9,500			$9,500		$9,500	
19	Costs							
20	Transferred-in costs, $85, $79.80, $82							
21	× 100 barrels of crude oil	8,500			7,980		8,200	
22	Division variable costs, $8 × 50 barrels of gasoline	400			400		400	
23	Division fixed costs, $6 × 50 barrels of gasoline	300			300		300	
24	Total division costs	9,200			8,680		8,900	
25	Division operating income	$ 300			$ 820		$ 600	
26	Operating income of both divisions together	$1,200			$1,200		$1,200	

income the same, we focus attention on the effects of different transfer-pricing methods on the operating income of each division. Subsequent sections of this chapter show that different transfer-pricing methods can cause managers to take different actions leading to different total operating incomes.

Consider the two methods in the first two columns of Exhibit 22-2. The operating income of the transportation division is $520 more ($900 − $380) if transfer prices are based on market prices rather than on 105% of full cost. The operating income of the refining division is $520 more ($820 − $300) if transfer prices are based on 105% of full cost rather than market prices. If the transportation division's sole criterion were to maximize its own division operating income, it would favor transfer prices at market prices. In contrast, the refining division would prefer transfer prices at 105% of full cost to maximize its own division operating income. The hybrid transfer price of $82 is between the 105% of full cost and market-based transfer prices. It splits the $1,200 of operating income equally between the divisions, and could arise as a result of negotiations between the transportation and refining division managers.

It's not surprising that subunit managers, especially those whose compensation or promotion directly depends on subunit operating income, take considerable interest in setting transfer prices. To reduce the excessive focus of subunit managers on their own subunits, many companies compensate subunit managers on the basis of both subunit and company-wide operating incomes.

We next examine market-based, cost-based, and hybrid transfer prices in more detail. We show how the choice of transfer-pricing method combined with managers' sourcing decisions can determine the size of the company-wide operating-income pie itself.

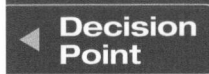

Decision Point

What are alternative ways of calculating transfer prices, and what criteria should be used to evaluate them?

Market-Based Transfer Prices

Learning Objective 4

Illustrate how market-based transfer prices promote goal congruence in perfectly competitive markets

... division managers transacting internally are motivated to take the same actions as if they were transacting externally

Transferring products or services at market prices generally leads to optimal decisions when three conditions are satisfied: (1) The market for the intermediate product is perfectly competitive, (2) interdependencies of subunits are minimal, and (3) there are no additional costs or benefits to the company as a whole from buying or selling in the external market instead of transacting internally.

Perfectly-Competitive-Market Case

A **perfectly competitive market** exists when there is a homogeneous product with buying prices equal to selling prices and no individual buyers or sellers can affect those prices by their own actions. By using market-based transfer prices in perfectly competitive markets, a company can (1) promote goal congruence, (2) motivate management effort, (3) evaluate subunit performance, and (4) preserve subunit autonomy.

Consider Horizon Petroleum again. Assume there is a perfectly competitive market for crude oil in the Houston area. As a result, the transportation division can sell and the refining division can buy as much crude oil as each wants at $85 per barrel. Horizon would prefer its managers to buy or sell crude oil internally. Think about the decisions that Horizon's division managers would make if each had the autonomy to sell or buy crude oil externally. If the transfer price between Horizon's transportation and refining divisions is set below $85, the manager of the transportation division will be motivated to sell all crude oil to external buyers in the Houston area at $85 per barrel. If the transfer price is set above $85, the manager of the refining division will be motivated to purchase all crude oil requirements from external suppliers. Only an $85 transfer price will motivate the transportation division and the refining division to buy and sell internally. That's because neither division profits by buying or selling in the external market.

Suppose Horizon evaluates division managers on the basis of their individual division's operating income. The transportation division will sell, either internally or externally, as much crude oil as it can profitably transport, and the refining division will buy, either internally or externally, as much crude oil as it can profitably refine. An $85-per-barrel transfer price achieves goal congruence—the actions that maximize each division's operating income are also the actions that maximize operating income of Horizon Petroleum as a whole. Furthermore, because the transfer price is not based on costs, it motivates each division manager to exert management effort to maximize his or her own division's operating income. Market prices also serve to evaluate the economic viability and profitability of each division individually. For example, Koch Industries, the second-largest private company in the United States, uses market-based pricing for all internal transfers. As their CFO, Steve Feilmeier, notes, "We believe that the alternative for any given asset should always be considered in order to best optimize the profitability of the asset. If you simply transfer price between two different divisions at cost, then you may be subsidizing your whole operation and not know it." Returning to our Horizon example, suppose that under market-based transfer prices, the refining division consistently shows small or negative profits. Then, Horizon may consider shutting down the refining division and simply transport and sell the oil to other refineries in the Houston area.

Distress Prices

When supply outstrips demand, market prices may drop well below their historical averages. If the drop in prices is expected to be temporary, these low market prices are sometimes called "distress prices." Deciding whether a current market price is a distress price is often difficult. Prior to the worldwide spike in commodity prices in the 2006–2008 period, the market prices of several mineral and agricultural commodities, including nickel, uranium, and wheat, stayed for many years at what people initially believed were temporary distress levels!

Which transfer price should be used for judging performance if distress prices prevail? Some companies use the distress prices themselves, but others use long-run average prices, or "normal" market prices. In the short run, the manager of the selling subunit should supply the product or service at the distress price as long as it exceeds the *incremental costs* of supplying the product or service. If the distress price is used as the transfer price, the selling division will show a loss because the distress price will not exceed the *full cost* of the division. If the long-run average market price is used, forcing the manager to buy internally at a price above the current market price will hurt the buying division's short-run operating income. But the long-run average market price will provide a better measure of the long-run profitability and viability of the supplier division. Of course, if the price remains low in the long run, the company should use the low market price as the transfer price. If this price is lower than the variable and fixed costs that can be saved if manufacturing facilities are shut down, the production facilities of the selling subunit should be sold, and the buying subunit should purchase the product from an external supplier.

Imperfect Competition

If markets are not perfectly competitive, selling prices affect the quantity of product sold. If the selling division sells its product in the external market, the selling division manager would choose a price and quantity combination that would maximize the division's operating income. If the transfer price is set at this selling price, the buying division may find that acquiring the product is too costly and results in a loss. It may decide not to purchase the product. Yet, from the point of view of the company as a whole, it may well be that profits are maximized if the selling division transfers the product to the buying division for further processing and sale. For this reason, when the market for the intermediate good is imperfectly competitive, the transfer price must generally be set below the external market price (but above the selling division's variable cost) in order to induce efficient transfers.[5]

> **Decision Point**
>
> Under what market conditions do market-based transfer prices promote goal congruence?

Cost-Based Transfer Prices

Cost-based transfer prices are helpful when market prices are unavailable, inappropriate, or too costly to obtain, such as when markets are not perfectly competitive, when the product is specialized, or when the internal product is different from the products available externally in terms of quality and customer service.

> **Learning Objective 5**
>
> Understand how to avoid making suboptimal decisions when transfer prices are based on full cost plus a markup
>
> ... in situations when buying divisions regard the fixed costs and the markup as variable costs

Full-Cost Bases

In practice, many companies use transfer prices based on full cost. To approximate market prices, cost-based transfer prices are sometimes set at full cost plus a margin. These transfer prices, however, can lead to suboptimal decisions. Suppose Horizon Petroleum makes internal transfers at 105% of full cost. Recall that the refining division purchases, on average, 20,000 barrels of crude oil per day from a local Houston supplier, who delivers the crude oil to the refinery at a price of $85 per barrel. To reduce crude oil costs, the refining division has located an independent producer in Matamoros—Gulfmex Corporation—that is willing to sell 20,000 barrels of crude oil per day at $79 per barrel, delivered to Horizon's pipeline in Matamoros. Given Horizon's organization structure, the transportation division would purchase the 20,000 barrels of crude oil in Matamoros from Gulfmex, transport it to Houston, and then sell it to the refining division. The pipeline has unused capacity and can ship the 20,000 barrels per day at its variable cost of $1 per barrel without affecting the shipment of the 10,000 barrels of crude oil per day acquired under its existing long-term contract arrangement. Will Horizon Petroleum incur lower costs by

---

[5] Consider a firm where division S produces the intermediate product. S has a capacity of 15 units and a variable cost per unit of $2. The imperfect competition is reflected in a downward-sloping demand curve for the intermediate product—if S wants to sell Q units, it has to lower the market price to P = 20 − Q. The division's profit function is therefore given by Q × (20 − Q) − 2Q = $18Q − Q^2$. Simple calculus reveals that it is optimal for S to sell 9 units of the intermediate product at a price of $11, thereby making a profit of $81. Now, suppose that division B in the same firm can take the intermediate product, incur an additional variable cost of $4 and sell it in the external market for $12. Since S has surplus capacity (it only uses 9 of its 15 units of capacity), it is clearly in the firm's interest to have S make additional units and transfer them to B. The firm makes an incremental profit of $12 − $2 − $4 = $6 for each transferred unit. However, if the transfer price for the intermediate product were set equal to the market price of $11, B would reject the transaction since it would lose money on it ($12 − $11 − $4 = − $3 per unit).
To resolve this conflict, the transfer price should be set at a suitable *discount* to the external price in order to induce the buying division to seek internal transfers. In our example, the selling price must be greater than S's variable cost of $2, but less than B's contribution margin of $8. That is, the transfer price has to be discounted relative to the market price ($11) by a minimum of $3. We explore the issue of feasible transfer pricing ranges further in the section on hybrid transfer prices.

purchasing crude oil from Gulfmex in Matamoros or by purchasing crude oil from the Houston supplier? Will the refining division show lower crude oil purchasing costs by acquiring oil from Gulfmex or by acquiring oil from its current Houston supplier?

The following analysis shows that Horizon Petroleum's operating income would be maximized by purchasing oil from Gulfmex. The analysis compares the incremental costs in both divisions under the two alternatives. The analysis assumes the fixed costs of the transportation division will be the same regardless of the alternative chosen. That is, the transportation division cannot save any of its fixed costs if it does not transport Gulfmex's 20,000 barrels of crude oil per day.

- **Alternative 1:** Buy 20,000 barrels from the Houston supplier at $85 per barrel. Total costs to Horizon Petroleum are 20,000 barrels × $85 per barrel = $1,700,000.
- **Alternative 2:** Buy 20,000 barrels in Matamoros at $79 per barrel and transport them to Houston at a variable cost of $1 per barrel. Total costs to Horizon Petroleum are 20,000 barrels × ($79 + $1) per barrel = $1,600,000.

There is a reduction in total costs to Horizon Petroleum of $100,000 ($1,700,000 − $1,600,000) by acquiring oil from Gulfmex.

Suppose the transportation division's transfer price to the refining division is 105% of full cost. The refining division will see its reported division costs increase if the crude oil is purchased from Gulfmex:

$$\text{Transfer price} = 1.05 \times \left(\begin{array}{c} \text{Purchase price} \\ \text{from} \\ \text{Gulfmex} \end{array} + \begin{array}{c} \text{Variable cost per unit} \\ \text{of Transportation} \\ \text{Division} \end{array} + \begin{array}{c} \text{Fixed cost per unit} \\ \text{of Transportation} \\ \text{Division} \end{array} \right)$$

$$= 1.05 \times (\$79 + \$1 + \$3) = 1.05 \times \$83 = \$87.15 \text{ per barrel}$$

- **Alternative 1:** Buy 20,000 barrels from Houston supplier at $85 per barrel. Total costs to refining division are 20,000 barrels × $85 per barrel = $1,700,000.
- **Alternative 2:** Buy 20,000 barrels from the transportation division of Horizon Petroleum that were purchased from Gulfmex. Total costs to refining division are 20,000 barrels × $87.15 per barrel = $1,743,000.

As a profit center, the refining division can maximize its short-run division operating income by purchasing from the Houston supplier at $1,700,000.

The refining division looks at each barrel that it obtains from the transportation division as a variable cost of $87.15 per barrel; if 10 barrels are transferred, it costs the refining division $871.50; if 100 barrels are transferred, it costs $8,715. In fact, the variable cost per barrel is $80 ($79 to purchase the oil from Gulfmex plus $1 to transport it to Houston). The remaining $7.15 ($87.15 − $80) per barrel is the transportation division's fixed cost and markup. *The full cost plus a markup transfer-pricing method causes the refining division to regard the fixed cost (and the 5% markup) of the transportation division as a variable cost and leads to goal incongruence.*

Should Horizon's top management interfere and force the refining division to buy from the transportation division? Top management interference would undercut the philosophy of decentralization, so Horizon's top management would probably view the decision by the refining division to purchase crude oil from external suppliers as an inevitable cost of decentralization and not interfere. Of course, some interference may occasionally be necessary to prevent costly blunders. But recurring interference and constraints would simply transform Horizon from a decentralized company into a centralized company.

What transfer price will promote goal congruence for both the transportation and refining divisions? The minimum transfer price is $80 per barrel. A transfer price below $80 does not provide the transportation division with an incentive to purchase crude oil from Gulfmex in Matamoros because it is below the transportation division's incremental costs. The maximum transfer price is $85 per barrel. A transfer price above $85 will cause the refining division to purchase crude oil from the external market rather than from the transportation division. A transfer price between the minimum and maximum transfer prices of $80 and $85 will promote goal congruence: Each division will increase its own reported operating income while increasing Horizon Petroleum's operating income if the refining division purchases crude oil from Gulfmex in Matamoros.

In the absence of a market-based transfer price, senior management at Horizon Petroleum cannot easily determine the profitability of the investment made in the transportation division and hence whether Horizon should keep or sell the pipeline. Furthermore, if the transfer price had been based on the actual costs of the transportation division, it would provide the division with no incentive to control costs. That's because all cost inefficiencies of the transportation division would get passed along as part of the actual full-cost transfer price. In fact, every additional dollar of cost arising from wastefulness in the transportation division would generate an additional five cents in profit for the division under the "105% of full cost" rule!

Surveys indicate that, despite the limitations, managers generally prefer to use full-cost-based transfer prices. That's because these transfer prices represent relevant costs for long-run decisions, they facilitate external pricing based on variable and fixed costs, and they are the least costly to administer. However, full-cost transfer pricing does raise many issues. How are each subunit's indirect costs allocated to products? Have the correct activities, cost pools, and cost-allocation bases been identified? Should the chosen fixed-cost rates be actual or budgeted? The issues here are similar to the issues that arise in allocating fixed costs, which were introduced in Chapter 14. Many companies determine the transfer price based on budgeted rates and practical capacity because it overcomes the problem of inefficiencies in actual costs and costs of unused capacity getting passed along to the buying division.

Variable-Cost Bases

Transferring 20,000 barrels of crude oil from the transportation division to the refining division at the variable cost of $80 per barrel achieves goal congruence, as shown in the preceding section. The refining division would buy from the transportation division because the transportation division's variable cost is less than the $85 price charged by external suppliers. Setting the transfer price equal to the variable cost has other benefits. Knowledge of the variable cost per barrel of crude oil is very helpful to the refining division for many decisions such as the short-run pricing decisions discussed in Chapters 11 and 12. However, at the $80-per-barrel transfer price, the transportation division would record an operating loss, and the refining division would show large profits because it would be charged only for the variable costs of the transportation division. One approach to addressing this problem is to have the refining division make a lump-sum transfer payment to cover fixed costs and generate some operating income for the transportation division while the transportation division continues to make transfers at variable cost. The fixed payment is the price the refining division pays for using the capacity of the transportation division. The income earned by each division can then be used to evaluate the performance of each division and its manager.

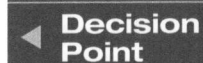

Decision Point

What problems can arise when full cost plus a markup is used as the transfer price?

Hybrid Transfer Prices

Consider again Horizon Petroleum. As we saw earlier, the transportation division has unused capacity it can use to transport oil from Matamoros to Houston at an incremental cost of $80 per barrel of crude oil. Horizon Petroleum, as a whole, maximizes operating income if the refining division purchases crude oil from the transportation division rather than from the Houston market (incremental cost per barrel of $80 versus price per barrel of $85). Both divisions would be interested in transacting with each other (and the firm achieves goal congruence) if the transfer price is between $80 and $85.

For any internal transaction, there is generally a minimum transfer price the selling division will not go below, based on its cost structure. In the Horizon Petroleum example, the minimum price acceptable to the transportation division is $80. There is also a maximum price the buying division will not wish to exceed, given by the lower of two quantities—the eventual contribution it generates from an internal transaction and the price of purchasing a comparable intermediate product from an outside party. For the

Learning Objective 6

Describe the range of feasible transfer prices when there is unused capacity

... from variable cost to market price of the product transferred

refining division, each barrel of gasoline sold to external parties generates $182 in contribution (the $190 price less the $8 variable cost of refining). Since it takes two barrels of crude oil to generate a barrel of gasoline, this is equivalent to a contribution of $91 per barrel of crude. For any price higher than $91, the refining division would lose money for each barrel of crude it takes from the transportation division. On the other hand, the refining division can purchase crude oil on the open market for $85 rather than having it transported internally. The maximum feasible transfer price is thus the lower of $91 and $85, or $85 in this instance. We saw previously that a transfer price between the minimum price ($80) and the maximum ($85) would promote goal congruence. We now describe three different ways in which firms attempt to determine the specific transfer price within these bounds.

Prorating the Difference Between Maximum and Minimum Transfer Prices

One approach that Horizon Petroleum could pursue is to choose a transfer price that splits, on some fair basis, the $5 difference between the $85-per-barrel market-based maximum price the refining division is willing to pay and the $80-per-barrel variable cost-based minimum price the transportation division wants to receive. An easy solution is to split the difference equally, resulting in a transfer price of $82.50. However, this solution ignores the relative costs incurred by the two divisions and might lead to disparate profit margins on the work contributed by each division to the final product. As an alternative approach, Horizon Petroleum could allocate the $5 difference on the basis of the variable costs of the two divisions. Using the data in Exhibit 22-1 (p. 804), variable costs are as follows:

Transportation division's variable costs to transport 100 barrels of crude oil ($1 × 100)	$100
Refining division's variable costs to refine 100 barrels of crude oil and produce 50 barrels of gasoline ($8 × 50)	400
Total variable costs	$500

Of the $5 difference, the transportation division gets to keep ($100 ÷ $500) × $5.00 = $1.00, and the refining division gets to keep ($400 ÷ $500) × $5.00 = $4.00. That is, the transfer price is $81 per barrel of crude oil ($79 purchase cost + $1 variable cost + $1 that the transportation division gets to keep). In effect, this approach results in a budgeted variable-cost-plus transfer price. The "plus" indicates the setting of a transfer price above variable cost.

To decide on the $1 and $4 allocations of the $5 incremental benefit to total company operating income per barrel, the divisions must share information about their variable costs. In effect, each division does not operate (at least for this transaction) in a totally decentralized manner. Furthermore, each division has an incentive to overstate its variable costs to receive a more-favorable transfer price. In the preceding example, suppose the transportation division claims a cost of $2 per barrel to ship crude oil from Gulfmex to Houston. This increased cost raises the variable cost-based minimum price to $79 + $2 = $81 per barrel; the maximum price remains $85. Of the $4 difference between the minimum and maximum, the transportation division now gets to keep ($200 ÷ ($200 + $400)) × $4.00 = $1.33, resulting in a higher transfer price of $82.33. The refining division similarly benefits from asserting that its variable cost to refine 100 barrels of crude oil is greater than $400. As a consequence, proration methods either require a high degree of trust and information exchange among divisions or include provisions for objective audits of cost information in order to be successful.

Negotiated Pricing

This is the most common hybrid method. Under this approach, top management does not administer a specific split of the eventual profits across the transacting divisions. Rather, the eventual transfer price results from a bargaining process between the selling and buying subunits. In the Horizon Petroleum case, for example, the transportation division and the refining division would be free to negotiate a price that is mutually acceptable to both.

As described earlier, the minimum and maximum feasible transfer prices are $80 and $85, respectively, per barrel of crude oil. Where between $80 and $85 will the transfer price per barrel be set? Under a negotiated transfer price, the answer depends on several things: the bargaining strengths of the two divisions; information the transportation division has about the price minus incremental marketing costs of supplying crude oil to outside refineries; and the information the refining division has about its other available sources of crude oil. Negotiations become particularly sensitive because Horizon Petroleum can now evaluate each division's performance on the basis of division operating income. The price negotiated by the two divisions will, in general, have no specific relationship to either costs or market price. But cost and price information is often the starting point in the negotiation process.

Consider the following situation: Suppose the refining division receives an order to supply specially processed gasoline. The incremental cost to purchase and supply crude oil is still $80 per barrel. However, suppose the refining division will profit from this order only if the transportation division can supply crude oil at a price not exceeding $82 per barrel.[6] In this case, the transfer price that would benefit both divisions must be greater than $80 but less than $82. Negotiations would allow the two divisions to achieve an acceptable transfer price. By contrast, a rule-based transfer price, such as a market-based price of $85 or a 105% of full-cost-based price of $87.15, would result in Horizon passing up a profitable opportunity.

A negotiated transfer price strongly preserves division autonomy. It also has the advantage that each division manager is motivated to put forth effort to increase division operating income. Surveys have found that approximately 15%–20% of firms set transfer prices based on negotiation among divisions. The key reason cited by firms that do not use negotiated prices is the cost of the bargaining process, that is, the time and energy spent by managers haggling over transfer prices.

Dual Pricing

There is seldom a single transfer price that simultaneously meets the criteria of promoting goal congruence, motivating management effort, evaluating subunit performance, and preserving subunit autonomy. As a result, some companies choose **dual pricing**, using two separate transfer-pricing methods to price each transfer from one subunit to another. An example of dual pricing arises when the selling division receives a full-cost-based price and the buying division pays the market price for the internally transferred products. Assume Horizon Petroleum purchases crude oil from Gulfmex in Matamoros at $79 per barrel. One way of recording the journal entry for the transfer between the transportation division and the refining division is as follows:

1. Debit the refining division (the buying division) with the market-based transfer price of $85 per barrel of crude oil.
2. Credit the transportation division (the selling division) with the 105%-of-full-cost transfer price of $87.15 per barrel of crude oil.
3. Debit a corporate cost account for the $2.15 ($87.15 − $85) per barrel difference between the two transfer prices.

The dual-pricing system promotes goal congruence because it makes the refining division no worse off if it purchases the crude oil from the transportation division rather than from the external supplier at $85 per barrel. The transportation division receives a corporate subsidy. In dual pricing, the operating income for Horizon Petroleum as a whole is less than the sum of the operating incomes of the divisions.

Dual pricing is not widely used in practice even though it reduces the goal incongruence associated with a pure cost-based transfer-pricing method. One concern with dual pricing is that it leads to problems in computing the taxable income of subunits located in different tax jurisdictions, such as in our example, where the transportation division is taxed in Mexico while the refining division is taxed in the United States. A second concern is that dual pricing insulates managers from the frictions of the marketplace because costs, not market prices, affect the revenues of the supplying division.

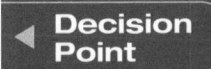

Within a range of feasible transfer prices, what are alternative ways for firms to arrive at the eventual price?

---

[6] For example, suppose a barrel of specially processed gasoline could be sold for $200 but also required a higher variable cost of refining of $36 per barrel. In this setting, the incremental contribution to the refining division is $164 per barrel of gasoline, which implies that it will pay at most $82 for a barrel of crude oil (since two barrels of crude are required for one barrel of gasoline).

A General Guideline for Transfer-Pricing Situations

Learning Objective 7

Apply a general guideline for determining a minimum transfer price

...incremental cost plus opportunity cost of supplying division

Exhibit 22-3 summarizes the properties of market-based, cost-based, and negotiated transfer-pricing methods using the criteria described in this chapter. As the exhibit indicates, it is difficult for a transfer-pricing method to meet all criteria. Market conditions, the goal of the transfer-pricing system, and the criteria of promoting goal congruence, motivating management effort, evaluating subunit performance, and preserving subunit autonomy (if desired) must all be considered simultaneously. The transfer price a company will eventually choose depends on the economic circumstances and the decision at hand. Surveys of company practice indicate that the full-cost-based transfer price is generally the most frequently used transfer-pricing method around the world, followed by market-based transfer price and negotiated transfer price.

Our discussion thus far highlight that, barring settings in which a perfectly competitive market exists for the intermediate product, there is generally a range of possible transfer prices that would induce goal congruence. We now provide a general guideline for determining the minimum price in that range. The following formula is a helpful first step in setting the minimum transfer price in many situations:

$$\text{Minimum transfer price} = \begin{array}{c}\text{Incremental cost}\\\text{per unit}\\\text{incurred up}\\\text{to the point of transfer}\end{array} + \begin{array}{c}\text{Opportunity cost}\\\text{per unit}\\\text{to the selling subunit}\end{array}$$

Incremental cost in this context means the additional cost of producing and transferring the product or service. Opportunity cost here is the maximum contribution margin forgone by the selling subunit if the product or service is transferred internally. For example, if the selling subunit is operating at capacity, the opportunity cost of transferring a unit internally rather than selling it externally is equal to the market price minus variable cost. That's because by transferring a unit internally, the subunit forgoes the contribution margin it could have obtained by selling the unit in the external market. We distinguish incremental cost from opportunity cost because financial accounting systems record incremental cost but do not record opportunity cost. The guideline measures a *minimum* transfer price because it represents the selling unit's cost of transferring the product. We illustrate the general guideline in some specific situations using data from Horizon Petroleum.

1. **A perfectly competitive market for the intermediate product exists, and the selling division has no unused capacity.** If the market for crude oil in Houston is perfectly

Exhibit 22-3
Comparison of Different Transfer-Pricing Methods

Criteria	Market-Based	Cost-Based	Negotiated
Achieves goal congruence	Yes, when markets are competitive	Often, but not always	Yes
Motivates management effort	Yes	Yes, when based on budgeted costs; less incentive to control costs if transfers are based on actual costs	Yes
Useful for evaluating subunit performance	Yes, when markets are competitive	Difficult unless transfer price exceeds full cost and even then is somewhat arbitrary	Yes, but transfer prices are affected by bargaining strengths of the buying and selling divisions
Preserves subunit autonomy	Yes, when markets are competitive	No, because it is rule-based	Yes, because it is based on negotiations between subunits
Other factors	Market may not exist, or markets may be imperfect or in distress	Useful for determining full cost of products and services; easy to implement	Bargaining and negotiations take time and may need to be reviewed repeatedly as conditions change

competitive, the transportation division can sell all the crude oil it transports to the external market at $85 per barrel, and it will have no unused capacity. The transportation division's incremental cost (as shown in Exhibit 22-1, p. 804) is $73 per barrel (purchase cost of $72 per barrel plus variable transportation cost of $1 per barrel) for oil purchased under the long-term contract or $80 per barrel (purchase cost of $79 plus variable transportation cost of $1) for oil purchased at current market prices from Gulfmex. The transportation division's opportunity cost per barrel of transferring the oil internally is the contribution margin per barrel forgone by not selling the crude oil in the external market: $12 for oil purchased under the long-term contract (market price, $85, minus variable cost, $73) and $5 for oil purchased from Gulfmex (market price, $85, minus variable cost, $80). In either case,

$$\text{Minimum transfer price per barrel} = \text{Incremental cost per barrel} + \text{Opportunity cost per barrel}$$

$$= \$73 + \$12 = \$85$$
or
$$= \$80 + \$5 = \$85$$

2. **An intermediate market exists that is not perfectly competitive, and the selling division has unused capacity.** In markets that are not perfectly competitive, capacity utilization can only be increased by decreasing prices. Unused capacity exists because decreasing prices is often not worthwhile—it decreases operating income.

    If the transportation division has unused capacity, its opportunity cost of transferring the oil internally is zero because the division does not forgo any external sales or contribution margin from internal transfers. In this case,

$$\text{Minimum transfer price per barrel} = \text{Incremental cost per barrel} = \begin{array}{l}\$73 \text{ per barrel for oil purchased under the} \\ \text{long-term contract or } \$80 \text{ per barrel for} \\ \text{oil purchased from Gulfmex in Matamoros}\end{array}$$

    In general, when markets are not perfectly competitive, the potential to influence demand and operating income through prices complicates the measurement of opportunity costs. The transfer price depends on constantly changing levels of supply and demand. There is not just one transfer price. Rather, the transfer prices for various quantities supplied and demanded depend on the incremental costs and opportunity costs of the units transferred.

3. **No market exists for the intermediate product.** This situation would occur for the Horizon Petroleum case if the crude oil transported by the transportation division could be used only by the Houston refinery (due to, say, its high tar content) and would not be wanted by external parties. Here, the opportunity cost of supplying crude oil internally is zero because the inability to sell crude oil externally means no contribution margin is forgone. For the transportation division of Horizon Petroleum, the minimum transfer price under the general guideline is the incremental cost per barrel (either $73 or $80). As in the previous case, any transfer price between the incremental cost and $85 will achieve goal congruence.

Decision Point

What is the general guideline for determining a minimum transfer price?

Multinational Transfer Pricing and Tax Considerations

Transfer pricing is an important accounting priority for managers around the world. A 2007 Ernst & Young survey of multinational enterprises in 24 countries found that 74% of parent firms and 81% of subsidiary respondents believed that transfer pricing was "absolutely critical" or "very important" to their organizations. The reason is that parent companies identify transfer pricing as the single most important tax issue they face. The sums of money involved are often staggering. Google, for example, has a 90% market share of UK internet searches and earned £1.6 billion in advertising revenues last year in Britain; yet, Google UK reported a pretax loss of £26 million. The reason is that revenues from customers in Britain are transferred to Google's European headquarters in Dublin. By paying the low Irish corporate tax rate of 12.5%, Google saved £450 million in UK taxes in 2009 alone. Transfer prices affect not just income taxes, but

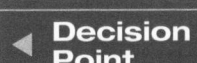

Learning Objective 8

Incorporate income tax considerations in multinational transfer pricing

... set transfer prices to minimize tax payments to the extent permitted by tax authorities

also payroll taxes, customs duties, tariffs, sales taxes, value-added taxes, environment-related taxes, and other government levies. Our aim here is to highlight tax factors, and in particular income taxes, as important considerations in determining transfer prices.

Transfer Pricing for Tax Minimization

Consider the Horizon Petroleum data in Exhibit 22-2 (p. 805). Assume that the transportation division based in Mexico pays Mexican income taxes at 30% of operating income and that the refining division based in the United States pays income taxes at 20% of operating income. Horizon Petroleum would minimize its total income tax payments with the 105%-of-full-cost transfer-pricing method, as shown in the following table, because this method minimizes income reported in Mexico, where income is taxed at a higher rate than in the United States.

Transfer-Pricing Method	Operating Income for 100 Barrels of Crude Oil			Income Tax on 100 Barrels of Crude Oil		
	Transportation Division (Mexico) (1)	Refining Division (United States) (2)	Total (3) = (1) + (2)	Transportation Division (Mexico) (4) = 0.30 × (1)	Refining Division (United States) (5) = 0.20 × (2)	Total (6) = (4) + (5)
Market price	$900	$300	$1,200	$270	$ 60	$330
105% of full costs	380	820	1,200	114	164	278
Hybrid price	600	600	1,200	180	120	300

Income tax considerations raise additional issues. Tax issues may conflict with other objectives of transfer pricing. Suppose the market for crude oil in Houston is perfectly competitive. In this case, the market-based transfer price achieves goal congruence, provides incentives for management effort, and helps Horizon to evaluate the economic profitability of the transportation division. But it is costly from the perspective of income taxes. To minimize income taxes, Horizon would favor using 105% of full cost for tax reporting. Tax laws in the United States and Mexico, however, constrain this option. In particular, the Mexican tax authorities, aware of Horizon's incentives to minimize income taxes by reducing the income reported in Mexico, would challenge any attempts to shift income to the refining division through an unreasonably low transfer price (see also Concepts in Action, p. 815).

Section 482 of the U.S. Internal Revenue Code governs taxation of multinational transfer pricing. Section 482 requires that transfer prices between a company and its foreign division or subsidiary, for both tangible and intangible property, equal the price that would be charged by an unrelated third party in a comparable transaction. Regulations related to Section 482 recognize that transfer prices can be market-based or cost-plus-based, where the plus represents margins on comparable transactions.[7]

If the market for crude oil in Houston is perfectly competitive, Horizon would be required to calculate taxes using the market price of $85 for transfers from the transportation division to the refining division. Horizon might successfully argue that the transfer price should be set below the market price because the transportation division incurs no marketing and distribution costs when selling crude oil to the refining division. For example, if marketing and distribution costs equal $2 per barrel, Horizon could set the transfer price at $83 ($85 − $2) per barrel, the selling price net of marketing and distribution costs. Under the U.S. Internal Revenue Code, Horizon could obtain advanced approval of the transfer-pricing arrangements from the tax authorities, called an *advanced pricing agreement* (*APA*). The APA is a binding agreement for a specified number of years. The goal of the APA program is to avoid costly transfer-pricing disputes between taxpayers and tax authorities. In 2007, there were 81 APAs executed, of which 54 were bilateral agreements with other tax treaty countries. Included in this was the completion of the first bilateral APA between the United States and China, involving Wal-Mart Stores.

The current global recession has pushed governments around the world to impose tighter trading rules and more aggressively pursue tax revenues. The number of countries

---

[7] J. Styron, "Transfer Pricing and Tax Planning: Opportunities for US Corporations Operating Abroad," *CPA Journal Online* (November 2007); R. Feinschreiber (Ed.), *Transfer Pricing Handbook*, 3rd ed. (New York: John Wiley & Sons, 2002).

Concepts in Action: Transfer Pricing Dispute Temporarily Stops the Flow of Fiji Water

Tax authorities and government officials across the globe pay close attention to taxes paid by multinational companies operating within their boundaries. At the heart of the issue are the transfer prices that companies use to transfer products from one country to another. Since 2008, Fiji Water, LLC, a U.S.-based company that markets its famous brand of bottled water in more than a dozen counties, has been engaged in a fierce transfer-pricing dispute with the government of the Fiji Islands, where its water bottling plant is located.

While Fiji Water is produced in the Fiji Islands, all other activities in the company's value chain—importing, distributing, and retailing—occur in the countries where Fiji Water is sold. Over time, the Fiji Islands government became concerned that Fiji Water was engaging in transfer price manipulations, selling the water shipments produced in the Fiji Islands at a very low price to the company headquarters in Los Angeles. It was feared that very little of the wealth generated by Fiji Water, the country's second largest exporter, was coming into the Fiji Islands as foreign reserves from export earnings, which Fiji badly needed to fund its imports. To the Fiji Islands government, Fiji Water was funneling most of its cash to the United States.

As a result of these concerns, the Fiji Islands Revenue and Customs Authority (FIRCA) decided to take action against Fiji Water. FIRCA halted exports in January 2008 at ports in the Fiji Islands by putting 200 containers loaded with Fiji Water bottled under armed guard, and issuing a statement accusing Fiji Water of transfer price manipulations. FIRCA's chief executive, Jitoko Tikolevu, said, "The wholly U.S.-owned Fijian subsidiary sold its water exclusively to its U.S. parent at the declared rate, in Fiji, of $4 a carton. In the U.S., though, the same company then sold it for up to $50 a carton."

Fiji Water immediately filed a lawsuit against FIRCA with the High Court of Fiji. The court issued an interim order, allowing the company to resume shipment of the embargoed containers upon payment of a bond to the court. In the media and subsequent court filings, the company stated that on a global basis it sold each carton of water for $20–28, and it did not make a profit due to "heavy investments in assets, employees, and marketing necessary to aggressively grow a successful branded product."

The dispute between FICRA and Fiji Water remains unresolved in the Fiji Islands court system. In the interim, Fiji Water has maintained its previous transfer price of $4 for water produced at its bottling plant in the Fiji Islands. To pressure the company to change its transfer pricing practices, the Fiji Islands government considered adding a 20-cents-per-litre excise tax on water produced in the country, but the tax was ultimately rejected as too draconian. As this high-profile case demonstrates, transfer pricing formulas and taxation details remain a contentious issue for governments and countries around the globe.

Source: Matau, Robert. 2008. Fiji water explains saga. *Fiji Times*, February 9; McMaster, James and Jan Novak. 2009. Fiji water and corporate social responsibility—Green makeover or 'green-washing'? The University of Western Ontario Richard Ivey School of Business No. 909A08, London, Ontario: Ivey Publishing.

---

that have imposed transfer pricing regulations has approximately quadrupled from 1995 to 2007, according to a 2008 KPMG report. Officials in China, where foreign businesses enjoyed favorable treatment until last year, recently issued new rules requiring multinationals to submit extensive transfer-pricing documentation. Countries such as India, Canada, Turkey, and Greece have brought greater scrutiny to bear on transfer pricing, focusing in particular on intellectual-property values, costs of back-office functions and losses of any type. In the United States, the Obama administration plans to shrink a "tax gap" the IRS estimates may be as high as $345 billion by restricting or closing several widely used tax loopholes. While the plan does not directly address transfer pricing practice, the IRS has become even more aggressive with enforcement. The agency added 1,200 people to its international staff in 2009, and the 2010 budget called for hiring another 800.

Transfer Prices Designed for Multiple Objectives

To meet multiple transfer-pricing objectives, such as minimizing income taxes, achieving goal congruence, and motivating management effort, a company may choose to keep one set of accounting records for tax reporting and a second set for internal management reporting.

Of course, it is costly to maintain two sets of books and companies such as Case New Holland, a world leader in the agricultural and construction equipment business, also oppose it for conceptual reasons. However, a survey by the AnswerThink Consulting Group of large companies (more than $2 billion in revenues) found that 77% used separate reporting systems to track internal pricing information, compared with about 25% of large companies outside that "best practices" group. Microsoft, for example, believes in "delinking" transfer pricing and employs an internal measurement system (Microsoft Accounting Principles, or MAPs) that uses a separate set of company-designed rules and accounts.[8] A key aspect of management control at Microsoft is the desire to hold local managers accountable for product profitability and to establish appropriate sales and marketing spending levels for every product line. To establish these sales and spending levels, the firm creates a profitability statement for every product in every region, and allocates G&A and R&D costs across sales divisions in ways that aren't necessarily the most tax efficient.

Even if a company does not have such formal separated reporting systems, it can still informally adjust transfer prices to satisfy the tradeoff between tax minimization and incentive provision. Consider a multinational firm that makes semiconductor products that it sells through its sales organization in a higher-tax country. To minimize taxes, the parent sets a high transfer price, thereby lowering the operating income of the foreign sales organization. It would be inappropriate to penalize the country sales manager for this low income since the sales organization has no say in determining the transfer price. As an alternative, the company can evaluate the sales manager on the direct contribution (revenues minus marketing costs) incurred in the country. That is, the transfer price incurred to acquire the semiconductor products is omitted for performance-evaluation purposes. Of course, this is not a perfect solution. By ignoring the cost of acquiring the products, the sales manager is given incentives to overspend on local marketing relative to what would be optimal from the firm's overall perspective. If the dysfunctional effects of this are suitably large, corporate managers must then step in and dictate specific operational decisions and goals for the manager based on the information available to them. More generally, adoption of a tax-compliant transfer pricing policy creates a need for nonfinancial performance indicators at lower management levels in order to better evaluate and reward performance.[9]

Additional Issues in Transfer Pricing

Additional factors that arise in multinational transfer pricing include tariffs and customs duties levied on imports of products into a country. The issues here are similar to income tax considerations; companies will have incentives to lower transfer prices for products imported into a country to reduce tariffs and customs duties charged on those products.

Decision Point

How do income tax considerations affect transfer pricing in multinationals?

In addition to the motivations for choosing transfer prices already described, multinational transfer prices are sometimes influenced by restrictions that some countries place on dividend- or income-related payments to parties outside their national borders. By increasing the prices of goods or services transferred into divisions in these countries, companies can seek to increase the cash paid out of these countries without violating dividend- or income-related restrictions.

Problem for Self-Study

The Pillercat Corporation is a highly decentralized company. Each division manager has full authority for sourcing decisions and selling decisions. The machining division of Pillercat has been the major supplier of the 2,000 crankshafts that the tractor division needs each year.

The tractor division, however, has just announced that it plans to purchase all its crankshafts in the forthcoming year from two external suppliers at $200 per crankshaft.

---

[8] For further details, see I. Springsteel, "Separate but Unequal," *CFO Magazine*, August 1999.

[9] Cools et al. "Management control in the transfer pricing tax compliant multinational enterprise," *Accounting, Organizations and Society*, August 2008 provides an illustrative case study of this issue in the context of a semiconductor product division of a multinational firm.

The machining division of Pillercat recently increased its selling price for the forthcoming year to $220 per unit (from $200 per unit in the current year).

Juan Gomez, manager of the machining division, feels that the 10% price increase is justified. It results from a higher depreciation charge on some new specialized equipment used to manufacture crankshafts and an increase in labor costs. Gomez wants the president of Pillercat Corporation to force the tractor division to buy all its crankshafts from the machining division at the price of $220. The following table summarizes the key data.

	A	B
1	Number of crankshafts purchased by tractor division	2,000
2	External supplier's market price per crankshaft	$ 200
3	Variable cost per crankshaft in machining division	$ 190
4	Fixed cost per crankshaft in machining division	$ 20

Required

1. Compute the advantage or disadvantage in terms of annual operating income to the Pillercat Corporation as a whole if the tractor division buys crankshafts internally from the machining division under each of the following cases:
   a. The machining division has no alternative use for the facilities used to manufacture crankshafts.
   b. The machining division can use the facilities for other production operations, which will result in annual cash operating savings of $29,000.
   c. The machining division has no alternative use for its facilities, and the external supplier drops the price to $185 per crankshaft.
2. As the president of Pillercat, how would you respond to Juan Gomez's request that you force the tractor division to purchase all of its crankshafts from the machining division? Would your response differ according to the three cases described in requirement 1? Explain.

Solution

1. Computations for the tractor division buying crankshafts internally for one year under cases **a**, **b**, and **c** are as follows:

	A	B	C	D
1			Case	
2		a	b	c
3	Number of crankshafts purchased by tractor division	2,000	2,000	2,000
4	External supplier's market price per crankshaft	$ 200	$ 200	$ 185
5	Variable cost per crankshaft in machining division	$ 190	$ 190	$ 190
6	Opportunity costs of the machining division supplying crankshafts to the tractor division	-	$ 29,000	-
7				
8	Total purchase costs if buying from an external supplier			
9	(2,000 shafts × $200, $200, $185 per shaft)	$400,000	$400,000	$370,000
10	Incremental cost of buying from the machining division			
11	(2,000 shafts × $190 per shaft)	380,000	380,000	380,000
12	Total opportunity costs of the machining division	-	29,000	-
13	Total relevant costs	380,000	409,000	380,000
14	Annual operating income advantage (disadvantage) to			
15	Pillercat of buying from the machining division	$ 20,000	$ (9,000)	$ (10,000)

The general guideline that was introduced in the chapter (p. 812) as a first step in setting a transfer price can be used to highlight the alternatives:

Case	Incremental Cost per Unit Incurred to Point of Transfer	+	Opportunity Cost per Unit to the Supplying Division	=	Transfer Price	External Market Price
a	$190	+	$0	=	$190.00	$200
b	$190	+	$14.50[a]	=	$204.50	$200
c	$190	+	$0	=	$190.00	$185

[a] Opportunity cost per unit = Total opportunity costs ÷ Number of crankshafts = $29,000 ÷ 2,000 = $14.50

Comparing transfer price to external-market price, the tractor division will maximize annual operating income of Pillercat Corporation as a whole by purchasing from the machining division in case **a** and by purchasing from the external supplier in cases **b** and **c**.

2. Pillercat Corporation is a highly decentralized company. If no forced transfer were made, the tractor division would use an external supplier, a decision that would be in the best interest of the company as a whole in cases **b** and **c** of requirement 1 but not in case **a**.

Suppose in case **a**, the machining division refuses to meet the price of $200. This decision means that the company will be $20,000 worse off in the short run. Should top management interfere and force a transfer at $200? This interference would undercut the philosophy of decentralization. Many top managers would not interfere because they would view the $20,000 as an inevitable cost of a suboptimal decision that can occur under decentralization. But how high must this cost be before the temptation to interfere would be irresistible? $30,000? $40,000?

Any top management interference with lower-level decision making weakens decentralization. Of course, Pillercat's management may occasionally interfere to prevent costly mistakes. But recurring interference and constraints would hurt Pillercat's attempts to operate as a decentralized company.

Decision Points

The following question-and-answer format summarizes the chapter's learning objectives. Each decision presents a key question related to a learning objective. The guidelines are the answer to that question.

Decision

1. What is a management control system and how should it be designed?

Guidelines

A management control system is a means of gathering and using information to aid and coordinate the planning and control decisions throughout the organization and to guide the behavior of managers and other employees. Effective management control systems (a) are closely aligned to the organization's strategy, (b) support the organizational responsibilities of individual managers, and (c) motivate managers and other employees to give effort to achieve the organization's goals.

2. What are the benefits and costs of decentralization?	The benefits of decentralization include (a) greater responsiveness to local needs, (b) gains from faster decision making, (c) increased motivation of subunit managers, (d) greater management development and learning, and (e) sharpened focus of subunit managers. The costs of decentralization include (a) suboptimal decision making, (b) excessive focus on the subunit rather than the company as a whole, (c) increased costs of information gathering, and (d) duplication of activities.
3. What are alternative ways of calculating transfer prices, and what criteria should be used to evaluate them?	A transfer price is the price one subunit charges for a product or service supplied to another subunit of the same organization. Transfer prices can be (a) market-based, (b) cost-based, or (c) hybrid. Different transfer-pricing methods produce different revenues and costs for individual subunits, and hence, different operating incomes for the subunits. Transfer prices seek to (a) promote goal congruence, (b) motivate management effort, (c) help evaluate subunit performance, and (d) preserve subunit autonomy (if desired).
4. Under what market conditions do market-based transfer prices promote goal congruence?	In perfectly competitive markets, there is no unused capacity, and division managers can buy and sell as much of a product or service as they want at the market price. In such settings, using the market price as the transfer price motivates division managers to transact internally and to take exactly the same actions as they would if they were transacting in the external market.
5. What problems can arise when full cost plus a markup is used as the transfer price?	A transfer price based on full cost plus a markup may lead to suboptimal decisions because it leads the buying division to regard the fixed costs and the markup of the selling division as a variable cost. The buying division may then purchase products from an external supplier expecting savings in costs that, in fact, will not occur.
6. Within a range of feasible transfer prices, what are alternative ways for firms to arrive at the eventual price?	When there is unused capacity, the transfer-price range lies between the minimum price at which the selling division is willing to sell (its variable cost per unit) and the maximum price the buying division is willing to pay (the lower of its contribution or price at which the product is available from external suppliers). Methods for arriving at a price in this range include proration (such as splitting the difference equally or on the basis of relative variable costs), negotiation between divisions, and dual pricing.
7. What is the general guideline for determining a minimum transfer price?	The general guideline states that the minimum transfer price equals the incremental cost per unit incurred up to the point of transfer plus the opportunity cost per unit to the selling division resulting from transferring products or services internally.
8. How do income tax considerations affect transfer pricing in multinationals?	Transfer prices can reduce income tax payments by reporting more income in low-tax-rate countries and less income in high-tax-rate countries. However, tax regulations of different countries restrict the transfer prices that companies can use.

Terms to Learn

This chapter and the Glossary at the end of the book contain definitions of the following important terms:

autonomy
decentralization
dual pricing
dysfunctional decision making
effort

goal congruence
incongruent decision making
intermediate product
management control system

motivation
perfectly competitive market
suboptimal decision making
transfer price

Assignment Material

Questions

22-1 What is a management control system?
22-2 Describe three criteria you would use to evaluate whether a management control system is effective.
22-3 What is the relationship among motivation, goal congruence, and effort?

22-4 Name three benefits and two costs of decentralization.

22-5 "Organizations typically adopt a consistent decentralization or centralization philosophy across all their business functions." Do you agree? Explain.

22-6 "Transfer pricing is confined to profit centers." Do you agree? Explain.

22-7 What are the three methods for determining transfer prices?

22-8 What properties should transfer-pricing systems have?

22-9 "All transfer-pricing methods give the same division operating income." Do you agree? Explain.

22-10 Under what conditions is a market-based transfer price optimal?

22-11 What is one potential limitation of full-cost-based transfer prices?

22-12 Give two reasons why the dual-pricing system of transfer pricing is not widely used.

22-13 "Cost and price information play no role in negotiated transfer prices." Do you agree? Explain.

22-14 "Under the general guideline for transfer pricing, the minimum transfer price will vary depending on whether the supplying division has unused capacity or not." Do you agree? Explain.

22-15 How should managers consider income tax issues when choosing a transfer-pricing method?

Exercises

22-16 Evaluating management control systems, balanced scorecard. Adventure Parks Inc. (API) operates ten theme parks throughout the United States. The company's slogan is "Name Your Adventure," and its mission is to offer an exciting theme park experience to visitors of all ages. API's corporate strategy supports this mission by stressing the importance of sparkling clean surroundings, efficient crowd management and, above all, cheerful employees. Of course, improved shareholder value drives this strategy.

Required

1. Assuming that API uses a balanced scorecard approach (see Chapter 13) to formulating its management control system. List three measures that API might use to evaluate each of the four balanced scorecard perspectives: financial perspective, customer perspective, internal-business-process perspective, and learning-and-growth perspective.
2. How would the management controls related to financial and customer perspectives at API differ between the following three managers: a souvenir shop manager, a park general manager, and the corporation's CEO?

22-17 Cost centers, profit centers, decentralization, transfer prices. Fenster Corporation manufactures windows with wood and metal frames. Fenster has three departments: glass, wood, and metal. The glass department makes the window glass and sends it to either the wood or metal department where the glass is framed. The window is then sold. Upper management sets the production schedules for the three departments and evaluates them on output quantity, cost variances, and product quality.

Required

1. Are the three departments cost centers, revenue centers, or profit centers?
2. Are the three departments centralized or decentralized?
3. Can a centralized department be a profit center? Why or why not?
4. Suppose the upper management of Fenster Corporation decides to let the three departments set their own production schedules, buy and sell products in the external market, and have the wood and metal departments negotiate with the glass department for the glass panes using a transfer price.
   a. Will this change your answers to requirements 1 and 2?
   b. How would you recommend upper management evaluate the three departments if this change is made?

22-18 Benefits and costs of decentralization. Jackson Markets, a chain of traditional supermarkets, is interested in gaining access to the organic and health food retail market by acquiring a regional company in that sector. Jackson intends to operate the newly-acquired stores independently from its supermarkets.

One of the prospects is Health Source, a chain of twenty stores in the mid-Atlantic. Buying for all twenty stores is done by the company's central office. Store managers must follow strict guidelines for all aspects of store management in an attempt to maintain consistency among stores. Store managers are evaluated on the basis of achieving profit goals developed by the central office.

The other prospect is Harvest Moon, a chain of thirty stores in the Northeast. Harvest Moon managers are given significant flexibility in product offerings, allowing them to negotiate purchases with local organic farmers. Store managers are rewarded for exceeding self-developed return on investment goals with company stock options. Some managers have become significant shareholders in the company, and have even decided on their own to open additional store locations to improve market penetration. However, the increased autonomy has led to competition and price cutting among Harvest Moon stores within the same geographic market, resulting in lower margins.

Required

1. Would you describe Health Source as having a centralized or a decentralized structure? Explain.
2. Would you describe Harvest Moon as having a centralized or a decentralized structure? Discuss some of the benefits and costs of that type of structure.

3. Would stores in each chain be considered cost centers, revenue centers, profit centers, or investment centers? How does that tie into the evaluation of store managers?
4. Assume that Jackson chooses to acquire Harvest Moon. What steps can Jackson take to improve goal congruence between store managers and the larger company?

22-19 Multinational transfer pricing, effect of alternative transfer-pricing methods, global income tax minimization. Tech Friendly Computer, Inc., with headquarters in San Francisco, manufactures and sells a desktop computer. Tech Friendly has three divisions, each of which is located in a different country:

a. China division—manufactures memory devices and keyboards
b. South Korea division—assembles desktop computers using locally manufactured parts, along with memory devices and keyboards from the China division
c. U.S. division—packages and distributes desktop computers

Each division is run as a profit center. The costs for the work done in each division for a single desktop computer are as follows:

China division: Variable cost = 900 yuan
Fixed cost = 1,980 yuan

South Korea division: Variable cost = 350,000 won
Fixed cost = 470,000 won

U.S. division: Variable cost = $125
Fixed cost = $325

- Chinese income tax rate on the China division's operating income: 40%
- South Korean income tax rate on the South Korea division's operating income: 20%
- U.S. income tax rate on the U.S. division's operating income: 30%

Each desktop computer is sold to retail outlets in the United States for $3,800. Assume that the current foreign exchange rates are as follows:

9 yuan = $1 U.S.

1,000 won = $1 U.S.

Both the China and the South Korea divisions sell part of their production under a private label. The China division sells the comparable memory/keyboard package used in each Tech Friendly desktop computer to a Chinese manufacturer for 4,500 yuan. The South Korea division sells the comparable desktop computer to a South Korean distributor for 1,340,000 won.

1. Calculate the after-tax operating income per unit earned by each division under the following transfer-pricing methods: (a) market price, (b) 200% of full cost, and (c) 350% of variable cost. (Income taxes are not included in the computation of the cost-based transfer prices.)
2. Which transfer-pricing method(s) will maximize the after-tax operating income per unit of Tech Friendly Computer?

Required

22-20 Transfer-pricing methods, goal congruence. British Columbia Lumber has a raw lumber division and a finished lumber division. The variable costs are as follows:

- Raw lumber division: $100 per 100 board-feet of raw lumber
- Finished lumber division: $125 per 100 board-feet of finished lumber

Assume that there is no board-feet loss in processing raw lumber into finished lumber. Raw lumber can be sold at $200 per 100 board-feet. Finished lumber can be sold at $275 per 100 board-feet.

1. Should British Columbia Lumber process raw lumber into its finished form? Show your calculations.
2. Assume that internal transfers are made at 110% of variable cost. Will each division maximize its division operating-income contribution by adopting the action that is in the best interest of British Columbia Lumber as a whole? Explain.
3. Assume that internal transfers are made at market prices. Will each division maximize its division operating-income contribution by adopting the action that is in the best interest of British Columbia Lumber as a whole? Explain.

Required

22-21 Effect of alternative transfer-pricing methods on division operating income. (CMA, adapted) Ajax Corporation has two divisions. The mining division makes toldine, which is then transferred to the metals division. The toldine is further processed by the metals division and is sold to customers at a price of $150 per unit. The mining division is currently required by Ajax to transfer its total yearly output of

200,000 units of toldine to the metals division at 110% of full manufacturing cost. Unlimited quantities of toldine can be purchased and sold on the outside market at $90 per unit.

The following table gives the manufacturing cost per unit in the mining and metals divisions for 2012:

	Mining Division	Metals Division
Direct material cost	$12	$ 6
Direct manufacturing labor cost	16	20
Manufacturing overhead cost	32[a]	25[b]
Total manufacturing cost per unit	$60	$51

[a]Manufacturing overhead costs in the mining division are 25% fixed and 75% variable.
[b]Manufacturing overhead costs in the metals division are 60% fixed and 40% variable.

Required

1. Calculate the operating incomes for the mining and metals divisions for the 200,000 units of toldine transferred under the following transfer-pricing methods: (a) market price and (b) 110% of full manufacturing cost.
2. Suppose Ajax rewards each division manager with a bonus, calculated as 1% of division operating income (if positive). What is the amount of bonus that will be paid to each division manager under the transfer-pricing methods in requirement 1? Which transfer-pricing method will each division manager prefer to use?
3. What arguments would Brian Jones, manager of the mining division, make to support the transfer-pricing method that he prefers?

22-22 Transfer pricing, general guideline, goal congruence. (CMA, adapted). Quest Motors, Inc., operates as a decentralized multidivision company. The Vivo division of Quest Motors purchases most of its airbags from the airbag division. The airbag division's incremental cost for manufacturing the airbags is $90 per unit. The airbag division is currently working at 80% of capacity. The current market price of the airbags is $125 per unit.

Required

1. Using the general guideline presented in the chapter, what is the minimum price at which the airbag division would sell airbags to the Vivo division?
2. Suppose that Quest Motors requires that whenever divisions with unused capacity sell products internally, they must do so at the incremental cost. Evaluate this transfer-pricing policy using the criteria of goal congruence, evaluating division performance, motivating management effort, and preserving division autonomy.
3. If the two divisions were to negotiate a transfer price, what is the range of possible transfer prices? Evaluate this negotiated transfer-pricing policy using the criteria of goal congruence, evaluating division performance, motivating management effort, and preserving division autonomy.
4. Instead of allowing negotiation, suppose that Quest specifies a hybrid transfer price that "splits the difference" between the minimum and maximum prices from the divisions' standpoint. What would be the resulting transfer price for airbags?

22-23 Multinational transfer pricing, global tax minimization. The Mornay Company manufactures telecommunications equipment at its plant in Toledo, Ohio. The company has marketing divisions throughout the world. A Mornay marketing division in Vienna, Austria, imports 10,000 units of Product 4A36 from the United States. The following information is available:

U.S. income tax rate on the U.S. division's operating income	35%
Austrian income tax rate on the Austrian division's operating income	40%
Austrian import duty	15%
Variable manufacturing cost per unit of Product 4A36	$ 550
Full manufacturing cost per unit of Product 4A36	$ 800
Selling price (net of marketing and distribution costs) in Austria	$1,150

Suppose the United States and Austrian tax authorities only allow transfer prices that are between the full manufacturing cost per unit of $800 and a market price of $950, based on comparable imports into Austria. The Austrian import duty is charged on the price at which the product is transferred into Austria. Any import duty paid to the Austrian authorities is a deductible expense for calculating Austrian income taxes due.

Required

1. Calculate the after-tax operating income earned by the United States and Austrian divisions from transferring 10,000 units of Product 4A36 (a) at full manufacturing cost per unit and (b) at market price of comparable imports. (Income taxes are not included in the computation of the cost-based transfer prices.)
2. Which transfer price should the Mornay Company select to minimize the total of company import duties and income taxes? Remember that the transfer price must be between the full manufacturing cost per unit of $800 and the market price of $950 of comparable imports into Austria. Explain your reasoning.

22-24 Multinational transfer pricing, goal congruence (continuation of 22-23). Suppose that the U.S. division could sell as many units of Product 4A36 as it makes at $900 per unit in the U.S. market, net of all marketing and distribution costs.

Required

1. From the viewpoint of the Mornay Company as a whole, would after-tax operating income be maximized if it sold the 10,000 units of Product 4A36 in the United States or in Austria? Show your computations.
2. Suppose division managers act autonomously to maximize their division's after-tax operating income. Will the transfer price calculated in requirement 2 of Exercise 22-23 result in the U.S. division manager taking the actions determined to be optimal in requirement 1 of this exercise? Explain.
3. What is the minimum transfer price that the U.S. division manager would agree to? Does this transfer price result in the Mornay Company as a whole paying more import duty and taxes than the answer to requirement 2 of Exercise 22-23? If so, by how much?

22-25 Transfer-pricing dispute. The Allison-Chambers Corporation, manufacturer of tractors and other heavy farm equipment, is organized along decentralized product lines, with each manufacturing division operating as a separate profit center. Each division manager has been delegated full authority on all decisions involving the sale of that division's output both to outsiders and to other divisions of Allison-Chambers. Division C has in the past always purchased its requirement of a particular tractor-engine component from division A. However, when informed that division A is increasing its selling price to $150, division C's manager decides to purchase the engine component from external suppliers.

Division C can purchase the component for $135 per unit in the open market. Division A insists that, because of the recent installation of some highly specialized equipment and the resulting high depreciation charges, it will not be able to earn an adequate return on its investment unless it raises its price. Division A's manager appeals to top management of Allison-Chambers for support in the dispute with division C and supplies the following operating data:

C's annual purchases of the tractor-engine component	1,000 units
A's variable cost per unit of the tractor-engine component	$120
A's fixed cost per unit of the tractor-engine component	$ 20

Required

1. Assume that there are no alternative uses for internal facilities of division A. Determine whether the company as a whole will benefit if division C purchases the component from external suppliers for $135 per unit. What should the transfer price for the component be set at so that division managers acting in their own divisions' best interests take actions that are also in the best interest of the company as a whole?
2. Assume that internal facilities of division A would not otherwise be idle. By not producing the 1,000 units for division C, division A's equipment and other facilities would be used for other production operations that would result in annual cash-operating savings of $18,000. Should division C purchase from external suppliers? Show your computations.
3. Assume that there are no alternative uses for division A's internal facilities and that the price from outsiders drops $20. Should division C purchase from external suppliers? What should the transfer price for the component be set at so that division managers acting in their own divisions' best interests take actions that are also in the best interest of the company as a whole?

22-26 Transfer-pricing problem (continuation of 22-25). Refer to Exercise 22-25. Assume that division A can sell the 1,000 units to other customers at $155 per unit, with variable marketing cost of $5 per unit.

Determine whether Allison-Chambers will benefit if division C purchases the 1,000 units from external suppliers at $135 per unit. Show your computations.

Required

Problems

MyAccountingLab

22-27 General guideline, transfer pricing. The Slate Company manufactures and sells television sets. Its assembly division (AD) buys television screens from the screen division (SD) and assembles the TV sets. The SD, which is operating at capacity, incurs an incremental manufacturing cost of $65 per screen. The SD can sell all its output to the outside market at a price of $100 per screen, after incurring a variable marketing and distribution cost of $8 per screen. If the AD purchases screens from outside suppliers at a price of $100 per screen, it will incur a variable purchasing cost of $7 per screen. Slate's division managers can act autonomously to maximize their own division's operating income.

Required

1. What is the minimum transfer price at which the SD manager would be willing to sell screens to the AD?
2. What is the maximum transfer price at which the AD manager would be willing to purchase screens from the SD?
3. Now suppose that the SD can sell only 70% of its output capacity of 20,000 screens per month on the open market. Capacity cannot be reduced in the short run. The AD can assemble and sell more than 20,000 TV sets per month.
   a. What is the minimum transfer price at which the SD manager would be willing to sell screens to the AD?

b. From the point of view of Slate's management, how much of the SD output should be transferred to the AD?

c. If Slate mandates the SD and AD managers to "split the difference" on the minimum and maximum transfer prices they would be willing to negotiate over, what would be the resulting transfer price? Does this price achieve the outcome desired in requirement 3b?

22-28 Pertinent transfer price. Europa, Inc., has two divisions, A and B, that manufacture expensive bicycles. Division A produces the bicycle frame, and division B assembles the rest of the bicycle onto the frame. There is a market for both the subassembly and the final product. Each division has been designated as a profit center. The transfer price for the subassembly has been set at the long-run average market price. The following data are available for each division:

Selling price for final product	$300
Long-run average selling price for intermediate product	200
Incremental cost per unit for completion in division B	150
Incremental cost per unit in division A	120

The manager of division B has made the following calculation:

Selling price for final product		$300
Transferred-in cost per unit (market)	$200	
Incremental cost per unit for completion	150	350
Contribution (loss) on product		$(50)

Required

1. Should transfers be made to division B if there is no unused capacity in division A? Is the market price the correct transfer price? Show your computations.
2. Assume that division A's maximum capacity for this product is 1,000 units per month and sales to the intermediate market are now 800 units. Should 200 units be transferred to division B? At what transfer price? Assume that for a variety of reasons, division A will maintain the $200 selling price indefinitely. That is, division A is not considering lowering the price to outsiders even if idle capacity exists.
3. Suppose division A quoted a transfer price of $150 for up to 200 units. What would be the contribution to the company as a whole if a transfer were made? As manager of division B, would you be inclined to buy at $150? Explain.

22-29 Pricing in imperfect markets (continuation of 22-28). Refer to Problem 22-28.

Required

1. Suppose the manager of division A has the option of (a) cutting the external price to $195, with the certainty that sales will rise to 1,000 units or (b) maintaining the external price of $200 for the 800 units and transferring the 200 units to division B at a price that would produce the same operating income for division A. What transfer price would produce the same operating income for division A? Is that price consistent with that recommended by the general guideline in the chapter so that the resulting decision would be desirable for the company as a whole?
2. Suppose that if the selling price for the intermediate product were dropped to $195, sales to external parties could be increased to 900 units. Division B wants to acquire as many as 200 units if the transfer price is acceptable. For simplicity, assume that there is no external market for the final 100 units of division A's capacity.
   a. Using the general guideline, what is (are) the minimum transfer price(s) that should lead to the correct economic decision? Ignore performance-evaluation considerations.
   b. Compare the total contributions under the alternatives to show why the transfer price(s) recommended lead(s) to the optimal economic decision.

22-30 Effect of alternative transfer-pricing methods on division operating income. Crango Products is a cranberry cooperative that operates two divisions, a harvesting division and a processing division. Currently, all of harvesting's output is converted into cranberry juice by the processing division, and the juice is sold to large beverage companies that produce cranberry juice blends. The processing division has a yield of 500 gallons of juice per 1,000 pounds of cranberries. Cost and market price data for the two divisions are as follows:

	A	B	C	D	E
1	Harvesting Division			Processing Division	
2	Variable cost per pound of cranberries	$0.10		Variable processing cost per gallon of juice produced	$0.20
3	Fixed cost per pound of cranberries	$0.25		Fixed cost per gallon of juice produced	$0.40
4	Selling price per pound of cranberries in outside market	$0.60		Selling price per gallon of juice	$2.10

Required

1. Compute Crango's operating income from harvesting 400,000 pounds of cranberries during June 2012 and processing them into juice.
2. Crango rewards its division managers with a bonus equal to 5% of operating income. Compute the bonus earned by each division manager in June 2012 for each of the following transfer pricing methods:
   a. 200% of full cost
   b. Market price
3. Which transfer-pricing method will each division manager prefer? How might Crango resolve any conflicts that may arise on the issue of transfer pricing?

22-31 Goal-congruence problems with cost-plus transfer-pricing methods, dual-pricing system (continuation of 22-30). Assume that Pat Borges, CEO of Crango, had mandated a transfer price equal to 200% of full cost. Now he decides to decentralize some management decisions and sends around a memo that states the following: "Effective immediately, each division of Crango is free to make its own decisions regarding the purchase of direct materials and the sale of finished products."

Required

1. Give an example of a goal-congruence problem that will arise if Crango continues to use a transfer price of 200% of full cost and Borges's decentralization policy is adopted.
2. Borges feels that a dual transfer-pricing policy will improve goal congruence. He suggests that transfers out of the harvesting division be made at 200% of full cost and transfers into the processing division be made at market price. Compute the operating income of each division under this dual transfer pricing method when 400,000 pounds of cranberries are harvested during June 2012 and processed into juice.
3. Why is the sum of the division operating incomes computed in requirement 2 different from Crango's operating income from harvesting and processing 400,000 pounds of cranberries?
4. Suggest two problems that may arise if Crango implements the dual transfer prices described in requirement 2.

22-32 Multinational transfer pricing, global tax minimization. Industrial Diamonds, Inc., based in Los Angeles, has two divisions:

- South African mining division, which mines a rich diamond vein in South Africa
- U.S. processing division, which polishes raw diamonds for use in industrial cutting tools

The processing division's yield is 50%: It takes 2 pounds of raw diamonds to produce 1 pound of top-quality polished industrial diamonds. Although all of the mining division's output of 8,000 pounds of raw diamonds is sent for processing in the United States, there is also an active market for raw diamonds in South Africa. The foreign exchange rate is 6 ZAR (South African Rand) = $1 U.S. The following information is known about the two divisions:

	A	B	C	D	F	G
1	South African Mining Division					
2	Variable cost per pound of raw diamonds				600	ZAR
3	Fixed cost per pound of raw diamonds				1,200	ZAR
4	Market price per pound of raw diamonds				3,600	ZAR
5	Tax rate				25%	
6						
7	U.S. Processing Division					
8	Variable cost per pound of polished diamonds				220	U.S. dollars
9	Fixed cost per pound of polished diamonds				850	U.S. dollars
10	Market price per pound of polished diamonds				3,500	U.S. dollars
11	Tax rate				40%	

Required

1. Compute the annual pretax operating income, in U.S. dollars, of each division under the following transfer-pricing methods: (a) 250% of full cost and (b) market price.
2. Compute the after-tax operating income, in U.S. dollars, for each division under the transfer-pricing methods in requirement 1. (Income taxes are not included in the computation of cost-based transfer price, and Industrial Diamonds does not pay U.S. income tax on income already taxed in South Africa.)
3. If the two division managers are compensated based on after-tax division operating income, which transfer-pricing method will each prefer? Which transfer-pricing method will maximize the total after-tax operating income of Industrial Diamonds?
4. In addition to tax minimization, what other factors might Industrial Diamonds consider in choosing a transfer-pricing method?

22-33 International transfer pricing, taxes, goal congruence. Argone division of Gemini Corporation is located in the United States. Its effective income tax rate is 30%. Another division of Gemini, Calcia, is located in Canada, where the income tax rate is 42%. Calcia manufactures, among other things, an intermediate product for Argone called IP-2007. Calcia operates at capacity and makes 15,000 units of IP-2007 for Argone each period, at a variable cost of $60 per unit. Assume that there are no outside customers for IP-2007. Because the IP-2007 must be shipped from Canada to the United States, it costs Calcia an additional $4 per unit to ship the IP-2007 to Argone. There are no direct fixed costs for IP-2007. Calcia also manufactures other products.

A product similar to IP-2007 that Argone could use as a substitute is available in the United States for $75 per unit.

Required

1. What is the minimum and maximum transfer price that would be acceptable to Argone and Calcia for IP-2007, and why?
2. What transfer price would minimize income taxes for Gemini Corporation as a whole? Would Calcia and Argone want to be evaluated on operating income using this transfer price?
3. Suppose Gemini uses the transfer price from requirement 2, and each division is evaluated on its own after-tax division operating income. Now suppose Calcia has an opportunity to sell 8,000 units of IP-2007 to an outside customer for $68 each. Calcia will not incur shipping costs because the customer is nearby and offers to pay for shipping. Assume that if Calcia accepts the special order, Argone will have to buy 8,000 units of the substitute product in the United States at $75 per unit.
   a. Will accepting the special order maximize after-tax operating income for Gemini Corporation as a whole?
   b. Will Argone want Calcia to accept this special order? Why or why not?
   c. Will Calcia want to accept this special order? Explain.
   d. Suppose Gemini Corporation wants to operate in a decentralized manner. What transfer price should Gemini set for IP-2007 so that each division acting in its own best interest takes actions with respect to the special order that are in the best interests of Gemini Corporation as a whole?

22-34 Transfer pricing, goal congruence. The Bosh Corporation makes and sells 20,000 multisystem music players each year. Its assembly division purchases components from other divisions of Bosh or from external suppliers and assembles the multisystem music players. In particular, the assembly division can purchase the CD player from the compact disc division of Bosh or from Hawei Corporation. Hawei agrees to meet all of Bosh's quality requirements and is currently negotiating with the assembly division to supply 20,000 CD players at a price between $44 and $52 per CD player.

A critical component of the CD player is the head mechanism that reads the disc. To ensure the quality of its multisystem music players, Bosh requires that if Hawei wins the contract to supply CD players, it must purchase the head mechanism from Bosh's compact disc division for $24 each.

The compact disc division can manufacture at most 22,000 CD players annually. It also manufactures as many additional head mechanisms as can be sold. The incremental cost of manufacturing the head mechanism is $18 per unit. The incremental cost of manufacturing a CD player (including the cost of the head mechanism) is $30 per unit, and any number of CD players can be sold for $45 each in the external market.

Required

1. What are the incremental costs minus revenues from sale to external buyers for the company as a whole if the compact disc division transfers 20,000 CD players to the assembly division and sells the remaining 2,000 CD players on the external market?
2. What are the incremental costs minus revenues from sales to external buyers for the company as a whole if the compact disc division sells 22,000 CD players on the external market and the assembly division accepts Hawei's offer at (a) $44 per CD player or (b) $52 per CD player?
3. What is the minimum transfer price per CD player at which the compact disc division would be willing to transfer 20,000 CD players to the assembly division?
4. Suppose that the transfer price is set to the minimum computed in requirement 3 plus $2, and the division managers at Bosh are free to make their own profit-maximizing sourcing and selling decisions. Now, Hawei offers 20,000 CD players for $52 each.
   a. What decisions will the managers of the compact disc division and assembly division make?
   b. Are these decisions optimal for Bosh as a whole?
   c. Based on this exercise, at what price would you recommend the transfer price be set?

22-35 Transfer pricing, goal congruence, ethics. Jeremiah Industries manufactures high-grade aluminum luggage made from recycled metal. The company operates two divisions: metal recycling and luggage fabrication. Each division operates as a decentralized entity. The metal recycling division is free to sell sheet aluminum to outside buyers, and the luggage fabrication division is free to purchase recycled sheet aluminum from other sources. Currently, however, the recycling division sells all of its output to the fabrication division, and the fabrication division does not purchase materials from any outside suppliers.

Aluminum is transferred from the recycling division to the fabrication division at 110% of full cost. The recycling division purchases recyclable aluminum for $0.50 per pound. The division's other variable costs equal $2.80 per pound, and fixed costs at a monthly production level of 50,000 pounds are $1.50 per pound.

During the most recent month, 50,000 pounds of aluminum were transferred between the two divisions. The recycling division's capacity is 70,000 pounds.

Due to increased demand, the fabrication division expects to use 60,000 pounds of aluminum next month. Metalife Corporation has offered to sell 10,000 pounds of recycled aluminum next month to the fabrication division for $5.00 per pound.

Required

1. Calculate the transfer price per pound of recycled aluminum. Assuming that each division is considered a profit center, would the fabrication manager choose to purchase 10,000 pounds next month from Metalife?
2. Is the purchase in the best interest of Jeremiah Industries? Show your calculations. What is the cause of this goal incongruence?
3. The fabrication division manager suggests that $5.00 is now the market price for recycled sheet aluminum, and that this should be the new transfer price. Jeremiah's corporate management tends to agree. The metal recycling manager is suspicious. Metalife's prices have always been considerably higher than $5.00 per pound. Why the sudden price cut? After further investigation by the recycling division manager, it is revealed that the $5.00 per pound price was a one-time-only offer made to the fabrication division due to excess inventory at Metalife. Future orders would be priced at $5.50 per pound. Comment on the validity of the $5.00 per pound market price and the ethics of the fabrication manager. Would changing the transfer price to $5.00 matter to Jeremiah Industries?

Collaborative Learning Problem

22-36 Transfer pricing, utilization of capacity. (J. Patell, adapted) The California Instrument Company (CIC) consists of the semiconductor division and the process-control division, each of which operates as an independent profit center. The semiconductor division employs craftsmen who produce two different electronic components: the new high-performance Super-chip and an older product called Okay-chip. These two products have the following cost characteristics:

	Super-chip	Okay-chip
Direct materials	$ 5	$ 2
Direct manufacturing labor, 3 hours × $20; 1 hour × $20	60	20

Due to the high skill level necessary for the craftsmen, the semiconductor division's capacity is set at 45,000 hours per year.

Maximum demand for the Super-chip is 15,000 units annually, at a price of $80 per chip. There is unlimited demand for the Okay-chip at $26 per chip.

The process-control division produces only one product, a process-control unit, with the following cost structure:

- Direct materials (circuit board): $70
- Direct manufacturing labor (3 hours × $15): $45

The current market price for the control unit is $132 per unit.

A joint research project has just revealed that a single Super-chip could be substituted for the circuit board currently used to make the process-control unit. Direct labor cost of the process-control unit would be unchanged. The improved process-control unit could be sold for $145.

Required

1. Calculate the contribution margin per direct-labor hour of selling Super-chip and Okay-chip. If no transfers of Super-chip are made to the process-control division, how many Super-chips and Okay-chips should the semiconductor division manufacture and sell? What would be the division's annual contribution margin? Show your computations.
2. The process-control division expects to sell 5,000 process-control units this year. From the viewpoint of California Instruments as a whole, should 5,000 Super-chips be transferred to the process-control division to replace circuit boards? Show your computations.
3. What transfer price, or range of prices, would ensure goal congruence among the division managers? Show your calculations.
4. If labor capacity in the semiconductor division were 60,000 hours instead of 45,000, would your answer to requirement 3 differ? Show your calculations.

23 Performance Measurement, Compensation, and Multinational Considerations

Learning Objectives

1. Select financial and nonfinancial performance measures to use in a balanced scorecard

2. Examine accounting-based measures for evaluating business unit performance, including return on investment (ROI), residual income (RI), and economic value added (EVA®)

3. Analyze the key measurement choices in the design of each performance measure

4. Study the choice of performance targets and design of feedback mechanisms

5. Indicate the difficulties that occur when the performance of divisions operating in different countries is compared

6. Understand the roles of salaries and incentives when rewarding managers

7. Describe the four levers of control and why they are necessary

At the end of this school term, you're going to receive a grade that represents a measure of your performance in this course.

Your grade will likely consist of four elements—homework, quizzes, exams, and class participation. Do some of these elements better reflect your knowledge of the material than others? Would the relative weights placed on the various elements when determining your final grade influence how much effort you expend to improve performance on the different elements? Would it be fair if you received a good grade regardless of your performance? The following article about former AIG chief executive Martin Sullivan examines that very situation in a corporate context. Sullivan continued to receive performance bonuses despite pushing AIG to the brink of bankruptcy. By failing to link pay to performance, the AIG board of directors rewarded behavior that led to a government takeover of the firm.

Misalignment Between CEO Compensation and Performance at AIG[1]

After the September 2008 collapse of AIG, many shareholders and observers focused on the company's executive compensation. Many believed that the incentive structures for executives helped fuel the real estate bubble. Though people were placing long-term bets on mortgage-backed securities, much of their compensation was in the form of short-term bonuses. This encouraged excessive risk without the fear of significant repercussions.

Executive compensation at AIG had been under fire for many years. The Corporate Library, an independent research firm specializing in corporate governance, called the company "a serial offender in the category of outrageous CEO compensation."

Judging solely by company financial measures, AIG's 2007 results were a failure. Driven by the write-down of $11.1 billion in fixed income guarantees, the company's revenue was down 56% from 2006 results. AIG also reported $5 billion in losses in the final quarter of 2007 and warned of possible future losses due to ill-advised investments. Despite this, AIG chief executive Martin Sullivan earned $14.3 million in salary, bonus, stock options, and other long-term

---

[1] *Source:* Blair, Nathan. 2009. AIG – Blame for the bailout. Stanford Graduate School of Business No. A-203, Stanford, CA: Stanford Graduate School of Business; Son, Hugh. 2008. AIG chief Sullivan's compensation fell 32 percent. *Bloomberg.com*, April 4; Son, Hugh and Erik Holm. 2008. AIG's former chief Sullivan gets $47 million package. *Bloomberg.com*, July 1.

incentives. Sullivan's compensation was in the 90th percentile for CEOs of S&P 500 firms for 2007.

On June 15, 2008, AIG replaced Sullivan as CEO. By then, AIG reported cumulative losses totaling $20 billion. During Sullivan's three-year tenure at the helm, AIG lost 46% of its market value. At the time of his dismissal, the AIG board of directors agreed to give the ousted CEO about $47 million in severance pay, bonus, and long-term compensation.

Two months later, on the verge of bankruptcy, the U.S. government nationalized AIG. At a Congressional hearing in the aftermath of AIG's failure, one witness testified on Sullivan's compensation stating, "I think it is fair to say by any standard of measurement that this pay plan is as uncorrelated to performance as it is possible to be."

Companies measure reward and performance to motivate managers to achieve company strategies and goals. As the AIG example illustrates, however, if the measures are inappropriate or not connected to sustained performance, managers may improve their performance evaluations and increase compensation without achieving company goals. This chapter discusses the general design, implementation, and uses of performance measures, part of the final step in the decision-making process.

Financial and Nonfinancial Performance Measures

Many organizations are increasingly presenting financial and nonfinancial performance measures for their subunits in a single report called the *balanced scorecard* (Chapter 13). Different organizations stress different measures in their scorecards, but the measures are always derived from a company's strategy. Consider the case of Hospitality Inns, a chain of hotels. Hospitality Inns' strategy is to provide excellent customer service and to charge a higher room rate than its competitors. Hospitality Inns uses the following measures in its balanced scorecard:

1. **Financial perspective**—stock price, net income, return on sales, return on investment, and economic value added
2. **Customer perspective**—market share in different geographic locations, customer satisfaction, and average number of repeat visits
3. **Internal-business-process perspective**—customer-service time for making reservations, for check-in, and in restaurants; cleanliness of hotel and room, quality of room service; time taken to clean rooms; quality of restaurant experience; number of new services provided to customers (fax, wireless Internet, video games); time taken to plan and build new hotels

Learning Objective 1

Select financial performance measures

. . . such as return on investment, residual income

and nonfinancial performance measures to use in a balanced scorecard

. . . such as customer-satisfaction, number of defects

4. **Learning-and-growth perspective**—employee education and skill levels, employee satisfaction, employee turnover, hours of employee training, and information-system availability

As in all balanced scorecard implementations, the goal is to make improvements in the learning-and-growth perspective that will lead to improvements in the internal-business-process perspective that, in turn, will result in improvements in the customer and financial perspectives. Hospitality Inns also uses balanced scorecard measures to evaluate and reward the performance of its managers.

Some performance measures, such as the time it takes to plan and build new hotels, have a long time horizon. Other measures, such as time taken to check in or quality of room service, have a short time horizon. In this chapter, we focus on *organization subunits'* most widely used performance measures that cover an intermediate-to-long time horizon. These are internal financial measures based on accounting numbers routinely reported by organizations. In later sections, we describe why companies use both financial and nonfinancial measures to evaluate performance.

Designing accounting-based performance measures requires several steps:

Step 1: **Choose Performance Measures That Align with Top Management's Financial Goals.** For example, is operating income, net income, return on assets, or revenues the best measure of a subunit's financial performance?

Step 2: **Choose the Details of Each Performance Measure in Step 1.** Once a firm has chosen a specific performance measure, it must make a variety of decisions about the precise way in which various components of the measure are to be calculated. For example, if the chosen performance measure is return on assets, should it be calculated for one year or for a multiyear period? Should assets be defined as total assets or net assets (total assets minus total liabilities)? Should assets be measured at historical cost or current cost?

Step 3: **Choose a Target Level of Performance and Feedback Mechanism for Each Performance Measure in Step 1.** For example, should all subunits have identical targets, such as the same required rate of return on assets? Should performance reports be sent to top management daily, weekly, or monthly?

These steps need not be done sequentially. The issues considered in each step are interdependent, and top management will often proceed through these steps several times before deciding on one or more accounting-based performance measures. The answers to the questions raised at each step depend on top management's beliefs about how well each alternative measure fulfills the behavioral criteria discussed in Chapter 22: promoting goal congruence, motivating management effort, evaluating subunit performance, and preserving subunit autonomy.

> **Decision Point** ▶
>
> What financial and nonfinancial performance measures do companies use in their balanced scorecards?

Learning Objective 2

Examine accounting-based measures for evaluating business unit performance, including return on investment (ROI),

... return on sales times investment turnover

residual income (RI),

... income minus a dollar amount for required return on investment

and economic value added (EVA®)

... a variation of residual income

Accounting-Based Measures for Business Units

Companies commonly use four measures to evaluate the economic performance of their subunits. We illustrate these measures for Hospitality Inns.

Hospitality Inns owns and operates three hotels: one each in San Francisco, Chicago, and New Orleans. Exhibit 23-1 summarizes data for each hotel for 2012. At present, Hospitality Inns does not allocate the total long-term debt of the company to the three separate hotels. The exhibit indicates that the New Orleans hotel generates the highest operating income, $510,000, compared with Chicago's $300,000 and San Francisco's $240,000. But does this comparison mean the New Orleans hotel is the most "successful"? The main weakness of comparing operating incomes alone is that differences in *the size of the investment* in each hotel are ignored. **Investment** refers to the resources or assets used to generate income. It is not sufficient to compare operating incomes alone. The real question is whether a division generates sufficient operating income relative to the investment made to earn it.

Three of the approaches to measuring performance include a measure of investment: return on investment, residual income, and economic value added. A fourth approach, return on sales, does not measure investment.

Exhibit 23-1

Financial Data for Hospitality Inns for 2012 (in thousands)

	A	B	C	D	E
1		San Francisco Hotel	Chicago Hotel	New Orleans Hotel	Total
2	Hotel revenues	$1,200,000	$1,400,000	$3,185,000	$5,785,000
3	Hotel variable costs	310,000	375,000	995,000	1,680,000
4	Hotel fixed costs	650,000	725,000	1,680,000	3,055,000
5	Hotel operating income	$ 240,000	$ 300,000	$ 510,000	1,050,000
6	Interest costs on long-term debt at 10%				450,000
7	Income before income taxes				600,000
8	Income taxes at 30%				180,000
9	Net income				$ 420,000
10	Net book value at the end of 2012:				
11	Current assets	$ 400,000	$ 500,000	$ 660,000	$1,560,000
12	Long-term assets	600,000	1,500,000	2,340,000	4,440,000
13	Total assets	$1,000,000	$2,000,000	$3,000,000	$6,000,000
14	Current liabilities	$ 50,000	$ 150,000	$ 300,000	$ 500,000
15	Long-term debt				4,500,000
16	Stockholders' equity				1,000,000
17	Total liabilities and stockholders' equity				$6,000,000

Return on Investment

Return on investment (ROI) is an accounting measure of income divided by an accounting measure of investment.

$$\text{Return on investment} = \frac{\text{Income}}{\text{Investment}}$$

Return on investment is the most popular approach to measure performance. ROI is popular for two reasons: it blends all the ingredients of profitability—revenues, costs, and investment—into a single percentage; and it can be compared with the rate of return on opportunities elsewhere, inside or outside the company. Like any single performance measure, however, ROI should be used cautiously and in conjunction with other measures.

ROI is also called the *accounting rate of return* or the *accrual accounting rate of return* (Chapter 21, pp. 771–772). Managers usually use the term "ROI" when evaluating the performance of an organization's subunit and the term "accrual accounting rate of return" when using an ROI measure to evaluate a project. Companies vary in the way they define income in the numerator and investment in the denominator of the ROI calculation. Some companies use operating income for the numerator; others prefer to calculate ROI on an after-tax basis and use net income. Some companies use total assets in the denominator; others prefer to focus on only those assets financed by long-term debt and stockholders' equity and use total assets minus current liabilities.

Consider the ROIs of each of the three Hospitality hotels in Exhibit 23-1. For our calculations, we use the operating income of each hotel for the numerator and total assets of each hotel for the denominator.

Using these ROI figures, the San Francisco hotel appears to make the best use of its total assets.

Hotel	Operating Income	÷	Total Assets	=	ROI
San Francisco	$240,000	÷	$1,000,000	=	24%
Chicago	$300,000	÷	$2,000,000	=	15%
New Orleans	$510,000	÷	$3,000,000	=	17%

Each hotel manager can increase ROI by increasing revenues or decreasing costs (each of which increases the numerator), or by decreasing investment (which decreases the denominator). A hotel manager can increase ROI even when operating income decreases by reducing total assets by a greater percentage. Suppose, for example, that operating income of the Chicago hotel decreases by 4% from $300,000 to $288,000 [$300,000 × (1 − 0.04)] and total assets decrease by 10% from $2,000,000 to $1,800,000 [$2,000,000 × (1 − 0.10)]. The ROI of the Chicago hotel would then increase from 15% to 16% ($288,000 ÷ $1,800,000).

ROI can provide more insight into performance when it is represented as two components:

$$\frac{\text{Income}}{\text{Investment}} = \frac{\text{Income}}{\text{Revenues}} \times \frac{\text{Revenues}}{\text{Investment}}$$

which is also written as,

$$ROI = \text{Return on sales} \times \text{Investment turnover}$$

This approach is known as the *DuPont method of profitability analysis*. The DuPont method recognizes the two basic ingredients in profit-making: increasing income per dollar of revenues and using assets to generate more revenues. An improvement in either ingredient without changing the other increases ROI.

Assume that top management at Hospitality Inns adopts a 30% target ROI for the San Francisco hotel. How can this return be attained? We illustrate the DuPont method for the San Francisco hotel and show how this method can be used to describe three alternative ways in which the San Francisco hotel can increase its ROI from 24% to 30%.

	Operating Income (1)	Revenues (2)	Total Assets (3)	Operating Income / Revenues (4) = (1) ÷ (2)	×	Revenues / Total Assets (5) = (2) ÷ (3)	=	Operating Income / Total Assets (6) = (4) × (5)
Current ROI	$240,000	$1,200,000	$1,000,000	20%	×	1.2	=	24%
Alternatives								
A. Decrease assets (such as receivables), keeping revenues and operating income per dollar of revenue constant	$240,000	$1,200,000	$800,000	20%	×	1.5	=	30%
B. Increase revenues (via higher occupancy rate), keeping assets and operating income per dollar of revenue constant	$300,000	$1,500,000	$1,000,000	20%	×	1.5	=	30%
C. Decrease costs (via, say, efficient maintenance) to increase operating income per dollar of revenue, keeping revenue and assets constant	$300,000	$1,200,000	$1,000,000	25%	×	1.2	=	30%

Other alternatives, such as increasing the selling price per room, could increase both the revenues per dollar of total assets and the operating income per dollar of revenues. ROI makes clear the benefits managers can obtain by reducing their investment in current or long-term assets. Some managers know the need to boost revenues or to control costs, but they pay less attention to reducing their investment base. Reducing the investment base involves decreasing idle cash, managing credit judiciously, determining proper inventory levels, and spending carefully on long-term assets.

Residual Income

Residual income (RI) is an accounting measure of income minus a dollar amount for required return on an accounting measure of investment.

$$\text{Residual income } (RI) = \text{Income} - (\text{Required rate of return} \times \text{Investment})$$

Required rate of return multiplied by the investment is the *imputed cost of the investment*. The **imputed cost** of the investment is a cost recognized in particular situations but not recorded in financial accounting systems because it is an opportunity cost. In this situation, the imputed cost refers to the return Hospitality Inns could have obtained by making an alternative investment with similar risk characteristics.

Assume each hotel faces similar risks, and that Hospitality Inns has a required rate of return of 12%. The RI for each hotel is calculated as the operating income minus the required rate of return of 12% of total assets:

Hotel	Operating Income	−	Required Rate of Return	×	Investment	=	Residual Income
San Francisco	$240,000	−	(12%	×	$1,000,000)	=	$120,000
Chicago	$300,000	−	(12%	×	$2,000,000)	=	$ 60,000
New Orleans	$510,000	−	(12%	×	$3,000,000)	=	$150,000

Note that the New Orleans hotel has the best RI.

Some companies favor the RI measure because managers will concentrate on maximizing an absolute amount, such as dollars of RI, rather than a percentage, such as ROI. The objective of maximizing RI means that as long as a subunit earns a return in excess of the required return for investments, that subunit should continue to invest.

The objective of maximizing ROI may induce managers of highly profitable subunits to reject projects that, from the viewpoint of the company as a whole, should be accepted. Suppose Hospitality Inns is considering upgrading room features and furnishings at the San Francisco hotel. The upgrade will increase operating income of the San Francisco hotel by $70,000 and increase its total assets by $400,000. The ROI for the expansion is 17.5% ($70,000 ÷ $400,000), which is attractive to Hospitality Inns because it exceeds the required rate of return of 12%. By making this expansion, however, the San Francisco hotel's ROI will decrease:

$$\text{Pre-upgrade } ROI = \frac{\$240,000}{\$1,000,000} = 0.24, \text{ or } 24\%$$

$$\text{Post-upgrade } ROI = \frac{\$240,000 + \$70,000}{\$1,000,000 + \$400,000} = \frac{\$310,000}{\$1,400,000} = 0.221, \text{ or } 22.1\%$$

The annual bonus paid to the San Francisco manager may decrease if ROI affects the bonus calculation and the upgrading option is selected. Consequently, the manager may shun the expansion. In contrast, if the annual bonus is a function of RI, the San Francisco manager will favor the expansion:

$$\text{Pre-upgrade } RI = \$240,000 - (0.12 \times \$1,000,000) = \$120,000$$

$$\text{Post-upgrade } RI = \$310,000 - (0.12 \times \$1,400,000) = \$142,000$$

Goal congruence (ensuring that subunit managers work toward achieving the company's goals) is thus more likely using RI rather than ROI as a measure of the subunit manager's performance.

To see that this is a general result, observe that the post-upgrade ROI is a weighted average of the pre-upgrade ROI and the ROI of the project under consideration. Therefore, whenever a new project has a return higher than the required rate of return (12% in our example) but below the current ROI of the division (24% in our example), the division manager is tempted to reject it even though it is a project the shareholders would like to pursue.[2] On the other hand, RI is a measure that aggregates linearly. Therefore, the post-upgrade RI always equals the pre-upgrade RI plus the RI of the project under consideration (in the preceding example, the project's RI is $70,000 − 12% × $400,000 = $22,000, which is the difference between the post-upgrade and pre-upgrade RI amounts). As a result, a manager who is evaluated on residual income will choose a new project if and only if it has a positive RI. But this is exactly the criterion shareholders want the manager to employ; in other words, RI achieves goal congruence.

---

[2] Analogously, the manager of an underperforming division with an ROI of 7%, say, may wish to accept projects with returns between 7% and 12% even though these opportunities do not meet the shareholders' required rate of return.

Economic Value Added[3]

Economic value added is a specific type of RI calculation that is used by many companies. **Economic value added (EVA®)** equals after-tax operating income *minus* the (after-tax) weighted-average cost of capital *multiplied* by total assets minus current liabilities.

$$\text{Economic value added (EVA)} = \text{After-tax operating income} - \left[\text{Weighted-average cost of capital} \times \left(\text{Total assets} - \text{Current liabilities} \right) \right]$$

EVA substitutes the following numbers in the RI calculations: (1) income equal to after-tax operating income, (2) required rate of return equal to the (after-tax) weighted-average cost of capital, and (3) investment equal to total assets minus current liabilities.[4]

We use the Hospitality Inns data in Exhibit 23-1 to illustrate the basic EVA calculations. The weighted-average cost of capital (WACC) equals the *after-tax* average cost of all the long-term funds used by Hospitality Inns. The company has two sources of long-term funds: (a) long-term debt with a market value and book value of $4.5 million issued at an interest rate of 10%, and (b) equity capital that also has a market value of $4.5 million (but a book value of $1 million).[5] Because interest costs are tax-deductible and the income tax rate is 30%, the after-tax cost of debt financing is $0.10 \times (1 - \text{Tax rate}) = 0.10 \times (1 - 0.30) = 0.10 \times 0.70 = 0.07$, or 7%. The cost of equity capital is the opportunity cost to investors of not investing their capital in another investment that is similar in risk to Hospitality Inns. Hospitality Inns' cost of equity capital is 14%.[6] The WACC computation, which uses market values of debt and equity, is as follows:

$$\text{WACC} = \frac{(7\% \times \text{Market value of debt}) + (14\% \times \text{Market value of equity})}{\text{Market value of debt} + \text{Market value of equity}}$$

$$= \frac{(0.07 \times \$4,500,000) + (0.14 \times \$4,500,000)}{\$4,500,000 + \$4,500,000}$$

$$= \frac{\$945,000}{\$9,000,000} = 0.105, \text{ or } 10.5\%$$

The company applies the same WACC to all its hotels because each hotel faces similar risks.
Total assets minus current liabilities (see Exhibit 23-1) can also be computed as follows:

$$\text{Total assets} - \text{Current liabilities} = \text{Long-term assets} + \text{Current assets} - \text{Current liabilities}$$
$$= \text{Long-term assets} + \text{Working capital}$$

where

$$\text{Working capital} = \text{Current assets} - \text{Current liabilities}$$

After-tax hotel operating income is:

$$\text{Hotel operating income} \times (1 - \text{Tax rate}) = \text{Hotel operating income} \times (1 - 0.30) = \text{Hotel operating income} \times 0.70$$

---

[3] S. O'Byrne and D. Young, *EVA and Value-Based Management: A Practical Guide to Implementation* (New York: McGraw-Hill, 2000); J. Stein, J. Shiely, and I. Ross, *The EVA Challenge: Implementing Value Added Change in an Organization* (New York: John Wiley and Sons, 2001).

[4] When implementing EVA, companies make several adjustments to the operating income and asset numbers reported under generally accepted accounting principles (GAAP). For example, when calculating EVA, costs such as R&D, restructuring costs, and leases that have long-run benefits are recorded as assets (which are then amortized), rather than as current operating costs. The goal of these adjustments is to obtain a better representation of the economic assets, particularly intangible assets, used to earn income. Of course, the specific adjustments applicable to a company will depend on its individual circumstances.

[5] The market value of Hospitality Inns' equity exceeds book value because book value, based on historical cost, does not measure the current value of the company's assets and because various intangible assets, such as the company's brand name, are not shown at current value in the balance sheet under GAAP.

[6] In practice, the most common method of calculating the cost of equity capital is by applying the capital asset pricing model (CAPM). For details, see J. Berk and P. DeMarzo, *Corporate Finance*, 2nd ed. (Upper Saddle River, NJ: Prentice Hall, 2010).

EVA calculations for Hospitality Inns are as follows:

Hotel	After-Tax Operating Income	−	[WACC ×	(Total Assets − Current Liabilities)]	=	EVA
San Francisco	$240,000 × 0.70	−	[10.50% ×	($1,000,000 − $ 50,000)]	=	$68,250
Chicago	$300,000 × 0.70	−	[10.50% ×	($2,000,000 − $150,000)]	=	$15,750
New Orleans	$510,000 × 0.70	−	[10.50% ×	($3,000,000 − $300,000)]	=	$73,500

The New Orleans hotel has the highest EVA. Economic value added, like residual income, charges managers for the cost of their investments in long-term assets and working capital. Value is created only if after-tax operating income exceeds the cost of investing the capital. To improve EVA, managers can, for example, (a) earn more after-tax operating income with the same capital, (b) use less capital to earn the same after-tax operating income, or (c) invest capital in high-return projects.[7]

Managers in companies such as Briggs and Stratton, Coca-Cola, CSX, Equifax, and FMC use the estimated impact on EVA to guide their decisions. Division managers find EVA helpful because it allows them to incorporate the cost of capital, which is generally only available at the company-wide level, into decisions at the division level. Comparing the actual EVA achieved to the estimated EVA is useful for evaluating performance and providing feedback to managers about performance. CSX, a railroad company, credits EVA for decisions such as to run trains with three locomotives instead of four and to schedule arrivals just in time for unloading rather than having trains arrive at their destination several hours in advance. The result? Higher income because of lower fuel costs and lower capital investments in locomotives.

Return on Sales

The income-to-revenues ratio (or sales ratio), often called *return on sales (ROS)*, is a frequently used financial performance measure. As we have seen, ROS is one component of ROI in the DuPont method of profitability analysis. To calculate ROS for each of Hospitality's hotels, we divide operating income by revenues:

Hotel	Operating Income	÷	Revenues (Sales)	=	ROS
San Francisco	$240,000	÷	$1,200,000	=	20.0%
Chicago	$300,000	÷	$1,400,000	=	21.4%
New Orleans	$510,000	÷	$3,185,000	=	16.0%

The Chicago hotel has the highest ROS, but its performance is rated worse than the other hotels using measures such as ROI, RI, and EVA.

Comparing Performance Measures

The following table summarizes the performance of each hotel and ranks it (in parentheses) under each of the four performance measures:

Hotel	ROI	RI	EVA	ROS
San Francisco	24% (1)	$120,000 (2)	$68,250 (2)	20.0% (2)
Chicago	15% (3)	$ 60,000 (3)	$15,750 (3)	21.4% (1)
New Orleans	17% (2)	$150,000 (1)	$73,500 (1)	16.0% (3)

The RI and EVA rankings are the same. They differ from the ROI and ROS rankings. Consider the ROI and RI rankings for the San Francisco and New Orleans hotels. The New Orleans hotel has a smaller ROI. Although its operating income is only slightly more than

---

[7] Observe that the sum of the divisional after-tax operating incomes used in the EVA calculation, ($240,000 + $300,000 + $510,000) × 0.7 = $735,000, exceeds the firm's net income of $420,000. The difference is due to the firm's after-tax interest expense on its long-term debt, which amounts to $450,000 × 0.7 = $315,000. Because the EVA measure includes a charge for the weighted average cost of capital, which includes the after-tax cost of debt, the income figure used in computing EVA should reflect the after-tax profit before interest payments on debt are considered. After-tax operating income (often referred to in practice as NOPAT, or net operating profit after taxes) is thus the relevant measure of divisional profit for EVA calculations.

twice the operating income of the San Francisco hotel—$510,000 versus $240,000—its total assets are three times as large—$3 million versus $1 million. The New Orleans hotel has a higher RI because it earns a higher income after covering the required rate of return on investment of 12%. The high ROI of the San Francisco hotel indicates that its assets are being used efficiently. Even though each dollar invested in the New Orleans hotel does not give the same return as the San Francisco hotel, this large investment creates considerable value because its return exceeds the required rate of return. The Chicago hotel has the highest ROS but the lowest ROI. The high ROS indicates that the Chicago hotel has the lowest cost structure per dollar of revenues of all of Hospitality Inns' hotels. The reason for Chicago's low ROI is that it generates very low revenues per dollar of assets invested. Is any method better than the others for measuring performance? No, because each evaluates a different aspect of performance.

ROS measures how effectively costs are managed. To evaluate overall aggregate performance, ROI, RI, or EVA measures are more appropriate than ROS because they consider both income and investment. ROI indicates which investment yields the highest return. RI and EVA measures overcome some of the goal-congruence problems of ROI. Some managers favor EVA because of the accounting adjustments related to the capitalization of investments in intangibles. Other managers favor RI because it is easier to calculate and because, in most cases, it leads to the same conclusions as EVA. Generally, companies use multiple financial measures to evaluate performance.

Decision Point

What are the relative merits of return on investment (ROI), residual income (RI), and economic value added (EVA) as performance measures for subunit managers?

Choosing the Details of the Performance Measures

It is not sufficient for a company to identify the set of performance measures it wishes to use. The company has to make several choices regarding the specific details of how the measures are computed. These range from decisions regarding the time frame over which the measures are computed, to the definition of key terms such as "investment" and the calculation of particular components of each performance measure.

Alternative Time Horizons

An important element in designing accounting-based performance measures is choosing the time horizon of the performance measures. The ROI, RI, EVA, and ROS calculations represent the results for a single period, one year in our example. Managers could take actions that cause short-run increases in these measures but that conflict with the long-run interest of the company. For example, managers may curtail R&D and plant maintenance in the last three months of a fiscal year to achieve a target level of annual operating income. For this reason, many companies evaluate subunits on the basis of ROI, RI, EVA, and ROS over multiple years.

Another reason to evaluate subunits over multiple years is that the benefits of actions taken in the current period may not show up in short-run performance measures, such as the current year's ROI or RI. For example, an investment in a new hotel may adversely affect ROI and RI in the short run but benefit ROI and RI in the long run.

A multiyear analysis highlights another advantage of the RI measure: Net present value of all cash flows over the life of an investment equals net present value of the RIs.[8]

Learning Objective 3

Analyze the key measurement choices in the design of each performance measure

... choice of time horizon, alternative definitions, and measurement of assets

---

[8] This equivalence, often referred to as the "Conservation Property" of residual income, was originally articulated by Gabriel Preinreich in 1938. To see the equivalence, suppose the $400,000 investment in the San Francisco hotel increases operating income by $70,000 per year as follows: Increase in operating cash flows of $150,000 each year for 5 years minus depreciation of $80,000 ($400,000 ÷ 5) per year, assuming straight-line depreciation and $0 terminal disposal value. Depreciation reduces the investment amount by $80,000 each year. Assuming a required rate of return of 12%, net present values of cash flows and residual incomes are as follows:

Year		0	1	2	3	4	5	Net Present Value
(1)	Cash flow	−$400,000	$150,000	$150,000	$150,000	$150,000	$150,000	
(2)	Present value of $1 discounted at 12%	1	0.89286	0.79719	0.71178	0.63552	0.56743	
(3)	Present value: (1) × (2)	−$400,000	$133,929	$119,578	$106,767	$ 95,328	$ 85,114	$140,716
(4)	Operating income		$ 70,000	$ 70,000	$ 70,000	$ 70,000	$ 70,000	
(5)	Assets at start of year		$400,000	$320,000	$240,000	$160,000	$ 80,000	
(6)	Capital charge: (5) × 12%		$ 48,000	$ 38,400	$ 28,800	$ 19,200	$ 9,600	
(7)	Residual income: (4) − (6)		$ 22,000	$ 31,600	$ 41,200	$ 50,800	$ 60,400	
(8)	Present value of RI: (7) × (2)		$ 19,643	$ 25,191	$ 29,325	$ 32,284	$ 34,273	$140,716

This characteristic means that if managers use the net present value method to make investment decisions (as advocated in Chapter 21), then using multiyear RI to evaluate managers' performances achieves goal congruence.

Another way to motivate managers to take a long-run perspective is by compensating them on the basis of changes in the market price of the company's stock, because stock prices incorporate the expected future effects of current decisions.

Alternative Definitions of Investment

Companies use a variety of definitions for measuring investment in divisions. Four common alternative definitions used in the construction of accounting-based performance measures are as follows:

1. **Total assets available**—includes all assets, regardless of their intended purpose.
2. **Total assets employed**—total assets available minus the sum of idle assets and assets purchased for future expansion. For example, if the New Orleans hotel in Exhibit 23-1 has unused land set aside for potential expansion, total assets employed by the hotel would exclude the cost of that land.
3. **Total assets employed minus current liabilities**—total assets employed, excluding assets financed by short-term creditors. One negative feature of defining investment in this way is that it may encourage subunit managers to use an excessive amount of short-term debt because short-term debt reduces the amount of investment.
4. **Stockholders' equity**—calculated by assigning liabilities among subunits and deducting these amounts from the total assets of each subunit. One drawback of this method is that it combines operating decisions made by hotel managers with financing decisions made by top management.

Companies that use ROI or RI generally define investment as the total assets available. When top management directs a subunit manager to carry extra or idle assets, total assets employed can be more informative than total assets available. Companies that adopt EVA define investment as total assets employed minus current liabilities. The most common rationale for using total assets employed minus current liabilities is that the subunit manager often influences decisions on current liabilities of the subunit.

Alternative Asset Measurements

To design accounting-based performance measures, we must consider different ways to measure assets included in the investment calculations. Should assets be measured at historical cost or current cost? Should gross book value (that is, original cost) or net book value (original cost minus accumulated depreciation) be used for depreciable assets?

Current Cost

Current cost is the cost of purchasing an asset today identical to the one currently held, or the cost of purchasing an asset that provides services like the one currently held if an identical asset cannot be purchased. Of course, measuring assets at current costs will result in different ROIs than the ROIs calculated on the basis of historical costs.

We illustrate the current-cost ROI calculations using the data for Hospitality Inns (Exhibit 23-1) and then compare current-cost-based ROIs and historical-cost-based ROIs. Assume the following information about the long-term assets of each hotel:

	San Francisco	Chicago	New Orleans
Age of facility in years (at end of 2012)	8	4	2
Gross book value (original cost)	$1,400,000	$2,100,000	$2,730,000
Accumulated depreciation	$ 800,000	$ 600,000	$ 390,000
Net book value (at end of 2012)	$ 600,000	$1,500,000	$2,340,000
Depreciation for 2012	$ 100,000	$ 150,000	$ 195,000

Hospitality Inns assumes a 14-year estimated useful life, zero terminal disposal value for the physical facilities, and straight-line depreciation.

An index of construction costs indicating how the cost of construction has changed over the eight-year period that Hospitality Inns has been operating (2004 year-end = 100) is as follows:

Year	2005	2006	2007	2008	2009	2010	2011	2012
Construction cost index	110	122	136	144	152	160	174	180

Earlier in this chapter, we computed an ROI of 24% for San Francisco, 15% for Chicago, and 17% for New Orleans (p. 831). One possible explanation of the high ROI for the San Francisco hotel is that its long-term assets are expressed in 2004 construction-price levels—prices that prevailed eight years ago—and the long-term assets for the Chicago and New Orleans hotels are expressed in terms of higher, more-recent construction-price levels, which depress ROIs for these two hotels.

Exhibit 23-2 illustrates a step-by-step approach for incorporating current-cost estimates of long-term assets and depreciation expense into the ROI calculation. We make these calculations to approximate what it would cost today to obtain assets that would produce the same expected operating income that the subunits currently earn. (Similar adjustments to represent the current costs of capital employed and depreciation expense can also be made in the RI and EVA calculations.) The current-cost adjustment reduces the ROI of the San Francisco hotel by more than half.

	Historical-Cost ROI	Current-Cost ROI
San Francisco	24%	10.8%
Chicago	15%	11.1%
New Orleans	17%	14.7%

Adjusting assets to recognize current costs negates differences in the investment base caused solely by differences in construction-price levels. Compared with historical-cost ROI, current-cost ROI better measures the current economic returns from the investment. If Hospitality Inns were to invest in a new hotel today, investing in one like the New Orleans hotel offers the best ROI.

Current cost estimates may be difficult to obtain for some assets. Why? Because the estimate requires a company to consider, in addition to increases in price levels, technological advances and processes that could reduce the current cost of assets needed to earn today's operating income.

Long-Term Assets: Gross or Net Book Value?

Historical cost of assets is often used to calculate ROI. There has been much discussion about whether gross book value or net book value of assets should be used. Using the data in Exhibit 23-1 (p. 831), we calculate ROI using net and gross book values of plant and equipment as follows:

	Operating Income (from Exhibit 23-1) (1)	Net Book Value of Total Assets (from Exhibit 23-1) (2)	Accumulated Depreciation (from p. 837) (3)	Gross Book Value of Total Assets (4) = (2) + (3)	2012 ROI Using Net Book Value of Total Assets (calculated earlier) (5) = (1) ÷ (2)	2012 ROI Using Gross Book Value of Total Assets (6) = (1) ÷ (4)
San Francisco	$240,000	$1,000,000	$800,000	$1,800,000	24%	13.3%
Chicago	$300,000	$2,000,000	$600,000	$2,600,000	15%	11.5%
New Orleans	$510,000	$3,000,000	$390,000	$3,390,000	17%	15.0%

Using gross book value, the 13.3% ROI of the older San Francisco hotel is lower than the 15.0% ROI of the newer New Orleans hotel. Those who favor using gross book value claim it enables more accurate comparisons of ROI across subunits. For example, using

Performance Measurement, Compensation, and Multinational Considerations   125

Exhibit 23-2 ROI for Hospitality Inns: Computed Using Current-Cost Estimates as of the End of 2012 for Depreciation Expense and Long-Term Assets

	A	B	C	D	E	F	G	H
1	Step 1: Restate long-term assets from gross book value at historical cost to gross book value at current cost as of the end of 2012.							
2		Gross book value of long-term assets at historical cost	×	Construction cost index in 2012	÷	Construction cost index in year of construction	=	Gross book value of long-term assets at current cost at end of 2012
3	San Francisco	$1,400,000	×	(180	÷	100)	=	$2,520,000
4	Chicago	$2,100,000	×	(180	÷	144)	=	$2,625,000
5	New Orleans	$2,730,000	×	(180	÷	160)	=	$3,071,250
6								
7	Step 2: Derive net book value of long-term assets at current cost as of the end of 2012. (Assume estimated useful life of each hotel is 14 years.)							
8		Gross book value of long-term assets at current cost at end of 2012	×	Estimated remaining useful life	÷	Estimated total useful life	=	Net book value of long-term assets at current cost at end of 2012
9	San Francisco	$2,520,000	×	(6	÷	14)	=	$1,080,000
10	Chicago	$2,625,000	×	(10	÷	14)	=	$1,875,000
11	New Orleans	$3,071,250	×	(12	÷	14)	=	$2,632,500
12								
13	Step 3: Compute current cost of total assets in 2012. (Assume current assets of each hotel are expressed in 2012 dollars.)							
14		Current assets at end of 2012 (from Exhibit 23-1)	+	Long-term assets from Step 2	=	Current cost of total assets at end of 2012		
15	San Francisco	$400,000	+	$1,080,000	=	$1,480,000		
16	Chicago	$500,000	+	$1,875,000	=	$2,375,000		
17	New Orleans	$660,000	+	$2,632,500	=	$3,292,500		
18								
19	Step 4: Compute current-cost depreciation expense in 2012 dollars.							
20		Gross book value of long-term assets at current cost at end of 2012 (from Step 1)	÷	Estimated total useful life	=	Current-cost depreciation expense in 2012 dollars		
21	San Francisco	$2,520,000	÷	14	=	$180,000		
22	Chicago	$2,625,000	÷	14	=	$187,500		
23	New Orleans	$3,071,250	÷	14	=	$219,375		
24								
25	Step 5: Compute 2012 operating income using 2012 current-cost depreciation expense.							
26		Historical-cost operating income	−	Current-cost depreciation expense in 2012 dollars (from Step 4)	−	Historical-cost depreciation expense	=	Operating income for 2012 using current-cost depreciation expense in 2012 dollars
27	San Francisco	$240,000	−	($180,000	−	$100,000)	=	$160,000
28	Chicago	$300,000	−	($187,500	−	$150,000)	=	$262,500
29	New Orleans	$510,000	−	($219,375	−	$195,000)	=	$485,625
30								
31	Step 6: Compute ROI using current-cost estimates for long-term assets and depreciation expense.							
32		Operating income for 2012 using current-cost depreciation expense in 2012 dollars (from Step 5)	÷	Current cost of total assets at end of 2012 (from Step 3)	=	ROI using current-cost estimate		
33	San Francisco	$160,000	÷	$1,480,000	=	10.8%		
34	Chicago	$262,500	÷	$2,375,000	=	11.1%		
35	New Orleans	$485,625	÷	$3,292,500	=	14.7%		

Decision Point

Over what time frame should companies measure performance, and what are the alternative choices for calculating the components of each performance measure?

gross-book-value calculations, the return on the original plant-and-equipment investment is higher for the newer New Orleans hotel than for the older San Francisco hotel. This difference probably reflects the decline in earning power of the San Francisco hotel. Using the net book value masks this decline in earning power because the constantly decreasing investment base results in a higher ROI for the San Francisco hotel—24% in this example. This higher rate may mislead decision makers into thinking that the earning power of the San Francisco hotel has not decreased.

The proponents of using net book value as an investment base maintain that it is less confusing because (1) it is consistent with the amount of total assets shown in the conventional balance sheet, and (2) it is consistent with income computations that include deductions for depreciation expense. Surveys report net book value to be the dominant measure of assets used by companies for internal performance evaluation.

Target Levels of Performance and Feedback

Now that we have covered the different types of measures and how to choose them, let us turn our attention to how mangers set and measure target levels of performance.

Learning Objective 4

Study the choice of performance targets and design of feedback mechanisms

. . . carefully crafted budgets and sufficient feedback for timely corrective action

Choosing Target Levels of Performance

We next consider target-setting for accounting-based measures of performance against which actual performance can be compared. Historical-cost-based accounting measures are usually inadequate for evaluating economic returns on new investments, and in some cases, they create disincentives for expansion. Despite these problems, historical-cost ROIs can be used to evaluate current performance by establishing *target* ROIs. For Hospitality Inns, we need to recognize that the hotels were built in different years, which means they were built at different construction-price levels. Top management could adjust the target historical-cost-based ROIs accordingly, say, by setting San Francisco's ROI at 26%, Chicago's at 18%, and New Orleans' at 19%.

This useful alternative of comparing actual results with target or budgeted performance is frequently overlooked. The budget should be carefully negotiated with full knowledge of historical-cost accounting pitfalls. *Companies should tailor a budget to a particular subunit, a particular accounting system, and a particular performance measure.* For example, many problems of asset valuation and income measurement can be resolved if top management can get subunit managers to focus on what is attainable in the forthcoming budget period—whether ROI, RI, or EVA is used and whether the financial measures are based on historical cost or some other measure, such as current cost.

A popular way to establish targets is to set continuous improvement targets. If a company is using EVA as a performance measure, top management can evaluate operations on year-to-year changes in EVA, rather than on absolute measures of EVA. Evaluating performance on the basis of *improvements* in EVA makes the initial method of calculating EVA less important.

In establishing targets for financial performance measures, companies using the balanced scorecard simultaneously determine targets in the customer, internal-business-process, and learning-and-growth perspectives. For example, Hospitality Inns will establish targets for employee training and employee satisfaction, customer-service time for reservations and check-in, quality of room service, and customer satisfaction that each hotel must reach to achieve its ROI and EVA targets.

Choosing the Timing of Feedback

A final critical step in designing accounting-based performance measures is the timing of feedback. Timing of feedback depends largely on (a) how critical the information is for the success of the organization, (b) the specific level of management receiving the feedback, and (c) the sophistication of the organization's information technology. For example, hotel managers responsible for room sales want information on the number of rooms sold (rented) on a daily or weekly basis, because a large percentage of hotel costs are fixed costs. Achieving high room sales and taking quick action to reverse any declining sales trends are critical to the financial success of each hotel. Supplying managers with daily information about room sales is much easier if Hospitality Inns has a computerized room-reservation and check-in system. Top management, however, may look at information about daily room sales only on a monthly basis. In some instances, for example, because of concern about the low sales-to-total-assets ratio of the Chicago hotel, management may want the information weekly.

The timing of feedback for measures in the balanced scorecard varies. For example, human resources managers at each hotel measure employee satisfaction annually because satisfaction is best measured over a longer horizon. However, housekeeping department managers measure the quality of room service over much shorter time horizons, such as a week, because poor levels of performance in these areas for even a short period of time can harm a hotel's reputation for a long period. Moreover, housekeeping problems can be detected and resolved over a short time period.

> **Decision Point**
>
> What targets should companies use and when should they give feedback to managers regarding their performance relative to these targets?

Performance Measurement in Multinational Companies

Our discussion so far has focused on performance evaluation of different divisions of a company operating within a single country. We next discuss the additional difficulties created when the performance of divisions of a company operating in different countries is compared. Several issues arise.[9]

- The economic, legal, political, social, and cultural environments differ significantly across countries.
- Governments in some countries may limit selling prices of, and impose controls on, a company's products. For example, some countries in Asia, Latin America, and Eastern Europe impose tariffs and custom duties to restrict imports of certain goods.
- Availability of materials and skilled labor, as well as costs of materials, labor, and infrastructure (power, transportation, and communication), may also differ significantly across countries.
- Divisions operating in different countries account for their performance in different currencies. Issues of inflation and fluctuations in foreign-currency exchange rates affect performance measures.

As a result of these differences, adjustments need to be made to compare performance measures across countries.

> **Learning Objective 5**
>
> Indicate the difficulties that occur when the performance of divisions operating in different countries is compared
>
> ... adjustments needed for differences in inflation rates and changes in exchange rates

Calculating the Foreign Division's ROI in the Foreign Currency

Suppose Hospitality Inns invests in a hotel in Mexico City. The investment consists mainly of the costs of buildings and furnishings. Also assume the following:

- The exchange rate at the time of Hospitality's investment on December 31, 2011, is 10 pesos = $1.
- During 2012, the Mexican peso suffers a steady decline in its value. The exchange rate on December 31, 2012, is 15 pesos = $1.
- The average exchange rate during 2012 is [(10 + 15) ÷ 2] = 12.5 pesos = $1.
- The investment (total assets) in the Mexico City hotel is 30,000,000 pesos.
- The operating income of the Mexico City hotel in 2012 is 6,000,000 pesos.

What is the historical-cost-based ROI for the Mexico City hotel in 2012?

To answer this question, Hospitality Inns' managers first have to determine if they should calculate the ROI in pesos or in dollars. If they calculate the ROI in dollars, what exchange rate should they use? The managers may also be interested in how the

---
[9] See M. Z. Iqbal, *International Accounting—A Global Perspective* (Cincinnati: South-Western College Publishing, 2002).

ROI of Hospitality Inns Mexico City (HIMC) compares with the ROI of Hospitality Inns New Orleans (HINO), which is also a relatively new hotel of approximately the same size. The answers to these questions yield information that will be helpful when making future investment decisions.

$$\text{HIMC's } ROI \text{ (calculated using pesos)} = \frac{\text{Operating income}}{\text{Total assets}} = \frac{6{,}000{,}000 \text{ pesos}}{30{,}000{,}000 \text{ pesos}} = 0.20, \text{ or } 20\%$$

HIMC's ROI of 20% is higher than HINO's ROI of 17% (p. 831). Does this mean that HIMC outperformed HINO based on the ROI criterion? Not necessarily. That's because HIMC operates in a very different economic environment than HINO.

The peso has declined in value relative to the dollar in 2012. This decline has led to higher inflation in Mexico than in the United States. As a result of the higher inflation in Mexico, HIMC will charge higher prices for its hotel rooms, which will increase HIMC's operating income and lead to a higher ROI. Inflation clouds the real economic returns on an asset and makes historical-cost-based ROI higher. Differences in inflation rates between the two countries make a direct comparison of HIMC's peso-denominated ROI with HINO's dollar-denominated ROI misleading.

Calculating the Foreign Division's ROI in U.S. Dollars

One way to make a comparison of historical-cost-based ROIs more meaningful is to restate HIMC's performance in U.S. dollars. But what exchange rate should be used to make the comparison meaningful? Assume operating income was earned evenly throughout 2012. Hospitality Inns' managers should use the average exchange rate of 12.5 pesos = $1 to convert operating income from pesos to dollars: 6,000,000 pesos ÷ 12.5 pesos per dollar = $480,000. The effect of dividing the operating income in pesos by the higher pesos-to-dollar exchange rate prevailing during 2012, rather than the 10 pesos = $1 exchange rate prevailing on December 31, 2011, is that any increase in operating income in pesos as a result of inflation during 2012 is eliminated when converting back to dollars.

At what rate should HIMC's total assets of 30,000,000 pesos be converted? The 10 pesos = $1 exchange rate prevailing when the assets were acquired on December 31, 2011, because HIMC's assets are recorded in pesos at the December 31, 2011, cost, and they are not revalued as a result of inflation in Mexico in 2012. Because the cost of assets in HIMC's financial accounting records is unaffected by subsequent inflation, the exchange rate prevailing when the assets were acquired should be used to convert the assets into dollars. Using exchange rates after December 31, 2011, would be incorrect because these exchange rates incorporate the higher inflation in Mexico in 2012. Total assets are converted to 30,000,000 pesos ÷ 10 pesos per dollar = $3,000,000.

Then,

$$\text{HIMC's } ROI \text{ (calculated using dollars)} = \frac{\text{Operating income}}{\text{Total assets}} = \frac{\$480{,}000}{\$3{,}000{,}000} = 0.16, \text{ or } 16\%$$

As we have discussed, these adjustments make the historical-cost-based ROIs of the Mexico City and New Orleans hotels comparable because they negate the effects of any differences in inflation rates between the two countries. HIMC's ROI of 16% is less than HINO's ROI of 17%.

Residual income calculated in pesos suffers from the same problems as ROI calculated using pesos. Calculating HIMC's RI in dollars adjusts for changes in exchange rates and makes for more-meaningful comparisons with Hospitality's other hotels:

$$\text{HIMC's } RI = \$480{,}000 - (0.12 \times \$3{,}000{,}000)$$
$$= \$480{,}000 - \$360{,}000 = \$120{,}000$$

How can companies compare the performance of divisions operating in different countries?

which is also less than HINO's RI of $150,000. In interpreting HIMC's and HINO's ROI and RI, keep in mind that they are historical-cost-based calculations. They do, however, pertain to relatively new hotels.

Distinction Between Managers and Organization Units[10]

Our focus has been on how to evaluate the performance of a subunit of a company, such as a division. However, is evaluating the performance of a subunit manager the same as evaluating the performance of the subunit? If the subunit performed well, does it mean the manager performed well? In this section, we argue that the performance evaluation of a *manager* should be distinguished from the performance evaluation of that manager's *subunit*. For example, companies often put the most skillful division manager in charge of the division producing the poorest economic return in an attempt to improve it. The division may take years to show improvement. Furthermore, the manager's efforts may result merely in bringing the division up to a minimum acceptable ROI. The division may continue to be a poor performer in comparison with other divisions, but it would be a mistake to conclude from the poor performance of the division that the manager is performing poorly. The division's performance may be adversely affected by economic conditions over which the manager has no control.

As another example, consider again the Hospitality Inns Mexico City (HIMC) hotel. Suppose, despite the high inflation in Mexico, HIMC could not increase room prices because of price-control regulations imposed by the government. HIMC's performance in dollar terms would be very poor because of the decline in the value of the peso. But should top management conclude from HIMC's poor performance that the HIMC manager performed poorly? Probably not. Most likely, the poor performance of HIMC is largely the result of regulatory factors beyond the manager's control.

In the following sections, we show the basic principles for evaluating the performance of an individual subunit manager. These principles apply to managers at all organization levels. Later sections consider examples at the individual-worker level and the top-management level. We illustrate these principles using the RI performance measure.

> **Learning Objective 6**
>
> Understand the roles of salaries and incentives when rewarding managers
>
> ... balancing risk and performance-based rewards

The Basic Trade-Off: Creating Incentives Versus Imposing Risk

How the performance of managers and other employees is measured and evaluated affects their rewards. Compensation arrangements range from a flat salary with no direct performance-based incentive (or bonus), as in the case of many government employees, to rewards based on only performance, as in the case of real estate agents who are compensated only via commissions paid on the properties they sell. Most managers' total compensation includes some combination of salary and performance-based incentive. In designing compensation arrangements, we need to consider the *trade-off between creating incentives and imposing risk*. We illustrate this trade-off in the context of our Hospitality Inns example.

Sally Fonda owns the Hospitality Inns chain of hotels. Roger Brett manages the Hospitality Inns San Francisco (HISF) hotel. Assume Fonda uses RI to measure performance. To improve RI, Fonda would like Brett to increase sales, control costs, provide prompt and courteous customer service, and reduce working capital. But even if Brett did all those things, high RI is not guaranteed. HISF's RI is affected by many factors beyond Fonda's and Brett's control, such as a recession in the San Francisco economy, an earthquake that might negatively affect HISF, or even road construction near competing hotels which would drive customers to HISF. Uncontrollable factors make HISF's profitability uncertain and, therefore, risky.

As an entrepreneur, Fonda expects to bear risk. But Brett does not like being subject to risk. One way of "insuring" Brett against risk is to pay Brett a flat salary, regardless of the actual amount of RI earned. All the risk would then be borne by Fonda. This arrangement creates a problem, however, because Brett's effort is difficult to monitor. The absence of performance-based compensation means that Brett has no direct incentive to work harder or to undertake extra physical and mental effort beyond what is necessary to retain his job or to uphold his own personal values.

---

[10] The presentations here draw (in part) from teaching notes prepared by S. Huddart, N. Melumad, and S. Reichelstein.

Moral hazard describes a situation in which an employee prefers to exert less effort (or to report distorted information) compared with the effort (or accurate information) desired by the owner, because the employee's effort (or validity of the reported information) cannot be accurately monitored and enforced.[11] In some repetitive jobs, such as in electronic assembly, a supervisor can monitor the workers' actions, and the moral-hazard problem may not arise. However, a manager's job is to gather and interpret information and to exercise judgment on the basis of the information obtained. Monitoring a manager's effort is more difficult.

Paying no salary and rewarding Brett *only* on the basis of some performance measure—RI in our example—raises different concerns. In this case, Brett would be motivated to strive to increase RI because his rewards would increase with increases in RI. But compensating Brett on RI also subjects him to risk, because HISF's RI depends not only on Brett's effort, but also on factors such as local economic conditions over which Brett has no control.

Brett does not like being subject to risk. To compensate Brett for taking risk, Fonda must pay him extra compensation. That is, using performance-based bonuses will cost Fonda more money, *on average*, than paying Brett a flat salary. Why "on average"? Because Fonda's compensation payment to Brett will vary with RI outcomes. When averaged over these outcomes, the RI-based compensation will cost Fonda more than paying Brett a flat salary. The motivation for having some salary and some performance-based bonus in compensation arrangements is to balance the benefit of incentives against the extra cost of imposing risk on the manager.

Intensity of Incentives and Financial and Nonfinancial Measurements

What affects the intensity of incentives? That is, how large should the incentive component of a manager's compensation be relative to the salary component? To answer these questions, we need to understand how much the performance measure is affected by actions the manager takes to further the owner's objectives.

Preferred performance measures are those that are sensitive to or that change significantly with the manager's performance. They do not change much with changes in factors that are beyond the manager's control. Sensitive performance measures motivate the manager as well as limit the manager's exposure to risk, reducing the cost of providing incentives. Less-sensitive performance measures are not affected by the manager's performance and fail to induce the manager to improve. The more that owners have sensitive performance measures available to them, the more they can rely on incentive compensation for their managers.

The salary component of compensation dominates when performance measures that are sensitive to managers' actions are not available. This is the case, for example, for some corporate staff and government employees. A high salary component, however, does not mean incentives are completely absent. Promotions and salary increases do depend on some overall measure of performance, but the incentives are less direct. The incentive component of compensation is high when sensitive performance measures are available and when monitoring the employee's effort is difficult, such as in real estate agencies.

In evaluating Brett, Fonda uses measures from multiple perspectives of the balanced scorecard because nonfinancial measures on the balanced scorecard—employee satisfaction and the time taken for check-in, cleaning rooms, and providing room service—are more sensitive to Brett's actions. Financial measures such as RI are less sensitive to Brett's actions because they are affected by external factors such as local economic conditions beyond Brett's control. Residual income may be a very good measure of the economic viability of the hotel, but it is only a partial measure of Brett's performance.

Another reason for using nonfinancial measures in the balanced scorecard is that these measures follow Hospitality Inns' strategy and are drivers of future performance. Evaluating managers on these nonfinancial measures motivates them to take actions that will sustain long-run performance. Therefore, evaluating performance in all four perspectives of the balanced scorecard promotes both short- and long-run actions.

---

[11] The term *moral hazard* originated in insurance contracts to represent situations in which insurance coverage caused insured parties to take less care of their properties than they might otherwise. One response to moral hazard in insurance contracts is the system of deductibles (that is, the insured parties pay for damages below a specified amount).

Benchmarks and Relative Performance Evaluation

Owners often use financial and nonfinancial benchmarks to evaluate performance. Benchmarks representing "best practice" may be available inside or outside an organization. For HISF, benchmarks could be from similar hotels, either within or outside the Hospitality Inns chain. Suppose Brett has responsibility for revenues, costs, and investments. In evaluating Brett's performance, Fonda would want to use as a benchmark a hotel of a similar size influenced by the same uncontrollable factors, such as location, demographic trends, or economic conditions, that affect HISF. If all these factors were the same, *differences* in performances of the two hotels would occur only because of differences in the two managers' performances. Benchmarking, which is also called *relative performance evaluation*, filters out the effects of the common uncontrollable factors.

Can the performance of two managers responsible for running similar operations within a company be benchmarked against each other? Yes, but this approach could create a problem: The use of these benchmarks may reduce incentives for these managers to help one another, because a manager's performance-evaluation measure improves either by doing a better job or as a result of the other manager doing poorly. When managers do not cooperate, the company suffers. In this case, using internal benchmarks for performance evaluation may not lead to goal congruence.

Performance Measures at the Individual Activity Level

There are two issues when evaluating performance at the individual-activity level:

1. Designing performance measures for activities that require multiple tasks
2. Designing performance measures for activities done in teams

Performing Multiple Tasks

Most employees perform more than one task as part of their jobs. Marketing representatives sell products, provide customer support, and gather market information. Manufacturing workers are responsible for both the quantity and quality of their output. Employers want employees to allocate their time and effort intelligently among various tasks or aspects of their jobs.

Consider mechanics at an auto repair shop. Their jobs have two distinct aspects: repair work—performing more repair work generates more revenues for the shop—and customer satisfaction—the higher the quality of the job, the more likely the customer will be pleased. If the employer wants an employee to focus on both aspects, then the employer must measure and compensate performance on both aspects.

Suppose that the employer can easily measure the quantity, but not the quality, of auto repairs. If the employer rewards workers on a by-the-job rate, which pays workers only on the basis of the number of repairs actually performed, mechanics will likely increase the number of repairs they make and quality will likely suffer. Sears experienced this problem when it introduced by-the-job rates for its mechanics. To resolve the problem, Sears' managers took three steps to motivate workers to balance both quantity and quality: (1) They dropped the by-the-job rate system and paid mechanics an hourly salary, a step that deemphasized the quantity of repairs. Management determined mechanics' bonuses, promotions, and pay increases on the basis of an assessment of each mechanic's overall performance regarding quantity and quality of repairs. (2) Sears evaluated employees, in part, using data such as customer-satisfaction surveys, the number of dissatisfied customers, and the number of customer complaints. (3) Finally, Sears used staff from an independent outside agency to randomly monitor whether the repairs performed were of high quality.

Team-Based Compensation Arrangements

Many manufacturing, marketing, and design problems can be resolved when employees with multiple skills, knowledge, experiences, and perceptions pool their talents. A team achieves better results than individual employees acting alone.[12] Companies reward

---
[12] *Teams That Click: The Results-Driven Manager Series* (Boston: Harvard Business School Press, 2004).

individuals on a team based on team performance. Such team-based incentives encourage individuals to help one another as they strive toward a common goal.

The specific forms of team-based compensation vary across companies. Colgate-Palmolive rewards teams on the basis of each team's performance. Novartis, the Swiss pharmaceutical company, rewards teams on company-wide performance; a certain amount of team-based bonuses are paid only if the company reaches certain goals. To encourage the development of team skills, Eastman Chemical Company rewards team members using a checklist of team skills, such as communication and willingness to help one another. Whether team-based compensation is desirable depends, to a large extent, on the culture and management style of a particular organization. For example, one criticism of team-based compensation, especially in the United States, is that incentives for individual employees to excel are diminished, harming overall performance. Another problem is how to manage team members who are not productive contributors to the team's success but who, nevertheless, share in the team's rewards.

Executive Performance Measures and Compensation

The principles of performance evaluation described in the previous sections also apply to executive compensation plans. These plans are based on both financial and nonfinancial performance measures and consist of a mix of (1) base salary; (2) annual incentives, such as a cash bonus based on achieving a target annual RI; (3) long-run incentives, such as stock options (described later in this section) based on stock performance over, say, a five-year period; and (4) other benefits, such as medical benefits, pensions plans, and life insurance.

Well-designed plans use a compensation mix that balances risk (the effect of uncontrollable factors on the performance measure and hence compensation) with short-run and long-run incentives to achieve the organization's goals. For example, evaluating performance on the basis of annual EVA sharpens an executive's short-run focus. And using EVA and stock option plans over, say, five years motivates the executive to take a long-run view as well.

Stock options give executives the right to buy company stock at a specified price (called the exercise price) within a specified period. Suppose that on September 16, 2011, Hospitality Inns gave its CEO the option to buy 200,000 shares of the company's stock at any time before June 30, 2019, at the September 16, 2011, market price of $49 per share. Let's say Hospitality Inns' stock price rises to $69 per share on March 24, 2017, and the CEO exercises his options on all 200,000 shares. The CEO would earn $20 ($69 − $49) per share on 200,000 shares, or $4 million. If Hospitality Inns' stock price stays below $49 during the entire period, the CEO will simply forgo his right to buy the shares. By linking CEO compensation to increases in the company's stock price, the stock option plan motivates the CEO to improve the company's long-run performance and stock price. (See also the Concepts in Action feature, p. 847.)[13]

The Securities and Exchange Commission (SEC) requires detailed disclosures of the compensation arrangements of top-level executives. In complying with these rules in 2010, Starwood Hotels and Resorts, for example, disclosed a compensation table showing the salaries, bonuses, stock options, other stock awards, and other compensation earned by its top five executives during the 2007, 2008, and 2009 fiscal years. Starwood, whose brands include Sheraton, Westin, and the W Hotels, also disclosed the peer companies that it uses to set executive pay and conduct performance comparisons. These include competitors in the hotel and hospitality industry (such as Host, Marriott, and Wyndham), as well as companies with similar revenues in other industries relevant to key talent recruitment needs (including Colgate-Palmolive, Nike, and Starbucks). Investors use this information to evaluate the relationship between compensation and performance across companies generally, and across companies operating in similar industries.

---

[13] Although stock options can improve incentives by linking CEO pay to improvements in stock price, they have been criticized for promoting improper or illegal activities by CEOs to increase the options' value. See J. Fox, "Sleazy CEOs Have Even More Options Tricks," www.money.cnn.com/2006/11/13/magazines/fortune/options_scandals.fortune/index.htm (accessed September 5, 2007).

Concepts in Action: Government Bailouts, Record Profits, and the 2009 Wall Street Compensation Dilemma

Wall Street firms paid out near-record bonuses to their employees for 2009 and many in the public were furious, given Wall Street's role in triggering the recent economic crisis. After losing $42.8 billion in 2008 and requiring a government bailout, Wall Street firms recorded $55 billion in 2009 profits, a sum nearly three times greater than the previous record. These results begged a serious question for managers at Goldman Sachs, Morgan Stanley, JPMorgan Chase, and leading financial institutions: After requiring public support just a year earlier, just how big should bankers' paydays be?

Highly paid executives on Wall Street are virtually always investment bankers or the top executives of the firms that employ them. Wall Street firms traditionally paid their investment bankers a share of the total revenue garnered by their unit. While this system worked in previous years, many argued it led to bankers taking the excessive risks that pushed the U.S. financial system to the brink of collapse.

Moreover, 2008 Wall Street bonuses infuriated the public. Just months after government intervention totaling $700 billion, the largest Wall Street banks paid out $56.9 billion in bonuses, or 45.4% of their 2008 revenues. As a result, President Barack Obama laid out strict new regulations on compensation for the 100 highest-paid employees at firms that the government deemed "exceptional assistance recipients" (i.e., firms receiving the largest bailouts). Further, there is little question that without the government intervening to save the financial sector in late 2008, the investment banks would have had a much worse year in 2009. This created a difficult situation for the banks. As one observer noted, "It is fair to say that some of the pay schemes promoted bad behavior and led to excessive risk, but you still need some sort of short-term incentive" for good performance, which Wall Street produced in 2009.

Wall Street firms tried to find some middle ground in 2009 by reducing bonus pools, or the amount of revenues allocated to bonuses, and introducing more long-term compensation into the bonus mix. At Goldman Sachs, for example, top executives received no cash bonuses in 2009, and instead received shares in the company that must be held for five years. For investment bankers and other employees, the company reduced its bonus pool to 36% of company revenue (down from 44% in 2008) and increased the stock-to-cash compensation ratio. Despite these changes, the average Wall Street bonus jumped 25% in 2009 to $123,850. At Goldman Sachs, where profits hit an all-time high, employees made an average of $500,000 each in 2009, including salary and bonus.

While many observers lauded the movement towards having a higher-percentage of bonuses be deferred, the size of 2009 Wall Street bonuses outraged others and ensured that investment banker compensation will remain a hot-button issue on Wall Street, Main Street, and in Washington, DC, for many years to come.

Source: Corkery, Michael. 2009. Goldman bows to pressure, makes changes to compensation. *Wall Street Journal* "Deal Journal," blog December 10; Elliott, Douglas J. 2010. *Wall Street Pay: A Primer.* Washington, DC: The Brookings Institution; Gandel, Stephen. 2009. Wall Street, meet Ken Feinberg, the pay czar. *Time*, November 2; Phillips, Matt. 2010. Goldman: Employees don't mind record low pay ratios. *Wall Street Journal.* "MarketBeat," blog February 3; Shell, Adam. 2010. Despite recession, average Wall Street bonus leaps 25%. *USA*, February 24; *Wall Street Journal.* 2010. The easy guide to Wall Street pay and bonuses. January 20; Weisman, Jonathan and Joanna S. Lublin. 2009. Obama lays out limits on executive pay. *Wall Street Journal*, February 5.

The SEC rules also require companies to disclose the principles underlying their executive compensation plans and the performance criteria—such as profitability, revenue growth, and market share—used in determining compensation. In its financial statements, Starwood described some of these principles as promoting the company's competitive position, providing a balanced approach to incentivizing and retaining employees, and aligning senior management's interests with those of shareholders. Starwood uses earnings per share and EBITDA as performance criteria to determine annual incentives for all of its executives. In addition, each executive has an individual scorecard of financial and nonfinancial performance measures. The company's board of directors creates the overall strategic direction of the company. Individual and strategic goals for executives are then established to support the overall company goals but are tailored to each executive's area of control.

Decision Point

Why are managers compensated based on a mix of salary and incentives?

> **Learning Objective 7**
>
> Describe the four levers of control and why they are necessary
>
> ...boundary, belief, and interactive control systems counterbalance diagnostic control systems

Strategy and Levers of Control[14]

Given the management accounting focus of this book, this chapter has emphasized the role of quantitative financial and nonfinancial performance-evaluation measures that companies use to implement their strategies. These measures, such as ROI, RI, EVA, customer satisfaction, and employee satisfaction, monitor critical performance variables that help managers track progress toward achieving a company's strategic goals. Because these measures help diagnose whether a company is performing to expectations, they are collectively called **diagnostic control systems**. Companies motivate managers to achieve goals by holding them accountable for and by rewarding them for meeting these goals. The concern, however, is that the pressure to perform may cause managers to cut corners and misreport numbers to make their performance look better than it is, as happened at companies such as Enron, WorldCom, Tyco, and Health South. To prevent unethical and outright fraudulent behavior, companies need to balance the push for performance resulting from diagnostic control systems, the first of four levers of control, with three other levers: *boundary systems*, *belief systems*, and *interactive control systems*.

Boundary Systems

Boundary systems describe standards of behavior and codes of conduct expected of all employees, especially actions that are off-limits. Ethical behavior on the part of managers is paramount. In particular, numbers that subunit managers report should not be tainted by "cooking the books." They should be free of, for example, overstated assets, understated liabilities, fictitious revenues, and understated costs.

Codes of business conduct signal appropriate and inappropriate individual behaviors. The following are excerpts from Caterpillar's "Worldwide Code of Conduct":

> *While we conduct our business within the framework of applicable laws and regulations, for us, mere compliance with the law is not enough. We strive for more than that. . . . We must not engage in activities that create, or even appear to create, conflict between our personal interests and the interests of the company.*

Division managers often cite enormous pressure from top management "to make the budget" as excuses or rationalizations for not adhering to legal or ethical accounting policies and procedures. A healthy amount of motivational pressure is desirable, as long as the "tone from the top" and the code of conduct simultaneously communicate the absolute need for all managers to behave ethically at all times. Managers should train employees to behave ethically. They should promptly and severely reprimand unethical conduct, regardless of the benefits that might accrue to the company from unethical actions. Some companies, such as Lockheed-Martin, emphasize ethical behavior by routinely evaluating employees against a business code of ethics.

Many organizations also set explicit boundaries precluding actions that harm the environment. Environmental violations (such as water and air pollution) carry heavy fines and prison terms under the laws of the United States and other countries. But in many companies, environmental responsibilities extend beyond legal requirements.

Socially responsible companies set aggressive environmental goals and measure and report their performance against them. German, Swiss, Dutch, and Scandinavian companies report on environmental performance as part of a larger set of social responsibility disclosures (such as employee welfare and community development activities). Some companies, such as DuPont, make environmental performance a line item on every employee's salary appraisal report. Duke Power Company appraises employees on their performance in reducing solid waste, cutting emissions and discharges, and implementing environmental plans. The result? Duke Power has met all of its environmental goals.

---

[14] For a more-detailed discussion see R. Simons, *Levers of Control: How Managers Use Innovative Control Systems to Drive Strategic Renewal* (Boston: Harvard Business School Press, 1995).

Belief Systems

Belief systems articulate the mission, purpose, and core values of a company. They describe the accepted norms and patterns of behavior expected of all managers and other employees with respect to one another, shareholders, customers, and communities. For example, Johnson & Johnson describes its values and norms in a credo statement that is intended to inspire all managers and other employees to do their best.[15] Belief systems play to employees' *intrinsic motivation*, the desire to achieve self-satisfaction from good performance regardless of external rewards such as bonuses or promotion. Intrinsic motivation comes from being given greater responsibility, doing interesting and creative work, having pride in doing that work, establishing commitment to the organization, and developing personal bonds with coworkers. High intrinsic motivation enhances performance because managers and workers have a sense of achievement in doing something important, feel satisfied with their jobs, and see opportunities for personal growth.

Interactive Control Systems

Interactive control systems are formal information systems that managers use to focus the company's attention and learning on key strategic issues. Managers use interactive control systems to create an ongoing dialogue around these key issues and to personally involve themselves in subordinates' decision-making activities. An excessive focus on diagnostic control systems and critical performance variables can cause an organization to ignore emerging threats and opportunities—changes in technology, customer preferences, regulations, and industry competition that can undercut a business. Interactive control systems help prevent this problem by highlighting and tracking strategic uncertainties that businesses face, such as the emergence of digital imaging in the case of Kodak and Fujifilm, airline deregulation in the case of American Airlines, and the shift in customer preferences for mini- and microcomputers in the case of IBM. The key to this control lever is frequent face-to-face communications regarding these critical uncertainties. The result is ongoing discussion and debate about assumptions and action plans. New strategies emerge from the dialogue and debate surrounding the interactive process. Interactive control systems force busy managers to step back from the actions needed to manage the business today and to shift their focus forward to positioning the organization for the opportunities and threats of tomorrow.

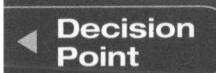

Decision Point

What are the four levers of control, and why does a company need to implement them?

Measuring and rewarding managers for achieving critical performance variables is an important driver of corporate performance. But these diagnostic control systems must be counterbalanced by the other levers of control, boundary systems, belief systems, and interactive control systems, to ensure that proper business ethics, inspirational values, and attention to future threats and opportunities are not sacrificed while achieving business results.

Problems for Self-Study

The baseball division of Home Run Sports manufactures and sells baseballs. Assume production equals sales. Budgeted data for February 2011 are as follows:

Current assets	$ 400,000
Long-term assets	600,000
Total assets	$1,000,000
Production output	200,000 baseballs per month
Target ROI (Operating income ÷ Total assets)	30%
Fixed costs	$400,000 per month
Variable cost	$4 per baseball

Required

1. Compute the minimum selling price per baseball necessary to achieve the target ROI of 30%.

---
[15]A full statement of the credo can be accessed at www.jnj.com/connect/about-jnj/jnj-credo/.

2. Using the selling price from requirement 1, separate the target ROI into its two components using the DuPont method.
3. Compute the RI of the baseball division for February 2011, using the selling price from requirement 1. Home Run Sports uses a required rate of return of 12% on total division assets when computing division RI.
4. In addition to her salary, Pamela Stephenson, the division manager, receives 3% of the monthly RI of the baseball division as a bonus. Compute Stephenson's bonus. Why do you think Stephenson is rewarded using both salary and a performance-based bonus? Stephenson does not like bearing risk.

Solution

1.
Target operating income = 30% of $1,000,000 of total assets
= $300,000

Let P = Selling price

Revenues − Variable costs − Fixed costs = Operating income

$200,000P - (200,000 \times \$4) - \$400,000 = \$300,000$

$200,000P = \$300,000 + \$800,000 + \$400,000$

$= \$1,500,000$

$P = \$7.50$ per baseball

Proof:
Revenues, 200,000 baseballs × $7.50/baseball		$1,500,000
Variable costs, 200,000 baseballs × $4/baseball		800,000
Contribution margin		700,000
Fixed costs		400,000
Operating income		$ 300,000

2. The DuPont method describes ROI as the product of two components: return on sales (income ÷ revenues) and investment turnover (revenues ÷ investment).

$$\frac{\text{Income}}{\text{Revenues}} \times \frac{\text{Revenues}}{\text{Investment}} = \frac{\text{Income}}{\text{Investment}}$$

$$\frac{\$300,000}{\$1,500,000} \times \frac{\$1,500,000}{\$1,000,000} = \frac{\$300,000}{\$1,000,000}$$

$$0.2 \times 1.5 = 0.30, \text{ or } 30\%$$

3. RI = Operating income − Required return on investment
= $300,000 − (0.12 × $1,000,000)
= $300,000 − $120,000
= $180,000

4. Stephensons bonus = 3% of RI
= 0.03 × $180,000 = $5,400

The baseball division's RI is affected by many factors, such as general economic conditions, beyond Stephenson's control. These uncontrollable factors make the baseball division's profitability uncertain and risky. Because Stephenson does not like bearing risk, paying her a flat salary, regardless of RI, would shield her from this risk. But there is a moral-hazard problem with this compensation arrangement. Because Stephenson's effort is difficult to monitor, the absence of performance-based compensation will provide her with no incentive to undertake extra physical and mental effort beyond what is necessary to retain her job or to uphold her personal values.

Paying no salary and rewarding Stephenson only on the basis of RI provides her with incentives to work hard but also subjects her to excessive risk because of uncontrollable factors that will affect RI and hence Stephenson's compensation. A compensation arrangement based only on RI would be more costly for Home Run Sports because it would have to compensate Stephenson for taking on uncontrollable risk. A compensation arrangement that consists of both a salary and an RI-based performance bonus balances the benefits of incentives against the extra costs of imposing uncontrollable risk

Performance Measurement, Compensation, and Multinational Considerations 137

Decision Points

The following question-and-answer format summarizes the chapter's learning objectives. Each decision presents a key question related to a learning objective. The guidelines are the answer to that question.

Decision	Guidelines
1. What financial and nonfinancial performance measures do companies use in their balanced scorecards?	Financial measures such as return on investment and residual income measure aspects of both manager performance and organization-subunit performance. In many cases, financial measures are supplemented with nonfinancial measures of performance from the customer, internal-business-process, and learning-and-growth perspectives of the balanced scorecard—for example, customer-satisfaction, quality of products and services, and employee satisfaction.
2. What are the relative merits of return on investment (ROI), residual income (RI), and economic-value added (EVA) as performance measures for subunit managers?	Return on investment (ROI) is the product of two components: income divided by revenues (return on sales) and revenues divided by investment (investment turnover). Managers can increase ROI by increasing revenues, decreasing costs, and decreasing investment. But, ROI may induce managers of highly profitable divisions to reject projects that are in the firm's best interest because accepting the project reduces divisional ROI. Residual income (RI) is income minus a dollar amount of required return on investment. RI is more likely than ROI to promote goal congruence. Evaluating managers on RI is also consistent with the use of discounted cash flow to choose long-term projects. Economic value added (EVA) is a variation of the RI calculation. It equals after-tax operating income minus the product of (after-tax) weighted-average cost of capital and total assets minus current liabilities.
3. Over what timeframe should companies measure performance, and what are the alternative choices for calculating the components of each performance measure?	A multiyear perspective induces managers to consider the long-term consequences of their actions and prevents a myopic focus on short-run profits. When constructing accounting-based performance measures, firms must first decide on a definition of investment. They must also choose whether assets included in the investment calculations are measured at historical cost or current cost, and whether depreciable assets are calculated at gross or net book value.
4. What targets should companies use and when should they give feedback to managers regarding their performance relative to these targets?	Companies should tailor a budget to a particular subunit, a particular accounting system, and a particular performance measure. In general, problems of asset valuation and income measurement in a performance measure can be overcome by emphasizing budgets and targets that stress continuous improvement. Timely feedback is critical to enable managers to implement actions that correct deviations from target performance.
5. How can companies compare the performance of divisions operating in different countries?	Comparing the performance of divisions operating in different countries is difficult because of legal, political, social, economic, and currency differences. ROI and RI calculations for subunits operating in different countries need to be adjusted for differences in inflation between the two countries and changes in exchange rates.
6. Why are managers compensated based on a mix of salary and incentives?	Companies create incentives by rewarding managers on the basis of performance. But managers face risks because factors beyond their control may also affect their performance. Owners choose a mix of salary and incentive compensation to trade off the incentive benefit against the cost of imposing risk.
7. What are the four levers of control, and why does a company need to implement them?	The four levers of control are diagnostic control systems, boundary systems, belief systems, and interactive control systems. Implementing the four levers of control helps a company simultaneously strive for performance, behave ethically, inspire employees, and respond to strategic threats and opportunities.

138 IBO Financial Management & Currency Risk

Terms to Learn

This chapter and the Glossary at the end of the book contain definitions of the following important terms:

- belief systems
- boundary systems
- current cost
- diagnostic control systems
- economic value added (EVA®)
- imputed cost
- interactive control systems
- investment
- moral hazard
- residual income (RI)
- return on investment (ROI)

Assignment Material

Questions

23-1 Give examples of financial and nonfinancial performance measures that can be found in each of the four perspectives of the balanced scorecard.

23-2 What are the three steps in designing accounting-based performance measures?

23-3 What factors affecting ROI does the DuPont method of profitability analysis highlight?

23-4 "RI is not identical to ROI, although both measures incorporate income and investment into their computations." Do you agree? Explain.

23-5 Describe EVA.

23-6 Give three definitions of investment used in practice when computing ROI.

23-7 Distinguish between measuring assets based on current cost and historical cost.

23-8 What special problems arise when evaluating performance in multinational companies?

23-9 Why is it important to distinguish between the performance of a manager and the performance of the organization subunit for which the manager is responsible? Give an example.

23-10 Describe moral hazard.

23-11 "Managers should be rewarded only on the basis of their performance measures. They should be paid no salary." Do you agree? Explain.

23-12 Explain the role of benchmarking in evaluating managers.

23-13 Explain the incentive problems that can arise when employees must perform multiple tasks as part of their jobs.

23-14 Describe two disclosures required by the SEC with respect to executive compensation.

23-15 Describe the four levers of control.

Exercises

23-16 ROI, comparisons of three companies. (CMA, adapted) Return on investment (ROI) is often expressed as follows:

$$\frac{\text{Income}}{\text{Investment}} = \frac{\text{Income}}{\text{Revenues}} \times \frac{\text{Revenues}}{\text{Investment}}$$

Required

1. What advantages are there in the breakdown of the computation into two separate components?
2. Fill in the following blanks:

	Companies in Same Industry		
	A	B	C
Revenues	$1,000,000	$500,000	?
Income	$ 100,000	$ 50,000	?
Investment	$ 500,000	?	$5,000,000
Income as a percentage of revenues	?	?	0.5%
Investment turnover	?	?	2
ROI	?	1%	?

After filling in the blanks, comment on the relative performance of these companies as thoroughly as the data permit.

23-17 Analysis of return on invested assets, comparison of two divisions, DuPont method. Global Data, Inc., has two divisions: Test Preparation and Language Arts. Results (in millions) for the past three years are partially displayed here:

	A	B	C	D	E	F	G
1		Operating Income	Operating Revenues	Total Assets	Operating Income/ Operating Revenues	Operating Revenues/ Total Assets	Operating Income/ Total Assets
2	Test Preparation Division						
3	2011	$ 720	$ 9,000	$1,800	?	?	?
4	2012	920	?	?	11.5%	?	46%
5	2013	1,140	?	?	9.5%	6	?
6	Language Arts Division						
7	2011	$ 660	$ 3,000	$2,000	?	?	?
8	2012	?	3,525	2,350	20%	?	?
9	2013	?	?	2,900	?	1.6	20%
10	Global Data, Inc.						
11	2011	$1,380	$12,000	$3,800	?	?	?
12	2012	?	?	?	?	?	?
13	2013	?	?	?	?	?	?

Required

1. Complete the table by filling in the blanks.
2. Use the DuPont method of profitability analysis to explain changes in the operating-income-to-total-assets ratios over the 2011–2013 period for each division and for Global Data as a whole. Comment on the results.

23-18 ROI and RI. (D. Kleespie, adapted) The Outdoor Sports Company produces a wide variety of outdoor sports equipment. Its newest division, Golf Technology, manufactures and sells a single product—AccuDriver, a golf club that uses global positioning satellite technology to improve the accuracy of golfers' shots. The demand for AccuDriver is relatively insensitive to price changes. The following data are available for Golf Technology, which is an investment center for Outdoor Sports:

Total annual fixed costs	$30,000,000
Variable cost per AccuDriver	$ 500
Number of AccuDrivers sold each year	150,000
Average operating assets invested in the division	$48,000,000

Required

1. Compute Golf Technology's ROI if the selling price of AccuDrivers is $720 per club.
2. If management requires an ROI of at least 25% from the division, what is the minimum selling price that the Golf Technology Division should charge per AccuDriver club?
3. Assume that Outdoor Sports judges the performance of its investment centers on the basis of RI rather than ROI. What is the minimum selling price that Golf Technology should charge per AccuDriver if the company's required rate of return is 20%?

23-19 ROI and RI with manufacturing costs. Superior Motor Company makes electric cars and has only two products, the Simplegreen and the Superiorgreen. To produce the Simplegreen, Superior Motor employed assets of $13,500,000 at the beginning of the period, and $13,400,000 of assets at the end of the period. Other costs to manufacture the Simplegreen include the following:

Direct materials	$3,000 per unit
Setup	$1,300 per setup-hour
Production	$415 per machine-hour

General administration and selling costs total $7,340,000 for the period. In the current period, Superior Motor produced 10,000 Simplegreen cars using 6,000 setup-hours and 175,200 machine-hours. Superior Motor sold these cars for $12,000 each.

Required

1. Assuming that Superior Motor defines investment as average assets during the period, what is the return on investment for the Simplegreen division?
2. Calculate the residual income for the Simplegreen if Superior Motor has a required rate of return of 12% on investments.

23-20 Financial and nonfinancial performance measures, goal congruence. (CMA, adapted) Summit Equipment specializes in the manufacture of medical equipment, a field that has become increasingly competitive. Approximately two years ago, Ben Harrington, president of Summit, decided to revise the bonus plan (based, at the time, entirely on operating income) to encourage division managers to focus on areas that were important to customers and that added value without increasing cost. In addition to a profitability incentive, the revised plan includes incentives for reduced rework costs, reduced sales returns, and on-time deliveries. Bonuses are calculated and awarded semiannually on the following basis: A base bonus is calculated at 2% of operating income; this amount is then adjusted as follows:

a. (i) Reduced by excess of rework costs over and above 2% of operating income
   (ii) No adjustment if rework costs are less than or equal to 2% of operating income
b. (i) Increased by $5,000 if more than 98% of deliveries are on time, and by $2,000 if 96% to 98% of deliveries are on time
   (ii) No adjustment if on-time deliveries are below 96%
c. (i) Increased by $3,000 if sales returns are less than or equal to 1.5% of sales
   (ii) Decreased by 50% of excess of sales returns over 1.5% of sales

Note: If the calculation of the bonus results in a negative amount for a particular period, the manager simply receives no bonus, and the negative amount is not carried forward to the next period.

Results for Summit's Charter division and Mesa division for 2012, the first year under the new bonus plan, follow. In 2011, under the old bonus plan, the Charter division manager earned a bonus of $27,060 and the Mesa division manager, a bonus of $22,440.

	Charter Division		Mesa Division	
	January 1, 2012, to June 30, 2012	July 1, 2012, to Dec. 31, 2012	January 1, 2012, to June 30, 2012	July 1, 2012, to Dec. 31, 2012
Revenues	$4,200,000	$4,400,000	$2,850,000	$2,900,000
Operating income	$462,000	$440,000	$342,000	$406,000
On-time delivery	95.4%	97.3%	98.2%	94.6%
Rework costs	$11,500	$11,000	$6,000	$8,000
Sales returns	$84,000	$70,000	$44,750	$42,500

Required

1. Why did Harrington need to introduce these new performance measures? That is, why does Harrington need to use these performance measures in addition to the operating-income numbers for the period?
2. Calculate the bonus earned by each manager for each six-month period and for 2012.
3. What effect did the change in the bonus plan have on each manager's behavior? Did the new bonus plan achieve what Harrington desired? What changes, if any, would you make to the new bonus plan?

23-21 Goal incongruence and ROI. Bleefl Corporation manufactures furniture in several divisions, including the patio furniture division. The manager of the patio furniture division plans to retire in two years. The manager receives a bonus based on the division's ROI, which is currently 11%.

One of the machines that the patio furniture division uses to manufacture the furniture is rather old, and the manager must decide whether to replace it. The new machine would cost $30,000 and would last 10 years. It would have no salvage value. The old machine is fully depreciated and has no trade-in value. Bleefl uses straight-line depreciation for all assets. The new machine, being new and more efficient, would save the company $5,000 per year in cash operating costs. The only difference between cash flow and net income is depreciation. The internal rate of return of the project is approximately 11%. Bleefl Corporation's weighted average cost of capital is 6%. Bleefl is not subject to any income taxes.

Required

1. Should Bleefl Corporation replace the machine? Why or why not?
2. Assume that "investment" is defined as average net long-term assets after depreciation. Compute the project's ROI for each of its first five years. If the patio furniture manager is interested in maximizing his or her bonus, would the manager replace the machine before he or she retires? Why or why not?
3. What can Bleefl do to entice the manager to replace the machine before retiring?

23-22 ROI, RI, EVA. Performance Auto Company operates a new car division (that sells high performance sports cars) and a performance parts division (that sells performance improvement parts for family cars). Some division financial measures for 2011 are as follows:

	A	B	C
1		New Car Division	Performance Parts Division
2	Total assets	$33,000,000	$28,500,000
3	Current liabilities	$ 6,600,000	$ 8,400,000
4	Operating income	$ 2,475,000	$ 2,565,000
5	Required rate of return	12%	12%

Required

1. Calculate return on investment (ROI) for each division using operating income as a measure of income and total assets as a measure of investment.
2. Calculate residual income (RI) for each division using operating income as a measure of income and total assets minus current liabilities as a measure of investment.
3. William Abraham, the New Car Division manager, argues that the performance parts division has "loaded up on a lot of short-term debt" to boost its RI. Calculate an alternative RI for each division that is not sensitive to the amount of short-term debt taken on by the performance parts division. Comment on the result.
4. Performance Auto Company, whose tax rate is 40%, has two sources of funds: long-term debt with a market value of $18,000,000 at an interest rate of 10%, and equity capital with a market value of $12,000,000 and a cost of equity of 15%. Applying the same weighted-average cost of capital (WACC) to each division, calculate EVA for each division.
5. Use your preceding calculations to comment on the relative performance of each division.

23-23 ROI, RI, measurement of assets. (CMA, adapted) Carter Corporation recently announced a bonus plan to be awarded to the manager of the most profitable division. The three division managers are to choose whether ROI or RI will be used to measure profitability. In addition, they must decide whether investment will be measured using gross book value or net book value of assets. Carter defines income as operating income and investment as total assets. The following information is available for the year just ended:

Division	Gross Book Value of Assets	Accumulated Depreciation	Operating Income
Radnor	$1,200,000	$645,000	$142,050
Easttown	1,140,000	615,000	137,550
Marion	750,000	420,000	92,100

Carter uses a required rate of return of 10% on investment to calculate RI.

Required

Each division manager has selected a method of bonus calculation that ranks his or her division number one. Identify the method for calculating profitability that each manager selected, supporting your answer with appropriate calculations. Comment on the strengths and weaknesses of the methods chosen by each manager.

23-24 Multinational performance measurement, ROI, RI. The Seaside Corporation manufactures similar products in the United States and Norway. The U.S. and Norwegian operations are organized as decentralized divisions. The following information is available for 2012; ROI is calculated as operating income divided by total assets:

	U.S. Division	Norwegian Division
Operating income	?	6,840,000 kroner
Total assets	$7,500,000	72,000,000 kroner
ROI	9.3%	?

Both investments were made on December 31, 2011. The exchange rate at the time of Seaside's investment in Norway on December 31, 2011, was 9 kroner = $1. During 2012, the Norwegian kroner decreased steadily in value so that the exchange rate on December 31, 2012, is 10 kroner = $1. The average exchange rate during 2012 is [(9 + 10) ÷ 2] = 9.5 kroner = $1.

Required

1a. Calculate the U.S. division's operating income for 2012.
 b. Calculate the Norwegian division's ROI for 2012 in kroner.
2. Top management wants to know which division earned a better ROI in 2012. What would you tell them? Explain your answer.
3. Which division do you think had the better RI performance? Explain your answer. The required rate of return on investment (calculated in U.S. dollars) is 8%.

23-25 ROI, RI, EVA and Performance Evaluation. Eva Manufacturing makes fashion products and competes on the basis of quality and leading-edge designs. The company has $3,000,000 invested in assets in its clothing manufacturing division. After-tax operating income from sales of clothing this year is $600,000. The cosmetics division has $10,000,000 invested in assets and an after-tax operating income this year of $1,600,000. Income for the clothing division has grown steadily over the last few years. The weighted-average cost of capital for Eva is 10% and the previous period's after-tax return on investment for each division was 15%. The CEO of Eva has told the manager of each division that the division that "performs best" this year will get a bonus.

Required

1. Calculate the ROI and residual income for each division of Eva Manufacturing, and briefly explain which manager will get the bonus. What are the advantages and disadvantages of each measure?
2. The CEO of Eva Manufacturing has recently heard of another measure similar to residual income called EVA. The CEO has the accountant calculate EVA adjusted incomes of clothing and cosmetics, and finds that the adjusted after-tax operating incomes are $720,000 and $1,430,000, respectively. Also, the clothing division

has $400,000 of current liabilities, while the cosmetics division has only $200,000 of current liabilities. Using the preceding information, calculate EVA, and discuss which division manager will get the bonus.

3. What nonfinancial measures could Eva use to evaluate divisional performances?

23-26 Risk sharing, incentives, benchmarking, multiple tasks. The Dexter division of AMCO sells car batteries. AMCO's corporate management gives Dexter management considerable operating and investment autonomy in running the division. AMCO is considering how it should compensate Jim Marks, the general manager of the Dexter division. Proposal 1 calls for paying Marks a fixed salary. Proposal 2 calls for paying Marks no salary and compensating him only on the basis of the division's ROI, calculated based on operating income before any bonus payments. Proposal 3 calls for paying Marks some salary and some bonus based on ROI. Assume that Marks does not like bearing risk.

Required

1. Evaluate the three proposals, specifying the advantages and disadvantages of each.
2. Suppose that AMCO competes against Tiara Industries in the car battery business. Tiara is approximately the same size as the Dexter division and operates in a business environment that is similar to Dexter's. The top management of AMCO is considering evaluating Marks on the basis of Dexter's ROI minus Tiara's ROI. Marks complains that this approach is unfair because the performance of another company, over which he has no control, is included in his performance-evaluation measure. Is Marks' complaint valid? Why or why not?
3. Now suppose that Marks has no authority for making capital-investment decisions. Corporate management makes these decisions. Is ROI a good performance measure to use to evaluate Marks? Is ROI a good measure to evaluate the economic viability of the Dexter division? Explain.
4. Dexter's salespersons are responsible for selling and providing customer service and support. Sales are easy to measure. Although customer service is important to Dexter in the long run, it has not yet implemented customer-service measures. Marks wants to compensate his sales force only on the basis of sales commissions paid for each unit of product sold. He cites two advantages to this plan: (a) It creates strong incentives for the sales force to work hard, and (b) the company pays salespersons only when the company itself is earning revenues. Do you like his plan? Why or why not?

Problems

23-27 Residual Income and EVA; timing issues. Doorchime Company makes doorbells. It has a weighted average cost of capital of 9%, and total assets of $5,550,000. Doorchime has current liabilities of $800,000. Its operating income for the year was $630,000. Doorchime does not have to pay any income taxes. One of the expenses for accounting purposes was a $90,000 advertising campaign. The entire amount was deducted this year, although the Doorchime CEO believes the beneficial effects of this advertising will last four years.

Required

1. Calculate residual income, assuming Doorchime defines investment as total assets.
2. Calculate EVA for the year. Adjust both the assets and operating income for advertising assuming that for the purposes of economic value added the advertising is capitalized and amortized on a straight-line basis over four years.
3. Discuss the difference between the outcomes of requirements 1 and 2 and which measure is preferred.

23-28 ROI performance measures based on historical cost and current cost. Nature's Elixir Corporation operates three divisions that process and bottle natural fruit juices. The historical-cost accounting system reports the following information for 2011:

	Passion Fruit Division	Kiwi Fruit Division	Mango Fruit Division
Revenues	$1,000,000	$1,400,000	$2,200,000
Operating costs (excluding plant depreciation)	600,000	760,000	1,200,000
Plant depreciation	140,000	200,000	240,000
Operating income	$ 260,000	$ 440,000	$ 760,000
Current assets	$ 400,000	$ 500,000	$ 600,000
Long-term assets—plant	280,000	1,800,000	2,640,000
Total assets	$ 680,000	$2,300,000	$3,240,000

Nature's Elixir estimates the useful life of each plant to be 12 years, with no terminal disposal value. The straight-line depreciation method is used. At the end of 2011, the passion fruit plant is 10 years old, the kiwi fruit plant is 3 years old, and the mango fruit plant is 1 year old. An index of construction costs over the 10-year period that Nature's Elixir has been operating (2001 year-end = 100) is as follows:

2001	2008	2010	2011
100	136	160	170

Given the high turnover of current assets, management believes that the historical-cost and current-cost measures of current assets are approximately the same.

1. Compute the ROI ratio (operating income to total assets) of each division using historical-cost measures. Comment on the results.
2. Use the approach in Exhibit 23-2 (p. 839) to compute the ROI of each division, incorporating current-cost estimates as of 2011 for depreciation expense and long-term assets. Comment on the results.
3. What advantages might arise from using current-cost asset measures as compared with historical-cost measures for evaluating the performance of the managers of the three divisions?

23-29 ROI, measurement alternatives for performance measures P. F. Skidaddle's operates casual dining restaurants in three regions: Denver, Seattle, and Sacramento. Each geographic market is considered a separate division. The Denver division is made up of four restaurants, each built in early 2002. The Seattle division is made up of three restaurants, each built in January 2006. The Sacramento division is the newest, consisting of three restaurants built four years ago. Division managers at P. F. Skidaddle's are evaluated on the basis of ROI. The following information refers to the three divisions at the end of 2012:

	Denver	Seattle	Sacramento	Total
Division revenues	$8,365,000	$6,025,000	$5,445,000	$20,138,000
Division expenses	7,945,000	5,521,000	4,979,000	18,445,000
Division operating income	723,000	504,000	466,000	1,693,000
Gross book value of long-term assets	4,750,000	3,750,000	4,050,000	12,300,000
Accumulated depreciation	3,300,000	1,750,000	1,080,000	6,130,000
Current assets	999,800	768,200	824,600	2,592,600
Depreciation expense	300,000	250,000	270,000	820,000
Construction cost index for year of construction	100	110	118	

1. Calculate ROI for each division using net book value of total assets.
2. Using the technique in Exhibit 23-2, compute ROI using current-cost estimates for long-term assets and depreciation expense. Construction cost index for 2012 is 122. Estimated useful life of operational assets is 15 years.
3. How does the choice of long-term asset valuation affect management decisions regarding new capital investments? Why might this be more significant to the Denver division manager than to the Sacramento division manager?

23-30 ROI, RI, and Multinational Firms. Konekopf Corporation has a division in the United States, and another in France. The investment in the French assets was made when the exchange rate was $1.30 per euro. The average exchange rate for the year was $1.40 per euro. The exchange rate at the end of the fiscal year was $1.45 per euro. Income and investment for the two divisions are as follows:

	United States	France
Investment in assets	$5,450,000	3,800,000 euro
Income for current year	$ 681,250	486,400 euro

1. The required return for Konekopf is 12%. Calculate ROI and RI for the two divisions. For the French division, calculate these measures using both dollars and euro. Which division is doing better?
2. What are the advantages and disadvantages of translating the French division information from euro to dollars?

23-31 Multinational firms, differing risk, comparison of profit, ROI and RI. Zynga Multinational, Inc., has divisions in the United States, Germany, and New Zealand. The U.S. division is the oldest and most established of the three, and has a cost of capital of 8%. The German division was started three years ago when the exchange rate for euro was 1 euro = $1.25. It is a large and powerful division of Zynga, Inc., with a cost of capital of 12%. The New Zealand division was started this year, when the exchange rate was 1 New Zealand Dollar (NZD) = $0.60. Its cost of capital is 14%. Average exchange rates for the current year are 1 euro = $1.40 and 1 NZD = $0.64. Other information for the three divisions includes the following:

	United States	Germany	New Zealand
Long term assets	$23,246,112	11,939,200 euro	9,400,000 NZD
Operating revenues	$13,362,940	5,250,000 euros	4,718,750 NZD
Operating expenses	$ 8,520,000	3,200,000 euros	3,250,000 NZD
Income tax rate	40%	35%	25%

Required

1. Translate the German and New Zealand information into dollars to make the divisions comparable. Find the after-tax operating income for each division and compare the profits.
2. Calculate ROI using after-tax operating income. Compare among divisions.
3. Use after-tax operating income and the individual cost of capital of each division to calculate residual income and compare.
4. Redo requirement 2 using pretax operating income instead of net income. Why is there a big difference, and what does it mean for performance evaluation?

23-32 ROI, RI, DuPont method, investment decisions, balanced scorecard. Global Event Group has two major divisions: print and Internet. Summary financial data (in millions) for 2011 and 2012 are as follows:

	A	B	C	D	E	F	G	H	I
1		Operating Income			Revenues			Total Assets	
2		2011	2012		2011	2012		2011	2012
3	Print	$3,740	$6,120		$18,300	$20,400		$18,650	$24,000
4	Internet	565	780		25,900	30,000		11,200	12,000

The two division managers' annual bonuses are based on division ROI (defined as operating income divided by total assets). If a division reports an increase in ROI from the previous year, its management is automatically eligible for a bonus; however, the management of a division reporting a decline in ROI has to present an explanation to the Global Event Group board and is unlikely to get any bonus.

Carol Mays, manager of the print division, is considering a proposal to invest $960 million in a new computerized news reporting and printing system. It is estimated that the new system's state-of-the-art graphics and ability to quickly incorporate late-breaking news into papers will increase 2013 division operating income by $144 million. Global Event Group uses a 12% required rate of return on investment for each division.

Required

1. Use the DuPont method of profitability analysis to explain differences in 2012 ROIs between the two divisions. Use 2012 total assets as the investment base.
2. Why might Mays be less than enthusiastic about accepting the investment proposal for the new system, despite her belief in the benefits of the new technology?
3. Chris Moreno, CEO of Global Event Group, is considering a proposal to base division executive compensation on division RI.
   a. Compute the 2012 RI of each division.
   b. Would adoption of an RI measure reduce Mays' reluctance to adopt the new computerized system investment proposal?
4. Moreno is concerned that the focus on annual ROI could have an adverse long-run effect on Global Event Group's customers. What other measurements, if any, do you recommend that Moreno use? Explain briefly.

23-33 Division managers' compensation, levers of control (continuation of 23-32). Chris Moreno seeks your advice on revising the existing bonus plan for division managers of Global Event Group. Assume division managers do not like bearing risk. Moreno is considering three ideas:

- Make each division manager's compensation depend on division RI.
- Make each division manager's compensation depend on company-wide RI.
- Use benchmarking, and compensate division managers on the basis of their division's RI minus the RI of the other division.

Required

1. Evaluate the three ideas Moreno has put forth using performance-evaluation concepts described in this chapter. Indicate the positive and negative features of each proposal.
2. Moreno is concerned that the pressure for short-run performance may cause managers to cut corners. What systems might Moreno introduce to avoid this problem? Explain briefly.

3. Moreno is also concerned that the pressure for short-run performance might cause managers to ignore emerging threats and opportunities. What system might Moreno introduce to prevent this problem? Explain briefly.

23-34 Executive compensation, balanced scorecard. Community Bank recently introduced a new bonus plan for its business unit executives. The company believes that current profitability and customer satisfaction levels are equally important to the bank's long-term success. As a result, the new plan awards a bonus equal to 1% of salary for each 1% increase in business unit net income or 1% increase in the business unit's customer satisfaction index. For example, increasing net income from $3 million to $3.3 million (or 10% from its initial value) leads to a bonus of 10% of salary, while increasing the business unit's customer satisfaction index from 70 to 73.5 (or 5% from its initial value) leads to a bonus of 5% of salary. There is no bonus penalty when net income or customer satisfaction declines. In 2011 and 2012, Community Bank's three business units reported the following performance results:

	Retail Banking		Business Banking		Credit Cards	
	2011	2012	2011	2012	2011	2012
Net income	$2,600,000	$2,912,000	$2,800,000	$2,940,000	$2,550,000	$2,499,000
Customer satisfaction	74	75.48	69	75.9	68	78.88

1. Compute the bonus as a percent of salary earned by each business unit executive in 2012.
2. What factors might explain the differences between improvement rates for net income and those for customer satisfaction in the three units? Are increases in customer satisfaction likely to result in increased net income right away?
3. Community Bank's board of directors is concerned that the 2012 bonus awards may not actually reflect the executives' overall performance. In particular, it is concerned that executives can earn large bonuses by doing well on one performance dimension but underperforming on the other. What changes can it make to the bonus plan to prevent this from happening in the future? Explain briefly.

23-35 Ethics, manager's performance evaluation. (A. Spero, adapted) Hamilton Semiconductors manufactures specialized chips that sell for $25 each. Hamilton's manufacturing costs consist of variable cost of $3 per chip and fixed costs of $8,000,000. Hamilton also incurs $900,000 in fixed marketing costs each year.

Hamilton calculates operating income using absorption costing—that is, Hamilton calculates manufacturing cost per unit by dividing total manufacturing costs by actual production. Hamilton costs all units in inventory at this rate and expenses the costs in the income statement at the time when the units in inventory are sold. Next year, 2012, appears to be a difficult year for Hamilton. It expects to sell only 400,000 units. The demand for these chips fluctuates considerably, so Hamilton usually holds minimal inventory.

1. Calculate Hamilton's operating income in 2012 (a) if Hamilton manufactures 400,000 units and (b) if Hamilton manufactures 500,000 units.
2. Would it be unethical for Randy Jones, the general manager of Hamilton Semiconductors, to produce more units than can be sold in order to show better operating results? Jones' compensation has a bonus component based on operating income. Explain your answer.
3. Would it be unethical for Jones to ask distributors to buy more product than they need? Hamilton follows the industry practice of booking sales when products are shipped to distributors. Explain your answer.

23-36 Ethics, levers of control. Monroe Moulding is a large manufacturer of wood picture frame moulding. The company operates distribution centers in Dallas and Philadelphia. The distribution centers cut frames to size (called "chops") and ship them to custom picture framers. Because of the exacting standards and natural flaws of wood picture frame moulding, the company typically produces a large amount of waste in cutting chops. In recent years, the company's average yield has been 76% of length moulding. The remaining 24% is sent to a wood recycler. Monroe's performance-evaluation system pays its distribution center managers substantial bonuses if the company achieves annual budgeted profit numbers. In the last quarter of 2010, Frank Jessup, Monroe's controller, noted a significant increase in yield percentage of the Dallas distribution center, from 74% to 85%. This increase resulted in a 5% increase in the center's profits.

During a recent trip to the Dallas center, Jessup wandered into the moulding warehouse. He noticed that much of the scrap moulding was being returned to the inventory bins rather than being placed in the discard pile. Upon further inspection, he determined that the moulding was in fact unusable. When he asked one of the workers, he was told that the center's manager had directed workers to stop scrapping all but the very shortest pieces. This practice resulted in the center over-reporting both yield and ending inventory. The overstatement of Dallas inventory will have a significant impact on Monroe's financial statements.

1. What should Jessup do? You may want to refer to the *IMA Statement of Ethical Professional Practice*, p. 38.
2. Which lever of control is Monroe emphasizing? What changes, if any, should be made?

Collaborative Learning Problem

23-37 RI, EVA, Measurement alternatives, Goal congruence. Renewal Resorts, Inc., operates health spas in Ft. Meyers, Florida, Scottsdale, Arizona, and Monterey, California. The Ft. Meyers spa was the company's first, opened in 1986. The Scottsdale spa opened in 1999, and the Monterey spa opened in 2008. Renewal Resorts has previously evaluated divisions based on residual income (RI), but the company is considering changing to an economic value added (EVA) approach. All spas are assumed to face similar risks. Data for 2012 follow:

	A	B	C	D	E
1		Ft. Meyers Spa	Scottsdale Spa	Monterey Spa	Total
2	Revenues	$4,100,000	$4,380,000	$3,230,000	$11,710,000
3	Variable costs	1,600,000	1,630,000	955,000	4,185,000
4	Fixed costs	1,280,000	1,560,000	980,000	3,820,000
5	Operating income	1,220,000	1,190,000	1,295,000	3,705,000
6	Interest costs on long-term debt at 8%	368,000	416,000	440,000	1,224,000
5	Income before taxes at 35%	852,000	774,000	855,000	2,481,000
6	Net income	553,800	503,100	555,750	1,612,650
7					
8	Net book value at 2012 year-end:				
9	Current assets	$1,280,000	$ 850,000	$ 600,000	$ 2,730,000
10	Long-term assets	4,875,000	5,462,000	6,835,000	17,172,000
11	Total assets	6,155,000	6,312,000	7,435,000	19,902,000
12	Current liabilities	330,000	265,000	84,000	679,000
13	Long-term debt	4,600,000	5,200,000	5,500,000	15,300,000
14	Stockholders' equity	1,225,000	847,000	1,851,000	3,923,000
15	Total liabilities and stockholders' equity	6,155,000	6,312,000	7,435,000	19,902,000
16					
17	Market value of debt	$4,600,000	$5,200,000	$5,500,000	$15,300,000
18	Market value of equity	2,400,000	2,660,000	2,590,000	7,650,000
19	Cost of equity capital				17%
20	Required rate of return				11%
21	Accumulated depreciation on long-term assets	2,200,000	1,510,000	220,000	

Required

1. Calculate RI for each of the spas based on operating income and using total assets as the measure of investment. Suppose that the Ft. Meyers spa is considering adding a new group of saunas from Finland that will cost $225,000. The saunas are expected to bring in operating income of $22,000. What effect would this project have on the RI of the Ft. Meyers spa? Based on RI, would the Ft. Meyers manager accept or reject this project? Why? Without resorting to calculations, would the other managers accept or reject the project? Why?

2. Why might Renewal Resorts want to use EVA instead of RI for evaluating the performance of the three spas?
3. Refer back to the original data. Calculate the WACC for Renewal Resorts.
4. Refer back to the original data. Calculate EVA for each of the spas, using net book value of long-term assets. Calculate EVA again, this time using gross book value of long-term assets. Comment on the differences between the two methods.
5. How is goal congruence affected by the selection of asset measurement method?

CHAPTER 6

The Foreign Exchange Market

The best way to destroy the capitalist system is to debauch the currency. By a continuing process of inflation, governments can confiscate, secretly and unobserved, an important part of the wealth of their citizens. —John Maynard Keynes.

LEARNING OBJECTIVES

◆ Examine the what, when, where, and why of currency trading in the global marketplace.

◆ Understand the definitions and distinctions between spot, forward, swaps, and other types of foreign exchange financial instruments.

◆ Learn the forms of currency quotations used by currency dealers, financial institutions, and agents of all kinds when conducting foreign exchange transactions.

◆ Analyze the interaction between changing currency values, cross exchange rates, and the opportunities arising from intermarket arbitrage.

The foreign exchange market provides the physical and institutional structure through which the money of one country is exchanged for that of another country, the rate of exchange between currencies is determined, and foreign exchange transactions are physically completed. *Foreign exchange* means the money of a foreign country; that is, foreign currency bank balances, banknotes, checks, and drafts. A *foreign exchange transaction* is an agreement between a buyer and seller that a fixed amount of one currency will be delivered for some other currency at a specified rate. This chapter describes the following features of the foreign exchange market:

◆ Its geographical extent
◆ Its three main functions
◆ Its participants
◆ Its immense daily transaction volume
◆ Types of transactions, including spot, forward, and swap transactions
◆ Methods of stating exchange rates, quotations, and changes in exchange rates

The chapter concludes with the Mini-Case, ***The Saga of the Venezuelan Bolivar Fuerte***, which details the continuing devaluation of the Venezuelan currency in 2010 and 2011.

Geographical Extent of the Foreign Exchange Market

The foreign exchange market spans the globe, with prices moving and currencies trading somewhere every hour of every business day. Major world trading starts each morning in Sydney and Tokyo, moves west to Hong Kong and Singapore, passes on to Bahrain, shifts to the main European markets of Frankfurt, Zurich, and London, jumps the Atlantic to New York, goes west to Chicago, and ends in San Francisco and Los Angeles. Many large international banks operate foreign exchange trading rooms in each major geographic trading center in order to serve important commercial accounts on a 24-hour-a-day basis. Global currency trading is indeed a 24-hour-a-day process. As shown in Exhibit 6.1, the volume of currency transactions ebbs and flows across the globe as the major currency trading centers of London, New York, and Tokyo open and close throughout the day. Exhibit 6.2 provides a general mapping of which trading centers are open when, and which centers do and do not overlap with other city markets.

In some countries, a portion of foreign exchange trading is conducted on an official trading floor by open bidding. Closing prices are published as the official price, or "fixing," for the day, and certain commercial and investment transactions are based on this official price. Business firms in countries with exchange controls, for example, China (mainland), often must surrender foreign exchange earned from exports to the central bank at the daily fixing price.

Banks engaged in foreign exchange trading are connected by highly sophisticated telecommunications networks, with dealers and brokers exchanging currency quotes instantaneously. The foreign exchange departments of many nonbank business firms also use Internet-based networks, but often access trading through the major bank trading rooms. Reuters, Telerate, and Bloomberg are the leading suppliers of foreign exchange rate information and trading systems. A growing part of the industry is automated trading, in which corporate buyers and sellers trade currencies through Internet-based platforms provided or hosted by major money center banks. Although the largest currency transactions are still handled by humans via telephone, the use of computer trading has grown dramatically in recent years.

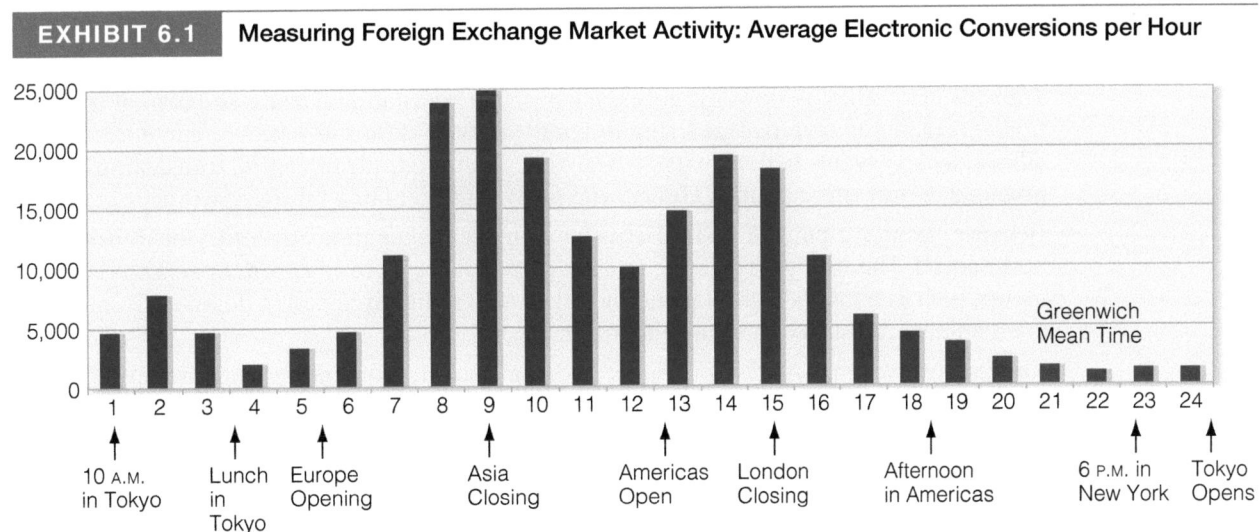

EXHIBIT 6.1 Measuring Foreign Exchange Market Activity: Average Electronic Conversions per Hour

Source: Federal Reserve Bank of New York, "The Foreign Exchange Market in the United States," 2001, www.ny.frb.org.

EXHIBIT 6.2   Global Currency Trading: The Trading Day

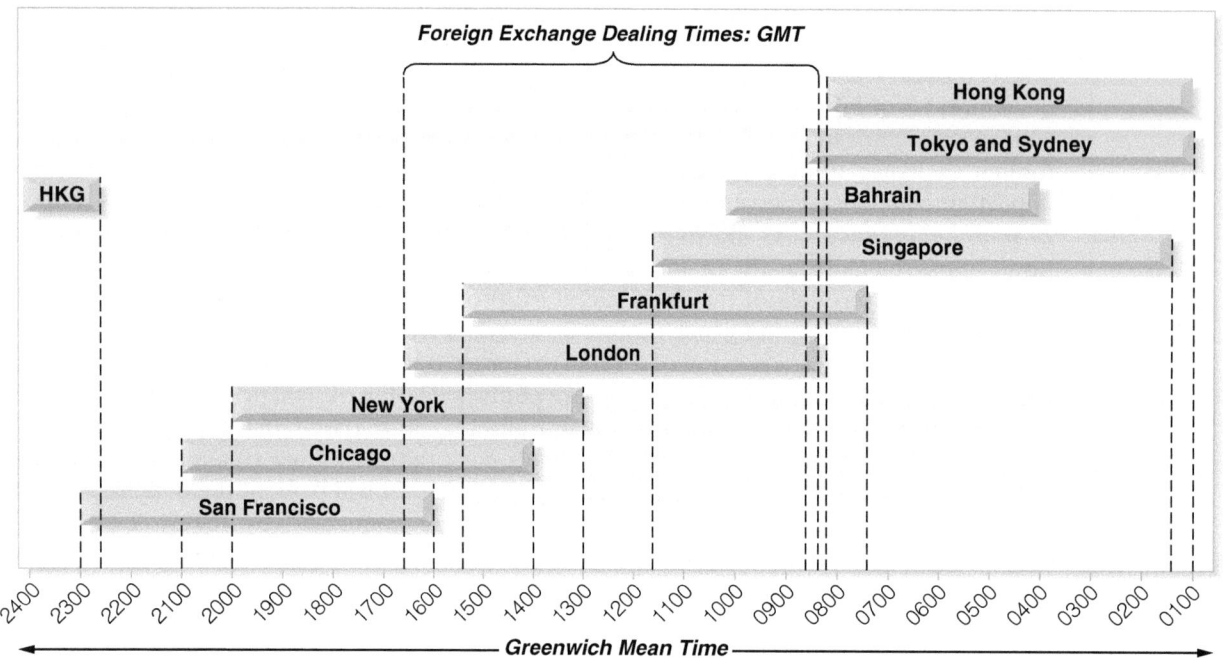

The currency trading day literally extends 24 hours per day. The busiest time of the day, however, is when New York and London overlap, the world's most liquid time of day.

Functions of the Foreign Exchange Market

The foreign exchange market is the mechanism by which participants transfer purchasing power between countries, obtain or provide credit for international trade transactions, and minimize exposure to the risks of exchange rate changes.

♦ Transfer of purchasing power is necessary because international trade and capital transactions normally involve parties living in countries with different national currencies. Usually each party, wants to deal in its own currency, but the trade or capital transaction can be invoiced in only one currency. Hence, one party must deal in a foreign currency.

♦ Because the movement of goods between countries takes time, inventory in transit must be financed. The foreign exchange market provides a source of credit. Specialized instruments, such as bankers' acceptances and letters of credit, discussed in detail in Chapter 19, are available to finance international trade.

♦ The foreign exchange market provides "hedging" facilities for transferring foreign exchange risk to someone else more willing to carry risk. These facilities are explained in Chapter 10.

Market Participants

The foreign exchange market consists of two tiers: the interbank or wholesale market, and the client or retail market. Individual transactions in the interbank market are usually for large sums that are multiples of a million U.S. dollars or the equivalent value in other currencies. By contrast, contracts between a bank and its clients are usually for specific amounts.

Five broad categories of participants operate within these two tiers: 1) bank and nonbank foreign exchange dealers; 2) individuals and firms conducting commercial or investment transactions; 3) speculators and arbitragers; 4) central banks and treasuries; and 5) foreign exchange brokers.

Bank and Nonbank Foreign Exchange Dealers

Banks, and a few nonbank foreign exchange dealers, operate in both the interbank and client markets. They profit from buying foreign exchange at a "bid" price and reselling it at a slightly higher "offer" (also called an "ask") price. Competition among dealers worldwide narrows the spread between bids and offers and so contributes to making the foreign exchange market "efficient" in the same sense as in securities markets.

Dealers in the foreign exchange departments of large international banks often function as "market makers." Such dealers stand willing at all times to buy and sell those currencies in which they specialize and thus maintain an "inventory" position in those currencies. They trade with other banks in their own monetary centers and with other centers around the world in order to maintain inventories within the trading limits set by bank policy. Trading limits are important because foreign exchange departments of many banks operate as profit centers, and individual dealers are compensated on a profit incentive basis.

Currency trading is quite profitable for commercial and investment banks. Many of the major currency-trading banks in the United States derive between 10% and 20% on average of their annual net income from currency trading. But currency trading is also very profitable for the bank's traders who typically earn a bonus based on the profitability to the bank of their individual trading activities.

Small- to medium-size banks are likely to participate but not be market makers in the interbank market. Instead of maintaining significant inventory positions, they buy from and sell to larger banks to offset retail transactions with their own customers. Of course, even market-making banks do not make markets in every currency. They trade for their own account in those currencies of most interest to their customers and become participants when filling customer needs in less important currencies. *Global Finance in Practice 6.1* describes a typical foreign exchange dealer's day on the job.

GLOBAL FINANCE IN PRACTICE 6.1

The Foreign Exchange Dealer's Day

How do foreign exchange dealers prepare for their working day? Foreign exchange dealing in Europe is officially opened at 8 A.M., but the dealer's work starts at least one hour earlier. Every morning, the chief dealers give their staff guidelines for their dealing activities. They will reassess their strategy on the basis of their estimation of the market over the next few months. They will also decide their tactics for the day, based on the following factors:

- ◆ **Trading Activities in the Past Few Hours in New York and the Far East.** Because of the time difference, banks in New York will have continued trading for several hours longer than the banks in Europe, while in the Far East the working day is already closing when the European day begins.

- ◆ **New Economic and Political Developments.** Following the theoretical forces that determine exchange rates, changes in interest rates, economic indicators, and monetary aggregates are the fundamental factors influencing exchange rates. Political events such as military conflicts, social unrest, the fall of a government, and so on, can also influence and sometimes even dominate the market scene.

- ◆ **The Bank's Own Foreign Exchange Position.** Early in the morning, market makers use electronic information systems to catch up on any events of the past night which might impact exchange rates. Charts (graphic presentations of rate movements) and screen-based rate boards allow dealers to study the latest developments in foreign exchange rates in New York and the Far East. As soon as this preparatory work is completed, the dealers will be ready for international trades (between 8 A.M. and 5 P.M.). The day starts with a series of telephone calls between the key market players, the aim being to sound out what intentions are. Until recently, brokers also acted as intermediaries in foreign exchange and money market operations.

Source: Foreign Exchange and Money Market Transactions, UBS Investment Bank, pp. 54–55.

Individuals and Firms Conducting Commercial and Investment Transactions

Importers and exporters, international portfolio investors, MNEs, tourists, and others use the foreign exchange market to facilitate execution of commercial or investment transactions. Their use of the foreign exchange market is necessary, but nevertheless incidental, to their underlying commercial or investment purpose. Some of these participants use the market to hedge foreign exchange risk as well.

Speculators and Arbitragers

Speculators and arbitragers seek to profit from trading in the market itself. They operate in their own interest, without a need or obligation to serve clients or to ensure a continuous market. Whereas dealers seek profit from the spread between bids and offers in addition to what they might gain from changes in exchange rates, speculators seek all of their profit from exchange rate changes. Arbitragers try to profit from simultaneous exchange rate differences in different markets.

A large proportion of speculation and arbitrage is conducted on behalf of major banks by traders employed by those banks. Thus, banks act both as exchange dealers and as speculators and arbitragers. (However, banks seldom admit to speculating; they characterize themselves as "taking an aggressive position"!) As described in *Global Finance in Practice 6.2*, however, trading is not for the weak of heart.

GLOBAL FINANCE IN PRACTICE 6.2

My First Day of Foreign Exchange Trading

For my internship I was working for the Treasury Front and Back Office of a major investment bank's New York branch on Wall Street. I was, for the first half of my internship, responsible for the timely input and verification of all foreign exchange, money market, securities, and derivative products. My job consisted of the input of all types of trades into the back office systems, the verification through confirmation or documentation of trade details, the verification and payment/receipt of funds regarding variation margins on future transactions, interest rate swaps, caps, floors, FRAs and options, and the maintenance of U.S. dollar positions for the end of day settlement. That was the boring part of my internship.

The second half was much more interesting. I received training in currency trading. I started on the spot desk, worked there for two weeks, and then moved to the swap desk for the remaining three weeks of my internship. From the first day of training in the front office I knew I would have to stay on my toes. The first two weeks of my training I was assigned to the spot desk where my supervisor was a senior trader, female, 23 years old, blonde, blue eyes, and extremely ambitious.

On the very first day, about 11 A.M., she bet on the rise of the Japanese yen after the elections of the new Japanese Prime Minister. She had a long position on the yen and was short on the dollar. Unfortunately she lost $700,000 in less than 10 minutes. It is still unclear for me why she made such a bet. The *Wall Street Journal* and the *Financial Times* (both papers were used heavily in the trading room) were very negative regarding the new Prime Minister's ability to reverse the financial crisis in Japan. It was clear that her position was based purely on emotions, instinct, savvy—anything but fundamentals.

To understand the impact of a $700,000 loss that my blonde *alien* made, you must understand that every trader on a spot desk has to make eight times his or her wage in commission. Let's say that my supervisor was making $80,000 a year. She would then need to make $640,000 in commission on spreads during that year to keep her job. A loss of $700,000 put her in a very bad position, and she knew it. But to her credit, she remained quite confident and did not appear shaken.

But after my first day I was pretty shaken. I understood after this that being a trader was not my cup of tea. It is not because of the stress of the job—and it is obviously very stressful. It was more that most of the skills of the job had nothing to do with what I had been learning in school for many years. And when I saw and experienced how hard these people partied up and down the streets of New York many nights—and then traded hundreds of millions of dollars in minutes the following day, well, I just did not see this as my career track.

Source: Reminiscences of an anonymous intern.

Central Banks and Treasuries

Central banks and treasuries use the market to acquire or spend their country's foreign exchange reserves as well as to influence the price at which their own currency is traded. They may act to support the value of their own currency because of policies adopted at the national level or because of commitments entered into through membership in joint float agreements, such as that of the European Monetary System (EMS) central banks that preceded introduction of the euro. Consequently, motive is not to earn a profit as such, but rather to influence the foreign exchange value of their currency in a manner that will benefit the interests of their citizens. In many instances they do their job best when they willingly take a loss on their foreign exchange transactions. As willing loss takers, central banks and treasuries differ in motive and behavior from all other market participants.

Foreign Exchange Brokers

Foreign exchange brokers are agents who facilitate trading between dealers without themselves becoming principals in the transaction. They charge a small commission for this service. They maintain instant access to hundreds of dealers worldwide via open telephone lines. At times a broker may maintain a dozen or more such lines to a single client bank, with separate lines for different currencies and for spot and forward markets.

It is a broker's business to know at any moment exactly which dealers want to buy or sell any currency. This knowledge enables the broker to find an opposite party for a client without revealing the identity of either party until after a transaction has been agreed upon. Dealers use brokers to expedite the transaction and to remain anonymous, since the identity of participants may influence short-term quotes.

Continuous Linked Settlement and Fraud

In 2002, the Continuous Linked Settlement (CLS) system was introduced. The CLS system eliminates losses if either party of a foreign exchange transaction is unable to settle with the other party. It links the Real-Time Gross Settlement (RTGS) systems in seven major currencies. It is expected eventually to result in a same-day settlement which will replace the traditional two-day transaction period.

The CLS system should help counteract fraud in the foreign exchange markets as well. In the United States, the Commodity Futures Modernization Act of 2000 gives the responsibility for regulating foreign exchange trading fraud to the U.S. Commodity Futures Trading Commission (CFTC).

Transactions in the Interbank Market

Transactions in the foreign exchange market can be executed on a *spot, forward,* or *swap* basis. A broader definition of the foreign exchange market includes foreign currency options, futures, and swaps, which are covered in Chapter 8. A *spot* transaction requires almost immediate delivery of foreign exchange. A *forward* transaction requires delivery of foreign exchange at some future date, either on an "outright" basis or through a "futures" contract. A *swap* transaction is the simultaneous exchange of one foreign currency for another.

Spot Transactions

A *spot* transaction in the interbank market is the purchase of foreign exchange, with delivery and payment between banks to take place, normally, on the second following business day. The Canadian dollar settles with the U.S. dollar on the first following business day. Exhibit 6.3 provides a structured map of when settlement occurs within the European market.

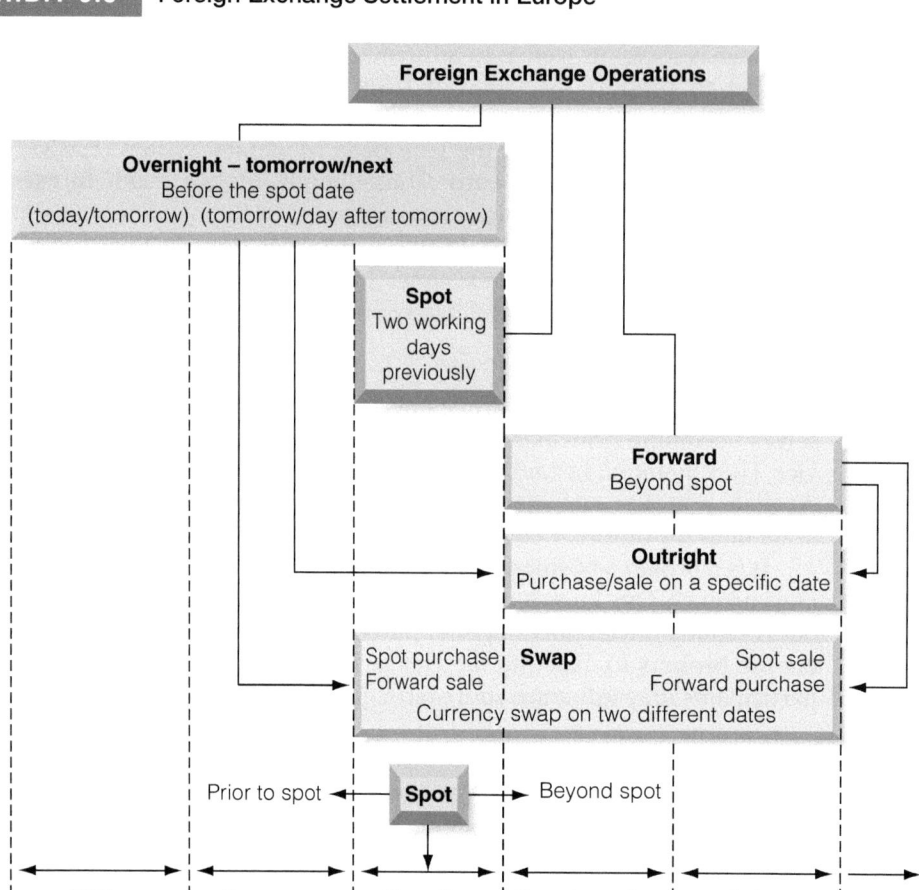

EXHIBIT 6.3 Foreign Exchange Settlement in Europe

Source: *Foreign Exchange and Money Market Transactions*, UBS Investment Bank, p. 58.

The date of settlement is referred to as the "value date." On the value date, most dollar transactions in the world are settled through the computerized Clearing House Interbank Payments System (CHIPS) in New York, which provides for calculation of net balances owed by any one bank to another and for payment by 6:00 P.M. that same day in Federal Reserve Bank of New York funds. Other central banks and settlement services providers operate similarly in other currencies around the world.

A typical spot transaction in the interbank market might involve a U.S. bank contracting on a Monday for the transfer of £10,000,000 to the account of a London bank. If the spot exchange rate were $1.8420/£, the U.S. bank would transfer £10,000,000 to the London bank on Wednesday, and the London bank would transfer $18,420,000 to the U.S. bank at the same time. A spot transaction between a bank and its commercial customer would not necessarily involve a wait of two days for settlement.

Outright Forward Transactions

An *outright forward* transaction (usually called just "forward") requires delivery at a future value date of a specified amount of one currency for a specified amount of another currency. The exchange rate is established at the time of the agreement, but payment and delivery are not required until maturity. Forward exchange rates are normally quoted for value dates of one, two, three, six, and twelve months. Actual contracts can be arranged for other numbers of months or, on occasion, for periods of more than one year. Payment is on the second business day after the even-month anniversary of the trade. Thus, a 2-month forward transaction entered into on March 18 will be for a value date of May 20, or the next business day if May 20 falls on a weekend or holiday.

Note that as a matter of terminology we can speak of "buying forward" or "selling forward" to describe the same transaction. A contract to deliver dollars for euros in six months is both "buying euros forward for dollars" and "selling dollars forward for euros."

Swap Transactions

A *swap* transaction in the interbank market is the simultaneous purchase and sale of a given amount of foreign exchange for two different value dates. Both purchase and sale are conducted with the same counterparty. A common type of swap is a "spot against forward." The dealer buys a currency in the spot market and simultaneously sells the same amount back to the same bank in the forward market. Since this is executed as a single transaction with one counterparty, the dealer incurs no unexpected foreign exchange risk. Swap transactions and outright forwards combined made up 57% of all foreign exchange market activity in April 2010.

Forward-Forward Swaps. A more sophisticated swap transaction is called a "forward-forward" swap. A dealer sells £20,000,000 forward for dollars for delivery in, say, two months at $1.8420/£ and simultaneously buys £20,000,000 forward for delivery in three months at $1.8400/£. The difference between the buying price and the selling price is equivalent to the interest rate differential, that is the *interest rate parity* described in Chapter 7, between the two currencies. Thus, a swap can be viewed as a technique for borrowing another currency on a fully collateralized basis.

Nondeliverable Forwards (NDFs). Created in the early 1990s, the *nondeliverable forward* (NDF), is now a relatively common derivative offered by the largest providers of foreign exchange derivatives. NDFs possess the same characteristics and documentation requirements as traditional forward contracts, except that they are settled only in U.S. dollars; the foreign currency being sold forward or bought forward is not delivered. The dollar-settlement feature reflects the fact that NDFs are contracted offshore—for example, in New York for a Mexican investor—and so are beyond the reach and regulatory frameworks of the home country governments (Mexico in this case). NDFs are traded internationally using standards set by the International Swaps and Derivatives Association (ISDA). Although originally envisioned to be a method of currency hedging, it is now estimated that more than 70% of all NDF trading is for speculation purposes.

NDFs are used primarily for emerging market currencies, currencies that typically do not have open spot market currency trading, liquid money markets, or quoted Eurocurrency interest rates. Although most NDF trading focused on Latin America in the 1990s, many Asian currencies have been very widely traded in the post-1997 Asian crisis era. In general, NDF markets normally develop for country currencies having large cross-border capital movements, but still being subject to convertibility restrictions. Trading in recent years has been dominated by the Korean won, Chilean peso, Taiwanese dollar, Brazilian reais, and Chinese renminbi.

Pricing of NDFs reflects basic interest differentials, as with regular forward contracts, plus some additional premium charged by the bank for dollar settlement. If, however, there is no accessible or developed money market for interest rate setting, the pricing of the NDF takes on a much more speculative element. Without true interest rates, traders often price on the basis of what they believe spot rates may be at the time of settlement.

NDFs are traded and settled outside the country of the subject currency, and therefore are beyond the control of the country's government. In the past this has created a difficult situation, in which the NDF market then serves as something of a gray market in the trading of that currency. For example, in late 2001, Argentina was under increasing pressure to abandon its fixed exchange rate regime of one peso equaling one U.S. dollar. The NDF market began quoting rates of ARS1.05/USD and ARS1.10/USD, in effect a devalued peso, for NDFs settling within the next year. This led to increasing speculative pressure against the peso (and to the ire of the Argentine government).

NDFs, however, have proven to be something of an imperfect replacement for traditional forward contracts. The problems with NDFs typically involve its "fixing of spot rate on the fixing date," the spot rate at the end of the contract used to calculate the settlement. In times of financial crisis, for example, with the Venezuelan bolivar in 2003, the government of the subject currency may suspend foreign exchange trading in the spot market for an extended period of time. Without an official fixing rate, the NDF cannot be settled. In the case of Venezuela, the problem was compounded when a new official "devalued bolivar" was announced, but still not traded.

Size of the Foreign Exchange Market

The Bank for International Settlements (BIS), in conjunction with central banks around the world, conducts a survey of currency trading activity every three years. The most recent survey, conducted in April 2010, estimated *daily* global net turnover in the foreign exchange market to be $3.2 trillion. The BIS data for surveys between 1989 and 2010 is shown in Exhibit 6.4.

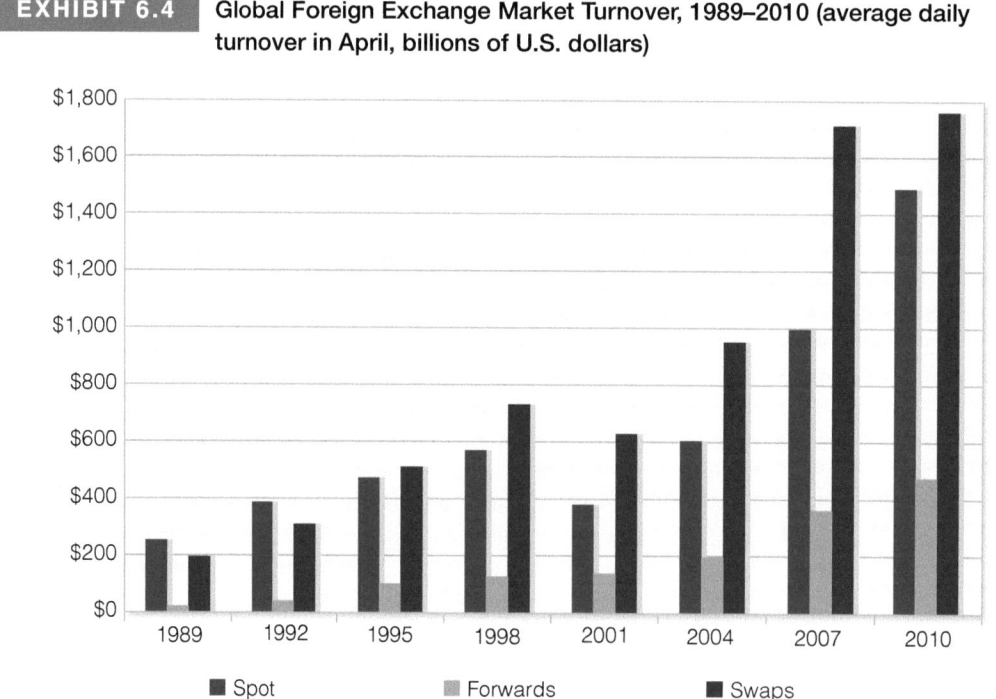

EXHIBIT 6.4 Global Foreign Exchange Market Turnover, 1989–2010 (average daily turnover in April, billions of U.S. dollars)

Source: Bank for International Settlements, "Triennial Central Bank Survey: Foreign Exchange and Derivatives Market Activity in April 2010: Preliminary Results," September 2010, www.bis.org.

Global foreign exchange turnover in Exhibit 6.4 is divided into three categories of currency instruments: spot transactions, forward transactions, and swap transactions. While spot market growth between 2007 and 2010 was dramatic, rising from $1.005 trillion to $1.495 trillion (48% growth in only three years), outright forwards rose from $0.362 trillion to $0.475 trillion (30% growth), with swaps growing only marginally, from $1.714 to $1.765 trillion. As we will discuss in Chapter 8, the low level of interest rates around the globe in recent years, combined with slowing economic growth and new debt issuances, has obviously had a dampening impact on the swap market.

Geographical Distribution

Exhibit 6.5 shows the proportionate share of foreign exchange trading for the most important national markets in the world between 1992 and 2010. (Note that although the data is collected and reported on a national basis, "United States" should largely be interpreted as "New York" because the great majority of foreign exchange trading takes place in the major city of each country. This is most true for "United Kingdom" and "London.")

EXHIBIT 6.5 Top 10 Geographic Trading Centers in the Foreign Exchange Market, 1992–2010 (average daily turnover in April)

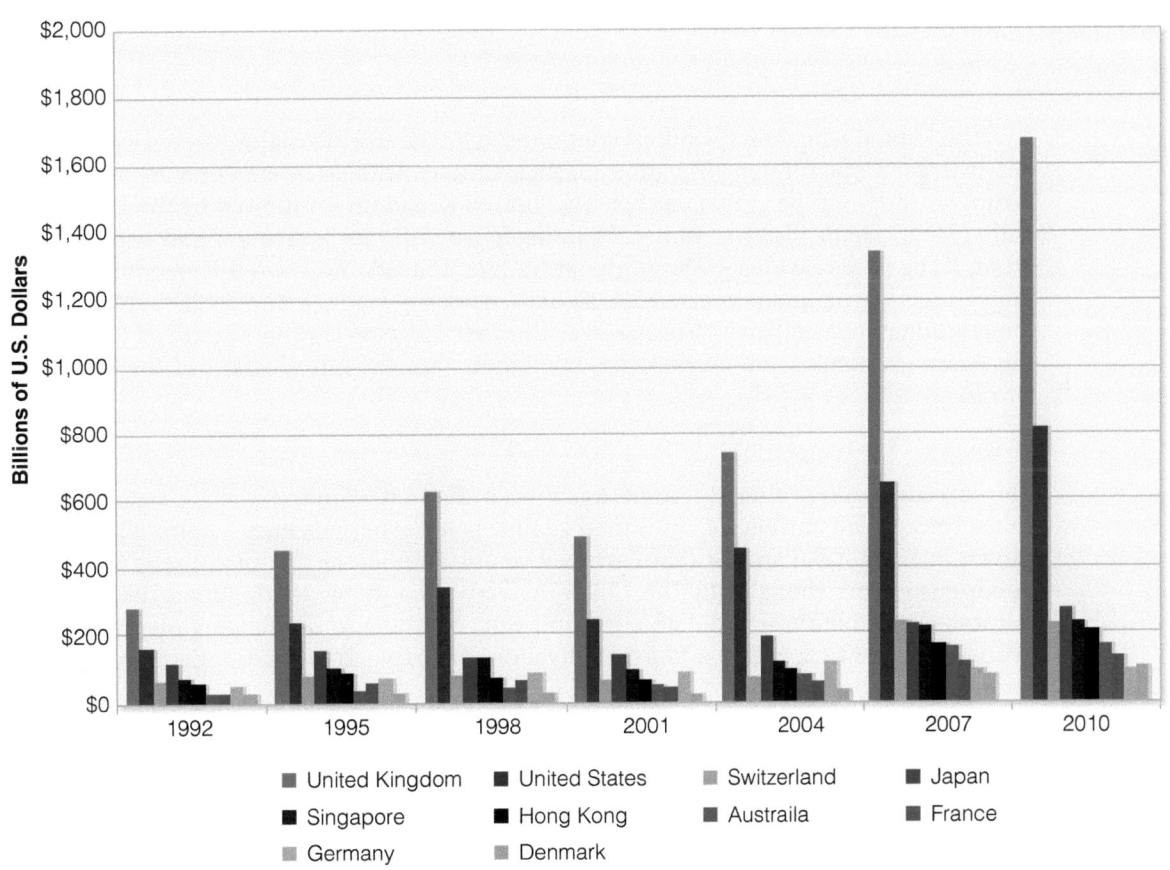

Source: Bank for International Settlements, "Triennial Central Bank Survey: Foreign Exchange and Derivatives Market Activity in April 2010: Preliminary Results," September 2010, www.bis.org.

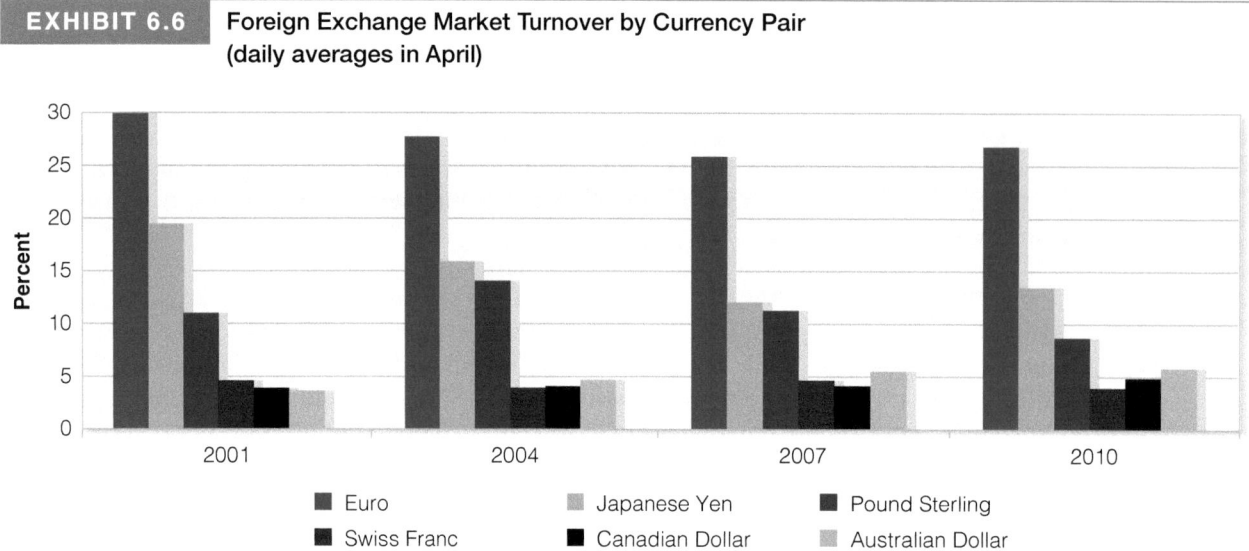

EXHIBIT 6.6 Foreign Exchange Market Turnover by Currency Pair (daily averages in April)

Source: Bank for International Settlements, "Triennial Central Bank Survey: Foreign Exchange and Derivatives Market Activity in April 2010: Preliminary Results," September 2010, www.bis.org.

The United Kingdom (London) continues to be the world's major foreign exchange market in traditional foreign exchange market activity with $1,854 billion in average daily turnover, 36.7% of the global market. The United Kingdom is followed by the United States with 17.9%, Japan (Tokyo) with 6.2%, Singapore with 5.3%, Switzerland with 5.2%, and Hong Kong now reaching 4.7% of global trading. Indeed, the United Kingdom and United States together make up nearly 55% of daily currency trading. The relative growth of currency trading in Asia versus Europe over the past 15 years is pronounced, as the growth of the Asian economies and markets has combined with the introduction of the euro to shift currency exchange activity.

Currency Composition

The currency composition of trading, as shown in Exhibit 6.6, also indicates significant global shifts. Because all currencies are traded against some other currency—pairs, all percentages shown in Exhibit 6.6 are for that currency versus another; in this case, the U.S. dollar. The dollar/euro cross along with the dollar/yen cross continue to dominate global trading. Although the "big three" (dollar, euro, and yen) continue to dominate global trades, it will probably not be long before a fourth, not yet on the map—the Chinese renminbi—will move into greater prominence.

Foreign Exchange Rates and Quotations

A *foreign exchange rate* is the price of one currency expressed in terms of another currency. A *foreign exchange quotation* (or *quote*) is a statement of willingness to buy or sell at an announced rate. As we delve into the terminology of currency trading, keep in mind basic pricing, say the price of an orange. If the price is $1.20/orange, the "price" is $1.20, the "unit" is the orange.

Currency Symbols

Quotations may be designated by traditional currency symbols or by ISO 4217 codes. The latter were developed in recent decades for use in electronic communications. Both traditional symbols and currency codes are given in full at the end of this book, but the major ones used throughout this chapter are the following:

Currency	Traditional Symbol	ISO 4217 Code
U.S. dollar	$	USD
European euro	€	EUR
Great Britain pound	£	GBP
Japanese yen	¥	JPY
Mexican peso	Ps	MXN

Today, all wholesale trading, that is, the trading of currencies between major banks in the global marketplace, uses the three-letter ISO codes. Although there are no hard and fast rules in the retail markets and in business periodicals, European and American periodicals have a tendency to use the traditional currency symbols, while many publications in Asia and the Middle East have embraced the use of ISO codes. The physical paper currency (banknotes) of most countries continue to use the country's traditional currency symbol.

Spot Market Quotes

Foreign exchange quotations follow a number of different systems and abbreviations (many are quite confusing, so stay focused). Exhibit 6.7 provides a brief overview of the most common quotation conventions, in this case, focusing on the European euro and U.S. dollar.

Dollar Rates. The *base currency* used to quote a currency's value is typically the U.S. dollar. Termed *European terms*, this means that whenever a currency's value is quoted, it is quoted in terms of number of units of currency to equal one U.S. dollar.

For example, if a trader in Zurich, whose home currency is the Swiss franc (CHF), were to request a quote from an Oslo-based trader on the Norwegian krone (NOK), the Norwegian trader will quote the value of the NOK against the USD, not the CHF. The result is that most currencies are quoted per dollar—Japanese yen per U.S. dollar, Norwegian krone per U.S. dollar, Mexican pesos per U.S. dollar, Brazilian real per U.S. dollar, Malaysian ringgit per U.S. dollar, Chinese renminbi per U.S. dollar, and so on.

EXHIBIT 6.7 Foreign Currency Quotations Convention

European terms	*American terms*
Foreign currency price of one dollar (USD)	U.S. dollar price of one euro (EUR)
EUR0.8214 = USD1.00	**USD1.2174 = EUR1.00**
Called:	*Called*:
"Direct quote" on the USD in Europe	"Direct quote" on the EUR in the United States
"Indirect quote" on the USD outside Europe	"Indirect quote" on the EUR in Europe
EUR is the *base*, or *price*, currency	USD is the *base*, or *price*, currency
USD is the *foreign*, or *unit*, currency	EUR is the *foreign*, or *unit*, currency

These quotes are reciprocals:

$$\frac{1}{EUR0.8214/USD} = USD1.2714/EUR$$

American terms are used in quoting rates for most foreign currency options and futures, as well as in retail markets that deal with tourists and personal remittances. Foreign exchange traders may also use nicknames for major currencies. "Cable" means the exchange rate between U.S. dollars and U.K. pound sterling, the name dating from the time when transactions in dollars and pounds were carried out over the Transatlantic telegraph cable. A Canadian dollar is a "loonie," named after the water fowl on Canada's one-dollar coin. "Kiwi" stands for the New Zealand dollar, "Aussie" for the Australian dollar, "Swissie" for Swiss francs, and "Sing dollar" for the Singapore dollar.

There are two major exceptions to this rule of using European terms: the euro and the U.K.'s pound sterling. The euro and the U.K. pound sterling are both normally quoted in *American terms*; the U.S. dollar price of one euro and the U.S. dollar price of one pound sterling. Additionally, Australian dollars and New Zealand dollars are normally quoted on American terms. Sterling is quoted as the foreign currency price of one pound for historical reasons. For centuries, the British pound sterling consisted of 20 shillings, each of which equaled 12 pence. Multiplication and division with the nondecimal currency were difficult. The custom evolved for foreign exchange prices in London, then the undisputed financial capital of the world, to be stated in foreign currency units per pound. This practice remained even after sterling changed to decimals in 1971.

The euro was first introduced as a substitute or replacement for domestic currencies like the Deutsche mark and French franc. To make the transition simple for the residents and users of these historical currencies, all quotes were made on a "domestic currency per euro" basis. This held true for its quotation against the U.S. dollar; hence, "U.S. dollars per euro" being the common quotation used today.

Direct and Indirect Quotations. A *direct quote* is the price of a foreign currency in domestic currency units. An *indirect quote* is the price of the domestic currency in foreign currency units.

In retail exchange in many countries (such as currency exchanged in hotels or airports) it is common practice to quote the *home currency* as the *price* and the *foreign currency* as the *unit*. A woman walking down the Avenue des Champs-Elysèes in Paris might see the following quote:

$$EUR0.8214 = USD1.00$$

In France, the home currency is the euro and the foreign currency is the dollar. This quotation in France is termed a *direct quote on the dollar* or a *price quote on the dollar*. Verbally, she might say to herself "0.8214 euros per dollar," or "it will cost me 0.8214 euros to get one dollar."

At the same time a man walking down Broadway in New York City may see the following quote in a bank window:

$$USD1.2174 = EUR1.00$$

The *home currency* is the dollar (the *price*), the *foreign currency* is the euro (the *unit*). In New York, this would be a *direct quote on the euro* (the home currency price of one unit of foreign currency) and an *indirect quote on the dollar* (the foreign currency price of one unit of home currency). Again, verbally, he would probably say "I will pay $1.2174 dollars per euro." These are *American terms*.

The two quotes are obviously equivalent (at least to four decimal places), one being the reciprocal of the other:

$$\frac{1}{EUR0.8214/USD} = USD1.2174/EUR$$

Bid and Ask Rates. Although a newspaper or magazine article will state an exchange rate as a single value, the market for buying and selling currencies, whether it be retail or wholesale, uses two different rates, one for buying and one for selling. Exhibit 6.8 provides a sample of how these quotations may be seen in the market for the dollar/euro.

A *bid* is the price (i.e., exchange rate) in one currency at which a dealer will buy another currency. An *ask* is the price (i.e., exchange rate) at which a dealer will sell the other currency. Dealers *bid* (buy) at one price and *ask* (sell) at a slightly higher price, making their profit from the spread between the buying and selling prices. The bid-ask spread may be quite large for currencies that are traded infrequently, in small volumes, or both.

Bid and ask quotations in the foreign exchange markets are superficially complicated by the fact that the bid for one currency is also the offer for the opposite currency. A trader seeking to buy dollars with euros is simultaneously offering to sell euros for dollars.

As illustrated in Exhibit 6.8, however, the full outright quotation (the full price to all of its decimal points) is typically shown only for the bid rate. Traders, however, tend to abbreviate when talking on the phone or putting quotations on a video screen. The first term, the *bid*, of a spot quotation may be given in full: that is, "1.2170." However, the second term, the *ask*, will probably be expressed only as the digits that differ from the bid. Hence, the bid and ask for spot euros would probably be shown "1.2170/78" on a video screen. In some cases between professional traders, they may only quote the last two digits of both the bid and ask, "70-78", because they know what the other figures are. Closing rates for 47 currencies (plus the SDR) as quoted by the *Wall Street Journal* are presented in Exhibit 6.9.

The *Wall Street Journal* gives American terms quotes under the heading "USD equivalent" and European terms quotes under the heading "Currency per USD." Quotes are given on an outright basis for spot, with forwards of one, three, and six months provided for a few select currencies. Quotes are for trading among banks in amounts of $1 million or more, as quoted at 4 P.M. EST by Reuters. The *Journal* does not state whether these are bid, ask, or mid-rate quotations.

EXHIBIT 6.8 Bid, Ask, and Mid-Point Quotations

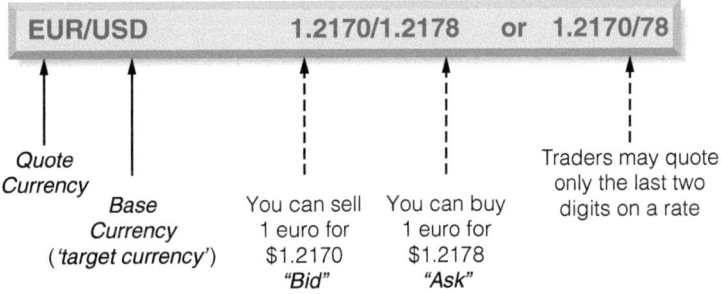

For example, the *Wall Street Journal* would quote the following currencies as follows:				
	Last Bid			Last Bid
Euro (EUR/USD)	1.2170	Brazilian Real (USD/BRL)		1.6827
Japanese Yen (USD/JPY)	83.16	Canadian Dollar (USD/CAD)		0.9930
U.K. Pound (GBP/USD)	1.5552	Mexican Peso (USD/MXN)		12.2365

EXHIBIT 6.9 — Exchange Rates: New York Closing Snapshot

U.S.-dollar foreign-exchange rates in late New York trading, Tuesday, January 4, 2011

Country	Currency	Symbol	Code	USD Equivalent	Currency per USD
Americas					
Argentina*	peso	Ps	ARS	0.252	3.9683
Brazil	real	R$	BRL	0.602	1.6611
Canada	dollar	C$	CAD	1.0015	0.9985
1-month forward				1.0009	0.9991
3-months forward				0.9995	1.0005
6-months forward				0.9968	1.0032
Chile	peso	$	CLP	0.00205	487.8
Colombia	peso	Col$	COP	0.0005276	1895.38
Ecuador	U.S. dollar	$	USD	1	1
Mexico*	new peso	$	MXN	0.0818	12.2324
Peru	new sol	S/.	PEN	0.3568	2.8027
Uruguay†	peso	$U	UYU	0.0502	19.92
Venezuela	boliviar fuerte	Bs	VND	0.23285056	4.2946
Asia-Pacific					
Australia	dollar	A$	AUD	1.0055	0.9945
China	yuan	¥	CNY	0.1514	6.607
Hong Kong	dollar	HK$	HKG	0.1287	7.7695
India	rupee	Rs	INR	0.02226	44.9236
Indonesia	rupiah	Rp	IDR	0.0001113	8985
Japan	yen	¥	JPY	0.012189	82.04
1-month forward				0.012193	82.01
3-months forward				0.012201	81.96
6-months forward				0.012215	81.87
Malaysia §	ringgit	RM	MYR	0.3263	3.0647
New Zealand	dollar	NZ$	NZD	0.7666	1.3045
Pakistan	rupee	Rs.	PKR	0.01166	85.763
Philippines	peso	₱	PHP	0.023	43.554
Singapore	dollar	S$	SGD	0.7765	1.2878
South Korea	won	W	KRW	0.0008885	1125.49
Taiwan	dollar	T$	TWD	0.03428	29.172
Thailand	baht	B	THB	0.03324	30.084
Vietnam	dong	d	VND	0.00005	19499
Europe					
Czech Republic**	koruna	Kc	CZK	0.05343	18.716
Denmark	krone	Dkr	DKK	0.1784	5.6054
Euro area	euro	€	EUR	1.3297	0.752
Hungary	forint	Ft	HUF	0.00482	207.47
Norway	krone	NKr	NOK	0.1705	5.8651
Poland	zloty	—	PLN	0.342	2.924
Romania	leu	L	RON	0.3112	3.2131
Russia ‡	ruble	R	RUB	0.03268	30.6
Sweden	krona	SKr	SEK	0.1487	6.7249
Switzerland	franc	Fr.	CHF	1.0537	0.949
1-month forward				1.0541	0.9487
3-months forward				1.0548	0.948
6-months forward				1.056	0.947
Turkey**	lira	YTL	TRY	0.6483	1.5426
United Kingdom	pound	£	GBP	1.5585	0.6416
1-month forward				1.5581	0.6418
3-months forward				1.5573	0.6421
6-months forward				1.5557	0.6428
Middle East/Africa					
Bahrain	dinar	—	BHD	2.6524	0.377
Egypt*	pound	£	EGP	0.1727	5.7921
Israel	shekel	Shk	ILS	0.2841	3.5199
Jordan	dinar	—	JOD	1.4109	0.7088
Kenya	shilling	KSh	KES	0.01234	81.05
Kuwait	dinar	—	KWD	3.5564	0.2812
Lebanon	pound	—	LBP	0.000666	1501.5
Saudi Arabia	riyal	SR	SAR	0.2667	3.7495
South Africa	rand	R	ZAR	0.1498	6.6756
United Arab Emirates	dirham	—	AED	0.2723	3.6724
IMF ††	special drawing right	—	SDR	1.5464	0.6467

Notes: *Floating rate †Financial §Government rate and ‡Russian Central Bank rate **Commercial rate ††Special Drawing Rights (SDR); from the International Monetary Fund; based on exchange rates for U.S., British and Japanese currencies. Based on trading among banks of $1 million and more, as quoted at 4 p.m. ET by Reuters. Rates are drawn from the *Wall Street Journal* for January 5, 2011.

A final note. The order of currencies in quotations used by traders can be quite confusing (at least the authors of this book think so). As noted by one major international banking publication:

The notation EUR/USD is the system used by traders, although mathematically it would be more correct to express the exchange rate the other way around, as it shows how many USD have to be paid to obtain EUR 1.

This is why the currency quotes in Exhibit 6.8—EUR/USD, USD/JPY, or GBP/USD—are quoted and used in business and the rest of this text as $1.2170/€, ¥83.16/$, and $1.5552/£. International finance is not for the weak of heart!

Cross Rates

Many currency pairs are only inactively traded, so their exchange rate is determined through their relationship to a widely traded third currency. For example, a Mexican importer needs Japanese yen to pay for purchases in Tokyo. Both the Mexican peso (MXN) and the Japanese yen (JPY) are commonly quoted against the U.S. dollar (USD). Using the following quotes from Exhibit 6.9:

$$\text{Japanese yen} \quad \text{JPY82.04/USD}$$
$$\text{Mexican peso} \quad \text{MXN12.2324/USD}$$

the Mexican importer can buy one U.S. dollar for MXN12.2324, and with that dollar can buy JPY 82.04. The cross rate calculation would be as follows:

$$\frac{\text{Japanese yen/U.S. dollar}}{\text{Mexican pesos/U.S. dollar}} = \frac{\text{JPY82.04/USD}}{\text{MXN12.2324/USD}} = \text{JPY6.7068/MXN}$$

The cross rate could also be calculated as the reciprocal:

$$\frac{\text{Mexican peso/U.S. dollar}}{\text{Japanese yen/U.S. dollar}} = \frac{\text{MXN12.2324/USD}}{\text{JPY82.04/USD}} = \text{MXN0.1491/JPY}$$

Cross rates often appear in financial publications in the form of a matrix, as shown in Exhibit 6.10 from the *Wall Street Journal* (same day quotes as in Exhibit 6.9). This matrix shows the amount of each currency (rows) needed to buy a unit of the currency—*bid rates*—of

EXHIBIT 6.10 Key Currency Cross Rates, Tuesday, January 4, 2011

Snapshot of foreign exchange cross rates at 4 P.M. EST.

	Dollar	Euro	Pound	Sfranc	Peso	Yen	CdnDlr
Canada	0.9985	1.3277	1.5562	1.0521	0.0816	0.0122	....
Japan	82.041	109.09	127.86	86.447	6.7069	....	82.164
Mexico	12.232	16.265	19.064	12.889	....	0.1491	12.251
Switzerland	0.949	1.2619	1.4791	....	0.0776	0.0116	0.9505
U.K.	0.6416	0.8532	....	0.6761	0.0525	0.0078	0.6426
Euro	0.752	....	1.1721	0.7924	0.0615	0.0092	0.7532
U.S.	....	1.3297	1.5585	1.0537	0.0818	0.0122	1.0015

Source: Thomson Reuters.

the country on the column. For example, reading across the row labeled "Japan," it takes 82.041 Japanese yen to buy one U.S. dollar, 109.09 yen to buy one euro, and 6.7069 yen to buy one Mexican peso.

Intermarket Arbitrage

Cross rates can be used to check on opportunities for intermarket arbitrage. Suppose the following exchange rates are quoted:

Citibank quotes U.S. dollars per euro	USD1.3297/EUR
Barclays Bank quotes U.S. dollars per pound sterling	USD1.5585/GBP
Dresdner Bank quotes euros per pound sterling	EUR1.1722/GBP

The cross rate between Citibank and Barclays Bank is

$$\frac{\text{USD1.5585/GBP}}{\text{USD1.3297/EUR}} = \text{EUR1.1721/GBP}$$

This cross rate is not the same as Dresdner Bank's quotation of EUR1.1722/GBP, so an opportunity exists to profit from arbitrage between the three markets. Exhibit 6.11 shows the steps in what is called *triangular arbitrage*.

A market trader at Citibank New York, with USD1,000,000, can sell that sum spot to Barclays Bank for USD1,000,000 ÷ USD1.5585/GBP = GBP641,643. Simultaneously, these pounds can be sold to Dresdner Bank for GBP641,643 × EUR1.1722/GBP = EUR752,133, and the trader can then immediately sell these euros to Citibank for dollars: EUR752,133 × USD1.3297/EUR = USD1,000,112. The profit on one such "turn" is a risk-free USD112 (not much, but it's digital!). Such triangular arbitrage can continue until exchange rate equilibrium is reestablished; that is, until the calculated cross rate equals the actual quotation, less any tiny margin for transaction costs.

EXHIBIT 6.11 Triangular Arbitrage by a Market Trader

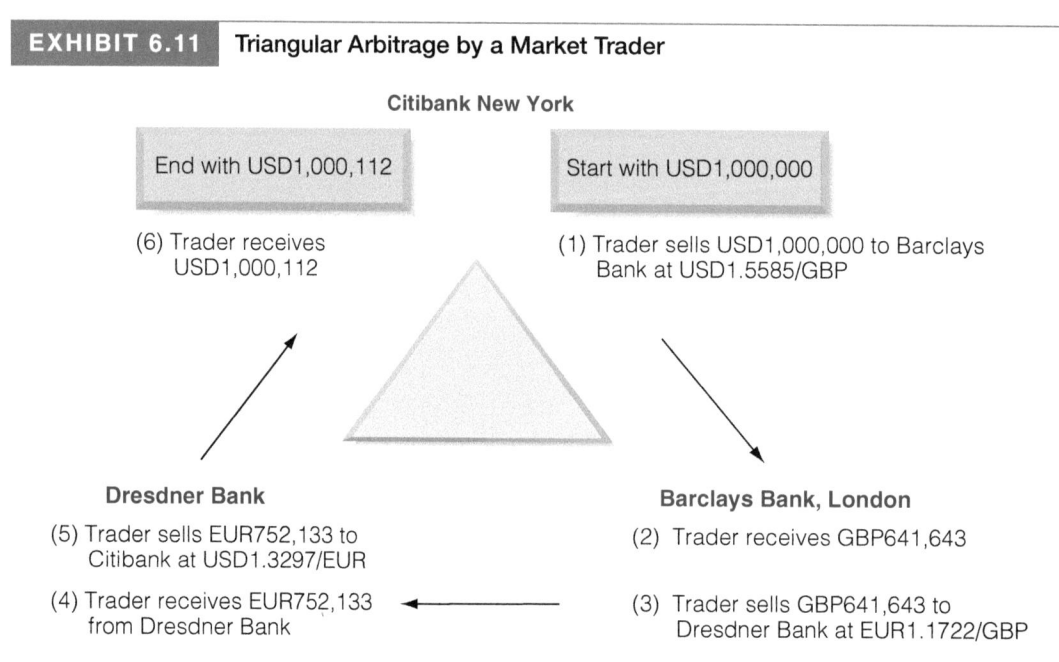

Percentage Change in Spot Rates

Assume that the Mexican peso has recently changed in value from MXP10.00/USD to MXP11.00/USD. Your home currency is the U.S. dollar. What is the percent change in the value of the Mexican peso? The calculation depends upon the designated home currency.

Foreign Currency Terms. When the foreign currency price (the price) of the home currency (the unit) is used, Mexican pesos per U.S. dollar in this case, the formula for the percent change in the foreign currency becomes

$$\%\Delta = \frac{\text{Beginning rate} - \text{Ending rate}}{\text{Ending rate}} \times 100 = \frac{\text{MXP10.00/USD} - \text{MXP11.00/USD}}{\text{MXP11.00/USD}} \times 100 = -9.09\%$$

The Mexican peso fell in value 9.09% against the dollar. Note that it takes more pesos per dollar, and the calculation resulted in a negative value, both characteristics of a fall in value.

Home Currency Terms. When the home currency price (the price) for a foreign currency (the unit) is used, therefore the reciprocals of the numbers used above, the formula for the percent change in the foreign currency is

$$\%\Delta = \frac{\text{Ending rate} - \text{Beginning rate}}{\text{Beginning rate}} \times 100 = \frac{\text{USD0.09091/MXP} - \text{USD0.1000/MXP}}{\text{USD0.1000/MXP}} \times 100 = -9.09\%$$

The calculation yields the identical percentage change, a fall in the value of the peso by 9.09%. Although many people find the second calculation, the home currency term calculation, as the more "intuitive" because it reminds them of many percentage change calculations, one must be careful to remember that these are exchanges of currency for currency, and which currency is designated as home currency matters.

Forward Quotations

Although spot rates are typically quoted on an outright basis, meaning all digits expressed, forward rates are typically quoted in terms of points or *pips*, the last digits of a currency quotation, depending on currency quotation convention. Forward rates of one year or less maturity are termed *cash rates*, longer than one-year *swap rates*. A forward quotation expressed in points is not a foreign exchange rate as such. Rather it is the *difference* between the forward rate and the spot rate. Consequently, the spot rate itself can never be given on a points basis.

Consider the spot and forward point quotes in Exhibit 6.12. The bid and ask spot quotes are outright quotes, but the forwards are stated as points from the spot rate. The 3-month points quotations for the Japanese yen in Exhibit 6.12 are "−143" *bid* and "−140" *ask*. The first number ("−143") refers to points away from the spot *bid*, and the second number ("−140") to points away from the spot *ask*. Given the outright quotes of 118.27 *bid* and 118.37 *ask*, the outright 3-month forward rates are calculated as follows:

	Bid	**Ask**
Outright spot	JPY118.27	JPY118.37
Plus points (3 months)	−1.43	−1.40
Outright forward	JPY116.84	JPY116.97

EXHIBIT 6.12 Spot and Forward Quotations for the Euro and Japanese yen

		Euro: Spot and Forward ($/€)				Japanese yen: Spot and Forward (¥/$)			
		Bid		Ask		Bid		Ask	
	Term	Points	Rate	Points	Rate	Points	Rate	Points	Rate
	Spot		1.0897		1.0901		118.27		118.37
Cash rates	1 week	3	1.0900	4	1.0905	−10	118.17	−9	118.28
	1 month	17	1.0914	19	1.0920	−51	117.76	−50	117.87
	2 months	35	1.0932	36	1.0937	−95	117.32	−93	117.44
	3 months	53	1.0950	54	1.0955	−143	116.84	−140	116.97
	4 months	72	1.0969	76	1.0977	−195	116.32	−190	116.47
	5 months	90	1.0987	95	1.0996	−240	115.87	−237	116.00
	6 months	112	1.1009	113	1.1014	−288	115.39	−287	115.50
	9 months	175	1.1072	177	1.1078	−435	113.92	−429	114.08
	1 year	242	1.1139	245	1.1146	−584	112.43	−581	112.56
Swap rates	2 years	481	1.1378	522	1.1423	−1150	106.77	−1129	107.08
	3 years	750	1.1647	810	1.1711	−1748	100.79	−1698	101.39
	4 years	960	1.1857	1039	1.1940	−2185	96.42	−2115	97.22
	5 years	1129	1.2026	1276	1.2177	−2592	92.35	−2490	93.47

The forward *bid* and *ask* quotations in Exhibit 6.12 longer than two years are called *swap rates*. As mentioned earlier, many forward exchange transactions in the interbank market involve a simultaneous purchase for one date and sale (reversing the transaction) for another date. This "swap" is a way to borrow one currency for a limited time while giving up the use of another currency for the same time. In other words, it is a short-term borrowing of one currency combined with a short-term loan of an equivalent amount of another currency. The two parties could, if they wanted, charge each other interest at the going rate for each of the currencies. However, it is easier for the party with the higher-interest currency to simply pay the net interest differential to the other. The swap rate expresses this net interest differential on a points basis rather than as an interest rate.

Forward Quotations in Percentage Terms

The percent per annum deviation of the forward from the spot rate is termed the *forward premium*. However, the *forward premium*—which may be either a positive (a premium) or negative value (a discount)—depends on which currency is the home, or base currency as with the calculation of percentage changes in spot rates. Assume the following spot rate for our discussion of *foreign currency terms* and *home currency terms*.

	Foreign currency (price)/ home currency (unit)	Home currency (price)/ foreign currency (unit)
Spot rate	¥118.27/$	USD0.0084552/JPY
3-month forward	¥116.84/$	USD0.0085587/JPY

Foreign Currency Terms. When the foreign currency is used as the price of the home currency (the unit), and substituting JPY/USD spot and forward rates, as well as the number of days forward (90), the forward premium on the yen (f^{JPY}) is calculated as follows:

$$f^{\text{JPY}} = \frac{\text{Spot} - \text{Forward}}{\text{Forward}} \times \frac{360}{90} \times 100 = \frac{118.27 - 116.84}{116.84} \times \frac{360}{90} \times 100 = +4.90\%$$

The sign is positive indicating that the Japanese yen is selling forward at a premium of 4.90% against the U.S. dollar.

Home Currency Terms. When the home currency (the dollar) is used as the price for the foreign currency (the yen), the reciprocals of the spot and forward rates used in the previous calculation, the calculation of the forward premium on the yen (f^{JPY}) is

$$f^{\text{JPY}} = \frac{\text{Forward} - \text{Spot}}{\text{Spot}} \times \frac{360}{90} \times 100 = \frac{0.0084552 - 0.0085587}{0.0085587} \times \frac{360}{90} \times 100 = +4.90\%$$

Again, result is identical to the previous premium calculation: a positive 4.90% premium of the yen against the dollar.

Summary of Learning Objectives

Examine the what, when, where, and why of currency trading in the global marketplace

- The three functions of the foreign exchange market are to transfer purchasing power, provide credit, and minimize foreign exchange risk.
- The foreign exchange market is composed of two tiers: the interbank market and the client market. Participants within these tiers include bank and nonbank foreign exchange dealers, individuals and firms conducting commercial and investment transactions, speculators and arbitragers, central banks and treasuries, and foreign exchange brokers.
- Geographically the foreign exchange market spans the globe, with prices moving and currencies traded somewhere every hour of every business day.

Understand the definitions and distinctions between spot, forward, swaps, and other types of foreign exchange financial instruments

- A foreign exchange *rate* is the price of one currency expressed in terms of another currency. A foreign exchange *quotation* is a statement of willingness to buy or sell currency at an announced price.
- Transactions within the foreign exchange market are executed either on a spot basis, requiring settlement two days after the transaction, or on a forward or swap basis, which requires settlement at some designated future date.

Learn the forms of currency quotations used by currency dealers, financial institutions, and agents of all kinds when conducting foreign exchange transactions

- *European terms* quotations are the foreign currency price of a U.S. dollar. *American terms* quotations are the dollar price of a foreign currency.
- Quotations can also be *direct* or *indirect*. A direct quote is the home currency price of a unit of foreign currency, while an indirect quote is the foreign currency price of a unit of home currency.
- Direct and indirect are *not* synonyms for American and European terms, because the home currency will change depending on who is doing the calculation, while European terms are always the foreign currency price of a dollar.

Analyze the interaction between changing currency values, cross exchange rates, and the possible opportunities arising from intermarket arbitrage

- A cross rate is an exchange rate between two currencies, calculated from their common relationships with a third currency. When cross rates differ from the direct rates between two currencies, intermarket arbitrage is possible.

MINI-CASE

The Saga of the Venezuelan Bolivar Fuerte

Una economía fuerte, un bolívar fuerte, un país fuerte.
Translation: A strong economy, a strong bolívar, a strong country.

The Venezuelan bolivar dropped in the country's parallel currency market Monday after the government's official devaluation late last week. The value of the bolivar fell to VEF9.25 to the dollar, according to LechugaVerde.com, a website widely used by locals to track the rate of the Venezuelan currency in the black market.
— "Venezuela Bolivar Falls In Parallel Market After Devaluation," by Kejal Vyas, *Wall Street Journal*, January 3, 2011.

Unfortunately for the Venezuelan people, their currency, the Venezuelan *bolivar fuerte*, had proven anything but strong. On January 1, 2011, President Hugo Chávez devalued the bolivar fuerte—the "strong bolivar"—again, the fifth time in the past decade.

Current Regime

This last devaluation was more of an adjustment. The previous devaluation, January 1, 2008, had fixed the bolivar fuerte (BsF) at BsF4.30/$ for general economic and exchange purposes, but a preferred rate of BsF2.60/$ for food, medicine, and heavy machinery imports considered essential.[1] The 2011 devaluation eliminated the preferred rate, moving all import transactions to BsF4.30/$. This was not a minor elimination, as many analysts believed that in 2010 alone roughly 40% of all dollar-transactions were at the 2.6 rate. Even with this magnitude of change the bolivar fuerte is still considered overvalued; the black market rate of BsF8/$ was the current exchange as the devaluation occurred. The bolivar's history is detailed in Exhibit 1.

EXHIBIT 1 The Venezuelan Bolivar's Decline, 1996–2011

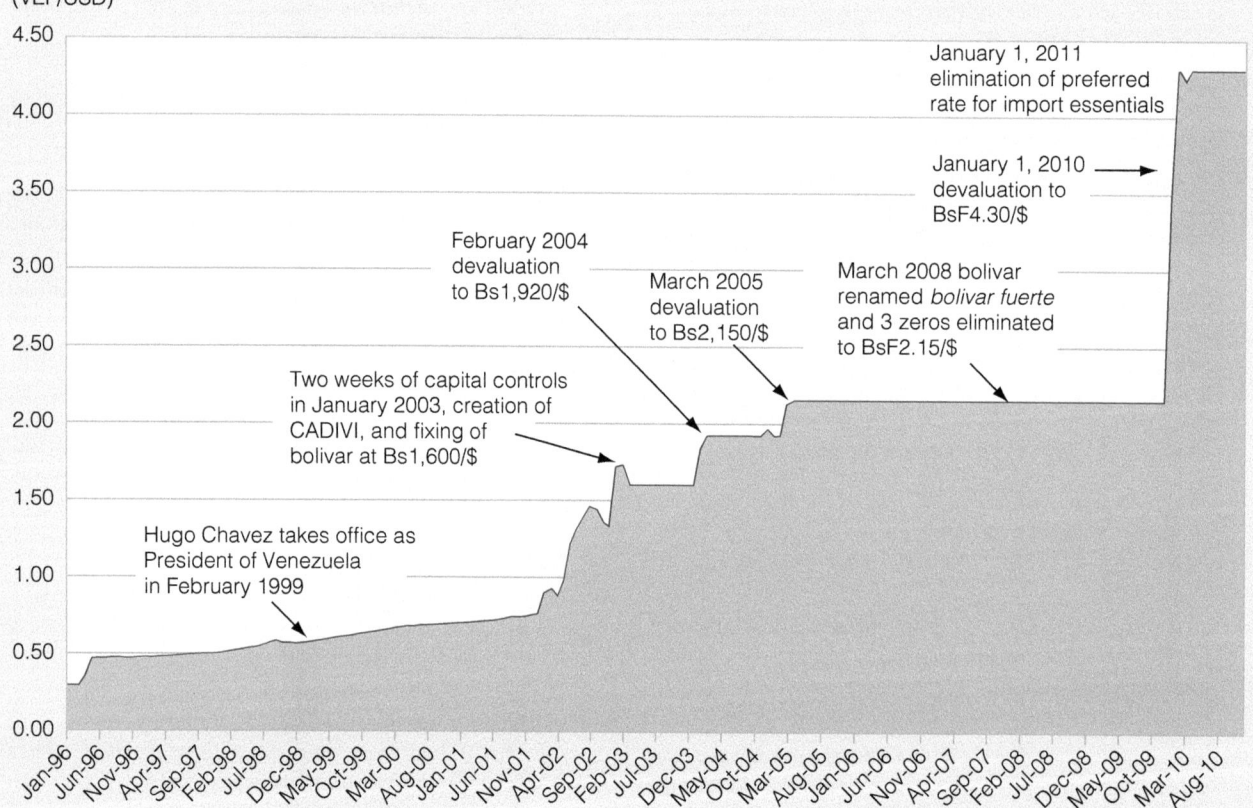

[1] "Venezuela to Devalue Currency," by Kejal Vyas and David Luhnow, *Wall Street Journal*, December 31, 2010.

Even this fixed exchange rate was subject to significant restrictions. CADIVI (Comisión de Administración de Divisas), the official government agency for the exchange of currency, limited Venezuelan residents to an annual total of $3,000 when traveling abroad, and $400 for Internet-based electronic purchases. Although the country had managed to go a number of years between devaluations, the 2008 and 2010 devaluations were clear losses for the purchasing power of the richest oil exporting country in South America.

The fight by the Venezuelan government and the Venezuelan Central Bank (BCV) to assert its independence from the manipulation of the outside world, specifically the United States, knew few bounds. When Hugo Chávez signed into law the currency reform measures in May 2010 to stop speculation of any kind, including foreign currency bonds in the form of equity securities on the Venezuelan stock exchange, it was made very clear what the objective was:[2]

> *Whoever, in one or multiple transactions, within one calendar year, without intervention of the BCV, buys, sells, or in any way offers, transfers, or receives foreign currency between an amount of 10,000 dollars to 20,000 dollars, of the United States of America or their equivalent ... will be sanctioned with a fine valued at double the amount of the operation, in bolivars.*

Chávez had repeatedly devalued the bolivar during his reign in office. In 2003, after the imposition of currency controls, the bolivar was fixed at Bs1,600/$. In February 2004, the bolivar was devalued from Bs1,600/$ to Bs1,920/$. In 2005, it experienced another devaluation, to Bs2,150/$. In January 2008, the bolivar was replaced with the *bolivar fuerte* (BsF) and re-denominated, knocking off three zeros from the currency value, from Bs2,150/$ to BsF2.15/$. All bank accounts and business agreements and contracts were instantly re-denominated into bolivar fuertes by decree. January 1, 2010, a full five years later, saw the bolivar devalued massively, from BsF2.15/$ to BsF4.3/$.

Of course this did not eliminate a third exchange rate in effect, the Transaction System for Foreign Currency Denominated Securities (SITME), another government organization established to set the rate used by businesses to gain access to critical hard currency like the U.S. dollar in order to pay for inputs and other imported components. That rate, set at an even more costly BsF5.30/$, allowed commercial business to gain limited access to foreign currency—at a very high price.

Alternative Markets

The Venezuelan people had struggled so long with an artificially valued currency that they had become some of the most adept in the world at working through *black markets* and *alternative markets*. The "black" or parallel market was a semi-legal market that used brokered desk trading, yet was still not formally authorized much less regulated by the Venezuelan government.

The black market for bolivars, quoted in newspapers until recently, served a major purpose. Although the government set the official exchange rate, it still did not meet all of the demand for dollars even at that rate. As a result, the black market rate became the key indicator of value changes from supply and demand. Grocery stores, restaurants, merchants of all kinds used the black market rates to base their prices and price changes. When the black market rate started rising rapidly, business owners started increasing prices to make up for the loss in value of receiving what they considered discounted bolivars. Chávez and the Venezuelan government then, repeatedly, chastised business and threatened business owners raising prices with losing their companies. Despite all official efforts, black market trading was estimated at an astounding $100 million per day.[3]

One of the most innovative developments in this dysfunctional marketplace had been the selective use of alternative currencies throughout Venezuela. One such example was the *cimarón*, a round piece of stamped cardboard, introduced in a number of rural markets in exchange for goods. The principle was that someone coming to the country markets with goods for barter could exchange them for cimarón, then the cimarón for other goods. What the cimarón could not be exchanged for was bolivar fuertes. According to José Guerra, the former head of research at the country's Central Bank, the cimarón was a relic from Venezuela's past in which landowners paid their peasant workers, their serfs, in tokens which could only be used for goods on their own estates.[4] Although promoted by the government as another step in being "freed" from capitalist ways, the alternative currencies had seen only limited use.

The Chávez Objective

Venezuela's constant battle with inflation has been the underlying economic force driving official devaluation and black market depreciation. Averaging anywhere between 20% and 35% per year over the past decade, inflation has undermined all attempts by the government to reign in the value of its own currency. The devaluations alone contribute to inflation, as more and more domestic

---

[2]"Venezuela Temporarily Closes Parallel Currency Market," by Tamara Pearson, Venezuelanalysis.com, May 18, 2010.

[3]"Currency Woes Dog Venezuelans After Devaluation," by Darcy Crowe, *Wall Street Journal*, May 10, 2010.

[4]"Venezuela's Alternative Currencies," *The Economist*, December 18, 2008, print edition.

currency must then be used to buy the same—or fewer goods—following devaluation. The poor typically suffer the brunt of the devaluation, as they spend the greatest percentages of their incomes on food and other basic necessities, the majority of which are imported.

The Chávez regime, however, has repeatedly used the devaluation of the bolivar to increase the domestic monetary resources it earns from its oil exports. Oil, priced in dollars on the world market, generates U.S. dollar earnings. After each devaluation, each dollar of oil export revenue generates more bolivars or bolivar fuerte for government spending within Venezuela.

South America's largest oil-producing nation will devalue its currency by weakening the exchange rate used in the central bank-administered bond trading market, or Sitme, by 18.5 percent to 6.50 bolivars per U.S. dollar from 5.30 at present, according to the median estimate of eight analysts surveyed by Bloomberg. Five of the analysts said the adjustment, which helps boost government revenue from oil exports, will occur by March 31.
—"Venezuela to Devalue Bolivar for Second Time This Quarter," By Charlie Devereux and Dominic Carey, *Bloomberg*, January 7, 2011.

CASE QUESTIONS

1. Why must a country's currency be devalued? What is failing in the economy?
2. What benefit did the Venezuelan regime in power gain from the repeated devaluation of the bolivar?
3. By the time you read this you will know whether the analysts predicting the future of the bolivar were correct. How did they do?

Questions

1. **Definitions.** Define the following terms:
   a. Foreign exchange market
   b. Foreign exchange transaction
   c. Foreign exchange

2. **Functions of the Foreign Exchange Market.** What are the three major functions of the foreign exchange market?

3. **Market Participants.** For each of the foreign exchange market participants, identify their motive for buying or selling foreign exchange.

4. **Transaction.** Define each of the following types of foreign exchange transactions:
   a. Spot
   b. Outright forward
   c. Forward-forward swaps

5. **Foreign Exchange Market Characteristics.** With reference to foreign exchange turnover in 2001 rank the following:
   a. The relative size of spot, forwards, and swaps as of 2001
   b. The five most important geographic locations for foreign exchange turnover
   c. The three most important currencies of denomination

6. **Foreign Exchange Rate Quotations.** Define and give an example of the following:
   a. Bid quote
   b. Ask quote

7. **Reciprocals.** Convert the following indirect quotes to direct quotes and direct quotes to indirect quotes:
   a. Euro: €1.22/$ (indirect quote)
   b. Russia: Rbl30/$ (indirect quote)
   c. Canada: $0.72/C$ (direct quote)
   d. Denmark: $0.1644/DKr (direct quote)

8. **Geographical Extent of the Foreign Exchange Market.**
   a. What is the geographical location of the foreign exchange market?
   b. What are the two main types of trading systems for foreign exchange?
   c. How are foreign exchange markets connected for trading activities?

9. **American and European Terms.** With reference to interbank quotations, what is the difference between American terms and European terms?

10. **Direct and Indirect Quotes.**
    a. Define and give an example of a direct quote between the U.S. dollar and the Mexican peso, where the United States is designated as the home country.
    b. Define and give an example of an indirect quote between the Japanese yen and the Chinese renminbi (yuan), where China is designated as the home country.

Problems

1. **Munich to Moscow.** On your post-graduation celebratory trip you decide to travel from Munich, Germany to Moscow, Russia. You leave Munich with

15,000 euros in your wallet. Wanting to exchange all of them for Russian rubles, you obtain the following quotes:

Spot rate on the dollar/euro cross rate	$1.3214/€
Spot rate on the ruble/dollar cross rate	Rbl 30.96/$

a. What is the Russian ruble/euro cross rate?
b. How many rubles will you obtain for your euros?

2. **Jumping to Japan.** After spending a week in Moscow you get an email from your friend in Japan. He can get you a very good deal on a plane ticket and wants you to meet him in Osaka next week to continue your post-graduation celebratory trip. You have 450,000 rubles left in your money pouch. In preparation for the trip you want to exchange your Russian rubles for Japanese yen so you get the following quotes:

Spot rate on the rubles/dollar cross rate	Rbl 30.96/$
Spot rate on the yen/dollar cross rate	¥ 84.02/$

a. What is the Russian ruble/euro cross rate?
b. How many rubles will you obtain for your euros?

3. **Visiting Guatemala.** Isaac Díez Peris lives in Rio de Janeiro. While attending school in Spain he meets Juan Carlos Cordero from Guatemala. Over the summer holiday Isaac decides to visit Juan Carlos in Guatemala City for a couple of weeks. Isaac's parents give him some spending money, R$4,500. Isaac wants to exchange it for Guatemalan quetzals (GTQ). He collects the following rates:

Spot rate on the GTQ/€ cross rate	GTQ 10.5799/€
Spot rate on the €/reais cross rate	€0.4462/R$

a. What is the Brazilian reais/Guatemalan quetzal cross rate?
b. How many quetzals will Isaac get for his reais?

4. **Trading in Zurich.** Andreas Broszio just started as an analyst for Credit Suisse in Zurich, Switzerland. He receives the following quotes for Swiss francs against the dollar for spot, 1-month forward, 3-months forward, and six months forward.

Spot exchange rate:

Bid rate	SF 1.2575/$
Ask rate	SF 1.2585/S
1-month forward	10 to 15
3-months forward	14 to 22
6-months forward	20 to 30

a. Calculate outright quotes for bid and ask, and the number of points spread between each.
b. What do you notice about the spread as quotes evolve from spot toward six months?
c. What is the 6-month Swiss bill rate?

5. **Crisis in the Pacific.** The Asian financial crisis which began in July 1997 wreaked havoc throughout the currency markets of East Asia.
a. Which of the following currencies had the largest depreciations or devaluations during the July to November period?
b. Which seemingly survived the first five months of the crisis with the least impact on their currencies?

Country	Currency	July 1997 (per US$)	November 1997 (per US$)
China	yuan	8.40	8.40
Hong Kong	dollar	7.75	7.73
Indonesia	rupiah	2,400	3,600
Korea	won	900	1,100
Malaysia	ringgit	2.50	3.50
Philippines	peso	27	34
Singapore	dollar	1.43	1.60
Taiwan	dollar	27.80	32.70
Thailand	baht	25.0	40.0

6. **Forward Premiums on the Japanese Yen.** Use the following spot and forward bid-ask rates for the Japanese yen/U.S. dollar (¥/$) exchange rate from September 16, 2010, to answer the following questions:
a. What is the mid-rate for each maturity?
b. What is the annual forward premium for all maturities?
c. Which maturities have the smallest and largest forward premiums?

Period	¥/$ Bid Rate	¥/$ Ask Rate
spot	85.41	85.46
1 month	85.02	85.05
2 months	84.86	84.90
3 months	84.37	84.42
6 months	83.17	83.20
12 months	82.87	82.91
24 months	81.79	81.82

7. **Bloomberg Currency Cross Rates.** Use the following cross rate table from Bloomberg to answer the following questions.
a. Japanese yen per U.S. dollar?
b. U.S. dollars per Japanese yen?
c. U.S. dollars per euro?
d. Euros per U.S. dollar?
e. Japanese yen per euro?
f. Euros per Japanese yen?

Currency	USD	EUR	JPY	GBP	CHF	CAD	AUD	HKD
HKD	7.7736	10.2976	0.0928	12.2853	7.9165	7.6987	7.6584	
AUD	1.015	1.3446	0.0121	1.6042	1.0337	1.0053		0.1306
CAD	1.0097	1.3376	0.0121	1.5958	1.0283		0.9948	0.1299
CHF	0.9819	1.3008	0.0117	1.5519		0.9725	0.9674	0.1263
GBP	0.6328	0.8382	0.0076		0.6444	0.6267	0.6234	0.0814
JPY	83.735	110.9238		132.3348	85.2751	82.9281	82.4949	10.7718
EUR	0.7549		0.009	1.193	0.7688	0.7476	0.7437	0.0971
USD		1.3247	0.0119	1.5804	1.0184	0.9904	0.9852	0.1286

g. Canadian dollars per U.S. dollar?
h. U.S. dollars per Canadian dollar?
i. Australian dollars per U.S. dollar?
j. U.S. dollars per Australian dollar?
k. British pounds per U.S. dollar?
l. U.S. dollars per British pound?
m. U.S. dollars per Swiss franc?
n. Swiss francs per U.S. dollar?

8. **Forward Premiums on the Dollar/Euro ($/€).** Use the following spot and forward bid-ask rates for the U.S. dollar/euro (US$/€) exchange rate from December 10, 2010, to answer the following questions:
   a. What is the mid-rate for each maturity?
   b. What is the annual forward premium for all maturities?
   c. Which maturities have the smallest and largest forward premiums?

Period	US$/€ Bid Rate	US$/€ Ask Rate
spot	1.3231	1.3232
1 month	1.3230	1.3231
2 months	1.3228	1.3229
3 months	1.3224	1.3227
6 months	1.3215	1.3218
12 months	1.3194	1.3198
24 months	1.3147	1.3176

9. **Triangular Arbitrage Using the Swiss Franc.** The following exchange rates are available to you. (You can buy or sell at the stated rates.) Assume you have an initial SF12,000,000. Can you make a profit via triangular arbitrage? If so, show the steps and calculate the amount of profit in Swiss francs.

Mt. Fuji Bank	¥ 92.00/$
Mt. Rushmore Bank	SF1.02/$
Mt Blanc Bank	¥ 90.00/SF

10. **Forward Premiums on the Australian Dollar.** Use the following spot and forward bid-ask rates for the U.S. dollar/Australian dollar (US$/A$) exchange rate from December 10, 2010, to answer the following questions:
    a. What is the mid-rate for each maturity?
    b. What is the annual forward premium for all maturities?
    c. Which maturities have the smallest and largest forward premiums?

Period	US$/A$ Bid Rate	US$/A$ Ask Rate
spot	0.98510	0.98540
1 month	0.98131	0.98165
2 months	0.97745	0.97786
3 months	0.97397	0.97441
6 months	0.96241	0.96295
12 months	0.93960	0.94045
24 months	0.89770	0.89900

11. **Transatlantic Arbitrage.** A corporate treasury working out of Vienna with operations in New York simultaneously calls Citibank in New York City and Barclays in London. The banks give the following quotes on the euro simultaneously.

Citibank NYC	Barclays London
$0.7551-61/€	$0.7545-75/€

    Using $1 million or its euro equivalent, show how the corporate treasury could make geographic arbitrage profit with the two different exchange rate quotes.

12. **Canuck Exports.** A Canadian exporter, Canuck Exports, will be receiving six payments of €12,000, ranging from now to 12 months in the future. Since the company keeps cash balances in both Canadian dollars and U.S. dollars, it can choose which currency

to change the euros to at the end of the various periods. Which currency appears to offer the better rates in the forward market?

Period	Days Forward	C$/euro	US$/euro
spot		1.3360	1.3221
1 month	30	1.3368	1.3230
2 months	60	1.3376	1.3228
3 months	90	1.3382	1.3224
6 months	180	1.3406	1.3215
12 months	360	1.3462	1.3194

13. **Venezuelan Bolivar (A).** The Venezuelan government officially floated the Venezuelan bolivar (Bs) in February 2002. Within weeks, its value had moved from the pre-float fix of Bs778/$ to Bs1025/$.
    a. Is this a devaluation or depreciation?
    b. By what percentage did its value change?

14. **Venezuelan Bolivar (B).** The Venezuelan political and economic crisis deepened in late 2002 and early 2003. On January 1, 2003, the bolivar was trading at Bs1400/$. By February 1, its value had fallen to Bs1950/$. Many currency analysts and forecasters were predicting that the bolivar would fall an additional 40% from its February 1 value by early summer 2003.
    a. What was the percentage change in January?
    b. Its forecast value for June 2003?

15. **Indirect Quotation on the Dollar.** Calculate the forward premium on the dollar (the dollar is the home currency) if the spot rate is €1.3300/$ and the 3-month forward rate is €1.3400/$.

16. **Direct Quotation on the Dollar.** Calculate the forward discount on the dollar (the dollar is the home currency) if the spot rate is $1.5800/£ and the 6-month forward rate is $1.5550/£.

17. **Mexican Peso - European Euro Cross Rate.** Calculate the cross rate between the Mexican peso (Ps) and the euro (€) from the following spot rates: Ps12.45/$ and €0.7550/$.

18. **Pura Vida.** Calculate the cross rate between the Costa Rican colón (₡) and the Canadian dollar (C$) from the following spot rates: C500.29/$ and C$1.02/$.

19. **Around the Horn.** Assuming the following quotes, calculate how a market trader at Citibank with $1,000,000 can make an intermarket arbitrage profit.

Citibank quotes U.S. dollar per pound	$1.5900/£
National Westminster quotes euros per pound	€1.2000/£
Deutschebank quotes U.S. dollar per euro	$0.7550/€

20. **Great Pyramids.** Inspired by his recent trip to the Great Pyramids, Citibank trader Ruminder Dhillon wonders if he can make an intermarket arbitrage profit using Libyan dinars and Saudi riyals. He has $1,000,000 to work with so he gathers the following quotes:

Citibank quotes U.S. dollar per Libyan dinar	$1.9324/LYD
National Bank of Kuwait quotes Saudi riyal per Libyan dinar	SAR1.9405/LYD
Barclay quotes U.S. dollar per Saudi riyal	$0.2667/SAR

Internet Exercises

1. **Bank for International Settlements.** The Bank for International Settlements (BIS) publishes a wealth of effective exchange rate indices. Use its database and analyses to determine the degree to which the dollar, the euro, and the yen (the "big three currencies") are currently overvalued or undervalued.

    Bank for International Settlements   bis.org/statistics/eer/index.htm

2. **Bank of Canada Exchange Rate Index (CERI).** The Bank of Canada regularly publishes an index of the Canadian dollar's value, the CERI. The CERI is a multilateral trade-weighted index of the Canadian dollar's value against other major global currencies relevant to the Canadian economy and business landscape. Use the CERI from the Bank of Canada's Web site to evaluate the relative strength of the *loonie* in recent years.

    Bank of Canada exchange rates   www.bankofcanada.ca/en/rates/ceri.html

3. **Forward Quotes.** OzForex Foreign Exchange Services provides representative forward rates on a multitude of currencies online. Use the following Web site to search out forward exchange rate quotations on a variety of currencies. (Note the London, New York, and Sydney times listed on the quotation screen.)

    OzForex   ozforex.com.au/fxoptions/optiondynamics.htm

4. **Federal Reserve Statistical Release.** The United States Federal Reserve provides daily updates of the value of the major currencies traded against the U.S. dollar on its Web site. Use the Fed's Web site to determine the relative weights used by the Fed to determine the index of the dollar's value.

    Federal Reserve   www.federalreserve.gov/releases/h10/update/

5. **Exotic Currencies.** Although major currencies like the U.S. dollar and the Japanese yen dominate the headlines, there are nearly as many currencies as countries in the world. Many of these currencies are traded in extremely thin and highly regulated markets, making their convertibility suspect. Finding quotations for these currencies is sometimes very difficult. Use the following Web pages to see how many African currency quotes you can find.

   Forex-Markets.com   www.forex-markets.com/quotes_exotic.htm

   Oanda.com   oanda.com

6. **Daily Market Commentary.** Many different online currency trading and consulting services provide daily assessments of global currency market activity. Use the following GCI site to find the market's current assessment of how the euro is trading against both the U.S. dollar and the Canadian dollar.

   GCI Financial Ltd   www.gcitrading.com/fxnews/

7. **Pacific Exchange Rate Service.** The Pacific Exchange Rate Service Web site, managed by Professor Werner Antweiler of the University of British Columbia, possesses a wealth of current information on currency exchange rates and related statistics. Use the service to plot the recent performance of currencies which have recently suffered significant devaluations or depreciations, such as the Argentine peso, the Venezuelan bolivar, the Turkish lira, and the Egyptian pound.

   Pacific Exchange Rate Service   fx.sauder.ubc.ca/plot.html

International Parity Conditions

CHAPTER 7

... if capital freely flowed towards those countries where it could be most profitably employed, there could be no difference in the rate of profit, and no other difference in the real or labour price of commodities, than the additional quantity of labour required to convey them to the various markets where they were to be sold.
—David Ricardo, *On the Principles of Political Economy and Taxation*, 1817, Chapter 7.

LEARNING OBJECTIVES

◆ Examine how price levels and price level changes (inflation) in countries determine the exchange rate at which their currencies are traded.

◆ Show how interest rates reflect inflationary forces within each country and currency.

◆ Explain how forward markets for currencies reflect expectations held by market participants about the future spot exchange rate.

◆ Analyze how, in equilibrium, the spot and forward currency markets are aligned with interest differentials and differentials in expected inflation.

What are the determinants of exchange rates? Are changes in exchange rates predictable? These are fundamental questions that managers of MNEs, international portfolio investors, importers and exporters, and government officials must deal with every day. This chapter describes the core financial theories surrounding the determination of exchange rates. Chapter 9 will introduce two other major theoretical schools of thought regarding currency valuation, and combine the three different theories in a variety of real-world applications.

The economic theories that link exchange rates, price levels, and interest rates are called *international parity conditions*. In the eyes of many, these international parity conditions form the core of the financial theory that is considered unique to the field of international finance. These theories do not always work out to be "true" when compared to what students and practitioners observe in the real world, but they are central to any understanding of how multinational business is conducted and funded in the world today. And, as is often the case, the mistake is not always in the theory itself, but in the way it is interpreted or applied in practice. This chapter concludes with a Mini-Case, *Emerging Market Carry-Trades*, which demonstrates how both the theory and practice of international parity conditions sometimes combine to form unusual opportunities for profit.

Prices and Exchange Rates

If identical products or services can be sold in two different markets, and no restrictions exist on the sale or transportation costs of moving the product between markets, the product's price should be the same in both markets. This is called the *law of one price*.

A primary principle of competitive markets is that prices will equalize across markets if frictions or costs of moving the products or services between markets do not exist. If the two markets are in two different countries, the product's price may be stated in different currency terms, but the price of the product should still be the same. Comparing prices would require only a conversion from one currency to the other. For example,

$$P^\$ \times S = P^\text{¥}$$

where the price of the product in U.S. dollars ($P^\$$), multiplied by the spot exchange rate (S, yen per U.S. dollar), equals the price of the product in Japanese yen ($P^\text{¥}$). Conversely, if the prices of the two products were stated in local currencies, and markets were efficient at competing away a higher price in one market relative to the other, the exchange rate could be deduced from the relative local product prices:

$$S = \frac{P^\text{¥}}{P^\$}$$

Purchasing Power Parity and the Law of One Price

If the law of one price were true for all goods and services, the *purchasing power parity* (PPP) exchange rate could be found from any individual set of prices. By comparing the prices of identical products denominated in different currencies, one could determine the "real" or PPP exchange rate that should exist if markets were efficient. This is the absolute version of the theory of purchasing power parity. Absolute PPP states that the spot exchange rate is determined by the relative prices of similar baskets of goods.

The "Big Mac Index," as it has been christened by *The Economist* (see Exhibit 7.1) and calculated regularly since 1986, is a prime example of the law of one price. Assuming that the Big Mac is indeed identical in all countries listed, it serves as one form of comparison of whether currencies are currently trading at market rates which are close to the exchange rate implied by Big Macs in local currencies.

For example, using Exhibit 7.1, in China a Big Mac costs yuan 13.2 (local currency), while in the United States the same Big Mac costs $3.73. The actual spot exchange rate was yuan 6.78/$ at this time. The price of a Big Mac in China in U.S. dollar terms was therefore

$$\frac{\text{Price of Big Mac in China in Yuan}}{\text{Yuan/\$ spot rate}} = \frac{\text{Yuan } 13.2}{\text{Yuan } 6.78/\$} = \$1.95$$

This is the value in column 2 of Exhibit 7.1 for China. *The Economist* then calculates the *implied purchasing power parity rate of exchange* using the actual price of the Big Mac in China (yuan 13.2) over the price of the Big Mac in the United States in U.S. dollars ($3.73):

$$\frac{\text{Price of Big Mac in China in Yuan}}{\text{Price of Big Mac in the U.S. in \$}} = \frac{\text{Yuan } 13.2}{\$3.73} = \text{Yuan } 3.54/\$$$

This is the value in column 4 of Exhibit 7.1 for China. In principle, this is what the Big Mac Index is saying the exchange rate between the yuan and the dollar should be according to the theory.

EXHIBIT 7.1 Selected Rates from the Big Mac Index

Country and Currency		(1) Big Mac Price in Local Currency	(2) Actual Dollar Exchange Rate on July 1	(3) Big Mac Price in Dollars	(4) Implied PPP of the Dollar	(5) Under/over Valuation against Dollar
United States	$	3.73	—	3.73	—	—
Britain	£	2.29	1.52	3.48*	1.63*	−7%
Canada	C$	4.17	1.04	4.01	1.12	7%
China	Yuan	13.2	6.78	1.95	3.54	−48%
Denmark	DK	28.50	5.81	4.91	7.64	32%
Euro area	€	3.38	1.28	4.33*	1.10*	16%
Japan	¥	320	87.2	3.67	85.8	−2%
Russia	Rouble	71.0	30.4	2.34	19.0	−37%
Switzerland	SFr	6.50	1.05	6.19	1.74	66%
Thailand	Baht	70.0	32.3	2.17	18.8	−42%

*These exchange rates are stated in US$ per unit of local currency, $/£ and $/€.

**Percentage under/over valuation against the dollar is calculated as (Implied−Actual)/(Actual), except for the Britain and Euro area calculations, which are (Actual−Implied)/(Implied)

Source: Data drawn from "The Big Mac Index," *The Economist*, July 22, 2010.

Now comparing this implied PPP rate of exchange, yuan 3.54/$, with the actual market rate of exchange at that time, yuan 6.78/$, the degree to which the yuan is either *undervalued* (−%) or *overvalued* (+%) versus the U.S. dollar is calculated as follows:

$$\frac{\text{Implied Rate} - \text{Actual Rate}}{\text{Actual Rate}} = \frac{\text{Yuan } 3.54/\$ - \text{Yuan } 6.78/\$}{\text{Yuan } 6.78/\$} = -48\%$$

In this case, the Big Mac Index indicates that the Chinese yuan is undervalued by 48% versus the U.S. dollar as indicated in the far right-hand column for China in Exhibit 7.1. *The Economist* is also quick to note that although this indicates a sizable undervaluation of the managed value of the Chinese yuan versus the dollar, the theory of purchasing power parity is supposed to indicate where the value of currencies should go over the long-term, and not necessarily its value today.

It is important to understand why the Big Mac may be a good candidate for the application of the law of one price and measurement of under or overvaluation. First, the product itself is nearly identical in each and every market. This is the result of product consistency, process excellence, and McDonald's brand image and pride. Second, and just as important, the product is a result of predominantly local materials and input costs. This means that its price in each country is representative of domestic costs and prices and not imported ones—which would be influenced by exchange rates themselves. But as *The Economist* points out, the Big Mac Index is not perfect.

> The index was never intended to be a precise predictor of currency movements, simply a take-away guide to whether currencies are at their "correct" long-run level. Curiously, however, burgernomics has an impressive record in predicting exchange rates: currencies that show up as overvalued often tend to weaken in later years. But you must always remember

the Big Mac's limitations. Burgers cannot sensibly be traded across borders and prices are distorted by differences in taxes and the cost of non-tradable inputs, such as rents.
— "Happy 20th Anniversary," *The Economist*, May 25, 2006.

A less extreme form of this principle would be that in relatively efficient markets the price of a basket of goods would be the same in each market. Replacing the price of a single product with a price index allows the PPP exchange rate between two countries to be stated as

$$S = \frac{PI^¥}{PI^\$}$$

where $PI^¥$ and $PI^\$$ are price indices expressed in local currency for Japan and the United States, respectively. For example, if the identical basket of goods cost ¥1,000 in Japan and $10 in the United States, the PPP exchange rate would be

$$\frac{¥1000}{\$10} = ¥100/\$.$$

Just in case you are starting to believe that PPP is just about numbers, *Global Finance in Practice 7.1* reminds you of the human side of the equation.

Relative Purchasing Power Parity

If the assumptions of the absolute version of PPP theory are relaxed a bit, we observe what is termed *relative purchasing power parity*. Relative PPP holds that PPP is not particularly helpful in determining what the spot rate is today, but that the relative change in prices between

---

GLOBAL FINANCE IN PRACTICE 7.1

The Immiseration of the North Korean People—The "Revaluation" of the North Korean Won

The principles of purchasing power are not just a theoretical principle, they can also capture the problems, poverty, and misery of a people. The devaluation of the North Korean won (KPW) in November 2009 was one such case.

The North Korean government has been trying to stop the growth and activity in the street markets of its country for decades. For many years the street markets have been the lone opportunity for most of the Korean people to earn a living. Under the communist state's stewardship, the quality of life for its 24 million people has continued to deteriorate. Between 1990 and 2008, the country's infant mortality rate had increased 30%, and life expectancy had fallen by three years. The United Nations estimated that one in three children under the age of five suffered malnutrition. Although most of the working population worked officially for the government, many were underpaid (or in many cases not paid), that they often bribed their bosses to allow them to leave work early to try to scrape out a living in the street markets of the underground economy.

But it was this very basic market economy which President Kim Jong-il and the governing regime wished to stamp out. On November 30, 2009, the Korean government made a surprise announcement to its people: a new, more valuable Korean won would replace the old one. "You have until the end of the day to exchange your old won for new won." All old 1,000 won notes would be replaced with 10 won notes, knocking off two zeros from the officially recognized value of the currency. This meant that everyone holding old won, their cash and savings, would now officially be worth 1/100th of what it was previously. Exchange was limited to 100,000 old won. People who had worked and saved for decades to accumulate what was roughly $200 or $300 in savings outside of North Korea were wiped out; their total life savings were essentially worthless. By officially denouncing the old currency, the North Korean people would be forced to exchange their holdings for new won. The government would indeed undermine the underground economy.

The results were devastating. After days of street protests, the government raised the 100,000 ceiling to 150,000. By late January 2010, inflation was rising so rapidly that Kim Jong-il apologized to the people for the revaluation's impact on their lives. The government administrator who had led the revaluation was arrested, and in February 2010, executed "for his treason."

two countries over a period of time determines the change in the exchange rate over that period. More specifically, *if the spot exchange rate between two countries starts in equilibrium, any change in the differential rate of inflation between them tends to be offset over the long run by an equal but opposite change in the spot exchange rate.*

Exhibit 7.2 shows a general case of relative PPP. The vertical axis shows the percentage change in the spot exchange rate for foreign currency, and the horizontal axis shows the percentage difference in expected rates of inflation (foreign relative to home country). The diagonal parity line shows the equilibrium position between a change in the exchange rate and relative inflation rates. For instance, point P represents an equilibrium point where inflation in the foreign country, Japan, is 4% lower than in the home country, the United States. Therefore, relative PPP would predict that the yen would appreciate by 4% per annum with respect to the U.S. dollar.

The main justification for purchasing power parity is that if a country experiences inflation rates higher than those of its main trading partners, and its exchange rate does not change, its exports of goods and services become less competitive with comparable products produced elsewhere. Imports from abroad become more price-competitive with higher-priced domestic products. These price changes lead to a deficit on current account in the balance of payments unless offset by capital and financial flows.

Empirical Tests of Purchasing Power Parity

Extensive testing of both the absolute and relative versions of purchasing power parity and the law of one price has been done.[1] These tests have, for the most part, not proved PPP to be accurate in predicting future exchange rates. Goods and services do not in

EXHIBIT 7.2 Relative Purchasing Power Parity (PPP)

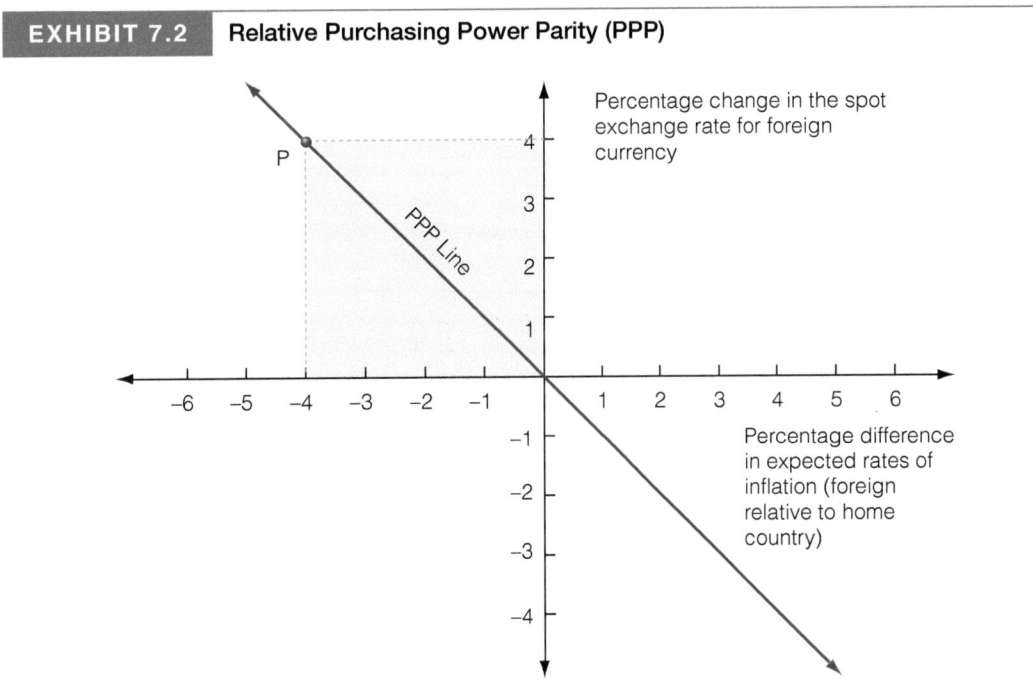

---

[1]See, for example, Kenneth Rogoff, "The Purchasing Power Parity Puzzle," *Journal of Economic Literature*, Volume 34, Number 2, June 1996, pp. 647–668; and Barry K. Goodwin, Thomas Greenes, and Michael K. Wohlgenant, "Testing the Law of One Price When Trade Takes Time," *Journal of International Money and Finance*, March 1990, pp. 21–40.

reality move at zero cost between countries, and in fact many services are not "tradable" — for example, haircuts. Many goods and services are not of the same quality across countries, reflecting differences in the tastes and resources of the countries of their manufacture and consumption.

Two general conclusions can be made from these tests: 1) PPP holds up well over the very long run but poorly for shorter time periods and 2) the theory holds better for countries with relatively high rates of inflation and underdeveloped capital markets.

Exchange Rate Indices: Real and Nominal

Because any single country trades with numerous partners, we need to track and evaluate its individual currency value against all other currency values in order to determine relative purchasing power. The objective is to discover whether its exchange rate is "overvalued" or "undervalued" in terms of PPP. One of the primary methods of dealing with this problem is the calculation of *exchange rate indices*. These indices are formed by trade-weighting the bilateral exchange rates between the home country and its trading partners.

The *nominal effective exchange rate index* uses actual exchange rates to create an index, on a weighted average basis, of the value of the subject currency over time. It does not really indicate anything about the "true value" of the currency, or anything related to PPP. The nominal index simply calculates how the currency value relates to some arbitrarily chosen base period, but it is used in the formation of the real effective exchange rate index. The *real effective exchange rate index* indicates how the weighted average purchasing power of the currency has changed relative to some arbitrarily selected base period. Exhibit 7.3 plots the real effective exchange rate indexes for the United States and Japan over the past 22 years.

EXHIBIT 7.3 IMF's Real Effective Exchange Rate Indexes for the United States, Japan, and the Euro Area

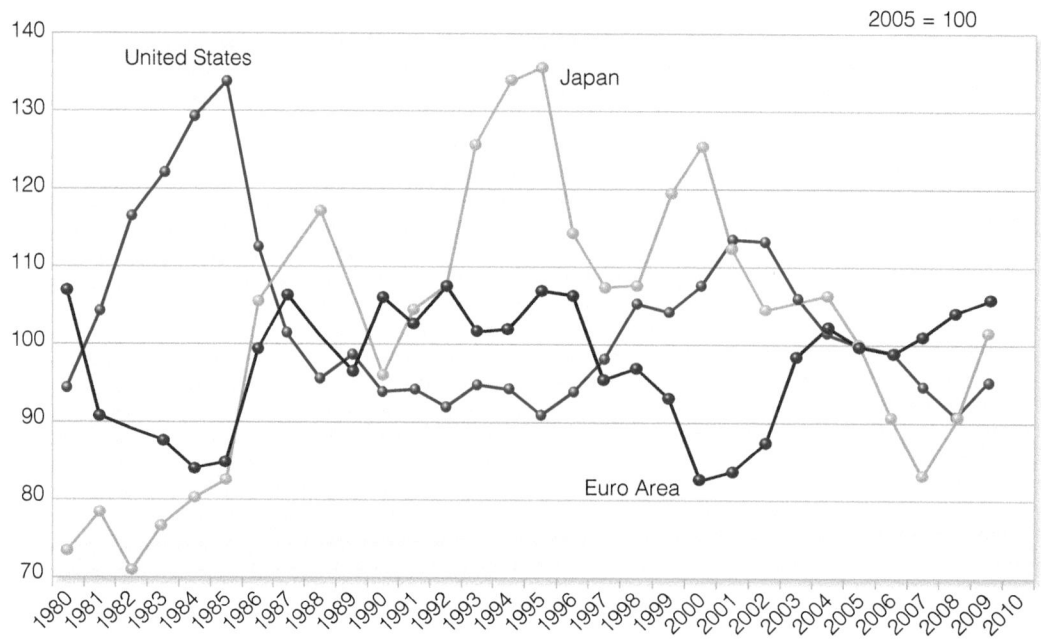

Source: *International Financial Statistics*, IMF, annual, CPI-weighted real effective exchange rates, series RECZF.

The real effective exchange rate index for the U.S. dollar, $E_R^\$$, is found by multiplying the nominal effective exchange rate index, $E_N^\$$ by the ratio of U.S. dollar costs, $C^\$$, over foreign currency costs, C^{FC}, both in index form:

$$E_R^\$ = E_N^\$ \times \frac{C^\$}{C^{FC}}$$

If changes in exchange rates just offset differential inflation rates—if purchasing power parity holds—all the real effective exchange rate indices would stay at 100. If an exchange rate strengthened more than was justified by differential inflation, its index would rise above 100. If the real effective exchange rate index is above 100, the currency would be considered "overvalued" from a competitive perspective. An index value below 100 would suggest an "undervalued" currency.

Exhibit 7.3 shows that the real effective exchange rate of the dollar, yen, and euro have changed over the past three decades. The dollar's index value was substantially above 100 in the 1980s (overvalued), but has remained below 100 (undervalued) since the late 1980s (it did rise slightly above 100 briefly in 1995–1996 and again in 2001–2002). The Japanese yen's real effective rate has remained above 100 for nearly the entire 1980 to 2006 period (overvalued). The euro, whose value has been back-calculated for the years prior to its introduction in 1999, has been largely below 100 and undervalued in its real lifetime.

Apart from measuring deviations from PPP, a country's real effective exchange rate is an important tool for management when predicting upward or downward pressure on a country's balance of payments and exchange rate, as well as an indicator of the desirability to produce for export from that country. *Global Finance in Practice 7.2* shows deviations from PPP in the twentieth century.

Exchange Rate Pass-Through

Incomplete *exchange rate pass-through* is one reason that a country's real effective exchange rate index can deviate for lengthy periods from its PPP-equilibrium level of 100. The degree to which the prices of imported and exported goods change as a result of exchange rate changes is termed *pass-through*. Although PPP implies that all exchange rate changes are passed-through by equivalent changes in prices to trading partners, empirical research in the 1980s questioned this long-held assumption. For example, sizable current account deficits of the United States in the 1980s and 1990s did not respond to changes in the value of the dollar.

To illustrate exchange rate pass-through, assume that BMW produces an automobile in Germany and pays all production expenses in euros. When the firm exports the auto to the United States, the price of the BMW in the U.S. market should simply be the euro value converted to dollars at the spot exchange rate:

$$P_{BMW}^\$ = P_{BMW}^{\euro} \times S$$

where $P_{BMW}^\$$ is the BMW price in dollars, $P_{BMW}^{\euro}$ is the BMW price in euros, and S is the number of dollars per euro. If the euro appreciated 10% versus the U.S. dollar, the new spot exchange rate should result in the price of the BMW in the United States rising a proportional 10%. If the price in dollars increases by the same percentage change as the exchange rate, the pass-through of exchange rate changes is complete (or 100%).

However, if the price in dollars rises by less than the percentage change in exchange rates (as is often the case in international trade), the pass-through is *partial*, as illustrated in

GLOBAL FINANCE IN PRACTICE 7.2

Deviations from Purchasing Power Parity in the Twentieth Century

The recent seminal work by Dimson, Marsh, and Staunton (2002) found that for the 1900–2000 period, relative purchasing power parity generally held. They noted also, however, that significant short-run deviations from PPP did occur. "When deviations from PPP appear to be present, it is likely that exchange rates are responding not only to relative inflation but also to other economic and political factors. Changes in productivity differentials, such as Japan's post-war productivity growth in the traded-goods sector, can bring similar wealth effects, with domestic inflation that does not endanger the country's exchange rate."

"While real exchange rates do not appear to exhibit a long-term upward or downward trend, they are clearly volatile, and on a year-to-year basis, PPP explains little of the fluctuations in foreign exchange rates. Some of the extreme changes (in the table) reflect exchange rates or inflation indexes that are not representative, typically (as in Germany) because of wartime controls, and this may amplify the volatility of real exchange rate changes. Given the potential measurement error in inflation indexes, and the fact that real exchange rates involve a ratio of two different price index series, it is all the more striking that, with the exception of South Africa, all real exchange rates appreciate or depreciate annually by no more than a fraction of one percentage point."

Source: Elroy Dimson, Paul Marsh, and Mike Staunton, *Triumph of the Optimists: 101 Years of Global Investment Returns,* Princeton University Press, 2002, pp. 97–98.

Real Exchange Rate Changes against the U.S. Dollar, Annually 1900–2000

Country	Geometric Mean (%)	Arithmetic Mean (%)	Standard Deviation (%)	Minimum Change (Year, %)	Maximum Change (Year, %)
Australia	−0.6	−0.1	10.7	1931: −39.0	1933: 54.2
Belgium	0.2	1.0	13.3	1919: −32.1	1933: 54.2
Canada	−0.5	−0.4	4.6	1931: −18.1	1933: 12.9
Denmark	0.1	1.0	12.7	1946: −50.3	1933: 37.2
France	−0.4	2.5	24.0	1946: −78.3	1943: 141.5
Germany	−0.1	15.1	134.8	1945: −75.0	1948: 1302.0
Ireland	−0.1	0.5	11.2	1946: −37.0	1933: 56.6
Italy	−0.2	4.0	39.5	1946: −64.9	1944: 335.2
Japan	0.2	3.2	29.5	1945: −78.3	1946: 253.0
The Netherlands	−0.1	0.8	12.6	1946: −61.6	1933: 55.7
South Africa	−1.3	−0.7	10.5	1946: −35.3	1986: 37.3
Spain	−0.4	1.1	18.8	1946: −56.4	1939: 128.7
Sweden	−0.4	0.2	10.7	1919: −38.0	1933: 43.5
Switzerland	0.2	0.8	11.2	1936: −29.0	1933: 53.3
United Kingdom	−0.3	0.3	11.7	1946: −36.7	1933: 55.2

Exhibit 7.4. The 71% pass-through (U.S. dollar prices rose only 14.29% when the euro appreciated 20%) implies that BMW is absorbing a portion of the adverse exchange rate change. This absorption could result from smaller profit margins, cost reductions, or both. For example, components and raw materials imported to Germany cost less in euros when the euro appreciates. It is also likely that some time may pass before all exchange rate changes are finally reflected in the prices of traded goods, including the period over which previously signed contracts are delivered upon. It is obviously in the interest of BMW to keep the appreciation of the euro from raising the price of its automobiles in major export markets.

The concept of *price elasticity of demand* is useful when determining the desired level of pass-through. Recall that the own-price elasticity of demand for any good is the percentage

> **EXHIBIT 7.4** Exchange Rate Pass-Through
>
> *Pass-through* is the measure of response of imported and exported product prices to exchange rate changes. Assume that the price in dollars and euros of a BMW automobile produced in Germany and sold in the United States at the spot exchange rate is
>
> $$P^\$_{BMW} = P^{\euro}_{BMW} \times (\$/\euro) = \euro 35{,}000 \times \$1{,}000/\euro = \$35{,}000$$
>
> If the euro were to appreciate 20% versus the U.S. dollar, from $\$1.0000/\euro$ to $\$1.2000/\euro$, the price of the BMW in the U.S. market should theoretically be $42,000. But if the price of the BMW in the U.S. does not rise by 20%—for example, it rises only to $40,000—then the degree of pass-through is partial;
>
> $$\frac{P^\$_{BMW,2}}{P^\$_{BMW,1}} = \frac{\$40{,}000}{\$35{,}000} = 1.1429, \text{ or a } 14.29\% \text{ increase.}$$
>
> The degree of pass-through is measured by the proportion of the exchange rate change reflected in dollar prices. In this example, the dollar price of the BMW rose only 14.29%, while the euro appreciated 20% against the U.S. dollar. The degree of pass-through is partial: 14.29% ÷ 20.00%, or approximately 0.71. Only 71% of the exchange rate change was passed-through to the U.S. dollar price. The remaining 29% of the exchange rate change has been absorbed by BMW.

change in quantity of the good demanded as a result of the percentage change in the good's own price:

$$\text{Price elasticity of demand} = e_p = \frac{\%\Delta Q_d}{\%\Delta P}$$

where Q_d is quantity demanded and P is product price. If the absolute value of e_p is less than 1.0, then the good is relatively "inelastic." If it is greater than 1.0, it is a relatively "elastic" good.

A German product that is relatively price-inelastic, meaning that the quantity demanded is relatively unresponsive to price changes, may often demonstrate a high degree of pass-through. This is because a higher dollar price in the United States market would have little noticeable effect on the quantity of the product demanded by consumers. Dollar revenue would increase, but euro revenue would remain the same. However, products that are relatively price-elastic would respond in the opposite way. If the 20% euro appreciation resulted in 20% higher dollar prices, U.S. consumers would decrease the number of BMWs purchased. If the price elasticity of demand for BMWs in the United States were greater than one, total dollar sales revenue of BMWs would decline.

Interest Rates and Exchange Rates

We have already seen how prices of goods in different countries should be related through exchange rates. We now consider how interest rates are linked to exchange rates.

The Fisher Effect

The Fisher effect, named after economist Irving Fisher, states that nominal interest rates in each country are equal to the required real rate of return plus compensation for expected inflation. More formally, this is derived from $(1 + r)(1 + \pi) - 1$:

$$i = r + \pi + r\pi$$

where i is the nominal rate of interest, r is the real rate of interest, and π is the expected rate of inflation over the period of time for which funds are to be lent. The final compound term,

$r\pi$, is frequently dropped from consideration due to its relatively minor value. The Fisher effect then reduces to (approximate form):

$$i = r + \pi$$

The Fisher effect applied to the United States and Japan would be as follows:

$$i^\$ = r^\$ + \pi^\$; i^¥ = r^¥ + \pi^¥$$

where the superscripts $ and ¥ pertain to the respective nominal (i), real r, and expected inflation (π) components of financial instruments denominated in dollars and yen, respectively. We need to forecast the future rate of inflation, not what inflation has been. Predicting the future can be difficult.

Empirical tests using *ex-post* national inflation rates have shown that the Fisher effect usually exists for short-maturity government securities such as Treasury bills and notes. Comparisons based on longer maturities suffer from the increased financial risk inherent in fluctuations of the market value of the bonds prior to maturity. Comparisons of private sector securities are influenced by unequal creditworthiness of the issuers. All the tests are inconclusive to the extent that recent past rates of inflation are not a correct measure of future expected inflation.

The International Fisher Effect

The relationship between the percentage change in the spot exchange rate over time and the differential between comparable interest rates in different national capital markets is known as the *international Fisher effect*. "Fisher-open," as it is often termed, states that the spot exchange rate should change in an equal amount but in the opposite direction to the difference in interest rates between two countries. More formally,

$$\frac{S_1 - S_2}{S_2} = i^\$ - i^¥$$

where $i^\$$ and $i^¥$ are the respective national interest rates, and S is the spot exchange rate using indirect quotes (an indirect quote on the dollar is, for example, ¥/$) at the beginning of the period (S_1) and the end of the period (S_2). This is the approximation form commonly used in industry. The precise formulation is as follows:

$$\frac{S_1 - S_2}{S_2} = \frac{i^\$ - i^¥}{1 + i^¥}$$

Justification for the international Fisher effect is that investors must be rewarded or penalized to offset the expected change in exchange rates. For example, if a dollar-based investor buys a 10-year yen bond earning 4% interest, instead of a 10-year dollar bond earning 6% interest, the investor must be expecting the yen to appreciate vis-à-vis the dollar by at least 2% per year during the 10 years. If not, the dollar-based investor would be better off remaining in dollars. If the yen appreciates 3% during the 10-year period, the dollar-based investor would earn a bonus of 1% higher return. However, the international Fisher effect predicts that with unrestricted capital flows, an investor should be indifferent to whether his bond is in dollars or yen, because investors worldwide would see the same opportunity and compete it away.

Empirical tests lend some support to the relationship postulated by the international Fisher effect, although considerable short-run deviations occur. A more serious criticism has been posed, however, by recent studies that suggest the existence of a foreign exchange risk premium for most major currencies. Also, speculation in uncovered interest arbitrage (on pages 187–188) creates distortions in currency markets. Thus, the expected change in exchange rates might consistently be more than the difference in interest rates.

The Forward Rate

A *forward rate* is an exchange rate quoted today for settlement at some future date. A forward exchange agreement between currencies states the rate of exchange at which a foreign currency will be *bought forward* or *sold forward* at a specific date in the future (typically after 30, 60, 90, 180, 270, or 360 days).

The forward rate is calculated for any specific maturity by adjusting the current spot exchange rate by the ratio of euro currency interest rates of the same maturity for the two subject currencies. For example, the 90-day forward rate for the Swiss franc/U.S. dollar exchange rate ($F_{90}^{SF/\$}$) is found by multiplying the current spot rate ($S^{SF/\$}$) by the ratio of the 90-day euro-Swiss franc deposit rate (i^{SF}) over the 90-day Eurodollar deposit rate ($i^{\$}$):

$$F_{90}^{SF/\$} = S^{SF/\$} \times \frac{\left[1 + \left(i^{SF} \times \frac{90}{360}\right)\right]}{\left[1 + \left(i^{\$} \times \frac{90}{360}\right)\right]}$$

Assuming a spot rate of SF1.4800/$, a 90-day euro Swiss franc deposit rate of 4.00% per annum, and a 90-day Eurodollar deposit rate of 8.00% per annum, the 90-day forward rate is SF1.4655/$:

$$F_{90}^{SF/\$} = \text{SF}1.4800/\$ \times \frac{\left[1 + \left(0.0400 \times \frac{90}{360}\right)\right]}{\left[1 + \left(0.0800 \times \frac{90}{360}\right)\right]} = \text{SF}1.4800/\$ \times \frac{1.01}{1.02} = \text{SF}1.4655/\$$$

The *forward premium* or *discount* is the percentage difference between the spot and forward exchange rate, stated in annual percentage terms. When the foreign currency price of the home currency is used, as in this case of SF/$, the formula for the percent-per-annum premium or discount becomes

$$f^{SF} = \frac{\text{Spot} - \text{Forward}}{\text{Forward}} \times \frac{360}{\text{days}} \times 100$$

Substituting the SF/$ spot and forward rates, as well as the number of days forward (90),

$$f^{SF} = \frac{\text{SF}1.4800/\$ - \text{SF}1.4655/\$}{\text{SF}1.4655/\$} \times \frac{360}{90} \times 100 = +3.96\% \text{ per annum}$$

The sign is positive, indicating that the Swiss franc is *selling forward at a 3.96% per annum premium* over the dollar (it takes 3.96% more dollars to get a franc at the 90-day forward rate).

As illustrated in Exhibit 7.5, the forward premium on the Eurodollar forward exchange rate series arises from the differential between Eurodollar interest rates and Swiss franc interest rates. Because the forward rate for any particular maturity utilizes the specific interest rates for that term, the forward premium or discount on a currency is visually obvious — the currency with the higher interest rate (in this case the U.S. dollar) will sell forward at a discount, and the currency with the lower interest rate (in this case the Swiss franc) will sell forward at a premium.

The forward rate is calculated from three observable data items — the spot rate, the foreign currency deposit rate, and the home currency deposit rate — and is not a forecast of the future spot exchange. It is, however, frequently used by managers within MNEs as a forecast, with mixed results, as the following section describes.

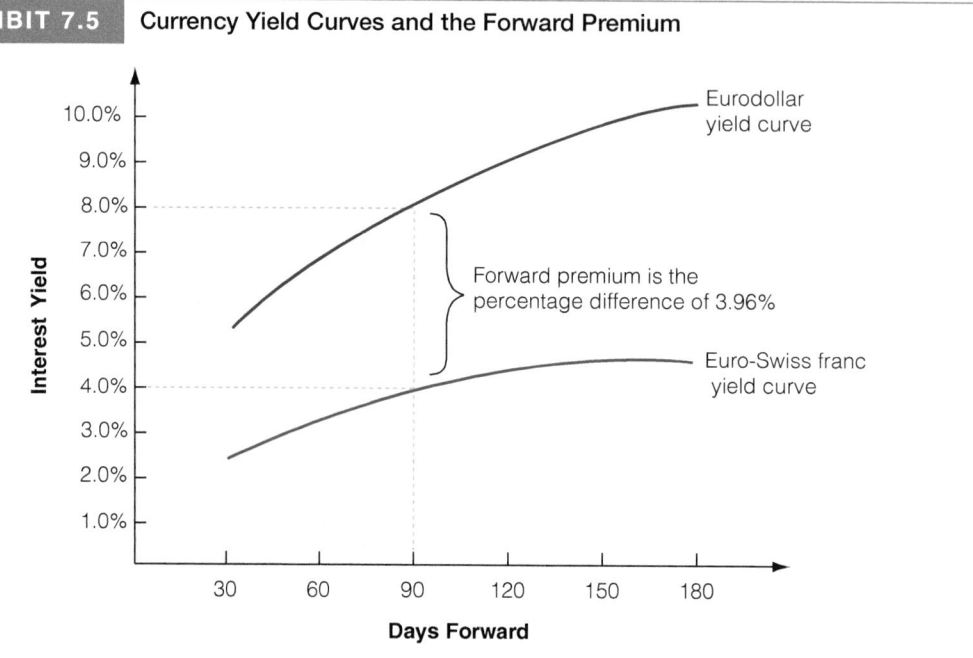

EXHIBIT 7.5 Currency Yield Curves and the Forward Premium

Interest Rate Parity (IRP)

The theory of *interest rate parity* (IRP) provides the link between the foreign exchange markets and the international money markets. The theory states: *The difference in the national interest rates for securities of similar risk and maturity should be equal to, but opposite in sign to, the forward rate discount or premium for the foreign currency, except for transaction costs.*

Exhibit 7.6 shows how the theory of interest rate parity works. Assume that an investor has $1,000,000 and several alternative but comparable Swiss franc (SF) monetary investments. If the investor chooses to invest in a dollar money market instrument, the investor would earn the dollar rate of interest. This results in $(1 + i^\$)$ at the end of the period, where $i^\$$ is the dollar rate of interest in decimal form. The investor may, however, choose to invest in a Swiss franc money market instrument of identical risk and maturity for the same period. This action would require that the investor exchange the dollars for francs at the spot rate of exchange, invest the francs in a money market instrument, sell the francs forward (in order to avoid any risk that the exchange rate would change), and at the end of the period convert the resulting proceeds back to dollars.

A dollar-based investor would evaluate the relative returns of starting in the top-left corner and investing in the dollar market (straight across the top of the box) compared to investing in the Swiss franc market (going down and then around the box to the top-right corner). The comparison of returns would be as follows:

$$(1 + i^\$) = S^{SF/\$} \times (1 + i^{SF}) \times \frac{1}{F^{SF/\$}}$$

where S = the spot rate of exchange and F = the forward rate of exchange. Substituting in the spot rate (SF1.4800/$) and forward rate (SF1.4655/$) and respective interest rates ($i^\$ = 0.02$, $i^{SF} = 0.01$) from Exhibit 7.6, the interest rate parity condition is as follows:

$$(1 + 0.02) = 1.4800 \times (1 + 0.01) \times \frac{1}{1.4655}$$

| EXHIBIT 7.6 | Interest Rate Parity (IRP) |

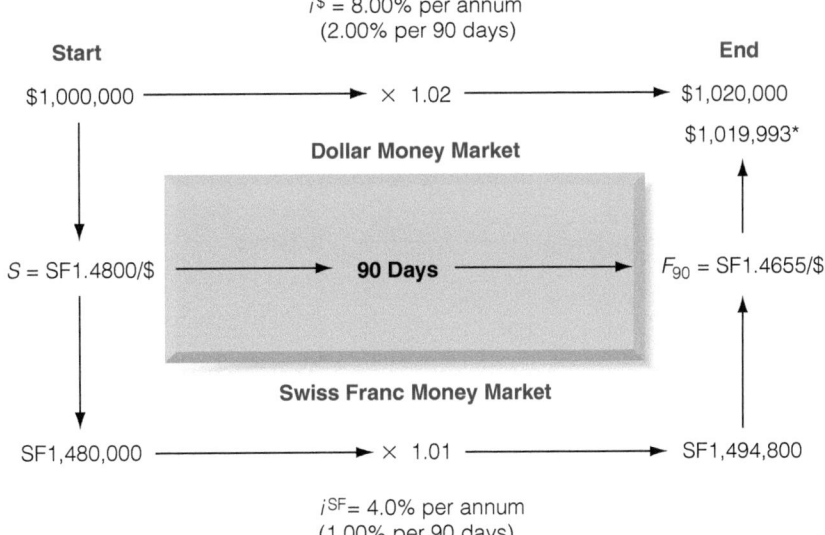

*Note that the Swiss franc investment yields $1,019,993, $7 less on a $1 million investment.

The left-hand side of the equation is the gross return the investor would earn by investing in dollars. The right-hand side is the gross return the investor would earn by exchanging dollars for Swiss francs at the spot rate, investing the franc proceeds in the Swiss franc money market, and simultaneously selling the principal plus interest in Swiss francs forward for dollars at the current 90-day forward rate.

Ignoring transaction costs, if the returns in dollars are equal between the two alternative money market investments, the spot and forward rates are considered to be at IRP. The transaction is "covered," because the exchange rate back to dollars is guaranteed at the end of the 90-day period. Therefore, as shown in Exhibit 7.6, in order for the two alternatives to be equal, any differences in interest rates must be offset by the difference between the spot and forward exchange rates (in approximate form):

$$\frac{F}{S} = \frac{(1 + i^{SF})}{(1 + i^{\$})} \text{ or } \frac{SF1.4655/\$}{SF1.4800/\$} = \frac{1.01}{1.02} = 0.9902 \approx 1\%$$

Covered Interest Arbitrage (CIA)

The spot and forward exchange markets are not constantly in the state of equilibrium described by interest rate parity. When the market is not in equilibrium, the potential for "riskless" or arbitrage profit exists. The arbitrager who recognizes such an imbalance will move to take advantage of the disequilibrium by investing in whichever currency offers the higher return on a covered basis. This is called *covered interest arbitrage* (CIA).

Exhibit 7.7 describes the steps that a currency trader, most likely working in the arbitrage division of a large international bank, would implement to perform a CIA transaction. The currency trader, Fye Hong, may utilize any of a number of major eurocurrencies that his bank holds to conduct arbitrage investments. The morning conditions indicate to Fye Hong that a CIA transaction that exchanges 1 million U.S. dollars for Japanese yen,

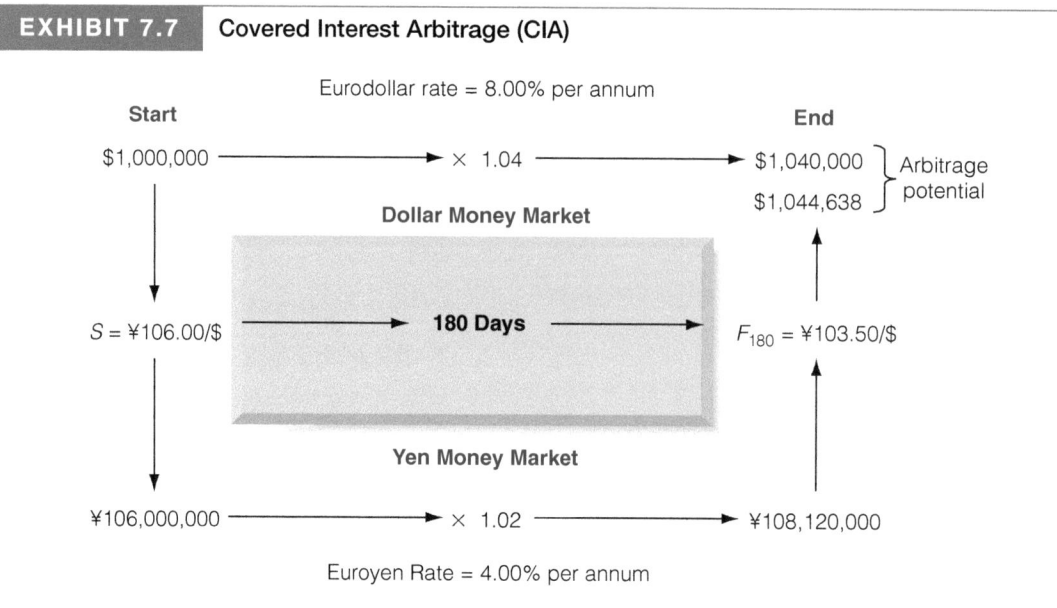

EXHIBIT 7.7 Covered Interest Arbitrage (CIA)

invested in a six month euroyen account and sold forward back to dollars, will yield a profit of $4,638 ($1,044,638 − $1,040,000) over and above that available from a eurodollar investment. Conditions in the exchange markets and euromarkets change rapidly however, so if Fye Hong waits even a few minutes, the profit opportunity may disappear. Fye Hong executes the following transaction:

Step 1: Convert $1,000,000 at the spot rate of ¥106.00/$ to ¥106,000,000 (see "Start" in Exhibit 7.7).

Step 2: Invest the proceeds, ¥106,000,000, in a euroyen account for six months, earning 4.00% per annum, or 2% for 180 days.

Step 3: Simultaneously sell the future yen proceeds (¥108,120,000) forward for dollars at the 180-day forward rate of ¥103.50/$. This action "locks in" gross dollar revenues of $1,044,638 (see "End" in Exhibit 7.7).

Step 4: Calculate the cost (opportunity cost) of funds used at the eurodollar rate of 8.00% per annum, or 4% for 180 days, with principal and interest then totaling $1,040,000. Profit on CIA ("End") is $4,638 ($1,044,638 − $1,040,000).

Note that all profits are stated in terms of the currency in which the transaction was initialized, but that a trader may conduct investments denominated in U.S. dollars, Japanese yen, or any other major currency.

Rule of Thumb. All that is required to make a covered interest arbitrage profit is for interest rate parity not to hold. Depending on the relative interest rates and forward premium, Fye Hong would have started in Japanese yen, invested in U.S. dollars, and sold the dollars forward for yen. The profit would then end up denominated in yen. But how would Fye Hong decide in which direction to go around the box in Exhibit 7.7?

The key to determining whether to start in dollars or yen is to compare the differences in interest rates to the forward premium on the yen (the *cost of cover*). For example, in

Exhibit 7.7, the difference in 180-day interest rates is 2.00% (dollar interest rates are higher by 2.00%). The premium on the yen for 180 days forward is as follows:

$$f^{¥} = \frac{\text{Spot} - \text{Forward}}{\text{Forward}} \times \frac{360}{180} \times 100 = \frac{¥106.00/\$ - ¥103.50/\$}{¥103.50/\$} \times 200 = 4.8309\%$$

In other words, by investing in yen and selling the yen proceeds forward at the forward rate, Fye Hong earns 4.83% per annum, whereas he would earn only 4% per annum if he continues to invest in dollars.

> ***Arbitrage Rule of Thumb:*** *If the difference in interest rates is greater than the forward premium (or expected change in the spot rate), invest in the higher interest yielding currency. If the difference in interest rates is less than the forward premium (or expected change in the spot rate), invest in the lower interest yielding currency.*

Using this rule of thumb should enable Fye Hong to choose in which direction to go around the box in Exhibit 7.7. It also guarantees that he will always make a profit if he goes in the right direction. This rule assumes that the profit is greater than any transaction costs incurred.

This process of CIA drives the international currency and money markets toward the equilibrium described by interest rate parity. Slight deviations from equilibrium provide opportunities for arbitragers to make small riskless profits. Such deviations provide the supply and demand forces that will move the market back toward parity (equilibrium).

Covered interest arbitrage opportunities continue until interest rate parity is reestablished, because the arbitragers are able to earn risk-free profits by repeating the cycle as often as possible. Their actions, however, nudge the foreign exchange and money markets back toward equilibrium for the following reasons:

1. The purchase of yen in the spot market and the sale of yen in the forward market narrows the premium on the forward yen. This is because the spot yen strengthens from the extra demand and the forward yen weakens because of the extra sales. A narrower premium on the forward yen reduces the foreign exchange gain previously captured by investing in yen.

2. The demand for yen-denominated securities causes yen interest rates to fall, and the higher level of borrowing in the United States causes dollar interest rates to rise. The net result is a wider interest differential in favor of investing in the dollar.

Uncovered Interest Arbitrage (UIA)

A deviation from covered interest arbitrage is *uncovered interest arbitrage* (UIA), wherein investors borrow in countries and currencies exhibiting relatively low interest rates and convert the proceeds into currencies that offer much higher interest rates. The transaction is "uncovered," because the investor does not sell the higher yielding currency proceeds forward, choosing to remain uncovered and accept the currency risk of exchanging the higher yield currency into the lower yielding currency at the end of the period. Exhibit 7.8 demonstrates the steps an uncovered interest arbitrager takes when undertaking what is termed the "yen carry-trade."

The "yen carry-trade" is an age-old application of UIA. Investors, from both inside and outside Japan, take advantage of extremely low interest rates in Japanese yen (0.40% per annum) to raise capital. Investors exchange the capital they raise for other currencies like U.S. dollars or euros. Then they reinvest these dollar or euro proceeds in dollar or euro money markets where the funds earn substantially higher rates of return (5.00% per annum

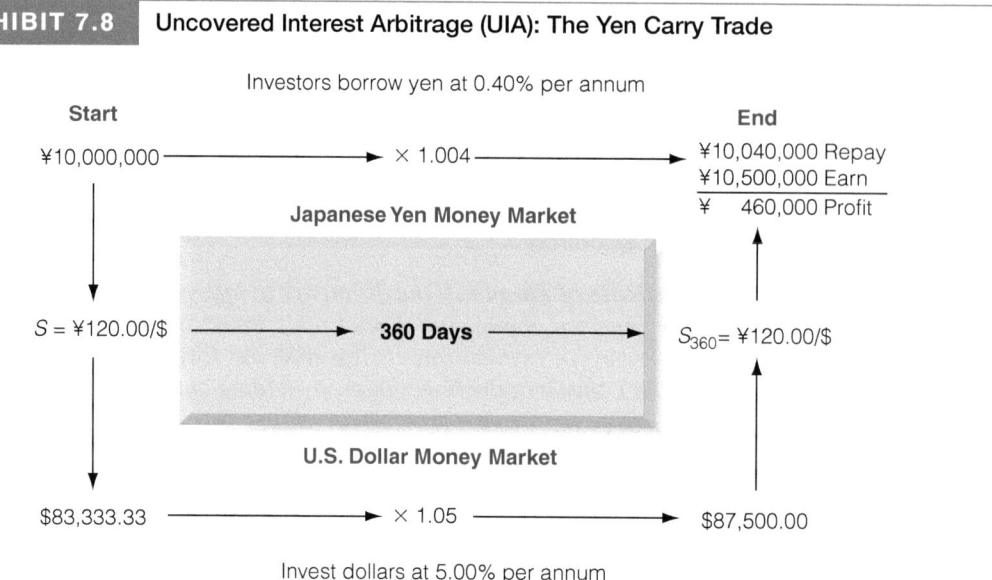

EXHIBIT 7.8 Uncovered Interest Arbitrage (UIA): The Yen Carry Trade

in Exhibit 7.8). At the end of the period—a year, in this case—they convert the dollar proceeds back into Japanese yen in the spot market. The result is a tidy profit over what it costs to repay the initial loan.

The trick, however, is that the spot exchange rate at the end of the year must not change significantly from what it was at the beginning of the year. If the yen were to appreciate significantly against the dollar, as it did in late 1999, moving from ¥120/$ to ¥105/$, these "uncovered" investors would suffer sizable losses when they convert their dollars into yen to repay the yen they borrowed. The higher return does indeed come at higher risk!

Equilibrium between Interest Rates and Exchange Rates

Exhibit 7.9 illustrates the conditions necessary for equilibrium between interest rates and exchange rates. The vertical axis shows the difference in interest rates in favor of the foreign currency, and the horizontal axis shows the forward premium or discount on that currency. The interest rate parity line shows the equilibrium state, but transaction costs cause the line to be a band rather than a thin line. Transaction costs arise from foreign exchange and investment brokerage costs on buying and selling securities. Typical transaction costs in recent years have been in the range of 0.18% to 0.25% on an annual basis. For individual transactions like Fye Hong's arbitrage activities in the previous example on covered interest arbitrage (CIA), there is no explicit transaction cost per trade; rather, the costs of the bank in supporting Fye Hong's activities are the transaction costs. Point X shows one possible equilibrium position, where a 4% lower rate of interest on yen securities would be offset by a 4% premium on the forward yen.

The disequilibrium situation, which encouraged the interest rate arbitrage in the previous CIA example, is illustrated by point U. It is located off the interest rate parity line because the lower interest on the yen is −4% (annual basis), whereas the premium on the forward yen is slightly over 4.8% (annual basis). Using the formula for forward premium presented earlier, we find the premium on the yen thus:

$$\frac{¥106.00/\$ - 103.50/\$}{¥103.50/\$} \times \frac{360 \text{ days}}{180 \text{ days}} \times 100 = 4.83\%$$

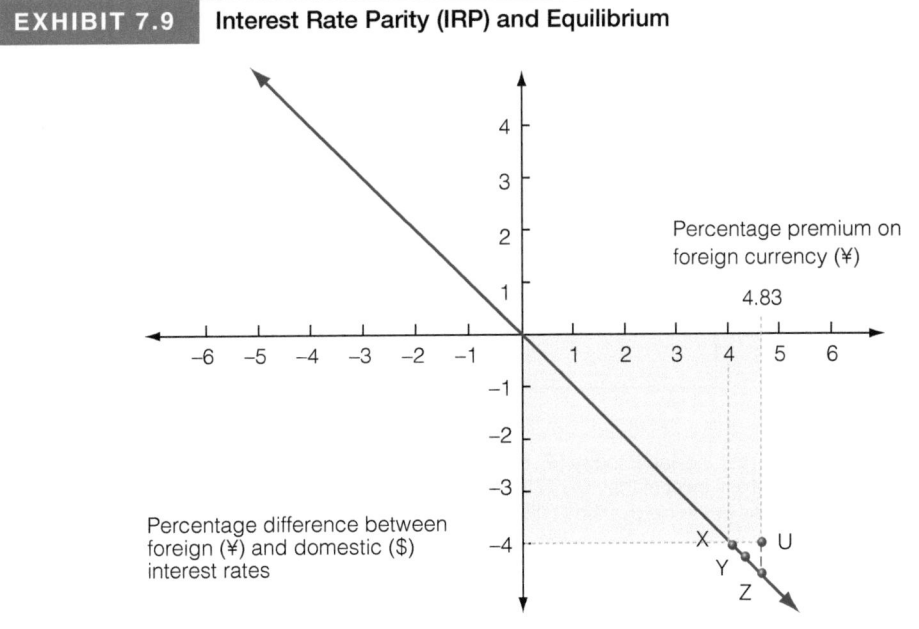

EXHIBIT 7.9 Interest Rate Parity (IRP) and Equilibrium

The situation depicted by point U is unstable, because all investors have an incentive to execute the same covered interest arbitrage. Except for a bank failure, the arbitrage gain is virtually risk-free.

Some observers have suggested that political risk does exist, because one of the governments might apply capital controls that would prevent execution of the forward contract. This risk is fairly remote for covered interest arbitrage between major financial centers of the world, especially because a large portion of funds used for covered interest arbitrage is in Eurodollars. The concern may be valid for pairings with countries not noted for political and fiscal stability.

The net result of the disequilibrium is that fund flows will narrow the gap in interest rates and/or decrease the premium on the forward yen. In other words, market pressures will cause point U in Exhibit 7.9 to move toward the interest rate parity band. Equilibrium might be reached at point Y, or at any other locus between X and Z, depending on whether forward market premiums are more or less easily shifted than interest rate differentials.

Forward Rate as an Unbiased Predictor of the Future Spot Rate

Some forecasters believe that foreign exchange markets for the major floating currencies are "efficient" and forward exchange rates are *unbiased predictors* of future spot exchange rates.

Exhibit 7.10 demonstrates the meaning of "unbiased prediction" in terms of how the forward rate performs in estimating future spot exchange rates. If the forward rate is an unbiased predictor of the future spot rate, the expected value of the future spot rate at time 2 equals the present forward rate for time 2 delivery, available now, $E_1(S_2) = F_{1,2}$.

Intuitively, this means that the distribution of possible actual spot rates in the future is centered on the forward rate. The fact that it is an unbiased predictor, however, does not mean that the future spot rate will actually be equal to what the forward rate predicts. Unbiased prediction simply means that the forward rate will, on average, overestimate and

> **EXHIBIT 7.10** Forward Rate as Unbiased Predictor for Future Spot Rate 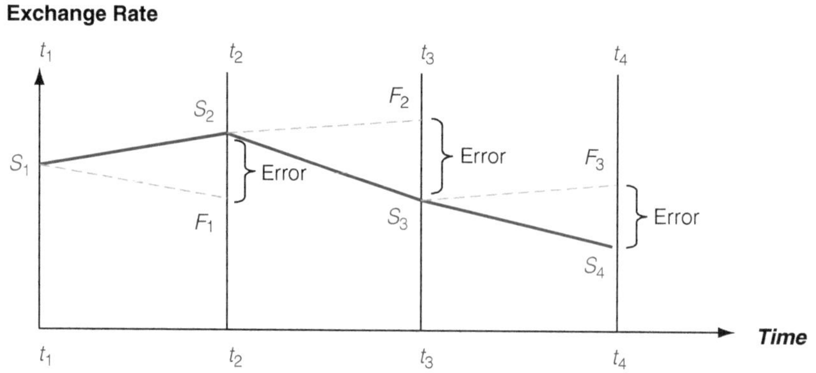
>
> The forward rate available today (F_t, $t + 1$), time t, for delivery at future time $t + 1$, is used as a "predictor" of the spot rate that will exist at that day in the future. Therefore, the forecast spot rate for time S_{t2} is F_1; the actual spot rate turns out to be S_2. The vertical distance between the prediction and the actual spot rate is the forecast error.
>
> When the forward rate is termed an "unbiased predictor of the future spot rate," it means that the forward rate overestimates or underestimates the future spot rate with relatively equal frequency and amount. It therefore "misses the mark" in a regular and orderly manner. The sum of the errors equals zero.

underestimate the actual future spot rate in equal frequency and degree. The forward rate may, in fact, never actually equal the future spot rate.

The rationale for this relationship is based on the hypothesis that the foreign exchange market is reasonably efficient. Market efficiency assumes that 1) all relevant information is quickly reflected in both the spot and forward exchange markets; 2) transaction costs are low; and 3) instruments denominated in different currencies are perfect substitutes for one another.

Empirical studies of the efficient foreign exchange market hypothesis have yielded conflicting results. Nevertheless, a consensus is developing that rejects the efficient market hypothesis. It appears that the forward rate is not an unbiased predictor of the future spot rate and that it does pay to use resources to attempt to forecast exchange rates.

If the efficient market hypothesis is correct, a financial executive cannot expect to profit in any consistent manner from forecasting future exchange rates, because current quotations in the forward market reflect all that is presently known about likely future rates. Although future exchange rates may well differ from the expectation implicit in the present forward market quotation, we cannot know today which way actual future quotations will differ from today's forward rate. The expected mean value of deviations is zero. The forward rate is therefore an "unbiased" estimator of the future spot rate.

Tests of foreign exchange market efficiency, using longer time periods of analysis, conclude that either exchange market efficiency is untestable or, if it is testable, that the market is not efficient. Furthermore, the existence and success of foreign exchange forecasting services suggest that managers are willing to pay a price for forecast information even though they can use the forward rate as a forecast at no cost. The "cost" of buying this information is, in many circumstances, an "insurance premium" for financial managers who might get fired for using their own forecast, including forward rates, when that forecast proves incorrect. If they "bought" professional advice that turned out wrong, the fault was not in their forecast!

If the exchange market is not efficient, it would be sensible for a firm to spend resources on forecasting exchange rates. This is the opposite conclusion to the one in which exchange markets are deemed efficient.

Prices, Interest Rates, and Exchange Rates in Equilibrium

Exhibit 7.11 illustrates all of the fundamental parity relations simultaneously, in equilibrium, using the U.S. dollar and the Japanese yen. The forecasted inflation rates for Japan and the United States are 1% and 5%, respectively; a 4% differential. The nominal interest rate in the U.S. dollar market (1-year government security) is 8%, a differential of 4% over the Japanese nominal interest rate of 4%. The spot rate, S_1, is ¥104/$, and the 1-year forward rate is ¥100/$.

- **Relation A: Purchasing Power Parity (PPP).** According to the relative version of purchasing power parity, the spot exchange rate one year from now, S_2, is expected to be ¥100/$:

$$S_2 = S_1 \times \frac{1 + \pi^¥}{1 + \pi^\$} = ¥104/\$ \times \frac{1.01}{1.05} = ¥100/\$$$

This is a 4% change and equal, but opposite in sign, to the difference in expected rates of inflation (1% − 5% or 4%).

- **Relation B: The Fisher Effect.** The real rate of return is the nominal rate of interest less the expected rate of inflation. Assuming efficient and open markets, the real rates of return should be equal across currencies. Here, the real rate is 3% in U.S. dollar markets ($r = i - \pi = 8\% - 5\%$), and in Japanese yen markets (4% − 1%). Note that the 3% real rate of return is not in Exhibit 7.11, but rather the Fisher effect's relationship—that nominal interest rate differentials equal the difference in expected rates of inflation, −4%.

EXHIBIT 7.11 International Parity Conditions in Equilibrium (Approximate Form)

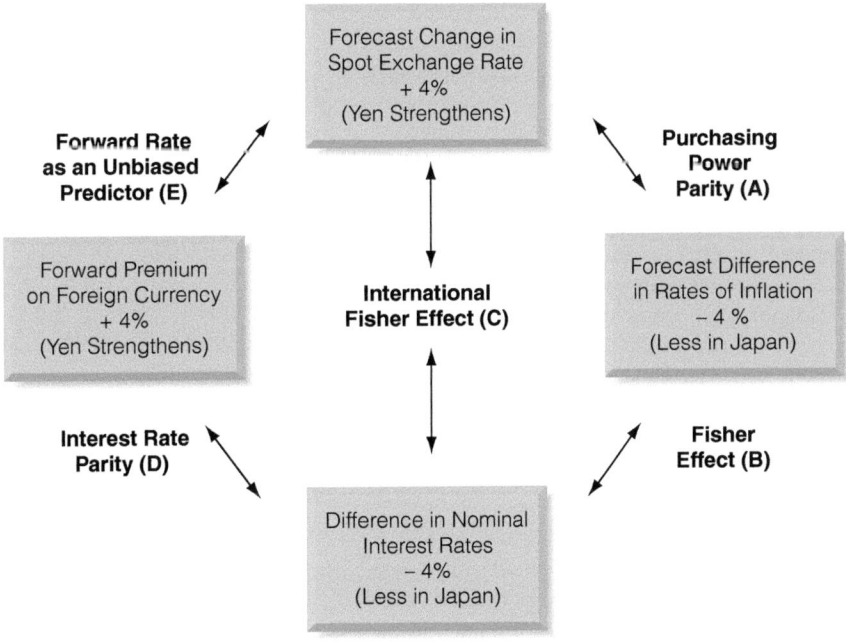

◆ **Relation C: International Fisher Effect.** The forecast change in the spot exchange rate, in this case 4%, is equal to, but opposite in sign to, the differential between nominal interest rates:

$$\frac{S_1 - S_2}{S_2} \times 100 = i^¥ - i^\$ = 4\% - 8\% = -4\%$$

◆ **Relation D: Interest Rate Parity (IRP).** According to the theory of interest rate parity, the difference in nominal interest rates is equal to, but opposite in sign to, the forward premium. For this numerical example, the nominal yen interest rate (4%) is 4% less than the nominal dollar interest rate (8%):

$$i^¥ - i^\$ = 4\% - 8\% = -4\%$$

and the forward premium is a positive 4%:

$$f^¥ = \frac{S_1 - F}{F} \times 100 = \frac{¥104/\$ - ¥100/\$}{¥100/\$} \times 100 = 4\%$$

◆ **Relation E: Forward Rate as an Unbiased Predictor.** Finally, the 1-year forward rate on the Japanese yen, ¥100/$, if assumed to be an unbiased predictor of the future spot rate, also forecasts ¥100/$.

Summary of Learning Objectives

Examine how price levels and price level changes (inflation) in countries determine the exchange rate at which their currencies are traded.

◆ Parity conditions have traditionally been used by economists to help explain the long-run trend in an exchange rate.

◆ Under conditions of freely floating rates, the expected rate of change in the spot exchange rate, differential rates of national inflation and interest, and the forward discount or premium are all directly proportional to each other and mutually determined. A change in one of these variables has a tendency to change all of them with a feedback on the variable that changes first.

◆ If the identical product or service can be sold in two different markets, and there are no restrictions on its sale or transportation costs of moving the product between markets, the product's price should be the same in both markets. This is called the law of one price.

◆ The absolute version of the theory of purchasing power parity states that the spot exchange rate is determined by the relative prices of similar baskets of goods.

◆ The relative version of the theory of purchasing power parity states that if the spot exchange rate between two countries starts in equilibrium, any change in the differential rate of inflation between them tends to be offset over the long run by an equal but opposite change in the spot exchange rate.

Show how interest rates reflect inflationary forces within each country and currency.

◆ The Fisher effect, named after economist Irving Fisher, states that nominal interest rates in each country are equal to the required real rate of return plus compensation for expected inflation.

Explain how forward markets for currencies reflect expectations held by market participants about the future spot exchange rate.

◆ The international Fisher effect, "Fisher-open" as it is often termed, states that the spot exchange rate should change in an equal amount but in the opposite direction to the difference in interest rates between two countries.

Analyze how, in equilibrium, the spot and forward currency markets are aligned with interest differentials and differentials in expected inflation.

◆ The theory of interest rate parity (IRP) states that the difference in the national interest rates for securities of similar risk and maturity should be equal to, but opposite in sign to, the forward rate discount or premium for the foreign currency, except for transaction costs.

- When the spot and forward exchange markets are not in equilibrium as described by interest rate parity, the potential for "riskless" or arbitrage profit exists. This is called covered interest arbitrage (CIA).

- Some forecasters believe that for the major floating currencies, foreign exchange markets are "efficient" and forward exchange rates are unbiased predictors of future spot exchange rates.

MINI-CASE

Emerging Market Carry Trades

The weak economic outlook for the euro zone is the primary factor driving the change in that trade. Minor differences in interest rates between the euro and either the dollar or the Japanese yen are less important right now, strategists said. Rates in the U.S. and Japan are near 0%, while they are at 1% in Europe.

— "Euro Becomes Increasingly Popular Choice to Fund Carry Trades," The *Wall Street Journal*, December 21, 2010.

Incredibly low interest rates in both the United States and Europe, accompanied by dim economic performance and continuing concern over fiscal deficits, has led to a most unexpected outcome: a new form of carry trade which shorts the dollar and euro.

The *carry trade* has long been associated with Japan and the relatively low interest rates which its financial community has made available to multinational investors. A form of uncovered interest rate arbitrage (UIA), the Japanese carry trade was based on an investor raising funds in Japan at low interest rates and then exchanging the proceeds for a foreign currency in which the interest rates promised higher relative returns. Then, at the end of the term, the investor could potentially exchange the foreign currency returns, plus interest, back to Japanese yen to settle the obligation and also, hopefully, a profit. The entire risk-return profile of the strategy, however, was based on the exchange rate at the end of the period being relatively unchanged from the initial spot rate.

The global financial crisis of 2007–2009 has left a marketplace in which the U.S. Federal Reserve and the European Central Bank have pursued easy money policies. Both central banks, in an effort to maintain high levels of liquidity and support fragile commercial banking systems, have kept interest rates at near-zero levels. Now global investors, those who see opportunities for profit in an anemic global economy, are using those same low-cost funds in the U.S. and Europe to fund uncovered interest arbitrage activities. But what is making this "emerging market carry trade" so unique is not the interest rates, but the fact that investors are shorting two of the world's core currencies: the dollar and the euro.

Consider the strategy outlined in Exhibit 1. An investor borrows EUR 20 million at an incredibly low rate, say 1.00% per annum or 0.50% for 180 days. The EUR 20 million are then exchanged for Indian rupees (INR), the current spot rate being INR 60.4672 = EUR 1.00. The resulting INR

EXHIBIT 1   The Euro/Emerging Market Carry Trade

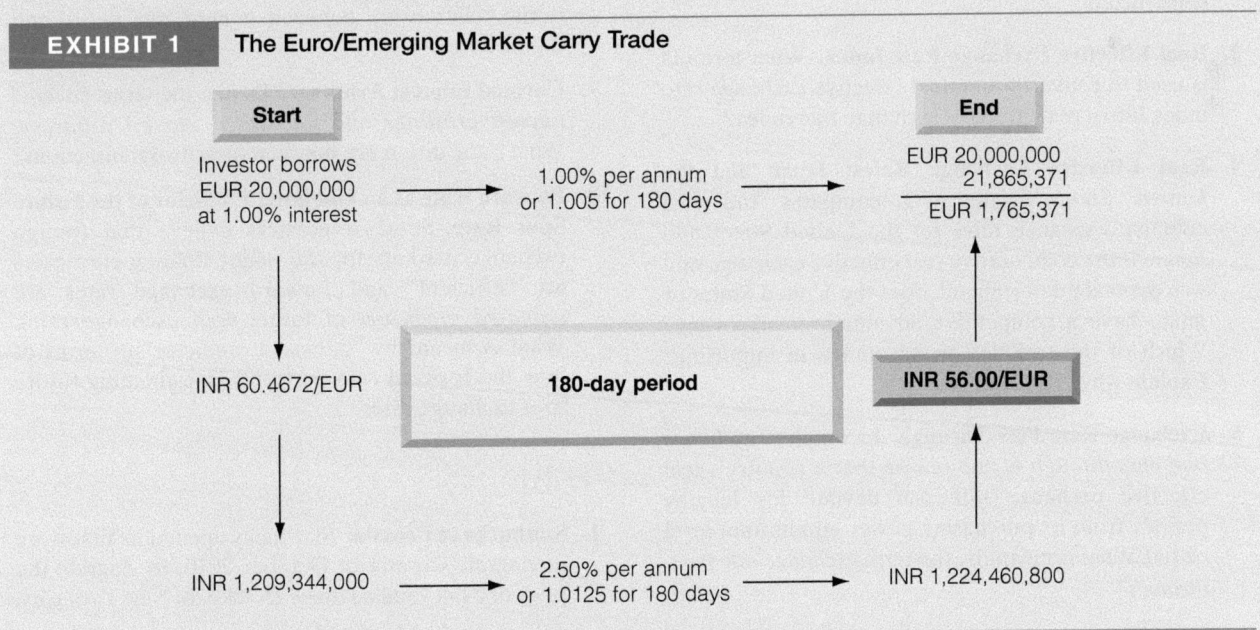

1,209,344,000 are put into an interest bearing deposit with any of a number of Indian banks attempting to attract capital. The rate of interest offered, 2.50%, is not particularly high, but is greater than that available in the dollar, euro, or even yen markets. But the critical component of the strategy is not to earn the higher rupee interest (although that does help), it is the expectations of the investor over the direction of the INR per EUR exchange rate.

The European economy yielded very weak economic growth in 2010, and all indications were that 2011 would not be much better. Low interest rates, although expected to persist, had not done much to support the euro's value. Like the dollar, many forecasts were for the euro to fall against many of the world's currencies—including the Indian rupee. The Indian economy, however, had been growing rapidly; in fact, nearly too fast. Inflationary pressures had kept inflation for 2010 at just under 10%, and it was expected to remain at 7% or higher throughout 2011. The State Bank of India, India's central bank, was expected to tighten monetary growth to fight inflationary pressures, sending rupee interest rates—and the rupee itself, higher on world markets. In the exhibit the investor is shown expecting a spot rate at the end of the 180-day arbitrage position at INR 56.00/EUR. The expected yield on position, a whopping 8.83% (EUR 1,765,371 profit on an initial investment of EUR 20 million). An extremely attractive rate of return in a global marketplace of sub-5% investment yields.

CASE QUESTIONS

1. Why are interest rates so low in the traditional core markets of USD and EUR?
2. What makes this "emerging market carry trade" so different from traditional forms of uncovered interest arbitrage?
3. Why are many investors shorting the dollar and the euro?

Questions

1. **Purchasing Power Parity.** Define the following terms:
   a. The law of one price
   b. Absolute purchasing power parity
   c. Relative purchasing power parity

2. **Nominal Effective Exchange Rate Index.** Explain how a nominal effective exchange rate index is constructed.

3. **Real Effective Exchange Rate Index.** What formula is used to convert a nominal effective exchange rate index into a real effective exchange rate index?

4. **Real Effective Exchange Rates: Japan and the United States.** Exhibit 7.3 compares the real effective exchange rates for the United States and Japan. If the comparative real effective exchange rate was the main determinant, does the United States or Japan have a competitive advantage in exporting? Which of the two has an advantage in importing? Explain why.

5. **Exchange Rate Pass-Through.** Incomplete *exchange rate pass-through* is one reason that a country's real effective exchange rate can deviate for lengthy periods from its purchasing power equilibrium level of 100. What is meant by the term *exchange rate pass-through*?

6. **The Fisher Effect.** Define the *Fisher effect*. To what extent do empirical tests confirm that the *Fisher effect* exists in practice?

7. **The International Fisher Effect.** Define the *international Fisher effect*. To what extent do empirical tests confirm that the *international Fisher effect* exists in practice?

8. **Interest Rate Parity.** Define *interest rate parity*. What is the relationship between *interest rate parity* and forward rates?

9. **Covered Interest Arbitrage.** Define the terms *covered interest arbitrage* and *uncovered interest arbitrage*. What is the difference between these two transactions?

10. **Forward Rate as an Unbiased Predictor of the Future Spot Rate.** Some forecasters believe that foreign exchange markets for the major floating currencies are "efficient" and forward exchange rates are *unbiased predictors* of future spot exchange rates. What is meant by "unbiased predictor" in terms of how the forward rate performs in estimating future spot exchange rates?

Problems

1. **Starbucks in Croatia.** Starbucks opened its first store in Zagreb, Croatia in October 2010. In Zagreb, the price of a tall vanilla latte is 25.70kn. In New York City,

the price of a tall vanilla latte is $2.65. The exchange rate between Croatian kunas (kn) and U.S. dollars is kn5.6288/$. According to purchasing power parity, is the Croatian kuna overvalued or undervalued?

2. **Crisis at the Heart of Carnaval.** The Argentine peso was fixed through a currency board at Ps1.00/$ throughout the 1990s. In January 2002, the Argentine peso was floated. On January 29, 2003, it was trading at Ps3.20/$. During that one year period, Argentina's inflation rate was 20% on an annualized basis. Inflation in the United States during that same period was 2.2% annualized.
   a. What should have been the exchange rate in January 2003 if PPP held?
   b. By what percentage was the Argentine peso undervalued on an annualized basis?
   c. What were the probable causes of undervaluation?

3. **Traveling Down Under.** Terry Lamoreaux owns homes in Sydney, Australia and Phoenix, Arizona. He travels between the two cities at least twice a year. Because of his frequent trips he wants to buy some new, high-quality luggage. He's done his research and has decided to purchase a Briggs and Riley three-piece luggage set. There are retail stores in Phoenix and Sydney. Terry was a finance major and wants to use purchasing power parity to determine if he is paying the same price regardless of where he makes his purchase.
   a. If the price of the three-piece luggage set in Phoenix is $850 and the price of the same three-piece set in Sydney is $930, using purchasing power parity, is the price of the luggage truly equal if the spot rate is A$1.0941/$?
   b. If the price of the luggage remains the same in Phoenix one year from now, determine the price of the luggage in Sydney in one year's time if PPP holds true. The U.S. Inflation rate is 1.15% and the Australian inflation rate is 3.13%.

4. **Takeshi Kamada—CIA Japan.** Takeshi Kamada, a foreign exchange trader at Credit Suisse (Tokyo), is exploring covered interest arbitrage possibilities. He wants to invest $5,000,000 or its yen equivalent, in a covered interest arbitrage between U.S. dollars and Japanese yen. He faced the following exchange rate and interest rate quotes.

Arbitrage funds available	$5,000,000
Spot rate (¥/$)	118.60
180-day forward rate (¥/$)	117.80
180-day U.S. dollar interest rate	4.800%
180-day Japanese yen interest rate	3.400%

5. **Takeshi Kamada—UIA Japan.** Takeshi Kamada, Credit Suisse (Tokyo), observes that the ¥/$ spot rate has been holding steady, and both dollar and yen interest rates have remained relatively fixed over the past week. Takeshi wonders if he should try an uncovered interest arbitrage (UIA) and thereby save the cost of forward cover. Many of Takeshi's research associates—and their computer models—are predicting the spot rate to remain close to ¥118.00/$ for the coming 180 days. Using the same data as in problem 4, analyze the UIA potential.

6. **Japanese/United States Parity Conditions.** Derek Tosh is attempting to determine whether U.S./Japanese financial conditions are at parity. The current spot rate is a flat ¥89.00/$, while the 360-day forward rate is ¥84.90/$. Forecast inflation is 1.100% for Japan, and 5.900% for the United States. The 360-day euro yen deposit rate is 4.700%, and the 360-day euro dollar deposit rate is 9.500%.
   a. Diagram and calculate whether international parity conditions hold between Japan and the United States.
   b. Find the forecasted change in the Japanese yen/U.S. dollar (¥/$) exchange rate one year from now.

7. **Corolla Exports and Pass-Through.** Assume that the export price of a Toyota Corolla from Osaka, Japan is ¥2,150,000. The exchange rate is ¥87.60/$. The forecast rate of inflation in the United States is 2.2% per year and in Japan is 0.0% per year. Use this data to answer the following questions on exchange rate pass-through.
   a. What was the export price for the Corolla at the beginning of the year expressed in U.S. dollars?
   b. Assuming purchasing power parity holds, what should be the exchange rate at the end of the year?
   c. Assuming 100% pass-through of exchange rate, what will be the dollar price of a Corolla at the end of the year?
   d. Assuming 75% pass-through, what will be the dollar price of a Corolla at the end of the year?

8. **Copenhagen Covered (A).** Heidi Høi Jensen, a foreign exchange trader at J.P.Morgan Chase, can invest $5 million, or the foreign currency equivalent of the bank's short-term funds, in a covered interest arbitrage with Denmark. Using the following quotes, can Heidi make a covered interest arbitrage (CIA) profit?

Arbitrage funds available	$5,000,000
Spot exchange rate (kr/$)	6.1720
3-month forward rate (kr/$)	6.1980
U.S. dollar 3-month interest rate	3.000%
Danish kroner 3-month interest rate	5.000%

9. **Copenhagen Covered (B) — Part a.** Heidi Høi Jensen is now evaluating the arbitrage profit potential in the same market after interest rates change. (Note that any time the difference in interest rates does not exactly equal the forward premium, it must be possible to make a CIA profit one way or another.)

Arbitrage funds available	$5,000,000
Spot exchange rate (kr/$)	6.1720
3-month forward rate (kr/$)	6.1980
U.S. dollar 3-month interest rate	4.000%
Danish kroner 3-month interest rate	5.000%

10. **Copenhagen Covered (B) — Part b.** Heidi Høi Jensen is now evaluating the arbitrage profit potential in the same market after interest rates change. (Note that any time the difference in interest rates does not exactly equal the forward premium, it must be possible to make a CIA profit one way or another.)

Arbitrage funds available	$5,000,000
Spot exchange rate (kr/$)	6.1720
3-month forward rate (kr/$)	6.1980
U.S. dollar 3-month interest rate	3.000%
Danish kroner 3-month interest rate	6.000%

11. **Casper Landsten — CIA.** Casper Landsten is a foreign exchange trader for a bank in New York. He has $1 million (or its Swiss franc equivalent) for a short term money market investment and wonders if he should invest in U.S. dollars for three months, or make a CIA investment in the Swiss franc. He faces the following quotes:

Arbitrage funds available	$1,000,000
Spot exchange rate (SFr/$)	1.2810
3-month forward rate (SFr/$)	1.2740
U.S. dollar 3-month interest rate	4.800%
Swiss franc 3-month interest rate	3.200%

12. **Casper Landsten — UIA.** Casper Landsten, using the same values and assumptions as in problem 11, decides to seek the full 4.800% return available in U.S. dollars by not covering his forward dollar receipts — an uncovered interest arbitrage (UIA) transaction. Assess this decision.

13. **Casper Landsten — Thirty Days Later.** One month after the events described in problems 10 and 11, Casper Landsten once again has $1 million (or its Swiss franc equivalent) to invest for three months. He now faces the following rates. Should he again enter into a covered interest arbitrage (CIA) investment?

Arbitrage funds available	$1,000,000
Spot exchange rate (SFr/$)	1.3392
3-month forward rate (SFr/$)	1.3286
U.S. dollar 3-month interest rate	4.750%
Swiss franc 3-month interest rate	3.625%

14. **Pulau Penang Island Resort.** Theresa Nunn is planning a 30-day vacation on Pulau Penang, Malaysia, one year from now. The present charge for a luxury suite plus meals in Malaysian ringgit (RM) is RM1,045/day. The Malaysian ringgit presently trades at RM3.1350/$. She determines that the dollar cost today for a 30-day stay would be $10,000. The hotel informs her that any increase in its room charges will be limited to any increase in the Malaysian cost of living. Malaysian inflation is expected to be 2.75% per annum, while U.S. inflation is expected to be 1.25%.
    a. How many dollars might Theresa expect to need one year hence to pay for her 30-day vacation?
    b. By what percent will the dollar cost have gone up? Why?

15. **Statoil of Norway's Arbitrage.** Statoil, the national oil company of Norway, is a large, sophisticated, and active participant in both the currency and petrochemical markets. Although it is a Norwegian company, because it operates within the global oil market, it considers the U.S. dollar as its functional currency, not the Norwegian krone. Ari Karlsen is a currency trader for Statoil, and has immediate use of either $3 million (or the Norwegian krone equivalent). He is faced with the following market rates, and wonders whether he can make some arbitrage profits in the coming 90 days.

Arbitrage funds available	$3,000,000
Spot exchange rate (Nok/$)	6.0312
3-month forward rate (Nok/$)	6.0186
U.S. dollar 3-month interest rate	5.000%
Norwegian krone 3-month interest rate	4.450%

16. **Separated by the Atlantic.** Separated by more than 3,000 nautical miles and five time zones, money and foreign exchange markets in both London and New York are very efficient. The following information has been collected from the respective areas:

Assumptions	London	New York
Spot exchange rate ($/€)	1.3264	1.3264
1-year Treasury bill rate	3.900%	4.500%
Expected inflation rate	Unknown	1.250%

a. What do the financial markets suggest for inflation in Europe next year?
b. Estimate today's 1-year forward exchange rate between the dollar and the euro?

17. **Chamonix Chateau Rentals.** You are planning a ski vacation to Mt. Blanc in Chamonix, France, one year from now. You are negotiating the rental of a chateau. The chateau's owner wishes to preserve his real income against both inflation and exchange rate changes, and so the present weekly rent of €9,800 (Christmas season) will be adjusted upward or downward for any change in the French cost of living between now and then. You are basing your budgeting on purchasing power parity (PPP). French inflation is expected to average 3.5% for the coming year, while U.S. dollar inflation is expected to be 2.5%. The current spot rate is $1.3620/€. What should you budget as the U.S. dollar cost of the 1-week rental?

Spot exchange rate ($/€)	$1.3620
Expected US inflation for coming year	2.500%
Expected French inflation for coming year	3.500%
Current chateau nominal weekly rent (€)	€ 9,800.00

18. **East Asiatic Company—Thailand.** The East Asiatic Company (EAC), a Danish company with subsidiaries throughout Asia, has been funding its Bangkok subsidiary primarily with U.S. dollar debt because of the cost and availability of dollar capital as opposed to Thai baht-denominated (B) debt. The treasurer of EAC-Thailand is considering a 1-year bank loan for $250,000. The current spot rate is B32.06/$, and the dollar-based interest is 6.75% for the 1-year period. 1-year loans are 12.00% in baht.
   a. Assuming expected inflation rates of 4.3% and 1.25% in Thailand and the United States, repectively, for the coming year, according to purchase power parity, what would be the effective cost of funds in Thai baht terms?
   b. If EAC's foreign exchange advisers believe strongly that the Thai government wants to push the value of the baht down against the dollar by 5% over the coming year (to promote its export competitiveness in dollar markets), what might be the effective cost of funds in baht terms?
   c. If EAC could borrow Thai baht at 13% per annum, would this be cheaper than either part (a) or part (b)?

19. **Maltese Falcon.** The infamous solid gold falcon, initially intended as a tribute by the Knights of Rhodes to the King of Spain in appreciation for his gift of the island of Malta to the order in 1530, has recently been recovered. The falcon is 14 inches high and solid gold, weighing approximately 48 pounds. Assume that gold prices have risen to $440/ounce, primarily as a result of increasing political tensions. The falcon is currently held by a private investor in Istanbul, who is actively negotiating with the Maltese government on its purchase and prospective return to its island home. The sale and payment are to take place in March 2004, and the parties are negotiating over the price and currency of payment. The investor has decided, in a show of goodwill, to base the sales price only on the falcon's specie value—its gold value.

The current spot exchange rate is 0.39 Maltese lira (ML) per U.S. dollar. Maltese inflation is expected to be about 8.5% for the coming year, while U.S. inflation, on the heels of a double-dip recession, is expected to come in at only 1.5%. If the investor bases value in the U.S. dollar, would he be better off receiving Maltese lira in one year—assuming purchasing power parity, or receiving a guaranteed dollar payment assuming a gold price of $420 per ounce.

20. **Malaysian Risk.** Clayton Moore is the manager of an international money market fund managed out of London. Unlike many money funds that guarantee their investors a near risk-free investment with variable interest earnings, Clayton Moore's fund is a very aggressive fund that searches out relatively high interest earnings around the globe, but at some risk. The fund is pound-denominated. Clayton is currently evaluating a rather interesting opportunity in Malaysia. Since the Asian Crisis of 1997, the Malaysian government enforced a number of currency and capital restrictions to protect and preserve the value of the Malaysian ringgit. The ringgit was fixed to the U.S. dollar at RM3.80/$ for seven years. In 2005, the Malaysian government allowed the currency to float against several major currencies. The current spot rate today is RM3.13485/$. Local currency time deposits of

180-day maturities are earning 8.900% per annum. The London eurocurrency market for pounds is yielding 4.200% per annum on similar 180-day maturities. The current spot rate on the British pound is $1.5820/£, and the 180-day forward rate is $1.5561/£.

21. **The Beer Standard.** In 1999, *The Economist* reported the creation of an index, or standard, for the evaluation of African currency values using the local prices of beer. Beer, instead of Big Macs, was chosen as the product for comparison because McDonald's had not penetrated the African continent beyond South Africa, and beer met most of the same product and market characteristics required for the construction of a proper currency index. Investec, a South African investment banking firm, has replicated the process of creating a measure of purchasing power parity (PPP) like that of the Big Mac Index of *The Economist*, for Africa.

The index compares the cost of a 375 milliliter bottle of clear lager beer across Sub-Sahara Africa. As a measure of PPP, the beer needs to be relatively homogeneous in quality across countries, and must possess substantial elements of local manufacturing, inputs, distribution, and service, in order to actually provide a measure of relative purchasing power. The beer is first priced in local currency (purchased in the taverns of the locals, and not in the high-priced tourist centers), then converted to South African rand. The price of the beer in rand is then compared to form one measure of whether the local currency is under-valued (−%) or overvalued (+%) versus the South African rand. Use the data in the table and complete the calculation of whether the individual currencies are undervalued or overvalued.

		Beer Prices				
Country	Beer	Local Currency	Local Currency	In rand	Implied PPP Rate	Spot Rate (3/15/99)
South Africa	Castle	Rand	2.30	—	—	—
Botswana	Castle	Pula	2.20	2.94	0.96	0.75
Ghana	Star	Cedi	1,200.00	3.17	521.74	379.10
Kenya	Tusker	Shilling	41.25	4.02	17.93	10.27
Malawi	Carlsberg	Kwacha	18.50	2.66	8.04	6.96
Mauritius	Phoenix	Rupee	15.00	3.72	6.52	4.03
Namibia	Windhoek	N$	2.50	2.50	1.09	1.00
Zambia	Castle	Kwacha	1,200.00	3.52	521.74	340.68
Zimbabwe	Castle	Z$	9.00	1.46	3.91	6.15

Internet Exercises

1. **Big Mac Index Updated.** Use *The Economist*'s Web site to find the latest edition of the Big Mac Index of currency overvaluation and undervaluation. (You will need to do a search for "Big Mac Currencies.") Create a worksheet to compare how the British pound, the euro, the Swiss franc, and the Canadian dollar have changed from the version presented in this chapter.

    The Economist   www.economist.com/markets/Bigmac/Index.cfm

2. **Purchasing Power Parity Statistics.** The Organization for Economic Cooperation and Development (OECD) publishes detailed measures of prices and purchasing power for its member countries. Go to the OECD's Web site and download the spreadsheet file with the historical data for purchasing power for the member countries.

    OECD Purchasing Power   www.oecd.org/department/0,3355,en_2649_34357_1_1_1_1_1,00.html

3. **International Interest Rates.** A number of Web sites publish current interest rates by currency and maturity. Use the *Financial Times* Web site listed here to isolate the interest rate differentials between the U.S. dollar, the British pound, and the euro for all maturities up to and including one year.

    Financial Times Market Data   www.ft.com/markets

    Data Listed by the *Financial Times*:

    International money rates (bank call rates for major currency deposits)

    Money rates (LIBOR and CD rates, etc.)

10-year spreads (individual country spreads versus the euro and U.S. 10-year treasuries) *Note*: Which countries actually have lower 10-year government bond rates than the United States and the euro? Probably Switzerland and Japan. Check.

Benchmark government bonds (sampling of representative government issuances by major countries and recent price movements) Note which countries are showing longer maturity benchmark rates.

Emerging market bonds (government issuances, Brady bonds, etc.)

Eurozone rates (miscellaneous bond rates for assorted European-based companies; includes debt ratings by Moodys and S&P)

4. **World Bank's International Comparison Program.** The World Bank has an ongoing research program that focuses on the relative purchasing power of 107 different economies globally, specifically in terms of household consumption. Download the latest data tables and highlight which economies seem to be showing the greatest growth in recent years in relative purchasing power.

World Bank International Comparison Program
web.worldbank.org/WBSITE/EXTERNAL/
DATASTATISTICS/ICPEXT/0,,pagePK:62002243~
theSitePK:270065,00.html

CHAPTER 7 APPENDIX
An Algebraic Primer to International Parity Conditions

The following is a purely algebraic presentation of the parity conditions explained in this chapter. It is offered to provide those who wish additional theoretical detail and definition ready access to the step-by-step derivation of the various conditions.

The Law of One Price

The *law of one price* refers to the state in which, in the presence of free trade, perfect substitutability of goods, and costless transactions, the equilibrium exchange rate between two currencies is determined by the ratio of the price of any commodity i denominated in two different currencies. For example,

$$S_t = \frac{P_{i,t}^{\$}}{P_{i,t}^{SF}}$$

where $P_i^{\$}$ and P_i^{SF} refer to the prices of the same commodity i, at time t, denominated in U.S. dollars and Swiss francs, respectively. The spot exchange rate, S_t, is simply the ratio of the two currency prices.

Purchasing Power Parity

The more general form in which the exchange rate is determined by the ratio of two price indexes is termed the absolute version of purchasing power parity (PPP). Each price index reflects the currency cost of the identical "basket" of goods across countries. The exchange rate that equates purchasing power for the identical collection of goods is then stated as follows:

$$S_t = \frac{P_t^{\$}}{P_t^{SF}}$$

where $P_t^{\$}$ and P_t^{SF} are the price index values in U.S. dollars and Swiss francs at time t, respectively. If π represents the rate of inflation in each country, the spot exchange rate at time $t + 1$ would be

$$S_{t+1} = \frac{P_t^{\$}(1 + \pi^{\$})}{P_t^{SF}(1 + \pi^{SF})} = S_t \left[\frac{(1 + \pi^{\$})}{(1 + \pi^{SF})} \right]$$

The change from period t to $t + 1$ is then

$$\frac{S_{t+1}}{S_t} = \frac{\dfrac{P_t^{\$}(1 + \pi^{\$})}{P_t^{SF}(1 + \pi^{SF})}}{\dfrac{P_t^{\$}}{P_t^{SF}}} = \frac{S_t \left[\dfrac{(1 + \pi^{\$})}{(1 + \pi^{SF})} \right]}{S_t} = \frac{(1 + \pi^{\$})}{(1 + \pi^{SF})}$$

Isolating the percentage change in the spot exchange rate between periods t and $t+1$ is then

$$\frac{S_{t+1} - S_t}{S_t} = \frac{S_t\left[\frac{(1+\pi^\$)}{(1+\pi^{SF})}\right] - S_t}{S_t} = \frac{(1+\pi^\$) - (1+\pi^{SF})}{(1+\pi^{SF})}$$

This equation is often approximated by dropping the denominator of the right-hand side if it is considered to be relatively small. It is then stated as

$$\frac{S_{t+1} - S_t}{S_t} = (1+\pi^\$) - (1+\pi^{SF}) = \pi^\$ - \pi^{SF}$$

Forward Rates

The forward exchange rate is that contractual rate which is available to private agents through banking institutions and other financial intermediaries who deal in foreign currencies and debt instruments. The annualized percentage difference between the forward rate and the spot rate is termed the forward premium,

$$f^{SF} = \left[\frac{F_{t,t+1} - S_t}{S_t}\right] \times \left[\frac{360}{n_{t,t+1}}\right]$$

where f^{SF} is the forward premium on the Swiss franc, $F_{t,t+1}$ is the forward rate contracted at time t for delivery at time $t+1$, S_t is the current spot rate, and $n_{t,t+1}$ is the number of days between the contract date (t) and the delivery date ($t+1$).

Covered Interest Arbitrage (CIA) and Interest Rate Parity (IRP)

The process of covered interest arbitrage is when an investor exchanges domestic currency for foreign currency in the spot market, invests that currency in an interest-bearing instrument, and signs a forward contract to "lock in" a future exchange rate at which to convert the foreign currency proceeds (gross) back to domestic currency. The net return on CIA is

$$\text{Net return} = \left[\frac{(1+i^{SF}) F_{t,t+1}}{S_t}\right] - (1+i^\$)$$

where S_t and $F_{t,t+1}$ are the spot and forward rates (\$/SF), i^{SF} is the nominal interest rate (or yield) on a Swiss franc-denominated monetary instrument, and $i^\$$ is the nominal return on a similar dollar-denominated instrument.

If they possess exactly equal rates of return—that is, if CIA results in zero riskless profit—interest rate parity (IRP) holds, and appears as

$$(1 + i^\$) = \left[\frac{(1+i^{SF}) F_{t,t+1}}{S_t}\right]$$

or alternatively as

$$\frac{(1+i^\$)}{(1+i^{SF})} = \frac{F_{t,t+1}}{S_t}$$

If the percent difference of both sides of this equation is found (the percentage difference between the spot and forward rate is the forward premium), then the relationship between the forward premium and relative interest rate differentials is

$$\frac{F_{t,t+1} - S_t}{S_t} = f^{SF} = \frac{i^\$ - i^{SF}}{i^\$ + i^{SF}}$$

If these values are not equal (thus, the markets are not in equilibrium), there exists a potential for riskless profit. The market will then be driven back to equilibrium through CIA by agents attempting to exploit such arbitrage potential, until CIA yields no positive return.

Fisher Effect

The Fisher effect states that all nominal interest rates can be decomposed into an implied real rate of interest (return) and an expected rate of inflation:

$$i^\$ = [(1 + r^\$)(1 + \pi^\$)] - 1$$

where $r^\$$ is the real rate of return, and $\pi^\$$ is the expected rate of inflation, for dollar-denominated assets. The subcomponents are then identifiable:

$$i^\$ = r^\$ + \pi^\$ + r^\$ \pi^\$$$

As with PPP, there is an approximation of this function that has gained wide acceptance. The cross-product term of $r^\$ \pi^\$$ is often very small and therefore dropped altogether:

$$i^\$ = r^\$ + \pi^\$$$

International Fisher Effect

The international Fisher effect is the extension of this domestic interest rate relationship to the international currency markets. If capital, by way of covered interest arbitrage (CIA), attempts to find higher rates of return internationally resulting from current interest rate differentials, the real rates of return between currencies are equalized (e.g., $r^\$ = r^{SF}$):

$$\frac{S_{t+1} - S_t}{S_t} = \frac{(1 + i^\$) - (1 + i^{SF})}{(1 + i^{SF})} = \frac{i^\$ - i^{SF}}{(1 + i^{SF})}$$

If the nominal interest rates are then decomposed into their respective real and expected inflation components, the percentage change in the spot exchange rate is

$$\frac{S_{t+1} - S_t}{S_t} = \frac{(r^\$ + \pi^\$ + r^\$\pi^\$) - (r^{SF} + \pi^{SF} + r^{SF}\pi^{SF})}{1 + r^{SF} + \pi^{SF} + r^{SF}\pi^{SF}}$$

The international Fisher effect has a number of additional implications, if the following requirements are met: (1) capital markets can be freely entered and exited; (2) capital markets possess investment opportunities that are acceptable substitutes; and (3) market agents have complete and equal information regarding these possibilities.

Given these conditions, international arbitragers are capable of exploiting all potential riskless profit opportunities, until real rates of return between markets are equalized

($r^\$ = r^{SF}$). Thus, the expected rate of change in the spot exchange rate reduces to the differential in the expected rates of inflation:

$$\frac{S_{t+1} - S_t}{S_t} = \frac{\pi^\$ + r^\$\pi^\$ - \pi^{SF} - r^{SF}\pi^{SF}}{1 + r^{SF} + \pi^{SF} + r^{SF}\pi^{SF}}$$

If the approximation forms are combined (through the elimination of the denominator and the elimination of the interactive terms of r and π), the change in the spot rate is simply

$$\frac{S_{t+1} - S_t}{S_t} = \pi^\$ - \pi^{SF}$$

Note the similarity (identical in equation form) of the approximate form of the international Fisher effect to purchasing power parity, discussed previously (the only potential difference is that between *ex post* and *ex ante*, or expected, inflation).

CHAPTER 8

Foreign Currency Derivatives and Swaps

Unless derivatives contracts are collateralized or guaranteed, their ultimate value also depends on the creditworthiness of the counterparties to them. In the meantime, though, before a contract is settled, the counterparties record profits and losses—often huge in amount—in their current earnings statements without so much as a penny changing hands. The range of derivatives contracts is limited only by the imagination of man (or sometimes, so it seems, madmen). — Warren Buffett, Berkshire Hathaway Annual Report, 2002.

LEARNING OBJECTIVES

- Explain how foreign currency futures are quoted, valued, and used for speculation purposes.
- Illustrate how foreign currency futures differ from forward contracts.
- Analyze how foreign currency options are quoted, valued, and used for speculation purposes.
- Explain how foreign currency options are valued.
- Define interest rate risk, and examine how can it be managed.
- Explain interest rate swaps and how they can be used to manage interest rate risk.
- Analyze how interest rate swaps and cross currency swaps can be used to manage both foreign exchange risk and interest rate risk simultaneously.

Financial management of the multinational enterprise in the twenty-first century will certainly include the use of *financial derivatives*. These *derivatives*, so named because their values are derived from an underlying asset like a stock or a currency, are powerful tools used in business today for two very distinct management objectives, *speculation* and *hedging*. The financial manager of an MNE may purchase these financial derivatives in order to take positions in the expectation of profit, speculation, or may use these instruments to reduce the risks associated with the everyday management of corporate cash flow, hedging. Before these financial instruments can be used effectively, however, the financial manager must understand certain basics about their structure and pricing.

In this chapter, we cover the primary foreign currency financial derivatives used today in multinational financial management: *foreign currency futures, foreign currency options, interest rate swaps, and cross currency interest rate swaps*. We focus on the fundamentals of their valuation and their use for speculative purposes. Chapter 10 will describe how these foreign currency derivatives can be used to hedge commercial transactions, hedging. The Mini-Case at the end of this chapter, ***McDonald's Corporation British Pound Exposure*** illustrates how one major multinational company, McDonald's, has used currency derivatives quite successfully over time.

A word of caution—of reservation—before proceeding further. Financial derivatives are powerful tools in the hands of careful and competent financial managers. They can also be destructive devices when used recklessly and carelessly. The history of finance is littered with cases in which financial managers—either intentionally or unintentionally—took huge positions resulting in significant losses for their companies, and occasionally, their outright collapse. In the right hands and with the proper controls, however, financial derivatives may provide management with opportunities to enhance and protect their corporate financial performance. User beware.

Foreign Currency Futures

A *foreign currency futures contract* is an alternative to a forward contract that calls for future delivery of a standard amount of foreign exchange at a fixed time, place, and price. It is similar to futures contracts that exist for commodities (hogs, cattle, lumber, etc.), interest-bearing deposits, and gold.

Most world money centers have established foreign currency futures markets. In the United States, the most important market for foreign currency futures is the International Monetary Market (IMM) of Chicago, a division of the Chicago Mercantile Exchange.

Contract Specifications

Contract specifications are established by the exchange on which futures are traded. Using the Chicago IMM as an example, the major features of standardized futures trading are illustrated by the Mexican peso futures traded on the Chicago Mercantile Exchange (CME), as shown in Exhibit 8.1. These are taken from the *Wall Street Journal*.

Each futures contract is for 500,000 Mexican pesos, this is the *notional principal*. Trading in each currency must be done in an even multiple of currency units. The method of stating exchange rates is in American terms, the U.S. dollar cost (price) of a foreign currency (unit), $/MXN, where the CME is mixing the old dollar symbol with the ISO 4217 code for the peso, MXN. In Exhibit 8.1 this is U.S. dollars per Mexican peso. Contracts mature on the third Wednesday of January, March, April, June, July, September, October, or December.

EXHIBIT 8.1 Mexican Peso (CME)—MXN 500,000; $ per 10MXN

Maturity	Open	High	Low	Settle	Change	Lifetime High	Lifetime Low	Open Interest
Mar	.10953	.10988	.10930	.10958	...	.11000	.09770	34,481
June	.10790	.10795	.10778	.10773	...	.10800	.09730	3,405
Sept	.10615	.10615	.10610	.10573	...	.10615	.09930	1,481

All contracts are for 500,000 Mexican pesos. "Open" means the opening price on the day. "High" means the high price on the day. "Low" indicates the lowest price on the day. "Settle" is the closing price on the day. "Change" indicates the change in the settle price from the previous day's close. "High" and "Low" to the right of Change indicate the highest and lowest prices this specific contract (as defined by its maturity) has experienced over its trading history. "Open Interest" indicates the number of contracts outstanding.

Contracts may be traded through the second business day prior to the Wednesday on which they mature. Unless holidays interfere, the last trading day is the Monday preceding the maturity date.

One of the defining characteristics of futures is the requirement that the purchaser deposits a sum as an initial *margin* or *collateral*. This requirement is similar to requiring a performance bond, and it can be met by a letter of credit from a bank, Treasury bills, or cash. In addition, a *maintenance margin* is required. The value of the contract is marked to market daily, and all changes in value are paid in cash daily. *Marked to market* means that the value of the contract is revalued using the closing price for the day. The amount to be paid is called the *variation margin*.

Only about 5% of all futures contracts are settled by the physical delivery of foreign exchange between buyer and seller. Most often, buyers and sellers offset their original position prior to delivery date by taking an opposite position. That is, an investor will normally close out a futures position by selling a futures contract for the same delivery date. The complete buy/sell or sell/buy is called a "round turn."

Customers pay a commission to their broker to execute a round turn and a single price is quoted. This practice differs from that of the interbank market, where dealers quote a bid and an offer and do not charge a commission. All contracts are agreements between the client and the exchange clearinghouse, rather than between the two clients involved. Consequently, clients need not worry that a specific counterparty in the market will fail to honor an agreement (counterparty risk). The clearinghouse is owned and guaranteed by all members of the exchange.

Using Foreign Currency Futures

Any investor wishing to speculate on the movement of the Mexican peso versus the U.S. dollar could pursue one of the following strategies. Keep in mind that the principle of a futures contract is that if a speculator buys a futures contract, they are locking in the price at which they must buy that currency on the specified future date, and if they sell a futures contract, they are locking in the price at which they must sell that currency on that future date.

Short Positions. If Amber McClain, a speculator working for International Currency Traders, believes that the Mexican peso will fall in value versus the U.S. dollar by March, she could sell a March futures contract, taking a short position. By selling a March contract, Amber locks in the right to sell 500,000 Mexican pesos at a set price. If the price of the peso falls by the maturity date as she expects, Amber has a contract to sell pesos at a price above their current price on the spot market. Hence, she makes a profit.

Using the quotes on Mexican peso (MXN) futures in Exhibit 8.1, Amber sells one March futures contract for 500,000 pesos at the closing price, termed the settle price, of $.10958/MXN. The value of her position at maturity—at the expiration of the futures contract in March—is then

$$\text{Value at maturity (Short position)} = -\text{Notional principal} \times (\text{Spot} - \text{Futures})$$

Note that the short position is entered into the valuation as a negative notional principal. If the spot exchange rate at maturity is $.09500/MXN, the value of her position on settlement is

$$\text{Value} = -\text{MXN } 500{,}000 \times (\$.09500/\text{MXN} - \$.10958/\text{MXN}) = \$7{,}290$$

Amber's expectation proved correct; the Mexican peso fell in value versus the U.S. dollar. We could say that "Amber ends up buying at $.09500 and sells at $.10958 per peso."

All that was really required of Amber to speculate on the Mexican peso's value was that she formed an opinion on the Mexican peso's future exchange value versus the U.S. dollar. In this case, she opined that it would fall in value by the March maturity date of the futures contract.

Long Positions. If Amber McClain expected the peso to rise in value versus the dollar in the near term, she could take a long position, by buying a March future on the Mexican peso. Buying a March future means that Amber is locking in the price at which she must buy Mexican pesos at the future's maturity date. Amber's futures contract at maturity would have the following value:

$$\text{Value at maturity (Long position)} = \text{Notional principal} \times (\text{Spot} - \text{Futures})$$

Again using the March settle price on Mexican peso futures in Exhibit 8.1, $.10958/MXN, if the spot exchange rate at maturity is $.1100/MXN, Amber has indeed guessed right. The value of her position on settlement is then

$$\text{Value} = \text{MXN}500{,}000 \times (\$.11000/\text{MXN} - \$.10958/\text{MXN}) = \$210$$

In this case, Amber makes a profit in a matter of months of $210 on the single futures contract. We could say that "Amber buys at $.10958 and sells at $.11000 per peso."

But what happens if Amber's expectation about the future value of the Mexican peso proves wrong? For example, if the Mexican government announces that the rate of inflation in Mexico has suddenly risen dramatically, and the peso falls to $.08000/MXN by the March maturity date, the value of Amber's futures contract on settlement is

$$\text{Value} = \text{MXN}500{,}000 \times (\$.08000/\text{MXN} - \$.10958/\text{MXN}) = (\$14{,}790)$$

In this case, Amber McClain suffers a speculative loss.

Futures contracts could obviously be used in combinations to form a variety of more complex positions. When we are combining contracts, however, valuation is fairly straightforward and additive in character.

Foreign Currency Futures versus Forward Contracts

Foreign currency futures contracts differ from forward contracts in a number of important ways. Individuals find futures contracts useful for speculation because they usually do not have access to forward contracts. For businesses, futures contracts are often considered inefficient and burdensome because the futures position is marked to market on a daily basis over the life of the contract. Although this does not require the business to pay or receive cash daily, it does result in more frequent margin calls from its financial service providers than the business typically wants.

Currency Options

A *foreign currency option* is a contract that gives the option purchaser (the buyer) the right, but not the obligation, to buy or sell a given amount of foreign exchange at a fixed price per unit for a specified time period (until the maturity date). The most important phrase in this definition is "but not the obligation"; this means that the owner of an option possesses a valuable choice.

In many ways buying an option is like buying a ticket to a benefit concert. The buyer has the right to attend the concert, but does not have to. The buyer of the concert ticket risks nothing more than what she pays for the ticket. Similarly, the buyer of an option cannot lose more than what he pays for the option. If the buyer of the ticket decides later not to attend the concert—prior to the day of the concert, the ticket can be sold to someone else who wishes to go.

- There are two basic types of options, *calls* and *puts*. A call is an option to buy foreign currency, and a *put* is an option to sell foreign currency.
- The buyer of an option is termed the *holder*, while the seller of an option is referred to as the *writer* or *grantor*.

Every option has three different price elements: 1) the *exercise* or *strike price*, the exchange rate at which the foreign currency can be purchased (call) or sold (put); 2) the *premium*, the cost, price, or value of the option itself; and 3) the underlying or actual spot exchange rate in the market.

An *American option* gives the buyer the right to exercise the option at any time between the date of writing and the expiration or maturity date. A *European option* can be exercised only on its expiration date, not before. Nevertheless, American and European options are priced almost the same because the option holder would normally sell the option itself before maturity. The option would then still have some "time value" above its "intrinsic value" if exercised (explained later in this chapter).

◆ The *premium* or option price is the cost of the option, usually paid in advance by the buyer to the seller. In the *over-the-counter market* (options offered by banks), premiums are quoted as a percentage of the transaction amount. Premiums on exchange-traded options are quoted as a domestic currency amount per unit of foreign currency.

◆ An option whose exercise price is the same as the spot price of the underlying currency is said to be *at-the-money* (ATM). An option that would be profitable, excluding the cost of the premium, if exercised immediately is said to be *in-the-money* (ITM). An option that would not be profitable, again excluding the cost of the premium, if exercised immediately is referred to as *out-of-the-money* (OTM).

Foreign Currency Options Markets

In the past three decades the use of foreign currency options as a hedging tool and for speculative purposes has blossomed into a major foreign exchange activity. A number of banks in the United States and other capital markets offer flexible foreign currency options on transactions of $1 million or more. The bank market, or over-the-counter market as it is called, offers custom-tailored options on all major trading currencies for any period up to one year, and in some cases, two to three years.

In December 1982, the Philadelphia Stock Exchange introduced trading in standardized foreign currency option contracts in the United States. The Chicago Mercantile Exchange and other exchanges in the United States and abroad have followed suit. Exchange-traded contracts are particularly appealing to speculators and individuals who do not normally have access to the over-the-counter market. Banks also trade on the exchanges because it is one of several ways they can offset the risk of options they have transacted with clients or other banks.

Increased use of foreign currency options is a reflection of the explosive growth in the use of other kinds of options and the resultant improvements in option pricing models. The original option pricing model developed by Black and Scholes in 1973 has been commercialized since then by numerous firms offering software programs and even built-in routines for handheld calculators. Several commercial programs are available for option writers and traders to utilize.

Options on the Over-the-Counter Market. Over-the-counter (OTC) options are most frequently written by banks for U.S. dollars against British pounds sterling, Swiss francs, Japanese yen, Canadian dollars, and most recently, the euro.

The main advantage of over-the-counter options is that they are tailored to the specific needs of the firm. Financial institutions are willing to write or buy options that vary by amount (notional principal), strike price, and maturity. Although the over-the-counter markets were relatively illiquid in the early years, the market has grown to such proportions that liquidity is now quite good. On the other hand, the buyer must assess the writing bank's ability to fulfill the option contract. Termed counterparty risk, the financial risk associated with the counterparty is an increasing issue in international markets as a result of the increasing use of financial contracts like options and swaps by MNE management. Exchange-traded options are more the territory of individuals and financial institutions themselves than of business firms.

If an investor wishes to purchase an option in the over-the-counter market, the investor will normally place a call to the currency option desk of a major money center bank, specify the currencies, maturity, strike rate(s), and ask for an *indication*—a bid-offer quote. The bank will normally take a few minutes to a few hours to price the option and return the call.

Options on Organized Exchanges. Options on the physical (underlying) currency are traded on a number of organized exchanges worldwide, including the Philadelphia Stock Exchange (PHLX) and the Chicago Mercantile Exchange.

Exchange-traded options are settled through a clearinghouse, so that buyers do not deal directly with sellers. The clearinghouse is the counterparty to every option contract and it guarantees fulfillment. Clearinghouse obligations are in turn the obligation of all members of the exchange, including a large number of banks. In the case of the Philadelphia Stock Exchange, clearinghouse services are provided by the Options Clearing Corporation (OCC).

Currency Option Quotations and Prices

Typical quotes in the *Wall Street Journal* for options on Swiss francs are shown in Exhibit 8.2. The *Journal*'s quotes refer to transactions completed on the Philadelphia Stock Exchange on the previous day. Quotations usually are available for more combinations of strike prices and expiration dates than were actually traded and thus reported in the newspaper. Currency option strike prices and premiums on the U.S. dollar are typically quoted as direct quotations on the U.S. dollar and indirect quotations on the foreign currency ($/SF, $/¥, etc.).

Exhibit 8.2 illustrates the three different prices that characterize any foreign currency option. The three prices that characterize an "August 58.5 call option" (highlighted in Exhibit 8.2) are the following:

1. **Spot Rate.** In Exhibit 8.2, "Option and Underlying" means that 58.51 cents, or $0.5851, was the spot dollar price of one Swiss franc at the close of trading on the preceding day.

EXHIBIT 8.2 Swiss Franc Option Quotations (U.S. cents/SF)

Option and Underlying	Strike Price	Calls—Last			Puts—Last		
		Aug	Sep	Dec	Aug	Sep	Dec
58.51	56.0	–	–	2.76	0.04	0.22	1.16
58.51	56.5	–	–	–	0.06	0.30	–
58.51	57.0	1.13	–	1.74	0.10	0.38	1.27
58.51	57.5	0.75	–	–	0.17	0.55	–
58.51	58.0	0.71	1.05	1.28	0.27	0.89	1.81
58.51	58.5	0.50	–	–	0.50	0.99	–
58.51	59.0	0.30	0.66	1.21	0.90	1.36	–
58.51	59.5	0.15	0.40	–	2.32	–	–
58.51	60.0	–	0.31	–	2.32	2.62	3.30

Each option = 62,500 Swiss francs. The August, September, and December listings are the option maturities or expiration dates.

2. **Exercise Price.** The exercise price, or "Strike price" listed in Exhibit 8.2, means the price per franc that must be paid if the option is exercised. The August call option on francs of 58.5 means $0.5850/SF. Exhibit 8.2 lists nine different strike prices, ranging from $0.5600/SF to $0.6000/SF, although more were available on that date than are listed here.

3. **Premium.** The premium is the cost or price of the option. The price of the August 58.5 call option on Swiss francs was 0.50 U.S. cents per franc, or $0.0050/SF. There was no trading of the September and December 58.5 call on that day. The premium is the market value of the option, and therefore the terms premium, cost, price, and value are all interchangeable when referring to an option.

The August 58.5 call option premium is 0.50 cents per franc, and in this case, the August 58.5 put's premium is also 0.50 cents per franc. Since one option contract on the Philadelphia Stock Exchange consists of 62,500 francs, the total cost of one option contract for the call (or put in this case) is SF62,500 × $0.0050/SF = $312.50.

Buyer of a Call

Options differ from all other types of financial instruments in the patterns of risk they produce. The option owner, the holder, has the choice of exercising the option or allowing it to expire unused. The owner will exercise it only when exercising is profitable, which means only when the option is in the money. In the case of a call option, as the spot price of the underlying currency moves up, the holder has the possibility of unlimited profit. On the down side, however, the holder can abandon the option and walk away with a loss never greater than the premium paid.

Hans Schmidt is a currency speculator in Zurich, Switzerland. The position of Hans as a buyer of a call is illustrated in Exhibit 8.3. Assume he purchases the August call option on

EXHIBIT 8.3 Profit and Loss for the Buyer of a Call Option

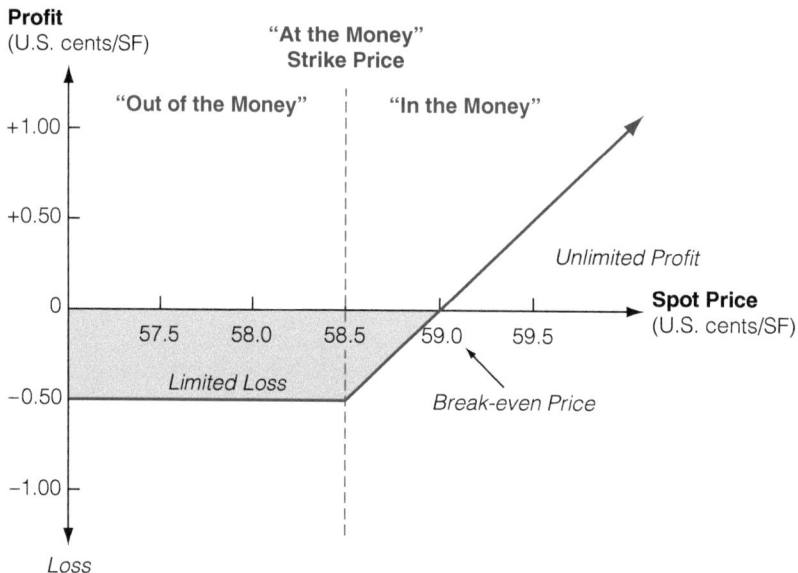

The buyer of a call option on SF, with a strike price of 58.5 cents/SF, has a limited loss of 0.50 cents/SF at spot rates less than 58.5 ("out of the money"), and an unlimited profit potential at spot rates above 58.5 cents/SF ("in the money").

Swiss francs described previously, the one with a strike price of 58.5 ($0.5850/SF), and a premium of $0.005/SF. The vertical axis measures profit or loss for the option buyer at each of several different spot prices for the franc up to the time of maturity.

At all spot rates below the strike price of 58.5, Hans would choose not to exercise his option. This is obvious because at a spot rate of 58.0 for example, he would prefer to buy a Swiss franc for $.580 on the spot market rather than exercising his option to buy a franc at $0.585. If the spot rate remains below 58.0 until August when the option expired, Hans would not exercise the option. His total loss would be limited to only what he paid for the option, the $0.005/SF purchase price. At any lower price for the franc, his loss would similarly be limited to the original $0.005/SF cost.

Alternatively, at all spot rates above the strike price of 58.5, Hans would exercise the option, paying only the strike price for each Swiss franc. For example, if the spot rate were 59.5 cents per franc at maturity, he would exercise his call option, buying Swiss francs for $0.585 each instead of purchasing them on the spot market at $0.595 each. He could sell the Swiss francs immediately in the spot market for $0.595 each, pocketing a gross profit of $0.010/SF, or a net profit of $0.005/SF after deducting the original cost of the option of $0.005/SF. Hans' profit, if the spot rate is greater than the strike price, with strike price $0.585, a premium of $0.005, and a spot rate of $0.595, is

$$\begin{aligned} \text{Profit} &= \text{Spot Rate} - (\text{Strike Price} + \text{Premium}) \\ &= \$0.595/\text{SF} - (\$0.585/\text{SF} + \$0.005/\text{SF}) \\ &= \$0.005/\text{SF} \end{aligned}$$

More likely, Hans would realize the profit through executing an offsetting contract on the options exchange rather than taking delivery of the currency. Because the dollar price of a franc could rise to an infinite level (off the upper right-hand side of Exhibit 8.3), maximum profit is unlimited. The buyer of a call option thus possesses an attractive combination of outcomes: limited loss and unlimited profit potential.

Note that *break-even price* of $0.590/SF is the price at which Hans neither gains nor loses on exercising the option. The premium cost of $0.005, combined with the cost of exercising the option of $0.585, is exactly equal to the proceeds from selling the francs in the spot market at $0.590. Note that he will still exercise the call option at the break-even price. This is because by exercising it he at least recoups the premium paid for the option. At any spot price above the exercise price but below the break-even price, the gross profit earned on exercising the option and selling the underlying currency covers part (but not all) of the premium cost.

Writer of a Call

The position of the writer (seller) of the same call option is illustrated in Exhibit 8.4. If the option expires when the spot price of the underlying currency is below the exercise price of 58.5, the option holder does not exercise. What the holder loses, the writer gains. The writer keeps as profit the entire premium paid of $0.005/SF. Above the exercise price of 58.5, the writer of the call must deliver the underlying currency for $0.585/SF at a time when the value of the franc is above $0.585. If the writer wrote the option "naked," that is, without owning the currency, that writer will now have to buy the currency at spot and take the loss. The amount of such a loss is unlimited and increases as the price of the underlying currency rises. Once again, what the holder gains, the writer loses, and vice versa. Even if the writer already owns the currency, the writer will experience an opportunity loss, surrendering against the option the same currency that could have been sold for more in the open market.

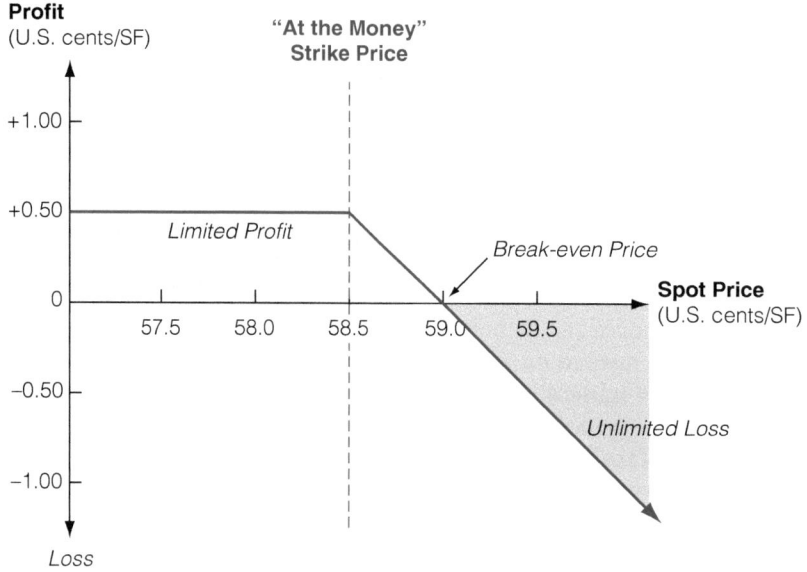

The writer of a call option on SF, with a strike price of 58.5 cents/SF, has a limited profit of 0.50 cents/SF at spot rates less than 58.5, and an unlimited loss potential at spot rates above (to the right of) 59.0 cents/SF.

For example, the profit to the writer of a call option of strike price $0.585, premium $0.005, a spot rate of $0.595/SF is

$$\begin{aligned} \text{Profit} &= \text{Premium} - (\text{Spot Rate} - \text{Strike Price}) \\ &= \$0.005/\text{SF} - (\$0.595/\text{SF} - \$0.585/\text{SF}) \\ &= -\$0.005/\text{SF} \end{aligned}$$

but only if the spot rate is greater than or equal to the strike rate. At spot rates less than the strike price, the option will expire worthless and the writer of the call option will keep the premium earned. The maximum profit that the writer of the call option can make is limited to the premium. The writer of a call option would have a rather unattractive combination of potential outcomes: limited profit potential and unlimited loss potential, but there are ways to limit such losses through other offsetting techniques.

Buyer of a Put

Hans' position as buyer of a put is illustrated in Exhibit 8.5. The basic terms of this put are similar to those we just used to illustrate a call. The buyer of a put option, however, wants to be able to sell the underlying currency at the exercise price when the market price of that currency drops (not rises as in the case of a call option). If the spot price of a franc drops to, say, $0.575/SF, Hans will deliver francs to the writer and receive $0.585/SF. The francs can now be purchased on the spot market for $0.575 each and the cost of the option was $0.005/SF, so he will have a net gain of $0.005/SF.

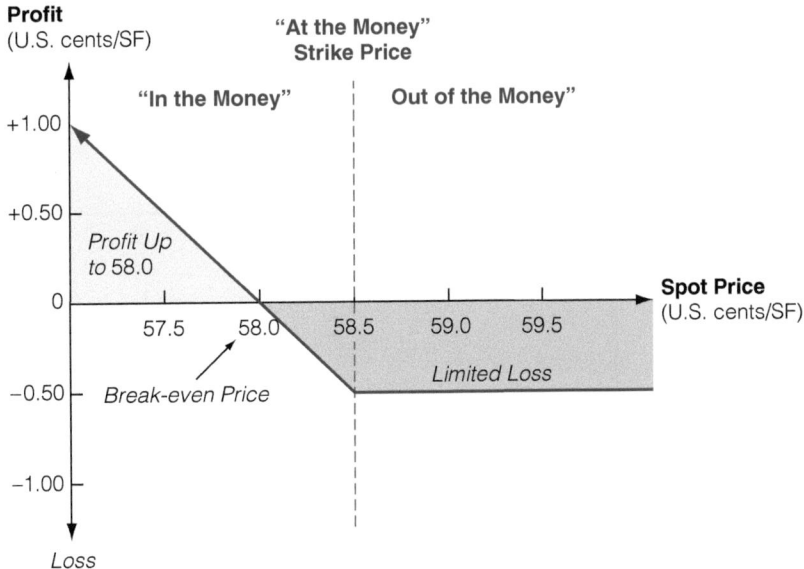

EXHIBIT 8.5 Profit and Loss for the Buyer of a Put Option

The buyer of a put option on SF, with a strike price of 58.5 cents/SF, has a limited loss of 0.50 cents/SF at spot rates greater than 58.5 ("out of the money"), and an unlimited profit potential at spot rates less than 58.5 cents/SF ("in the money") up to 58.0 cents.

Explicitly, the profit to the holder of a put option if the spot rate is less than the strike price, with a strike price $0.585/SF, premium of $0.005/SF, and a spot rate of $0.575/SF, is

$$\begin{aligned}\text{Profit} &= \text{Strike Price} - (\text{Spot Rate} + \text{Premium})\\ &= \$0.585/\text{SF} - (\$0.575/\text{SF} + \$0.005/\text{SF})\\ &= \$0.005/\text{SF}\end{aligned}$$

The break-even price for the put option is the strike price less the premium, or $0.580/SF in this case. As the spot rate falls further and further below the strike price, the profit potential would continually increase, and Hans' profit could be unlimited (up to a maximum of $0.580/SF, when the price of a franc would be zero). At any exchange rate above the strike price of 58.5, Hans would not exercise the option, and so would lose only the $0.005/SF premium paid for the put option. The buyer of a put option has an almost unlimited profit potential with a limited loss potential. Like the buyer of a call, the buyer of a put can never lose more than the premium paid up front.

Writer of a Put

The position of the writer who sold the put to Hans is shown in Exhibit 8.6. Note the symmetry of profit/loss, strike price, and break-even prices between the buyer and the writer of the put. If the spot price of francs drops below 58.5 cents per franc, Hans will exercise the option. Below a price of 58.5 cents per franc, the writer will lose more than the premium received from writing the option ($0.005/SF), falling below break-even. Between $0.580/SF and $0.585/SF the writer will lose part, but not all, of the premium received. If the spot price is above $0.585/SF, Hans will not exercise the option, and the option writer will pocket the entire premium of $0.005/SF.

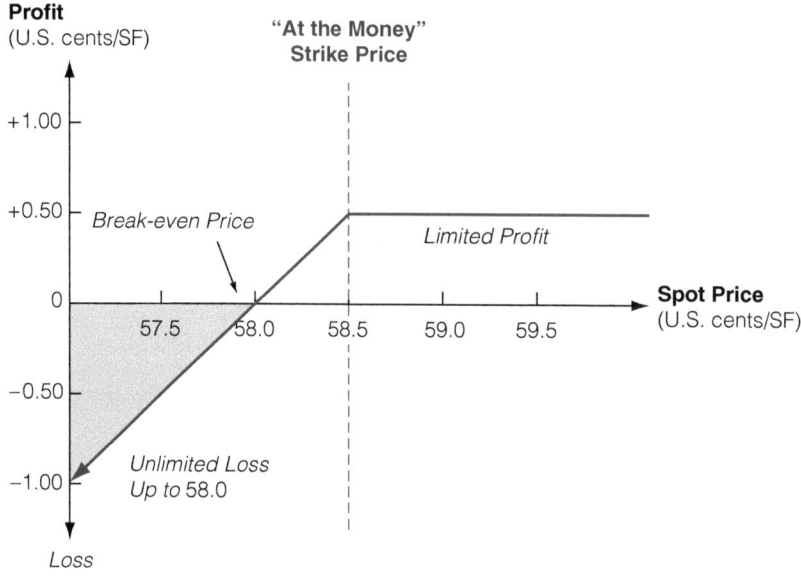

EXHIBIT 8.6 Profit and Loss for the Writer of a Put Option

The writer of a put option on SF, with a strike price of 58.5 cents/SF, has a limited profit of 0.50 cents/SF at spot rates greater than 58.5, and an unlimited loss potential at spot rates less than 58.5 cents/SF up to 58.0 cents.

The profit (loss) earned by the writer of a $0.585 strike price put, premium $0.005, at a spot rate of $0.575, is

$$\text{Profit (loss)} = \text{Premium} - (\text{Strike Price} - \text{Spot Rate})$$
$$= \$0.005/\text{SF} - (\$0.585/\text{SF} - \$0.575/\text{SF})$$
$$= -\$0.005/\text{SF}$$

but only for spot rates that are less than or equal to the strike price. At spot rates greater than the strike price, the option expires out-of-the-money and the writer keeps the premium. The writer of the put option has the same basic combination of outcomes available to the writer of a call: limited profit potential and unlimited loss potential. *Global Finance in Practice 8.1* describes one of the largest, and most successful, currency option speculations ever made—that by Andrew Krieger against the New Zealand kiwi.

GLOBAL FINANCE IN PRACTICE 8.1

The New Zealand Kiwi, Key, and Krieger

What has long been considered one of the most dramatic currency plays in history has moved back into the limelight. New Zealand elected Mr. John Key as its new Prime Minister in November 2008. Key's career has been a long and storied one, a large part of it involving speculation on foreign currencies. Strangely enough, Key had at one time worked with another currency speculator, Andrew Krieger, who is believed to have single-handedly caused the fall of the New Zealand dollar, the kiwi, in 1987.

Then, Andrew Krieger was a 31-year-old currency trader for Bankers Trust of New York (BT). Following the U.S. stock market crash in October 1987, the world's currency markets moved rapidly to exit the dollar. Many of the world's other currencies—including small ones which were in stable, open, industrialized markets like that of New Zealand—became the subject of interest. As the world's currency traders dumped dollars and bought kiwis, the value of the kiwi rose rapidly.

Krieger believed that the markets were overreacting, and would overvalue the kiwi. So he took a short position on the kiwi, betting on its eventual fall. And he did so in a big way, not limiting his positions to simple spot or forward market positions, but through currency options as well. (Krieger supposedly had approval for positions rising to nearly $700 million in size, while all other BT traders were restricted to $50 million.) Krieger, on behalf of BT, is purported to have shorted 200 million kiwi—more than the entire New Zealand money supply at the time. His view proved correct. The kiwi fell, and Krieger was able to earn millions in currency gains for BT. Ironically, only months later, Krieger resigned from BT when annual bonuses were announced and he reportedly earned only $3 million on the more than $300 million he had made for the bank.

Eventually, the New Zealand central bank lodged complaints with BT, in which the CEO at the time, Charles S. Sanford Jr., seemingly added insult to injury when he reportedly remarked "We didn't take too big a position for Bankers Trust, but we may have taken too big a position for that market."

Option Pricing and Valuation

Exhibit 8.7 illustrates the profit/loss profile of a European-style call option on British pounds. The call option allows the holder to buy British pounds at a strike price of $1.70/£. It has a 90-day maturity.

The value of this call option is actually the sum of two components:

$$\text{Total Value (premium)} = \text{Intrinsic Value} + \text{Time Value}$$

The pricing of any currency option combines six elements. For example, this European style call option on British pounds has a premium of $0.033/£ (3.3 cents per pound) at a spot rate of $1.70/£. This premium is calculated using the following assumptions: a spot rate of $1.70/£, a 90-day maturity, a $1.70/£ forward rate, both U.S. dollar and British pound interest rates of 8.00% per annum, and an option volatility for the 90-day period of 10.00% per annum.

EXHIBIT 8.7 Option Intrinsic Value, Time Value, and Total Value

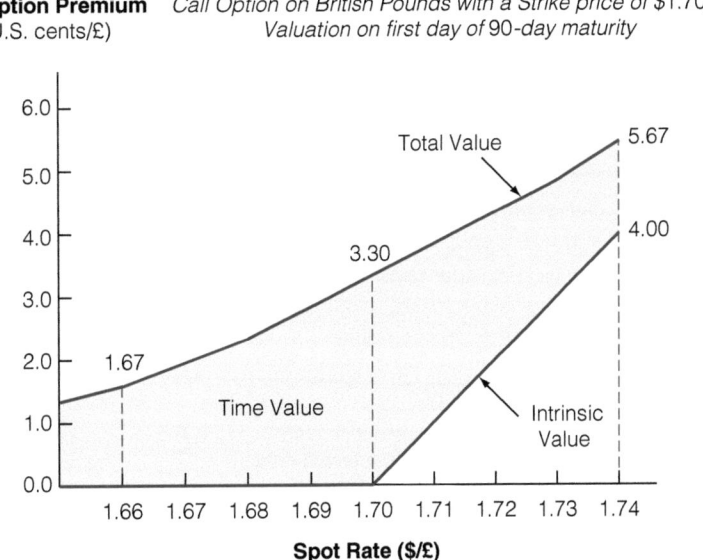

Intrinsic value is the financial gain if the option is exercised immediately. It is shown by the solid line in Exhibit 8.7, which is zero until it reaches the strike price, then rises linearly (1 cent for each 1-cent increase in the spot rate). Intrinsic value will be zero when the option is *out-of-the-money*—that is, when the strike price is above the market price—as no gain can be derived from exercising the option. When the spot rate rises above the strike price, the intrinsic value becomes positive because the option is always worth at least this value if exercised. On the date of maturity an option will have a value equal to its intrinsic value (zero time remaining means zero time value).

- When the spot rate is $1.74/£, the option is *in-the-money* and has an *intrinsic value* of $1.74–$1.70/£, or 4 cents per pound.

- When the spot rate is $1.70/£, the option is *at-the-money* and has an *intrinsic value* of $1.70–$1.70/£, or zero cents per pound.

- When the spot rate is $1.66/£, the option is *out-of-the-money* and has no intrinsic value. This is shown by the intrinsic value lying on the horizontal axis. Only a fool would exercise this call option at this spot rate instead of buying pounds more cheaply on the spot market.

The *time value* of an option exists because the price of the underlying currency, the spot rate, can potentially move further and further into the money before the option's expiration. Time value is shown in Exhibit 8.7 as the area between the *total value* of the option and its intrinsic value. An investor will pay something today for an out-of-the-money option (i.e., zero intrinsic value) on the chance that the spot rate will move far enough before maturity to move the option in-the-money. Consequently, the price of an option is always somewhat greater than its intrinsic value, since there is always some chance that the intrinsic value will rise between the present and the expiration date.

If currency options are to be used effectively, either for the purposes of speculation or risk management (covered in Chapters 10 and 11), the individual trader needs to know how option values—premiums—react to their various components. Exhibit 8.8 summarizes six basic sensitivities.

Although rarely noted, standard foreign currency options are priced around the forward rate because the current spot rate and both the domestic and foreign interest rates (home currency and foreign currency rates) are included in the option premium calculation. Regardless of the specific strike rate chosen and priced, the forward rate is central to valuation. The option-pricing formula calculates a subjective probability distribution centered on

EXHIBIT 8.8 Summary of Option Premium Components

Greek	Definition	Interpretation
Delta	Expected change in the option premium for a small change in the **spot rate**	The higher the delta, the more likely the option will move in-the-money
Theta	Expected change in the option premium for a small change in **time to expiration**	Premiums are relatively insensitive until the final 30 or so days
Lambda	Expected change in the option premium for a small change in **volatility**	Premiums rise with increases in volatility
Rho	Expected change in the option premium for a small change in the **domestic interest rate**	Increases in domestic interest rates cause increasing call option premiums
Phi	Expected change in the option premium for a small change in the **foreign interest rate**	Increases in foreign interest rates cause decreasing call option premiums

the forward rate. This approach does not mean that the market expects the forward rate to be equal to the future spot rate, it is simply a result of the arbitrage-pricing structure of options.

The forward rate focus also provides helpful information for the trader managing a position. When the market prices a foreign currency option, it does so without any bullish or bearish sentiment on the direction of the foreign currency's value relative to the domestic currency. If the trader has specific expectations about the future spot rate's direction, those expectations can be put to work. A trader will not be inherently betting against the market.

Interest Rate Risk

All firms—domestic or multinational, small or large, leveraged or unleveraged—are sensitive to interest rate movements in one way or another. Although a variety of interest rate risks exist in theory and industry, this book focuses on the financial management of the nonfinancial firm. Hence, our discussion is limited to the interest rate risks associated with the multinational firm. The interest rate risks of financial firms, such as banks, are not covered here.

The single largest interest rate risk of the nonfinancial firm is debt service. The debt structure of the MNE will possess differing maturities of debt, different interest rate structures (such as fixed versus floating-rate), and different currencies of denomination. Interest rates are currency-specific. Each currency has its own interest rate yield curve and credit spreads for borrowers. Therefore, the multicurrency dimension of interest rate risk for the MNE is a serious concern. As illustrated in Exhibit 8.9, even the interest rate calculations vary on occasion across currencies and countries. *Global Finance in Practice 8.2* provides additional evidence on the use of fixed versus floating-rate instruments in today's marketplace.

The second most prevalent source of interest rate risk for the MNE lies in its holdings of interest-sensitive securities. Unlike debt, which is recorded on the right-hand side of the firm's balance sheet, the marketable securities portfolio of the firm appears on the left-hand side. Marketable securities represent potential earnings or interest inflows to the firm. Ever-increasing competitive pressures have pushed financial managers to tighten their management of both the left and right sides of the firm's balance sheet.

EXHIBIT 8.9 International Interest Rate Calculations

International interest rate calculations differ by the number of days used in the period's calculation and their definition of how many days there are in a year (for financial purposes). The following example highlights how the different methods result in different 1-month payments of interest on a $10 million loan, 5.500% per annum interest, for an exact period of 28 days.

Practice	Day Count in Period	Days/Year	$10 million @ 5.500% per annum	
			Days Used	Interest Payment
International	Exact number of days	360	28	$42,777.78
British	Exact number of days	365	28	$42,191.78
Swiss (Eurobond)	Assumed 30 days/month	360	30	$45,833.33

> **GLOBAL FINANCE IN PRACTICE 8.2**
>
> **A Fixed-Rate or Floating-Rate World?**
>
> The *BIS Quarterly Review* of March 2009 provides a detailed statistical breakdown of the types of international notes and bonds newly issued and outstanding, by issuer, by type of instrument, and by currency of denomination. The data provides some interesting insights into the international securities market.
>
> - At of end of year 2008 there were $22.7 trillion outstanding in international notes and bonds issued by all types of institutions.
> - The market continues to be dominated by issuances of financial institutions. The issuers by dollar value were as follows: financial institutions, $17.9 trillion or 79%; governments, $1.8 trillion or 8%; international organizations, $0.6 trillion or 3%; and corporate issuers, $2.4 trillion or 10% of the total outstanding.
> - The instruments are still largely fixed-rate issuances, with 64% of all outstanding issuances being fixed-rate, 34% floating-rate, and roughly 2% equity-related.
> - The euro continues to dominate international note and bond issuances, making up more than 48% of the total. The euro is followed by the dollar, 36%, the pound sterling, 8%, the Japanese yen, 3%, and the Swiss franc, just under 2%.
>
> The data continues to support two long-standing fundamental properties of the international debt markets.
>
> - First, that the euro's domination reflects the long-term use of the international security markets by the institutions in the countries constituting the euro—Western Europe.
> - Second, that fixed-rate issuances are still the foundation of the market. Although floating-rate issuances did rise marginally in the 2003–2006 period, the international credit crisis of 2007–2008 and the response by central banks to push interest rates downwards created new opportunities for the issuance of longer-term fixed-rate issuances by issuers of all kinds.
>
> *Source*: Data drawn from Table 13B, *BIS Quarterly Review*, March 2009, p. 91, www.bis.org/statistics/secstats.htm.

Credit Risk and Repricing Risk

Prior to describing the management of the most common interest rate pricing risks, it is important to distinguish between credit risk and repricing risk. Credit risk, sometimes termed roll-over risk, is the possibility that a borrower's creditworth, at the time of renewing a credit, is reclassified by the lender. This can result in changing fees, changing interest rates, altered credit line commitments, or even denial. Repricing risk is the risk of changes in interest rates charged (earned) at the time a financial contract's rate is reset.

Consider the following debt strategies being considered by a corporate borrower. Each is intended to provide $1 million in financing for a 3-year period.

Strategy 1: Borrow $1 million for three years at a fixed rate of interest.

Strategy 2: Borrow $1 million for three years at a floating rate, LIBOR + 2%, to be reset annually.

Strategy 3: Borrow $1 million for one year at a fixed rate, then renew the credit annually.

Although the lowest cost of funds is always a major selection criteria, it is not the only one. If the firm chooses strategy 1, it assures itself of the funding for the full three years at a known interest rate. It has maximized the predictability of cash flows for the debt obligation. What it has sacrificed, to some degree, is the ability to enjoy a lower interest rate in the event that interest rates fall over the period. Of course, it has also eliminated the risk that interest rates could rise over the period, increasing debt servicing costs.

Strategy 2 offers what strategy 1 did not, flexibility (repricing risk). It too assures the firm of full funding for the 3-year period. This eliminates credit risk. Repricing risk is, however, alive and well in strategy 2. If LIBOR changes dramatically by the second or third year, the LIBOR rate change is passed through fully to the borrower. The spread, however, remains fixed (reflecting the credit standing that has been locked in for the full three years). Flexibility comes at a cost in this case, the risk that interest rates could go up as well as down.

Strategy 3 offers more flexibility and more risk. First, the firm is borrowing at the shorter end of the yield curve. If the yield curve is positively sloped, as is commonly the case in major industrial markets, the base interest rate should be lower. But the short end of the yield curve is also the more volatile. It responds to short-term events in a much more pronounced fashion than longer-term rates. The strategy also exposes the firm to the possibility that its credit rating may change dramatically by the time for credit renewal, for better or worse. Noting that credit ratings in general are established on the premise that a firm can meet its debt-service obligations under worsening economic conditions, firms that are highly creditworthy (investment-rated grades) may view strategy 3 as a more relevant alternative than do firms of lower quality (speculative grades). This is not a strategy for firms that are financially weak.

Although the previous example gives only a partial picture of the complexity of funding decisions within the firm, it demonstrates the many ways credit risks and repricing risks are inextricably intertwined. The expression *interest rate exposure* is a complex concept, and the proper measurement of the exposure prior to its management is critical. We now proceed to describe the interest rate risk of the most common form of corporate debt, floating-rate loans.

Interest Rate Derivatives

Like foreign currency, interest rates have derivatives in the form of futures, forwards, and options. In addition, and likely of more importance, is the interest rate swap.

Interest Rate Futures

Unlike foreign currency futures, *interest rate futures* are relatively widely used by financial managers and treasurers of nonfinancial companies. Their popularity stems from the relatively high liquidity of the interest rate futures markets, their simplicity in use, and the rather standardized interest rate exposures most firms possess. The two most widely used futures contracts are the Eurodollar futures traded on the Chicago Mercantile Exchange (CME) and the U.S. Treasury Bond Futures of the Chicago Board of Trade (CBOT). Interestingly, the third-largest volume of a traded futures contract in the latter 1990s was the U.S. dollar/Brazilian *real* currency futures contract traded on the Bolsa de Mercadorias y Futuros in Brazil.

To illustrate the use of futures for managing interest rate risks we will focus on the 3-month Eurodollar futures contracts. Exhibit 8.10 presents Eurodollar futures for two years (they actually trade 10 years into the future).

EXHIBIT 8.10 Eurodollar Futures Prices

Maturity	Open	High	Low	Settle	Yield	Open Interest
June 10	94.99	95.01	94.98	95.01	4.99	455,763
Sept	94.87	94.97	94.87	94.96	5.04	535,932
Dec	94.60	94.70	94.60	94.68	5.32	367,036
Mar 11	94.67	94.77	94.66	94.76	5.24	299,993
June	94.55	94.68	94.54	94.63	5.37	208,949
Sept	94.43	94.54	94.43	94.53	5.47	168,961
Dec	94.27	94.38	94.27	94.36	5.64	130,824

Typical presentation by the *Wall Street Journal*. Only regular quarterly maturities shown. All contracts are for $1 million; points of 100%. Open interest is number of contracts outstanding.

The yield of a futures contract is calculated from the *settlement price*, which is the closing price for that trading day. For example, a financial manager examining the Eurodollar quotes in Exhibit 8.10 for a March 2011 contract would see that the *settlement price* on the previous day was 94.76, an annual yield of 5.24%:

$$\text{Yield} = (100.00 - 94.76) = 5.24\%$$

Since each contract is for a 3-month period (quarter) and a notional principal of $1 million, each basis point is actually worth $2,500 (.01 × $1,000,000 × 90/360).

If a financial manager were interested in hedging a floating-rate interest payment due in March 2011, she would need to *sell a future*, to take a short position. This strategy is referred to as a short position because the manager is selling something she does not own (as in shorting common stock). If interest rates rise by March—as the manager fears—the futures price will fall and she will be able to close the position at a profit. This profit will roughly offset the losses associated with rising interest payments on her debt. If the manager is wrong, however, and interest rates actually fall by the maturity date, causing the futures price to rise, she will suffer a loss that will wipe out the "savings" derived by making a lower floating-rate interest payment than she expected. So by selling the March 2011 futures contract, the manager will be locking in an interest rate of 5.24%.

Obviously interest rate futures positions could be—and are on a regular basis—purchased purely for speculative purposes. Although that is not the focus of the managerial context here, the example shows how any speculator with a directional view on interest rates could take positions in expectations of profit.

As mentioned previously, the most common interest rate exposure of the nonfinancial firm is interest payable on debt. Such exposure is not, however, the only interest rate risk. As more and more firms aggressively manage their entire balance sheet, the interest earnings from the left-hand side are under increasing scrutiny. If financial managers are expected to earn higher interest on interest-bearing securities, they may well find a second use of the interest rate futures market: to lock in future interest earnings. Exhibit 8.11 provides an overview of these two basic interest rate exposures and the strategies needed to manage interest rate futures.

Forward Rate Agreements

A *forward rate agreement* (FRA) is an interbank-traded contract to buy or sell interest rate payments on a notional principal. These contracts are settled in cash. The buyer of an FRA obtains the right to lock in an interest rate for a desired term that begins at a future date. The contract specifies that the seller of the FRA will pay the buyer the increased interest expense

EXHIBIT 8.11 Interest Rate Futures Strategies for Common Exposures

Exposure or Position	Futures Action	Interest Rates	Position Outcome
Paying interest on future date	Sell a Futures (short position)	If rates go up	Futures price falls; short earns a profit
		If rates go down	Futures price rises; short earns a loss
Earning interest on future date	Buy a Futures (long position)	If rates go up	Futures price falls; long earns a loss
		If rates go down	Futures price rises; long earns a profit

on a nominal sum (the notional principal) of money if interest rates rise above the agreed rate, but the buyer will pay the seller the differential interest expense if interest rates fall below the agreed rate. Maturities available are typically 1, 3, 6, 9, and 12 months, much like traditional forward contracts for currencies.

Like foreign currency forward contracts, FRAs are useful on individual exposures. They are contractual commitments of the firm that allow little flexibility to enjoy favorable movements, such as when LIBOR is falling as described above. Firms also use FRAs if they plan to invest in securities at future dates but fear that interest rates might fall prior to the investment date. Because of the limited maturities and currencies available, however, FRAs are not widely used outside the largest industrial economies and currencies.

Interest Rate Swaps

Swaps are contractual agreements to exchange or swap a series of cash flows. These cash flows are most commonly the interest payments associated with debt service, such as the floating-rate loan described above.

- If the agreement is for one party to swap its fixed interest rate payment for the floating interest rate payments of another, it is termed an *interest rate swap*.
- If the agreement is to swap currencies of debt service obligation—for example, Swiss franc interest payments in exchange for U.S. dollar interest payments—it is termed a *currency swap*.
- A single swap may combine elements of both interest rate and currency swaps.

In any case, however, the swap serves to alter the firm's cash flow obligations, as in changing floating-rate payments into fixed-rate payments associated with an existing debt obligation. The swap itself is not a source of capital, but rather an alteration of the cash flows associated with payment. What is often termed the *plain vanilla swap* is an agreement between two parties to exchange fixed-rate for floating-rate financial obligations. This type of swap forms the largest single financial derivative market in the world.

The two parties may have various motivations for entering into the agreement. For example, a very common position is as follows. A corporate borrower of good credit standing has existing floating-rate debt service payments. The borrower, after reviewing current market conditions and forming expectations about the future, may conclude that interest rates are about to rise. In order to protect the firm against rising debt-service payments, the company's treasury may enter into a swap agreement to pay *fixed/receive floating*. This means the firm will now make fixed interest rate payments and receive from the swap counterparty floating interest rate payments. The floating-rate payments that the firm receives are used to service the debt obligation of the firm, so the firm, on a net basis, is now making fixed interest rate payments. Using derivatives it has synthetically changed floating-rate debt into fixed-rate debt. It has done so without going through the costs and intricacies of refinancing existing debt obligations.

Similarly, a firm with fixed-rate debt that expects interest rates to fall can change fixed-rate debt to floating-rate debt. In this case, the firm would enter into a *pay floating/receive fixed* interest rate swap. Exhibit 8.12 presents a summary table of the recommended interest rate swap strategies for firms holding either fixed-rate debt or floating-rate debt.

The cash flows of an interest rate swap are interest rates applied to a set amount of capital (*notional principal*). For this reason they are also referred to as *coupon swaps*. Firms entering into interest rate swaps set the notional principal so that the cash flows resulting from the interest rate swap cover their interest rate management needs.

Interest rate swaps are contractual commitments between a firm and a swap dealer and are completely independent of the interest rate exposure of the firm. That is, the firm may

EXHIBIT 8.12 Interest Rate Swap Strategies

Position	Expectation	Interest Rate Swap Strategy
Fixed-Rate Debt	Rates to go up	Do nothing
	Rates to go down	Pay floating/Receive fixed
Floating-Rate Debt	Rates to go up	Pay fixed/Receive floating
	Rates to go down	Do nothing

enter into a swap for any reason it sees fit and then swap a notional principal that is less than, equal to, or even greater than the total position being managed. For example, a firm with a variety of floating-rate loans on its books may enter into interest rate swaps for only 70% of the existing principal, if it wishes. The reason for entering into a swap, and the swap position the firm enters into, is purely at management's discretion. It should also be noted that the interest rate swap market is filling a gap in market efficiency. If all firms had free and equal access to capital markets, regardless of interest rate structure or currency of denomination, the swap market would most likely not exist. The fact that the swap market not only exists but flourishes and provides benefits to all parties is in some ways the proverbial "free lunch."

Currency Swaps

Since all swap rates are derived from the yield curve in each major currency, the fixed-to floating-rate interest rate swap existing in each currency allows firms to swap across currencies. Exhibit 8.13 lists typical swap rates for the euro, the U.S. dollar, the Japanese yen, and the

EXHIBIT 8.13 Interest Rate and Currency Swap Quotes

Years	Euro-E Bid	Euro-E Ask	Swiss franc Bid	Swiss franc Ask	U.S. dollar Bid	U.S. dollar Ask	Japanese yen Bid	Japanese yen Ask
1	2.99	3.02	1.43	1.47	5.24	5.26	0.23	0.26
2	3.08	3.12	1.68	1.76	5.43	5.46	0.36	0.39
3	3.24	3.28	1.93	2.01	5.56	5.59	0.56	0.59
4	3.44	3.48	2.15	2.23	5.65	5.68	0.82	0.85
5	3.63	3.67	2.35	2.43	5.73	5.76	1.09	1.12
6	3.83	3.87	2.54	2.62	5.80	5.83	1.33	1.36
7	4.01	4.05	2.73	2.81	5.86	5.89	1.55	1.58
8	4.18	4.22	2.91	2.99	5.92	5.95	1.75	1.78
9	4.32	4.36	3.08	3.16	5.96	5.99	1.90	1.93
10	4.42	4.46	3.22	3.30	6.01	6.04	2.04	2.07
12	4.58	4.62	3.45	3.55	6.10	6.13	2.28	2.32
15	4.78	4.82	3.71	3.81	6.20	6.23	2.51	2.56
20	5.00	5.04	3.96	4.06	6.29	6.32	2.71	2.76
25	5.13	5.17	4.07	4.17	6.29	6.32	2.77	2.82
30	5.19	5.23	4.16	4.26	6.28	6.31	2.82	2.88
LIBOR	3.0313	3.0938	1.3125	1.4375	4.9375	5.0625	0.1250	0.2188

Typical presentation by the *Financial Times*. Bid and ask spreads as of close of London business. US$ is quoted against 3-month LIBOR; Japanese yen against 6-month LIBOR; Euro and Swiss franc against 6-month LIBOR.

Swiss franc. These swap rates are based on the government security yields in each of the individual currency markets, plus a credit spread applicable to investment grade borrowers in the respective markets.

Note that the swap rates in Exhibit 8.13 are not rated or categorized by credit ratings. This is because the swap market itself does not carry the credit risk associated with individual borrowers. Individual borrowers with obligations priced at LIBOR plus a spread will keep the spread. The fixed spread, a credit risk premium, is still borne by the firm itself. For example, lower-rated firms may pay spreads of 3% or 4% over LIBOR, while some of the world's largest and most financially sound MNEs may actually raise capital at rates of LIBOR −0.40%. The swap market does not differentiate the rate by the participant; all swap at fixed rates versus LIBOR in the respective currency.

The usual motivation for a currency swap is to replace cash flows scheduled in an undesired currency with flows in a desired currency. The desired currency is probably the currency in which the firm's future operating revenues (inflows) will be generated. Firms often raise capital in currencies in which they do not possess significant revenues or other natural cash flows. The reason they do so is cost; specific firms may find capital costs in specific currencies attractively priced to them under special conditions. Having raised the capital, however, the firm may wish to swap its repayment into a currency in which it has future operating revenues.

The utility of the currency swap market to an MNE is significant. An MNE wishing to swap a 10-year fixed 6.04% U.S. dollar cash flow stream could swap to 4.46% fixed in euro, 3.30% fixed in Swiss francs, or 2.07% fixed in Japanese yen. It could swap from fixed dollars not only to fixed rates, but also to floating LIBOR rates in the various currencies as well. All are possible at the rates quoted in Exhibit 8.13.

Prudence in Practice

In the following chapters we will illustrate how derivatives can be used to reduce the risks associated with the conduct of multinational financial management. It is critical, however, that the user of any financial tool or technique—including financial derivatives—follow sound principles and practices. Many a firm has been ruined as a result of the misuse of derivatives. A word to the wise: Do not fall victim to what many refer to as the *gambler's dilemma*—confusing luck with talent.

Major corporate financial disasters related to financial derivatives continue to be a problem in global business. As is the case with so many issues in modern society, technology is not at fault, rather human error in its use. We conclude our discussion of financial derivatives with a note of caution and humility from an essay in the *Harvard Business Review* by Peter Bernstein:

> *More than any other development, the quantification of risk defines the boundary between modern times and the rest of history. The speed, power, movement, and instant communication that characterize our age would have been inconceivable before science replaced superstition as a bulwark against risks of all kinds.*
>
> *It is hubris that we believe that we can put reliable and stable numbers on the impact of a politician's power, on the probability of a takeover boom like the one that occurred in the 1980s, on the return on the stock market over the next 2, 20, or 50 years, or on subjective factors like utility and risk aversion. It is equally silly to limit our deliberations only to those variables that do lend themselves to quantification, excluding all serious consideration of the unquantifiable. It is irrational to confuse probability with timing and to assume that an event with low probability is therefore not imminent. Such confusion, however, is by*

no means unusual. And it surely is naive to define discontinuity as anomaly instead of as normality; only the shape and the timing of the disturbances are hidden from us, not their inevitability.

Finally, the science of risk management is capable of creating new risks even as it brings old risk under control. Our faith in risk management encourages us to take risk we otherwise would not take. On most counts, that is beneficial. But we should be wary of increasing the total amount of risk in the system. Research shows that the security of seat belts encourages drivers to behave more aggressively, with the result that the number of accidents rises even as the seriousness of injury in any one accident may diminish.[1]

Summary of Learning Objectives

Explain how foreign currency futures are quoted, valued, and used for speculation purposes.

◆ A foreign currency futures contract is an exchange-traded agreement calling for future delivery of a standard amount of foreign exchange at a fixed time, place, and price.

◆ Foreign currency futures contracts are in reality standardized forward contracts. Unlike forward contracts, however, trading occurs on the floor of an organized exchange rather than between banks and customers. Futures also require collateral and are normally settled through the purchase of an offsetting position.

Illustrate how foreign currency futures differ from forward contracts.

◆ Futures differ from forward contracts by size of contract, maturity, location of trading, pricing, collateral/margin requirements, method of settlement, commissions, trading hours, counterparties, and liquidity.

◆ Financial managers typically prefer foreign currency forwards over futures out of simplicity of use and position maintenance. Financial speculators typically prefer foreign currency futures over forwards because of the liquidity of the futures markets.

Analyze how foreign currency options are quoted, valued, and used for speculation purposes.

◆ Foreign currency options are financial contracts that give the holder the right, but not the obligation, to buy (in the case of calls) or sell (in the case of puts) a specified amount of foreign exchange at a predetermined price on or before a specified maturity date.

◆ The use of a currency option as a speculative device for the buyer of an option arises from the fact that an option gains in value as the underlying currency rises (for calls) or falls (for puts). The amount of loss when the underlying currency moves opposite to the desired direction is limited to the premium of the option.

◆ The use of a currency option as a speculative device for the writer (seller) of an option arises from the option premium. If the option—either a put or call—expires out-of-the-money (valueless), the writer of the option has earned, and retains, the entire premium.

◆ Speculation is an attempt to profit by trading on expectations about prices in the future. In the foreign exchange market, one speculates by taking a position in a foreign currency and then closing that position after the exchange rate has moved; a profit results only if the rate moves in the direction that the speculator expected.

Explain how foreign currency options are valued.

◆ Currency option valuation, the determination of the option's premium, is a complex combination of the current spot rate, the specific strike rate, the forward rate (which itself is dependent on the current spot rate and interest differentials), currency volatility, and time to maturity.

◆ The total value of an option is the sum of its intrinsic value and time value. Intrinsic value depends on the relationship between the option's strike price and the current spot rate at any single point in time, whereas time value estimates how this current intrinsic value may change—for the better—prior to the option's maturity or expiration.

---

[1]Reprinted by permission of *Harvard Business Review*. Excerpt from "The New Religion of Risk Management" by Peter L. Bernstein, March–April 1996. Copyright 1996 by the Harvard Business School Publishing Corporation; all rights reserved.

Define interest rate risk, and examine how can it be managed.

♦ The single largest interest rate risk of the nonfinancial firm is debt-service. The debt structure of the MNE will possess differing maturities of debt, different interest rate structures (such as fixed versus floating-rate), and different currencies of denomination.

♦ The increasing volatility of world interest rates, combined with the increasing use of short-term and variable-rate debt by firms worldwide, has led many firms to actively manage their *interest rate risks*.

♦ The primary sources of interest rate risk to a multinational nonfinancial firm are short-term borrowing and investing, as well as long-term sources of debt.

♦ The techniques and instruments used in interest rate risk management in many ways resemble those used in currency risk management: the old tried and true methods of lending and borrowing.

♦ The primary instruments and techniques used for interest rate risk management include forward rate agreements (FRAs), forward swaps, interest rate futures, and interest rate swaps.

Explain interest rate swaps and how they can be used to manage interest rate risk.

♦ The interest rate and currency swap markets allow firms that have limited access to specific currencies and interest rate structures to gain access at relatively low costs. This in turn allows these firms to manage their currency and interest rate risks more effectively.

Analyze how interest rate swaps and cross currency swaps can be used to manage both foreign exchange risk and interest rate risk simultaneously.

♦ A cross currency interest rate swap allows a firm to alter both the currency of denomination of cash flows in debt service, but also to alter the fixed-to-floating or floating-to-fixed interest rate structure.

MINI-CASE

McDonald's Corporation's British Pound Exposure

McDonald's Corporation has investments in more than 100 countries. It considers its equity investment in foreign affiliates capital which is at risk, subject to hedging depending on the individual country, currency, and market.

British Subsidiary as an Exposure

McDonald's parent company has three different pound-denominated exposures arising from its ownership and operation of its British subsidiary.

1. The British subsidiary has equity capital which is a pound-denominated asset of the parent company.

2. In addition to the equity capital invested in the British affiliate, the parent company provides intra-company debt in the form of a 4-year £125 million loan. The loan is denominated in British pounds and carries a fixed 5.30% per annum interest payment.

3. The British subsidiary pays a fixed percentage of gross sales in royalties to the parent company. This too is pound-denominated. The three different exposures sum to a significant exposure problem for McDonald's.

An additional technical detail further complicates the situation. When the parent company makes an intra-company loan as that to the British subsidiary, it must designate—according to U.S. accounting and tax law practices—whether the loan is considered to be *permanently invested* in that country. (Although on the surface it seems illogical to consider four years "permanent," the loan itself could simply be continually rolled-over by the parent company and never actually be repaid.) If not considered permanent, the foreign exchange gains and losses related to the loan flow directly to the parent company's profit and loss statement (P&L), according to FAS #52. If, however, the loan is designated as permanent, the foreign exchange gains and losses related to the intracompany loan would flow only to the CTA (cumulative translation adjustment) on the consolidated balance sheet. To date, McDonald's has chosen to designate the loan as *permanent*. The functional currency of the British affiliate for consolidation purposes is the local currency, the British pound.

Anka Gopi is both the Manager for Financial Markets/Treasury and a McDonald's shareholder. She is currently reviewing the existing hedging strategy employed by McDonald's against the pound exposure. The company has been hedging the pound exposure by entering into a cross-currency U.S. dollar/British pound sterling swap. The current swap is a 7-year swap to receive dollars and pay pounds. Like all cross-currency swaps, the agreement requires McDonald's-U.S. to make regular pound-denominated interest payments and a bullet principal repayment (notional principal) at the end of the swap agreement. McDonald's considers the large notional principal payment a hedge against the equity investment in its British affiliate.

According to accounting practice, a company may elect to take the interest associated with a foreign currency-denominated loan and carry that directly to the parent company's P&L This has been done in the past, and McDonald's has benefited from the inclusion of this interest payment.

FAS #133, *Accounting for Derivative Instruments and Hedging Activities*, issued in June 1998, was originally intended to be effective for all fiscal quarters within fiscal years beginning after June 15, 1999 (for most firms this meant January 1, 2000). The new standard, however, was so complex and potentially of such material influence to U.S.-based MNEs, that the Financial Accounting Standards Board has been approached by dozens of major firms and asked to postpone mandatory implementation. The standard's complexity, combined with the workloads associated with Y2K (year 2000) risk controls, persuaded the Financial Accounting Standards Board to delay FAS #133's mandatory implementation date indefinitely.

Issues for Discussion. Anka Gopi, however, still wishes to consider the impact of FAS #133 on the hedging strategy currently employed. Under FAS #133, the firm will have to mark-to-market the entire cross-currency swap position, including principal, and carry this to *other comprehensive income* (OCI). OCI, however, is actually a form of income required under U.S. GAAP and reported in the footnotes to the financial statements, but not the income measure used in reported earnings per share. Although McDonald's has been carrying the interest payments on the swap to income, it has not previously had to carry the present value of the swap principal to OCI. In Anka Gopi's eyes, this poses a substantial material risk to OCI.

Anka Gopi also wished to reconsider the current strategy. She began by listing the pros and cons of the current strategy, comparing these to alternative strategies, and then deciding what if anything should be done about it at this time.

CASE QUESTIONS

1. How does the cross-currency swap effectively hedge the three primary exposures McDonald's has relative to its British subsidiary?
2. How does the cross-currency swap hedge the long-term equity position in the foreign subsidiary?
3. Should Anka—and McDonald's—worry about OCI?

Questions

1. **Options versus Futures.** Explain the difference between foreign currency *options* and *futures* and when either might be most appropriately used.
2. **Trading Location for Futures.** Check the *Wall Street Journal* to find where in the United States foreign exchange future contracts are traded.
3. **Futures Terminology.** Explain the meaning and probable significance for international business of the following contract specifications:
   a. Specific-sized contract
   b. Standard method of stating exchange rates
   c. Standard maturity date
   d. Collateral and maintenance margins
   e. Counterparty
4. **A Futures Trade.** A newspaper shows the prices below for the previous day's trading in U.S. dollar-euro currency futures. What do the terms shown indicate?

Month:	December
Open:	0.9124
Settlement:	0.9136
Change:	+0.0027
High:	0.9147
Low:	0.9098
Estimated volume	29,763
Open interest:	111,360
Contract size:	€125,000

5. **Puts and Calls.** What is the basic difference between a *put* on British pounds sterling and a *call* on sterling?
6. **Call Contract Elements.** You read that exchange-traded American call options on pounds sterling having a strike price of 1.460 and a maturity of next March are now quoted at 3.67. What does this mean if you are a potential buyer?
7. **The Option Cost.** What happens to the premium you paid for the above option in the event you decide to let the option expire unexercised? What happens to this amount in the event you do decide to exercise the option?
8. **Buying a European Option.** You have the same information as in question 4, except that the pricing is for a European option. What is different?
9. **Writing Options.** Why would anyone write an option, knowing that the gain from receiving the option premium is fixed but the loss if the underlying price goes in the wrong direction can be extremely large?
10. **Option Valuation.** The value of an option is stated to be the sum of its *intrinsic value* and its *time value*. Explain what is meant by these terms.
11. **Reference Rates.** What is an interest "reference rate" and how is it used to set rates for individual borrowers?

12. **Risk and Return.** Some corporate treasury departments are organized as a service center (cost center), while others are set up as profit centers. What is the difference and what are the implications for the firm?

13. **Forecast Types.** What is the difference between a specific forecast and a directional forecast?

14. **Policy Statements.** Explain the difference between a goal statement and a policy statement?

15. **Credit and Repricing Risk.** From the point of view of a borrowing corporation, what are credit and repricing risks. Explain steps a company might take to minimize both.

16. **Forward Rate Agreement.** How can a business firm that has borrowed on a floating rate basis use a forward rate agreement to reduce interest rate risk?

17. **Eurodollar Futures.** A newspaper reports that a given June Eurodollar futures settled at 93.55. What was the annual yield? How many dollars does this represent?

18. **Defaulting on an Interest Rate Swap.** Smith Company and Jones Company enter into an interest rate swap, with Smith paying fixed interest to Jones, and Jones paying floating interest to Smith. Smith now goes bankrupt and so defaults on its remaining interest payments. What is the financial damage to Jones Company?

19. **Currency Swaps.** Why would one company, with interest payments due in pounds sterling, want to swap those payments for interest payments due in U.S. dollars?

20. **Counterparty Risk.** How does exchange trading in swaps remove any risk that the counterparty in a swap agreement will not complete the agreement?

Problems

1. **Peleh's Puts.** Peleh writes a put option on Japanese yen with a strike price of $0.008000/¥ (¥125.00/$) at a premium of 0.0080¢ per yen and with an expiration date six months from now. The option is for ¥12,500,000. What is Peleh's profit or loss at maturity if the ending spot rates are ¥110/$, ¥115/$, ¥120/$, ¥125/$, ¥130/$, ¥135/$, and ¥140/$?

2. **Sallie Schnudel.** Sallie Schnudel trades currencies for Keystone Funds in Jakarta. She focuses nearly all of her time and attention on the U.S. dollar/Singapore dollar ($/S$) cross-rate. The current spot rate is $0.6000/S$. After considerable study, she has concluded that the Singapore dollar will appreciate versus the U.S. dollar in the coming 90 days, probably to about $0.7000/S$. She has the following options on the Singapore dollar to choose from:

Option	Strike Price	Premium
Put on Sing $	$0.6500/S$	$0.00003/S$
Call on Sing $	$0.6500/S$	$0.00046/S$

   a. Should Sallie buy a put on Singapore dollars or a call on Singapore dollars?
   b. What is Sallie's break-even price on the option purchased in part (a)?
   c. Using your answer from part (a), what is Sallie's gross profit and net profit (including premium) if the spot rate at the end of 90 days is indeed $0.7000/S$?
   d. Using your answer from part (a), what is Sallie's gross profit and net profit (including premium) if the spot rate at the end of 90 days is $0.8000/S$?

3. **Ventosa Investments.** Jamie Rodriguez, a currency trader for Chicago-based Ventosa Investments, uses the futures quotes on the British pound (£) shown at the bottom of the page to speculate on the value of the pound.
   a. If Jamie buys 5 June pound futures, and the spot rate at maturity is $1.3980/£, what is the value of her position?
   b. If Jamie sells 12 March pound futures, and the spot rate at maturity is $1.4560/£, what is the value of her position?
   c. If Jamie buys 3 March pound futures, and the spot rate at maturity is $1.4560/£, what is the value of her position?
   d. If Jamie sells 12 June pound futures, and the spot rate at maturity is $1.3980/£, what is the value of her position?

British Pound Futures, US$/pound (CME) Contract = 62,500 pounds

Maturity	Open	High	Low	Settle	Change	High	Open Interest
March	1.4246	1.4268	1.4214	1.4228	0.0032	1.4700	25,605
June	1.4164	1.4188	1.4146	1.4162	0.0030	1.4550	809

4. **Amber McClain.** Amber McClain, the currency speculator we met in the chapter, sells eight June futures contracts for 500,000 pesos at the closing price quoted in Exhibit 8.1.
   a. What is the value of her position at maturity if the ending spot rate is $0.12000/Ps?
   b. What is the value of her position at maturity if the ending spot rate is $0.09800/Ps?
   c. What is the value of her position at maturity if the ending spot rate is $0.11000/Ps?

5. **Blade Capital (A).** Christoph Hoffeman trades currency for Blade Capital of Geneva. Christoph has $10 million to begin with, and he must state all profits at the end of any speculation in U.S. dollars. The spot rate on the euro is $1.3358/€, while the 30-day forward rate is $1.3350/€.
   a. If Christoph believes the euro will continue to rise in value against the U.S. dollar, so that he expects the spot rate to be $1.3600/€ at the end of 30 days, what should he do?
   b. If Christoph believes the euro will depreciate in value against the U.S. dollar, so that he expects the spot rate to be $1.2800/€ at the end of 30 days, what should he do?

6. **Blade Capital (B).** Christoph Hoffeman of Blade Capital now believes the Swiss franc will appreciate versus the U.S. dollar in the coming 3-month period. He has $100,000 to invest. The current spot rate is $0.5820/SF, the 3-month forward rate is $0.5640/SF, and he expects the spot rates to reach $0.6250/SF in three months.
   a. Calculate Christoph's expected profit assuming a pure spot market speculation strategy.
   b. Calculate Christoph's expected profit assuming he buys or sells SF three months forward.

7. **Vatic Capital.** Cachita Haynes works as a currency speculator for Vatic Capital of Los Angeles. Her latest speculative position is to profit from her expectation that the U.S. dollar will rise significantly against the Japanese yen. The current spot rate is ¥120.00/$. She must choose between the following 90-day options on the Japanese yen:

Option	Strike Price	Premium
Put on yen	¥125/$	$0.00003/S$
Call on yen	¥125/$	$0.00046/S$

   a. Should Cachita buy a put on yen or a call on yen?
   b. What is Cachita's break-even price on the option purchased in part (a)?
   c. Using your answer from part (a), what is Cachita's gross profit and net profit (including premium) if the spot rate at the end of 90 days is ¥140/$?

8. **Calling All Profits.** Assume a call option on euros is written with a strike price of $1.2500/€ at a premium of 3.80¢ per euro ($0.0380/€) and with an expiration date three months from now. The option is for €100,000. Calculate your profit or loss should you exercise before maturity at a time when the euro is traded spot at the following:
   a. $1.10/€
   b. $1.15/€
   c. $1.20/€
   d. $1.25/€
   e. $1.30/€
   f. $1.35/€
   g. $1.40/€

9. **Mystery at Baker Street.** Arthur Doyle is a currency trader for Baker Street, a private investment house in London. Baker Street's clients are a collection of wealthy private investors who, with a minimum stake of £250,000 each, wish to speculate on the movement of currencies. The investors expect annual returns in excess of 25%. Although officed in London, all accounts and expectations are based in U.S. dollars.

   Arthur is convinced that the British pound will slide significantly—possibly to $1.3200/£—in the coming 30 to 60 days. The current spot rate is $1.4260/£. Arthur wishes to buy a put on pounds which will yield the 25% return expected by his investors. Which of the following put options would you recommend he purchase? Prove your choice is the preferable combination of strike price, maturity, and up-front premium expense.

Strike Price	Maturity	Premium
$1.36/£	30 days	$0.00081/£
$1.34/£	30 days	$0.00021/£
$1.32/£	30 days	$0.00004/£
$1.36/£	60 days	$0.00333/£
$1.34/£	60 days	$0.00150/£
$1.32/£	60 days	$0.00060/£

10. **Contrarious Calandra.** Calandra Panagakos works for CIBC Currency Funds in Toronto. Calandra is something of a contrarian—as opposed to most of the forecasts, she believes the Canadian dollar (C$) will appreciate versus the U.S. dollar over the coming 90 days. The current spot rate is $0.6750/C$. Calandra

may choose between the following options on the Canadian dollar.

Option	Strike Price	Premium
Put on C$	$0.7000	$0.00003/S$
Call on C$	$0.7000	$0.00049/S$

   a. Should Calandra buy a put on Canadian dollars or a call on Canadian dollars?
   b. What is Calandra's break-even price on the option purchased in part (a)?
   c. Using your answer from part (a), what is Calandra's gross profit and net profit (including premium) if the spot rate at the end of 90 days is indeed $0.7600?
   d. Using your answer from part (a), what is Calandra's gross profit and net profit (including premium) if the spot rate at the end of 90 days is $0.8250?

11. **Chavez S.A.** Chavez S.A., a Venezuelan company, wishes to borrow $8,000,000 for eight weeks. A rate of 6.250% per annum is quoted by potential lenders in New York, Great Britain, and Switzerland using, respectively, international, British, and the Swiss-Eurobond definitions of interest (day count conventions). From which source should Chavez borrow?

12. **Botany Bay Corporation.** Botany Bay Corporation of Australia seeks to borrow US$30,000,000 in the Eurodollar market. Funding is needed for two years. Investigation leads to three possibilities. Compare the alternatives and make a recommendation.
   1. Botany Bay could borrow the US$30,000,000 for two years at a fixed 5% rate of interest.
   2. Botany Bay could borrow the US$30,000,000 at LIBOR + 1.5%. LIBOR is currently 3.5%, and the rate would be reset every six months.
   3. Botany Bay could borrow the US$30,000,000 for one year only at 4.5%. At the end of the first year Botany Bay Corporation would have to negotiate for a new 1-year loan.

13. **Raid Gauloises.** Raid Gauloises is a rapidly growing French sporting goods and adventure racing outfitter. The company has decided to borrow €20,000,000 via a euro-euro floating rate loan for four years. Raid must decide between two competing loan offers from two of its banks.

   Banque de Paris has offered the 4-year debt at euro-LIBOR + 2.00% with an up-front initiation fee of 1.8%. Banque de Sorbonne, however, has offered euro-LIBOR + 2.5%, a higher spread, but with no loan initiation fees up front, for the same term and principal. Both banks reset the interest rate at the end of each year.

   Euro-LIBOR is currently 4.00%. Raid's economist forecasts that LIBOR will rise by 0.5 percentage points each year. Banque de Sorbonne, however, officially forecasts euro-LIBOR to begin trending upward at the rate of 0.25 percentage points per year. Raid Gauloises's cost of capital is 11%. Which loan proposal do you recommend for Raid Gauloises?

14. **Schifano Motors.** Schifano Motors of Italy recently took out a 4-year €5 million loan on a floating rate basis. It is now worried, however, about rising interest costs. Although it had initially believed interest rates in the Euro-zone would be trending downward when taking out the loan, recent economic indicators show growing inflationary pressures. Analysts are predicting that the European Central Bank will slow monetary growth driving interest rates up.

   Schifano is now considering whether to seek some protection against a rise in euro-LIBOR, and is considering a forward rate agreement (FRA) with an insurance company. According to the agreement, Schifano would pay to the insurance company at the end of each year the difference between its initial interest cost at LIBOR + 2.50% (6.50%) and any fall in interest cost due to a fall in LIBOR. Conversely, the insurance company would pay to Schifano 70% of the difference between Schifano's initial interest cost and any increase in interest costs caused by a rise in LIBOR.

   Purchase of the floating rate agreement will cost €100,000, paid at the time of the initial loan. What are Schifano's annual financing costs now if LIBOR rises and if LIBOR falls? Schifano uses 12% as its weighted average cost of capital. Do you recommend that Schifano purchase the FRA?

15. **Chrysler LLC.** Chrysler LLC, the now privately held company sold off by DaimlerChrysler, must pay floating rate interest three months from now. It wants

Assumptions	Values	Swap Rates	3-year Bid	3-year Ask
Notional principal	$ 10,000,000	U.S. dollar	5.56%	5.59%
Spot exchange rate, SFr/$	1.5000	Swiss franc—SFr	1.93%	2.01%
Spot exchange rate, $/euro	1.1200			

to lock in these interest payments by buying an interest rate futures contract. Interest rate futures for three months from now settled at 93.07, for a yield of 6.93% per annum.

a. If the floating interest rate three months from now is 6.00%, what did Chrysler gain or lose?

b. If the floating interest rate three months from now is 8.00%, what did Chrysler gain or lose?

16. **CB Solutions.** Heather O'Reilly, the treasurer of CB Solutions, believes interest rates are going to rise, so she wants to swap her future floating rate interest payments for fixed rates. Presently, she is paying LIBOR + 2% per annum on $5,000,000 of debt for the next two years, with payments due semiannually. LIBOR is currently 4.00% per annum. Heather has just made an interest payment today, so the next payment is due six months from today.

    Heather finds that she can swap her current floating rate payments for fixed payments of 7.00% per annum. (CB Solution's weighted average cost of capital is 12%, which Heather calculates to be 6% per 6-month period, compounded semiannually).

    a. If LIBOR rises at the rate of 50 basis points per 6-month period, starting tomorrow, how much does Heather save or cost her company by making this swap?

    b. If LIBOR falls at the rate of 25 basis points per 6-month period, starting tomorrow, how much does Heather save or cost her company by making this swap?

17. **Lluvia and Paraguas.** Lluvia Manufacturing and Paraguas Products both seek funding at the lowest possible cost. Lluvia would prefer the flexibility of floating rate borrowing, while Paraguas wants the security of fixed rate borrowing. Lluvia is the more creditworthy company. They face the following rate structure. Lluvia, with the better credit rating, has lower borrowing costs in both types of borrowing.

    Lluvia wants floating rate debt, so it could borrow at LIBOR + 1%. However it could borrow fixed at 8% and swap for floating rate debt. Paraguas wants fixed rate debt, so it could borrow fixed at 12%. However, it could borrow floating at LIBOR +2% and swap for fixed rate debt. What should they do?

18. **Trident's Cross Currency Swap: SFr for US$.** Trident Corporation entered into a 3-year cross currency interest rate swap to receive U.S. dollars and pay Swiss francs. Trident, however, decided to unwind the swap after one year—thereby having two years left on the settlement costs of unwinding the swap after one year. Repeat the calculations for unwinding, but assume that the rates shown above now apply.

19. **Trident's Cross Currency Swap: Yen for Euros.** Use the table of swap rates in the chapter (Exhibit 8.13), and assume Trident enters into a swap agreement to receive euros and pay Japanese yen, on a notional

principal of €5,000,000. The spot exchange rate at the time of the swap is ¥104/€.

a. Calculate all principal and interest payments, in both euros and Swiss francs, for the life of the swap agreement.

b. Assume that one year into the swap agreement Trident decides it wants to unwind the swap agreement and settle it in euros. Assuming that a 2-year fixed rate of interest on the Japanese yen is now 0.80%, and a 2-year fixed rate of interest on the euro is now 3.60%, and the spot rate of exchange is now ¥114/€, what is the net present value of the swap agreement? Who pays whom what?

20. **Falcor.** Falcor is the U.S.-based automotive parts supplier that was spun-off from General Motors in 2000. With annual sales of over $26 billion, the company has expanded its markets far beyond traditional automobile manufacturers in the pursuit of a more diversified sales base. As part of the general diversification effort, the company wishes to diversify the currency of denomination of its debt portfolio as well. Assume Falcor enters into a $50 million 7-year cross currency interest rate swap to do just that—pay euros and receive dollars. Using the data in Exhibit 8.13,

a. Calculate all principal and interest payments in both currencies for the life of the swap.

b. Assume that three years later Falcor decides to unwind the swap agreement. If 4-year fixed rates of interest in euros have now risen to 5.35%, 4-year fixed rate dollars have fallen to 4.40%, and the current spot exchange rate is $1.02/€, what is the net present value of the swap agreement? Who pays whom what?

Pricing Your Own Options

An Excel workbook entitled FX Option Pricing *is downloadable from the book's Web site. The workbook has five spreadsheets constructed for pricing currency options for the following five currency pairs: U.S. dollar/euro, U.S. dollar/ Japanese yen, euro/Japanese yen, U.S. dollar/British pound, and euro/British pound. The dollar/euro pair is shown in the table at the top of the next page. Use the appropriate spreadsheet from the workbook to answer questions 21–25.*

Pricing Currency Options on the Euro

	A U.S.-based firm wishing to buy or sell euros (the foreign currency)		A European firm wishing to buy or sell dollars (the foreign currency)	
	Variable	Value	Variable	Value
Spot rate (domestic/foreign)	S_0	$1.2480	S_0	€0.8013
Strike rate (domestic/foreign)	X	$1.2500	X	€0.8000
Domestic interest rate (%p.a.)	r_d	1.453%	r_d	2.187%
Foreign interest rate (%p.a.)	r_f	2.187%	r_f	1.453%
Time (years, 365 days)	T	1.000	T	1.000
Days equivalent		365.00		365.00
Volatility (%p.a.)	s	10.500%	s	10.500%
Call option premium (per unit fc)	c	$0.0461	c	€0.0366
Put option premium (per unit fc)	p	$0.0570	p	€0.0295
(European pricing)				
Call option premium (%)	c	3.69%	c	4.56%
Put option premium (%)	p	4.57%	p	3.68%

21. **U.S. Dollar/Euro.** The table above indicates that a 1-year call option on euros at a strike rate of $1.25/€ will cost the buyer $0.0632/€, or 4.99%. But that assumed a volatility of 12.000% when the spot rate was $1.2674/€. What would that same call option cost if the volatility was reduced to 10.500% when the spot rate fell to $1.2480/€?

22. **U.S. Dollar/Japanese Yen.** What would be the premium expense, in home currency, for a Japanese firm to purchase an option to sell 750,000 U.S. dollars, assuming the initial values listed in the FX Option Pricing workbook?

23. **Euro/Japanese Yen.** A French firm is expecting to receive JPY 10.4 million in 90 days as a result of an export sale to a Japanese semiconductor firm. What will it cost, in total, to purchase an option to sell the yen at €0.0072/JPY?

24. **U.S. Dollar/British Pound.** Assuming the same initial values for the dollar/pound cross rate in the FX Option Pricing workbook, how much more would a call option on pounds be if the maturity was doubled from 90 to 180 days? What percentage increase is this for twice the length of maturity?

25. **Euro/British Pound.** How would the call option premium change on the right to buy pounds with euros if the euro interest rate changed to 4.000% from the initial values listed in the FX Option Pricing workbook?

Internet Exercises

1. **Financial Derivatives and the ISDA.** The International Swaps and Derivatives Association (ISDA) publishes a wealth of information about financial derivatives, their valuation and their use, in addition to providing master documents for their contractual use between parties. Use the following ISDA Internet site to find the definitions to 31 basic financial derivative questions and terms:

    ISDA   www.isda.org/educat/faqs.html

2. **Risk Management of Financial Derivatives.** If you think this book is long, take a look at the freely downloadable U.S. Comptroller of the Currency's handbook on risk management related to the care and use of financial derivatives!

    Comptroller of the Currency   www.occ.treas.gov/handbook/deriv.pdf

3. **Option Pricing.** OzForex Foreign Exchange Services is a private firm with an enormously powerful foreign currency derivative-enabled Web site. Use the following site to evaluate the various "Greeks" related to currency option pricing.

    OzForex   www.ozforex.com.au/reference/fxoptions/

4. **Garman-Kohlhagen Option Formulation.** For those brave of heart and quantitatively adept, check out the following Internet site's detailed presentation of the Garman-Kohlhagen option formulation used widely in business and finance today.

    Riskglossary.com   www.riskglossary.com/link/garman_kohlhagen_1983.htm

5. **Chicago Mercantile Exchange.** The Chicago Mercantile Exchange trades futures and options on a variety of currencies, including the Brazilian real. Use the following site to evaluate the uses of these currency derivatives:

    Chicago Mercantile Exchange   www.cme.com/trading/dta/del/product_list.html?ProductType=cur

6. **Implied Currency Volatilities.** The single unobservable variable in currency option pricing is the volatility, since volatility inputs are the expected standard deviation of the daily spot rate for the coming period of the option's maturity. Use the New York Federal Reserve's Web site to obtain current implied currency volatilities for major trading cross-rate pairs.

   Federal Reserve Bank of New York   www.ny.frb.org/markets/impliedvolatility.html

7. **Montreal Exchange.** The Montreal Exchange is a Canadian exchange devoted to the support of financial derivatives in Canada. Use its Web site to view the latest on MV volatility—the volatility of the Montreal Exchange Index itself—in recent trading hours and days.

   Montreal Exchange   www.m-x.ca/marc_options_en.php

CHAPTER 9

Foreign Exchange Rate Determination and Forecasting

The herd instinct among forecasters makes sheep look like independent thinkers. —Edgar R. Fiedler.

LEARNING OBJECTIVES

◆ Examine how the supply and demand for any currency can be viewed as an asset choice issue within the portfolio of investors.

◆ Explore how the three major approaches to exchange rate determination—parity conditions, the balance of payments, and the asset approach—combine to explain the numerous emerging market currency crises experienced in recent years.

◆ Observe how forecasters combine technical analysis with the three major theoretical approaches to forecasting exchange rates.

What determines the exchange rate between currencies? This has proven to be a very difficult question to answer. Companies and agents need foreign currency for buying imports, or may earn foreign currency by exporting. Investors, investing in interest-bearing instruments in foreign countries and currencies, fixed-income securities like bonds, shares in publicly traded companies, or other new types of hybrid instruments in foreign markets, all need foreign currency. Tourists, migrant workers, speculators on currency movements—all of these economic agents buy and sell and supply and demand currencies every day. This chapter offers some basic theoretical frameworks to try to organize these elements, forces, and principles.

Chapter 7 described the international parity conditions that integrate exchange rates with inflation and interest rates and provided a theoretical framework for both the global financial markets and the management of international financial business. Chapter 4 provided a detailed analysis of how an individual country's international economic activity, its balance of payments, can impact exchange rates. This chapter extends those discussions of exchange rate determination to the third school, the asset market approach.

Exhibit 9.1 provides an overview of the many determinants of exchange rates. This road map is first organized by the three major schools of thought (parity conditions, balance of payments approach, asset market approach), and second by the individual drivers within those approaches. At first glance the idea that there are three sets of theories may appear daunting, but it is important to remember that these are not *competing theories*, but rather *complementary theories*. Without the depth and breadth of the various approaches combined, our ability to capture the complexity of the global market for currencies is lost. The chapter concludes with the Mini-Case, ***The Japanese Yen Intervention of 2010***, detailing Japan's return to its guidance of market value.

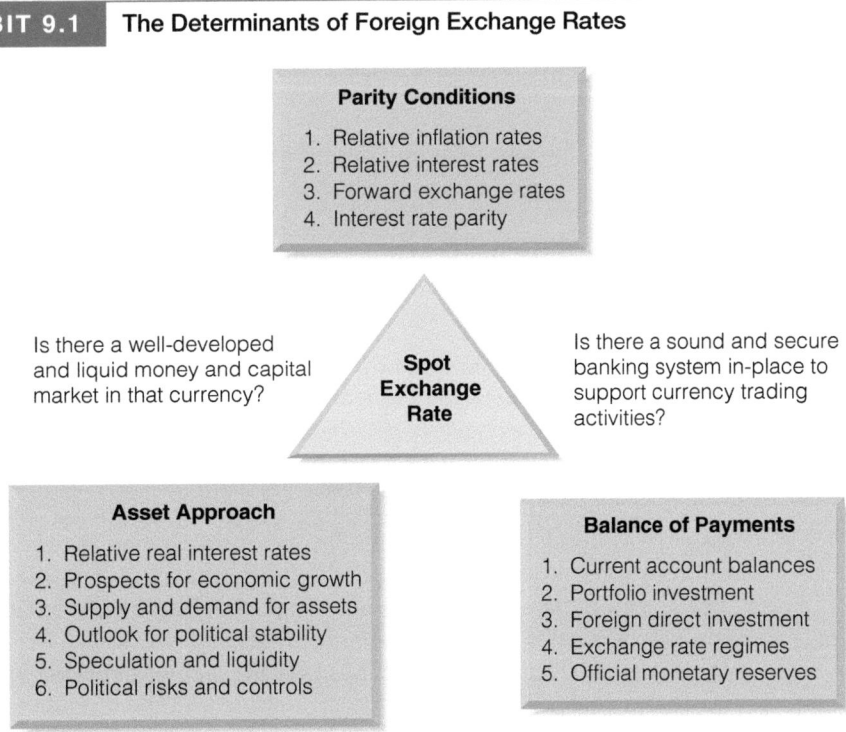

EXHIBIT 9.1 The Determinants of Foreign Exchange Rates

In addition to gaining an understanding of the basic theories, it is equally important to gain a working knowledge of how the complexities of international political economy, societal and economic infrastructures, and random political, economic, or social events affect the exchange rate markets. Here are a few examples:

◆ *Infrastructure weaknesses* were among the major causes of the exchange rate collapses in emerging markets in the late 1990s. On the other hand, infrastructure strengths help explain why the U.S. dollar continued to be strong, at least until the September 11, 2001 terrorist attack on the United States, despite record balance of payments deficits on current account.

◆ *Speculation* contributed greatly to the emerging market crises. Some characteristics of speculation are hot money flowing into and out of currencies, securities, real estate, and commodities. Uncovered interest arbitrage caused by exceptionally low borrowing interest rates in Japan coupled with high real interest rates in the United States was a problem in much of the 1990s. Borrowing yen to invest in safe U.S. government securities, hoping that the exchange rate did not change, was popular.

◆ *Cross-border foreign direct investment and international portfolio investment* into the emerging markets dried up during the recent crises. This has proven to be a very serious issue both for MNEs from the industrialized countries operating in emerging markets, and even more serious for the multinationals that call these emerging market countries home.

◆ *Foreign political risks* were much reduced in recent years as capital markets became less segmented from each other and more liquid. More countries adopted democratic forms of government. However, recent occurrences of terrorism within the U.S. may be changing perceptions of political risk.

Finally, note that most *determinants* of the spot exchange rate are also in turn *affected by* changes in the spot rate. In other words, they are not only linked but also mutually determined.

Exchange Rate Determination: The Theoretical Thread

Under the skin of an international economist lies a deep-seated belief in some variant of the PPP theory of the exchange rate.
—Paul Krugman, 1976.

There are basically three views of the exchange rate. The first takes the exchange rate as the relative price of monies (the monetary approach); the second, as the relative price of goods (the purchasing-power-parity approach); and the third, the relative price of bonds.
—Rudiger Dornbusch, "Exchange Rate Economics: Where Do We Stand?, *Brookings Papers on Economic Activity* 1, 1980, pp. 143–194.

Professor Dornbusch's tripartite categorization of exchange rate theory is a good starting point, but in some ways not robust enough—in our humble opinion—to capture the multitude of theories and approaches. So, in the spirit of both tradition and completeness, we have amended Dornbusch's three categories with several additional streams of thought in the following discussion. The next section will provide a brief overview of the many different, but related, theories of exchange rate determination, and their relative usefulness in forecasting for business purposes.

Purchasing Power Parity Approaches

The most widely accepted for all exchange rate determination theories, the theory of *purchasing power parity* (PPP) states that the long-run equilibrium exchange rate is determined by the ratio of domestic prices relative to foreign prices, as explained in Chapter 7. PPP is both the oldest and most widely followed of the exchange rate theories, as most theories of exchange rate determination have PPP elements embedded within their frameworks.

There are a number of different versions of PPP, the *Law of One Price, Absolute Purchasing Power Parity*, and *Relative Purchasing Power Parity* (discussed in detail in Chapter 7). The latter of the three theories, *Relative Purchasing Power Parity*, is thought to be the most relevant to possibly explaining what drives exchange rate values. In essence, it states that changes in relative prices between countries drive the change in exchange rates over time.

If, for example, the current spot exchange rate between the Japanese yen and U.S. dollar was ¥90.00 = $1.00, and Japanese and U.S. prices were to change at 2% and 1% over the coming period, respectively, the spot exchange rate next period would be ¥90.89/$.

$$S_{t+1} = S_t \times \frac{1 + \Delta \text{ in Japanese prices}}{1 + \Delta \text{ in U.S. prices}} = ¥90.00/\$ \times \frac{1.02}{1.01} = ¥90.89/\$.$$

Although PPP seems to possess a core element of common sense, it has proven to be quite poor at forecasting exchange rates. The problems are both theoretical and empirical. The theoretical problems lie primarily with its basic assumption that the *only thing* that matters is relative price changes. Yet many currency supply and demand forces are driven by other forces including investment incentives and economic growth. The empirical issues are primarily in deciding which measures or indexes of prices to use across countries, in addition to the ability to provide a "predicted change in prices" with the chosen indexes.

Balance of Payments (Flows) Approaches

After purchasing power parity, the most frequently used theoretical approach to exchange rate determination is probably that involving the supply and demand for currencies in the foreign exchange market. These exchange rate *flows* reflect current account and financial account transactions recorded in a nation's balance of payments, as described in Chapter 4. The basic *balance of payments approach* argues that the equilibrium exchange rate is found when the net inflow (outflow) of foreign exchange arising from current account activities matches the net outflow (inflow) of foreign exchange arising from financial account activities.

The balance of payments approach continues to enjoy a wide degree of appeal as the balance of payments transactions are one of the most frequently captured and reported of international economic activity. Trade surpluses and deficits, current account growth in service activity, and recently the growth and significance of international capital flows continue to fuel this theoretical fire.

Criticisms of the balance of payments approach arise from the theory's emphasis on *flows* of currency and capital rather than *stocks* of money or financial assets. Relative stocks of money or financial assets play no role in exchange rate determination in this theory, a weakness explored in the following monetary and asset market approaches.

Curiously, the balance of payments approach is largely dismissed by the academic community today, while the practitioner public—market participants including currency traders themselves—still rely on different variations of the theory for much of their decision making.

Monetary Approaches

The *monetary approach* in its simplest form states that the exchange rate is determined by the supply and demand for national monetary stocks, as well as the expected future levels and rates of growth of monetary stocks. Other financial assets, such as bonds, are not considered relevant for exchange rate determination as both domestic and foreign bonds are viewed as perfect substitutes. It is all about money stocks.

The monetary approach focuses on changes in the supply and demand for money as the primary determinant of inflation. Changes in relative inflation rates in turn are expected to alter exchange rates through a purchasing power parity affect. The monetary approach then assumes that prices are flexible in the short run as well as the long run, so that the transmission mechanism of inflationary pressure is immediate in impact.

In monetary models of exchange rate determination, real economic activity is relegated to a role in which it only influences exchange rates through any alterations to the demand for money. The theory is also criticized on its omission of a number of factors which generally are agreed by area experts as important to exchange rate determination, including 1) the failure of PPP to hold in the short to medium term; 2) money demand appears to be relatively unstable over time; and 3) the level of economic activity and the money supply appear to be interdependent, not independent. Therefore, we will not pursue the monetary approach further.

Asset Market Approach (Relative Price of Bonds)

The *asset market approach*, sometimes called the *relative price of bonds* or *portfolio balance approach*, argues that exchange rates are determined by the supply and demand for financial assets of a wide variety. Shifts in the supply and demand for financial assets alter exchange rates. Changes in monetary and fiscal policy alter expected returns and perceived relative risks of financial assets, which in turn alter rates.

Many of the macroeconomic theoretical developments in the 1980s and 1990s focused on how monetary and fiscal policy changes altered the relative perceptions of return and risk to the stocks of financial assets driving exchange rate changes. The frequently cited works of Mundell-Fleming are in this genre. Theories of *currency substitution*, the ability of individual and commercial investors to alter the composition of their monetary holdings in their portfolios, follow the same basic premises of the portfolio balance and re-balance framework.

Unfortunately, for all of the good work and research over the past 50 years, the ability to forecast exchange rate values in the short term to long term is—in the words of the authors below—*sorry*. Although academics and practitioners alike agree that in the long-run fundamental principles such as purchasing power and external balances drive currency values, none of the fundamental theories has proven that useful in the short to medium term.

> *... the case for macroeconomic determinants of exchange rates is in a sorry state ... [The] results indicate that no model based on such standard fundamentals like money supplies, real income, interest rates, inflation rates and current account balances will ever succeed in explaining or predicting a high percentage of the variation in the exchange rate, at least at short- or medium-term frequencies.*
> —Jeffrey A. Frankel and Andrew K. Rose, "A Survey of Empirical Research on Nominal Exchange Rates," *NBER Working Paper* no. 4865, 1994.

Technical Analysis

The forecasting inadequacies of fundamental theories has led to the growth and popularity of *technical analysis*, the belief that the study of past price behavior provides insights into future price movements. The primary feature of technical analysis is the assumption that exchange rates, or for that matter any market-driven price, follows trends. And those trends may be analyzed and projected to provide insights into short-term and medium-term price movements in the future.

Most theories of technical analysis differentiate fair value from market value. Fair value is the true long-term value which the price will eventually retain. The market value is subject to a multitude of changes and behaviors arising from widespread market participant perceptions and beliefs.

The Asset Market Approach to Forecasting

The *asset market approach* assumes that whether foreigners are willing to hold claims in monetary form depends on an extensive set of investment considerations or drivers. These drivers, as previously depicted in Exhibit 9.1, include the following elements:

- Relative real interest rates are a major consideration for investors in foreign bonds and short-term money market instruments.
- Prospects for economic growth and profitability are an important determinant of cross-border equity investment in both securities and foreign direct investment.
- Capital market liquidity is particularly important to foreign institutional investors. Cross-border investors are not only interested in the ease of buying assets, but also in the ease of selling those assets quickly for fair market value if desired.
- A country's economic and social infrastructure is an important indicator of its ability to survive unexpected external shocks and to prosper in a rapidly changing world economic environment.
- Political safety is exceptionally important to both foreign portfolio and direct investors. The outlook for political safety is usually reflected in political risk premiums for a country's securities and for purposes of evaluating foreign direct investment in that country.
- The credibility of corporate governance practices is important to cross-border portfolio investors. A firm's poor corporate governance practices can reduce foreign investors' influence and cause subsequent loss of the firm's focus on shareholder wealth objectives.
- *Contagion* is defined as the spread of a crisis in one country to its neighboring countries and other countries with similar characteristics—at least in the eyes of cross-border

investors. Contagion can cause an "innocent" country to experience capital flight with a resulting depreciation of its currency.
- ◆ Speculation can both cause a foreign exchange crisis or make an existing crisis worse. We will observe this effect through the three illustrative cases that follow shortly.

Foreign investors are willing to hold securities and undertake foreign direct investment in highly developed countries based primarily on relative real interest rates and the outlook for economic growth and profitability. All the other drivers described in Exhibit 9.1 are assumed to be satisfied.

For example, during the 1981–1985 period, the U.S. dollar strengthened despite growing current account deficits. This strength was due partly to relatively high real interest rates in the United States. Another factor, however, was the heavy inflow of foreign capital into the U.S. stock market and real estate, motivated by good long-run prospects for growth and profitability in the United States.

The same cycle was repeated in the United States in the period between 1990 and 2000. Despite continued worsening balances on current account, the U.S. dollar strengthened in both nominal and real terms due to foreign capital inflow motivated by rising stock and real estate prices, a low rate of inflation, high real interest returns, and a seemingly endless "irrational exuberance" about future economic prospects. This time the "bubble" burst following the September 11, 2001 terrorist attacks on the United States. The attack and its aftermath caused a negative reassessment of long-term growth and profitability prospects in the United States (as well as a newly formed level of political risk for the United States itself). This negative outlook was reinforced by a very sharp drop in the U.S. stock markets based on lower expected earnings. Further damage to the economy was caused by a series of revelations about failures in corporate governance of several large corporations (including overstatement of earnings, insider trading, and self-serving executives).

Loss of confidence in the U.S. economy led to a large withdrawal of foreign capital from U.S. security markets. As would be predicted by both the balance of payments and asset market approaches, the U.S. dollar depreciated. Indeed, its nominal rate depreciated by 18% between mid-January and mid-July 2002 relative to the euro alone.

The experience of the United States, as well as other highly developed countries, illustrates why some forecasters believe that exchange rates are more heavily influenced by economic prospects than by the current account. One scholar summarizes this belief using an interesting anecdote.

Many economists reject the view that the short-term behavior of exchange rates is determined in flow markets. Exchange rates are asset prices traded in an efficient financial market. Indeed, an exchange rate is the relative price of two currencies and therefore is determined by the willingness to hold each currency. Like other asset prices, the exchange rate is determined by expectations about the future, not current trade flows.

A parallel with other asset prices may illustrate the approach. Let's consider the stock price of a winery traded on the Bordeaux stock exchange. A frost in late spring results in a poor harvest, in terms of both quantity and quality. After the harvest the wine is finally sold, and the income is much less than the previous year. On the day of the final sale there is no reason for the stock price to be influenced by this flow. First, the poor income has already been discounted for several months in the winery stock price. Second, the stock price is affected by future, in addition to current, prospects. The stock price is based on expectations of future earnings, and the major cause for a change in stock price is a revision of these expectations.

A similar reasoning applies to exchange rates: Contemporaneous international flows should have little effect on exchange rates to the extent they have already been expected.

> *Only news about future economic prospects will affect exchange rates. Since economic expectations are potentially volatile and influenced by many variables, especially variables of a political nature, the short-run behavior of exchange rates is volatile.*
> —Bruno Solnik, *International Investments*, 3rd Edition, Reading, MA: Addison Wesley, 1996, p. 58. Reprinted with permission of Pearson Education, Inc.

The asset market approach to forecasting is also applicable to emerging markets. In this case, however, a number of additional variables contribute to exchange rate determination. These variables, as described previously, are illiquid capital markets, weak economic and social infrastructure, political instability, corporate governance, contagion effects, and speculation. These variables will be illustrated in the sections on crises that follow.

Currency Market Intervention

> *A fundamental problem with exchange rates is that no commonly accepted method exists to estimate the effectiveness of official intervention into foreign exchange markets. Many interrelated factors affect the exchange rate at any given time, and no quantitative model exists that is able to provide the magnitude of any causal relationship between intervention and an exchange rate when so many interdependent variables are acting simultaneously.*
> —"Japan's Currency Intervention: Policy Issues," Dick K. Nanto, CRS Report to Congress, July 13, 2007, CRS-7.

The value of a country's currency is of significant interest to an individual government's economic and political policies and objectives. Those interests sometimes extend beyond the individual country, but may actually reflect some form of collective country interest. Although many countries have moved from fixed exchange rate values long ago, the governments and central bank authorities of the multitude of floating rate currencies still privately and publicly profess what value their currency "should hold" in their eyes, regardless of whether the market for that currency agrees at that time. *Foreign currency intervention*, the active management, manipulation, or intervention in the market's valuation of a country's currency, is a component of currency valuation and forecast that cannot be overlooked.

Motivations for Intervention

There is a long-standing saying that "what worries bankers is inflation, but what worries elected officials is unemployment." The principle is actually quite useful in understanding the various motives for currency market intervention. Depending upon whether a country's central bank is an independent institution (e.g., the U.S. Federal Reserve), or a subsidiary of its elected government (as the Bank of England was for many years), the bank's policies may either fight inflation or fight slow economic growth.

Historically, a primary motive for a government to pursue currency value change was to keep the country's currency cheap so that foreign buyers would find its exports cheap. This policy, long referred to as "beggar-thy-neighbor," gave rise to several competitive devaluations over the years. It has not, however, fallen out of fashion. The Asian financial crisis of 1997 (discussed in detail in the following section), resulted in a number of countries devaluing their currency when they did not have to; they devalued their currencies intentionally to remain competitive with neighboring countries with competing export products. The slow economic growth and continuing employment problems in many countries in 2010 and 2011 led to some countries, the United States and the European Union being prime examples, working to hold their currency values down.

Alternatively, the fall in the value of the domestic currency will sharply reduce the purchasing power of its people. If the economy is forced, for a variety of reasons, to continue to purchase imported products (e.g., petroleum imports because of no domestic substitute), a currency devaluation or depreciation may prove highly inflationary—and in the extreme, impoverish the country's people. This was a partial outcome of the Argentine crisis of 1999 discussed in the following section, and a result of the multitude of devaluations which President Hugo Chavez of Venezuela has directed over the past decade.

It is frequently noted that most countries would like to see stable exchange rates, to not get into the entanglements associated with manipulating currency values. Unfortunately, that would also imply that not only are they happy with the current level, but also that the level or rate of exchange is existing within a global economy which itself is not changing. One must look no further than the continuing highly public debate between the United States and China over the value of the yuan. The U.S. believes it is undervalued, making Chinese exports to the United States overly cheap, which in turn, results in a growing current account deficit of the United States and current account surplus of China.

The International Monetary Fund, as one of its basic principles (Article IV), encourages members to avoid pursuing "currency manipulation" to gain competitive advantages over other members. The IMF defines manipulation as "protracted large-scale intervention in one direction in the exchange market."

Intervention Methods

There are a multitude of ways in which an individual or collective set of governments and central banks can alter the value of their currencies. It should be noted, however, that the methods of market intervention used are very much determined by the size of the country's economy, the magnitude of global trading in its currency, and the depth and breadth of development in its domestic financial markets. A short list of the intervention methods would include the following:

Direct Intervention. This is the active buying and selling of the domestic currency against foreign currencies. This traditionally required a central bank to act like any other trader in the currency market—albeit a big one. If the goal was to increase the value of the domestic currency, the central bank would purchase its own currency using its foreign exchange reserves, at least to the acceptable limits of depleting its reserves that it could endure.

If the goal was to decrease the value of its currency—to fight an appreciation of its currency's value on the foreign exchange market—it would sell its own currency in exchange for foreign currency, typically major hard currencies like the dollar and euro. Although there are no physical limits to its ability to sell its own currency (it could theoretically continue to "print money" endlessly), central banks are cautious to the degree to which they may potentially change their monetary supplies through intervention.

Direct intervention was the primary method used for many years, but beginning in the 1970s, the world's currency markets grew enough that any individual player, even a central bank, may find itself insufficient in resources to move the market. As one trader stated a number of years ago, "We at the bank found ourselves little more than a grain of sand on the beach of the market." *Global Finance in Practice 9.1* provides one suggested strategy for this lack of market-weight.

One solution to the market size challenge has been the occasional use of *coordinated intervention*, in which several major countries, or a collective such as the G8 of industrialized countries, agree that a specific currency's value is out of alignment with their collective interests. In that situation, they may work collectively, to intervene and push a currency's value in a desired direction. The September 1985 Plaza Agreement, an agreement signed at the Plaza Hotel in New York City by the members of the Group of Ten, was one such coordinated intervention agreement. The members, collectively, had concluded that currency values had

> **GLOBAL FINANCE IN PRACTICE 9.1**
>
> **Rules of Thumb for Effective Intervention**
>
> There are a number of factors, features, and tactics, according to many currency traders that determine the effectiveness of an intervention effort.
>
> - **Don't Lean Into the Wind.** Markets that are moving significantly in one direction, like the strengthening of the Japanese yen in the fall of 2010, are very tough to turn. Termed "leaning into the wind," intervention during a strong market movement will most likely result in a very expensive failure. Currency traders argue that central banks should time their intervention very carefully, choosing moments when trading volumes are light and direction nearly flat. Don't lean into the wind, read it.
> - **Coordinate Timing and Activity.** Use traders or associates in a variety of geographic markets and trading centers, possibly other central banks, if at all possible. The markets are much more likely to be influenced if they believe the intervention activity is reflecting a grassroots movement, and not the singular activity of a single trading entity or bank.
> - **Use Good News.** Particularly when trying to quell a currency fall, time the intervention to coincide with positive economic, financial, or business news closely associated with a country's currency market. Traders often argue that 'markets wish to celebrate good news,' and currencies may be no different.
> - **Don't Be Cheap.** Overwhelm them. Traders fear missing the moment, and a large, coordinated, well-timed intervention can make them fear they are leaning in the wrong direction. A successful intervention is in many ways a battle of psychology; play on their insecurities. If it appears the intervention is gradually having the desired impact, throw ever-increasing assets into the battle. Don't get cheap.

become too volatile or too extreme in movement for sound economic policy management. The problem with coordinated intervention is, of course, reaching agreement between nations. This has proven to be a major sticking point in the principle's use.

Indirect Intervention. This is the alteration of economic or financial fundamentals which are thought to be drivers of capital to flow in and out of specific currencies. This was a logical development for market manipulation given the growth in size of the global currency markets relative to the financial resources of central banks.

The most obvious and widely used factor here is interest rates. Following the financial principles outlined previously in parity conditions, higher real rates of interest attract capital. If a central bank wishes to "defend its currency" for example, it might follow a restrictive monetary policy which would drive real rates of interest up. The method is therefore no longer limited to the quantity of foreign exchange reserves held by the country, but only by its willingness to suffer the domestic impacts of higher real interest rates in order to attract capital inflows and therefore drive up the demand for its currency.

Alternatively, a country wishing for its currency to fall in value, particularly when confronted with a continual appreciation of its value against major trading partner currencies, the central bank may work to lower real interest rates, reducing the returns to capital.

Because indirect intervention uses tools of monetary policy, a fundamental dimension of economic policy, the magnitude and extent of impacts may reach far beyond currency value. Overly stimulating economic activity, or increasing money supply growth beyond real economic activity, may prove inflationary. The use of such broad-based tools like interest rates to manipulate currency values requires a determination of importance, in many cases the choice to pursue international economic goals at the expense of domestic economic policy goals.

It is also important to remember that intervention may fail. One very real example of intervention failure occurred in 1992 when the United Kingdom attempted to defend the value of the British pound against a rapidly rising Deutsche Mark. As a member of the European Exchange Rate Mechanism (ERM) of the EMS of the time, the pound's value against the Deutsche Mark had to be maintained within a narrow band. The Bank of England, after increasing key interest rates three times in six hours on one day, pulled the currency from the ERM. (A global currency speculator of significance at the time, George Soros, is reported to have made millions of dollars betting against the pound.) The United Kingdom was said to have suffered a "humiliating defeat," although it was a currency war, not a military one.

Capital Controls. This is the restriction of access to foreign currency by government. This involves limiting the ability to exchange domestic currency for foreign currency. When access and exchange is permitted, trading often takes place only with official designees of the government or central bank, and only at dictated exchange rates.

Often, governments will limit access to foreign currencies to commercial trade: for example, allowing access to hard currency for the purchase of imports "of import" only. Access for investment purposes, particularly short-term portfolio purposes in which investors are investing in and out of interest-bearing accounts, purchasing or selling fixed income or equity securities or other funds, is often prohibited or limited.

The Chinese regulation of access and trading of the Chinese yuan is a prime example over the use of capital controls over currency value. In addition to the government's setting of the daily rate of exchange, access to the exchange is limited by a difficult and timely bureaucratic process for approval, and is limited to commercial trade transactions alone.

Understanding the motivations and methods for currency market intervention are critical to any analysis of the determination of future exchange rates. And although it is often impossible to determine, in the end, whether subtle intervention was successful, it appears to be an area of growing market activity, particularly for countries trying to "emerge" to higher levels of economic income and wealth.

Disequilibrium: Exchange Rates in Emerging Markets

Although the three different schools of thought on exchange rate determination (*parity conditions*, *balance of payments approach*, and *asset approach*) described earlier make understanding exchange rates appear to be straightforward, that is rarely the case. The large and liquid capital and currency markets follow many of the principles outlined so far relatively well in the medium to long term. The smaller and less liquid markets, however, frequently demonstrate behaviors that seemingly contradict theory. The problem lies not in the theory, but in the relevance of the assumptions underlying the theory. An analysis of the emerging market crises illustrates a number of these seeming contradictions.

After a number of years of relative global economic tranquility, the second half of the 1990s was racked by a series of currency crises that shook all emerging markets. The devaluation of the Mexican peso in December 1994 was a harbinger. The Asian crisis of July 1997, the Russian ruble's collapse in August 1998, and the fall of the Argentine peso in 2002 provide a spectrum of emerging market economic failures, each with its own complex causes and unknown outlooks. These crises also illustrated the growing problem of capital flight and short-run international speculation in currency and securities markets. We will use each of the individual crises to focus on a specific dimension of the causes and consequences.

The Asian Crisis of 1997

The roots of the Asian currency crisis extended from a fundamental change in the economics of the region, the transition of many Asian nations from being net exporters to net importers. Starting as early as 1990 in Thailand, the rapidly expanding economies of the Far East began importing more than they exported, requiring major net capital inflows to support their currencies. As long as the capital continued to flow in—capital for manufacturing plants, dam projects, infrastructure development, and even real estate speculation—the pegged exchange rates of the region could be maintained. When the investment capital inflows stopped, however, crisis was inevitable.

The most visible roots of the crisis were in the excesses of capital inflows into Thailand in 1996 and early 1997. With rapid economic growth and rising profits forming the backdrop,

Thai firms, banks, and finance companies had ready access to capital on the international markets, finding U.S. dollar debt cheap offshore. Thai banks continued to raise capital internationally, extending credit to a variety of domestic investments and enterprises beyond what the Thai economy could support. As capital flows into the Thai market hit record rates, financial flows poured into investments of all kinds, including manufacturing, real estate, and even equity market margin-lending. As the investment "bubble" expanded, some participants raised questions about the economy's ability to repay the rising debt. The baht came under attack.

Currency Collapse. In May and June 1997, more and more rumors circulated throughout the globe's currency traders that the Thai baht was weak, and that a number of major investors were now speculating on its fall. The Thai government and central bank quickly intervened in the foreign exchange markets directly (using up precious hard currency reserves) and indirectly (by raising interest rates to attempt to stop the continual outflow). Thai investment ground quickly to a halt. Foreign capital, which had flowed into Thailand freely in the months and years previous, stopped.

A second round of speculative attacks in late June and early July proved too much for the Thai authorities. On July 2, 1997, the Thai central bank finally allowed the baht to float (or sink in this case). The baht fell 17% against the U.S. dollar and more than 12% against the Japanese yen in a matter of hours. By November, the baht had fallen from THB25/USD to nearly THB40/USD, a fall of about 38%, as illustrated in Exhibit 9.2.

Within days, in Asia's own version of what is called the *tequila effect*, a number of neighboring Asian nations, some with and some without similar characteristics to Thailand, came under speculative attack by currency traders and capital markets. ("Tequila effect" is the term used to describe how the Mexican peso crisis of December 1994 quickly spread to other Latin American currency and equity markets, a form of financial panic termed *contagion*.)

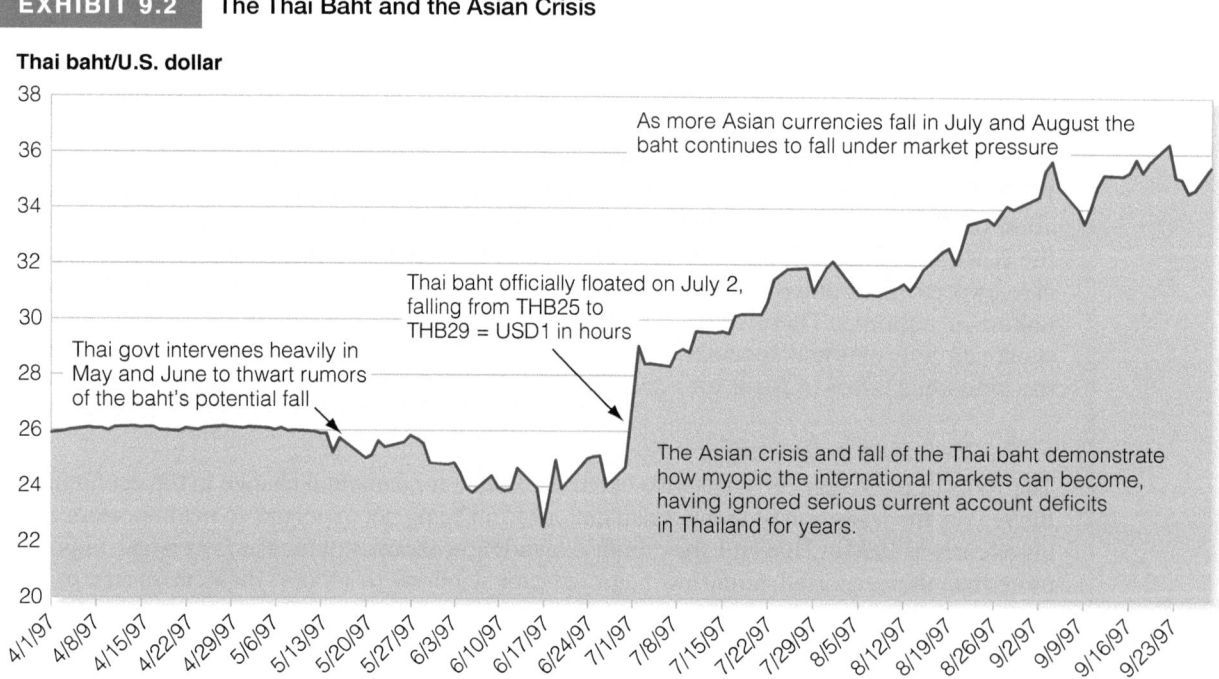

EXHIBIT 9.2 The Thai Baht and the Asian Crisis

The Philippine peso, the Malaysian ringgit, and the Indonesian rupiah all fell in the months following the July baht devaluation.

In late October 1997, Taiwan caught the markets off balance with a surprise competitive devaluation of 15%. The Taiwanese devaluation seemed only to renew the momentum of the crisis. Although the Hong Kong dollar survived (at great expense to the central bank's foreign exchange reserves), the Korean won (KRW) was not so lucky. In November 1997, the historically stable won also fell victim, falling from KRW900/USD to more than KRW1100. The only currency that had not fallen besides the Hong Kong dollar was the Chinese renminbi, which was not freely convertible. Although the renminbi was not devalued, there was rising speculation that the Chinese government would soon devalue it for competitive reasons. It did not.

Causal Complexities. The Asian economic crisis—for it was more than just a currency collapse—had many roots besides traditional balance of payments difficulties. The causes were different in each country, yet, there are specific underlying similarities which allow comparison: corporate socialism, corporate governance, banking stability, and management.

Although Western markets have long known the volatility of the free market, the countries of the post–World War II Asia have largely known only stability. Because of the influence of government and politics in the business arena, even in the event of failure, it was believed that government would not allow firms to fail, workers to lose their jobs, or banks to close. Practices that had persisted for decades without challenge, such as lifetime employment, were now no longer sustainable.

Little doubt exists that many local firms operating within the Far Eastern business environments were often largely controlled either by families or by groups related to the governing party or body of the country. This tendency has been labeled *cronyism*. Cronyism means that the interests of minority stockholders and creditors are often secondary at best to the primary motivations of corporate management. When management did not focus on "the bottom line," the bottom line deteriorated.

The banking sector has fallen behind. Bank regulatory structures and markets have been deregulated nearly without exception across the globe. The central role played by banks in the conduct of business, however, had largely been ignored and underestimated. As firms across Asia collapsed, government coffers were emptied and speculative investments made by the banks themselves failed. Without banks, the "plumbing" of business conduct was shut down.

The Asian economic crisis had global impacts. What started as a currency crisis quickly became a regionwide recession. (The magnitude of economic devastation in Asia is still largely unappreciated by Westerners. At a 1998 conference sponsored by the Milken Institute, a speaker noted that the world's preoccupation with the economic problems of Indonesia was incomprehensible because "the total gross domestic product of Indonesia is roughly the size of North Carolina." The following speaker observed, however, that the last time he had checked, "North Carolina did not have a population of 220 million people.") The slowed economies of the region quickly caused major reductions in world demands for many products, especially commodities. World oil, metal, and agricultural products markets all saw severe price falls as demand fell. These price drops were immediately noticeable in declining earnings and growth prospects for other emerging economies. The problems of Russia in 1998 were reflections of those declines.

In the aftermath, the international speculator and philanthropist George Soros was the object of much criticism, primarily by the Prime Minister of Malaysia, Dr. Mahathir Mohamad, for being the cause of the crisis because of massive speculation by his and other hedge funds. Soros, however, was likely only the messenger. *Global Finance in Practice 9.2* details the Soros debate.

GLOBAL FINANCE IN PRACTICE 9.2

Was George Soros to Blame for the Asian Crisis?

We have worked 30 to 40 years to develop our countries to this level, but along comes a man with a few billion dollars, and who in a period of just two weeks, has undone most of the work we have done. As a result, the people of our countries suffer. You talk about human rights and protecting people. But they must be protected from people like Soros who has so much money and so much power and totally thoughtless because he is not only hurting the people of Myanmar, but the poor people in Indonesia, Malaysia, the Philippines and Thailand.
—Prime Minister Datuk Seri Dr. Mahathir Mohamad of Malaysia *New Straits Times*, Kuala Lumpur, July 27, 1997.

For Thailand to blame Mr Soros for its plight is rather like condemning an undertaker for burying a suicide.
—*The Economist*, August 2, 1997, p. 57.

George Soros is probably the most famous currency speculator—and possibly the most successful—in global history. Admittedly responsible for much of the European financial crisis of 1992 and the fall of the French franc in 1993, he once again was the recipient of critical attention in 1997 following the fall of the Thai baht and Malaysian ringgit. Prime Minister Mahathir of Malaysia blamed Soros for the collapse of the ringgit, as the quote indicates.

Nine years later, in 2006, Mahathir and Soros met for the first time. Mahathir apologized and withdrew his previous accusations. In Soros's book published in 1998, *The Crisis of Global Capitalism: Open Society Endangered*, Soros explained his role in the crisis as follows:

The financial crisis that originated in Thailand in 1997 was particularly unnerving because of its scope and severity. . . . By the beginning of 1997, it was clear to Soros Fund Management that the discrepancy between the trade account and the capital account was becoming untenable. We sold short the Thai baht and the Malaysian ringgit early in 1997 with maturities ranging from six months to a year. (That is, we entered into contracts to deliver at future dates Thai Baht and Malaysian ringgit that we did not currently hold.) Subsequently Prime Minister Mahathir of Malaysia accused me of causing the crisis, a wholly unfounded accusation. We were not sellers of the currency during or several months before the crisis; on the contrary, we were buyers when the currencies began to decline—we were purchasing ringgit to realize the profits on our earlier speculation. (Much too soon, as it turned out. We left most of the potential gain on the table because we were afraid that Mahathir would impose capital controls. He did so, but much later.)

The Russian Crisis of 1998

"A stable ruble is the anchor of an inflation-free economy," according to Alexander Livshits, deputy head of President Boris Yeltsin's administration. He added that the loss of a stable ruble *"will start rocking our ship again. The result is well known—nausea."*

The crisis of August 1998 was the culmination of a continuing deterioration in general economic conditions in Russia. During the period from 1995 to 1998, Russian borrowers—both governmental and nongovernmental—had borrowed heavily on the international capital markets. Servicing this debt soon became a growing problem, as servicing dollar debt requires earning dollars. The Russian current account, a surprisingly healthy surplus, was not finding its way into internal investment and external debt service. Capital flight accelerated, as hard-currency earnings flowed out as fast as they found their way in. Finally, in the spring of 1998, even Russian export earnings began to decline. Russian exports were predominantly commodity-based, and global commodity prices had been falling since the start of the Asian crisis in 1997.

The Russian currency, the ruble (RUB), operated under a managed float. This meant that the Central Bank of Russia allowed the ruble to trade within a band. The exchange rate band had been adjusted continually throughout 1996, 1997, and the first half of 1998. Theoretically, the Central Bank allowed the exchange rate and associated band to slide daily at a 1.5% per month rate. Automatically, the Central Bank announced an official exchange rate each day at which it was willing to buy and sell rubles, always within the official band. In the event that the ruble's rate came under pressure at the limits of the band, the Central Bank intervened in the market by buying and selling rubles, usually buying, using the country's foreign exchange reserves.

The August Collapse. On August 7, 1998, the Russian Central Bank announced that its currency reserves had fallen by $800 million in the last week of July. Prime Minister Kiriyenko said that Russia would issue an additional $3 billion in foreign bonds to help pay its rising debt, a full $1 billion more than had been previously scheduled. The ruble, however, continued to trade within a very narrow range.

On August 10, Russian stocks fell more than 5% as investors feared a Chinese currency (renminbi) devaluation. The Chinese currency was the only Asian currency of size not devalued in 1997 and 1998. Devaluation would aid Chinese exports in cutting into Russian export sales. Analysts worldwide speculated that international markets were waiting to see if the Russian government would increase its tax revenues as it had promised the IMF throughout the year. Russian oil companies were publicly warned by the Russian government to pay past due taxes. (Russian tax collections averaged $1 billion per month in 1998, less than those of New York City.) By Wednesday of that week, Russian financing choices narrowed further as the government canceled the government debt auction for the third week in a row.

The following days saw a continuing series of press releases assuring the markets and general population that the government had everything under control. The government stated that the "panic" was psychological, not fiscal, and repeated, as it had in recent days, that it had money to meet its obligations through the fall of the year. The Russian Central Bank continued to trade rubles throughout Friday at RUB6.30/USD, but at many unofficial exchanges throughout Moscow the rate was RUB7.00/USD or more. President Boris Yeltsin, in a speech in the ancient city of Novgorode, stated

"There will be no devaluation—that's firm and definite."

He went on to add,

"That would signify that there was a disaster and that everything was collapsing. On the contrary, everything is going as it should."

"As it should" turned out to mean devaluation. On Monday, August 17, the floodgates were released. The Russian Central Bank announced that the ruble would be allowed to fall by 34% this year, from RUB6.30/USD to about RUB9.50. The government then announced a 90-day moratorium on all repayment of foreign debt, debt owed by Russian banks and all private borrowers, in order to avert a banking collapse.

The currency's fall continued into the following week, as illustrated in Exhibit 9.3. On Thursday, August 27, Acting Prime Minister Viktor Chernomyrdin traveled to the Ukraine to meet with the visiting head of the IMF, Michael Camdessus. A sense of urgency was felt after the ruble fell from RUB10.0/USD to RUB13.0 the previous day alone. In related matters, the Central Bank of Russia, in an attempt to defray criticism of its management of the ruble's devaluation, disclosed that it had expended $8.8 billion in the preceding eight weeks defending the ruble's value. On August 28, the Moscow currency exchange closed after 10 minutes of trading as the ruble continued to fall.

The Aftermath. It is hard to say when a crisis begins or ends, but for the Russian people and the Russian economy, the deterioration of the economic conditions continued. What is likely of more substantial concern is the toll the crisis has taken on Russian society. For many, the collapse of the ruble and the loss of Russia's access to the international capital markets brought into question the benefits of a free-market economy, long championed by the advocates of Western-style democracy.

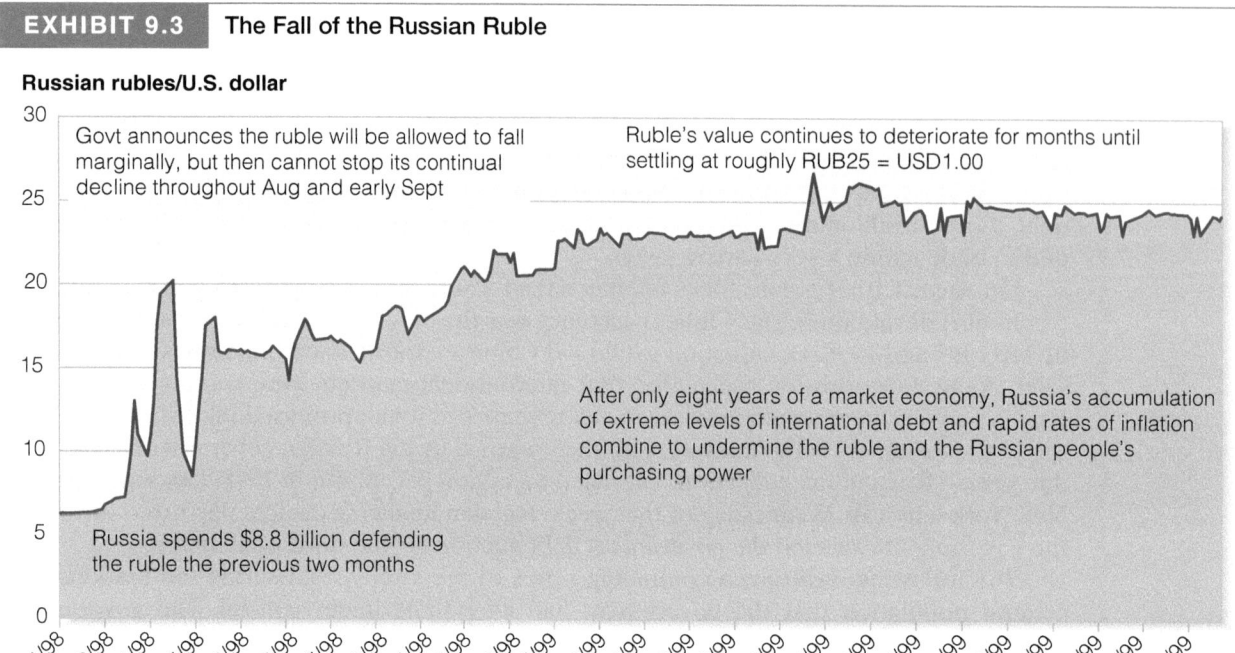

EXHIBIT 9.3 The Fall of the Russian Ruble

The Argentine Crisis of 2002

> *Now, most Argentines are blaming corrupt politicians and foreign devils for their ills. But few are looking inward, at mainstream societal concepts such as viveza criolla, an Argentine cultural quirk that applauds anyone sly enough to get away with a fast one. It is one reason behind massive tax evasion here: One of every three Argentines does so—and many like to brag about it.*
>
> —"Once-Haughty Nation's Swagger Loses Its Currency,"
> Anthony Faiola, *The Washington Post*, March 13, 2002.

Argentina's economic ups and downs have historically been tied to the health of the Argentine peso. South America's southernmost resident—which oftentimes considered itself more European than Latin American—had been wracked by hyperinflation, international indebtedness, and economic collapse in the 1980s. By early 1991 the people of Argentina had had enough. Economic reform in the early 1990s was a common goal of the Argentine people. They were not interested in quick fixes, but lasting change and a stable future. They nearly got it.

The Currency Board. In 1991, the Argentine peso had been fixed to the U.S. dollar at a one-to-one rate of exchange. The policy was a radical departure from traditional methods of fixing the rate of a currency's value. Argentina adopted a *currency board*, a structure—rather than merely a commitment—to limiting the growth of money in the economy. Under a currency board, the central bank may increase the money supply in the banking system only with increases in its holdings of hard currency reserves. The reserves were in this case U.S. dollars. By removing the ability of government to expand the rate of growth of the money supply, Argentina believed it was eliminating the source of inflation which had devastated its standard of living.

The idea was simple: limit the rate of growth in the country's money supply to the rate at which the country receives net inflows of U.S. dollars as a result of trade growth and general surplus. It was both a recipe for conservative and prudent financial management, and a decision to eliminate the power of politicians, elected and unelected, to exercise judgment both good and bad. It was an automatic and unbendable rule. And from the beginning, it had shown the costs and benefits of its rigor.

Although hyperinflation had indeed been the problem, the "cure" was a restrictive monetary policy which slowed economic growth. The first and foremost cost of the slower economic growth had been in unemployment. Beginning with a decade low unemployment rate in 1991, unemployment rose to double-digit levels in 1994 and stayed there. The real GDP growth rate, which opened the decade with booming levels over 10%, settled into recession in late 1998. GDP growth "shrank" in 1999 (−3.5%) and 2000 (−0.4%).

As part of the continuing governmental commitment to the currency board's fixed exchange rate for the peso, Argentine banks allowed depositors to hold their money in either form—pesos or dollars. This was intended to provide a market-based discipline to the banking and political systems, and to demonstrate the government's unwavering commitment to maintaining the peso's value parity with the dollar. Although intended to build confidence in the system, in the end it proved disastrous to the Argentine banking system.

Economic Crisis of 2001. The 1998 recession proved to be unending. Three and a half years later, Argentina was still in recession. By 2001, crisis conditions had revealed three very important underlying problems with Argentina's economy: 1) the Argentine peso was overvalued; 2) the currency board regime had eliminated monetary policy alternatives for macroeconomic policy; and 3) the Argentine government budget deficit—and deficit spending—was out of control. The peso had indeed been stabilized. But inflation had not been eliminated, and the other factors which are important in the global market's evaluation of a currency's value—economic growth, corporate profitability, etc.—had not necessarily always been positive. The inability of the peso's value to change with market forces led many to believe increasingly that it was overvalued, and that the overvaluation gap was rising as time passed.

Argentina's large neighbor to the north, Brazil, had also suffered many of the economic ills of hyperinflation and international indebtedness. Brazil's response, the *Real Plan*, was introduced in July 1994. The real plan worked, for a while, but eventually collapsed in January 1999 as a result of the rising gap between the real's official value and the market's assessment of its true value. With the fall of the Brazilian real, however, Brazilian consumers could no longer afford Argentine exports. Argentine exports became some of the most expensive in all of South America as other countries saw their currencies slide marginally against the dollar over the decade. But not the Argentine peso.

The Currency Board and Monetary Policy. The increasingly sluggish economic growth in Argentina warranted expansionary economic policies argued many policymakers in and out of the country. But the currency board's basic premise was that the money supply to the financial system could not be expanded any further or faster than the ability of the economy to capture dollar reserves. This eliminated monetary policy as an avenue for macroeconomic policy formulation, leaving only fiscal policy for economic stimulation.

Government spending was not slowing, however. As the unemployment rate grew higher, as poverty and social unrest grew, government—both in the civil center of Argentina, Buenos Aires, and in the outer provinces—was faced with growing expansionary spending needs to close the economic and social gaps. Government spending continued to increase, but tax receipts did not. Lower income led to lower taxes on income. Argentina turned to the international markets to aid in the financing of its government's deficit spending. The total foreign debt of the country began rising dramatically. Only a number of IMF capital injections prevented the total foreign debt of the country from skyrocketing. When the decade was over, however, total foreign debt had effectively doubled, and the economy's earning power had not.

Social Repercussions. As economic conditions continued to deteriorate, banks suffered increasing runs. Depositors, fearing that the peso would be devalued, lined up to withdraw their money, both Argentine peso cash balances and U.S. dollar cash balances. Pesos were converted to dollars, once again adding fuel to the growing fire of currency collapse. The government, fearing that the increasing financial drain on banks would cause their collapse, closed the banks. Consumers, unable to withdrawal more than $250 per week, were instructed to use debit cards and credit cards to make purchases and conduct the everyday transactions required by society.

Riots in the streets of Buenos Aires in December 2001 intensified the need for rapid change. As the new year of 2002 arrived, the second president in two weeks, Fernando de la Rua, was driven from office. He was succeeded by a Peronist, President Adolfo Rodriguez Saa, who lasted all of one week as president before he too was driven from office. President Saa did, however, leave his legacy. In his one week as President of Argentina, President Adolfo Rodriguez Saa declared the largest sovereign debt default in history. Argentina announced it would not be able to make interest payments due on $155 billion in government debt.

Devaluation. On Sunday, January 6, 2002, in the first act of his presidency, President Eduardo Duhalde devalued the peso from ARS1.00/USD to ARS1.40. But the economic pain continued. Two weeks after the devaluation, the banks were still closed. Most of the state governments outside of Buenos Aires, basically broke and without access to financing resources, began printing their own money—*script*—promissary notes of the provincial governments. The provincial governments were left with little choice as the economy of Argentina was nearing complete collapse as people and businesses could not obtain money to conduct the day-to-day commercial transactions of life.

On February 3, 2002, the Argentine government announced that the peso would be floated, as seen in Exhibit 9.4. The government would no longer attempt to fix or manage its value to any specific level, allowing the market to find or set the exchange rate. The value of the peso now began a slow but gradual depreciation.[1] As the year wore on the country was confronted with issue after issue of social, political, and economic collapse.

A former Harvard professor and member of the U.S. President's Council of Economic Advisors summed up the hard lessons of the Argentine story.

In reality, the Argentines understood the risk that they were taking at least as well as the IMF staff did. Theirs was a calculated risk that might have produced good results. It is true, however, that the IMF staff did encourage Argentina to continue with the fixed exchange rate and currency board. Although the IMF and virtually all outside economists believe that a floating exchange rate is preferable to a "fixed but adjustable" system, in which the government recognizes that it will have to devalue occasionally, the IMF (as well as some outside economists) came to believe that the currency board system of a firmly fixed exchange rate (a "hard peg" in the jargon of international finance) is a viable long-term policy for an economy. Argentina's experience has proved that wrong.[2]

---

[1] When a currency that is under a fixed exchange rate regime is officially altered in its value—downward—it is termed a *devaluation*. When a currency which is freely floated on exchange markets moves downward in value it is termed *depreciation*.

[2] "Argentina's Fall," Martin Feldstein, *Foreign Affairs*, March/April 2002.

| EXHIBIT 9.4 | The Collapse of the Argentine Peso |

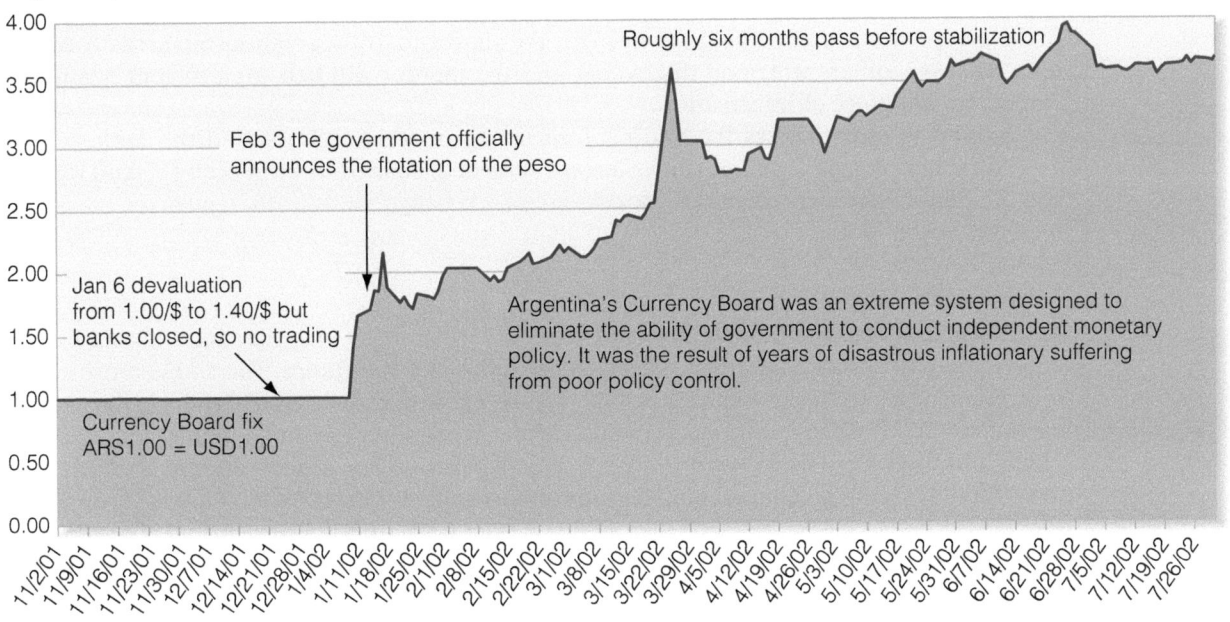

Forecasting in Practice

Numerous foreign exchange forecasting services exist, many of which are provided by banks and independent consultants. In addition, some multinational firms have their own in-house forecasting capabilities. Predictions can be based on elaborate econometric models, technical analysis of charts and trends, intuition, and a certain measure of gall.

Whether any of the forecasting services are worth their cost depends partly on our motive for forecasting as well as the required accuracy of the forecast. For example, long-run forecasts may be motivated by a multinational firm's desire to initiate a foreign investment in Japan, or perhaps to raise long-term funds denominated in Japanese yen. Or a portfolio manager may be considering diversifying for the long term in Japanese securities. The longer the time horizon of the forecast, the more inaccurate but also the less critical the forecast is likely to be. The forecaster will typically use annual data to display long-run trends in such economic fundamentals as Japanese inflation, growth, and BOP.

Short-term forecasts are typically motivated by a desire to hedge a receivable, payable, or dividend for perhaps a period of three months. In this case, the long-run economic fundamentals may not be as important as technical factors in the marketplace, government intervention, news, and passing whims of traders and investors. Accuracy of the forecast is critical, since most of the exchange rate changes are relatively small even though the day-to-day volatility may be high.

Forecasting services normally undertake fundamental economic analysis for long-term forecasts, and some base their short-term forecasts on the same basic model. Others base their short-term forecasts on technical analysis similar to that conducted in security analysis. They attempt to correlate exchange rate changes with various other variables, regardless of whether there is any economic rationale for the correlation. The chances of these forecasts being consistently useful or profitable depend on whether one believes the foreign exchange market is efficient. The more efficient the market is, the more likely it is that exchange rates are "random walks," with past price behavior providing no clues to the future. The less efficient the foreign exchange market is, the better the chance that forecasters may get lucky and find a key relationship that holds, at least for the short run. If the relationship is really consistent, however, others will soon discover it and the market will become efficient again with respect to that piece of information.

Exhibit 9.5 summarizes the various forecasting periods, regimes, and the authors' suggested methodologies. Opinions, however, are subject to change without notice! (And remember, if authors could predict the movement of exchange rates with regularity, we surely wouldn't write books.)

Technical Analysis

Technical analysts, traditionally referred to as *chartists*, focus on price and volume data to determine past trends that are expected to continue into the future. The single most important element of technical analysis is that future exchange rates are based on the current exchange rate. Exchange rate movements, similar to equity price movements, can be subdivided into three periods: 1) day-to-day movement, which is seemingly random; 2) short-term movements extending from several days to trends lasting several months; 3) long-term movements, which are characterized by up and down long-term trends. Long-term technical analysis has gained new popularity as a result of recent research into the possibility that long-term "waves" in currency movements exist under floating exchange rates.

The longer the time horizon of the forecast, the more inaccurate the forecast is likely to be. Whereas forecasting for the long run must depend on economic fundamentals of exchange rate determination, many of the forecast needs of the firm are short- to medium-term in their

EXHIBIT 9.5   Exchange Rate Forecasting in Practice

Forecast Period	Regime	Recommended Forecast Methods
SHORT-RUN	Fixed-Rate	1. Assume the fixed rate is maintained 2. Indications of stress on fixed rate? 3. Capital controls; black market rates 4. Indicators of government's capability to maintain fixed-rate? 5. Changes in official foreign currency reserves

	Floating-Rate	1. Technical methods which capture trend
		2. Forward rates as forecasts
		   (a) <30 days, assume a random walk
		   (b) 30–90 days, forward rates
		3. 90–360 days, combine trend with fundamental analysis
		4. Fundamental analysis of inflationary concerns
		5. Government declarations and agreements regarding exchange rate goals
		6. Cooperative agreements with other countries

LONG-RUN	Fixed-Rate	1. Fundamental analysis 2. BOP management 3. Ability to control domestic inflation 4. Ability to generate hard currency reserves to use for intervention 5. Ability to run trade surpluses
	Floating-Rate	1. Focus on inflationary fundamentals and PPP 2. Indicators of general economic health such as economic growth and stability 3. Technical analysis of long-term trends; new research indicates possibility of long-term technical "waves"

time horizon and can be addressed with less theoretical approaches. Time series techniques infer no theory or causality but simply predict future values from the recent past. Forecasters freely mix fundamental and technical analysis, presumably because forecasting is like playing horseshoes—getting close is all that counts. *Global Finance in Practice 9.3* provides a short analysis of how accurate one very prestigious currency forecaster was over a 3-year period.

Cross-Rate Consistency in Forecasting

International financial managers must often forecast their home currency exchange rates for the set of countries in which the firm operates, not only to decide whether to hedge or to make an investment, but also as part of preparing multicountry operating budgets in the home country's currency. These are the operating budgets against which the performance of foreign subsidiary managers will be judged. Checking the reasonableness of the cross rates implicit in individual forecasts acts as a reality check to the original forecasts.

GLOBAL FINANCE IN PRACTICE 9.3

JPMorgan Chase Forecast of the Dollar/Euro

There are many different foreign exchange forecasting services and service providers. JPMorgan Chase (JPMC) is one of the most prestigious and widely used.[1] A review of JPMC's forecasting accuracy for the U.S. dollar/euro spot exchange rate ($/€) for the 2002 to 2005 period, in 90-day increments, is presented in the exhibit. The graph shows the actual spot exchange rate for the period and JPMC's forecast for the spot exchange rate for the same period.

There is good news and there is bad news. The good news is that JPMC hit the actual spot rate dead on in both May and November 2002. The bad news is that after that, they missed. Somewhat worrisome is when the forecast got the direction wrong. For example, in February 2004, JPMC had forecast the spot rate to move from the current rate of $1.27/€ to $1.32/€, but in fact, the dollar had appreciated dramatically in the following 3-month period to close at $1.19/€. This was in fact a massive difference. Again, in November 2004, JPMC had forecast the spot rate to move from the current spot rate of $1.30/€ to $1.23/€, but in fact, the actual spot rate proved to be $1.32/€.

The lesson learned is probably that regardless of how professional and prestigious a forecaster may be, and how accurate they may have been in the past, forecasting the future—by anyone for anything—is challenging to say the least.

[1]This analysis uses exchange rate data as published in the print edition of *The Economist*, appearing quarterly. The source of the exchange rate forecasts, as noted in *The Economist*, is JPMorgan Chase.

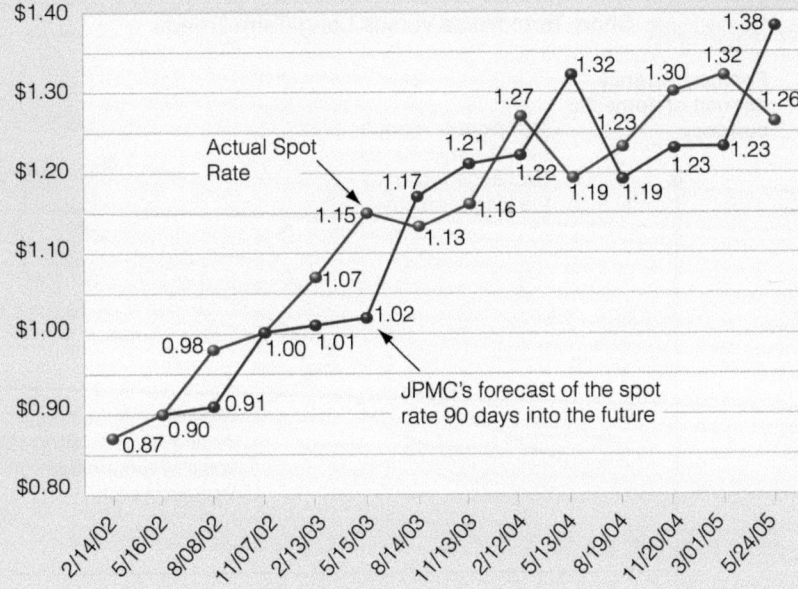

To illustrate, assume the U.S. parent home office forecasts the yen-to-dollar exchange rate a year hence to be ¥120/$ and the U.K. pound sterling rate to be $1.50/£. This creates an implied spot rate one year hence of ¥180/£. However, both the Japanese and the British financial managers, with good reason, have forecast a spot rate one year hence of ¥150/£.

Obviously the two foreign subsidiary managers (forecasting ¥150/£) and the home office (with an implicit forecast of ¥180/£) cannot both be correct. The time to reconcile these conflicting forecasts is the present, not one year hence when managers in Japan or the United Kingdom claim that their performance against budget is better than measured by the U.S. parent. Additionally, checking the reasonableness of implied cross rates is an exercise in improving the accuracy of the forecasting process.

Forecasting: What to Think?

Obviously, with the variety of theories and practices, forecasting exchange rates into the future is a daunting task. Here is a synthesis of our thoughts and experience:

◆ It appears from decades of theoretical and empirical studies that exchange rates do adhere to the fundamental principles and theories outlined in the previous sections. Fundamentals do apply in the long term. There is, therefore, something of a *fundamental equilibrium path* for a currency's value.

◆ It also seems that in the short term, a variety of random events, institutional frictions, and technical factors may cause currency values to deviate significantly from their long-term fundamental path. This is sometimes referred to as *noise*. Clearly, therefore, we might expect deviations from the long-term path not only to occur, but also to occur with some regularity and relative longevity.

Exhibit 9.6 illustrates this synthesis of forecasting thought. The long-term equilibrium path of the currency—although relatively well defined in retrospect—is not always apparent in the short term. The exchange rate itself may deviate in something of a cycle or wave about the long-term path.

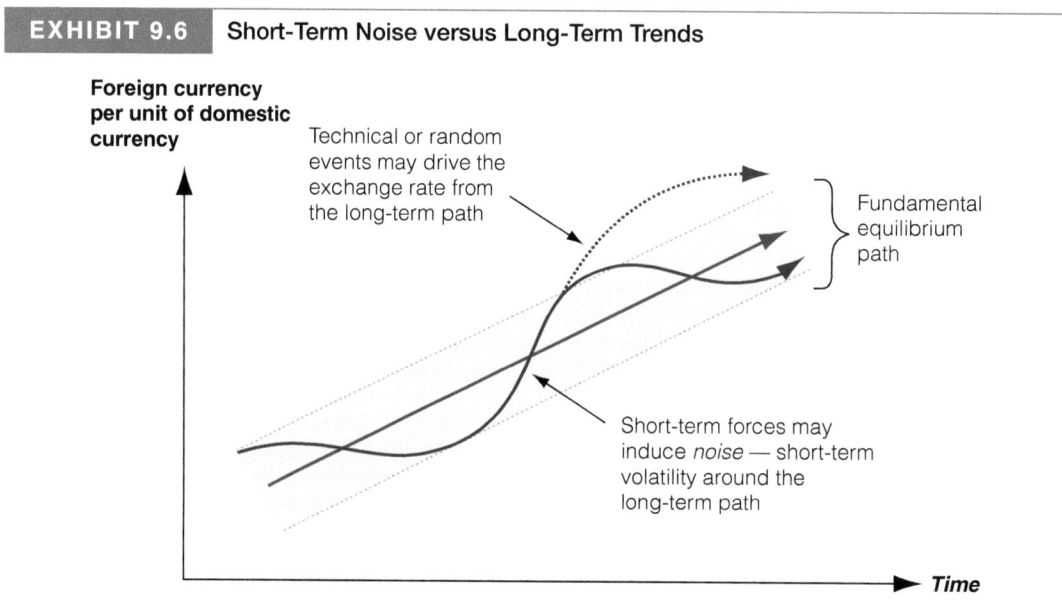

EXHIBIT 9.6 Short-Term Noise versus Long-Term Trends

If market participants both agree on the general long-term path and possess *stabilizing expectations*, the currency's value will periodically return to the long-term path. It is critical, however, that when the currency's value rises above the long-term path, most market participants see it as being overvalued and respond by selling the currency—causing its price to fall. Similarly, when the currency's value falls below the long-term path, market participants respond by buying the currency driving its value up. This is what is meant by *stabilizing expectations*: Market participants continually respond to deviations from the long-term path by buying or selling to drive the currency back to the long-term path.

If, for some reason, the market becomes unstable, as illustrated by the dotted deviation path in Exhibit 9.6, the exchange rate may move significantly away from the long-term path for longer periods of time. Causes of these destabilizing markets, weak infrastructure (such as the banking system), and political or social events that dictate economic behaviors, are often the actions of speculators and inefficient markets.

Exchange Rate Dynamics: Making Sense of Market Movements

Although the various theories surrounding exchange rate determination are clear and sound, it may appear on a day-to-day basis that the currency markets do not pay much attention to the theories, they don't read the books! The difficulty is understanding which fundamentals are driving markets at which points in time.

One example of this relative confusion over exchange rate dynamics is the phenomenon known as *overshooting*. Assume that the current spot rate between the dollar and the euro, as illustrated in Exhibit 9.7, is S_0. The U.S. Federal Reserve announces an expansionary monetary policy which cuts U.S. dollar interest rates. If euro-denominated interest rates remain unchanged, the new spot rate expected by the exchange markets on the basis of interest differentials is S_1. This immediate change in the exchange rate is typical

EXHIBIT 9.7 Exchange Rate Dynamics: Overshooting

If the U.S. Federal Reserve were to announce a change in monetary policy, an expansion in money supply growth, it could potentially result in an "overshooting" exchange rate change.

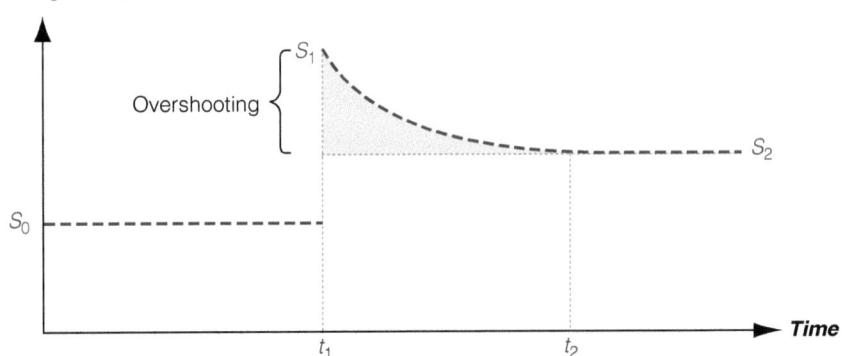

The Fed announces a monetary expansion at a time t_1. This results immediately in lower dollar interest rates. The foreign exchange markets immediately respond to the lower dollar interest rates by driving the value of the dollar down from S_0 to S_1. This new rate is based on *interest differentials*. However, in the coming days and weeks, as the fundamental price effects of the monetary policy actions work their way through the economy, *purchasing power parity* takes hold and the market moves toward a longer term valuation of the dollar—by time t_2—of S_2, a weaker dollar than S_0, but not as weak as initially set at S_1.

of how the markets react to *news*, distinct economic and political events which are observable. The immediate change in the value of the dollar/euro is therefore based on interest differentials.

As time passes, however, the price impacts of the monetary policy change start working their way through the economy. As price changes occur over the medium to long term, purchasing power parity forces drive the market dynamics, and the spot rate moves from S_1 toward S_2. Although both S_1 and S_2 were rates determined by the market, they reflected the dominance of different theoretical principles. As a result, the initial lower value of the dollar of S_1 is often explained as an *overshooting* of the longer-term equilibrium value of S_2.

This is of course only one possible series of events and market reactions. Currency markets are subject to new *news* every hour of every day, making it very difficult to forecast exchange rate movements in short periods of time. In the longer term, as shown here, the markets do customarily return to fundamentals of exchange rate determination.

Summary of Learning Objectives

Examine how the supply and demand for any currency can be viewed as an asset choice issue within the portfolio of investors.

◆ The asset approach to forecasting suggests that whether foreigners are willing to hold claims in monetary form depends partly on relative real interest rates and partly on a country's outlook for economic growth and profitability.

◆ Longer-term forecasting, over one year, requires a return to the basic analysis of exchange rate fundamentals such as BOP, relative inflation rates, relative interest rates, and the long-run properties of purchasing power parity.

◆ Technical analysts (chartists) focus on price and volume data to determine past trends that are expected to continue into the future.

◆ Exchange rate forecasting in practice is a mix of both fundamental and technical forms of exchange rate analysis.

Explore how the three major approaches to exchange rate determination—parity conditions, the balance of payments, and the asset approach—combine to explain the numerous emerging market currency crises experienced in recent years.

◆ The Asian currency crisis was primarily a balance of payments crisis in its origins and impacts on exchange rate determination. A weak economic and financial infrastructure, corporate governance problems and speculation were also contributing factors.

◆ The Russian ruble crisis of 1998 was a complex combination of speculative pressures best explained by the asset approach to exchange rate determination.

◆ The Argentine crisis of 2002 was probably a combination of a disequilibrium in international parity conditions (differential rates of inflation) and balance of payments disequilibrium (current account deficits combined with financial account outflows).

Observe how forecasters combine technical analysis with the three major theoretical approaches to forecasting exchange rates.

◆ In the long term, it does appear that exchange rates follow a fundamental equilibrium path, one consistent with the fundamental theories of exchange rate determination.

◆ In the short term, however, a variety of random events, institutional frictions, and technical factors may cause currency values to deviate significantly from their long-term fundamental path.

MINI-CASE

The Japanese Yen Intervention of 2010[1]

We will take decisive steps if necessary, including intervention, while continuing to closely watch currency market moves from now on.
— Yoshihiko Noda, Finance Minister of Japan, September 13, 2010.

Japan has been the subject of continued criticism for nearly two decades over its frequent intervention in the foreign exchange markets. Trading partners have accused it of market manipulation, while Japan has argued that it is a country and economy which is inherently global in its economic structure, relying on its international competitiveness for its livelihood, and currency stability is its only desire.

The debate was renewed in September 2010 when Japan intervened in the foreign exchange markets for the first time in nearly six years. Japan reportedly bought nearly 20 billion U.S. dollars in exchange for Japanese yen in an attempt to stop the continuing appreciation of the yen. Finance Ministry officials had stated publicly that 82 yen per dollar was probably the limit of their tolerance for yen appreciation.

As illustrated in Exhibit 1, the Bank of Japan intervened on September 13 as the yen approached 82 yen per dollar. (The Bank of Japan is independent in its ability to conduct Japanese monetary policy, but as the organizational subsidiary of the Japanese Ministry of Finance, it must conduct foreign exchange operations on behalf of the Japanese government.) Japanese officials reportedly notified authorities in both the United States and the European Union of their activity, but noted that they had not asked for permission or support.

The intervention resulted in public outcry from Beijing to Washington to London over the "new era of currency intervention." Although market intervention is always looked down upon by free market proponents, the move by Japan was seen as particularly frustrating as it came at a time when the United States was continuing to pressure China to revalue its currency, the renminbi. As noted by economist Nouriel Roubini, "We are in a world where everyone wants

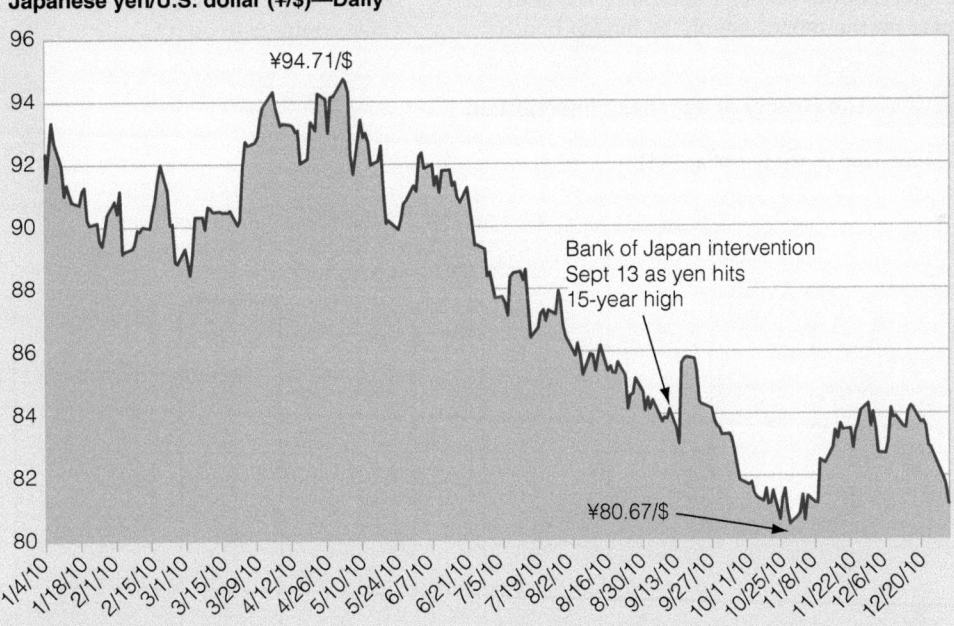

EXHIBIT 1   Intervention and the Japanese Yen, 2010

[1]This Mini-Case draws from a number of sources including "Japan's Currency Intervention: Policy Issues," Dick K. Nanto, CRS Report for Congress, July 13, 2007; IMF Country Report No. 05/273, Japan: 2005 Article IV Consultation Staff Report, August 2005; "Interventions and the Japanese Economic Recovery," Takatoshi Ito, paper presented at the University of Michigan Conference on Policy Options for Japan and the United States, October 2004; "Towards a New Era of Currency Intervention," Mansoor Mohi-Uddin, *Financial Times*, September 22, 2010; "Currency Intervention's Mixed Record of Success," Russell Hotten, *BBC News*, September 16, 2010.

a weak currency," a marketplace in which all countries are looking to stimulate their domestic economies through exceptionally low interest rates and corresponding weak currency values—"a global race to the bottom."

Ironically, as illustrated in Exhibit 1, it appears that the intervention was largely unsuccessful. When the Bank of Japan started buying dollars in an appreciating yen market—the so-called "leaning into the wind" strategy—it was hoping to either stop the appreciation, change the direction of the spot rate movement, or both. In either pursuit, it appears to have failed. As one analyst commented, it turned out to be a "short-term fix to a long-term problem." Although the yen spiked downward (more yen per dollar) for a few days, it returned once again to an appreciating path within a week.

Japan's frequent interventions, described in Exhibit 2, have been the subject of much study. In an August 2005 study by the IMF, it was noted that between 1991 and 2005, the Bank of Japan had intervened on 340 days, the European Central Bank on 4 days (since its inception in 1998), and the U.S. Federal Reserve on 22 days. Although the IMF has never found Japanese intervention to be officially "currency manipulation," an analysis by Takatoshi Ito in 2004 concluded that there was on average a one-yen per dollar change in market rates, roughly 1%, as a result of Japanese intervention over time.

It is not clear at this time whether or not Japan will "sterilize" the intervention, meaning neutralize the additional yen impact on the money supply by buying bonds domestically. Although this has been the tendency historically, given the current deflation forces in Japan, it may not be necessary.

Japan's interventions are not, however, a lone example of attempted market manipulation. The Swiss National Bank repeatedly intervened in 2009 to stop the appreciation of the Swiss franc against both the dollar and the euro, and recently, in January 2011, Chile had aggressively sold Chilean pesos against the U.S. dollar to stop its continued appreciation.

> *There is no historical case in which [yen] selling intervention succeeded in immediately stopping the pre-existing long term uptrend in the Japanese yen.*
> —Tohru Sasaki, Currency Strategist, JPMorgan.

CASE QUESTIONS

1. Could the Bank of Japan continually intervene to try to stop the appreciation of the yen? Is there any limit to its ability to intervene?

2. Why is a stronger yen such a bad thing for Japan? Isn't a stronger currency value an indication of confidence by the global markets in the economy and policies of a country?

3. If currency intervention has such a poor record, why do you think countries like Japan or Switzerland or Chile continue to do it?

EXHIBIT 2 The History of Japanese Intervention

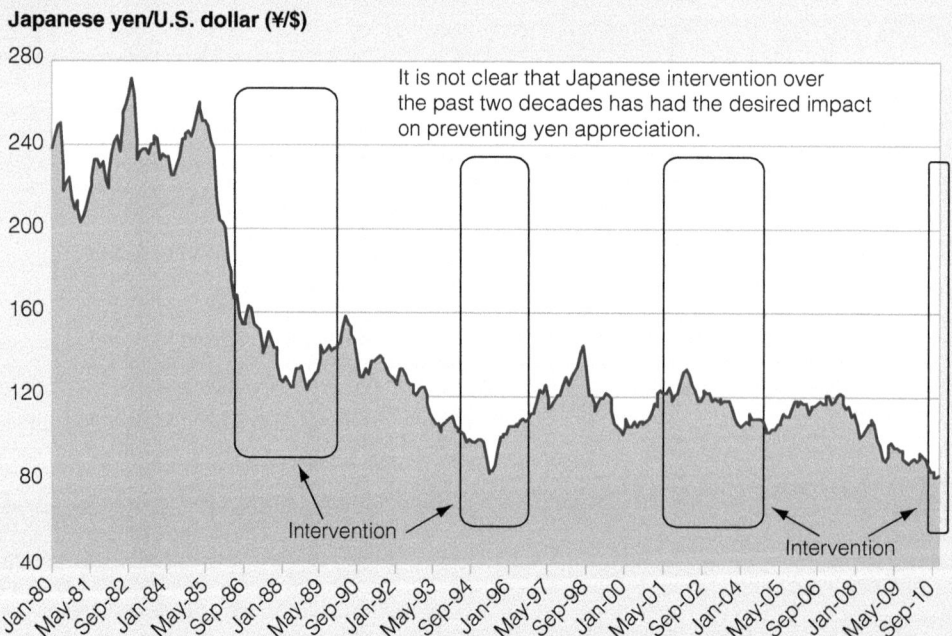

Questions

1. **Term Forecasting.** What are the major differences between short-term and long-term forecasts for the following:
   a. A fixed exchange rate
   b. A floating exchange rate

2. **Exchange Rate Dynamics.** What is meant by the term "overshooting"? What causes it and how is it corrected?

3. **Fundamental Equilibrium.** What is meant by the term "fundamental equilibrium path" for a currency value? What is "noise"?

4. **Asset Market Approach to Forecasting.** Explain how the asset market approach can be used to forecast future spot exchange rates. How does the asset market approach differ from the BOP approach to forecasting?

5. **Technical Analysis.** Explain how technical analysis can be used to forecast future spot exchange rates. How does technical analysis differ from the BOP and asset market approaches to forecasting?

6. **Forecasting Services.** Numerous exchange rate forecasting services exist. Trident's CFO Maria Gonzalez is considering whether to subscribe to one of these services at a cost of $20,000 per year. The price includes online access to the forecasting services' computerized econometric exchange rate prediction model. What factors should Maria consider when deciding whether or not to subscribe?

7. **Cross-Rate Consistency in Forecasting.** Explain the meaning of "*cross-rate consistency*" as used by MNEs. How do MNEs use a check of cross-rate consistency in practice?

8. **Infrastructure Weakness.** *Infrastructure weakness* was one of the causes of the emerging market crisis in Thailand in 1997. Define infrastructure weakness and explain how it could affect a country's exchange rate.

9. **Infrastructure Strength.** Explain why infrastructure strengths have helped to offset the large BOP deficits on current account in the United States.

10. **Speculation.** The emerging market crises of 1997–2002 were worsened because of rampant speculation. Do speculators cause such crisis or do they simply respond to market signals of weakness? How can a government manage foreign exchange speculation?

11. **Foreign Direct Investment.** Swings in foreign direct investment flows into and out of emerging markets contribute to exchange rate volatility. Describe one concrete historical example of this phenomenon during the last 10 years.

12. **Thailand's Crisis of 1997.** What were the main causes of Thailand's crisis of 1997? What lessons were learned and what steps were eventually taken to normalize Thailand's economy?

13. **Russia's Crisis of 1998.** What were the main causes of Russia's crisis of 1998? What lessons were learned and what steps were taken to normalize Russia's economy?

14. **Argentina's Crisis of 2001–2002.** What were the main causes of Argentina's crisis of 2001–2002? What lessons were learned and what steps were taken to normalize Argentina's economy?

Problems

1. **Trepak (The Russian Dance).** The Russian ruble (RUB) traded at RUB 29.00/USD on January 2, 2009. On December 11, 2010, its value had fallen to RUB 31.45/USD. What was the percentage change in its value?

2. **Center of the World.** The Ecuadorian sucre (S) suffered from hyper-inflationary forces throughout 1999. Its value moved from S5,000/$ to S25,000/$. What was the percentage change in its value?

3. **Reais Reality.** The Brazilian reais' (R$) value was R$1.80/$ on Thursday, January 24, 2008. Its value fell to R$2.39/$ on Monday, January 26, 2009. What was the percentage change in its value?

4. **That's Loonie.** The Canadian dollar's value against the U.S. dollar has seen some significant changes over recent history. Use the following graph of the C$/US$ exchange rate for the 30-year period between 1980 and end-of-year 2010 to estimate the percentage change in the Canadian dollar's value (it's affectionately known as the "loonie") versus the dollar for the following periods.
   a. January 1980–December 1985
   b. January 1986–December 1991
   c. January 1992–December 2001
   d. January 2002–December 2006
   e. January 2007–December 2008
   f. January 2009–December 2010

**Monthly Average Exchange Rates:
Canadian Dollars/U.S. Dollar**

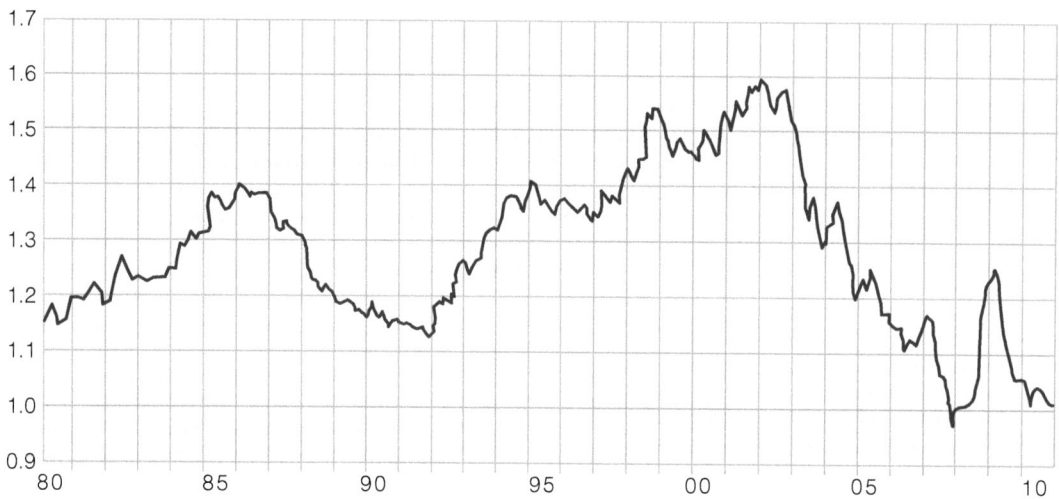

Source: PACIFIC Exchange Rates © 2010 by Prof. Werner Antweiler, University of British Columbia, Vancouver BC, Canada.

5. **Paris to Tokyo.** The Japanese yen-euro cross rate is one of the more significant currency values for global trade and commerce. The graph below shows this cross rate from when the euro was launched in January 1999 through the end-of-year 2010. Estimate the change in the value of the yen over the following three periods of change.
   a. Jan 1999–Aug 2001
   b. Sep 2001–June 2008
   c. July 2008–Dec 2010

6. **Lowering the Lira.** The Turkish lira (TL) was officially devalued by the Turkish government in February 2001 during a severe political and economic crisis. The Turkish government announced on February 21 that the lira would be devalued by 20%. The spot exchange rate on February 20 was TL68,000/$.
   a. What was the exchange rate after devaluation?
   b. What was percentage change after falling to TL100,000/$?

**Monthly Average Exchange Rates:
Japanese Yen/European Euro**

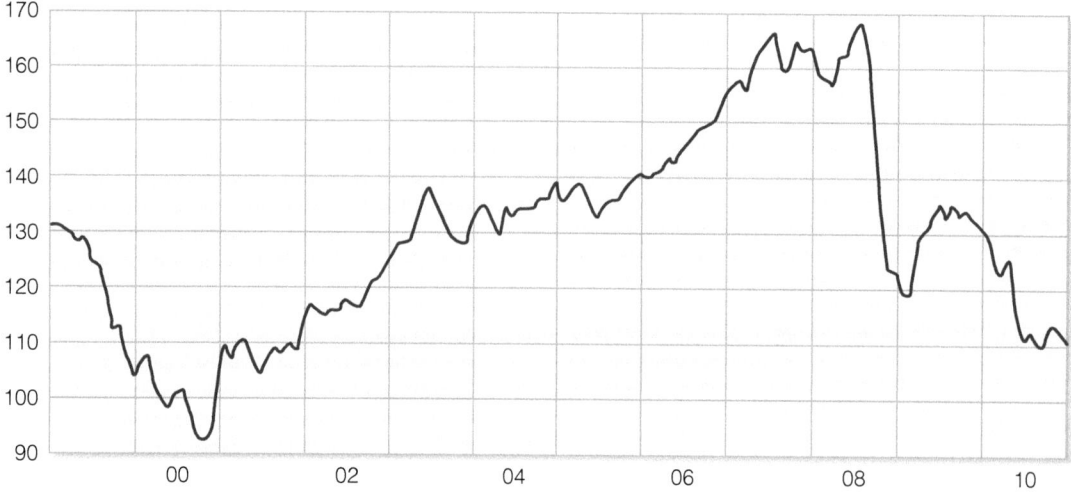

Source: PACIFIC Exchange Rates © 2010 by Prof. Werner Antweiler, University of British Columbia, Vancouver BC, Canada.

7. **Cada Seis Años.** Mexico was famous—or infamous—for many years in having two things every six years (*cada seis años* in Spanish): a presidential election and a currency devaluation. This was the case in 1976, 1982, 1988, and 1994. In its last devaluation on December 20, 1994, the value of the Mexican peso (Ps) was officially changed from Ps3.30/$ to Ps5.50/$. What was the percentage devaluation?

8. **Brokedown Palace.** The Thai baht (THB) was devalued by the Thai government from THB25/$ to THB29/$ on July 2, 1997. What was the percentage devaluation of the baht?

9. **Forecasting the Argentine Peso.** As illustrated in the graph on the next page, the Argentine peso moved from its fixed exchange rate of Ps1.00/$ to over Ps2.00/$ in a matter of days in early January 2002. After a brief period of high volatility, the peso's value appeared to settled down into a range varying between 2.0 and 2.5 pesos per dollar. If you were forecasting the Argentine peso further into the future, how would you use the information in the graphic—the value of the peso freely floating in the weeks following devaluation—to forecast its future value?

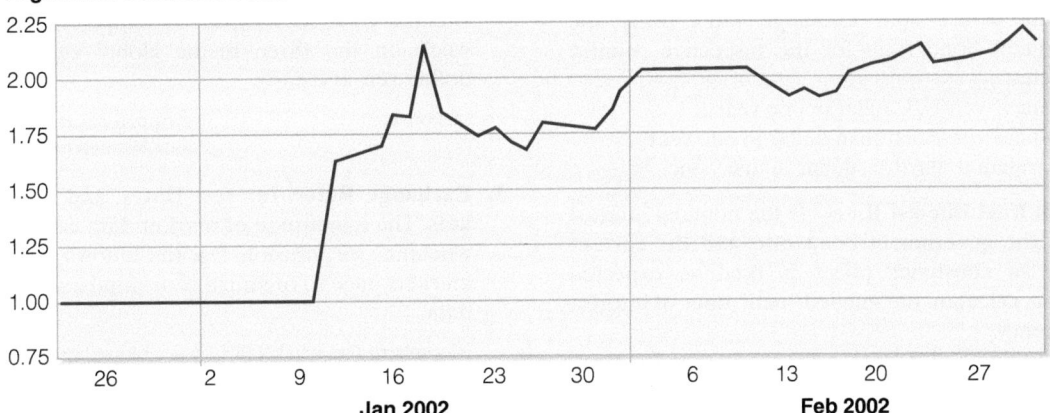

Daily Exchange Rates: Argentine Pesos/U.S. Dollar

Forecasting the Pan-Pacific Pyramid

Using the table below containing economic, financial, and business indicators from October 20, 2007, issue of *The Economist* (print edition) to answer problems 10 through 15.

Country	Gross Domestic Product				Industrial Production	Unemployment Rate
	Latest Qtr	Qtr*	Forecast 2007e	Forecast 2008e	Recent Qtr	Latest
Australia	4.3%	3.8%	4.1%	3.5%	4.6%	4.2%
Japan	1.6%	−1.2%	2.0%	1.9%	4.3%	3.8%
United States	1.9%	3.8%	2.0%	2.2%	1.9%	4.7%

Country	Consumer Prices			Interest Rates	
	Year Ago	Latest	Forecast 2007e	3-month Latest	1-yr Govt Latest
Australia	4.0%	2.1%	2.4%	6.90%	6.23%
Japan	0.9%	−0.2%	0.0%	0.73%	1.65%
United States	2.1%	2.8%	2.8%	4.72%	4.54%

Country	Trade Balance Last 12 mos (billion $)	Current Account		Current Units (per US$)	
		Last 12 mos (billion $)	Forecast 07 (% of GDP)	Oct 17th	Year Ago
Australia	−13.0	−$47.0	−5.7%	1.12	1.33
Japan	98.1	$197.5	4.6%	117	119
United States	−810.7	−$793.2	−5.6%	1.00	1.00

Source: Data abstracted from *The Economist*, October 20, 2007, print edition. Unless otherwise noted, percentages are percentage changes over one year. Rec Qtr = recent quarter. Values for 2007e are estimates or forecasts.

10. **Current Spot Rates.** What are the current spot exchange rates for the following cross rates?
    a. Japanese yen/U.S. dollar exchange rate
    b. Japanese yen/Australian dollar exchange rate
    c. Australian dollar/U.S. dollar exchange rate

11. **Purchasing Power Parity Forecasts.** Assuming purchasing power parity, and assuming that the forecasted change in consumer prices is a good proxy of predicted inflation, forecast the following cross rates:
    a. Japanese yen/U.S. dollar in one year
    b. Japanese yen/Australian dollar in one year
    c. Australian dollar/U.S. dollar in one year

12. **International Fischer Forecasts.** Assuming International Fisher applies to the coming year, forecast the following future spot exchange rates using the government bond rates for the respective country currencies:
    a. Japanese yen/U.S. dollar in one year
    b. Japanese yen/Australian dollar in one year
    c. Australian dollar/U.S. dollar in one year

13. **Implied Real Interest Rates.** If the nominal interest rate is the government bond rate, and the current change in consumer prices is used as expected inflation, calculate the implied "real" rates of interest by currency.
    a. Australian dollar "real" rate
    b. Japanese yen "real" rate
    c. U.S. dollar "real" rate

14. **Forward Rates.** Using the spot rates and 3-month interest rates above, calculate the 90-day forward rates for:
    a. Japanese yen/U.S. dollar exchange rate
    b. Japanese yen/Australian dollar exchange rate
    c. Australian dollar/U.S. dollar exchange rate

15. **Real Economic Activity and Misery.** Calculate the country's Misery Index (unemployment + inflation) and then use it like interest differentials to forecast the future spot exchange rate, one year into the future.
    a. Japanese yen/U.S. dollar exchange rate in one year
    b. Japanese yen/Australian dollar exchange rate in one year
    c. Australian dollar/U.S. dollar exchange rate in one year

Internet Exercises

1. **Recent Economic and Financial Data.** Use the following Web sites to obtain recent economic and financial data used for all approaches to forecasting presented in this chapter.

   Economist.com   www.economist.com
   FT.com   www.ft.com
   EconEdLink   www.econedlink.org/datalinks/index.cfm

2. **OzForex Weekly Comment.** The OzForex Foreign Exchange Services Web site provides a weekly commentary on major political and economic factors and events which move current markets. Using their Web site, see what they expect to happen in the coming week on the three major global currencies—the dollar, yen, and euro.

   OzForex   www.ozforex.com.au/marketwatch.htm

3. **Exchange Rates, Interest Rates, and Global Markets.** The magnitude of market data can seem overwhelming on occasion. Use the following Bloomberg markets page to organize your mind and your global data.

   Bloomberg Financial News   www.bloomberg.com/markets

4. **National Bank of Slovakia and the Slovakia Koruna.** The National Bank of Slovakia has been publishing spot and forward rates of selected currencies versus the Slovakia koruna for several years. Using the following Web site, compile spot rates, 3-month forward rates, and 6-month forward rates for a recent 2-year period. After graphing the data, does it appear that the forward rate has predicted the future direction of the spot rate?

   National Bank of Slovakia   www.nbs.sk/KL/INDEXA.HTM

5. **Banque Canada and the Canadian Dollar Forward Market.** Using the following Web site to find the latest spot and forward quotes of the Canadian dollar against the Bahamian dollar and the Brazilian real.

   Banque Canada   www.bank-banque-canada.ca/fmd/exchange.htm

Transaction and Translation Exposure

CHAPTER 10

There are two times in a man's life when he should not speculate: when he can't afford it and when he can.
—"Following the Equator," *Pudd'nhead Wilson's New Calendar*, Mark Twain.

LEARNING OBJECTIVES

- Distinguish between the three major foreign exchange exposures experienced by firms.
- Analyze the pros and cons of hedging foreign exchange transaction exposure.
- Examine the alternatives available to a firm to manage a large and significant transaction exposure.
- Evaluate the institutional practices and concerns of conducting foreign exchange risk management.
- Demonstrate how translation practices result in a foreign exchange exposure for the multinational enterprise.
- Explain the meaning behind the designation of a foreign subsidiary's "functional currency."
- Illustrate both the theoretical and practical differences between the two primary methods of translating foreign currency denominated financial statements into the currency reporting of the parent company.
- Compare translation exposure with operating expense.
- Analyze the costs and benefits of managing translation exposure.

Foreign exchange exposure is a measure of the potential for a firm's profitability, net cash flow, and market value to change because of a change in exchange rates. An important task of the financial manager is to measure foreign exchange exposure and to manage it so as to maximize the profitability, net cash flow, and market value of the firm. This chapter describes and details both types of accounting exposure: transaction exposure and translation exposure. The chapter concludes with a Mini-Case, **Banbury Impex (India)**, which involves a recent exposure management problem in India.

Types of Foreign Exchange Exposure

What happens to a firm when foreign exchange rates change? There are two distinct categories of foreign exchange exposure for the firm, those that are based in accounting and those that arise from economic competitiveness. The accounting exposures, specifically described as *transaction exposure* and *translation exposure*, arise from contracts and accounts being denominated in foreign currency. The economic exposure, which we will describe as *operating exposure*, is the potential change in the value of the firm from its changing global competitiveness as determined by exchange rates. Exhibit 10.1 shows schematically the three main types of foreign exchange exposure: *transaction*, *translation*, and *operating*.

Transaction Exposure

Transaction exposure measures changes in the value of outstanding financial obligations incurred prior to a change in exchange rates but not due to be settled until after the exchange rates change. Thus, it deals with changes in cash flows that result from existing contractual obligations.

Translation Exposure

Translation exposure is the potential for accounting-derived changes in owner's equity to occur because of the need to "translate" foreign currency financial statements of foreign subsidiaries into a single reporting currency to prepare worldwide consolidated financial statements.

Operating Exposure

Operating exposure, also called *economic exposure*, *competitive exposure*, or *strategic exposure*, measures the change in the present value of the firm resulting from any change in future operating cash flows of the firm caused by an *unexpected* change in exchange rates. The change in value depends on the effect of the exchange rate change on future sales volume, prices, and costs.

Transaction exposure and operating exposure exist because of unexpected changes in future cash flows. The difference between the two is that transaction exposure is concerned with future cash flows already contracted for, while operating exposure focuses on expected (not yet contracted for) future cash flows that might change because a change in exchange rates has altered international competitiveness.

EXHIBIT 10.1 Corporate Foreign Exchange Exposure

Resulting from Accounting	Resulting from Economics
Transaction Exposure	Operating Exposure
Impact of settling outstanding obligations entered into before change in exchange rates but to be settled after change in exchange rates	Change in expected future cash flows arising from an unexpected change in exchange rates
Translation Exposure	Changes in future cash flows arising from firm and competitor firm responses
Changes in income and owners' equity in consolidated financial statements caused by a change in exchange rates	

Time and Exchange Rate Changes →

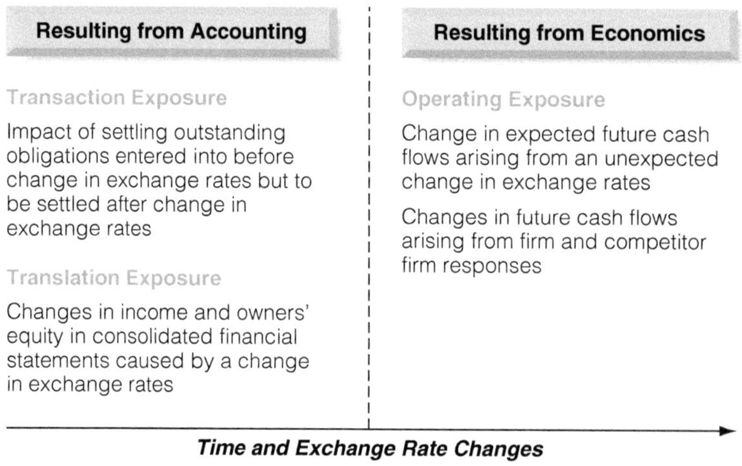

Why Hedge?

MNEs possess a multitude of cash flows that are sensitive to changes in exchange rates, interest rates, and commodity prices. Chapters 10 and 11 focus exclusively on the sensitivity of the individual firm's value and future cash flows to exchange rates. We begin by exploring the question of whether exchange rate risk should or should not be managed.

Hedging Defined

Many firms attempt to manage their currency exposures through *hedging*, which is the taking of a position, either acquiring a cash flow, an asset, or a contract that will rise (fall) in value and offset a fall (rise) in the value of an existing position. Hedging protects the owner of the existing asset from loss. However, it also eliminates any gain from an increase in the value of the asset hedged against. The question remains: What is to be gained by the firm from hedging?

According to financial theory, the value of a firm is the net present value of all expected future cash flows. The fact that these cash flows are *expected* emphasizes that nothing about the future is certain. If the reporting currency value of many of these cash flows is altered by exchange rates changes, a firm that hedges its currency exposures reduces some of the variance in the value of its future expected cash flows. *Currency risk* can then be defined as the variance in expected cash flows arising from unexpected exchange rate changes.

Exhibit 10.2 illustrates the distribution of expected net cash flows of the individual firm. Hedging these cash flows narrows the distribution of the cash flows about the mean of the distribution. Currency hedging reduces risk. Reduction of risk is not, however, the same as adding value or return. The value of the firm depicted in Exhibit 10.2 would be increased only if hedging actually shifted the mean of the distribution to the right. In fact, if hedging is not

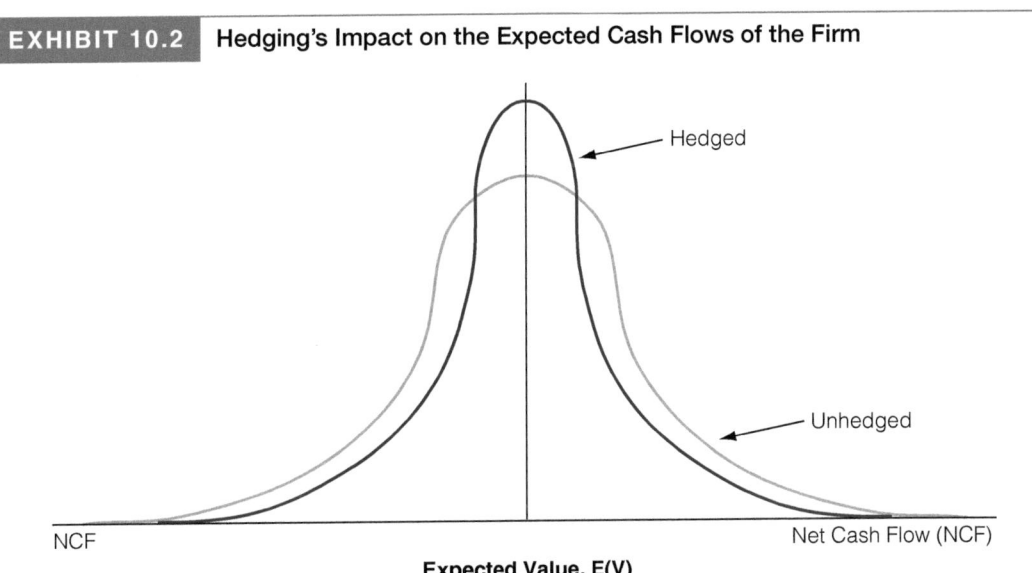

EXHIBIT 10.2 Hedging's Impact on the Expected Cash Flows of the Firm

Hedging reduces the variability of expected cash flows about the mean of the distribution. This reduction of distribution variance is a reduction of risk.

"free," meaning that the firm must expend resources to hedge, then hedging will add value only if the rightward shift is sufficiently large to compensate for the cost of hedging.

The Pros and Cons of Hedging

Is a reduction in the variability of cash flows sufficient reason for currency risk management? Opponents of currency hedging commonly make the following arguments:

- Shareholders are more capable of diversifying currency risk than is the management of the firm. If stockholders do not wish to accept the currency risk of any specific firm, they can diversify their portfolios to manage the risk in a way that satisfies their individual preferences and risk tolerance.
- Currency risk management does not increase the expected cash flows of the firm. Currency risk management does, however, consume firm resources and so reduces cash flow. The impact on value is a combination of the reduction of cash flow (which lowers value) and the reduction in variance (which increases value).
- Management often conducts hedging activities that benefit management at the expense of the shareholders. The field of finance called *agency theory* frequently argues that management is generally more risk-averse than are shareholders.
- Managers cannot outguess the market. If and when markets are in equilibrium with respect to parity conditions, the expected net present value of hedging should be zero.
- Management's motivation to reduce variability is sometimes driven by accounting reasons. Management may believe that it will be criticized more severely for incurring foreign exchange losses than for incurring similar or even higher cash costs in avoiding the foreign exchange loss. Foreign exchange losses appear in the income statement as a highly visible separate line item or as a footnote, but the higher costs of protection are buried in operating or interest expenses.
- Efficient market theorists believe that investors can see through the "accounting veil" and therefore have already factored the foreign exchange effect into a firm's market valuation. Hedging would only add cost.

Proponents of hedging cite the following arguments:

- Reduction in risk of future cash flows improves the planning capability of the firm. If the firm can more accurately predict future cash flows, it may be able to undertake specific investments or activities that it might otherwise not consider.
- Reduction of risk in future cash flows reduces the likelihood that the firm's cash flows will fall below a level sufficient to make debt-service payments in order for its continued operation. This minimum cash flow point, often referred to as the point of *financial distress*, lies left of the center of the distribution of expected cash flows. Hedging reduces the likelihood of the firm's cash flows falling to this level.
- Management has a comparative advantage over the individual shareholder in knowing the actual currency risk of the firm. Regardless of the level of disclosure provided by the firm to the public, management always possesses an advantage in the depth and breadth of knowledge concerning the real risks.
- Markets are usually in disequilibrium because of structural and institutional imperfections, as well as unexpected external shocks (such as an oil crisis or war). Management is in a better position than shareholders to recognize disequilibrium conditions and to take advantage of single opportunities to enhance firm value through *selective hedging* (the hedging of exceptional exposures or the occasional use of hedging when management has a definite expectation of the direction of exchange rates).

Measurement of Transaction Exposure

Transaction exposure measures gains or losses that arise from the settlement of existing financial obligations whose terms are stated in a foreign currency. Transaction exposure arises from any of the following:

- Purchasing or selling on credit goods or services when prices are stated in foreign currencies
- Borrowing or lending funds when repayment is to be made in a foreign currency
- Being a party to an unperformed foreign exchange forward contract
- Otherwise acquiring assets or incurring liabilities denominated in foreign currencies

The most common example of transaction exposure arises when a firm has a receivable or payable denominated in a foreign currency. Exhibit 10.3 demonstrates how this exposure is born. The total transaction exposure consists of *quotation, backlog,* and *billing exposures*.

A transaction exposure is created at the first moment the seller quotes a price in foreign currency terms to a potential buyer (t_1). The quote can be either verbal, as in a telephone quote, or, as in written bid or a printed price list. With the placing of an order (t_2), the potential exposure created at the time of the quotation (t_1) is converted into actual exposure, called *backlog exposure* because the product has not yet been shipped or billed. Backlog exposure lasts until the goods are shipped and billed (t_3), at which time it becomes *billing exposure*. Billing exposure remains until payment is received by the seller (t_4).

Purchasing or Selling on Open Account. Suppose that Trident Corporation, a U.S. firm, sells merchandise on open account to a Belgian buyer for €1,800,000, with payment to be made in 60 days. The spot exchange rate on the date of the sale is \$1.1200/€, and the seller expects to exchange the euros received for €1,800,000 × \$1.1200/€ = \$2,016,000 when payment is received. The \$2,016,000 is the value of the sale which is posted to the firm's books. Accounting practices stipulate that the foreign currency transaction be listed at the spot exchange rate in effect on the date of the transaction.

Transaction exposure arises because of the risk that Trident will receive something other than the \$2,016,000 expected and booked. For example, if the euro weakens to \$1.1000/€ when

EXHIBIT 10.3 The Life Span of Transaction Exposure

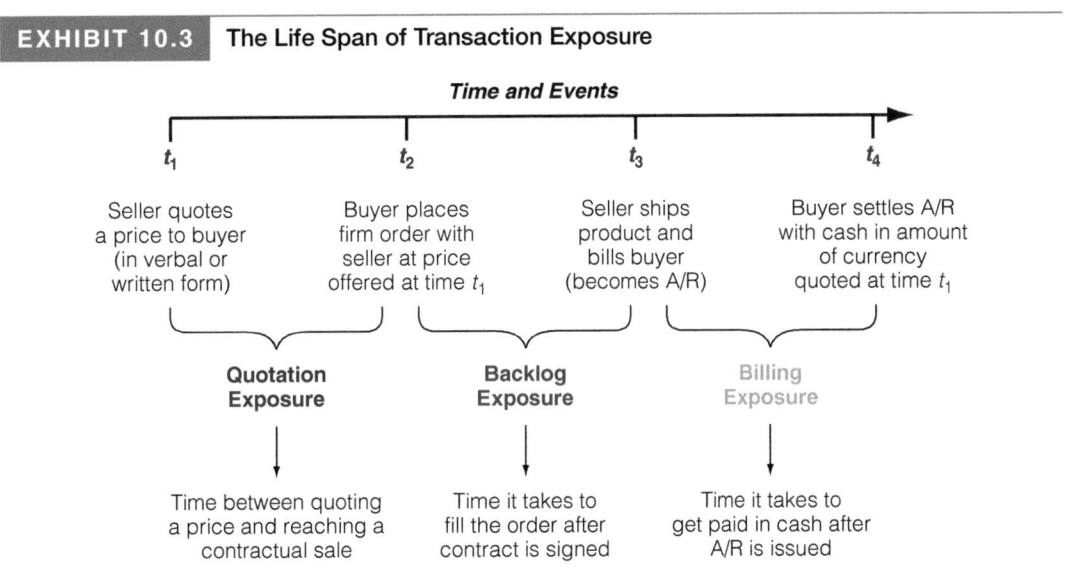

payment is received, the U.S. seller will receive only €1,800,000 × $1.1000/€ = $1,980,000, or some $180,000 less.

Transaction settlement: €1,800,000 × $1.1000/€ =	$1,980,000
Transaction booked: €1,800,000 × $1.1200/€ =	$2,016,000
Foreign exchange gain (loss) on sale =	($180,000)

If the euro should strengthen to $1.3000/€, however, Trident receives €1,800,000 × $1.3000/€ = $2,340,000, an increase of $180,000 over the amount expected. Thus, exposure is the chance of either a loss or a gain on the resulting dollar settlement versus what the sale was booked at.

The U.S. seller might have avoided transaction exposure by invoicing the Belgian buyer in dollars. Of course, if the U.S. company attempted to sell only in dollars it might not have obtained the sale in the first place. Even if the Belgian buyer agrees to pay in dollars, transaction exposure is not eliminated. Instead, it is transferred to the Belgian buyer, whose dollar account payable has an unknown cost—to it—60 days hence.

Borrowing and Lending. A second example of transaction exposure arises when funds are borrowed or loaned, and the amount involved is denominated in a foreign currency. For example, in 1994, PepsiCo's largest bottler outside of the United States was Grupo Embotellador de Mexico (Gemex). In mid-December 1994, Gemex, a Mexican company, had U.S. dollar debt of $264 million. At that time, Mexico's *new peso* ("Ps") was traded at Ps3.45/US$, a pegged rate that had been maintained with minor variations since January 1, 1993, when the new currency unit had been created. On December 22, 1994, the peso was allowed to float because of economic and political events within Mexico, and in one day it sank to Ps4.65/US$. For most of the following January it traded in a range near Ps5.50/US$.

Dollar debt in mid-December 1994: US$264,000,000 × Ps3.45/US$ =	Ps910,800,000
Dollar debt in mid-January 1995: US$264,000,000 × Ps5.50/US$ =	Ps1,452,000,000
Dollar debt increase measure in Mexican pesos	Ps541,200,000

The number of pesos needed to repay the dollar debt increased by 59%! In U.S. dollar terms, the drop in the value of the pesos caused Gemex of Mexico to need the peso-equivalent of an additional US$98,400,000 to repay its debt.

Other Causes of Transaction Exposure. When a firm enters into a forward exchange contract, it deliberately creates transaction exposure. This risk is usually incurred to hedge an existing transaction exposure. For example, a U.S. firm might want to offset an existing obligation to purchase ¥100 million to pay for an import from Japan in 90 days. One way to offset this payment is to purchase ¥100 million in the forward market today for delivery in 90 days. In this manner any change in value of the Japanese yen relative to the dollar is neutralized. Thus, the potential transaction loss (or gain) on the account payable is offset by the transaction gain (or loss) on the forward contract.

Note that foreign currency cash balances do not create transaction exposure, even though their home currency value changes immediately with a change in exchange rates. No legal obligation exists to move the cash from one country and currency to another at a future date. If such an obligation did exist, it would show on the books as a payable (e.g., dividends declared and payable) or receivable and then be counted as part of transaction exposure. Nevertheless, the foreign exchange value of cash balances does change when exchange rates change. Such a change is reflected in the consolidated statement of cash flows and the consolidated balance sheet.

Contractual Hedges. Foreign exchange transaction exposure can be managed by *contractual*, *operating*, and *financial hedges*. The main contractual hedges employ the forward, money, futures, and options markets. Operating and financial hedges employ the use of risk-sharing agreements, leads and lags in payment terms, swaps, and other strategies to be discussed in later chapters.

The term *natural hedge* refers to an offsetting operating cash flow, a payable arising from the conduct of business. A *financial hedge* refers to either an offsetting debt obligation (such as a loan) or some type of financial derivative such as an interest rate swap. Care should be taken to distinguish hedges in the same way finance distinguishes cash flows—*operating* from *financing*. The following case illustrates how contractual hedging techniques may be used to protect against transaction exposure.

Trident's Transaction Exposure

Maria Gonzalez is the chief financial officer of Trident. She has just concluded negotiations for the sale of a turbine generator to Regency, a British firm, for £1,000,000. This single sale is quite large in relation to Trident's present business. Trident has no other current foreign customers, so the currency risk of this sale is of particular concern. The sale is made in March with payment due three months later in June. Exhibit 10.4 summarizes the financial and market information Maria has collected for the analysis of her currency exposure problem. The unknown—the *transaction exposure*—is the actual realized value of the receivable in U.S. dollars at the end of 90 days.

Trident operates on relatively narrow margins. Although Maria and Trident would be very happy if the pound appreciated versus the dollar, concerns center on the possibility that

EXHIBIT 10.4 Trident's Transaction Exposure

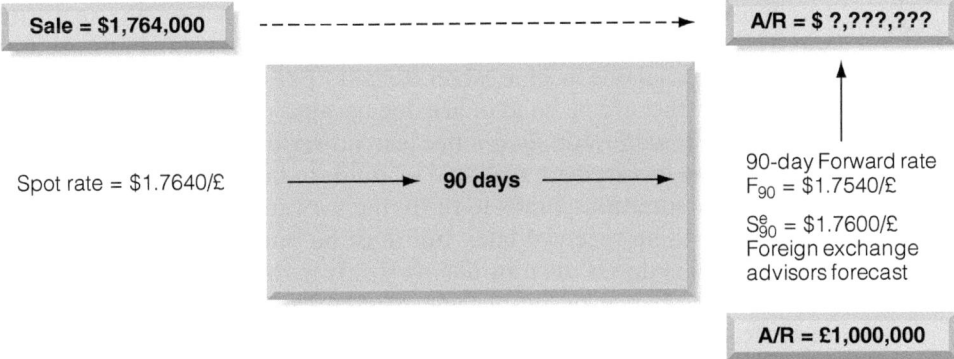

U.S. Dollar Market

Trident's weighted average cost of capital = 12.00% (3.00% for 90 days)
US$ 3-month borrowing rate = 8.00% per annum (2.00% for 90 days)
US$ 3-month investment rate = 6.00% per annum (1.50% for 90 days)

Sale = $1,764,000

A/R = $?,???,???

Spot rate = $1.7640/£

90 days

90-day Forward rate
F_{90} = $1.7540/£

S^e_{90} = $1.7600/£
Foreign exchange
advisors forecast

A/R = £1,000,000

UK£ 3-month investment rate = 8.00% per annum (2.00% for 90 days)
UK£ 3-month borrowing rate = 10.00% per annum (2.50% for 90 days)

British Pound Market

June (3-month) put option for £1,000,000 with a strike rate of $1.75/£; premium of 1.5%

the pound will fall. When Trident had priced and budgeted this contract, it had set a very slim minimum acceptable margin at a sales price of $1,700,000; Trident wanted the deal for both financial and strategic purposes. The *budget rate*, the lowest acceptable dollar per pound exchange rate, was therefore established at $1.70/£. Any exchange rate below this budget rate would result in Trident realizing no profit on the deal.

Four alternatives are available to Trident to manage the exposure: 1) remain unhedged; 2) hedge in the forward market; 3) hedge in the money market; or 4) hedge in the options market.

Unhedged Position

Maria may decide to accept the transaction risk. If she believes the foreign exchange advisor, she expects to receive £1,000,000 × $1.76 = $1,760,000 in three months. However, that amount is at risk. If the pound should fall to, say, $1.65/£, she will receive only $1,650,000. Exchange risk is not one-sided, however; if the transaction is left uncovered and the pound strengthened even more than forecast by the advisor, Trident will receive considerably more than $1,760,000. The essence of an unhedged approach is as follows.

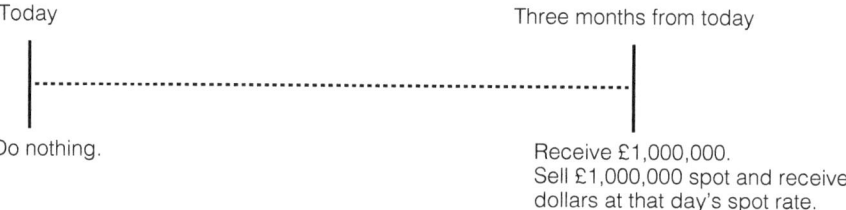

Forward Market Hedge

A *forward hedge* involves a forward (or futures) contract and a source of funds to fulfill that contract. The forward contract is entered into at the time the transaction exposure is created. In Trident's case, that would be in March, when the sale to Regency was booked as an account receivable.

When a foreign currency denominated sale such as this is made, it is booked at the spot rate of exchange existing on the booking date. In this case, the spot rate on the date of sale was $1.7640/£, so the receivable was booked as $1,764,000. Funds to fulfill the forward contract will be available in June, when Regency pays £1,000,000 to Trident. If funds to fulfill the forward contract are on hand or are due because of a business operation, the hedge is considered *covered*, *perfect*, or *square* because no residual foreign exchange risk exists. Funds on hand or to be received are matched by funds to be paid.

In some situations, funds to fulfill the forward exchange contract are not already available or due to be received later, but must be purchased in the spot market at some future date. Such a hedge is *open* or *uncovered*. It involves considerable risk because the hedger must take a chance on purchasing foreign exchange at an uncertain future spot rate in order to fulfill the forward contract. Purchase of such funds at a later date is referred to as *covering*.

Should Trident wish to hedge its transaction exposure with a forward, it will sell £1,000,000 forward today at the 3-month forward rate of $1.7540/£. This is a *covered transaction* in which the firm no longer has any foreign exchange risk. In three months the firm will receive £1,000,000 from the British buyer, deliver that sum to the bank against its forward sale, and receive $1,754,000. This would be recorded on Trident's income statement as a foreign exchange loss of $10,000 ($1,764,000 as booked, $1,754,000 as settled).

The essence of a forward hedge is as follows:

Today — Sell £1,000,000 forward @ $1.7540/£.

Three months from today — Receive £1,000,000. Deliver £1,000,000 against forward sale. Receive $1,754,000.

If Maria's forecast of future rates was identical to that implicit in the forward quotation, that is, $1.7540/£, expected receipts would be the same whether or not the firm hedges. However, realized receipts under the unhedged alternative could vary considerably from the certain receipts when the transaction is hedged. Never underestimate the value of predictability of outcomes (and 90 nights of solid sleep).

Money Market Hedge

Like a forward market hedge, a *money market hedge* also involves a contract and a source of funds to fulfill that contract. In this instance, the contract is a loan agreement. The firm seeking the money market hedge borrows in one currency and exchanges the proceeds for another currency. Funds to fulfill the contract—that is, to repay the loan—are generated from business operations, in this case, the account receivable.

A money market hedge can cover a single transaction, such as Trident's £1,000,000 receivable, or repeated transactions. Hedging repeated transactions is called *matching*. It requires the firm to match the expected foreign currency cash inflows and outflows by currency and maturity. For example, if Trident had numerous sales denominated in pounds to British customers over a long period of time, it would have somewhat predictable U.K. pound cash inflows. The appropriate money market hedge technique here would be to borrow U.K. pounds in an amount matching the typical size and maturity of expected pound inflows. Then, if the pound depreciated or appreciated, the foreign exchange effect on cash inflows in pounds would be offset by the effect on cash outflows in pounds from repaying the pound loan plus interest.

The structure of a money market hedge resembles that of a forward hedge. The difference is that the cost of the money market hedge is determined by different interest rates than the interest rates used in the formation of the forward rate. The difference in interest rates facing a private firm borrowing in two separate country markets may be different from the difference in risk-free government bill rates or Eurocurrency interest rates in these same markets. In efficient markets interest rate parity should ensure that these costs are nearly the same, but not all markets are efficient at all times.

To hedge in the money market, Maria will borrow pounds in London at once, immediately convert the borrowed pounds into dollars, and repay the pound loan in three months with the proceeds from the sale of the generator. She will need to borrow just enough to repay both the principal and interest with the sale proceeds. The borrowing interest rate will be 10% per annum, or 2.5% for three months. Therefore, the amount to borrow now for repayment in three months is

$$\frac{£1,000,000}{1 + 0.025} = £975,610$$

Maria would borrow £975,610 now, and in three months repay that amount plus £24,390 of interest with the account receivable. Trident would exchange the £975,610 loan proceeds for dollars at the current spot exchange rate of $1.7640/£, receiving $1,720,976 at once.

The money market hedge, if selected by Trident, creates a pound-denominated liability, the pound loan, to offset the pound-denominated asset, the account receivable. The money market hedge works as a hedge by matching assets and liabilities according to their currency of denomination. Using a simple T-account illustrating Trident's balance sheet, the loan in British pounds is seen to offset the pound-denominated account receivable:

Assets		Liabilities and Net Worth	
Account receivable	£1,000,000	Bank loan (principal)	£975,610
		Interest payable	24,390
	£1,000,000		£1,000,000

The loan acts as a *balance sheet hedge* against the pound-denominated account receivable.

To compare the forward hedge with the money market hedge one must analyze how Trident's loan proceeds will be utilized for the next three months. Remember that the loan proceeds are received today but the forward contract proceeds are received in three months. For comparison purposes, one must either calculate the future value of the loan proceeds or the present value of the forward contract proceeds. Since the primary uncertainty here is the dollar value in three months, we will use future value here.

As both the forward contract proceeds and the loan proceeds are relatively certain, it is possible to make a clear choice between the two alternatives based on the one that yields the higher dollar receipts. This result, in turn, depends on the assumed rate of investment or use of the loan proceeds.

At least three logical choices exist for an assumed investment rate for the loan proceeds for the next three months. First, if Trident is cash rich, the loan proceeds might be invested in U.S. dollar money market instruments that yield 6% per annum. Second, Maria might simply use the pound loan proceeds to pay down dollar loans that currently cost Trident 8% per annum. Third, Maria might invest the loan proceeds in the general operations of the firm, in which case the cost of capital of 12% per annum would be the appropriate rate. The field of finance generally uses the company's cost of capital to move capital forward and backward in time, and we will therefore use the WACC of 12% (3% for the 90-day period here) to calculate the future value of proceeds under the money market hedge:

$$\$1,720,976 \times 1.03 = \$1,772,605$$

A break-even rate can now be calculated between the forward hedge and the money market hedge. Assume that r is the unknown 3-month investment rate, expressed as a decimal, that would equalize the proceeds from the forward and money market hedges. We have

$$(\text{Loan proceeds}) \times (1 + \text{rate}) = (\text{forward proceeds})$$
$$\$1,720,976 \times (1 + r) = \$1,754,000$$
$$r = 0.0192$$

One can convert this 3-month (90 days) investment rate to an annual whole percentage equivalent, assuming a 360-day financial year, as follows:

$$0.0192 \times \frac{360}{90} \times 100 = 7.68\%$$

In other words, if Maria Gonzalez can invest the loan proceeds at a rate higher than 7.68% per annum, she would prefer the money market hedge. If she can only invest at a rate lower than 7.68%, she would prefer the forward hedge.

The essence of a money market hedge is as follows:

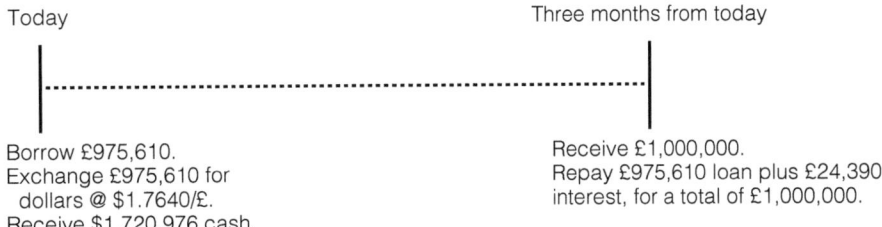

Today — Borrow £975,610. Exchange £975,610 for dollars @ $1.7640/£. Receive $1,720,976 cash.

Three months from today — Receive £1,000,000. Repay £975,610 loan plus £24,390 interest, for a total of £1,000,000.

The money market hedge therefore results in cash received up-front (at the start of the period), which can then be carried forward in time for comparison with the other hedging alternatives.

Options Market Hedge

Maria Gonzalez could also cover her £1,000,000 exposure by purchasing a put option. This technique allows her to speculate on the upside potential for appreciation of the pound while limiting downside risk to a known amount. Maria could purchase from her bank a 3-month put option on £1,000,000 at an at-the-money (ATM) strike price of $1.75/£ with a premium cost of 1.50%. The cost of the option—the premium—is

$$(\text{Size of option}) \times (\text{premium}) \times (\text{spot rate}) = \text{cost of option}$$
$$£1,000,000 \times 0.015 \times \$1.7640 = \$26,460$$

Because we are using future value to compare the various hedging alternatives, it is necessary to project the premium cost of the option forward three months. We will use the cost of capital of 12% per annum or 3% per quarter. Therefore, the premium cost of the put option as of June would be $26,460(1.03) = $27,254. This is equal to $0.0273 per pound ($27,254 ÷ £1,000,000).

When the £1,000,000 is received in June, the value in dollars depends on the spot rate at that time. The upside potential is unlimited, the same as in the unhedged alternative. At any exchange rate above $1.75/£, Trident would allow its option to expire unexercised and would exchange the pounds for dollars at the spot rate. If the expected rate of $1.76/£ materializes, Trident would exchange the £1,000,000 in the spot market for $1,760,000. Net proceeds would be $1,760,000 minus the $27,254 cost of the option, or $1,732,746.

In contrast to the unhedged alternative, downside risk is limited with an option. If the pound depreciates below $1.75/£, Maria would exercise her option to sell (put) £1,000,000 at $1.75/£, receiving $1,750,000 gross, but $1,722,746 net of the $27,254 cost of the option. Although this downside result is worse than the downside of the forward or money market hedges, the upside potential is unlimited.

The essence of the at-the-money (ATM) put option market hedge is as follows:

Today — Buy put option to sell pounds @ $1.75/£. Pay $26,460 for put option.

Three months hence — Receive £1,000,000. Either deliver £1,000,000 against put, receiving $1,750,000; or sell £1,000,000 spot if current spot rate is > $1.75/£.

We can calculate a trading range for the pound that defines the break-even points for the option compared with the other strategies. The upper bound of the range is determined by comparison with the forward rate. The pound must appreciate enough above the $1.7540 forward rate to cover the $0.0273/£ cost of the option. Therefore, the break-even upside spot price of the pound must be $1.7540 + $0.0273 = $1.7813. If the spot pound appreciates above $1.7813, proceeds under the option strategy will be greater than under the forward hedge. If the spot pound ends up below $1.7813, the forward hedge would be superior in retrospect.

The lower bound of the range is determined by the unhedged strategy. If the spot price falls below $1.75/£, Maria will exercise her put and sell the proceeds at $1.75/£. The net proceeds will be $1.75/£ less the $0.0273 cost of the option, or $1.7221/£. If the spot rate falls below $1.7221/£, the net proceeds from exercising the option will be greater than the net proceeds from selling the unhedged pounds in the spot market. At any spot rate above $1.7221/£, the spot proceeds from remaining unhedged will be greater.

Foreign currency options have a variety of hedging uses. A put option is useful to construction firms or other exporters when they must submit a fixed price bid in a foreign currency without knowing until some later date whether their bid is successful. Similarly, a call option is useful to hedge a bid for a foreign business or firm if a potential future foreign currency payment may be required. In either case, if the bid is rejected, the loss is limited to the cost of the option.

Comparison of Alternatives

Exhibit 10.5 shows the value of Trident's £1,000,000 account receivable over a range of possible ending spot exchange rates and hedging alternatives. This exhibit makes it clear that the firm's *view* of likely exchange rate changes aids in the hedging choice.

◆ If the exchange rate is expected to move against Trident—to the left of $1.76/£, the money market hedge is the clearly preferred alternative—a guaranteed value of $1,772,605.

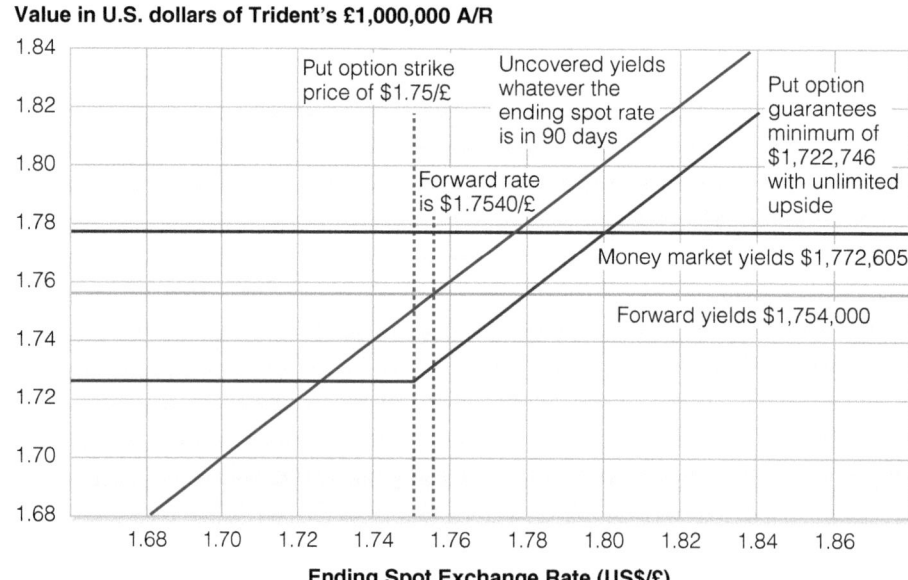

EXHIBIT 10.5 Valuation of Cash Flows under Hedging Alternatives for Trident with Option

♦ If the exchange rate is expected to move in Trident's favor, to the right of $1.76/£, the choice of the hedge is more complex, and lies between remaining unhedged, the money market hedge, or the put option.

Remaining unhedged is most likely an unacceptable choice. If Maria's expectations regarding the future spot rate proved wrong, and the spot rate fell below $1.70/£, she would not reach her budget rate. The put option offers a unique alternative. If the exchange rate moves in Trident's favor, the put option offers nearly the same upside potential as the unhedged alternative except for the up-front costs. If, however, the exchange rate moves against Trident, the put option limits the downside risk to $1,722,746.

Strategy Choice and Outcome

Trident, like all firms attempting to hedge transaction exposure, must decide on a strategy before the exchange rate changes occur. How will Maria Gonzalez choose among the alternative hedging strategies? She must select on the basis of two decision criteria: 1) the *risk tolerance* of Trident, as expressed in its stated policies; and 2) her own *view*, or expectation of the direction (and distance) the exchange rate will move over the coming 90-day period.

Trident's *risk tolerance* is a combination of management's philosophy toward transaction exposure and the specific goals of treasury activities. Many firms believe that currency risk is simply a part of doing business internationally, and therefore, start their analysis from an unhedged baseline. Other firms, however, view currency risk as unacceptable, and either start their analysis from a full forward contract cover baseline, or simply mandate that all transaction exposures be fully covered by forward contracts regardless of the value of other hedging alternatives. The treasury in most firms operates as a cost or *service center* for the firm. On the other hand, if the treasury operates as a *profit center*, it might tolerate taking more risk.

The final choice among hedges—if Maria Gonzalez does expect the pound to appreciate—combines both the firm's risk tolerance, its view, and its confidence in its view. Transaction exposure management with contractual hedges requires managerial judgment.

Management of an Account Payable

The management of an account payable, where the firm would be required to make a foreign currency payment at a future date, is similar but not identical in form. If Trident had a £1,000,000 account payable in 90 days, the hedging choices would appear as follows:

Remain Unhedged. Trident could wait 90 days, exchange dollars for pounds at that time, and make its payment. If Trident expects the spot rate in 90 days to be $1.7600/£, the payment would be expected to cost $1,760,000. This amount is, however, uncertain; the spot exchange rate in 90 days could be very different from that expected.

Forward Market Hedge. Trident could buy £1,000,000 forward, locking in a rate of $1.7540/£, and a total dollar cost of $1,754,000. This is $6,000 less than the expected cost of remaining unhedged, and therefore clearly preferable to the first alternative.

Money Market Hedge. The money market hedge is distinctly different for a payable as opposed to a receivable. To implement a money market hedge in this case, Trident would exchange U.S. dollars spot and invest them for 90 days in a pound-denominated interest-bearing account. The principal and interest in British pounds at the end of the 90-day period would be used to pay the £1,000,000 account payable.

In order to assure that the principal and interest exactly equal the £1,000,000 due in 90 days, Trident would discount the £1,000,000 by the pound investment interest rate of 8% for 90 days in order to determine the pounds needed today:

$$\frac{£1,000,000}{\left[1 + \left(.08 \times \frac{90}{360}\right)\right]} = £980,392.16$$

This £980,392.16 needed today would require $1,729,411.77 at the current spot rate of $1.7640/£:

$$£980,392.16 \times \$1.7640/£ = \$1,729,411.77$$

Finally, in order to compare the money market hedge outcome with the other hedging alternatives, the $1,729,411.77 cost today must be carried forward 90 days to the same future date as the other hedge choices. If the current dollar cost is carried forward at Trident's WACC of 12%, the total cost of the money market hedge is $1,781,294.12. This is higher than the forward hedge and therefore unattractive.

$$\$1,729,411.77 \times \left[1 + \left(.12 \times \frac{90}{360}\right)\right] = \$1,781,294.12$$

Option Hedge. Trident could cover its £1,000,000 account payable by purchasing a *call option* on £1,000,000. A June call option on British pounds with a near at-the-money strike price of $1.75/£ would cost 1.5% (premium) or

$$£1,000,000 \times 0.015 \times \$1.7640/£ = \$26,460$$

This premium, regardless of whether the call option is exercised or not, will be paid up-front. Its value carried forward 90 days at the WACC of 12%, would raise its end of period cost to $27,254.

If the spot rate in 90 days is less than $1.75/£, the option would be allowed to expire and the £1,000,000 for the payable purchased on the spot market. The total cost of the call option hedge if the option is not exercised is theoretically smaller than any other alternative (with the exception of remaining unhedged, because the option premium is still paid and lost). If the spot rate in 90 days exceeds $1.75/£, the call option would be exercised. The total cost of the call option hedge if exercised is as follows:

Exercise call option (£1,000,000 × $1.75/£)	$1,750,000
Call option premium (carried forward 90 days)	27,254
Total maximum expense of call option hedge	$1,777,254

The four hedging methods of managing a £1,000,000 account payable for Trident are summarized in Exhibit 10.6. The costs of the forward hedge and money market hedge are certain. The cost using the call option hedge is calculated as a maximum, and the cost of remaining unhedged is highly uncertain.

As with Trident's account receivable, the final hedging choice depends on the confidence of Maria's exchange rate expectations, and her willingness to bear risk. The forward hedge provides the lowest cost of making the account payable payment that is certain. If the dollar strengthens against the pound, ending up at a spot rate less than $1.75/£, the call option could potentially be the lowest cost hedge. Given an expected spot rate of $1.76/£, however, the forward hedge appears the preferred alternative.

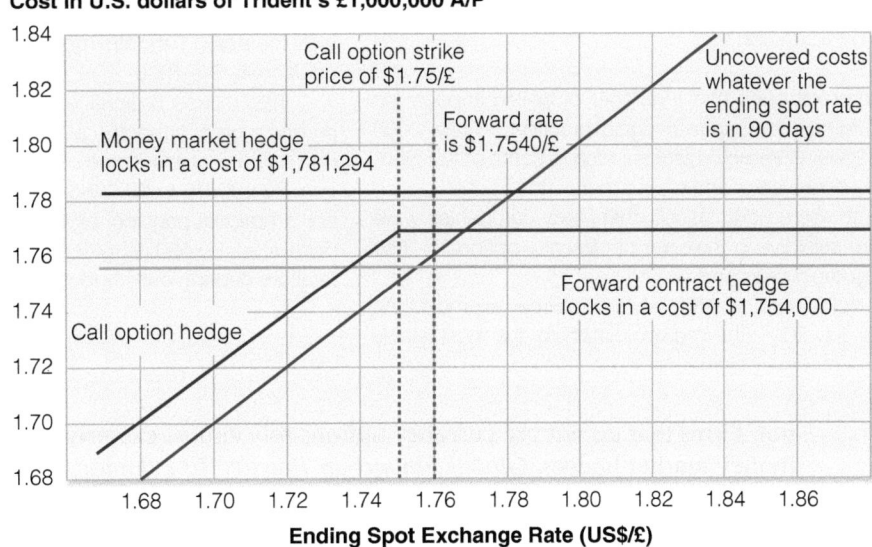

EXHIBIT 10.6 Valuation of Hedging Alternatives for an Account Payable

Risk Management in Practice

As many different approaches to exposure management exist as there are firms. A variety of surveys of corporate risk management practices in recent years in the United States, the United Kingdom, Finland, Australia, and Germany, indicate no real consensus exists regarding the best approach. The following is our attempt to assimilate the basic results of these surveys and combine them with our own personal experiences.

Which Goals? The treasury function of most private firms, the group typically responsible for transaction exposure management, is usually considered a cost center. It is not expected to add profit to the firm's bottom-line (which is not the same thing as saying it is not expected to add value to the firm). Currency risk managers are expected to err on the conservative side when managing the firm's money.

Which Exposures? Transaction exposures exist before they are actually booked as foreign currency-denominated receivables and payables. However, many firms do not allow the hedging of quotation exposure or backlog exposure as a matter of policy. The reasoning is straightforward: until the transaction exists on the accounting books of the firm, the probability of the exposure actually occurring is considered to be less than 100%. Conservative hedging policies dictate that contractual hedges be placed only on existing exposures.

An increasing number of firms, however, are actively hedging not only backlog exposures, but also selectively hedging quotation and *anticipated exposures. Anticipated exposures* are transactions for which there are—at present—no contracts or agreements between parties, but are anticipated on the basis of historical trends and continuing business relationships. Although this may appear to be overly speculative on the part of these firms, it may be that hedging expected foreign-currency payables and receivables for future periods is the most conservative approach to protect the firm's future operating revenues.

Which Contractual Hedges? As might be expected, transaction exposure management programs are generally divided along an "option-line," those that use options and those that do

> **GLOBAL FINANCE IN PRACTICE 10.1**
>
> **The Credit Crisis and Option Volatilities in 2009**
>
> The global credit crisis had a number of lasting impacts on corporate foreign exchange hedging practices in late 2008 and early 2009. Currency volatilities rose to some of the highest levels seen in years, and stayed there. This caused option premiums to rise so dramatically that many companies were much more selective in their use of currency options in their risk management programs.
>
> The dollar-euro volatility was a prime example. As recently as July 2007, the implied volatility for the most widely traded currency cross was below 7% for maturities from one week to three years. By October 31, 2008, the 1-month implied volatility had reached 29%. Although this was seemingly the peak, 1-month implied volatilities were still over 20% on January 30, 2009.
>
> This makes options very expensive. For example, the premium on a 1-month call option on the euro with a strike rate forward-at-the-money at the end of January 2009 rose from $0.0096/€ to $0.0286/€ when volatility is 20%, not 7%. For a notional principal of €1 million, that is an increase in price from $9,580 to $28,640. That will put a hole in any treasury department's budget.

not. Firms that do not use currency options rely almost exclusively on forward contracts and money market hedges. *Global Finance in Practice 10.1* demonstrates how market condition may change firm hedging choices.

Many MNEs have established rather rigid transaction exposure risk management policies which mandate *proportional hedging*. These policies generally require the use of forward contract hedges on a percentage (e.g., 50, 60, or 70%) of existing transaction exposures. As the maturity of the exposures lengthens, the percentage forward-cover required decreases. The remaining portion of the exposure is then selectively hedged on the basis of the firm's risk tolerance, view of exchange rate movements, and confidence level. Although rarely acknowledged by the firms themselves, selective hedging is essentially speculation. Significant question remains as to whether a firm or a financial manager can consistently predict the future direction of exchange rates.

Translation Exposure

Translation exposure, the second category of accounting exposures, arises because financial statements of foreign subsidiaries—which are stated in foreign currency—must be restated in the parent's reporting currency for the firm to prepare consolidated financial statements. Foreign subsidiaries of U.S. companies, for example, must restate local euro, pound, yen, etc., statements into U.S. dollars so the foreign values can be added to the parent's U.S. dollar-denominated balance sheet and income statement. This accounting process is called "translation." *Translation exposure* is the potential for an increase or decrease in the parent's net worth and reported net income caused by a change in exchange rates since the last translation.

Although the main purpose of translation is to prepare consolidated statements, translated statements are also used by management to assess the performance of foreign subsidiaries. Although such assessment might be performed from the local currency statements, restatement of all subsidiary statements into the single "common denominator" of one currency facilitates management comparison.

Overview of Translation

There are two financial statements for each subsidiary which must be translated for consolidation: the *income statement* and the *balance sheet*. (Statements of cash flow are not translated from the foreign subsidiaries.) The consolidated statement of cash flow is constructed from the consolidated statement of income and consolidated balance sheet. Because the consolidated results for any multinational firm are constructed from all of its subsidiary operations, including foreign subsidiaries, the possibility of a change in consolidated net income or consolidated net worth from period to period, as a result of a change in exchange rates, is high.

For any individual financial statement, internally, if the same exchange rate were used to remeasure each and every line item on the individual statement, the income statement and balance sheet, there would be no imbalances resulting from the remeasurement. But if a different exchange rate were used for different line items on an individual statement, an imbalance would result. Different exchange rates are used in remeasuring different line items because translation principles are a complex compromise between historical and current values. The question, then, is what is to be done with the imbalance?

Subsidiary Characterization. Most countries specify the translation method to be used by a foreign subsidiary based on its business operations. For example, a foreign subsidiary's business can be categorized as either an *integrated foreign entity* or a *self-sustaining foreign entity*. An *integrated foreign entity* is one which operates as an extension of the parent company, with cash flows and general business lines that are highly interrelated with those of the parent. A *self-sustaining foreign entity* is one which operates in the local economic environment independent of the parent company. The differentiation is important to the logic of translation. A foreign subsidiary should be valued principally in terms of the currency that is the basis of its economic viability.

It is not unusual for a single company to have both types of foreign subsidiaries, *integrated* and *self-sustaining*. For example, a U.S.-based manufacturer that produces subassemblies in the United States which are then shipped to a Spanish subsidiary for finishing and resale in the European Union would likely characterize the Spanish subsidiary as an *integrated foreign entity*. The dominant currency of economic operation is likely the U.S. dollar. That same U.S. parent may also own an agricultural marketing business in Venezuela that has few cash flows or operations related to the U.S. parent company or U.S. dollar. The Venezuelan subsidiary may source all inputs and sell all products in Venezuelan bolivar. Because the Venezuelan subsidiary's operations are independent of its parent, and its functional currency is the Venezuelan bolivar, it would be classified as a *self-sustaining foreign entity*.

Functional Currency. A foreign subsidiary's *functional currency* is the currency of the primary economic environment in which the subsidiary operates and in which it generates cash flows. In other words, it is the dominant currency used by that foreign subsidiary in its day-to-day operations. It is important to note that the geographic location of a foreign subsidiary and its functional currency may be different. The Singapore subsidiary of a U.S. firm may find that its functional currency is the U.S. dollar (*integrated* subsidiary), the Singapore dollar (*self-sustaining* subsidiary), or a third currency such as the British pound (also a *self-sustaining* subsidiary). The United States, rather than distinguishing a foreign subsidiary as either integrated or self-sustaining, requires that the functional currency of the subsidiary be determined.

Management must evaluate the nature and purpose of each of its individual foreign subsidiaries to determine the appropriate functional currency for each. If a foreign subsidiary of a U.S.-based company is determined to have the U.S. dollar as its functional currency, it is essentially an extension of the parent company (equivalent to the integrated foreign entity designation used by most countries). If, however, the functional currency of the foreign subsidiary is determined to be different from the U.S. dollar, the subsidiary is considered a separate entity from the parent (equivalent to the self-sustaining entity designation).

Translation Methods

Two basic methods for translation are employed worldwide, the *current rate method* and the *temporal method*. Regardless of which method is employed, a translation method must not only designate at what exchange rate individual balance sheet and income statement items are remeasured, but also designate where any imbalance is to be recorded, either in current income or in an equity reserve account in the balance sheet.

Current Rate Method. The current rate method is the most prevalent in the world today. Under this method, all financial statement line items are translated at the "current" exchange rate with few exceptions.

- *Assets and Liabilities.* All assets and liabilities are translated at the current rate of exchange; that is, at the rate of exchange in effect on the balance sheet date.
- *Income Statement Items.* All items, including depreciation and cost of goods sold, are translated at either the actual exchange rate on the dates the various revenues, expenses, gains, and losses were incurred or at an appropriately weighted average exchange rate for the period.
- *Distributions.* Dividends paid are translated at the exchange rate in effect on the date of payment.
- *Equity Items.* Common stock and paid-in capital accounts are translated at historical rates. Year-end retained earnings consist of the original year-beginning retained earnings plus or minus any income or loss for the year.

Gains or losses caused by translation adjustments are *not* included in the calculation of consolidated net income. Rather, translation gains or losses are reported separately and accumulated in a separate equity reserve account (on the consolidated balance sheet) with a title such as "cumulative translation adjustment" (CTA), but it depends on the country. If a foreign subsidiary is later sold or liquidated, translation gains or losses of past years accumulated in the CTA account are reported as one component of the total gain or loss on sale or liquidation. The total gain or loss is reported as part of the net income or loss for the time period in which the sale or liquidation occurs.

Temporal Method. Under the temporal method, specific assets and liabilities are translated at exchange rates consistent with the timing of the item's creation. The *temporal method* assumes that a number of individual line item assets such as inventory and net plant and equipment are restated regularly to reflect market value. If these items were not restated but were instead carried at historical cost, the temporal method becomes the *monetary/nonmonetary method* of translation, a form of translation that is still used by a number of countries today. Line items include the following:

- *Monetary assets* (primarily cash, marketable securities, accounts receivable, and long-term receivables) and *monetary liabilities* (primarily current liabilities and long-term debt). These are translated at current exchange rates. *Nonmonetary assets and liabilities* (primarily inventory and fixed assets) are translated at historical rates.
- *Income Statement Items.* These are translated at the average exchange rate for the period, except for items such as depreciation and cost of goods sold that are directly associated with nonmonetary assets or liabilities. These accounts are translated at their historical rate.
- *Distributions.* Dividends paid are translated at the exchange rate in effect on the date of payment.
- *Equity Items.* Common stock and paid-in capital accounts are translated at historical rates. Year-end retained earnings consist of the original year-beginning retained earnings plus or minus any income or loss for the year, plus or minus any imbalance from translation.

Under the temporal method, gains or losses resulting from remeasurement are carried directly to current consolidated income, and not to equity reserves. Hence, foreign exchange gains and losses arising from the translation process do introduce volatility to consolidated earnings.

U.S. Translation Procedures. The United States differentiates foreign subsidiaries on the basis of functional currency, not subsidiary characterization. A note on terminology: Under U.S. accounting and translation practices, use of the current rate method is termed "translation" while use of the temporal method is termed "remeasurement." The primary principles of U.S. translation are summarized as follows:

- If the financial statements of the foreign subsidiary of a U.S. company are maintained in U.S. dollars, translation is not required.
- If the financial statements of the foreign subsidiary are maintained in the local currency and the local currency is the *functional currency*, they are translated by the *current rate method*.
- If the financial statements of the foreign subsidiary are maintained in the local currency and the U.S. dollar is the *functional currency*, they are remeasured by the *temporal method*.
- If the financial statements of foreign subsidiaries are in the local currency and neither the local currency nor the dollar is the functional currency, then the statements must first be remeasured into the functional currency by the temporal method, and then translated into dollars by the current rate method.
- U.S. translation practices have a special provision for translating statements of foreign subsidiaries operating in *hyperinflation countries*. These are countries where cumulative inflation has been 100% or more over a 3-year period. In this case, the subsidiary must use the temporal method.

A final note: The selection of the functional currency is determined by the economic realities of the subsidiary's operations, and is not a discretionary management decision on preferred procedures or elective outcomes. Since many U.S.-based multinationals have numerous foreign subsidiaries, some dollar-functional and some foreign currency-functional, currency gains and losses may be passing through both current consolidated income and/or accruing in equity reserves.

International Translation Practices. Many of the world's largest industrial countries use International Accounting Standards Committee (IASC), and therefore the same basic translation procedure. A foreign subsidiary is an *integrated foreign entity* or a *self-sustaining foreign entity*; *integrated foreign entities* are typically remeasured using the *temporal method* (or some slight variation thereof); and *self-sustaining foreign entities* are translated at the *current rate method*, also termed the *closing-rate method*.

Trident Corporation's Translation Exposure

Trident Corporation, first introduced in Chapter 1 and shown in Exhibit 10.7, is a U.S.-based corporation, with a U.S. business unit, as well as foreign subsidiaries in both Europe and China. The company is publicly traded and its shares are traded on the New York Stock Exchange (NYSE).

Each subsidiary of Trident—the United States, Europe, and China—will have its own financial statement. Each set of financials will be constructed in the local currency (yuan, dollar, euro), but the subsidiary income statements and balance sheets will also be translated into U.S. dollars, the reporting currency of the company, for consolidation and reporting. As a

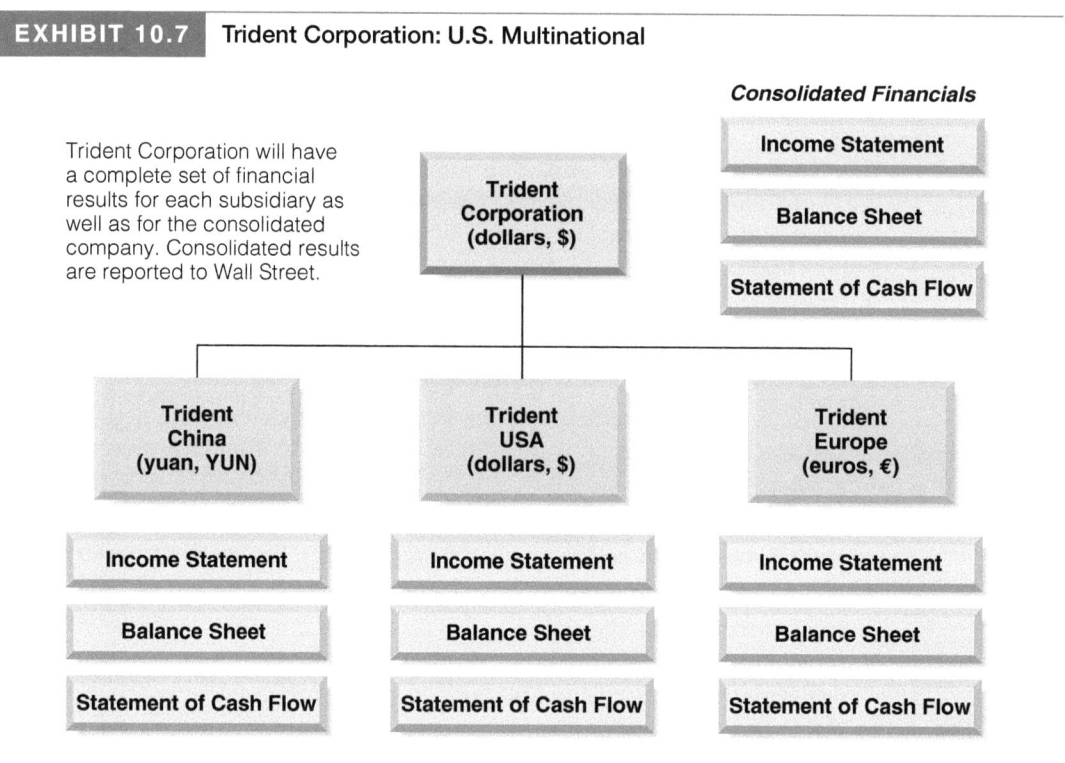

EXHIBIT 10.7 Trident Corporation: U.S. Multinational

Trident Corporation will have a complete set of financial results for each subsidiary as well as for the consolidated company. Consolidated results are reported to Wall Street.

U.S.-based corporation whose shares are traded on the NYSE, it will report all of its final results in U.S. dollars.

Trident Corporation's Translation Exposure: Income

Trident Corporation's sales and earnings by operating unit for 2009 and 2010 are described in Exhibit 10.8.

EXHIBIT 10.8 Trident Corporation, Selected Financial Results, 2009–2010

	Sales (millions, local currency)			Average Exchange Rate ($/€ and YUN/$)			Sales (millions of US$)		
	2009	2010	% Change	2009	2010	% Change	2009	2010	% Change
United States	$280	$300	7.1%	—	—		$280.0	$300.0	7.1%
Europe	€118	€120	1.7%	1.4000	1.3200	−5.71%	$165.2	$158.4	−4.1%
China	YUN600	YUN600	0.0%	6.8300	6.7000	1.94%	$87.8	$89.6	1.9%
Total							$533.0	$548.0	2.8%

	Earnings (millions, local currency)			Average Exchange Rate ($/€ and YUN/$)			Earnings (millions of US$)		
	2009	2010	% Change	2009	2010	% Change	2009	2010	% Change
United States	$28.2	$28.6	1.4%	—	—		$28.2	$28.6	1.4%
Europe	€10.4	€10.5	1.0%	1.4000	1.3200	−5.71%	$14.6	$13.9	−4.8%
China	YUN71.4	YUN71.4	0.0%	6.8300	6.7000	1.94%	$10.5	$10.7	1.9%
Total							$53.2	$53.1	−0.2%

- **Consolidated Sales.** For 2010, the company generated $300 million in sales in its U.S. unit, $158.4 million in its European subsidiary (€120 million at $1.32/€), and $89.6 million in its Chinese subsidiary (YUN600 million at YUN6.70/$). Total global sales for 2010 were $548.0 million. This constituted sales growth of 2.8% over 2009.
- **Consolidated Earnings.** The company's earnings (profits) fell in 2010, dropping to $53.1 million from $53.2 million in 2009. Although not a large fall, Wall Street would not react favorably to a fall in consolidated earnings.

A closer look at the sales and earnings by country, however, yields some interesting insights. Sales and earnings in the U.S. unit rose, sales growing 7.1% and earnings growing 1.4%. Since the U.S. unit makes up more than half of the total company's sales and profits, this is very important. The Chinese subsidiary's sales and earnings were identical in 2009 and 2010 when measured in local currency, Chinese yuan. The Chinese yuan, however, was revalued against the U.S. dollar by the Chinese government, from YUN6.83/$ to YUN6.70/$. The result was the dollar value of both Chinese sales and profits rose.

The European subsidiary's financial results are even more striking. Sales and earnings in Europe in euros grew from 2009 to 2010. Sales grew 1.7% while earnings increased 1.0%. But the euro depreciated against the dollar, falling from $1.40/€ to $1.32/€. This depreciation of 5.7% resulted in the financial results of European operations falling in dollar terms. As a result, Trident's consolidated earnings, as reported dollars, fell in 2010. One can imagine the discussion and debate within Trident, and with the analysts who follow the firm, of the fall in earnings reported to Wall Street.

Translation Exposure: Balance Sheet

Let us continue the example of Trident focusing here on the balance sheet of its European subsidiary. We will illustrate translation by both methods, the temporal method and current rate method, in order to show the very arbitrary nature of a translation gain or loss. The functional currency of Trident Europe is the euro, and the reporting currency of its parent, Trident Corporation, is the U.S. dollar.

Our analysis assumes that plant and equipment and long-term debt were acquired, and common stock issued, by Trident Europe some time in the past when the exchange rate was $1.2760/€. Inventory currently on hand was purchased or manufactured during the immediately prior quarter when the average exchange rate was $1.2180/€. At the close of business on Monday, December 31, 2010, the current spot exchange rate was $1.2000/€. When business reopened on January 3, 2011, after the New Year holiday, the euro had dropped in value versus the dollar to $1.0000/€.

Current Rate Method. Exhibit 10.9 illustrates translation loss using the current rate method. Assets and liabilities on the predepreciation balance sheet are translated at the current exchange rate of $1.2000/€. Capital stock is translated at the historical rate of $1.2760/€, and retained earnings are translated at a composite rate that is equivalent to having each past year's addition to retained earnings translated at the exchange rate in effect in that year.

The sum of retained earnings and the CTA account must "balance" the liabilities and net worth section of the balance sheet with the asset side. For this hypothetical example, we have assumed the two amounts used for the December 31 balance sheet. As shown in Exhibit 10.9, the "just before depreciation" dollar translation reports an accumulated translation loss from prior periods of $136,800. This balance is the cumulative gain or loss from translating euro statements into dollars in prior years.

After the depreciation, Trident Corporation translates assets and liabilities at the new exchange rate of $1.0000/€. Equity accounts, including retained earnings, are translated just as they were before depreciation, and as a result the cumulative translation loss

EXHIBIT 10.9   Trident Europe's Translation Loss after Depreciation of the Euro: Current Rate Method

		December 31, 2010		January 2, 2011	
Assets	In Euros (€)	Exchange Rate (US$/euro)	Translated Accounts (US$)	Exchange Rate (US$/euro)	Translated Accounts (US$)
Cash	1,600,000	1.2000	$ 1,920,000	1.0000	$ 1,600,000
Accounts receivable	3,200,000	1.2000	3,840,000	1.0000	3,200,000
Inventory	2,400,000	1.2000	2,880,000	1.0000	2,400,000
Net plant and equipment	4,800,000	1.2000	5,760,000	1.0000	4,800,000
Total	12,000,000		$14,400,000		$12,000,000
Liabilities and Net Worth					
Accounts payable	800,000	1.2000	$ 960,000	1.0000	$800,000
Short-term bank debt	1,600,000	1.2000	1,920,000	1.0000	1,600,000
Long-term debt	1,600,000	1.2000	1,920,000	1.0000	1,600,000
Common stock	1,800,000	1.2760	2,296,800	1.2760	2,296,800
Retained earnings	6,200,000	1.2000 (a)	7,440,000	1.2000 (b)	7,440,000
Translation adjustment (CTA)	—		$ (136,800)		$(1,736,800)
Total	12,000,000		$14,400,000		$12,000,000

(a) Dollar retained earnings before depreciation are the cumulative sum of additions to retained earnings of all prior years, translated at exchange rates in each year.
(b) Translated into dollars at the same rate as before depreciation of the euro.

increases to $1,736,800. The increase of $1,600,000 in this account (from a cumulative loss of $136,800 to a new cumulative loss of $1,736,800) is the translation loss measured by the current rate method.

This translation loss is a decrease in equity, measured in the parent's reporting currency, of "net exposed assets." An "exposed asset" is an asset whose value drops with the depreciation of the functional currency and rises with an appreciation of that currency. "Net" exposed assets in this context means exposed assets minus exposed liabilities. Net exposed assets are positive (that is, "long") if exposed assets exceed exposed liabilities. They are negative ("short") if exposed assets are smaller than exposed liabilities.

Temporal Method. Translation of the same accounts under the temporal method shows the arbitrary nature of any gain or loss from translation. This is illustrated in Exhibit 10.10. Monetary assets and monetary liabilities in the predepreciation euro balance sheet are translated at the current rate of exchange, but other assets and the equity accounts are translated at their historic rates. For Trident Europe, the historical rate for inventory differs from that for net plant and equipment because inventory was acquired more recently.

Under the temporal method, translation losses are not accumulated in a separate equity account but passed directly through each quarter's income statement. Thus, in the dollar balance sheet translated before depreciation, retained earnings were the cumulative result of earnings from all prior years translated at historical rates in effect each year, plus translation gains or losses from all prior years. In Exhibit 10.10, no translation loss appears in the predepreciation dollar balance sheet because any losses would have been closed to retained earnings.

The effect of the depreciation is to create an immediate translation loss of $160,000. This amount is shown as a separate line item in Exhibit 10.10 in order to focus attention on it for this example. Under the temporal method, this translation loss of $160,000 would pass

EXHIBIT 10.10 Trident Europe's Translation Loss after Depreciation of the Euro: Temporal Method

		December 31, 2010		January 2, 2011	
Assets	In Euros (€)	Exchange Rate (US$/euro)	Translated Accounts (US$)	Exchange Rate (US$/euro)	Translated Accounts (US$)
Cash	1,600,000	1.2000	$ 1,920,000	1.0000	$ 1,600,000
Accounts receivable	3,200,000	1.2000	3,840,000	1.0000	3,200,000
Inventory	2,400,000	1.2180	2,923,200	1.2180	2,923,200
Net plant and equipment	4,800,000	1.2760	6,124,800	1.2760	6,124,800
Total	12,000,000		$14,808,000		$13,848,000
Liabilities and Net Worth					
Accounts payable	800,000	1.2000	$ 960,000	1.0000	$ 800,000
Short-term bank debt	1,600,000	1.2000	1,920,000	1.0000	1,600,000
Long-term debt	1,600,000	1.2000	1,920,000	1.0000	1,600,000
Common stock	1,800,000	1.2760	2,296,800	1.2760	2,296,800
Retained earnings	6,200,000	1.2437 (a)	7,711,200	1.2437 (b)	7,711,200
Translation gain (loss)	—			(c)	$ (160,000)
Total	12,000,000		$14,808,000		$13,848,000

(a) Dollar retained earnings before depreciation are the cumulative sum of additions to retained earnings of all prior years, translated at exchange rates in each year.

(b) Translated into dollars at the same rate as before depreciation of the euro.

(c) Under the temporal method, the translation loss of $160,000 would be closed into retained earnings through the income statement rather than left as a separate line item as shown here. Ending retained earnings would actually be $7,711,200 − $160,000 = $7,551,200.

through the income statement, reducing reported net income and reducing retained earnings. Ending retained earnings would in fact be $7,711,200 minus $160,000, or $7,551,200. Whether gains and losses pass through the income statement under the temporal method depends upon the country.

Managerial Implications

In the case of Trident, the translation loss or gain was larger under the current rate method because inventory and net plant and equipment, as well as all monetary assets, are deemed exposed. When net exposed assets are larger, gains or losses from translation are also larger. If management expects a foreign currency to depreciate, it could minimize translation exposure by reducing net exposed assets. If management anticipates an appreciation of the foreign currency, it should increase net exposed assets to benefit from a gain.

Depending on the accounting method, management might select different assets and liabilities for reduction or increase. Thus, "real" decisions about investing and financing might be dictated by which accounting technique is required, when in fact, the method of reporting should be neutral in its influence on operating and financing decisions.

Managing Translation Exposure

The main technique to minimize translation exposure is called a *balance sheet hedge*. At times, some firms have attempted to hedge translation exposure in the forward market. Such action amounts to speculating in the forward market in the hope that a cash profit will be realized to offset the noncash loss from translation. Success depends on a precise prediction of future exchange rates, for such a hedge will not work over a range of possible future spot rates. In addition, the profit from the forward "hedge" (i.e., speculation) is taxable, but the translation loss does not reduce taxable income.

Balance Sheet Hedge Defined. A balance sheet hedge requires an equal amount of *exposed* foreign currency assets and liabilities on a firm's consolidated balance sheet. If this can be achieved for each foreign currency, net translation exposure will be zero. A change in exchange rates will change the value of exposed liabilities in an equal amount but in a direction opposite to the change in value of exposed assets. If a firm translates by the temporal method, a zero net exposed position is called *monetary balance*. Complete monetary balance cannot be achieved under the current rate method because total assets would have to be matched by an equal amount of debt, but the equity section of the balance sheet must still be translated at historic exchange rates.

The cost of a balance sheet hedge depends on relative borrowing costs. If foreign currency borrowing costs, after adjusting for foreign exchange risk, are higher than parent currency borrowing costs, the balance sheet hedge is costly, and vice versa. Normal operations, however, already require decisions about the magnitude and currency denomination of specific balance sheet accounts. Thus, balance sheet hedges are a compromise in which the denomination of balance sheet accounts is altered, perhaps at a cost in terms of interest expense or operating efficiency, to achieve some degree of foreign exchange protection.

To achieve a balance sheet hedge, Trident Corporation must either 1) reduce exposed euro assets without simultaneously reducing euro liabilities, or 2) increase euro liabilities without simultaneously increasing euro assets. One way to do this is to exchange existing euro cash for dollars. If Trident Europe does not have large euro cash balances, it can borrow euros and exchange the borrowed euros for dollars. Another subsidiary could borrow euros and exchange them for dollars. That is, the essence of the hedge is for the parent or any of its subsidiaries to create euro debt and exchange the proceeds for dollars.

Current Rate Method. Under the current rate method, Trident should borrow as much as €8,000,000. The initial effect of this first step is to increase both an exposed asset (cash) and an exposed liability (notes payable) on the balance sheet of Trident Europe, with no immediate effect on *net* exposed assets. The required follow-up step can take two forms: 1) Trident Europe could exchange the acquired euros for U.S. dollars and hold those dollars itself, or 2) it could transfer the borrowed euros to Trident Corporation, perhaps as a euro dividend or as repayment of intracompany debt. Trident Corporation could then exchange the euros for dollars. In some countries, local monetary authorities will not allow their currency to be so freely exchanged.

Another possibility would be for Trident Corporation or a sister subsidiary to borrow the euros, thus keeping the euro debt entirely off Trident's books. However, the second step is still essential to eliminate euro exposure; the borrowing entity must exchange the euros for dollars or other unexposed assets. Any such borrowing should be coordinated with all other euro borrowings to avoid the possibility that one subsidiary is borrowing euros to reduce translation exposure at the same time as another subsidiary is repaying euro debt. (Note that euros can be "borrowed," by simply delaying repayment of existing euro debt; the goal is to increase euro debt, not borrow in a literal sense.)

Temporal Method. If translation is by the temporal method, the much smaller amount of only €800,000 need be borrowed. As before, Trident Europe could use the proceeds of the loan to acquire U.S. dollars. However, Trident Europe could also use the proceeds to acquire inventory or fixed assets in Europe. Under the temporal method, these assets are not regarded as exposed and do not drop in dollar value when the euro depreciates.

When Is a Balance Sheet Hedge Justified?

If a firm's subsidiary is using the local currency as the functional currency, the following circumstances could justify when to use a balance sheet hedge:

- The foreign subsidiary is about to be liquidated, so that value of its CTA would be realized.
- The firm has debt covenants or bank agreements that state the firm's debt/equity ratios will be maintained within specific limits.
- Management is evaluated on the basis of certain income statement and balance sheet measures that are affected by translation losses or gains.
- The foreign subsidiary is operating in a hyperinflationary environment.

If a firm is using the parent's home currency as the functional currency of the foreign subsidiary, all transaction gains/losses are passed through to the income statement. Hedging this consolidated income to reduce its variability may be important to investors and bond rating agencies.

In the end, accounting exposure is a topic of great concern and complex choices for all multinationals. As demonstrated by *Global Finance in Practice 10.2*, despite the best of intentions and structures, business itself may dictate hedging outcomes.

GLOBAL FINANCE IN PRACTICE 10.2

When Business Dictates Hedging Results

GM Asia, a regional subsidiary of GM Corporation, U.S., held major corporate interests in a variety of countries and companies, including Daewoo Auto. GM had acquired control of Daewoo of South Korea's automobile operations in 2001. The following years had been very good for the Daewoo unit, and by 2009, GM Daewoo was selling automobile components and vehicles to more than 100 countries.

Daewoo's success meant that it had expected sales (receivables) from buyers all over the world. What was even more remarkable was that the global automobile industry now used the U.S. dollar more than ever as its currency of contract for cross-border transactions. This meant that Daewoo did not really have dozens of foreign currencies to manage, just one, the U.S. dollar. So Daewoo of Korea had, in late 2007 and early 2008, entered into a series of *forward exchange contracts*. These currency contracts locked in the Korean won value of the many dollar-denominated receivables the company *expected* to receive from international automobile sales in the coming year. In the eyes of many, this was a conservative and responsible currency hedging policy; that is, until the global financial crisis and the following collapse of global automobile sales.

The problem for Daewoo was not that the Korean won per U.S. dollar exchange rate had moved dramatically; it had not. The problem was that Daewoo's sales, like all other automobile industry participants, had collapsed. The sales had not taken place, and therefore the underlying exposures, the expected receivables in dollars by Daewoo, had not happened. But GM still had to contractually deliver on the forward contracts. It would cost GM Daewoo Won2,300 billion. GM's Daewoo unit was now broke, its equity wiped out by currency hedging gone bad. GM Asia needed money, quickly, and selling interests in its highly successful Chinese and Indian businesses was the only solution.

Summary of Learning Objectives

Distinguish between the three major foreign exchange exposures experienced by firms.

- MNEs encounter three types of currency exposure: transaction exposure; translation exposure, and operating exposure.
- *Transaction exposure* measures gains or losses that arise from the settlement of financial obligations whose terms are stated in a foreign currency.
- *Operating exposure*, also called *economic exposure*, measures the change in the present value of the firm resulting from any change in future operating cash flows of the firm caused by an *unexpected* change in exchange rates.
- *Translation exposure* is the potential for accounting-derived changes in owner's equity to occur because of the need to "translate" foreign currency financial statements of foreign affiliates into a single reporting

currency to prepare worldwide consolidated financial statements.

Analyze the pros and cons of hedging foreign exchange transaction exposure.

- Considerable theoretical debate exists as to whether firms should hedge currency risk. Theoretically, hedging reduces the variability of the cash flows to the firm. It does not increase the cash flows to the firm. In fact, the costs of hedging may potentially lower them.

Examine the alternatives available to a firm to manage a large and significant transaction exposure.

- Transaction exposure can be managed by contractual techniques and certain operating strategies. Contractual hedging techniques include forward, futures, money market, and option hedges.
- The choice of which contractual hedge to use depends on the individual firm's currency risk tolerance and its expectation of the probable movement of exchange rates over the transaction exposure period.
- In general, if an exchange rate is expected to move in a firm's favor, the preferred contractual hedges are probably those which allow it to participate in some up-side potential, but protect it against significant adverse exchange rate movements.
- In general, if the exchange rate is expected to move against the firm, the preferred contractual hedge is one which locks in an exchange rate, such as the forward contract hedge or money market hedge.

Evaluate the institutional practices and concerns of conducting foreign exchange risk management in practice.

- Risk management in practice requires a firm's treasury department to identify its goals. Is treasury a cost center or profit center?
- Treasury must also choose which contractual hedges it wishes to use and what proportion of the currency risk should be hedged. Additionally, treasury must determine whether the firm should buy and/or sell currency options, a strategy that has historically been risky for some firms and banks.

Demonstrate how translation practices result in a foreign exchange exposure for the multinational enterprise.

- Translation exposure results from translating foreign–currency-denominated statements of foreign subsidiaries into the parent's reporting currency so the parent can prepare consolidated financial statements. Translation exposure is the potential for loss or gain from this translation process.

Explain the meaning behind the designation of a foreign subsidiary's "functional currency."

- A foreign subsidiary's functional currency is the currency of the primary economic environment in which the subsidiary operates and in which it generates cash flows. In other words, it is the dominant currency used by that foreign subsidiary in its day-to-day operations.

Illustrate both the theoretical and practical differences between the two primary methods of converting foreign currency denominated financial statements into the reporting currency of the parent company.

- The two basic procedures for translation used in most countries today are the current rate method and the temporal method.
- Technical aspects of translation include questions about when to recognize gains or losses in the income statement, the distinction between functional and reporting currency, and the treatment of subsidiaries in hyperinflation countries.

Compare translation exposure with operating exposure.

- Translation gains and losses can be quite different from operating gains and losses, not only in magnitude but also in sign. Management may need to determine which is of greater significance prior to deciding which exposure is to be managed first.

Analyze the costs and benefits of managing translation exposure.

- The main technique for managing translation exposure is a balance sheet hedge. This calls for having an equal amount of exposed foreign currency assets and liabilities.
- Even if management chooses to follow an active policy of hedging translation exposure, it is nearly impossible to offset both transaction and translation exposure simultaneously. If forced to choose, most managers will protect against transaction losses because these are realized cash losses, rather than protect against translation losses.

MINI-CASE

Banbury Impex (India)[1]

As November 2010 came to a close, CEO Aadesh Lapura of Banbury Impex Private Limited, a textile company in India, sat in his office in solitude looking over his company's financial statements. It looked like 2010 would close with a small growth in sales and a small drop in profits. Although Banbury's profits were positive, the prospects of about 1.5% return on sales were simply not good enough moving forward. He now had two problems: negotiating a short-term prospective sale to a Turkish company, and increasing his overall profitability, which was a larger, long-term problem.

Lapura concluded that overall profitability—or lack thereof—was a result of two price forces. The first was the rapid rise in the price of cotton. A major cost driver in the textiles industry, cotton prices had risen dramatically in 2010. The second issue was clearly the rising value of the Indian rupee (INR) against the U.S. dollar (USD). Banbury's sales were all invoiced in U.S. dollars, and the dollar was falling. Profit margins were down, and he needed to move quickly.

Banbury Fabrics

Founded in 1997, Banbury Impex Private Ltd. was a family-owned enterprise that manufactured and exported apparel fabrics. The company expected sales close to INR 25.6 crores or USD 5.4 million (a *crore*, cr, is a unit in the Indian numbering system equal to 10 million) in 2010 as illustrated in Exhibit 1. Sales were flat, operating income was declining, and—to be honest—prospects bleak.

Banbury's sales were nearly all exported, mainly to the Middle East (50%), South America (30%), and Europe (10%). Banbury's products included a range of blended woven fabrics made from viscose, cotton, and wool. The company operated two weaving units based in India.

The company's sales growth had been slow over the past five years, averaging about 2.5% per year. However, management had been satisfied with 5% margins in 2006 and 2007 in a highly competitive business environment. Cash flows had remained relatively predictable as Lapura had managed foreign exchange risks by using forward contracts. Choosing to invoice all international sales in USD helped provide further stability in mitigating raw material costs as international cotton prices were priced in USD. All things considered, Banbury's profit projections for 2011 looked disastrously low.

The Indian Textile Industry

The Indian textile industry has been a major contributor to Indian GDP over the past several years. After dismantling the quota regime in 2005, the government had hoped

EXHIBIT 1 Banbury Impex Private Ltd—Sales and Income

	2006	2007	2008	2009	Expected 2010	Forecast 2011
Sales (USD)	5,000,000	5,100,000	5,202,000	5,306,040	5,412,161	5,520,404
Average rate (INR/USD)	44.6443	41.7548	43.6976	46.8997	44.8624	45.2500
Sales (INR)	223,221,500	212,949,480	227,314,915	248,851,684	242,802,523	249,798,282
Cost of goods sold (INR)	151,790,620	144,805,646	159,120,441	216,500,965	235,518,447	242,304,333
Cotton Costs	57,680,436	55,026,146	60,465,767	84,435,376	124,824,777	128,421,297
Direct Labor	19,732,781	28,961,129	38,188,906	47,630,212	49,458,874	48,460,867
Weaving Charges	44,019,280	40,545,581	31,824,088	47,630,212	32,972,583	33,922,607
Variable Overhead	30,358,124	20,272,790	28,641,679	36,805,164	28,262,214	31,499,563
Operating Income	71,430,880	68,143,834	68,194,475	32,350,719	7,284,076	7,493,948
Net Income	11,161,075	10,647,474	11,365,746	7,465,551	3,642,038	3,746,974
Return on Sales (% of sales)	5.0%	5.0%	5.0%	3.0%	1.5%	1.5%
COGS (% of Sales)	68%	68%	70%	87%	97%	97%
Cotton Costs (% of COGS)	38%	38%	38%	39%	53%	53%
Direct Labor (% of COGS)	13%	20%	24%	22%	21%	20%

[1]Copyright © 2010 Thunderbird, School of Global Management. All rights reserved. This case was prepared by Kyle Mineo, MBA '10, Saurabh Goyal, MBA '10, and Tim Erion, MBA '10, under the direction of Professor Michael Moffett for the purpose of classroom discussion only, and not to indicate either effective or ineffective management.

for textile exports to hit USD 50 billion by 2012, but as of 2010, they were only USD 22 billion.

The industry was both capital and labor intensive, as well as highly regulated. Companies operated on small margins in a highly competitive marketplace, and the global recession of 2008–2009 had battered the Indian industry even further. Challenges faced by the Indian textile industry included the following:

Rising Raw Material and Labor Costs. The chief raw materials used in textiles were cotton and other natural and poly-based yarn. Erratic monsoons, coupled with increased exports of cotton in the recent years, had caused the price of cotton to rise dramatically. During the past 12 months, cotton prices had increased more than 75%. A variety of government programs and restrictions had also contributed to a growing scarcity of skilled labor in the textile industry.

Competition from China and other Asian Countries. India and China account for the majority of global textile production. Due to low labor costs and strong government support and infrastructure, China had been able to stay ahead in competing with the BRIC (Brazil, Russia, India, and China) countries. As a consequence, Chinese textile products were priced more competitively in the global market, and prevented Indian companies from pushing through any price increases. Indian companies were now suffering falling margins and losing orders to other countries. Much of the Indian low-value market had already shifted to Bangladesh, as costs there were 50% cheaper than in India.

Appreciation of the Rupee. The rupee had grown increasingly volatile in recent years against the dollar, and over the past two years, appreciated by nearly 20%. This appreciation had made countries like Bangladesh and Vietnam more competitive on the global front. In early November, the rupee had risen to INR44/USD, the strongest in more than three years. It now hovered at 45. Further strengthening of the rupee against the dollar would most likely put many Indian textile companies out of business.

The Curious Case of High Cotton Prices
The cotton market had been nothing other than "crazy" recently. The monsoons in India had prompted many farmers to plant more cotton to meet the heightened demand. But, despite growing production, cotton prices had skyrocketed in the past year, reaching $1.50/lb, as illustrated in Exhibit 2. The increased demand from China

EXHIBIT 2 Curious Case of Rising Cotton Prices

and the reduced inventories in the United States had driven the price up.

Although most market analysts continued to argue that cotton prices were abnormally high—and must fall sooner rather than later—they remained high and only seemed to go higher as the soothsayers predicted their fall. What frightened Lapura even more, were the market analysts who were now arguing that cotton prices had moved to a higher level, permanently.

Lapura was considering the use of cotton futures, a practice some of his competitors were already using. A recent check of futures prices had provided him some data on what prices he may be able to lock in now for cotton in the coming year, in U.S. cents per pound: March 2011: 113.09; July 2011: 102.06/; October 2011: 95.03. Although futures would eliminate the risk of further increases in cotton prices, he was still afraid he would be locking in the price at the top.

Currency of Invoice

As an Indian textile exporter, Lapura had never had choice about the currency of invoice—it would be the U.S. dollar. But maybe times had changed? The dollar had been falling against the rupee for some time now (as seen in Exhibit 3), and as a result, the rupees generated from export sales were less and less. The problem was that as an exporter from what the world called an "emerging market," his hard currency choices were the U.S. dollar, the European euro, and the Japanese yen. And the rupee had been strengthening against all of them!

But what might the future bring? All three hard currencies were at record low rates of return—nominal interest rate yields—and not expected to change much in the immediate future. They were under careful watch by their central banks, with all three central banks pumping liquidity into the respective monetary systems following the credit crisis of 2008–2009. The most immediate likelihood was the rise of inflation in all three markets. Unfortunately, that would not help, as a rise in inflation would probably only drive their values down further against the rupee.

The Turkish Sale

Lapura's immediate problem was a $250,000 textile sale he had made to a Turkish customer. The contract allowed him to change the currency of invoice from the Turkish lira to the dollar or euro if he wished, but he had to decide by close of business day.

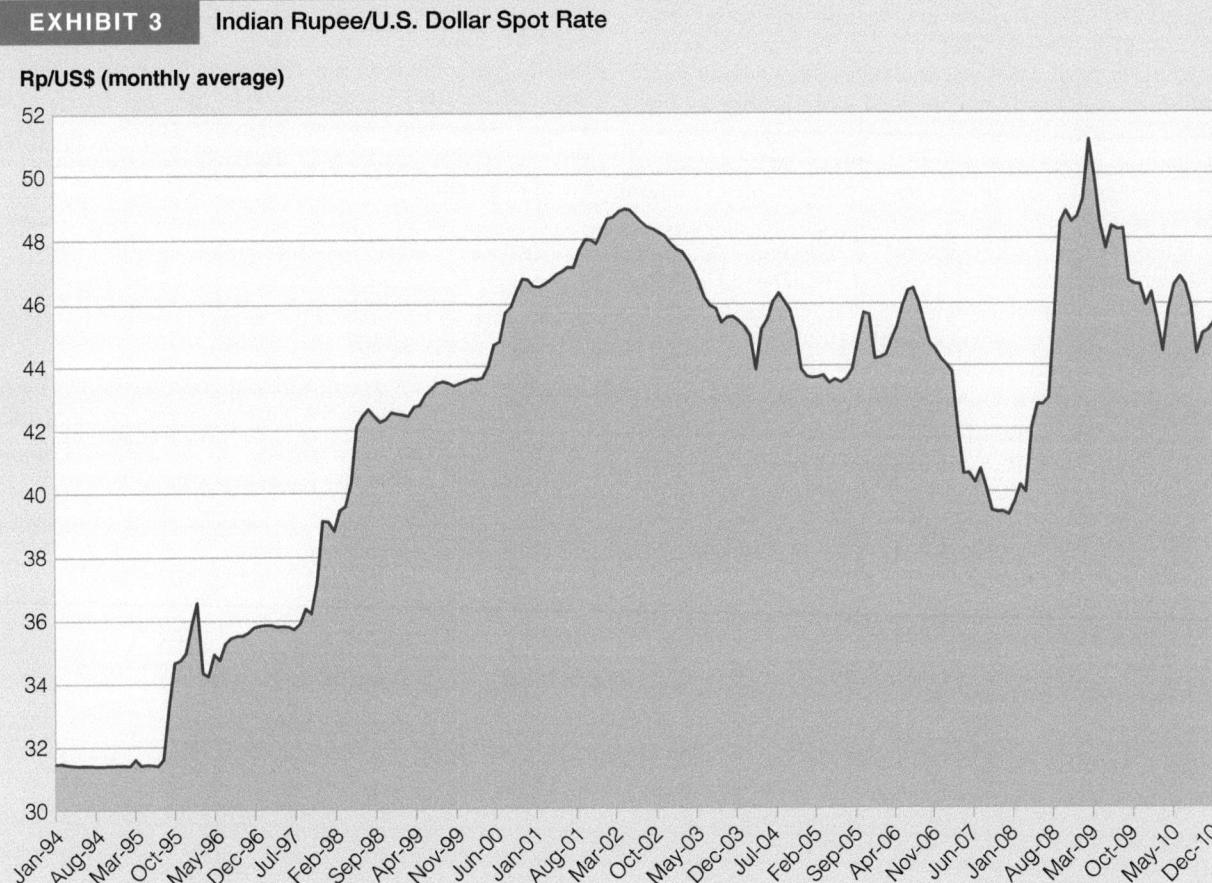

EXHIBIT 3 Indian Rupee/U.S. Dollar Spot Rate

EXHIBIT 4 Forward Rate Quotes

Currency Cross	Symbols	Spot	Bank Quotes on Forward Rates		
			30 days	60 days	90 days
Indian rupees per U.S. dollar	USD/INR	45.8300	46.12	46.70	46.11
Indian rupees per euro	EURO/INR	60.9611	61.70	61.90	62.20
Japanese yen per rupee	INR/JPY	1.8250	1.81	1.81	1.80
Indian rupees per Turkish lira	TRY/INR	30.7192	30.96	30.95	30.87
Turkish lira per U.S. dollar	USD/LIRA	1.4793	1.49	1.48	1.48

Expected settlement on the invoice was January 30, 2011. But regardless of which currency he chose (the rupee not being one of the choices), he still had to decide how to hedge it.

Lapura had collected a variety of forward rates from his local bank for the dollar, euro, and Turkish lira, as listed in Exhibit 4. He eyed the dollar quotes the closest. The forwards would lock him into a rupee rate, which was slightly better than the current spot rate. Of course if the forwards were considered indicators of likely rate movement, they did indicate what he had long hoped for—a rise in the dollar.

He had also considered some form of money market hedge—borrowing Turkish lira against the receivable. Although he had been selling in Turkey for over five years, he had never borrowed there, and only had one bank relationship in Ankara. If he provided sales history to the Turkish bank, he may be able to use his $250,000 receivable as collateral. Domestic loan rates in Turkey for companies with similar credit quality were about 14% according to his bankers. But his bankers also told him that as a small foreign business, the Turkish market would charge him an additional 300 basis point credit spread. But if he did indeed get the money sooner rather than later, domestic Indian deposit rates were averaging a healthy 10.4%.

Currency options had recently become a hedging alternative in India. The National Stock Exchange of India in Mumbai had opened a currency options market in October 2010. With no experience with options, Lapura wondered if an option would provide better protection than a forward contract. The options market, at least for now, was limited to INR/USD options. Although Mr. Lapura could see the upside potential that an options contract might provide, he wondered how much the contract would hurt his slim margins if he had to exercise his contract. Put and call option quotes on the dollar, considered by Mr. Lapura, are listed in Exhibit 5.

Out of Time

Aadesh Lapura picked up his notes and knew it was time to call a family meeting. Times were tough and the family's livelihood was being threatened. Two things needed to be sorted out and quickly. With the last major sale of 2010 on the books—the Turkish sale, he knew he needed to protect the value of this sale from currency losses. Secondly, he needed to find a sustainable path to protecting the business over the long term. With India's continued economic growth, many analysts are forecasting a stronger Indian Rupee versus USD exchange rate into the foreseeable future. Competition was fierce. Lapura wondered how much longer his Indian operations—the livelihood of the family—would be profitable.

CASE QUESTIONS

1. Which factor do you think is more threatening to Banbury's profitability, cotton prices or the rising value of the rupee?
2. Do you believe Lapura should hedge his cotton costs with cotton futures? What would you recommend?
3. Which currency of invoice do you think Lapura should choose for the Turkish sale?
4. What recommendation would you make in terms of hedging the Turkish sale receipts?

EXHIBIT 5 Currency Option Quotes on the USD

Strike Rate (Rupee/USD)	Put Premium (Rupee/USD)	Call Premium (Rupee/USD)
44.00	0.005	1.890
45.25	0.035	0.440

Quotes for 60-day maturity, USD 1000 per contract.
Source: National Stock Exchange of India, nseindia.com.

Questions

1. **Foreign Exchange.** Define the following terms:
   a. *Foreign exchange exposure*
   b. The four types of foreign exchange exposure

2. **Hedging and Currency Risk.** Define the following terms:
   a. *hedging*
   b. *currency risk*

3. **Arguments against Currency Risk Management.** Describe six arguments against a firm pursuing an active currency risk management program?

4. **Arguments for Currency Risk Management.** Describe four arguments in favor of a firm pursuing an active currency risk management program?

5. **Transaction Exposure.** What are the four main types of transactions from which transaction exposure arises?

6. **Life Span of a Transaction Exposure.** Diagram the life span of an exposure arising from selling a product on open account. On the diagram define and show *quotation*, *backlog*, and *billing* exposures.

7. **Borrowing Exposure.** Give an example of a transaction exposure that arises from borrowing in a foreign currency.

8. **Cash Balances.** Explain why foreign currency cash balances do not cause transaction exposure.

9. **Contractual Hedges.** What are the four main contractual instruments used to hedge transaction exposure?

10. **Decision Criteria.** Ultimately, a treasurer must chose among alternative strategies to manage transaction exposure. Explain the two main decision criteria that must be used.

11. **Proportional Hedge.** Many MNEs have established transaction exposure risk management policies that mandate proportional hedging. Explain and give an example of how proportional hedging can be implemented.

12. **By Any Other Name.** What does the word *translation* mean? Why is translation exposure sometimes called *accounting exposure*?

13. **Converting Financial Assets.** In the context of preparing consolidated financial statements, are the words *translate* and *convert* synonyms?

14. **The Central Problem.** What is the central problem involved in consolidating the financial statements of a foreign subsidiary?

15. **Self-Sustaining Subsidiaries.** What is the difference between a *self-sustaining foreign subsidiary* and an *integrated foreign subsidiary*?

16. **Functional Currency.** What is a *functional currency*? What is a nonfunctional currency?

17. **Translating Assets.** What are the major differences in translating assets between the current rate method and the temporal method?

18. **Translating Liabilities.** What are the major differences in translating liabilities between the current rate method and the temporal method?

19. **Hyperinflation.** What is *hyperinflation* and what are the consequences for translating foreign financial statements?

20. **Foreign Exchange Losses by Any Other Name.** What is the primary difference between losses from transaction exposure, operating exposure, and translation exposure?

Problems

1. **P & G India.** Proctor and Gamble's affiliate in India, P & G India, procures much of its toiletries product line from a Japanese company. Because of the shortage of working capital in India, payment terms by Indian importers are typically 180 days or longer. P & G India wishes to hedge an 8.5 million Japanese yen payable. Although options are not available on the Indian rupee (Rs), forward rates are available against the yen. Additionally, a common practice in India is for companies like P & G India to work with a currency agent who will, in this case, lock in the current spot exchange rate in exchange for a 4.85% fee. Using the following exchange rate and interest rate data, recommend a hedging strategy.

2. **Siam Cement.** Siam Cement, the Bangkok-based cement manufacturer, suffered enormous losses with the coming of the Asian crisis in 1997. The company had been pursuing a very aggressive growth strategy in the mid-1990s, taking on massive quantities of foreign–currency-denominated debt (primarily U.S. dollars). When the Thai baht (B) was devalued from its pegged rate of B25.0/$ in July 1997, Siam's interest payments alone were over $900 million on its outstanding dollar debt (with an average interest rate of 8.40% on its U.S. dollar debt at that time). Assuming Siam Cement took out $50 million in debt in June 1997 at 8.40% interest, and had to repay it in one year when the spot exchange rate had stabilized at B42.0/$, what was the foreign exchange loss incurred on the transaction?

3. **BioTron Medical, Inc.** Brent Bush, CFO of a medical device distributor, BioTron Medical, Inc., was approached by a Japanese customer, Numata, with a proposal to pay cash (in yen) for its typical orders of ¥12,500,000 every other month if it were given a 4.5% discount. Numata's current terms are 30 days with no discounts. Using the following quotes and estimated cost of capital for Numata, Bush will compare the proposal with covering yen payments with forward contracts.

Spot rate:	¥111.40/$
30-day forward rate:	¥111.00/$
90-day forward rate:	¥110.40/$
180-day forward rate:	¥109.20/$
Numata's WACC	8.850%
BioTron's WACC	9.200%

4. **Embraer of Brazil.** Embraer of Brazil is one of the two leading global manufacturers of regional jets (Bombardier of Canada is the other). Regional jets are smaller than the traditional civilian airliners produced by Airbus and Boeing, seating between 50 and 100 people on average. Embraer has concluded an agreement with a regional U.S. airline to produce and deliver four aircraft one year from now for $80 million. Although Embraer will be paid in U.S. dollars, it also possesses a currency exposure of inputs—it must pay foreign suppliers 20 million for inputs one year from now (but they will be delivering the subcomponents throughout the year). The current spot rate on the Brazilian real (R$) is R$1.8240/$, but it has been steadily appreciating against the U.S. dollar over the past three years. Forward contracts are difficult to acquire and considered expensive. Citibank Brasil has not explicitly provided Embraer a forward rate quote, but has stated that it will probably be pricing a forward off the current 4.00% U.S. dollar Eurocurrency rate and the 10.50% Brazilian government deposit note.

5. **Vizor Pharmaceuticals.** Vizor Pharmaceuticals, a U.S.-based multinational pharmaceutical company, is evaluating an export sale of its cholesterol-reduction drug with a prospective Indonesian distributor. The purchase would be for 1,650 million Indonesian rupiah (Rp), which at the current spot exchange rate of Rp9,450/$, translates into nearly $175,000. Although not a big sale by company standards, company policy dictates that sales must be settled for at least a minimum gross margin, in this case, a cash settlement of $168,000. The current 90-day forward rate is Rp9,950/$. Although this rate appeared unattractive, Vizor had to contact several major banks before even finding a forward quote on the rupiah. The consensus of currency forecasters at the moment, however, is that the rupiah will hold relatively steady, possibly falling to Rp9,400/$ over the coming 90 to 120 days. Analyze the prospective sale and make a hedging recommendation.

6. **Mattel Toys.** Mattel is a U.S.-based company whose sales are roughly two-thirds in dollars (Asia and the Americas) and one-third in euros (Europe). In September, Mattel delivers a large shipment of toys (primarily Barbies and Hot Wheels) to a major distributor in Antwerp. The receivable, €30 million, is due in 90 days, standard terms for the toy industry in Europe. Mattel's treasury team has collected the following currency and market quotes. The company's foreign exchange advisors believe the euro will be at about $1.4200/€ in 90 days. Mattel's management does not use currency options in currency risk management activities. Advise Mattel on which hedging alternative is probably preferable.

Current spot rate ($/€)	$1.4158
Credit Suisse 90-day forward rate ($/€)	$1.4172
Barclays 90-day forward rate ($/€)	$1.4195
Mattel Toys WACC ($)	9.600%
90-day eurodollar interest rate	4.000%
90-day euro interest rate	3.885%
90-day eurodollar borrowing rate	5.000%
90-day euro borrowing rate	5.000%

7. **Bobcat Company.** Bobcat Company, U.S.-based manufacturer of industrial equipment, just purchased a Korean company that produces plastic nuts and bolts for heavy equipment. The purchase price was Won7,500 million. Won1,000 million has already been paid, and the remaining Won6,500 million is due in six months. The current spot rate is Won1,110/$, and the 6-month forward rate is Won1,175/$. The 6-month Korean won interest rate is 16% per annum, the 6-month U.S. dollar rate is 4% per annum. Bobcat can invest at these interest rates, or borrow at 2% per annum above those rates. A 6-month call option on won with a 1200/$ strike rate has a 3.0% premium, while the 6-month put option at the same strike rate has a 2.4% premium.

Bobcat can invest at the rates given above, or borrow at 2% per annum above those rates. Bobcat's weighted average cost of capital is 10%. Compare alternate ways that Bobcat might deal with its foreign exchange exposure. What do you recommend and why?

8. **Aquatech.** Aquatech is a U.S.-based company that manufactures, sells, and installs water purification equipment. On April 11, the company sold a system to the City of Nagasaki, Japan, for installation in Nagasaki's famous Glover Gardens (where Puccini's *Madame Butterfly* waited for the return of Lt. Pinkerton). The sale was priced in yen at ¥20,000,000, with payment due in three months.

Spot exchange rate:	¥118.255/$ (closing mid-rates)
1-month forward rate:	¥117.760/$, a 5.04% p.a. premium
3-month forward:	¥116.830/$, a 4.88% p.a. premium
1-year forward:	¥112.450/$, a 5.16% p.a. premium

Money Rates	United States	Japan	Differential
One month	4.8750%	0.09375%	4.78125%
Three months	4.9375%	0.09375%	4.84375%
Twelve months	5.1875%	0.31250%	4.87500%

Note: The interest rate differentials vary slightly from the forward discounts on the yen because of time differences for the quotes. The spot ¥118.255/$, for example, is a mid-point range. On April 11, the spot yen traded in London from ¥118.30/$ to ¥117.550/$.

Additional information: Aquatech's Japanese competitors are currently borrowing yen from Japanese banks at a spread of two percentage points above the Japanese money rate. Aquatech's weighted average cost of capital is 16%, and the company wishes to protect the dollar value of this receivable.

3-month options from Kyushu Bank:
- Call option on ¥20,000,000 at exercise price of ¥118.00/$: a 1% premium.
- Put option on ¥20,000,000, at exercise price of ¥118.00/$: a 3% premium.

a. What are the costs and benefits of alternative hedges? Which would you recommend, and why?
b. What is the break-even reinvestment rate when comparing forward and money market alternatives?

9. **Compass Rose.** Compass Rose, Ltd., a Canadian manufacturer of raincoats, does not selectively hedge its transaction exposure. Instead, if the date of the transaction is known with certainty, all foreign currency-denominated cash flows must utilize the following mandatory forward cover formula:

Compass Rose's Manadatory Forward Cover	0–90 days	91–180 days	>180 days
Paying the points forward	75%	60%	50%
Receiving the points forward	100%	90%	50%

Compass Rose expects to receive multiple payments in Danish kroner over the next year. DKr 3,000,000 is due in 90 days; DKr 2,000,000 is due in 180 days; and DKr 1,000,000 is due in one year. Using the following spot and forward exchange rates, what would be the amount of forward cover required by company policy by period?

10. **Pupule Travel.** Pupule Travel, a Honolulu, Hawaii–based 100% privately owned travel company, has signed an agreement to acquire a 50% ownership share of Taichung Travel, a Taiwan–based privately owned travel agency specializing in servicing inbound customers from the United States and Canada. The acquisition price is 7 million Taiwan dollars (T$7,000,000) payable in cash in three months.

Thomas Carson, Pupule Travel's owner, believes the Taiwan dollar will either remain stable or decline a little over the next three months. At the present spot rate of T$35/$, the amount of cash required is only $200,000, but even this relatively modest amount will need to be borrowed personally by Thomas Carson. Taiwanese interest-bearing deposits by nonresidents are regulated by the government, and are currently set at 1.5% per year. He has a credit line with Bank of Hawaii for $200,000 with a current borrowing interest rate of 8% per year. He does not believe that he can calculate a credible weighted average cost of capital since he has no stock outstanding and his competitors are all also privately owned without disclosure of their financial results. Since the acquisition would use up all his available credit, he wonders if he should hedge this transaction exposure. He has quotes from Bank of Hawaii shown in the following table:

Spot rate (T$/$)	33.40
3-month forward rate (T$/$)	32.40
3-month Taiwan dollar deposit rate	1.500%
3-month dollar borrowing rate	6.500%
3-month call option on T$	not available

Analyze the costs and risks of each alternative, and then make a recommendation as to which alternative Thomas Carson should choose.

11. **Chronos Time Pieces.** Chronos Time Pieces of Boston exports watches to many countries, selling in local currencies to stores and distributors. Chronos prides itself on being financially conservative. At least 70% of each individual transaction exposure is hedged, mostly in the forward market, but occasionally with options. Chronos's foreign exchange policy is such that the 70%

hedge may be increased up to a 120% hedge if devaluation or depreciation appears imminent. Chronos has just shipped to its major North American distributor. It has issued a 90-day invoice to its buyer for €1,560,000. The current spot rate is $1.2224/€, the 90-day forward rate is $1.2270/€. Chronos's treasurer, Manny Hernandez, has a very good track record in predicting exchange rate movements. He currently believes the euro will weaken against the dollar in the coming 90 to 120 days, possibly to around $1.16/€.

12. **Lucky 13.** Lucky 13 Jeans of San Antonio, Texas, is completing a new assembly plant near Guatemala City. A final construction payment of Q8,400,000 is due in six months. ("Q" is the symbol for Guatemalan quetzals.) Lucky 13 uses 20% per annum as its weighted average cost of capital. Today's foreign exchange and interest rate quotations are as follows:

Construction payment due in 6-months (A/P, quetzals)	8,400,000
Present spot rate (quetzals/$)	7.0000
6-month forward rate (quetzals/$)	7.1000
Guatemalan 6-month interest rate (per annum)	14.000%
U.S. dollar 6-month interest rate (per annum)	6.000%
Lucky 13's weighted average cost of capital (WACC)	20.000%

Lucky 13's treasury manager, concerned about the Guatemalan economy, wonders if Lucky 13 should be hedging its foreign exchange risk. The manager's own forecast is as follows:

Expected spot rate in 6-months (quetzals/$):

Highest expected rate (reflecting a significant devaluation)	8.0000
Expected rate	7.3000
Lowest expected rate (reflecting a strengthening of the quetzal)	6.4000

What realistic alternatives are available to Lucky 13 for making payments? Which method would you select and why?

13. **Burton Manufacturing.** Jason Stedman is the director of finance for Burton Manufacturing, a U.S.-based manufacturer of handheld computer systems inventory management. Burton's system combines a low-cost active bar code used on inventory (the bar code tags emit an extremely low-grade radio frequency) with custom designed hardware and software which tracks the low-grade emissions for inventory control. Burton has completed the sale of a bar code system to a British firm, Pegg Metropolitan (UK), for a total payment of £1,000,000. The exchange rates shown at the bottom of this page were available to Burton on the following dates corresponding to the events of this specific export sale. Assume each month is 30 days.

14. **Micca Metals, Inc.** Micca Metals, Inc. is a specialty materials and metals company located in Detroit, Michigan. The company specializes in specific precious metals and materials which are used in a variety of pigment applications in many other industries including cosmetics, appliances, and a variety of high tinsel metal fabricating equipment. Micca just purchased a shipment of phosphates from Morocco for 6,000,000, dirhams, payable in six months. Micca's cost of capital is 8.600%.

Six-month call options on 6,000,000 dirhams at an exercise price of 10.00 dirhams per dollar are available from Bank Al-Maghrub at a premium of 2%. Six-month put options on 6,000,000 dirhams at an exercise price of 10.00 dirhams per dollar are available at a premium of 3%. Compare and contrast alternative ways that Micca might hedge its foreign exchange transaction exposure. What is your recommendation?

Assumptions	Values
Shipment of phosphates from Morocco, Moroccan dirhams	6,000,000
Micca's cost of capital (WACC)	14.000%
Spot exchange rate, dirhams/$	10.00
6-month forward rate, dirhams/$	10.40

15. **Maria Gonzalez and Trident.** Trident—the U.S.-based company discussed in this chapter, has concluded a second larger sale of telecommunications equipment

Date	Event	Spot Rate ($/£)	Forward Rate ($/£)	Days Forward of Forward Rate
February 1	Price quotation for Pegg	1.7850	1.7771	210
March 1	Contract signed for sale	1.7465	1.7381	180
	Contract amount, pounds	£1,000,000		
June 1	Product shipped to Pegg	1.7689	1.7602	90
August 1	Product received by Pegg	1.7840	1.7811	30
September 1	Grand Met makes payment	1.7290	—	—

to Regency (U.K.). Total payment of £3,000,000 is due in 90 days. Maria Gonzalez has also learned that Trident will only be able to borrow in the United Kingdom at 14% per annum (due to credit concerns of the British banks). Given the following exchange rates and interest rates, what transaction exposure hedge is now in Trident's best interest?

Assumptions	Value
90-day A/R in pounds	£3,000,000.00
Spot rate, US$ per pound ($/£)	$1.7620
90-day forward rate, US$ per pound ($/£)	$1.7550
3-month U.S. dollar investment rate	6.000%
3-month U.S. dollar borrowing rate	8.000%
3-month U.K. investment interest rate	8.000%
3-month U.K. borrowing interest rate	14.000%
Put options on the British pound: Strike rates, US$/pound ($/£)	
Strike rate ($/£)	$1.75
Put option premium	1.500%
Strike rate ($/£)	$1.71
Put option premium	1.000%
Trident's WACC	12.000%
Maria Gonzalez's expected spot rate in 90-day, US$ per pound ($/£)	$1.7850

16. **Larkin Hydraulics.** On May 1, Larkin Hydraulics, a wholly owned subsidiary of Caterpillar (U.S.), sold a 12-megawatt compression turbine to Rebecke-Terwilleger Company of the Netherlands for €4,000,000, payable €2,000,000 on August 1 and €2,000,000 on November 1. Larkin derived its price quote of €4,000,000 on April 1 by dividing its normal U.S. dollar sales price of $4,320,000 by the then current spot rate of $1.0800/€.

By the time the order was received and booked on May 1, the euro had strengthened to $1.1000/€, so the sale was in fact worth €4,000,000 × $1.1000/€ = $4,400,000. Larkin had already gained an extra $80,000 from favorable exchange rate movements. Nevertheless, Larkin's director of finance now wondered if the firm should hedge against a reversal of the recent trend of the euro. Four approaches were possible:

1. Hedge in the forward market: The 3-month forward exchange quote was $1.1060/€ and the 6-month forward quote was $1.1130/€.
2. Hedge in the money market: Larkin could borrow euros from the Frankfurt branch of its U.S. bank at 8.00% per annum.
3. Hedge with foreign currency options: August put options were available at strike price of $1.1000/€ for a premium of 2.0% per contract, and November put options were available at $1.1000/€ for a premium of 1.2%. August call options at $1.1000/€ could be purchased for a premium of 3.0%, and November call options at $1.1000/€ were available at a 2.6% premium.
4. Do nothing: Larkin could wait until the sales proceeds were received in August and November, hope the recent strengthening of the euro would continue, and sell the euros received for dollars in the spot market.

Larkin estimates the cost of equity capital to be 12% per annum. As a small firm, Larkin Hydraulics is unable to raise funds with long-term debt. U.S. T-bills yield 3.6% per annum. What should Larkin do?

17. **Tristan Narvaja, S.A. (A).** Tristan Narvaja, S.A., is the Uruguayan subsidiary of a U.S. manufacturing company. Its balance sheet for January 1 follows. The January 1 exchange rate between the U.S. dollar and the peso Uruguayo ($U) is $U20/$. Determine Tristan Narvaja's contribution to the translation exposure of its parent on January 1, using the current rate method.

Balance Sheet (thousands of pesos Uruguayo, $U)

Assets	January 1	Exchange Rate (U/US)
Cash	60,000	20.00
Accounts receivable	120,000	20.00
Inventory	120,000	20.00
Net plant and equipment	240,000	20.00
	540,000	
Liabilities and Net Worth		
Current liabilities	30,000	20.00
Long-term debt	90,000	20.00
Capital stock	300,000	15.00
Retained earnings	120,000	15.00
	540,000	

18. **Tristan Narvaja, S.A. (B).** Using the same balance sheet as in problem 17, calculate Tristan Narvaja's contribution to its parent's translation loss if the exchange rate on December 31 is $U22/$. Assume all peso accounts remain as they were at the beginning of the year.

19. **Tristan Narvaja, S.A. (C).** Calculate Tristan Narvaja's contribution to its parent's translation gain or loss using the current rate method if the exchange rate on December 31 is $U12/$. Assume all peso accounts remain as they were at the beginning of the year.

Balance Sheet of Cairo Ingot, Ltd.

		Before Exchange Rate Change	
Assets	Egyptian Pounds Statement	Exchange Rate (Egyptian £/UK£)	Translated Accounts British Pounds
Cash	16,500,000	5.50	£ 3,000,000.00
Accounts receivable	33,000,000	5.50	6,000,000
Inventory	49,500,000	5.50	9,000,000
Net plant and equipment	66,000,000	5.50	12,000,000
Total	165,000,000		£30,000,000.00
Liabilities and Net Worth			
Accounts payable	24,750,000	5.50	£ 4,500,000.00
Long-term debt	49,500,000	5.50	9,000,000
Invested capital	90,750,000	5.50	16,500,000
CTA account (loss)	—		—
Total	165,000,000		£30,000,000.00

20. **Cairo Ingot, Ltd.** Cairo Ingot, Ltd., is the Egyptian subsidiary of Trans-Mediterranean Aluminum, a British multinational that fashions automobile engine blocks from aluminum. Trans-Mediterranean's home reporting currency is the British pound. Cairo Ingot's December 31 balance sheet is shown at the top of this page. At the date of this balance sheet, the exchange rate between Egyptian pounds and British pounds sterling was £E5.50/UK£.
    a. What is Cairo Ingot's contribution to the translation exposure of Trans-Mediterranean on December 31, using the current rate method?
    b. Calculate the translation exposure loss to Trans-Mediterranean if the exchange rate at the end of the following quarter is £E6.00/£. Assume all balance sheet accounts are the same at the end of the quarter as they were at the beginning.

Internet Exercises

1. **Current Volatilities.** You wish to price your own options, but you need current volatilities on the euro, British pound, and Japanese yen. Using the following Web sites, collect spot rates and volatilities in order to price forward at-the-money put options for your option pricing analysis.

Federal Reserve Bank of New York	www.ny.frb.org/statistics
RatesFX.com	www.ratesfx.com/

2. **Hedging Objectives.** All multinational companies will state the goals and objectives of their currency risk management activities in their annual reports. Beginning with the following firms, collect samples of corporate "why hedge?" discussions for a contrast and comparison discussion.

Nestlé	www.nestle.com
Disney	www.disney.com
Nokia	www.nokia.com
BP	www.bp.com

3. **Changing Translation Practices: FASB.** The Financial Accounting Standards Board promulgates standard practices for the reporting of financial results by companies in the United States. It also, however, often leads the way in the development of new practices and emerging issues around the world. One major issue today is the valuation and reporting of financial derivatives and derivative agreements by firms. Use the FASB's home page and the Web pages of several of the major accounting firms and other interest groups around the world to see current proposed accounting standards and the current state of reaction to the proposed standards.

FASB home page	raw.rutgers.edu/raw/fasb/
Treasury Management Association	www.tma.org/

Operating Exposure

The essence of risk management lies in maximizing the areas where we have some control over the outcome while minimizing the areas where we have absolutely no control over the outcome and the linkage between effect and cause is hidden from us. —Peter Bernstein, *Against the Gods*, 1996.

LEARNING OBJECTIVES

◆ Examine how operating exposure arises through unexpected changes in both operating and financing cash flows.

◆ Analyze the sequence of how unexpected exchange rate changes alter the economic performance of a business unit through the sequence of volume, price, cost, and other key variable changes.

◆ Evaluate the strategic alternatives to managing operating exposure.

◆ Detail the proactive policies available to firms for managing operating exposure.

This chapter examines the economic exposure of a firm over time, what we term *operating exposure*. *Operating exposure*, also referred to as *economic exposure, competitive exposure,* or *strategic exposure*, measures any change in the present value of a firm resulting from changes in future operating cash flows caused by any unexpected change in exchange rates. Operating exposure analysis assesses the impact of changing exchange rates on a firm's own operations over coming months and years and on its competitive position vis-à-vis other firms. The goal is to identify strategic moves or operating techniques the firm might wish to adopt to enhance its value in the face of unexpected exchange rate changes.

Operating exposure and transaction exposure are related in that they both deal with future cash flows. They differ in terms of which cash flows management considers and why those cash flows change when exchange rates change. We begin by revisiting the structure of our firm, Trident Corporation, and how its structure dictates its likely operating exposure. The chapter continues with a series of strategies and structures used in the management of operating exposure, and concludes with a Mini-Case, ***Toyota's European Operating Exposure***.

Trident Corporation: A Multinational's Operating Exposure

The structure and operations of a multinational company determine the nature of its operating exposure. Trident Corporation's basic structure and currencies of operation are described in Exhibit 11.1. As a U.S.-based publicly traded company, ultimately all financial metrics and values have to be consolidated and expressed in U.S. dollars. That accounting exposure of the firm was described in Chapter 10. Operationally, however, the functional

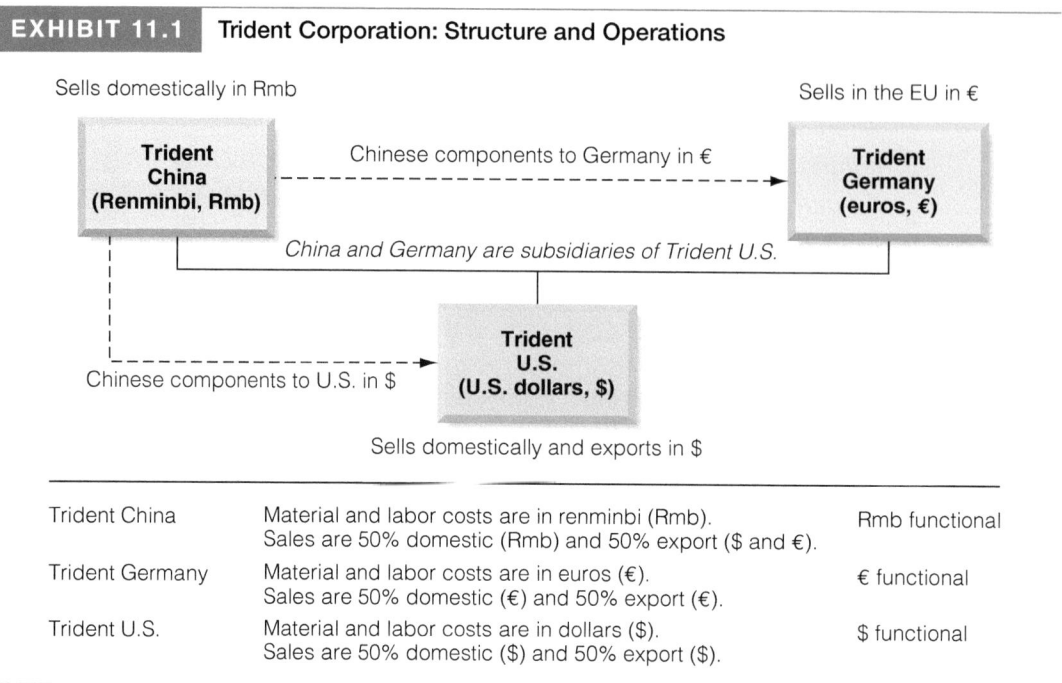

currencies of the individual subsidiaries in combination determine the overall operating exposure of the firm in total.

The net operating cash flows of any individual business unit reflects where and to whom it sells against from whom and from where it buys:

$$\begin{array}{c} \text{Net operating} \\ \text{cash flow} \end{array} = \begin{array}{c} \text{Receivables over time} \\ \text{from sales} \end{array} - \begin{array}{c} \text{Payables over time} \\ \text{for inputs and labor} \end{array}$$

For example, Trident Germany sells locally and exports, but all sales are invoiced in euros. All operating cash inflows are therefore in its home currency, the euro. On the cost side, labor costs are local and in euros, as well as many of its material input purchases being local and in euros. It also purchases components from Trident China, but those too are invoiced in euros. Trident Germany is clearly euro-functional, with all cash inflows and outflows in euros.

Trident Corporation U.S. is similar in structure to Trident Germany. All cash inflows from sales, domestic and international, are in U.S. dollars. All costs, labor and materials, sourced domestically and internationally, are invoiced in U.S. dollars. This includes purchases from Trident China. Trident U.S. is therefore obviously dollar functional.

Trident China is more complex. Cash outflows, labor and materials, are all domestic and paid in Chinese renminbi. Cash inflows, however, are generated across three different currencies as the company sells locally in renminbi, as well as exporting to both Germany in euros and the United States in dollars. On net, although having some cash inflows in both dollars and euros, the dominant currency cash flow is the renminbi.

Static versus Dynamic Operating Exposure

Measuring the operating exposure of a firm like Trident requires forecasting and analyzing all the firm's future individual transaction exposures together with the future exposures of all the firm's competitors and potential competitors worldwide. Exchange rate changes in the short term affect current and immediate contracts, generally termed *transactions*. But over the longer term, as prices change and competitors react, the more fundamental economic and competitive drivers of the business may alter all cash flows of all units. A simple example will clarify the point.

Assume Trident's three business units are roughly equal in size. In 2012, the dollar starts depreciating in the market against the euro at the same time the Chinese government continues the gradual revaluation of the renminbi. The operating exposure of each individual business unit then needs to be examined statically (transaction exposures) and dynamically (future business transactions not yet contracted for).

- ◆ **Trident China.** Sales in U.S. dollars will result in fewer renminbi proceeds in the immediate period. Sales in euros may stay roughly the same in renminbi proceeds depending on the relative movement of the Rmb against the euro. General profitability will fall in the short run. In the longer term, depending on the markets for its products and the nature of competition, it may need to raise the price it sells its export products for, even to its U.S. parent company.
- ◆ **Trident Germany.** Since this business unit's cash inflows and outflows are all in euros, there is no immediate transaction exposure or change. It may suffer some rising input costs in the future if Trident China does indeed eventually push through price increases of component sales. Profitability is unaffected in the short term.
- ◆ **Trident U.S.** Like Trident Germany, Trident U.S. has all local currency cash inflows and outflows. A fall in the value of the dollar will have no immediate (transaction exposure) impact, but may change over the medium to long term as input costs from China may rise over time as the Chinese subsidiary tries to regain prior profit margins. But, like Germany, short-term profitability is unaffected.

The net result for Trident is possibly a fall in the total profitability of the firm in the short term, primarily from the fall in profits of the Chinese subsidiary; that is, the short-term transaction/operating exposure impact. The fall in the dollar in the short term, however, is likely to have a positive impact on translation exposure, as profits and earnings in renminbi and euros translate into more and more dollars. Wall Street would likely like the results in the immediate quarter or two.

Operating and Financing Cash Flows

The cash flows of the MNE can be divided into *operating cash flows* and *financing cash flows*. Operating cash flows arise from intercompany (between unrelated companies) and intracompany (between units of the same company) receivables and payables, rent and lease payments for the use of facilities and equipment, royalty and license fees for the use of technology and intellectual property, and assorted management fees for services provided.

Financing cash flows are payments for the use of intercompany and intracompany loans (principal and interest) and stockholder equity (new equity investments and dividends). Each of these cash flows can occur at different time intervals, in different amounts, and in different currencies of denomination, and each has a different predictability of occurrence. We summarize cash flow possibilities in Exhibit 11.2 for Trident China and Trident U.S.

Expected versus Unexpected Changes in Cash Flow

Operating exposure is far more important for the long-run health of a business than changes caused by transaction or translation exposure. However, operating exposure is inevitably subjective because it depends on estimates of future cash flow changes over an

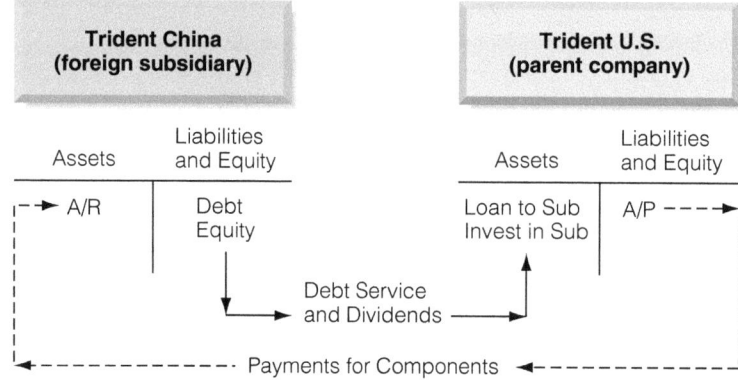

EXHIBIT 11.2 Financial and Operating Cash Flows between Parent and Subsidiary

arbitrary time horizon. Thus, it does not spring from the accounting process but rather from the operating analysis. Planning for operating exposure is a total management responsibility depending upon the interaction of strategies in finance, marketing, purchasing, and production.

An *expected* change in foreign exchange rates is not included in the definition of operating exposure, because both management and investors should have factored this information into their evaluation of anticipated operating results and market value.

- From a management perspective, budgeted financial statements already reflect information about the effect of an expected change in exchange rates.
- From a debt service perspective, expected cash flow to amortize debt should already reflect the international Fisher effect. The level of expected interest and principal repayment should be a function of expected exchange rates rather than existing spot rates.
- From an investor's perspective, if the foreign exchange market is efficient, information about expected changes in exchange rates should be widely known and thus reflected in a firm's market value. Only unexpected changes in exchange rates, or an inefficient foreign exchange market, should cause market value to change.
- From a broader macroeconomic perspective, operating exposure is not just the sensitivity of a firm's future cash flows to unexpected changes in foreign exchange rates, but also its sensitivity to other key macroeconomic variables. This factor has been labeled as *macroeconomic uncertainty*.

Chapter 7 described the parity relationships among exchange rates, interest rates, and inflation rates. However, these variables are often in disequilibrium with one another. Therefore, unexpected changes in interest rates and inflation rates could also have a simultaneous but differential impact on future cash flows. As discussed in *Global Finance in Practice 11.1*, fixed exchange rates obviously add an additional complexity to managing future cash flows and general corporate currency risk.

GLOBAL FINANCE IN PRACTICE 11.1

Do Fixed Exchange Rates Increase Corporate Currency Risk in Emerging Markets?

It has long been argued that when firms know the exchange rate cannot or will not change, they will conduct their business as if currency exposure—at least against the major currency(s) which their home currency is fixed—will not occur. As one study of currency risk in India noted: "These results support the hypothesis that pegged exchange rates induce moral hazard and increase financial fragility."[1]

Moral hazard is the concept that a party, an agent, an individual, or a firm will take on more risk when it either knows or believes that a second party will handle, accommodate, or insure the negative repercussions of the firm's risk-taking decisions. In other words, a firm may take more risk when it knows that someone else will pick up the tab. In a fixed or managed exchange rate regime, that party is represented by the central bank which tells all those undertaking cross-currency contractual obligations and exposures that the exchange rate will not change.

Although there is still scant research on this specific practice for most of the emerging markets, it could prove to be a significant issue in the years to come as many emerging markets become the object of major new international capital flows—the so-called globalization of finance. If commercial firms in those markets are not aware of the risk which the country itself may be taking in opening the door to international capital flows, both in and out of the country, and the impact they may have on the country's exchange rate, they may be in for a wild ride in the immediate years to come.

[1] "Does the currency regime shape unhedged currency exposure?," by Ila Patnaik and Ajay Shah, *Journal of International Money and Finance*, 29, 2010, pp. 760–769. See also "Moral Hazard, Financial Crises, and the Choice of Exchange Rate Regimes," Apanard Angkinand and Thomas Willett, June 2006; and "Exchange-Rate Regimes for Emerging Markets: Moral Hazard and International Borrowing," by Ronald I. McKinnon and Huw Pill, Oxford Review of Economic Policy, Vol. 15, No. 3, 1999.

Measuring Operating Exposure

An unexpected change in exchange rates impacts a firm's expected cash flows at four levels, depending on the time horizon used, as summarized in Exhibit 11.3.

1. **Short Run.** The first-level impact is on expected cash flows in the 1-year operating budget. The gain or loss depends on the currency of denomination of expected cash flows. These are both existing transaction exposures and anticipated exposures. The currency of denomination cannot be changed for existing obligations, or even for implied obligations such as purchase or sales commitments. Apart from real or implied obligations, in the short run it is difficult to change sales prices or renegotiate factor costs. Therefore, realized cash flows will differ from those expected in the budget. However, as time passes, prices and costs can be changed to reflect the new competitive realities caused by a change in exchange rates.

EXHIBIT 11.3 Operating Exposure's Phases of Adjustment and Response

Phase	Time	Price Changes	Volume Changes	Structural Changes
Short Run	Less than one year	Prices are fixed/contracted	Volumes are contracted	No competitive market changes
Medium Run: Equilibrium	Two to five years	Complete pass-through of exchange rate changes	Volumes begin a partial response to prices	Existing competitors begin partial responses
Medium Run: Disequilibrium	Two to five years	Partial pass-through of exchange rate changes	Volumes begin a partial response to prices	Existing competitors begin partial responses
Long Run	More than five years	Completely flexible	Completely flexible	Threat of new entrants and changing competitor responses

2. **Medium Run: Equilibrium.** The second-level impact is on expected medium-run cash flows, such as those expressed in 2- to 5-year budgets, assuming parity conditions hold among foreign exchange rates, national inflation rates, and national interest rates. Under equilibrium conditions, the firm should be able to adjust prices and factor costs over time to maintain the expected level of cash flows. In this case, the currency of denomination of expected cash flows is not as important as the countries in which cash flows originate. National monetary, fiscal, and balance of payments policies determine whether equilibrium conditions will exist and whether firms will be allowed to adjust prices and costs.

    If equilibrium exists continuously, and a firm is free to adjust its prices and costs to maintain its expected competitive position, its operating exposure may be zero. Its expected cash flows would be realized and therefore its market value unchanged since the exchange rate change was anticipated. However, it is also possible that equilibrium conditions exist but the firm is unwilling or unable to adjust operations to the new competitive environment. In such a case, the firm would experience operating exposure because its realized cash flows would differ from expected cash flows. As a result, its market value might also be altered.

3. **Medium Run: Disequilibrium.** The third-level impact is on expected medium-run cash flows assuming disequilibrium conditions. In this case, the firm may not be able to adjust prices and costs to reflect the new competitive realities caused by a change in exchange rates. The primary problem may be the reactions of existing competitors. The firm's realized cash flows will differ from its expected cash flows. The firm's market value may change because of the unanticipated results.

4. **Long Run.** The fourth-level impact is on expected long-run cash flows, meaning those beyond five years. At this strategic level, a firm's cash flows will be influenced by the reactions of both existing and potential competitors, possible new entrants, to exchange rate changes under disequilibrium conditions. In fact, all firms that are subject to international competition, whether they are purely domestic or multinational, are exposed to foreign exchange operating exposure in the long run whenever foreign exchange markets are not continuously in equilibrium.

Measuring Operating Exposure: Trident Germany

Exhibit 11.4 presents the dilemma facing Trident as a result of an unexpected change in the value of the euro, the currency of economic consequence for the German subsidiary. Trident derives much of its reported profits (earnings and earnings per share—EPS—as reported to Wall Street) from its European subsidiary. If the euro unexpectedly falls in value, how will Trident Germany's revenues change (prices, in euro terms, and volumes)? How will its costs change (primarily input costs, in euro terms)? How will competitors respond? We explain the sequence of likely events over the short and medium run in the following section.

Base Case. Trident Germany manufactures in Germany, sells domestically and exports, and all sales are invoiced in euros. Accounts receivable are equal to one-fourth of annual sales, the average collection period being 90 days. Inventory is equal to 25% of annual direct costs. Trident Germany can expand or contract production volume without any significant change in per-unit direct costs or in general and administrative expenses. Depreciation on plant and equipment is €600,000 per year, and the corporate tax rate is 34%.

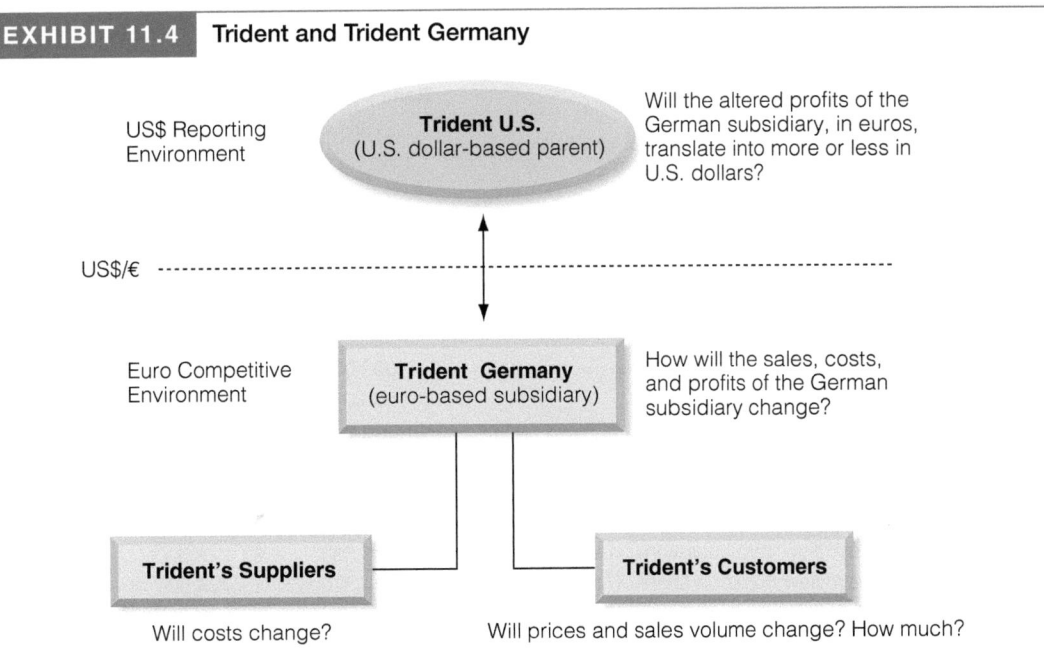

EXHIBIT 11.4 Trident and Trident Germany

An unexpected depreciation in the value of the euro alters both the competitiveness of the subsidiary and the financial results which are consolidated with the parent company.

The December 31, 2011, balance sheet and alternative scenarios are shown in Exhibit 11.5. We assume that on January 1, 2012, before any commercial activity begins, the euro unexpectedly drops from \$1.2000/€ to \$1.0000/€. If no depreciation had occurred, Trident Germany was expected to perform in 2012 as shown in the base case of Exhibit 11.5, generating a dollar cash flow from operations for Trident of \$2,074,320.

Operating exposure depends on whether an unexpected change in exchange rates causes unanticipated changes in sales volume, sales prices, or operating costs. Following a euro depreciation, Trident Germany might choose to maintain its domestic sales prices constant in euro terms, or it might try to raise domestic prices because competing imports are now priced higher in Europe. The firm might choose to keep export prices constant in terms of foreign currencies, in terms of euros, or somewhere in between (partial pass-through). The strategy undertaken depends to a large measure on management's opinion about the price elasticity of demand. On the cost side, Trident Germany might raise prices because of more expensive imported raw material or components, or perhaps because all domestic prices in Germany have risen and labor is now demanding higher wages to compensate for domestic inflation.

Trident Germany's domestic sales and costs might also be partly determined by the effect of the euro depreciation on demand. To the extent that the depreciation, by making prices of German goods initially more competitive, stimulates purchases of European goods in import-competing sectors of the economy as well as exports of German goods, German national income should increase. This assumes that the favorable effect of a euro depreciation on comparative prices is not immediately offset by higher domestic inflation. Thus, Trident Germany might be able to sell more goods domestically because of price and income effects and internationally because of price effects.

EXHIBIT 11.5   Trident Europe's Changing Cash Flows under Euro Depreciation

Assumptions	Base Case	Case 1	Case 2	Case 3
Exchange rate, $/€	1.2000	1.0000	1.0000	1.0000
Sales volume (units)	1,000,000	1,000,000	2,000,000	1,000,000
Sales price per unit	€12.80	€12.80	€12.80	€15.36
Direct cost per unit	€9.60	€9.60	€9.60	€9.60
Annual Cash Flows before Adjustments				
Sales revenue	€12,800,000	€12,800,000	€25,600,000	€15,360,000
Direct cost of goods sold	9,600,000	9,600,000	19,200,000	9,600,000
Cash operating expenses (fixed)	890,000	890,000	890,000	890,000
Depreciation	600,000	600,000	600,000	600,000
Pretax profit	€1,710,000	€1,710,000	€4,910,000	€4,270,000
Income tax expense	581,400	581,400	1,669,400	1,451,800
Profit after tax	€1,128,600	€1,128,600	€3,240,600	€2,818,200
Add back depreciation	600,000	600,000	600,000	600,000
Cash flow from operations, in euros	€1,728,600	€1,728,600	€3,840,600	€3,418,200
Cash flow from operations, in dollars	$2,074,320	$1,728,600	$3,840,600	$3,418,200
Adjustments to Working Capital for 2012 and 2016 Caused by Changes in Conditions				
Accounts receivable	€3,200,000	€3,200,000	€6,400,000	€3,840,000
Inventory	2,400,000	2,400,000	4,800,000	2,400,000
Sum	€5,600,000	€5,600,000	€11,200,000	€6,240,000
Change from base conditions in 2012	€0	€0	€5,600,000	€640,000

Year	Year-End Cash Flows			
1 (2012)	$2,074,320	$1,728,600	($1,759,400)	$2,778,200
2 (2013)	$2,074,320	$1,728,600	$3,840,600	$3,418,200
3 (2014)	$2,074,320	$1,728,600	$3,840,600	$3,418,200
4 (2015)	$2,074,320	$1,728,600	$3,840,600	$3,418,200
5 (2016)	$2,074,320	$1,728,600	$9,440,600	$4,058,200

Year	Change in Year-End Cash Flows from Base Conditions			
1 (2012)	na	($345,720)	($3,833,720)	$703,880
2 (2013)	na	($345,720)	$1,766,280	$1,343,880
3 (2014)	na	($345,720)	$1,766,280	$1,343,880
4 (2015)	na	($345,720)	$1,766,280	$1,343,880
5 (2016)	na	($345,720)	$7,366,280	$1,983,880

	Present Value of Incremental Year-End Cash Flows			
	na	($1,033,914)	$2,866,106	$3,742,892

Note: Initial balance sheet for Trident Germany is the same as that presented in Exhibit 10.9. Analysis assumes accounts receivable at 25% of sales, inventory of 25% of direct cost, German tax rate of 34%, and Trident Germany's cost of capital at 20%.

To illustrate the effect of various postdepreciation scenarios on Trident Germany's operating exposure, consider three simple cases:

Case 1: Depreciation, no change in any variable

Case 2: Increase in sales volume, other variables remain constant

Case 3: Increase in sales price, other variables remain constant

To calculate the net change in present value under each of the scenarios, we will use a 5-year horizon for any change in cash flow induced by the change in the dollar/euro exchange rate.

Case 1: Depreciation; No Change in Any Variable. Assume that in the five years ahead no changes occur in sales volume, sales price, or operating costs. Profits for the coming year in euros will be as expected, and cash flow from operations will be €1,728,600, as shown in Exhibit 11.5. With a new exchange rate of $1.0000/€, this cash flow measured in dollars during 2012 will be €1,728,600 × $1.0000/€ = $1,728,600. Exhibit 11.5 shows that the change in year-end cash flows from the base case is a negative $345,720 for each of the next five years (2012–2016). Exhibit 11.5 shows that the discounted present value of this series of diminished dollar value cash flows is $1,033,914.

Case 2: Volume Increases; Other Variables Remain Constant. Assume that sales within Europe double following the depreciation because German-made telecom components are now more competitive with imports. Additionally, export volume doubles because German-made components are now cheaper in countries whose currencies have not weakened. The sales price is kept constant in euro terms because management of Trident Germany has not observed any change in local German operating costs and because it sees an opportunity to increase market share.

Exhibit 11.5 shows expected cash flow for the first year (2012) would be $3,840,600. This amount, however, is not available because a doubling of sales volume will require additional investment in accounts receivable and in inventory. Although a portion of this additional investment might be financed by increasing accounts payable, we assume additional working capital is financed by cash flow from operations.

At the end of 2012, accounts receivable will be equal to one-fourth of annual sales, or €6,400,000. This amount is twice receivables of €3,200,000 at the end of 2011, and the incremental increase of €3,200,000 must be financed from available cash. Year-end inventory would be equal to one-fourth of annual direct costs, or €4,800,000, an increase of €2,400,000 over the year-beginning level. Receivables and inventory together increase by €5,600,000. At the end of five years (2016), these incremental cash outflows will be recaptured because any investment in current assets eventually rolls back into cash.

Assuming no further change in volume, price, or costs, cash inflows for the five years would be as described in Exhibit 11.5. In this instance, the depreciation causes a major drop in first-year cash flow from the $2,074,320 anticipated in 2012 without depreciation to a negative cash flow of $1,759,400. However, the remaining four years' cash flow is substantially enhanced by the operating effects of the depreciation. Over time, Trident Germany generates significantly more cash for its owners. The depreciation produces an operating gain over time, rather than an operating *loss*.

The reason that Trident Corporation is better off in Case 2 following the depreciation is that sales volume doubled while the per-unit dollar-equivalent sales price fell only 16.67%—the percent amount of the currency depreciation. In other words, the product faced a price elasticity of demand greater than one.

Case 3: Sales Price Increases, Other Variables Remain Constant. Assume the euro sales price is raised from €12.80 to €15.36 per unit to maintain the same U.S. dollar-equivalent price (the change offsets the depreciation of the euro). Assume further that volume remains constant in spite of this price increase; that is, customers expect to pay the same dollar-equivalent price, and local costs do not change.

Trident Germany is now better off following the depreciation than it was before because the sales price, which is pegged to the international price level, increased. However, volume did not drop. The new level of accounts receivable would be one-fourth of the new sales level of €15,360,000, or €3,840,000, an increase of €640,000 over the base case. The investment in inventory is $2,400,000, which is the same as the base case because annual direct costs did not change.

Expected dollar cash flow in every year exceeds the cash flow of $2,074,320 that had been originally expected. The increase in working capital causes net cash flow to be only $2,778,200 in 2012, but thereafter, the cash flow is $3,418,200 per year, with an additional $640,000 working capital recovered in the fifth year. The key to this improvement is operating leverage. If costs are incurred in euros and do not increase after a depreciation, an increase in the sales price by the amount of depreciation will lead to sharply higher profits.

Other Possibilities. If any portion of sales revenues were incurred in other currencies, the situation would be different. Trident Germany might leave the foreign sales price unchanged, in effect raising the euro-equivalent price. Alternatively, it might leave the euro-equivalent price unchanged, thus lowering the foreign sales price in an attempt to gain volume. Of course, it could also position itself between these two extremes. Depending on elasticities and the proportion of foreign to domestic sales, total sales revenue might rise or fall.

If some or all raw material or components were imported and paid for in hard currencies, euro operating costs would increase after the depreciation of the euro. Another possibility is that local (not imported) euro costs would rise after a depreciation.

Measurement of Loss. Exhibit 11.5 summarizes the change in expected year-end cash flows for the three cases and compares them with the cash flow expected should no depreciation occur (base case). These changes are then discounted by Trident's assumed weighted average cost of capital of 20% to obtain the present value of the gain (loss) on operating exposure.

In Case 1, in which nothing changes after the euro is devalued, Trident incurs an operating loss with a present value of ($1,033,914). In Case 2, in which volume doubled with no price change after depreciation, Trident experienced an operating gain with a present value of $2,866,106. In Case 3, in which the euro sales price was increased and volume did not change, the present value of the operating gain from depreciation was $3,742,892. An almost infinite number of combinations of volume, price, and cost could follow any depreciation, and any or all of them might take effect over time.

Strategic Management of Operating Exposure

The objective of both operating and transaction exposure management is to anticipate and influence the effect of unexpected changes in exchange rates on a firm's future cash flows, rather than merely hoping for the best. To meet this objective, management can *diversify the firm's operating and financing base. Management can also change the firm's operating and financing policies.*

The key to managing operating exposure at the strategic level is for management to recognize a disequilibrium in parity conditions when it occurs and to be pre-positioned to react most appropriately. This task can best be accomplished if a firm diversifies internationally both its operating and its financing bases. Diversifying operations means diversifying sales, location of production facilities, and raw material sources. Diversifying the financing base means raising funds in more than one capital market and in more than one currency.

A diversification strategy permits the firm to react either actively or passively, depending on management's risk preference, to opportunities presented by disequilibrium conditions in the foreign exchange, capital, and product markets. Such a strategy does not require management to predict disequilibrium but only to recognize it when it occurs. It does require management to consider how competitors are pre-positioned with respect to their own operating exposures. This knowledge should reveal which firms would be helped or hurt competitively by alternative disequilibrium scenarios.

Diversifying Operations

If a firm's operations are diversified internationally, management is pre-positioned both to recognize disequilibrium when it occurs and to react competitively. Consider the case where purchasing power parity is temporarily in disequilibrium. Although the disequilibrium may have been unpredictable, management can often recognize its symptoms as soon as they occur. For example, management might notice a change in comparative costs in the firm's own plants located in different countries. It might also observe changed profit margins or sales volume in one area compared to another, depending on price and income elasticities of demand and competitors' reactions.

Recognizing a temporary change in worldwide competitive conditions permits management to make changes in operating strategies. Management might make marginal shifts in sourcing raw materials, components, or finished products. If spare capacity exists, production runs can be lengthened in one country and reduced in another. The marketing effort can be strengthened in export markets where the firm's products have become more price competitive because of the disequilibrium condition.

Even if management does not actively distort normal operations when exchange rates change, the firm should experience some beneficial portfolio effects. The variability of its cash flows is probably reduced by international diversification of its production, sourcing, and sales because exchange rate changes under disequilibrium conditions are likely to increase the firm's competitiveness in some markets while reducing it in others. In that case, operating exposure would be neutralized.

In contrast to the internationally diversified MNE, a purely domestic firm might be subject to the full impact of foreign exchange operating exposure even though it does not have foreign currency cash flows. For example, it could experience intense import competition in its domestic market from competing firms producing in countries with undervalued currencies.

A purely domestic firm does not have the option to react to an international disequilibrium condition in the same manner as an MNE. In fact, a purely domestic firm will not be positioned to recognize that a disequilibrium exists because it lacks comparative data from its own internal sources. By the time external data are available, it is often too late to react. Even if a domestic firm recognizes the disequilibrium, it cannot quickly shift production and sales into foreign markets in which it has had no previous presence.

Constraints exist that may limit the feasibility of diversifying production locations. The technology of a particular industry may require large economies of scale. High tech firms, such as Intel, prefer to locate in places where they have easy access to other high tech suppliers, a highly educated workforce, and one or more leading universities. Their R&D efforts are closely tied to initial production and sales activities.

Diversifying Financing

If a firm diversifies its financing sources, it will be pre-positioned to take advantage of temporary deviations from the international Fisher effect. If interest rate differentials do not equal expected changes in exchange rates, opportunities to lower a firm's cost of capital will exist. However, to be able to switch financing sources, a firm must already be well known in the international investment community, with banking contacts firmly established. Again, this is not typically an option for a domestic firm.

As we will demonstrate in Chapter 12, diversifying sources of financing, regardless of the currency of denomination, can lower a firm's cost of capital and increase its availability of capital. It could also diversify such risks as restrictive capital market policies, and other constraints if the firm is located in a segmented capital market. This is especially important for firms resident in emerging markets.

Proactive Management of Operating Exposure

Operating and transaction exposures can be partially managed by adopting operating or financing policies that offset anticipated foreign exchange exposures. Four of the most commonly employed proactive policies are 1) matching currency cash flows; 2) risk-sharing agreements; 3) back-to-back or parallel loans; and 4) cross-currency swaps.

Matching Currency Cash Flows

One way to offset an anticipated continuous long exposure to a particular currency is to acquire debt denominated in that currency. Exhibit 11.6 depicts the exposure of a U.S. firm with continuing export sales to Canada. In order to compete effectively in Canadian markets, the firm invoices all export sales in Canadian dollars. This policy results in a continuing receipt of Canadian dollars month after month. If the export sales are part of a continuing supplier relationship, the long Canadian dollar position is relatively predictable and constant. This endless series of transaction exposures could of course be continually hedged with forward contracts or other contractual hedges, as discussed in Chapter 10.

But what if the firm sought out a continual use, an outflow, for its continual inflow of Canadian dollars? If the U.S. firm were to acquire part of its debt-capital in the Canadian dollar markets, it could use the relatively predictable Canadian dollar cash inflows from export sales to service the principal and interest payments on Canadian dollar debt and be cash *flow matched*. The U.S.-based firm has hedged an operational cash inflow by creating a financial cash outflow, and so it does not have to actively manage the exposure with contractual financial instruments such as forward contracts. This form of hedging, sometimes referred to as matching, is effective in eliminating currency exposure when the exposure cash flow is relatively constant and predictable over time.

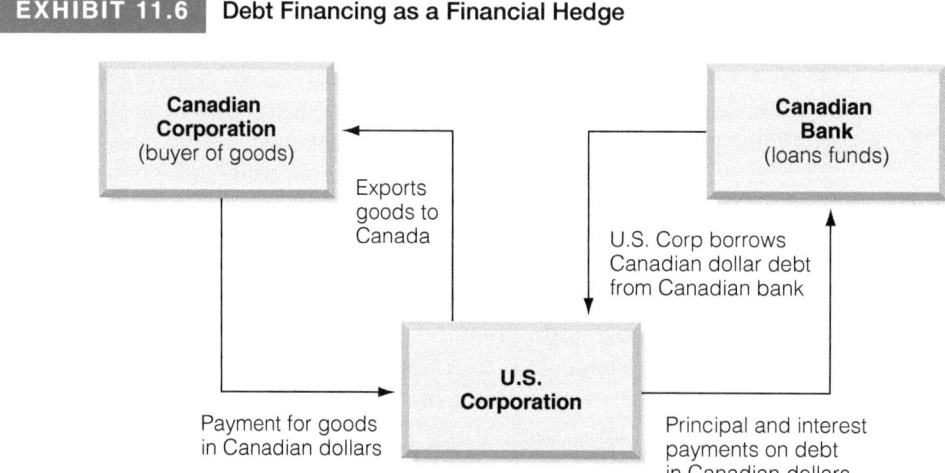

EXHIBIT 11.6 Debt Financing as a Financial Hedge

Exposure: The sale of goods to Canada creates a foreign currency exposure from the inflow of Canadian dollars.

Hedge: The Canadian dollar debt payments act as a financial hedge by requiring debt service, an outflow of Canadian dollars.

The list of potential matching strategies is nearly endless. A second alternative would be for the U.S. firm to seek out potential suppliers of raw materials or components in Canada as a substitute for U.S. or other foreign firms. The firm would then possess not only an operational Canadian dollar cash inflow, the receivable, but also a Canadian dollar operational cash outflow, a payable. If the cash flows were roughly the same in magnitude and timing, the strategy would be a natural hedge. The term "natural" refers to operating-based activities of the firm.

A third alternative, often referred to as currency switching, would be to pay foreign suppliers with Canadian dollars. For example, if the U.S. firm imported components from Mexico, the Mexican firms themselves might welcome payment in Canadian dollars because they are short Canadian dollars in their multinational cash flow network.

Currency Clauses: Risk-Sharing

An alternative arrangement for managing a long-term cash flow exposure between firms with a continuing buyer-supplier relationship is *risk-sharing*. Risk-sharing is a contractual arrangement in which the buyer and seller agree to "share" or split currency movement impacts on payments between them. If the two firms are interested in a long-term relationship based on product quality and supplier reliability and not on the whims of the currency markets, a cooperative agreement to share the burden of currency risk management may be in order.

If Ford's North American operations import automotive parts from Mazda (Japan) every month, year after year, major swings in exchange rates can benefit one party at the expense of the other. (Ford is a major stockholder of Mazda, but it does not exert control over its operations. Therefore, the risk-sharing agreement is particularly appropriate; transactions between the two are both intercompany and intracompany. A risk-sharing agreement solidifies the partnership.) One potential solution would be for Ford and Mazda to agree that all purchases by Ford will be made in Japanese yen at the current exchange rate, as long as the spot rate on the date of invoice is between, say, ¥115/$ and ¥125/$. If the exchange rate is between these values on the payment dates, Ford agrees to accept whatever transaction exposure exists (because it is paying in a foreign currency). If, however, the exchange rate falls outside this range on the payment date, Ford and Mazda will share the difference equally.

For example, Ford has an account payable of ¥25,000,000 for the month of March. If the spot rate on the date of invoice is ¥110/$, the Japanese yen would have appreciated versus the dollar, causing Ford's costs of purchasing automotive parts to rise. Since this rate falls outside the contractual range, Mazda would agree to accept a total payment in Japanese yen which would result from a difference of ¥5/$ (i.e., ¥115 − ¥110). Ford's payment would be

$$\left[\frac{\yen 25{,}000{,}000}{\yen 115.00/\$ - \left(\frac{\yen 5.00/\$}{2}\right)}\right] = \frac{\yen 25{,}000{,}000}{\yen 112.50/\$} = \$222{,}222.22$$

Ford's total payment in Japanese yen would be calculated using an exchange rate of ¥112.50/$, and saves Ford $5,050.51. At a spot rate of ¥110/$, Ford's costs for March would be $227,272.73. The risk-sharing agreement between Ford and Mazda allows Ford to pay $222,222.22, a savings of $5,050.51 over the cost without risk sharing (this "savings" is a reduction in an increased cost, not a true cost reduction). Both parties therefore incur costs and benefits from exchange rate movements outside the specified band. Note that the movement could just as easily have been in Mazda's favor if the spot rate had moved to ¥130/$.

The risk-sharing arrangement is intended to smooth the impact on both parties of volatile and unpredictable exchange rate movements. Of course, a sustained appreciation of one currency versus the other would require the negotiation of a new sharing agreement, but the ultimate goal of the agreement is to alleviate currency pressures on the continuing business relationship. Risk-sharing agreements like these have been in use for nearly 50 years on world markets. They became something of a rarity during the 1960s when exchange rates were relatively stable under the Bretton Woods Agreement. But with the return to floating exchange rates in the 1970s, firms with long-term customer-supplier relationships across borders have returned to some old ways of maintaining mutually beneficial long-term trade.

Back-to-Back Loans

A *back-to-back loan*, also referred to as a *parallel loan* or *credit swap*, occurs when two business firms in separate countries arrange to borrow each other's currency for a specific period of time. At an agreed terminal date they return the borrowed currencies. The operation is conducted outside the foreign exchange markets, although spot quotations may be used as the reference point for determining the amount of funds to be swapped. Such a swap creates a covered hedge against exchange loss, since each company, on its own books, borrows the same currency it repays. Back-to-back loans are also used at a time of actual or anticipated legal limitations on the transfer of investment funds to or from either country.

The structure of a typical back-to-back loan is illustrated in Exhibit 11.7. A British parent firm wanting to invest funds in its Dutch subsidiary locates a Dutch parent firm that wants to invest funds in the United Kingdom. Avoiding the exchange markets entirely, the British parent lends pounds to the Dutch subsidiary in the United Kingdom, while the Dutch parent lends euros to the British subsidiary in the Netherlands. The two loans would be for equal values at the current spot rate and for a specified maturity. At maturity, the two separate loans would each be repaid to the original lender, again without any need to use the foreign exchange markets. Neither loan carries any foreign exchange risk, and neither loan normally needs the approval of any governmental body regulating the availability of foreign exchange for investment purposes.

Parent company guarantees are not needed on the back-to-back loans because each loan carries the right of offset in the event of default of the other loan. A further agreement can

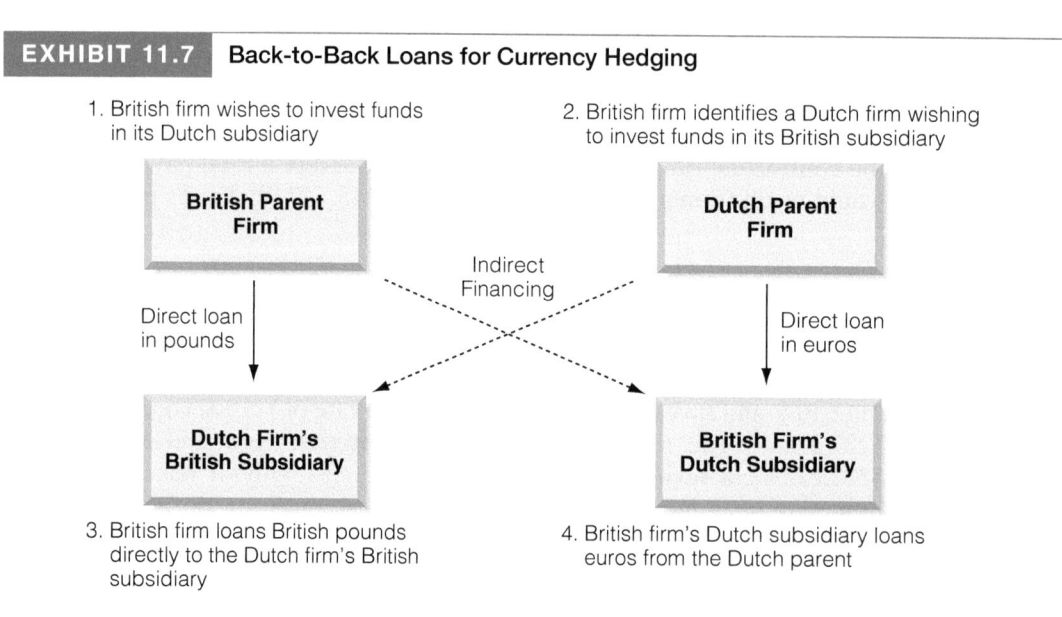

EXHIBIT 11.7 Back-to-Back Loans for Currency Hedging

The back-to-back loan provides a method for parent-subsidiary cross-border financing without incurring direct currency exposure.

provide for maintenance of principal parity in case of changes in the spot rate between the two countries. For example, if the pound dropped by more than, say, 6% for as long as 30 days, the British parent might have to advance additional pounds to the Dutch subsidiary to bring the principal value of the two loans back to parity. A similar provision would protect the British if the euro should weaken. Although this parity provision might lead to changes in the amount of home currency each party must lend during the period of the agreement, it does not increase foreign exchange risk, because at maturity all loans are repaid in the same currency loaned.

There are two fundamental impediments to widespread use of the back-to-back loan. First, it is difficult for a firm to find a partner, termed a *counterparty*, for the currency, amount, and timing desired. Secondly, a risk exists that one of the parties will fail to return the borrowed funds at the designated maturity—although this risk is minimized because each party to the loan has, in effect, 100% collateral, albeit in a different currency. These disadvantages have led to the rapid development and wide use of the currency swap.

Cross Currency Swaps

A *cross currency swap* resembles a back-to-back loan except that it does not appear on a firm's balance sheet. As we noted briefly in Chapter 6, the term swap is widely used to describe a foreign exchange agreement between two parties to exchange a given amount of one currency for another and, after a period of time, to give back the original amounts swapped. Care should be taken to clarify which of the many different swaps is being referred to in a specific case.

In a currency swap, a firm and a swap dealer or swap bank agree to exchange an equivalent amount of two different currencies for a specified period of time. Currency swaps can be negotiated for a wide range of maturities up to at least 10 years. If funds are more expensive in one country than another, a fee may be required to compensate for the interest differential. The swap dealer or swap bank acts as a middleman in setting up the swap agreement.

A typical currency swap first requires two firms to borrow funds in the markets and currencies in which they are best known. For example, a Japanese firm would typically borrow yen on a regular basis in its home market. If, however, the Japanese firm were exporting to the United States and earning U.S. dollars, it might wish to construct a *matching cash flow hedge* which would allow it to use the U.S. dollars earned to make regular debt-service payments on U.S. dollar debt. If, however, the Japanese firm is not well known in the U.S. financial markets, it may have no ready access to U.S. dollar debt.

One way in which it could, in effect, borrow dollars, is to participate in a *cross-currency swap* (see Exhibit 11.8). The Japanese firm could swap its yen-denominated debt service payments with another firm that has U.S. dollar-debt service payments. This swap would have the Japanese firm "paying dollars" and "receiving yen." The Japanese firm would then have dollar-debt service without actually borrowing U.S. dollars. Simultaneously, a U.S. corporation could actually be entering into a cross-currency swap in the opposite direction—"paying yen" and "receiving dollars." The swap dealer is taking the role of a middleman.

Swap dealers arrange most swaps on a "blind basis," meaning that the initiating firm does not know who is on the other side of the swap arrangement—the counterparty. The firm views the dealer or bank as its counterparty. Because the swap markets are dominated by the major money center banks worldwide, the counterparty risk is acceptable. Because the swap dealer's business is arranging swaps, the dealer can generally arrange for the currency, amount, and timing of the desired swap.

Accountants in the United States treat the currency swap as a foreign exchange transaction rather than as debt and treat the obligation to reverse the swap at some later date as a forward exchange contract. Forward exchange contracts can be matched against assets, but they are entered in a firm's footnotes rather than as balance sheet items. The result is that

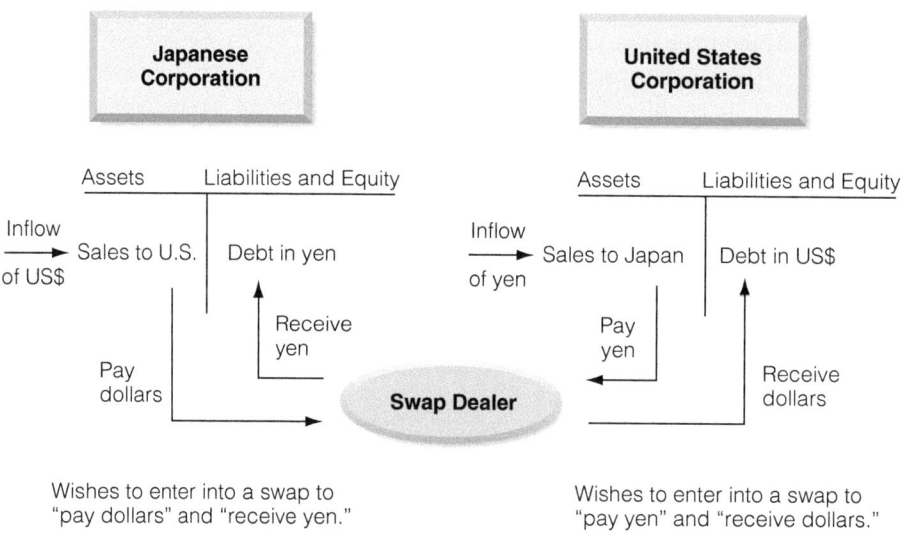

EXHIBIT 11.8 Using Cross-Currency Swaps

Both the Japanese corporation and the U.S. corporation would like to enter into a cross-currency swap which would allow them to use foreign currency cash inflows to service debt.

both translation and operating exposures are avoided, and neither a long-term receivable nor a long-term debt is created on the balance sheet.

Contractual Approaches: Hedging the Unhedgeable

Some MNEs now attempt to hedge their operating exposure with contractual strategies. A number of firms like Merck (U.S.) have undertaken long-term currency option positions, hedges designed to offset lost earnings from adverse exchange rate changes. This hedging of what many of these firms refer to as *strategic exposure or competitive exposure* seems to fly in the face of traditional theory.

The ability of firms to hedge the "unhedgeable" is dependent upon *predictability*: 1) the predictability of the firm's future cash flows, and 2) the predictability of the firm's competitor's responses to exchange rate changes. Although the management of many firms may believe they are capable of predicting their own cash flows, few in practice feel capable of accurately predicting competitor response. As illustrated by *Global Finance in Practice 11.2*, many firms still find even timely measurement of exposure a challenge.

Merck is an example of a firm whose management feels capable of both. The company possesses relatively predictable long-run revenue streams due to the product-niche nature of the pharmaceuticals industry. As a U.S.-based exporter to foreign markets, markets in which sales levels by product are relatively predictable and prices are often regulated by government, Merck can accurately predict net long-term cash flows in foreign currencies five and ten years into the future. Merck has a relatively undiversified operating structure. It is highly centralized in terms of where research, development, and production costs are located. Merck's managers feel Merck has no real alternatives but contractual hedging if it is to weather long-term unexpected exchange rate changes. Merck has purchased over-the-counter (OTC) long-term put options on foreign currencies versus the U.S. dollar as

> **GLOBAL FINANCE IN PRACTICE 11.2**
>
> **Key Challenges to Managing FX Risk**
>
> A global survey and study conducted in the first quarter of 2010, comprising 275 respondents from 16 primary industries and 17 global regions, provides some insight into the challenges companies perceive in measuring and managing their currency risk. The top FX management challenges according to the survey were, in order:
>
> - Difficult to quantify exposure
> - Confidence in data
> - Timely access to data
> - Lack of automated processes
> - Lack of relevant knowledge/skills
> - Lacks priority management
>
> The first three are obviously interrelated, and speak to the difficulty of firms in measuring their exposure to foreign exchange risk accurately and with confidence in time for proactive management.
>
> *Source*: "Foreign Exchange Exposure Management: A benchmark survey of foreign currency exposure and risk practices, challenges, and results," Fireapps Financial Risk Exposed, 2010, www.fireapps.com.

insurance against potential lost earnings from exchange rate changes. In Merck's case, the predictability of competitor response to exchange rate changes is less pertinent given the niche-market nature of pharmaceutical products.

A significant question remains as to the true effectiveness of hedging operating exposure with contractual hedges. The fact remains that even after feared exchange rate movements and put option position payoffs have occurred, the firm is competitively disadvantaged. The capital outlay required for the purchase of such sizable put option positions is capital not used for the potential diversification of operations, which in the long run might have more effectively maintained the firm's global market share and international competitiveness.

Summary of Learning Objectives

Examine how operating exposure arises through unexpected changes in operating and financing cash flows.

- *Foreign exchange exposure* is a measure of the potential for a firm's profitability, net cash flow, and market value to change because of a change in exchange rates. The three main types of foreign exchange risk are *operating*, *transaction*, and *translation* exposures.
- *Operating exposure* measures the change in value of the firm that results from changes in future operating cash flows caused by an unexpected change in exchange rates.

Analyze the sequence of how unexpected exchange rate changes alter the economic performance of a business unit through volume, price, cost and other key variable changes.

- An unexpected change in exchange rates impacts a firm's expected cash flow at four levels: 1) short run; 2) medium run, equilibrium case; 3) medium run, disequilibrium case; and 4) long run.

Evaluate the strategic alternatives to managing operating exposure.

- Operating strategies for the management of operating exposure emphasize the structuring of firm operations in order to create matching streams of cash flows by currency. This is termed natural hedging.
- The objective of operating exposure management is to anticipate and influence the effect of unexpected changes in exchange rates on a firm's future cash flow, rather than being forced into passive reaction to such changes as was described in the Trident Europe case. This task can best be accomplished if a firm diversifies internationally both its operations and its financing base.

Detail the proactive policies available to firms for managing operating exposure.

- Proactive policies include matching currency of cash flow, currency risk sharing clauses, back-to-back loan structures, and cross-currency swap agreements.
- Strategies to change financing policies include matching currency cash flows, back-to-back loans and currency swaps.
- Contractual approaches (i.e., options and forwards) have occasionally been used to hedge operating exposure but are costly and possibly ineffectual.

MINI-CASE

Toyota's European Operating Exposure

It was January 2002, and Toyota Motor Europe Manufacturing (TMEM) had a problem. More specifically, Mr. Toyoda Shuhei, the new President of TMEM, had a problem. He was on his way to Toyota Motor Company's (Japan) corporate offices outside Tokyo to explain the continuing losses of the European manufacturing and sales operations. The CEO of Toyota Motor Company, Mr. Hiroshi Okuda, was expecting a proposal from Mr. Shuhei to reduce and eventually eliminate the European losses. The situation was intense given that TMEM was the only major Toyota subsidiary suffering losses.

Toyota and Auto Manufacturing

Toyota Motor Company was the number one automobile manufacturer in Japan, the third largest manufacturer in the world by unit sales (5.5 million units or one auto every six seconds), but number eight in sales in Continental Europe. The global automobile manufacturing industry had been experiencing, like many industries, continued consolidation in recent years as margins were squeezed, economies of scale and scope pursued, and global sales slowed.

Toyota was no different. It had continued to rationalize its manufacturing along regional lines. Toyota had continued to increase the amount of local manufacturing in North America. In 2001, over 60% of Toyota's North American sales were locally manufactured. But Toyota's European sales were nowhere close to this yet. Most of Toyota's automobile and truck manufacturing for Europe was still done in Japan. In 2001, only 24% of the autos sold in Europe were manufactured in Europe (including the United Kingdom), the remainder were imported from Japan (see Exhibit 1).

Toyota Motor Europe sold 634,000 automobiles in 2000. This was the second largest foreign market for Toyota, second only to North America. TMEM expected significant growth in European sales, and was planning to expand European manufacturing and sales to 800,000 units by 2005. But for fiscal 2001, the unit reported operating losses of ¥9.897 billion ($82.5 million at ¥120/$). TMEM had three assembly plants in the United Kingdom, one plant in Turkey, and one plant in Portugal. In November 2000, Toyota Motor Europe announced publicly that it would not generate positive profits for the next two years due to the weakness of the euro.

Toyota had recently introduced a new model to the European market, the Yaris, which was proving very successful. The Yaris, a super-small vehicle with a 1,000cc engine, had sold more than 180,000 units in 2000.

EXHIBIT 1 Toyota Motor's European Currency Operating Structure

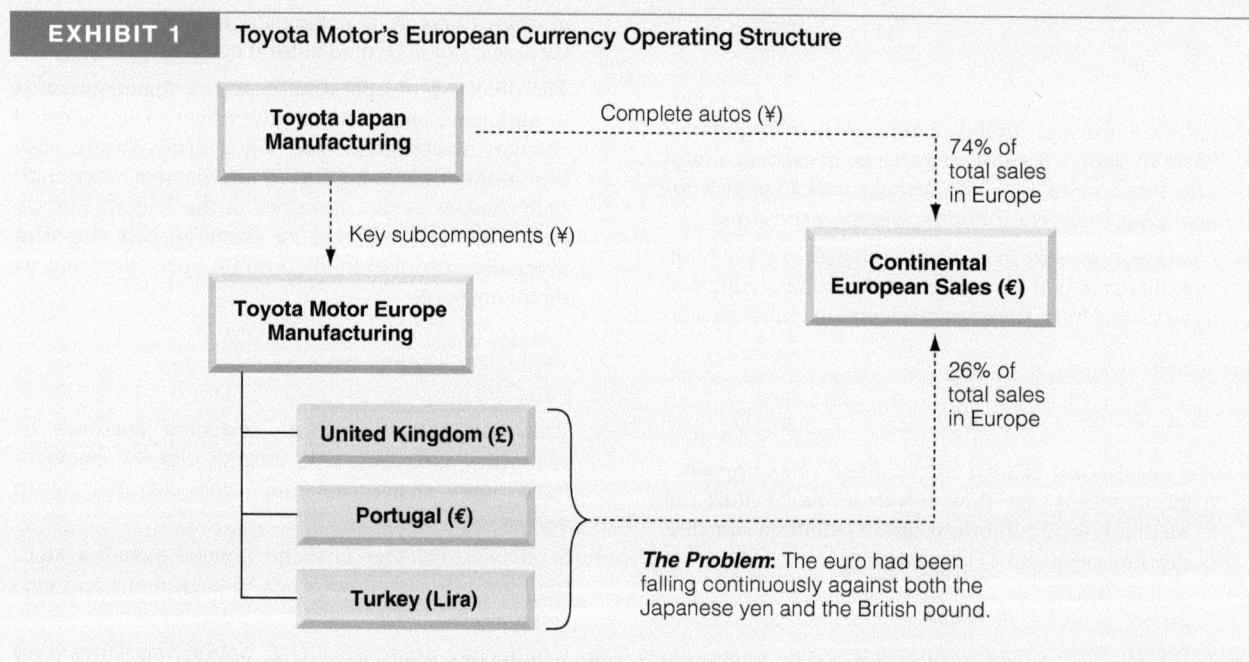

The Problem: The euro had been falling continuously against both the Japanese yen and the British pound.

Although the Yaris had been specifically designed for the European market, the decision had been made early on to manufacture it in Japan.

Currency Exposure

The primary source of the continuing operating losses suffered by TMEM was the falling value of the euro. Over the recent two year period, the euro had fallen in value against both the Japanese yen and the British pound. As demonstrated in Exhibit 1, the cost base for most of the autos sold within the Continental European market was the Japanese yen. Exhibit 2 illustrates the slide of the euro against the Japanese yen.

As the yen rose against the euro, costs increased significantly when measured in euro terms. If Toyota wished to preserve its price competitiveness in the European market, it had to absorb most of the exchange rate changes and suffer reduced or negative margins on both completed cars and key subcomponents shipped to its European manufacturing centers. Deciding to manufacture the Yaris in Japan had only exacerbated the situation.

Management Response

Toyota management was not sitting passively by. In 2001, they had initiated some assembly operations in Valenciennes, France. Although a relatively small percentage of total European sales as of January 2002, Toyota planned to continue to expand its capacity and capabilities to source about 25% of European sales by 2004. Assembly of the Yaris was scheduled to be moved to Valenciennes in 2002. The continuing problem, however, was that it was an assembly facility, meaning that much of the expensive value-added content of the autos being assembled was still based in either Japan or the United Kingdom.

Mr. Shuhei, with the approval of Mr. Okuda, had also initiated a local sourcing and procurement program for the United Kingdom manufacturing operations. TMEM wished to decrease the number of key components imported from Toyota Japan to reduce the currency exposure of the U.K. unit. But again, the continuing problem of the British pound's value against the euro, as shown in Exhibit 3, reduced even the effectiveness of this solution.

CASE QUESTIONS

1. Why do you think Toyota waited so long to move much of its manufacturing for European sales to Europe?
2. If the British pound were to join the European Monetary Union would the problem be resolved? How likely do you think this is?
3. If you were Mr. Shuhei, how would you categorize your problems and solutions? What was a short-term problem? What was a long-term problem?
4. What measures would you recommend that Toyota Europe take to resolve the continuing operating losses?

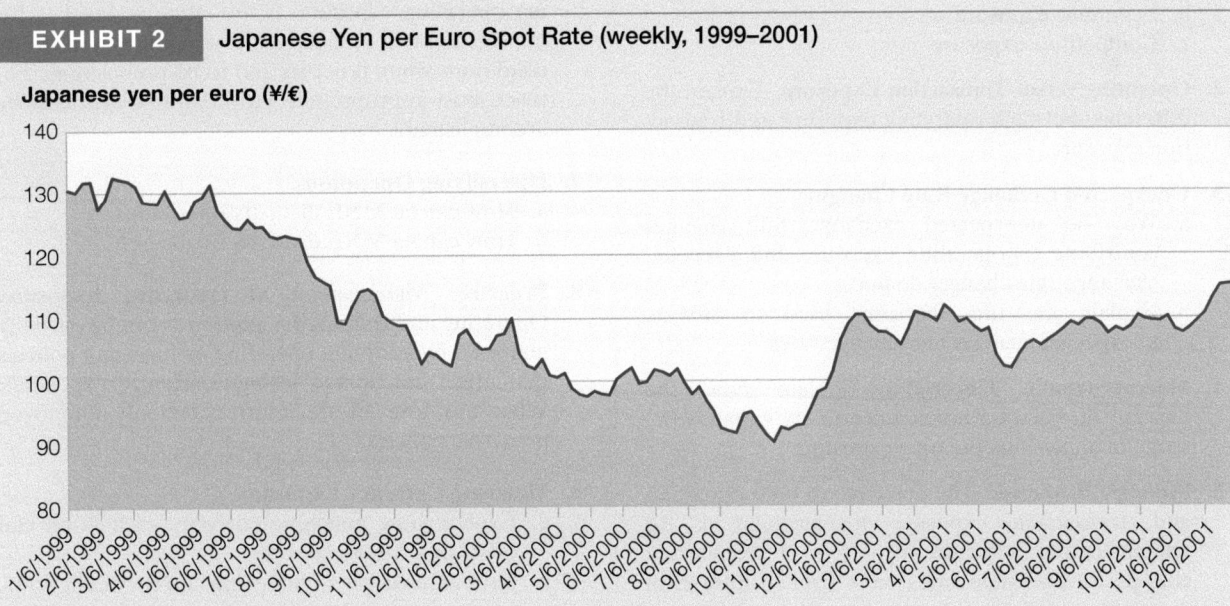

EXHIBIT 2 Japanese Yen per Euro Spot Rate (weekly, 1999–2001)

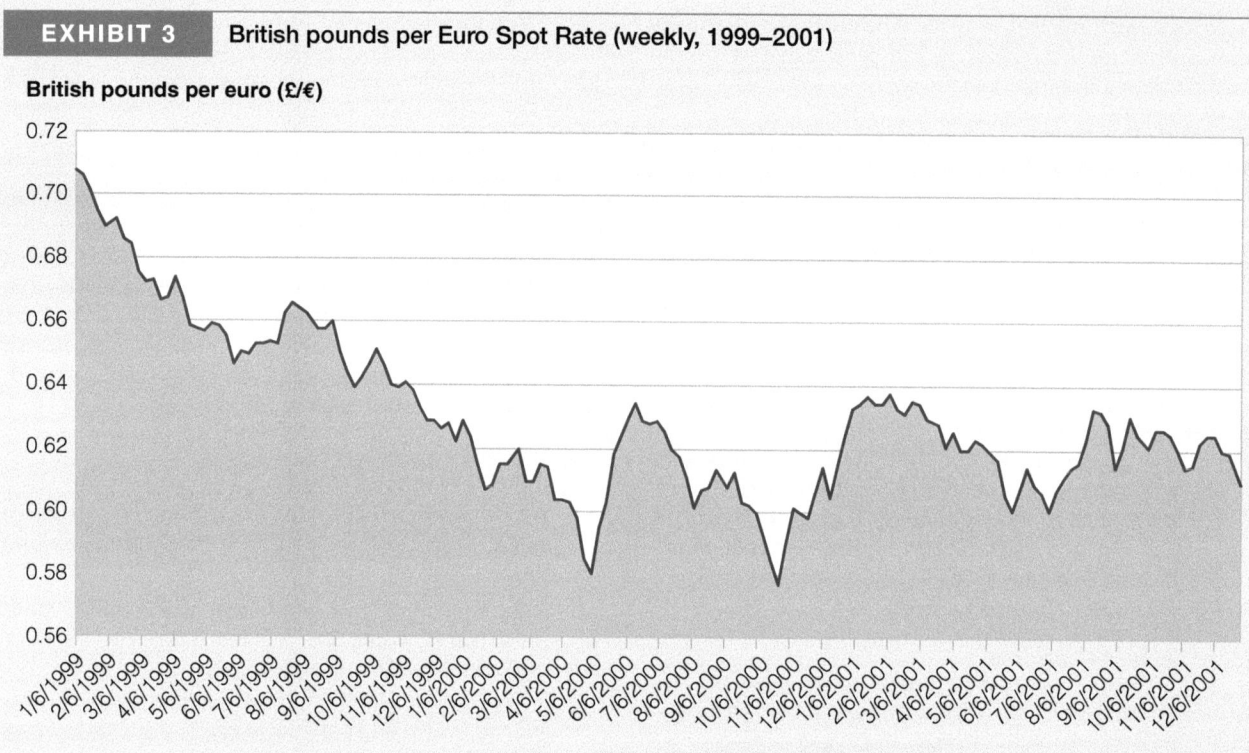

EXHIBIT 3 British pounds per Euro Spot Rate (weekly, 1999–2001)

Questions

1. **Definitions.** Define the following terms:
   a. Operating exposure
   b. Economic exposure
   c. Competitive exposure

2. **Operating versus Transaction Exposure.** Explain the difference between operating exposure and transaction exposure.

3. **Unexpected Exchange Rate Changes.**
   a. Why do unexpected exchange rate changes contribute to operating exposure, but expected exchange rate changes do not?
   b. Explain the time horizons used to analyze unexpected changes in exchange rates.

4. **Macroeconomic Uncertainty.** Explain how the concept of macroeconomic uncertainty expands the scope of analyzing operating exposure.

5. **Strategic Response.** The objective of both operating and transaction exposure management is to anticipate and influence the effect of unexpected changes in exchange rates on a firm's future cash flows. What strategic alternative policies exist to enable management to manage these exposures?

6. **Managing Operating Exposure.** The key to managing operating exposure at the strategic level is for management to recognize a disequilibrium in parity conditions when it occurs and to be prepositioned to react most appropriately. How can this task best be accomplished?

7. **Diversifying Operations.**
   a. How can an MNE diversify operations?
   b. How can an MNE diversify financing?

8. **Proactive Management of Operating Exposure.** Operating and transaction exposures can be partially managed by adopting operating or financing policies that offset anticipated foreign exchange exposures. What are four of the most commonly employed proactive policies?

9. **Matching Currency Exposure.**
   a. Explain how matching currency cash flows can offset operating exposure.
   b. Give an example of matching currency cash flows.

10. **Risk Sharing.** An alternative arrangement for managing operating exposure between firms with a continuing buyer-supplier relationship is risk sharing. Explain how risk sharing works.

11. **Back-to-Back Loans.** Explain how back-to-back loans can hedge foreign exchange operating exposure.

12. **Currency Swaps.** Explain how currency swaps can hedge foreign exchange operating exposure. What are the accounting advantages of currency swaps?

13. **Contractual Hedging.** Eastman Kodak is an MNE that has undertaken contractual hedging of its operating exposure.
    a. How do they accomplish this task?
    b. What assumptions do they make in order to justify contractual hedging of their operating exposure?
    c. How effective is such contractual hedging in your opinion? Explain your reasoning.

Problems

1. **DeMagistris Fashion Company.** DeMagistris Fashion Company, based in New York City, imports leather coats from Acuña Leather Goods, a reliable and longtime supplier, based in Buenos Aires, Argentina. Payment is in Argentine pesos. When the peso lost its parity with the U.S. dollar in January 2002, it collapsed in value to Ps4.0/$ by October 2002. The outlook was for a further decline in the peso's value. Since both DeMagistris and Acuña wanted to continue their longtime relationship, they agreed on a risk-sharing arrangement. As long as the spot rate on the date of an invoice is between Ps3.5/$ and Ps4.5/$ DeMagistris will pay based on the spot rate. If the exchange rate falls outside this range, they will share the difference equally with Acuña Leather Goods. The risk-sharing agreement will last for six months, at which time the exchange rate limits will be reevaluated. DeMagistris contracts to import leather coats from Acuña for Ps8,000,000 or $2,000,000 at the current spot rate of Ps4.0/$ during the next six months.
    a. If the exchange rate changes immediately to Ps6.00/$, what will be the dollar cost of six months of imports to DeMagistris?
    b. At Ps6.00/$, what will be the peso export sales in Acuña Leather Goods to DeMagistris Fashion Company?

2. **Mauna Loa.** Mauna Loa, a macadamia nut subsidiary of Hershey's with planations on the slopes of its namesake volcano in Hilo, Hawaii, exports macadamia nuts worldwide. The Japanese market is its biggest export market, with average annual sales invoiced in yen to Japanese customers of ¥1,200,000,000. At the present exchange rate of ¥125/$, this is equivalent to $9,600,000. Sales are relatively equally distributed during the year. They show up as a ¥250,00,000 account receivable on Mauna Loa's balance sheet. Credit terms to each customer allow for 60 days before payment is due. Monthly cash collections are typically ¥100,000,000.

   Mauna Loa would like to hedge its yen receipts, but it has too many customers and transactions to make it practical to sell each receivable forward. It does not want to use options because they are considered to be too expensive for this particular purpose. Therefore, they have decided to use a "matching" hedge by borrowing yen.
    a. How much should Mauna Loa borrow in yen?
    b. What should be the terms of payment on the yen loan?

3. **Murray Exports (A).** Murray Exports (U.S.) exports heavy crane equipment to several Chinese dock facilities. Sales are currently 10,000 units per year at the yuan equivalent of $24,000 each. The Chinese yuan (renminbi) has been trading at Yuan8.20/$, but a Hong Kong advisory service predicts the renminbi will drop in value next week to Yuan9.00/$, after which it will remain unchanged for at least a decade. Accepting this forecast as given, Murray Exports faces a pricing decision in the face of the impending devaluation. It may either 1) maintain the same yuan price and in effect sell for fewer dollars, in which case Chinese volume will not change; or 2) maintain the same dollar price, raise the yuan price in China to offset the devaluation, and experience a 10% drop in unit volume. Direct costs are 75% of the U.S. sales price.
    a. What would be the short-run (one year) impact of each pricing strategy?
    b. Which do you recommend?

4. **Murray Exports (B).** Assume the same facts as in Murray Exports (A). Additionally, financial management believes that if it maintains the same yuan sales price, volume will increase at 12% per annum for eight years. Dollar costs will not change. At the end of 10 years, Murray Exports' patent expires and it will no longer export to China. After the yuan is devalued to Yuan9.20/$, no further devaluations are expected. If Murray Exports raises the yuan price so as to maintain its dollar price,

volume will increase at only 1% per annum for eight years, starting from the lower initial base of 9,000 units. Again, dollar costs will not change, and at the end of eight years Murray Exports will stop exporting to China. Murray Exports' weighted average cost of capital is 10%. Given these considerations, what should be Murray Exports' pricing policy?

5. **MacLoren Automotive.** MacLoren Automtive manufactures British sports cars, a number of which are exported to New Zealand for payment in pounds sterling. The distributor sells the sports cars in New Zealand for New Zealand dollars. The New Zealand distributor is unable to carry all of the foreign exchange risk, and would not sell MacLoren models unless MacLoren could share some of the foreign exchange risk. MacLoren has agreed that sales for a given model year will initially be priced at a "base" spot rate between the New Zealand dollar and pound sterling set to be the spot mid-rate at the beginning of that model year. As long as the actual exchange rate is within ±5% of that base rate, payment will be made in pounds sterling. That is, the New Zealand distributor assumes all foreign exchange risk. However, if the spot rate at time of shipment falls outside of this ±5% range, MacLoren will share equally (i.e., 50/50) the difference between the actual spot rate and the base rate. For the current model year the base rate is NZ$1.6400/£.
   a. What are the outside ranges within which the New Zealand importer must pay at the then current spot rate?
   b. If MacLoren ships 10 sports cars to the New Zealand distributor at a time when the spot exchange rate is NZ$1.7000/£, and each car has an invoice cost £32,000, what will be the cost to the distributor in New Zealand dollars? How many pounds will MacLoren receive, and how does this compare with McLaren's expected sales receipt of £32,000 per car?
   c. If MacLoren Automotive ships the same 10 cars to New Zealand at a time when the spot exchange rate is NZ$1.6500/£, how many New Zealand dollars will the distributor pay? How many pounds will MacLoren Automotive receive?
   d. Does a risk-sharing agreement such as this one shift the currency exposure from one party of the transaction to the other?
   e. Why is such a risk-sharing agreement of benefit to MacLoren? To the New Zealand distributor?

6. **Trident Germany: Case 4.** Trident Germany decides not to change its domestic price of €12.80 per unit within Europe, but to raise its export price (in euros) from £12.80 per unit to €15.36 per unit, thus preserving its original dollar equivalent price of $15.36 per unit. Volume in both markets remains the same because no buyer perceives that the price has changed.

7. **Trident Germany: Case 5.** Trident Germany finds that domestic costs increase in proportion to the drop in value of the euro because of local inflation and a rise in the cost of imported raw materials and components. This rise in costs (+20%) applies to all cash costs, including direct costs and fixed cash operating costs. However, it does not apply to depreciation. Because of the increase in its costs, Trident Europe increases its sales price in euros from €12.80 per unit to €15.36 per unit.

8. **Risk-Sharing at Harley Davidson.** Harley-Davidson (U.S.) reportedly uses risk-sharing agreements with its own foreign subsidiaries and with independent foreign distributors. Because these foreign units typically sell to their local markets and earn local currency, Harley would like to ease their individual currency exposure problems by allowing them to pay for merchandise from Harley (U.S.) in their local functional currency. The spot rate between the U.S. dollar and the Australian dollar on January 1 is A$1.3052/US$. Assume that Harley uses this rate as the basis for setting its central rate or base exchange rate for the year at A$1.3000/US$. Harley agrees to price all contracts to Australian distributors at this exact exchange rate as long as the current spot rate on the order date is within ±2.5% of this rate. If the spot rate falls outside of this range, but is still within ±5% of the central rate, Harley will "share" equally (i.e., "50/50") the difference between the new spot rate and the neutral boundary with the distributor.

9. **Hurte-Paroxysm Products, Inc. (A).** Hurte-Paroxysm Products, Inc. (HP) of the United States, exports computer printers to Brazil, whose currency, the reais (symbol R$) has been trading at R$3.40/US$. Exports to Brazil are currently 50,000 printers per year at the reais equivalent of $200 each. A strong rumor exists that the reais will be devalued to R$4.00/$ within two weeks by the Brazilian government. Should the devaluation take place, the reais is expected to remain unchanged for another decade. Accepting this forecast as given, HP faces a pricing decision which must be made before any actual devaluation: HP may either 1) maintain the same reais price and in effect sell for fewer dollars, in which case Brazilian volume will not change, or 2) maintain the same dollar price, raise

the reais price in Brazil to compensate for the devaluation, and experience a 20% drop in volume. Direct costs in the United States are 60% of the U.S. sales price. What would be the short-run (1-year) implication of each pricing strategy? Which do you recommend?

10. **Hurte-Paroxysm Products, Inc. (B).** Assume the same facts as in Hurte-Paroxysm Products, Inc. (A). HP also believes that if it maintains the same price in Brazilian reais as a permanent policy, volume will increase at 10% per annum for six years, costs will not change. At the end of six years, HP's patent expires and it will no longer export to Brazil. After the reais is devalued to R$4.00/US$, no further devaluation is expected. If HP raises the price in reais so as to maintain its dollar price, volume will increase at only 4% per annum for six years, starting from the lower initial base of 40,000 units. Again, dollar costs will not change, and at the end of six years, HP will stop exporting to Brazil. HP's weighted average cost of capital is 12%. Given these considerations, what do you recommend for HP's pricing policy? Justify your recommendation.

Internet Exercises

1. **Operating Exposure: Recent Examples.** Using the following major periodicals as starting points, find a current example of a firm with a substantial operating exposure problem. To aid in your search, you might focus on businesses having major operations in countries with recent currency crises, either through depreciation or major home currency appreciation.

    Financial Times   www.ft.com/
    The Economist   www.economist.com/
    The *Wall Street Journal*   www.wsj.com/

2. **SEC Edgar Files.** To analyze an individual firm's operating exposure more carefully, it is necessary to have more detailed information available than in the normal annual report. Choose a specific firm with substantial international operations, for example, Coca-Cola or PepsiCo, and search the Security and Exchange Commission's Edgar Files for more detailed financial reports of their international operations.

    Search SEC EDGAR Archives   www.sec.gov/cgi-bin/srch-edgar